GW00391299

Ken Irwin was born in Liverpool on 1
Secondary Modern school at 15, he start
office, before getting into journalism.

He worked on a number of provincial papers including The Liverpolitan, the Journal of Commerce, Birkenhead News, Nottingham Evening Post and Gardian Journal, and Liverpool Evening Express, before joining the Daily Mirror in Manchester as Northern TV critic.

After moving to London, he worked in Fleet Street, becoming TV and Show Business Editor. He left the Mirror after 31 years to concentrate on freelance writing. During his years as a journalist, Ken was also a judge on ITV's top talent show New Faces, appeared on various TV shows, and worked as a football reporter and sports presenter for BBC radio. He has written radio plays and comedy scripts, as well as being the author of several books.

He is married, with a daughter and two sons, and now lives in Manchester.

In this autobiography, he traces the events and stories that shaped his life, his family and his career. Ken was four years old when World War 11 started. He recalls hiding under the stairs during the heavy German bombing raids on Liverpool, when his next-door neighbours were killed overnight; his illness as a child; his youthful years in the Methodist Church; how he got into journalism and his determination to get to the top in Fleet Street, starting as a local reporter writing sports stories at a penny-a-line, and ending up selling a single serie of articles to a national paper for £40,000.

He has interviewed some of the biggest stars in films, music and TV -- from Bing Crosby and Perry Como, Joan Collins and Judi Dench to the Beatles, Alice Cooper, Ozzy Osbourne, Neil Diamond, Tom Jones and Elton John. They're all here... Abba, The Carpenters, Tommy Steele, Cliff Richard, Liza Minnelli, Cilla Black, David Bowie, David Frost, Dudley Moore, Morecambe and Wise, Benny Hill, Les Dawson, Cannon and Ball, Des O'Connor, Tommy Cooper, Paul Daniels, David Jason, Roger Moore, Piers Brosnan, Anthony Hopkins, Daniel Craig, Shirley McLaine, Glenda Jackson, Ken Dodd, Jimmy Tarbuck, Bruce Forsyth, Terry Wogan, Engelbert Humperdink. And many more.

Plus behind-the-scenes stories and scandals from the TV soaps.

For my wife Betty, now Elizabeth.

For Amina, who encouraged me to write this and badgered
me until I'd finished it.

Technical Editor: Amina Helal

FOREWORD

When the Careers Officer asks you, when you're 14 or 15, what you want to do in life, it's very difficult, isn't it? I left school at 15. Breckfield Secondary Modern in Venice Street, Everton, in Liverpool. The school was still there until a few years ago, when the local authorities decided to knock it down in what was supposed to be a great slum clearance scheme and a regeneration of the whole district. But it hasn't happened. The area is still a run-down remnant of what used to be a life for decent, hard-working people.

In junior school, St. Saviours in Breckfield Road North, Everton, I didn't pass the scholarship, or the 11-plus as it was then called. I didn't even take it because I was absent from school so much as a kid - I suffered badly from asthma.

To be honest, I didn't particularly like school - not until the last year or two with the seniors in Venice Street. My favourite subjects were English and art. I always finished top of the class in both, and I was particularly good at writing essays, which I loved.

In fact, I won a prize for writing the best essay in Liverpool for my age group, when I was 14. I was supposed to be presented with a certificate and a book by the Lord Mayor at St. George's Hall, but I was too shy, or too sick to go. So, they sent me the book, instead. I've still got it.

In my last year at Venice Street, I started a school magazine and was made the first editor. I can vividly remember reading a story in one of the comics I bought, The Hotspur, about a newspaper reporter. And I remember seeing Humphrey Bogart in some black-and-white film, playing a reporter. And I thought "That's for me."

But when the Careers Officer came around, about six months before I was due to leave school and asked what I wanted to do as a job, I can remember telling him, "Please sir, I'd like to be a reporter." He just laughed and said, "Oh, I don't think so, lad." He then added quite simply and dogmatically, "It's either office or factory, make your choice."

Disappointed, I replied "Office." And on leaving school, I actually started work as a junior clerk in a shipping office in the Royal Liver

1

Buildings. Houlder Brothers. Earning 12s 6d a week. I was there for about two years and I quite enjoyed it and did well.

But I still yearned to be a reporter. I wrote to the Liverpool Echo, and went into their office. There were no vacancies. I then must have written to every newspaper I could think of - first the locals, then the nationals. Dozens of application letters, asking for a job. Back came the same replies. Sorry - No job without experience.

So, I then started writing articles on a freelance basis. The first piece I ever had published was for the shipping company's house magazine. Then I wrote sports stories and sent them off to a local magazine.

Eventually, I got my foot in the door with a magazine called The Liverpolitan. After writing the sports column for them, the Editor Peter Graham offered me a full-time job, as one of his staff, Richard Whittington-Egan, had gone down sick with TB. I went for an interview, was given the staff job, but then had to give in my notice at the shipping office.

My boss there – Mr Ted Brown, head of the Outward Freight department - was a little taken aback when I walked into his office and said I wanted to leave. He asked me why. "Because I want to be a journalist," I said rather pompously.

He said, "Is it the money? You can have a ten bob rise if you stay. We like you. You could do well here." No, it wasn't the money. I was actually taking less money than I was already earning to go and be a journalist.

So that was the end of my shipping career. The end of running up and down Water Street, Chapel Street and Old Hall Street every day, delivering shipping notes to various offices, as well as the Cunard Building and the Mersey Docks and Harbour Board building on the famous waterfront. The end of sitting on a high stool and writing out and checking Bills of Lading on distinctive smelling parchment. The end, as junior office boy, of making the tea, and being responsible for putting up the Union Jack flag on the front of the Liver Building every St. George's Day and King's Birthday (a task that particularly scared me, because I was always afraid the flag was going to be swept away by the wind and blown in to the nearby River Mersey before I could rig it up properly).

The Liverpolitan - a glossy monthly, rather posh magazine with a not very big circulation - had an office in Old Swan. A couple of rooms above a Post Office. We had an editorial staff of only four - the Editor Peter Graham, his girlfriend Ann Dutton, who was his assistant and woman's editor, a circulation manager, who was an Irishman with bad teeth who rolled his own cigarettes and chain-smoked all day. And me. I wrote the sports page and everything else they threw at me. A gossip column, news and society events. Anything new we could think of. But I loved it. I was with the magazine for nearly two years, before I started getting itchy feet and ambitions for something bigger.

Luck always has a lot to do with things, I suppose. After sending off applications to papers again, one paper, The Journal of Commerce, told me they had a vacancy for a shipping reporter. I jumped at it.

This meant going around all the docks every day, on the then dilapidated overhead railway, and reporting on ships' movements.

It was quite boring after a while. But it was a job. Quite well paid, good experience, and I became fascinated with shipping. And still am.

After that, though, it was all systems go. I went on to be a reporter on the Birkenhead News. I was there for about two years, and then moved to Nottingham, worked for the Evening Post and the daily Guardian Journal. They had a split shift system, which meant working four hours on the evening paper, four hours off, then another four hours back on for the daily paper.

Nottingham was my first job away from home, and I found lodgings with the local Methodist minister, the Rev. Walter Joyce and his family in Ruddington. But I was then engaged to be married, and moved back to Liverpool, got a job as a reporter on the Evening Express, got married and was happy being back on Merseyside with the family.

Then disaster struck. The paper closed. It was taken over and amalgamated with the Liverpool Echo. We were all made redundant. I was 23, married, one child and another on the way. And out of work. Most of the editorial staff of the Express scurried off to Manchester and London, all desperately looking for jobs.

Again, I suppose I was lucky. I had become quite well known on the Evening Express and I was doing some good stuff. As well as news reporting, I had done a lot of feature writing, and one day a week was writing the popular Over The Mersey Wall gossip column. I got a phone call from the Daily Mirror in Manchester, offering me a job as Northern TV Critic.

The pay was £19 a week, which was double what I was getting on the now defunct Evening Express, but it was on a three-month trial.

So, I moved to Manchester, with the family. And for my sins, I was then with the Daily Mirror for 31 years. They never did tell me if I'd passed the three-month trial!

After about seven years in Manchester, they offered me a job in the London office. That was every journalist's dream of success - Fleet Street! The Street of Ink! There was no place quite like it. It was everything I'd expected it to be. The Street of a Thousand Dreams. Full of eccentric characters and adventure.

When I moved to London to join the TV team, there were four of us. The first thing I knew was that on one side, next to the TV office, we had Marjorie Proops in the big office. And columnist Cassandra (Bill Connors) and Donald Zec, the show business writer, sharing an office on the other side. They just don't come any more famous than that. And there was I, working alongside them. Some days I'd feel like having to pinch myself to make sure it was real.

From then on, I decided to specialise in TV - and later show business. It's always good to become a specialist in something, instead of just being a reporter, chasing news stories every day.

To cut a long story short, I then went on, over the years, to become Chief Show Business Writer, then TV Editor, and finally TV and Show Business Editor, with a staff of 12 writers under me, and two secretaries. They included TV writers, theatre critics, film critics, pop music writers. And a big budget to look after.

I ran that department for more than three years. But there must be something in me which means I have to make changes in my life because I gave up being Show Business Editor, quite voluntarily. I got tired of running the office, signing expenses, sending other people out to do jobs which often I knew I could do better. I just missed being "out on the road" and got itchy feet. I grew disillusioned with London, was fed up being on the treadmill, and asked for a move back to Manchester.

Partly, this was due to domestic circumstances. My younger son Paul was suddenly taken seriously ill, and when we visited him in hospital, we thought we might actually lose him. He had to have an operation, and they took away half a lung.

Fortunately, he recovered. But I started to look at my own life and reflect on things. What was I doing - working around the clock? On call night and day, drinking far too much in the well-known watering holes of Fleet Street and in our office pub, which was ironically nicknamed The Stab In The Back. And for what?

Manchester was a backwater after London. But I had less responsibility as the chief Northern showbiz writer, and I could more or less please myself what I did.

4

But calamity struck again. Enter one Robert Maxwell, the tyrant who took over as owner of the Mirror group.

Fortunately, I didn't have to deal with him very much. But once Maxwell moved in as owner of the Mirror, the whole working atmosphere changed. A happy office became something of a nightmare. People were made redundant. The staff became disenchanted. Reporters left to go to other papers. A lot of them were fired. Maxwell was ruthless. He pruned the staff back to nothing.

He used to arrive at the office in London by helicopter on the roof of the High Holborn building, and the News Editor would immediately yell to the staff in the newsroom, "The EGO has landed!".

Having said that, I must recall that my dealings with Maxwell were unusual, to say the least.

After I'd moved back to Manchester - partly to get away from the London office and Maxwell - I was in Dublin, covering the Eurovision Song Contest, when I received a phone call from the News Editor in Manchester. "I think you should know, Ken, that Maxwell is closing down the Manchester office. We are all being sacked."

It was a complete bombshell. I couldn't believe it. But then, half an hour later, I got another call from the Mirror Editor, saying they wanted me back in London.

It was a great dilemma for me. While they were closing the Northern office and making everyone redundant, they kept me on. Maxwell fired everybody in Manchester (an editorial staff of 120 or so) except for a couple of news desk guys and a photographer. But didn't include me.

They wouldn't let me stay up North, and they wouldn't make me redundant and give me a pay-off like the others.

The Editor in London, Richard Stott, insisted, "You've got no choice. There's a job for you back here. Count yourself lucky. You should never have gone back to bloody Manchester in the first place."

Of, course I'd now sold my house in London, bought a new house, with my wife, in the North – in Disley, a nice part of Cheshire. But the office said: "Maxwell is offering you a flat in London. It's free, gratis and for nothing. You can have it for six months, until you find another house."

I had no choice. I went back to London, settled for being called Chief Show Business Writer, and moved into one of Maxwell's furnished flats in the heart of London, in fashionable Bloomsbury, only a ten-minute walk from the head office.

And that's another story. I happened to be in hospital, the first time I'd ever been off or in hospital in my life. I was in for three days. I even agreed to work from my hospital bed and I was writing the nightly TV crits. When I got a phone call from the office manager, saying, "I'm sorry to hear you are in hospital, Ken. But I've got bad news for you from Mr. Maxwell. Your six months in the flat are up. You've got to be out by next Monday."

Well, my wife didn't want to move back to London. Neither did I, really. I had to then buy a cheap house, a two-bed maisonette in Harrow. And I worked through the week in London and travelled home at weekends to Disley. I did that for two years, driving down to London on Sunday nights, and back North on Fridays.

It began to take its toll. I suddenly asked myself if I really wanted to do this for the next ten years. The answer was No.

So, I quit the Mirror. I asked if I could be made redundant. They said No. They thought I was bluffing, that I wanted more money. I told them I'd decided to go. I worked my three months' notice. And I left, after 31 years, and decided to set up on my own as a freelance, operating in the North.

My colleagues couldn't believe I was serious about leaving. I'd been there so long I was almost part of the office fabric. Some of them thought I was brave to give up a secure job, top money, good expenses, an office car if I wanted one, to go freelancing at the age of 54. But it was a gamble. Others thought I was quite mad.

Fortunately, it worked out okay for me. Because of my reputation in Fleet Street and on the Mirror, I had lots of showbiz contacts, and I got more work than I could handle - writing for all the National daily and Sunday papers, a lot of magazines, women's magazines, showbiz papers. And I managed to make a comfortable living. In fact, in my first year as a freelance, I trebled my earnings.

After about six years, however, I decided enough was enough. I didn't want to do it anymore. So, I retired early. I never did want to work until I was 65, anyway.

I couldn't complain about the Mirror. They'd treated me well over 31 years. And in return, I've had a career which I suppose would have been the envy of many young journalists today.

I was with the Mirror in its heyday. When it was a real, vibrant newspaper, selling more than five million copies a day, the biggest circulation in the world. When journalism was exciting and full of fun. It isn't today. It's now all computerised and pretty boring.

Looking back, I've no real regrets. I've done it all, really. And I've had a ball, as they say.

I've been arrested and locked up in jail with Derek Nimmo in the Vatican in Rome. I've played golf with the first man to play golf on the moon, Alan Shepard, and with people like Sean Connery, Jimmy Tarbuck and Burt Lancaster. I've been involved in one of the biggest libel trials, which went on for five days in the High Court - all for calling Ken Barlow boring. And I'm in the Guinness Book of Records as the TV Critic who said that Coronation Street wouldn't last - and it has now been running for well over 50 years.

I've met several members of the Royal family and become friends with so many stars and international names like Bing Crosby, Perry Como, Joan Collins, Eartha Kitt and Shirley McLaine. I was once banned from a TV studio by Ken Dodd - because I dared to criticise one of his shows. I was thrown out of his dressing room by Bruce Forsyth because he didn't like my line of questioning. And I've been out "busking" with the Goons, Peter Sellers, Harry Secombe and Spike Milligan in Oxford Street - just for an afternoon giggle.

But it's all been great fun. And I wouldn't change a thing. Well, not much, anyway.

THAT'S   SHOWBUSINESS!

CHAPTER 1: THE BEATLES

It was my wife Betty who first spotted the Beatles. I can't claim to have discovered the four lads from Liverpool, but I was the first to write about them in a national paper, and I gave them most of their early publicity.

But it was my wife, who knows nothing at all about pop music, who drew my attention to them and helped put them on the map, and make them into worldwide stars. I'd never heard of them, but she said to me one night, "You should see these four Liverpool lads in a pop group. They've been on Granada TV in an afternoon show. They've got funny haircuts with fringes."

So, I made a few enquiries. I was then the Northern TV critic with the Mirror. I discovered they'd been booked to appear on a programme called Scene at 6:30, having been spotted by TV producer Johnny Hamp.

They were also doing some shows for BBC radio in Manchester, so I went down to the BBC studios to see them. And my first encounter with them was quite funny.

When the producer took me up to interview them, we went upstairs into the gallery, and there were these four mop-haired lads. One was sitting down on the front row, another was six or seven seats behind, and two of them were spaced out on the back row, and they each had a girl with them, sort of snogging.

The producer said, "Come on, boys, I'd like you to meet Ken Irwin from the Daily Mirror. He wants to write a piece about you."

They all rather sheepishly put the girls down and gathered together in front of me. They weren't easy to interview because whatever questions I asked them, they tried to score points off each other with their answers. It was John Lennon and Paul McCartney who did most of the talking.

After I'd written that first piece on them, I followed up by going to Liverpool to meet their manager Brian Epstein, at his family's record shop in Whitechapel.

He was delighted that a paper like the Daily Mirror was taking an interest, and he couldn't stop talking about them. After we had run a big feature, Epstein became quite close. He had several other groups on his books, and it wasn't long before the Beatles suddenly exploded.

As we all know now, the whole pop scene in Liverpool took off in the early 60s, and because of our friendship Epstein gave me lots of stuff on his other groups. He wasted no time in ringing me up regularly with news stories about them.

At one time, Epstein had three of his groups in the Top Ten, the Beatles, Billy J. Kramer, and Gerry and the Pacemakers. And he suggested I should do a feature on all three of them. I asked him to get the three groups together for me for one big picture. But this took some time to organise because the groups were busy playing at different gigs all over the country.

Finally, he rang me up and said, "I've got them for next Thursday. All three groups will be at my house in Queen's Drive. Can you come and bring a photographer at, say, 11am?" I quickly agreed.

It was a memorable occasion - for the following reason. The night before I was due over in Liverpool, I was driving home from the office at night, about 10.30pm, it was raining heavily, I was probably driving too fast, and a car pulled out of a side road in front of me. I braked, skidded all over the road, and crashed my car. I ploughed through three or four parked cars, just opposite Belle View stadium in Manchester. My car was a write-off and I ended up in hospital.

Fortunately, I wasn't badly hurt. But I had a knee injury and couldn't walk properly. I discharged myself from the hospital and insisted on going home by taxi.

Next morning, I felt dreadful. But I just couldn't miss doing this job I'd lined up with Epstein. I had no car, so I phoned the Mirror photographer Johnny Walker, who picked me up at home and we drove to Liverpool.

I can remember, as we walked into Epstein's house in Queen's Drive, Childwall, all the pop lads were there. And as I hobbled in, my knee giving me excruciating pain, Ringo Starr said, "Oh, look at him. It's bloody Hopalong Cassidy."

Anyway, we took all three groups down the road to the Childwall Fiveways pub, only about 100 yards away and I lined them up, sitting on the wall, with Brian Epstein standing above them with his arms out wide. It made a super picture. And that week, I think, the Beatles, Billy J. Kramer and Gerry and the Pacemakers were 1, 2, and 3 in the singles pop charts, so we had a great piece and we carried this picture very big in the Mirror, with my story.

It became quite a classic photograph, which was later flogged around the world. It was the very first picture of the three top groups together.

I did lots of other pieces on them after that. And of course, the Beatles went on to become the greatest pop music group in history, as we all know.

Because of all that early publicity I gave them in the Mirror, Epstein became very friendly. He would often phone me up with exclusive news stories, as his pop empire grew into a global phenomenon.

In the early days, however, before Beatlemania really broke out, a friend of mine, Derek Taylor, asked me over a pint in the pub if I would introduce him to Brian Epstein.

Derek was then working for the Daily Express in Manchester, as their Northern show business correspondent. We were supposed to be deadly rivals, because the Mirror and the Express were always fighting each other for top circulation. But we were great mates because we had worked together in Birkenhead, Derek on the Advertiser and me on the Birkenhead News, both doing courts and councils together, as young reporters.

I took Derek over to Liverpool to meet Epstein, and he interviewed him and did a piece for the Express. The way things worked out, about six months later, Derek phoned me and said Brian Epstein had offered him a job as Press Officer to the Beatles. He had decided to leave the Express because Epstein was paying him £70 a week and that sort of money was too good to turn down.

At the time, I can remember feeling a bit peeved, because I had known Epstein much longer, and done a lot of stories with him, but he had never offered me such a plum job in his rapidly developing empire (Whether I would have taken it or not is another matter).

But ironically, as Derek told me some years later, Epstein had given him the job because he thought Derek (who was tall, very handsome and clean-cut) was queer - or gay, as we would say today.

Epstein couldn't have been more wrong about Derek, who was actually married with four kids. But although Derek stayed on and worked with the Beatles for some years, Epstein never quite forgave him for not being homosexual. And at one time he banned Derek from taking his wife Joan to any of the social functions, telling him he was there for work, not pleasure.

Derek and I used to laugh about it in later years, when he would recall some of the outrageous things he and the Beatles got up to when they were on the road on their worldwide travels.

Much as he loved his job, Derek unfortunately got into drugs and all that goes with it in the world of rock music. I recall him once telling me that it was part of his job, after every concert the Beatles did, to have to go out, to face the mob of screaming, hysterical girls outside, and then pick four of the best-looking girls and take them backstage to meet the Beatles, one for each of them. And sometimes, he confessed, he might even select five, to keep himself happy.

My friendship and association with Epstein came to an abrupt end, however. It was John Lennon's 21st birthday and they had a party for him at the Cavern Club in Liverpool. I was at home, watching TV and about to phone over my TV crit for the night, when the telephone rang. It was Brian Epstein. He told me that he suspected the Mirror had got hold of a story that John Lennon had been involved in a fight and had slugged the doorman at the Cavern.

He begged me to get the Mirror not to use the story. It had leaked out to our Mirror news man based in Liverpool. But Epstein said to me, "If you can get the Editor to drop this story, Ken, I'll be your friend for life. You'll get all the big stories on the Beatles. I promise you we'll always deal with the Mirror first on everything." He was desperately pleading with me.

"Look, I can't promise to drop a story like that," I told him. "But I will talk to the Editor and see what I can do."

He thanked me and said, "I'll wait for your call." I then phoned my Northern Editor, Bernard Shrimsley, and asked him if we had a story on John Lennon. He said, "Yes, it's going on Page 1 tomorrow. Lennon got drunk, turned nasty, and started punching the doorman, who was an old friend of his at the Cavern. There's no way we can drop it, Ken. We've got it exclusively. Give me Epstein's number, I'll phone him."

So, I gave him Brian's home number. Next day, the Mirror carried the story: "Lennon in Birthday Punch-up" all over the front page. And I never heard another word from Brian Epstein from that day till the day he died.

In my dealings with the Beatles, Paul McCartney was always nice and chatty and the most approachable. Ringo was thick, George Harrison was quiet, and it was John Lennon who liked to take over and do all the talking if you'd let him.

My final PS...I was in New York once, doing some interviews, and I thought wouldn't it be great if I could get an interview with John Lennon. He had become a recluse and wouldn't talk to the Press at all.

So I took a taxi to his apartment block, just off Central Park. I went in through the front door, and the caretaker stopped me. I said I wanted to see John Lennon and showed him my credentials.

It happened to be a Bank Holiday. The caretaker was very nice, but said that Mr. Lennon was away for a few days. I decided to leave a note, saying something like: "Hello, John, remember me? I'm in New York, staying at such a hotel, I'm only here until Thursday. I'd love to get together for a chat, either on or off the record. Just for old time's sake, as fellow Scousers." I left him with my hotel number.

Of course, he didn't phone. I left New York and came home. That was it. It would have been a nice scoop if I could have pulled it off, but I thought no more about it.

Six months later, the news broke… John Lennon had been shot dead outside his apartment block.

It was terribly sad, of course. I spent the whole day in the office, editing and co-ordinating an eight-page Special which the Mirror did on him, with reports and tributes coming in from all over the world.

CHAPTER 2: CORONATION STREET

When I wrote that very first TV crit on Coronation Street in the Daily Mirror - in December 1960 - I was a very young critic. But I can't make that an excuse. For those who can remember the first few episodes of Coronation Street, they were pretty awful. At least, I thought so.

Here's what I wrote: "Young scriptwriter Tony Warren claims to have spent a couple of months going around meeting the ordinary people of the North before he wrote the first episodes of Granada's serial Coronation Street. Frankly, I can't believe it. If he did, he certainly spent his time with the wrong folk. For there is little reality in his new serial, which, apparently, we will have to suffer twice a week. The programme is doomed from the outset - with its dreary signature tune and grim scene of a row of terraced houses and smoking chimneys."

It has since gone down in the Guinness Book of Records. And it's now one of those questions which comes up quite regularly on various quiz shows: Who was the critic who said Coronation Street would never last?

Pat Phoenix, who played Elsie Tanner, used to laugh about it. Every year, for quite a few years, she'd send me a card at the Mirror on the anniversary of the programme, saying, "Remember that crit, Ken? Well, we're still here!"

It grew into quite a joke. But over the years I became quite friendly with most of the Street cast. Dear old Violet Carson, who played Ena Sharples, was one I got on extremely well with. She invited me over to her house in Blackpool a few times. She didn't like doing interviews or talking to the Press, but she was always happy to meet with me.

And people like Liz Dawn, Bill Tarmey, Julie Goodyear in the early years, and Lynne Perry, they were all very friendly. But my favourite character was Jean Alexander, who played the wonderful Hilda Ogden. She was always very approachable. Very genuine. Never very starry.

After she left The Street, I was invited over to her house a few times, and she was happy to do interviews with me, for various magazines and on location for Last of the Summer Wine, which I know she loved doing.

Jean was one of the few who wasn't actually playing herself. Hilda Ogden was very different from Jean Alexander.

I also became very friendly with Pat Phoenix. And she taught me a lesson quite early on. Coronation Street had been running for about three or four years, and Pat was its biggest star. She phoned me up one day and said, "I'm thinking of quitting when my contract ends in a few months' time. I want to go into films." I told her I wanted to run the story, and she said it would be okay.

So we did. Next day, we ran a big news story in the Mirror: "Pat Phoenix wants to quit as Elsie Tanner. I want to go into films, she says."

Other papers followed it up. It was all denied by Granada TV, of course. But about a month later, I got a phone call from Pat, saying "Thanks, Ken. You did me a big favour. My contract was coming up for renewal and when they saw your story in the Mirror, Sidney Bernstein (the head of Granada) doubled my salary and extended my contract." She then had the best contract of the whole cast, because they didn't want to lose her. "Thanks," she said, "I owe you a lunch some time."

That taught me a lesson I wasn't to forget. How the stars can use us, the media, when they want to!

After she left, we met up many times, and I did stories and features on her various activities. But I remember Pat and Tony Booth touring in a stage play, and we got together for a lunch in Manchester. They were both very Left wing Socialists. And Pat told me, "You want to watch out for Tony Blair. the MP."

I'd never heard of him. But she said, "Tony Blair is my Tony's son-in-law. He's a rising star in the Labour party. He's going to be very big in the government. Don't be surprised if he isn't Prime Minister one day."

We laughed about it, over coffee. I didn't know just how serious they both were. But I took it all with a pinch of salt. Perhaps I should have listened to them. But I wonder if Pat would still be so proud of him today?

Old Jack Howarth, who played the grumpy Albert Tatlock, managed to die while I was away on holiday in Cornwall. We'd rented a cottage for a week in Rock, which didn't have a telephone. When I heard the news on the radio, I phoned the office from a local call box. And then I had to scribble away and write Jack's obituary, off the top of my head, and phone it over.

That's the trouble with being a Specialist in newspapers - you are never really off duty. At least, not when I was working. The office would ring night and day, whether you were on holiday or not. And that's something you had to learn to live with.

After that initial "clanger", if you like, in dismissing Coronation Street, it was obvious the programme was here to stay - for some years anyway. Although if anyone had dared to suggest that it would still be going, and on our TV screens in 50 years, they would have sent for the men in white coats to take them away!

However, I wrote all the early stories on The Street. Being based in Manchester, I made friends with some of the cast. And when the programme was coming up to its tenth birthday, I decided to write a book.

This covered the first ten years of the programme, how the show had started, and included all the hirings and firings, how many actors had come and gone. I insisted it should be a paperback, because it would sell better than a hardback. I took the idea of the book to the Mirror's own publishing company, but I was staggered when they turned it down because they said they couldn't guarantee enough sales in Canada and Australia to justify the costs of its publication.

I then managed to get myself a literary agent. It was Roger Hancock, the brother of Tony Hancock, Britain's top comedian. He found me a publisher, Corgi Books, and the book, which I titled The REAL Coronation Street, was planned to come out in December 1970, the tenth anniversary of the programme.

The publishers tried to keep it on the secret list, and I didn't tell anyone I was writing it. I wanted to do the real story, not a TV company PR job.

Unfortunately, the news leaked out, and Sidney Bernstein, the big boss at Granada TV, wanted to take legal action to try and stop the book coming out because he wanted full approval beforehand. I was determined not to give in. He was finally advised that if he did take legal action, he would only be giving us more publicity for the book.

The book came out. I sold the serial rights to TV Times and Corgi threw a massive launch party, at my suggestion, in Fleet Street, to which we invited not the current Coronation Street cast, but all the prominent actors who had left or been killed off over the previous ten years.

There was a story in almost every national paper and a big picture: "The Ghosts of Coronation Street!"

Everyone I had invited came. I even managed to get Arthur Lowe (who played the cantankerous Leonard Swindley) and he normally hated publicity. But he turned up. We got tremendous publicity. The book sold out within ten days and went into a second print.

And shortly after that, they published it in Holland as a new book. So, I've got a book which really is pure double Dutch!

This gave me an appetite to write more books. I wrote another book on The Comedians (which was another Granada show, but this time they were happy to give me permission, and in fact they invited me to write it).

16

Over the years, because of my close association with Coronation Street, and because of all the stories I wrote on the programme, I suppose I earned the reputation of having the best contacts on The Street.

And of course, because of that initial awful TV crit, I could never really get away from the programme. So rather than try to hide it, I decided to always laugh about it. And I suppose I have cashed in on it instead.

I remember, when the programme was 25 years old, the editor of the Mirror made me write a big double-page centre spread. The headline was: "Okay, so I was wrong!" with flashback pictures and an article pleading my defence.

And long after I'd left the Mirror, I was still being approached by other papers and magazines to write about the programme.

When I left the Mirror in 1990, I set up as a freelance. And when Coronation Street was then coming up to its 30th birthday, I got an approach not from the Mirror but from The Sun. Would I write a series of articles for them? I suggested, as it was 30 years old, why not a series of 30 articles? No one had ever written such a lengthy newspaper series before. But I was convinced I had enough material to do it.

I was called in to meet the Editor of The Sun, the legendary Kelvin McKenzie, the man who made The Sun such a success (whether you liked it or not, it was now the best-selling paper in Britain).

We negotiated a fee. I suggested an enormous fee. Kelvin halved it. And I agreed. I must admit it was the biggest fee I'd ever received for anything in my life. But then, there was a lot of work involved. Even McKenzie was staggered by the thought of 30 articles, but we both knew we were on to a winner.

It took me a few months to write it. The Sun ran the series to coincide with The Street's 30th birthday. They took out massive TV advertising, and splashed it all over their front pages.

Now, first, let me explain that everything I wrote in that series of articles was true and accurate. I have been in the game a long time. I know the laws of libel. I know just how far you can go in print. I also know that you cannot commit libel if what you write is the truth. And I was never, ever into making up stories, anyway.

Everything I wrote in those articles was true, based on what I had been told by others, and what these actors had actually told me themselves over the years I'd been dealing with them.

Unfortunately, when it came to the feature on Bill Roache (still better known as Ken Barlow, even after 50 years) I'd not only labelled him Boring, but The Sun put a very damning headline on the piece. This read: "Hated by his colleagues."

They also managed, much to my annoyance, to re-write one or two little things and twisted around some words in the piece I'd written.

The result was that Bill Roache decided to sue for libel. He sued The Sun, the editor Kelvin McKenzie, and me as the author. It took a year to get the case to court - in October 1991.

There's a lot I could say about that case, but it would take too long. But I spent five days in the High Court, in the notorious Court 13 in front of Chief Justice Waterhouse, and it became one of the biggest libel trials in show business history, I suppose.

The Sun insisted that we defend the libel action. They even had the Queen's lawyers, Farrar and Company, on our side. Roache turned up in court on the first day, with half a dozen members of the cast of Coronation Street in tow. They included Johnny Briggs (Mike Baldwin), Bill Waddington (Percy Sugden), Michael Le Velle (Kevin Webster), Betty Driver (Betty Turpin) and Amanda Barrie (Alma Sedgewick). Plus a producer or two.

They were all there to give him a good character reference and say what a lovely chap he was. They not only stopped the traffic outside the court, they got all the headlines. I think the trial was covered not only by every paper, but on BBC, ITV, and Sky who covered it worldwide.

It was hard to take in. I couldn't believe it when I had to face the TV cameras and the hoard of Pressmen. We were on the TV news every night. And I must confess what really hit me hardest was when a newspaper reporter (I think it was the Daily Mail) came to me in court on the first day and asked, "Is it true your house is on the line? If you lose this case, do you lose your house?"

That wasn't actually true. The Sun had agreed to pay all the costs and expenses, win or lose. I think they realised it was their mistake (that damning headline), and they were responsible for all of this, not me. But it was a frightening experience. I had to go into the witness box and face a dreadful interrogation by Roach's lawyers.

Of course, there was no way I could produce many of the witnesses I wanted. Most of the information had come from actors and scriptwriters who still worked for Granada on Coronation Street, and they couldn't risk losing their jobs. Nor would I have expected them to.

Privately though I did have the backing of some of The Street actors. I remember Lynne Perrie (who played Ivy Tilsley) coming on the phone to me and actually thanking me for the article I'd written on her in the same

Sun series. And saying that everything she'd read in the series had been accurate.

It was awfully lonely, sitting in that court for five days. Only a few yards away from Roache and his dreadful wife Sarah, who turned up in a different expensive designer label outfit every day. One of the papers, the Daily Telegraph I think, ran pictures of her in all her different outfits and called her Mrs. Jaeger!

In the end, when the jury came in with their verdict, they announced for Roache. His face lit up. Then they declared the damages: £50,000. You should have seen Roache's face change. His wife immediately went into tears. Because they both realised they had lost.

The Sun had already offered £50,000 before the case, to settle it. But Roache had refused. And because The Sun had already put that sum of £50,000 into court, it meant that Roache had to pay not only his own costs but The Sun's costs as well.

All hell broke loose outside the court. Roache appealed. And a year later his appeal was heard. The judge turned it down, found for The Sun this time, and the judge actually went on record and told Roache he was "a greedy man" and didn't deserve to win any more money.

He then, for some strange reason, decided to sue his own solicitor, Peter Carter-Ruck, claiming that he'd been wrongfully advised about going to court in the first place. And he lost that case as well, and had to fork out more, hefty legal costs.

He was declared bankrupt in 1999. And some years later he admitted that he regretted taking The Sun to court. "It was my ego speaking," he said.

The ironic thing to come out of all this was, about a year later, when Roache was pleading poverty and said that the legal action had ruined him, he dreamed up the idea of a board game, which he called Libel. And he actually marketed this as a Christmas game, with great publicity. It didn't really take off, though, and was never a viable commercial proposition.

Roache wrote his autobiography in a paperback, in 1993. He called it Ken And Me. In it, he had a go at me. His vicious attack on me went over several pages and he said some outrageous things, some blatant lies which if I'd wanted to, I could certainly have sued him for libel. But I'd decided that one appearance in court for libel in life was enough for me!

Then, as though one autobiography wasn't enough, Roache churned out another boring book in 2007, this time in hardback, which he called Soul On The Street. It was even more tedious than the first one and was full of pompous nonsense with Roache supposed to be looking into his own soul and fathoming out the meaning of life. It really was a yawn-stretcher.

He did, however, recall one true incident which, even now when I think about it, still makes me smile. It was on the first day he went to see his solicitor, Peter Carter-Ruck, then the UK's leading libel lawyer.

Roache wrote in his book: "I went to meet him at his offices in Holborn and an extraordinary thing happened on my way back to Manchester. I was taking the train from Euston, but when I got there the train was in but the gates leading down to the platform were closed, so I joined the queue. I was reading a newspaper when I heard someone come up behind me and say 'Hello.' It was Ken Irwin. I couldn't believe it.

"Was this strange meeting the universe throwing me a last chance to take a magnanimous view and shrug it off? If so, I didn't take it.

"I said, 'I was absolutely horrified by that article you wrote.' He said, 'What article?'

"You know full well what article. I think it's the worst thing that's ever been written about me and I'm taking action."

It was an amazing coincidence, I must admit. Not just that Roache and I should both, quite separately, be in London on the same day. But that we should meet, at the railway barrier at Euston, going for the same train back to Manchester. And on the very day he had been to his lawyers to start proceedings to sue me.

As it was, we then spent a very awkward five minutes or so, standing next to each other, waiting to get on the train. I tried to make idle conversation with him by saying something like, "I see Granada's shares have gone down today." But he was having none of it. He turned his back on me and ignored me. I was so relieved when we eventually moved forward and got onto the train, and we were in different carriages.

CHAPTER 3: KEN DODD

I've known Ken Dodd for more than fifty years. I first started interviewing him when he was an up-and-coming comedian in Liverpool and I was on the local paper, the Evening Express as a young reporter.

In fact, he once even invited me to his home to interview him, and I think I am probably the only journalist ever to have seen the inside of his house, for Ken was always a very private person.

It was when he was still living with his parents in the house they had occupied for years, in Thomas Lane, Knotty Ash, a not too smart suburb of Liverpool. His father, and later his brother, ran a coal merchant business from home. It was an odd sort of house. Nothing special to look at from the outside. But when inside, I found it very antiquated. I recall that the living room was decorated in old-fashioned, flowery wallpaper, which even then was out-dated.

But Ken has lived there all his life, long after his parents died. And despite his success and the fortune he must have made, he has never moved away from his beloved Knott Ash, and as far as I know he still lives there. Though it is a very unpretentious address for a big showbiz star. It could be that he is not interested in all the rich trappings usually associated with show business people. Or it could simply be that he is keen to hang on to his money, because he has certainly acquired a reputation for being rather mean.

However, I'm a great admirer of his and we've always got on well. Until one day, when I upset him with a TV crit I wrote. I was then the Northern TV critic with the Mirror, and Doddy was doing his own series for ITV.

Sitting quietly watching the TV rehearsals, as I often did at ABC's studios in Manchester, because they were a friendly bunch and they all knew me, I had Diddy David Hamilton sitting next to me. We were both chortling away at Doddy's rehearsal.

Suddenly, there was a message over the loudspeaker tannoy: "Will Mr. Ken Irwin please report to Reception. There's a phone call for you."

Well, Doddy heard this and stopped rehearsals immediately. He then looked up, saw me sitting halfway up the gallery, and marched up the stairs and confronted me,

"What do you think you're doing here?" he demanded.

"I'm watching you," I said.

"Well, get out, I'm not doing the show while you are here," he screamed. I thought he was joking. So I laughed. But I then quickly realised that he was very serious.

"Go on, get out," he shouted. I was so shocked that I stood my ground. I sat there, and said rather defiantly, "You can't throw me out. The floor manager is in charge of the studio. Only he can throw me out."

He marched down the stairs and started having a conference on the studio floor. David Hamilton asked me what it was all about. "I don't know," I said. "But keep talking to me" - because I was shaking like a leaf, and by now I was the attention of the whole studio.

Eventually the floor manager, Geoff, who I knew very well, came up and told me Doddy was refusing to do the show unless I left.

"Are you throwing me out, then?" I asked. Geoff said, "No, don't be silly."

"Then I'm not moving," I said. "Only you have the power to throw me out, and I've been invited here by your Press Office. So I'm not going."

This went on for about 20 minutes. The producer was sent for, and eventually the Head of Light Entertainment Philip Jones, who was quite a good friend of mine, came out of his office and pleaded with me, "Please, Ken, I don't know what all this is about. But Doddy won't do the show until you leave. We are already more than an hour behind schedule in rehearsals, and a studio audience is expected in here in an hour. I promise you I'll sort this out. Come and have a drink in my office."

Reluctantly, I agreed to go. Philip and I and Press Officer Mal Griffiths all went for a drink in the pub across the road. Doddy then resumed with the rehearsals.

I didn't go back to see the finished show. I went home instead. But I got a phone call next day from Philip Jones, telling me that what sparked it off was that when Ken Dodd was doing his last TV series, from Blackpool for the BBC, I had written a TV criticism in the Mirror which he did not like. I'd said something about him not being as funny on TV as he was in the theatre. And apparently just hearing my name over the studio tannoy system had struck a nerve.

Then I received a telegram from Philip Jones, by way of an apology. A jokey message saying: "We want to form the Ken Irwin Fan Club - and Ken Dodd wants to be the president."

Annoyed though I was at the time, I laughed it off. But the result was that I didn't speak to Doddy for three or four years. He ignored me and I ignored him.

It was rather funny really, because after I'd moved down to London with the Mirror, I was covering a TV Awards ceremony, and I went to the foyer to make a phone call, and there was Doddy, making a phone call at the next telephone cubicle. He looked at me, and said "Hello, Ken." I said, "Hello, Ken". And that was that. We had more or less called a truce.

Nothing more happened until a couple of years later and I got a phone call from the Press Office of ATV, telling me that they had just signed up Ken Dodd, having lured him away from the BBC, and he was being launched in a big new series for ITV. Would I like to be the first to interview him?

Mildly amused, I told the Press Officer the background, and said, "Look, I think you'd better ask Ken if he wants to do an interview with the Mirror and maybe he'd prefer someone else, not me, because of our past 'feud'.

She came back on and said, No, Ken laughed when she'd reminded him of our altercation, and said he would love to do an interview with me.

So we fixed a time and date. I was to meet him at the Adelphi Hotel in Liverpool at 7pm. I went up by train from London, and I even arranged to stay overnight at my mother's house after I'd done the interview.

Duly, I turned up at the Adelphi at 6 pm (I always like to be early, rather than late). I had a lager in the bar and waited for Doddy to arrive. At 7 o'clock, no Doddy. 7.30. 8 o'clock, no Mr. Dodd. So I phoned his home, and his father answered and said, "Ken has gone over to Birkenhead." I said, "Well, he's supposed to be meeting me at 7 o'clock. I'm at the Adelphi now." He said, "Oh, Ken's been on the phone and said he was running a bit late. I'm sure he'll be with you as soon as possible."

So I waited. 8.30 ticked by. I was now getting anxious, so I phoned his home again. His father said, "He's on his way. He's been on the phone and said he'll definitely be there by 9 o'clock."

Well, 9 o'clock came. Then 9.30. At ten o'clock I'd had enough. I can understand people being inadvertently late for an appointment. But I went to the doorman of the Adelphi and said, "Do you know Ken Dodd?" He said, of course. I said, "Well, let's synchronise watches. It's now 10 o'clock, and I'm leaving. If Mr. Dodd arrives, will you tell him I've been waiting for him for four hours, and I'm now going home." I gave him my card, and I walked out, took a taxi and stayed overnight at my mother's place.

Early next morning, I received a phone call from my boss Clifford Davis, in London, saying, "What happened last night? Ken Dodd has been on to the Editor, complaining that he turned up for an interview at the Adelphi Hotel and you weren't there." I couldn't believe it. I was furious. I phoned

Doddy at his home. This time he answered the phone. I said, "What's this about phoning my Editor to complain I wasn't there? I waited four hours - from 6 pm until 10 o'clock, and you didn't show up."

He said, "I got there about 10.15." Then he added, "Where you carrying a brown leather bag?" I said Yes. He said, "I saw someone I thought was you walking down Lime Street with a bag."

"Well, why didn't you say something? I asked. "To be honest, you had a face like thunder, and I didn't fancy tackling you," he said.

"Well, I wasn't too happy," I said. "But why did you phone up my editor this morning and tell him I hadn't turned up?" He said, "Well, when I got to the Adelphi, you weren't there, where you? And I didn't know how to get in touch with you."

Anyway, I said, "Well, do you still want to do this interview?" He said he did. "Why don't we meet at the Adelphi at 4 o'clock today?" he offered. I said, "Right, you're on. But I warn you now, Ken, I'll wait up to half an hour, and if you're not there then, I'm on the next train back to London."

It worked. He turned up, this time only 15 minutes late. We did the interview over tea and sandwiches, and I got a good feature out of him.

But I happened to be talking to Doddy's agent a few weeks later, and told him of the incident. He chuckled and said, "You should know Ken by now. He's not the most punctual of people. You're lucky, anyway. You only had to wait 24 hours to get him. With TV Times, the reporter had to wait a week being messed around!"

I've met Ken many times since. We've made it up now. We became friendly again. The biggest scandal to hit Ken Dodd though was the action taken by Inland Revenue when he was accused of defrauding the tax man. He was alleged to have tried to hide thousands of pounds of his income and not paid tax on it by taking suitcases of cash and investing it in the Isle of Man and other offshore banks.

On the final day of Ken's mammoth trial for Inland Revenue fraud, in July 1989, he was found not guilty of all charges, and there was a round of applause from everyone in the packed public gallery.

Dodd was defended by the great barrister George Carman, who at one time during the three-week trial, quipped, "Some accountants are comedians, but comedians are never accountants."

It was also revealed during the trial that Dodd had very little money in his bank account, but had £336,000 in cash stashed in suitcases in his attic. When the Judge asked him, "What does a hundred thousand pounds in a suitcase feel like?" Ken replied, "The notes are very light, m'Lord."

As the Show Business Editor, I was in the London office at that time, so I was not involved in actually reporting the case in court. We at the Mirror had several pages already prepared on Doddy for the end of the trial. And I had written a background piece on his career, etc.

We actually had a front-page prepared, declaring: "Doddy Jailed   For Fraud." But when the jury came in with a Not Guilty verdict, it really was a matter of "Change the Front Page!"

The Mirror Editor Richard Stott came marching down to my office, after the court result had been announced, and he was red faced with fury. In front of the whole of the News Room staff, he screamed at me, "It's all your bloody fault, Irwin. That's bloody Scousers for you. You all stick together. Only a Liverpool jury could have let Doddy off. Thanks to your lot, we've got to change the front page."

He then tore up the proof of the front page and threw the pieces at me.

"You'd better re-write the front page. And I want it in a hurry," he yelled, and strode angrily back to his office.

Apart from his court case which highlighted the fact that he certainly liked to stash his money away, Doddy had something of a reputation for being careful with his cash - a tight-wad in fact. Although he earned fantastically high sums, he didn't like to part with it.

One story I recall was when he was starring in a series of TV shows produced at ABC in Manchester. Working at the studios was a very nice middle-aged bloke called Frank who was employed as a minor production assistant, but generally referred to as a Gofor. ("Go for this. Go for that").

Usually after recording his show, Doddy would drive back home to Liverpool. One night, he was driving out of the studio car-park (with his girlfriend as his passenger) when he saw Frank standing in the drizzly rain at a nearby bus-stop. He wound down the window and asked him if he wanted a lift. Frank said he lived only a couple of miles away, so Ken said, "Jump in." And off they went.

When they arrived at Frank's road, he was about to get out when Ken said, "Is there a fish and chip shop around here?" Yes, there was, said Frank, just a few miles further down the road. So Ken asked him to stay with them and direct them, and Frank agreed. When they arrived at the chip shop, Ken turned to Frank and said, "I wonder if you'd mind going in and getting us a couple of portions of fish and chips, while we wait in the car? Here, I'll give you the money." He then handed Frank a five-pound note.

Being the nice boke that he was, Frank went into the Chippy and came out ten minutes later with a parcel of chips.

Ken wound the window down, took the wrapped-up supper from him, and said, "Thanks. That's very good of you." Then he said, "Is there any change?" Frank gave him the loose change from the fiver.

"You're a diamond," said Doddy. "Goodnight." And he drove off, leaving Frank further from home than he had been when he was waiting for his bus.

Frank then had to walk home in the rain. But he enjoyed telling the story next day when he was back in the studios.

Another occasion I went to see Doddy was when he was appearing in panto at Stockport. As I was then living only a few miles away, I arranged to go and interview him for a piece for one of the magazines.

As I drove into the theatre car-park, I was suddenly surrounded by a crowd of enthusiastic theatregoers on their way in to see the show. They were waving and shouting at me. But when I parked up and got out of the car, I was greeted by a mass look of disappointment. "Who are you?" said one woman. "We thought you were Ken Dodd."

It suddenly struck me why I was the focus of attention. I was driving my lovely gold-coloured Jaguar with its number plate KEN 11.

Then, just as I was walking away, Doddy drove in to the car-park – in a battered old mud-splattered Volvo (which he later told me had done 150,000 miles!).

Age has caught up with Doddy but he continues to work, even though he's now in his 90s. The thing about Ken is that he loves performing so much that he finds it difficult to stop. His stage shows go on forever. It's usually curtain up at 7.30pm., but it's well after midnight before the curtain comes down, and he waves farewell with his jaunty vocal version of "Happiness, Happiness."

Even Ken jokes to the audience about the length of his shows. "All the doors are locked. You can't get out," he screams. Or, "Hey, are you looking at your watch? A watch is no good to you here - you'll need a calendar. We might finish by next Tuesday."

And when people go to buy advance tickets, it's been known for some box-office staff to warn them, "Bring a blanket. Or even bring a breakfast."

The last time I saw him, live on stage, was when we lived on the banks of the River Mersey at New Brighton, and I took my wife to the local Floral Hall theatre to see him. She had never seen his stage show before, except on TV. I warned her it was going to be a long night.

26

However, we sat through a lot of Doddy, interspersed with other minor supporting acts. And at 10'clock the curtain came down. Betty said, "Right, let's get home." I said "No, it's only the interval. There's the second half of the show still to go." But she'd had enough. "I'll walk home, you stay," she said. But I couldn't let her walk the mile home on her own in the dark. So we left together, and I missed the second half. It didn't really bother me, because I knew most of the jokes and Ken's act anyway. And it hadn't changed much over the years.

He still makes me laugh, though. Only the other day I saw a flashback of him on TV, and he came out with this one: "This woman asked me did I know where an Erogenous Zone was. I said, Well, I know you can't park there until after six o'clock." And his more subtle gag: "Did you know that five out of every three people don't understand fractions?"

I can't leave Ken Dodd without recalling a very funny incident. It involved my good friend John Stevenson, a journalist who had just joined the staff of the Daily Mail in Manchester as their Northern show business correspondent. I was then already established on the Mirror. And one-day John said to me, "I was thinking of going over to see Ken Dodd in pantomime in Liverpool. I've never met him. Do you think he might do an interview with me?"

Not only had he not met Doddy, but John had never been to Liverpool before. (He must have led a sheltered life up in the wilds of Oldham, I thought). I suggested we have a night out together, go and see Dodd, who was playing at the Royal Court Theatre, and also pop in and see Jimmy Tarbuck, who was topping the bill in a rival panto at the Empire Theatre. He thought this a splendid idea. So off we went, in my car.

We sat through the early evening first-house performance at the Empire, and then went backstage to meet Tarbuck, who was in his usual jolly mood. I did the introductions and said to Jimmy, "This is John Stevenson, the new show business reporter with the Daily Mail." Jim shook hands and said, "Oh, you've taken over from that fellow Hilton Tims, have you?" John replied, "Yes. He's moved to London. And I'm the new guy in Manchester." Then Tarby chuckled and quipped, "To be honest, I never really liked him much. Hilton Tims was the kind of bloke who'd piss in anybody's lobby." It was such an odd and spontaneous thing to say that John and I both fell about laughing.

After chatting for a while, we left Jimmy and walked over to the Royal Court, where we presented our Press cards and were shown into Ken Dodd's dressing room.

Doddy was in good form. He made a fuss of us and then asked, "Would you like a drink? I've got some lager here." He then gave us a bottle each, from the fridge, and we sat down to talk. The trouble was, Ken's long-time girlfriend Anita Boutin was also there, and she was obviously suffering from a glass or two too many. Every few minutes, while we were talking, she would interrupt by saying something or other, only for Ken to tell her to shut up.

It became a little embarrassing. And then, quite suddenly, she picked up an empty gin bottle and hurled it at Doddy, followed by some obscenity. He ducked, and the bottle missed his head by a few feet. That's when John and I decided it was time to leave.

We thanked him for the drink, John said he would be in touch with Ken to do an interview, and we quickly departed.

Outside after the show, we were feeling peckish so decided to go and have dinner. It was about 10.30pm and we found a little restaurant on Lime Street, went in and ordered a meal and a bottle of wine.

Everything was fine until things got quite busy and the restaurant quickly filled up. Without so much as a "May we?" we were suddenly joined by two blokes who just staggered in and sat down on the two spare chairs at our table.

John and I looked at each other but said nothing. The two guys then tried to make conversation. They had obviously been drinking and were a little the worse for wear.

However, John and I had ordered steak and chips, and when our meal came, one of our table companions leaned over to John and said cheekily, "Giss a chip." He then tried to help himself to John's chips by grabbing at his plate. John's immediate reaction was to beat him off with his knife and fork. "No. Wait for your own meal," he said. And every time the guy tried to grab a chip, John stabbed him gently with his fork.

Unfortunately, the bloke was determined to cause trouble. "Right, do you want to settle this outside, Four Eyes?" he snarled. John sat there, adjusted his glasses and stared at the bloke, and continued quite calmly with his meal. I was feeling far less secure. I had the horrible feeling that we were going to be followed out when we left and it would all end in a fight.

Never have I been more relieved than when the waitress came over and served our two unwelcome table guests with their meals. At least John's chips were now safe.

As we left and got into my car to drive back to Manchester, John laughed and said, "Bloody hell, Ken, it's been a funny night, hasn't it?"

"Welcome to Liverpool," I said.

CHAPTER 4: DISCOVERIES

JIMMY TARBUCK

It gives you great satisfaction, when you're a showbiz reporter, to actually "discover" someone new. To spot an unknown artist, write about them, and watch them become a "star". It's happened a few times to me.

As I said earlier, I cannot claim to have discovered the Beatles, but spotting them in their early days and giving them all their first national Press publicity gave me a bit of a buzz.

But one person I really can claim to have discovered was Jimmy Tarbuck. I first saw Jimmy when he was doing an audience warm-up for a TV show in Manchester. He was then a club comic around Liverpool. But when I saw him, he was so funny that I wrote a piece in the Northern Mirror about this unknown warm-up comic. The TV producers then booked him to do a show for ABC. And I wrote a bigger piece which went into the Mirror's London edition, in which I raved about him: "The best young comedian in the North," I declared.

Well, this was seen in London by Val Parnell, who was then the head of ATV and the big boss of the London Palladium. On the strength of my piece in the Mirror, Tarbuck was booked for the Palladium the very next week. He couldn't believe it. Neither could I.

I went down to watch him on Sunday Night at the London Palladium. And, of course, he was a sensation. The cocky young kid with the Beatles-style haircut stole the show and made all the headlines next day. And later, when Val Parnell was looking for a new compere to take over the prestigious Palladium show, after Bruce Forsyth and Norman Vaughan, they signed up Tarbuck, and he knew then he was made for life.

Jimmy once told me he'd be forever grateful, and we became quite good friends.

Ten years after he first broke into show business as a teenager, I met up with him again. He was starring in a summer season at Great Yarmouth, had his own ITV series, Tarbuck's Back, and was going to America for guest spots on TV and cabaret in Las Vegas. "I've not changed very much. I'm still the same feller I was when I got my big break at the Palladium, except that I've improved," he told me.

One thing that did upset him was when people called him a big-head. "I'm not," he said. "I'm cocky, yes. That's just me, and I can't change. I'm confident, yes. But conceited? Definitely not."

30

He was driving around in a white Mercedes sports car (licence number COM 1C), had just bought a new £25,000 house near Coombe Hill, Surrey, so that he could be near the golf course, and was waiting to become a dad for the third time.

"I'm a very lucky bloke, I don't need anyone to tell me that," he smiled. "But money is secondary to my enjoyment of work. Honestly, if I didn't enjoy the work, I'd pack it all in tomorrow.

"When I finally kick the bucket, all I'd like people to say about me is 'What a character he was!' And if they add 'And he was always good for a laugh,' well, I'll be more than happy. I'll be dead chuffed."

Well, Tarby has certainly stayed the course and earned a lot of laughs along the way.

MICHAEL BARRYMORE

Another big star I helped discover was Michael Barrymore. It happened like this. The Editor of the Mirror came to me one day and said, "Ken, why don't we find an unknown entertainer who really has got talent, and give him a big boost and promote him to stardom. It would be great if we could do it."

So, I had the task of finding someone. I went on to several showbiz agents and producers. And one PR man, Clifford Elson, an old chum of mine, told me of this guy called Michael Barrymore. He was bottom of the bill at a summer show in Great Yarmouth.

Clifford said he was hilariously funny. His act was seven minutes, standing on his head, telling jokes. It was an act he'd devised whilst working in Australia. Down Under. Upside Down. Get it? Anyway, I was assured he really was a scream. I went to see him. And I was immediately convinced he could be "our man."

Barrymore was only too happy to co-operate. In fact, he jumped at the chance to be a Daily Mirror "discovery." He couldn't believe his luck when I met him and told him what we were going to do.

As the then Show Business Editor, I put one of our writers, Bill Marshall, with Michael and we published a double-page spread, with pictures, raving about this newcomer. We then followed him around, covering every new venue he played. And it wasn't long before Barrymore went from bottom of the bill to the top. He was soon headlining summer season bills in Blackpool, and really shot to the top when he started appearing in guest spots on TV and rapidly landed his own series.

Within a few years, Barrymore became just about the biggest star on TV, because he had what we call the Likeability factor. Everybody liked him. All ages - from kids to grannies. He was Mr. Versatility. His earnings must have made him a multi-millionaire.

Unfortunately, things later went downhill for Michael. His marriage broke up, he came out as being gay, he got into drugs. A lot of scandal and bad publicity led to him being dropped from TV and his career took a dive.

It was all rather sad, because I liked Michael. He had tremendous talent, and he let his whole career slip away from him.

NOEL EDMONDS

Another one I consider I helped to discover was Noel Edmonds. I was the first reporter to meet Noel when he came to London after working on one of the pop pirate ships. An agent got me to interview him. Shortly after, he was signed up by BBC Radio One as a disc-jockey. And it didn't take long before Noel was up alongside the big names.

He went on to become a multi-millionaire and one of the best-known faces on TV, with some of the most popular and innovative shows on the box. He's a nice guy, Noel, and personally I think the BBC were mad to fall out with him and drop him a few years ago.

GLORIA HUNNIFORD

Gloria Hunniford is another one who owes a lot to me. I first met Gloria when she came to the BBC in London to sit in for one week in place of the popular Jimmy Young on his Radio Two show.

She had never worked in England before, although she was quite a big name back in Ireland on the local Belfast radio station and as a singer.

I went along to meet her at the BBC, did an interview with her, and we used it quite big in the Mirror: "The woman taking over from Jimmy Young!"

The BBC then booked her for a second week while Jimmy was still on holiday. And with the publicity she got in the Mirror, she was suddenly a "celebrity". She became an immediate hit with the listeners.

The next thing was I got a phone call from Gloria saying, "Guess what - the BBC have given me a long-term contract."

She then moved to London from Ireland and landed her own radio show, and within a year or so she was a really big-name broadcaster.

Unfortunately, it had its down side. She left her husband, who was a radio producer in Ireland, and ended up divorcing him.

Her daughter, the lovely Caron Keating, then followed her to live in London, and I did a few pieces on them both - "Caron following in Mum Gloria's footsteps!" etc.

When I was having lunch with her once, a few years later, I said to Gloria, "What would have happened if I'd never have written that first piece about you? You'd probably still be happy and living in Ireland."

She laughed and said, "No, Ken, I don't think so. I was always very ambitious. I think I'd have ended up getting divorced, anyway. I don't think I can blame you or Jimmy Young or the BBC for any of that."

LENNY HENRY

Of course, the other discoveries I was involved with was when I became one of the judges on the ITV series New Faces in the 1970s.

I was one of the regular TV judges on some of those shows, which were televised from Birmingham. I used to sit on the panel, on a rota system, alongside such names as Micky Most, Tony Hatch, Jack Parnell, Terry Wogan, Tony Blackburn, and showbiz journalists from one or two other papers.

It was quite nerve-wracking, having to give your opinion on all the acts completely ad-lib. We saw them do a run-through at rehearsals, and then it was the show, live, in front of a studio audience. That programme was one of the top shows, and pulled in 14 million viewers every week.

Some of the "unknowns" discovered from New Faces went on to become huge stars. The first was Marti Caine, and others we discovered included Victoria Wood, Lenny Henry and Jim Davidson.

I became quite good friends with most of them. I particularly admire Victoria Wood. I thought she was tremendously talented.

Lenny Henry was quite a cheeky young kid when he first shot to fame. I can remember going to interview him at his home in Birmingham, and meeting his mum, a big, smiling woman with a tremendously loud laugh.

And as I left, Lenny came to the door to show me out, and as I got into my car, with its private number plate (KEN 11), he yelled, "Oh, you bloody great poseur."

It wasn't long before he had his own TV series and it was obvious he was going to be around for a long time. And it's great to see Lenny has now got into straight acting, and has even conquered Shakespeare. He has done a lot for charity of course, and his work for Comic Relief, in particular, brought him the ultimate Royal reward.

It was terrific when in 2015 he was knighted at Buckingham Palace and became Sir Lenny Henry.

Now I'll bet that big Mum of his, who made tea and sandwiches for me in their little house in Dudley, would have been really proud of her boy.

JIM DAVIDSON

After coming out of New Faces as a winner, Jim Davidson became quite chummy with me. He took me out on his boat for a day once when I went to interview him in Torquay in a summer season. We spent all afternoon on the boat, went off for lunch, and then he went to do his stage show at the theatre in the evening. I was with him as he parked his maroon Rolls Royce outside the theatre and didn't even bother locking it. I pointed this out to him, and Jim said, "Oh, it's not worth it, mate. People do damage to my Rolls all the time. Last week someone scratched all down the side, and it cost me a thousand pounds to get the scratches out. I leave it open now, it saves anyone breaking into it and having to smash the windows." He was slightly mad, Jim.

On another occasion, we had a bit of a fall-out, in Blackpool, when I went to interview him and to see his summer show. He was so blue on stage that I couldn't believe it. Some people were walking out because of the rude jokes and filthy language.

Later, I was invited to the after-show party by his agent. And Jim came up asked me what I thought of his show. I couldn't help it, I said, "A bit over the top, wasn't it, Jim? You can be funny without being so crude or filthy, y'know!"

He stormed off in a huff and complained to his agent. "Ken Irwin's been slagging me off. I'm going to ignore him from now on."

His agent came over and told me. I just said, "If that's the way he wants to play it, too bad." I finished my drink and walked out and went back to my hotel.

But that's Jim. Next time we met, I think he'd forgotten all about it.

CHAPTER 5: BOOKS & SCRIPTS

Over the years, I've dabbled quite a bit outside of journalism. In the early days, in Manchester, I used to do football reports for BBC radio, and was the anchor-man and presenter for a Saturday-afternoon radio sports programme for a short while - until the Northern editor of the Mirror Ted Fennah, called me into his office and told me I'd better decide what I wanted to do: Work for the Mirror, or for the BBC!

So I was more or less forced to give up the broadcasting and the football reporting, which I really enjoyed doing.

Then I tried my hand as a scriptwriter. While still working full-time for the Mirror, I wrote comedy scripts in my spare time and sent them off to various comedians.

Having sent one script off to Michael Bentine, who had a wacky but popular series on TV called The Square World, I was surprised one morning when the phone went at 8 o'clock at home. It was Michael Bentine, saying, "I've got this script of yours. I like it very much. I want to use it in next week's TV show. How much do you want for it?"

A little taken aback, I just hesitated. He said, "I usually pay about £25 a minute. This sketch runs for about three minutes, so I'll give you £75 for it. Okay?"

Yes, of course, I said. He used the sketch I'd written in his next show, and I duly received a cheque from him. That was long before I'd ever met Michael Bentine, and he didn't know who I was.

This encouraged me to try my hand at more scripts. I then wrote a full-length play for radio, which the BBC bought and produced. It was titled A Matter of Policy and it was broadcast in their peak Play of the Week slot.

I would have liked to have written more scripts, but again I had to make the decision of being a newspaperman or turning to scriptwriting. It was difficult finding time to do both. I decided to stick to newspapers.

THE COMEDIANS

When it came to books, when I wrote my first book on Coronation Street, I got myself a literary agent who encouraged me to write more. I did a book called The Comedians, which was based on The Comedians TV series, which was a big hit in the 1970s.

Granada invited me to write it (which was ironic, after the fuss they caused over my book The REAL Coronation, when they tried to stop me publishing without their approval). This meant me interviewing all the comedians separately, which was no problem but a bit of a chore. But it also meant me wading through some 72 hours of TV tapes, to give a sample of jokes, to show their individual styles of humour.

There was a lot of frustration involved, however. Having used some of their best jokes, I had to get permission from the individual comedians to use the jokes in book form. Most of them more or less agreed, with the exception of Ken Goodwin.

Remember him? He was the tall, gangly, daft one from Lancashire with the big, silly smile. Unfortunately, he emerged from The Comedians as the headliner, the best of the bunch. And when The Comedians were all booked to do a long run with a stage show at the London Palladium, it was Goodwin who was chosen as the top of the bill.

Out of the blue, I had a call from Johnny Hamp, the TV producer, saying that Goodwin was going mad at me for using his jokes in the book, and could I sort it out with him.

It seemed Ken wanted to know what the comedians were getting out of this book, and if they were going to get paid. And when Goodwin started playing up, one or two of the others started getting stroppy, too, and asked for money. I then had the awful job of trying to placate them.

First, I took Ken Goodwin to lunch at a nice restaurant in London. I showed him the pages I'd written about him, and he was quite pleased. Then I showed him the jokes we were going to print. He immediately objected, and said, "If these jokes appear in print, bang goes my act."

I said, "I don't agree. You've already admitted to me, in the piece I've written in the book, that you get most of your jokes from The Dandy and Beano comics, anyway."

Yes, that's right, he agreed. "Well, they're not your copyright then, are they? You pinched them from comics like the Beano," I pointed out.

He just sat there and chuckled. We then went through all these jokes I wanted to print. And we agreed, drop that one, I could keep this one. In the end, I lost about half a dozen of what he regarded as his best jokes, which he wanted to keep, and I promised I wouldn't print.

Finally, he agreed to accept my version and approved it all for the book. I ordered him a large brandy to wrap up our meal, and we shook hands on the deal.

There were still a couple of others to sort out, though. So I then went along to the Palladium theatre, and went backstage to confront the others who were moaning and complaining.

I saw Bernard Manning and Frank Carson, and I told them "Look, if any of you don't like it, too bad. I'm committed to doing the book. And if anyone doesn't want to appear in the book, that's fine by me, I'll just drop them. The book will come out, but they won't be part of it!"

Big Bernard said, "Leave this to me." He then marched backstage into the other dressing-rooms, and I heard doors banging, and raised voices.

Five minutes later, he came back. "It's all sorted, Ken. No worry. You'll have no more trouble from any of them"

When I asked him what he'd said to them, Bernard just grinned and said, "I told them that Ken Irwin needs you like he needs a fucking fire in his front parlour. So if you want to be in the book, you'd better shut your gobs. Just enjoy the publicity."

That was it. Sorted. I know Bernard wasn't everyone's cup of tea, but I always got on well with him. Now you know why.

We then sold the serial rights to the Sunday People, who ran excerpts from it for three weeks. The publicity helped promote the book and it was a big seller.

It became the ultimate joke book, and I can remember when I'd finished it and delivered the manuscript to the publishers, going into the BBC TV Centre club in London and saying to my Press Office mates, "Come on, ask me for a joke on any subject you like!" And they did. We were having such a giggle, because my head was still full of those thousands of jokes I'd been editing for some weeks. Then in walked Eric Morecambe and Ernie Wise who had just finished recording one of their TV shows and were having an after-show drink.

Eric heard me, came over and said, "Okay, Ken, how about this one?" They then joined us at our table, and it ended up with an hilarious exchange of jokes between me, Eric and Ernie, and anyone who wanted to join in.

TOP OF THE POPS

After the success of The Comedians book, I was then invited by the BBC to do a book on Top Of The Pops. So I devised and produced what became their Top of the Pops Annual, which I went on to do for about seven years, purely as a freelance, while still working for the Daily Mirror of course.

This meant me interviewing just about every top star who appeared on the show. Everyone from Elton John, Cliff Richard, to 10 cc, The Rolling Stones, the Beatles, Status Quo, Gary Glitter and all the up-and-coming groups, as well as the top American groups like the Jackson Five and The Osmond brothers.

And whenever I was asked who was my favourite pop star I ever interviewed, I think it had to be David Bowie. He had such a charisma about him. When he walked into the studio, everyone was in awe of him. And when I interviewed him for the first time, I was struck by how articulate and intelligent he was. He also had an amazing face, with different coloured eyes. One was bright blue, the other eye was brown. It made his face light up in a most magnetic way. On top of that, I think he was a great performer.

MAX BYGRAVES

Still on the subject of writing books, I once went to interview Max Bygraves, who I knew very well. We were down at his home in Bournemouth and sitting out by the swimming pool, chatting. I happened to say to him, "You've never written your life story, Max. Why?" He said, "I've never bothered. Is there any money in it?"

Yes, I told him, there can be, particularly if you sell the serial rights to a newspaper or magazine - that's where the money is, and it actually helps to sell the book. I told him I'd be happy to "ghost write" the book for him, if he was interested. He said, "Leave it with me. I'll think about it."

About a year later, I got a phone call at my office. It was Max Bygraves. He said, "Hey, Ken, are you busy? I want to discuss that idea of a book with you. Why not come down and have lunch?" I went over to his flat in London. He opened a bottle of wine and put two steaks on the grill, and we sat in the kitchen.

Max said, "Remember you talking to me about writing my life-story as a book?" I said Yes. He then said, "Well, I'd like you to have a look at this. I've been down in Australia for six months, working. And during the day I wrote 2,000 words a day. I've had it all typed out by my secretary. But I wanted your opinion on it before I send it off to a publisher."

I couldn't believe it. He handed me all these typed pages. I flipped through the first few pages, and I had to agree - it was very good.

"Thanks for the idea. I'll send you a copy when it's published," he said. And he did. I was later invited by the publishers to a book launch, and Max signed a copy of his book specially for me. It was titled I Wanna Tell You A Story, and I still have it somewhere at home.

Max came over to me and said, "Hey, Ken, there's more money than I thought in this book-writing lark. We've just sold the serial rights to a woman's magazine, and they've promised me a small fortune."

We laughed about it later. Although I was a bit peeved, I couldn't help but admire him. Max had more or less said, thanks for the idea, but I don't need you. I can write the book myself!

In fact, Max followed this up a few years later with a novel. It was called The Milkman's On His Way. It was pretty trashy, actually, which I couldn't even be bothered to read after the first half dozen pages. But again, he gave me a copy and signed it to me, so I suppose it was a gesture, in a way, that he appreciated my help in getting him started as a writer.

In fact, the next time I went down to see him, at home in Bournemouth, he told me that writing had given him a whole new interest in life. And he jokingly revealed, "I'll let you in on a secret. I am really thrilled because I recently wrote a short story for a women's magazine, sent it in under the pen-name of Mrs. Graves - and it won me an electric typewriter."

And he said, "Thanks to you, I now get a tremendous thrill out of stringing words together. I don't really care whether my books sell - I don't really need the money, anyway."

A canny bloke, Max. He was one of the richest men in show business, pulling in nearly a million pounds a year. And he loved boasting about his wealth and achievements. He showed me around his house, a ten-bedroomed mansion which his wife Blossom had been responsible for renovating. It had a basement billiard room, a gymnasium, a sauna, a bar, and a very big swimming pool set in acres of beautiful gardens. I know a lot of today's stars have now got all these luxury homes. But I'm talking about Max in the mid70s.

"I'm hotter now than I've ever been in my career," he boasted. "I've done 17 Royal Variety Shows and have 23 gold records for the sale of my Singalong albums. I sell more records over a year than Elton John. My last album sold half-a-million. My record company has just released three albums at once - something no one else has ever done."

He was so proud. And I don't suppose you could blame him. He was a cockney kid from Bermondsey, brought up in hard times, and was one of six children. His father was a boxer who fought for 30 shillings a fight, often three or four times a week.

"Dad wanted me to be a fighter. He used to tie my boot laces to my brother's and then make us stand toe to toe and punch the hell out of each other, learning to be proper fighters," he said.

Show business got Max out of poverty. He gave up as a £5-a-week carpenter to sing and do impressions, after being demobbed from the RAF after the war. He then spent years on radio, making a name for himself before making the big time on TV.

"Critics say I'm old-fashioned, but I know what audiences want," he would tell me. "Too many people in show business are happy to take the money and run. Not me. I give full value. Otherwise, I wouldn't have been around so long. I've got to know that an audience is enjoying what I do.

"Young comics tell me they get elated when they hear laughter. I don't have to worry about getting laughs any more. Only when you get silences from audiences need you worry!"

ERIC SYKES

Max wasn't the only big-name I had trouble with when it came to writing books. Well, not so much trouble, as frustration.

The wonderful Eric Sykes was another. When Eric was at the height of his fame, the star of one TV series after another, my literary agent suggested to me that he'd be a great subject for a book. I went along to see him, and Eric agreed he would be happy to work with me, as he had always been too busy to write his autobiography himself.

To tie in with his current TV series, which he was doing with Hattie Jacques, I suggested we have a simple working title of Sykes ...and a Book. The idea was that I was to interview all the people who had worked with Eric over the years, to get their anecdotes about him, and he would then chip in with his replies and come up with some amusing stories. He liked the idea and said we'd do it together.

I had no difficulty in finding a publisher who agreed to commission the book, and they offered quite a handsome up-front payment which they called advanced royalties. I gave all of this to Eric, and immediately started work, interviewing people like Jimmy Edwards, Spike Milligan, Hattie Jacques and others who were happy to talk about him.

After a few months, however, I realised it was not going to be as easy as I'd thought. The trouble was, Eric was always so busy working that he could never find time to work on the book. And I then had the publishers on my back, wanting to know when we could deliver.

In the end, I realised that Eric just wasn't able to meet up with me as often as we'd planned. Reluctantly, I had to tell the publishers that they'd have to wait much longer for the book. And we then mutually agreed to cancel it.

Of course, they wanted their advance payment back, and I had given all of this to Eric. But there was no problem. He immediately sent me a cheque, with his apologies. And I returned it to the publishers.

A very funny man, Eric. Not only a brilliant comedian but also a very fine comedy writer. If I had to single out someone I'd most like to spend an hour with over a pie and a pint, he would be very high on the list.

The funny thing is, many years later, in 2005, Eric did decide to eventually write his autobiography. Ironically, he titled it If I Don't Write It, Nobody Else Will. (He'd obviously forgotten my attempts to prompt him into writing it with me). And he thanked film actor Tom Courtenay for the title.

It was quite a hefty hardback. And I have a copy, which Eric signed, on my bookshelves. It's a terrific read. He dedicated the book to his mother, whom he never knew because she tragically died giving birth to him.

Born in Oldham, Eric had a very sad early life. With his mother dying in childbirth, Eric's elder brother was taken in by relatives, but his father had to give baby Eric away to a neighbour, who took it upon themselves to look after him.

And he recalls in the book that he was farmed out and left under the tender eye of a parrot that lived in a cage above his cot. Two years later, when his father came to collect him, "Neither he nor anyone else could understand what I was babbling about. Hardly surprising, as I'd never learned English, but spoke fluent parrot."

The truth, or an exaggeration, what a wonderful line. And it was so typical of the dry wit which made Sykes such a wonderful raconteur.

MIKE YARWOOD

My last attempt at a book was even more frustrating, however. When I left the Mirror to go freelancing in 1990, a top PR agent came on to me and told me Mike Yarwood had signed a contract with a publisher but needed someone to write the book for him - was I interested? Well, I said Yes, because I had just set up as a freelance, I was flattered to be asked, and it could also be a nice little earner.

Without hesitation, I agreed to do it. I knew Mike Yarwood quite well, though not really closely. I'd interviewed him on and off over the years, and we'd always got on well, so he trusted me.

But he was now living on his own, his marriage had broken up, he'd been divorced, his career had gone down the pan because of his heavy drinking. And he wanted to tell his whole life-story because he was trying to make a showbiz comeback.

When I went down to meet him, we discussed things. And we then set about doing a series of interviews. I spent a lot of time with him. I went over to his flat in Weybridge every day, and spent weeks doing interviews on tape, trying to get all these stories out of him. But it was hard going.

We did this for a few months. And I got more and more worried about it because he kept telling me the same things, over and over, and I knew it wasn't enough. We were still scratching at the surface. Somehow, Mike just wouldn't open up.

Eventually, the publishers were pushing me for the manuscript. And I had to go to Mike's agent and say, "Look, sorry, but this isn't going to work. I'm not getting enough out of Mike."

He was very disappointed, because he'd already been paid part of his fee up front. I'd been working with him for nothing. We'd agreed financial terms after the book was completed. But I'd wanted it to be Mike Yarwood's story, As Told to Ken Irwin, rather than me just being an anonymous silent "ghost writer," simply writing it but not having my name on it.

Anyway, in the end, I told the publishers straight that in my opinion it was not going to make a very interesting book. I certainly didn't want my name on it, anyway.

So, we agreed - that was it. I had spent three or four months, doing interviews, working quite hard, and all for nothing as it turned out.

Mike Yarwood then tried to make his comeback. He made one or two brief TV appearances and introduced the impersonation of Prime Minister John Major into his act. But it didn't work out. Impressionists like Rory Bremner had come along and taken over, and Yarwood was out of date and well past his best.

Mike is a very nice man, but he just didn't have the confidence to get up on stage in front of the cameras and perform any more.

PORRIDGE

I cannot finish this chapter without getting a little grudge out of my system. Well, not so much a grudge as a personal memory which occasionally haunts me.

Going back to the period when I was trying to write comedy scripts in my spare time as a young reporter in Manchester, I teamed up with my good chum John Stevenson, who was then on the Daily Mail and had similar ambitions to break into scriptwriting. He used to come over to my house a couple of mornings a week and we would put our heads together and try to think of funny ideas which could be expanded upon.

Making each other laugh wasn't difficult. But actually writing the scripts was. We hit on various ideas but dismissed them as too trivial. Then one day, we came up with what we thought was a brilliant idea – why not a comedy show set in a prison? It was John's idea, not mine. But I immediately saw the potential in it and we both became very keen to put it down on paper.

To our knowledge, no one had ever produced a sitcom for TV about prison life, and the more we thought about it, the more excited we became.

We quickly devised the plot and set about writing a script. It was to be about two prisoners sharing a cell. One an experienced old lag who'd been in and out of jail all his life, and the other a young, naive first-timer who wasn't really a villain but had been put away in more unfortunate circumstances. The comedy was to come from their new close relationship and their behaviour with other prisoners.

We even cast the characters. We had in our minds two ideal actors for the leading roles – veteran actor Bill Frazer as the old lag, and cockney actor Tony Selby as the innocent but cheeky younger jailbird. Frazer was already well known as the bullying Sgt. Snudge in the popular comedy series The Army Game. But I thought he would be ideal as our belligerent incarcerated anti-hero.

We not only started writing the first script but also devised the plots for six more episodes. Our idea was that one of the crimes our main character was convicted of was bigamy, and the last episode would have him being released – and walking out of jail to find not one but three wives waiting to greet him. He would then have to decide which one to go back to live with.

And then, without letting our ambitions runs away with us, we even planned a new spin-off series as a follow-up. This would have the old bloke living happily with one of the women, but then his young cellmate would come knocking on his door, having been released from prison with nowhere to go, and wanting to be his new lodger.

John and I thought it would be hilarious. And, of course, it would have been. The trouble was we were both busy with our journalistic careers, and in the end we simply didn't have time to continue with our script-writing activities.

I moved to London shortly after, and John stayed with the Mail for a few years before taking the plunge and becoming a full-time scriptwriter. He reckoned it was the best decision he ever made. I think so too, because he went on to become one of the best comedy writers in the country.

A few years later, however, I came across this half-written script which John and I had produced about a prison comedy. I thought it was too good to throw away, so I phoned him, asked his advice, and he suggested that I should finish the script and he would have no objection if I submitted it in my name to any company I thought might be interested.

That's what I did. It took me some weeks, but I completed the script and was quite pleased with the finished product. Now where should I go next? Instead of simply sending it off to the BBC or an ITV company and hoping for the best, I decided to approach a producer I knew at London Weekend TV. He was a well-known guy who had produced some good comedy series. I sent the script to him, complete with ideas for six more episodes, and even the idea for a follow-up series featuring the same characters.

He acknowledged receipt, then had it for a short while, and eventually sent me a very nice letter. It wasn't the usual standard reply, but was quite flattering. He said he thought the idea was a good one, and the writing was also very professional. But he didn't think it was quite right for production and needed more work on it. He was very encouraging, though, and suggested that sometime in the future I should pop in and see him, and he would be happy to discuss this script and any further ideas I might have.

Disappointed but not suicidal, I decided to forget it. I put the script into a drawer somewhere. It wasn't the end of the world. Just one of those things. I suppose I should have followed it up and pursued his invitation to go and discuss things, but I couldn't be bothered.

I never gave it another thought until a year or two later, when the BBC launched a brand-new comedy series. It was called Porridge, starred Ronnie Barker and Richard Beckinsale, and was all about a couple sharing a prison cell and trying to see the funny side of prison life. The sitcom was written by Dick Clement and Ian La Frenais, two well established scriptwriters.

Odd, I thought. That sounds exactly like our idea. I wonder how the BBC came up with it?

It has been said, of course, that there's no such thing as a new idea. Writers have often claimed that they have been ripped off by someone else cashing in on what was their original idea.

How Clement and La Frenais suddenly came up with this wonderful idea for Porridge we shall never know. It's not uncommon for producers to talk about these things over a drink in the studio bar. A script which has been rejected by a producer may well find its way into someone else's basket.

It could well be pure coincidence that La Frenais and Clement came up with the very same idea as the one John Stevenson and I worked on.

What we do know is that Porridge went on to become one of the best and most successful sitcoms in the history of television. Ronnie Barker was superb (and, on reflection, was probably much better than Bill Frazer would have been).

What makes it all the more galling, however, is that the BBC produced 20 episodes of Porridge and it ran from 1974 to 1977. And after it finished, Ronnie Barker and Richard Beckinsale went on to do a follow-up series. Wait for it. All about two convict chums being out of prison and rebuilding their lives together. This was called Going Straight. And it was written by – guess who? - Ian La Frenais and Dick Clement. What another amazing coincidence!

Now I may be cynical in my old age. I'm prepared to believe that one idea for a series being duplicated, could be accidental and unfortunate. But two ideas? Two very different series, with the same characters, and by the same writers? Doesn't that sound a little strange?

No one can ever prove these things of course. Clement and La Frenais both live and work in Hollywood now. Both are respected writers. And no doubt very rich. I've got nothing against them at all.

But I never did meet up again with that producer who sent me that very courteous and flattering letter, "rejecting" my script. I've still got the letter in my files. I have to be very careful about the laws of libel, though.

John and I have discussed it a few times over the passing years. We've laughed about it. And that's all we can do, really.

It's all water under the bridge now. Would we have been happier if we'd sold that first script together? And who wants to live in Hollywood, anyway?

CHAPTER 6: DEREK NIMMO

Derek Nimmo was one of the smartest, wittiest men around. A very funny bloke and very good company. I got to know him quite well over the years.

But I shall never forget what trouble we got into together once - in Rome. I was flying to Italy to cover a TV festival in Verona, in September 1969, and I learned that the BBC were filming scenes for Derek Nimmo's popular TV series Oh, Brother! in which he played a Catholic priest. I arranged with the BBC that it would be okay to interview him while he was on location filming.

I flew to Rome, met Derek and the producer Duncan Wood for lunch, just opposite the Coliseum. It was a very good lunch, and Derek seemed in no hurry to get back to work.

We had arranged after lunch, to take some pictures of him, to go with my article. I didn't have a Mirror photographer with me, but the office had arranged that I should team up with a French freelance photographer who was based in Rome.

He turned up, as agreed, and we went off, Derek, me and the photographer, to take some pictures around the city.

We went to St. Peter's and the photographer quickly got busy taking pictures of Derek, who was dressed as a Monk in a brown cassock and sandals.

All went well at first. Derek was sitting on the steps of St. Peter's, and the photographer was snapping away. There were a couple of English girls who recognised Derek and came over to chat to him. They were in their early twenties, and one was a particularly pretty blonde. Derek started fooling around and picked up this girl in his arms and started swinging her about, purely for picture purposes.

What happened next was completely unexpected. As we finished shooting and moved off to get into the photographer's car, we were suddenly surrounded and swooped upon by two giant Swiss Guards (those 6ft 6in Vatican guards, dressed in traditional garish uniforms) and a little fat man who turned out to be the head of police for the Vatican. And within five minutes we were all marched inside and down to the cells and were told we were being arrested.

The photographer, who was the only one who spoke Italian, tried to explain to them, but they snatched his camera from him. From what we gathered later, what had happened was that a couple of Nuns had been on the top of the steps when Derek had picked up the girl. And in horror, the Nuns had dashed inside and reported that there was a Monk who'd gone mad in the mid-day sun and was trying to molest a blonde tourist.

No matter how much we protested, we couldn't convince them of the truth. But my photographer then discreetly slipped something into my jacket top pocket - it was a roll of film. And he whispered, "I think you should have this, Ken. You'll probably get out of here before we do."

He then managed to convince the police chief that I was nothing more than an innocent bystander and had nothing to do with the incident. So they finally let me go. But not before they put both Derek and the photographer into two separate cells.

Derek pleaded his innocence and tried to explain that he was an actor, playing the part of a Monk. But when they asked for his identification, all he could do was lift up his cassock, showing only his Y-fronts, and say, "I've got no proof on me."

I didn't know quite what to do. But I ran, literally about a mile, to break the news to the BBC producer and the film crew who were anxiously waiting to re-start afternoon filming.

When I told them that Derek had been arrested, Duncan Wood went berserk. "Get everything packed into the vans and let's get out of here," he ordered the crew.

He turned to me and said, "Bloody hell, Ken, the Vatican authorities will confiscate all our film, and we are also going to lose half a day's filming because the sun's gone down and we are losing light."

To say he was not very happy with me is an understatement. I then jumped into a taxi. In those days, we had a Mirror office in Rome, and a Mirror correspondent based there. I produced the roll of film from my pocket, told him what had happened. He took the film off me, said he'd get the film back to London on the next plane.

Meanwhile, I sat down and wrote the story - and phoned it over to London. I then went back to join the BBC production team at their hotel.

It was about five hours later when Derek Nimmo finally arrived back. Still in his Monk's garb, he was grinning all over his face. And he quickly told us what had happened.

It seems they just couldn't convince the Vatican police. They thought he was some mad Monk - until late in the afternoon when a little Irish priest passed by, recognised Nimmo in the cell and told the police chief, "Oh yes, he's an English actor all right. He's the famous Derek Nimmo and he's always playing priests, monks or bishops on TV."

48

Eventually, they let him go, and my photographer as well. The photographer had been arrested, they said, because he was taking professional pictures, and although holidaymakers can take snaps on the steps of St. Peter's, you cannot take professional pictures anywhere in the Vatican without permission, which must be in writing.

Well, Derek was full of it. Although the BBC had lost half a day's filming, we all had dinner together, a lot of vino was consumed, and Nimmo regaled us all with these stories of what had happened.

I finished up at the Press Club, drinking with our Rome reporter until about midnight, and then gratefully got back to my hotel.

Next morning, I phoned the office and they told me I'd made the front page of the Mirror with the story, and the headline "Oh, Brother!"- and a big picture of Derek as the mad Monk swinging this blonde girl in the air.

The trouble was, I was supposed to catch a train to Verona to cover the TV festival. But I had such a hangover and I just couldn't face a long train journey. I checked out of my hotels and hailed a taxi to take me to the station. But on the way, I said, "Can you drive me to Verona instead?"

The cab driver happily agreed. And I ended up taking a taxi halfway across Italy, from Rome to Verona. The fare cost me over £80. But I knew I would get it back on expenses, as the office were rather pleased with me, because as well as a TV feature on the interview I'd got with Nimmo, we'd also managed to get a front-page exclusive news story, which was a bit of a bonus.

Derek often laughed about that incident. In fact, I once saw him tell the story on Michael Parkinson's TV chat show of his Vatican arrest and incarceration.

Sadly, Derek died quite prematurely. He somehow fell down the stairs at his home, and never recovered.

But he was a great character, and a wonderful raconteur.

CHAPTER 7: BING CROSBY & PERRY COMO

Of all the big names I've met and really liked, Perry Como and Bing Crosby, two of the all-time great crooners, must be pretty near the top of my list.

I first met Perry Como when I went up from London to Southport to see his stage show and do a feature on him. He was appearing in concert on a tour, and I booked into the same hotel as him on Lord Street.

After going to the show, I went back to the hotel, where we had dinner together. He was absolutely charming, talked a lot, and was good company. It was more like chatting to a friend than doing a newspaper interview.

One of the things he told me was that, earlier in the day, he'd slipped out of his hotel and gone over to Woolworths for some lemon drops which, apparently, he always liked to take, to soothe his throat before a concert. He was in Woollies, at the sweet counter. Nobody recognised him except this one woman who stopped to look at him, and said, "Aren't you? No, you're not, are you? Didn't you used to be Perry Como?"

He laughed and said, "No, I still am Perry Como." He bought his lemon drops and gave her an autograph. But he couldn't help smiling at the woman's face. Well, it's not every day you meet Perry Como buying sweets in Woolworths, is it?

Anyway, after dinner, it was quite late, about midnight, and Perry suddenly said, "Hey, I feel like some fresh air. Let's go and have a look around Southport. Come on, Ken, show me around town."

We were strolling around. It was deadly quiet; no one was around. Walking down the historic Lord Street about 1 am. He was admiring the buildings, when a police car drew up at the kerb. One of the guys we had with us was a big 6ft 6ins black bloke, with a shaven head. He was Perry's hired private bodyguard, who worked in London as a security guard with a lot of visiting stars in Britain.

The police car stopped, an officer got out, came over to us, looked up at this black guy and said, "Well, who have we got here? What are you lot up to?"

"We're just taking a stroll," said Perry. "Oh, just taking a stroll, eh - at one o'clock in the morning? And who are you? Where do you live?" said the policeman.

"The name's Como. Perry Como. Do you want my home address or just the hotel where I'm staying?"

Well, the officer's face was a picture. He went back to the car and said to his colleague, "Look who it is. It's Perry Como." Of course, they both wanted his autograph and all that stuff and were happy to break up their boring police shift with a chat. That was fine.

A couple of years later, Perry Como was back in London. I went along to a big record company reception for him. It was crowded. But Perry walked in, spotted me among the Press mob, came over and yelled, "Hey, how are you? How's that lovely little place Southport? Remember, we nearly got in trouble with the police?" I was just so surprised that he had such a good memory.

He was a very likeable bloke. He struck me as one of the really genuine guys around. And not at all "starry."

+   +   +

Then there was Bing Crosby. I listened to Bing on the radio with my mother when I was a kid. And then she used to take us to see all those Hollywood musical films, starring Crosby, Bob Hope and Fred Astaire.

I met Bing when I went up to Scotland to cover a Pro-Celebrity golf tournament which the BBC used to televise. This year it was at Gleneagles. The British team was captained by Sean Connery and had Bruce Forsyth, Jimmy Tarbuck, Val Doonican, Max Bygraves, boxer Henry Cooper, and racing drivers Jackie Stewart and James Hunt, as well as golf champion Tony Jacklin. And the American team was captained by Bing Crosby, and they had Burt Lancaster in the team, tough-guy film actor George C. Scott, and astronaut Alan Shepard, who had actually played golf on the moon.

We were there over the best part of a week and one day I got the chance, thanks to Jimmy Tarbuck, of joining him and some of the others for a round of golf, including Burt Lancaster and Alan Shepard, who was a very quiet, unassuming guy, and not like an astronaut superman at all.

But I really wanted to interview Bing Crosby, my childhood hero. The Americans had a personal PR man there, to look after them all, and I asked him the first day we were there if he could arrange an interview for me with Bing. He said he'd try.

Two or three days went by, and I kept seeing the PR man, and he was saying "Look, I'll try, but I can't promise anything. Bing doesn't like to be disturbed when he's on these golfing trips."

Another day, and I got tired of this, so I took matters into my own hands. I strolled over to the Royal Gleneagles Hotel, where they were all staying, and went into the lobby, got on the telephone and rang up the hotel, from an outside line, and asked to be put through to Mr. Bing

Crosby's suite. Surprisingly, they didn't ask me any questions, but rang his room and someone picked up the phone. I asked to speak to Bing Crosby. "This is he," said the voice, which was quite unmistakeable.

So, I told him who I was, said I'd like an interview with him. "Where are you?" he asked. "Downstairs in the lobby," I said. "Well, come on up." He gave me his room number.

I went up to his room. He shook my hand, sat me down, ordered coffee and we chatted away. I even name-dropped to him and said I'd met Perry Como, who as everyone knew was a junior to Bing but became something of a vocal rival. And Bing said, "Oh, so you know Perry, eh?".

"Well, I've met him and had dinner with him," I said. We then got on like a house on fire. He even introduced me to his 17-year-old grandson, his youngest, and said "This fellow is going to be the amateur golf champion of America next year."

All was fine, until there was a knock on the door and in walked this PR man. He saw me sitting there, drinking coffee. "Oh, this is Mr. Irwin," said Bing. "He says he's been trying to get an interview with me for several days now."

Well, the PR man's face went quite white, and he mumbled some sort of apology. But Bing dismissed him, and we continued in conversation for an hour or more.

He really was very charming. And I got a very good piece out of him. But I don't think that PR bloke talked to me for the rest of the week.

Public Relations people, I can tell you, are a pain in the backside to journalists. Most of them are either failed or would-be journalists, anyway.

The outcome of that week, however, produced another big story for me. And it was down to having good contacts, which every journalist thrives upon.

All the celebrity players were having dinner one night. A big private party at their hotel, to which I and the BBC had not been invited. Fair enough. I knew nothing about it until the next day, when I bumped into Jimmy Tarbuck, who came over to me quietly and said, "Have you heard what happened last night?" I said, "No. What?"

He said, "Oh, it was a riot. George C. Scott got so drunk at the dinner, he then went upstairs, threw the TV out of the window and smashed up his room. And this morning he's walked out and flown home back to America."

At first, I thought he was joking. "No," said Jimmy mischievously. "If you want to do a story, it's up to you. Only don't say I told you. They're all trying to keep it quiet. But Bing Crosby is furious because he's now a player short."

Somehow, I had to stand the story up. It was a tricky one. I didn't want to upset Bing by going on to him, or any of the other players and asking them.

Instead, I went around the corner, phoned up the Gleneagles Hotel and asked for the manager. I said it was the Daily Mirror and we'd got this story about George C. Scott smashing up his room - was it true?

And to my surprise, the hotel manager confirmed everything. He was so annoyed. "We have been assured by the TV producers and the BBC that they will pay for all the damage," he said.

So, there I had it. A big story - "Hollywood star smashes up hotel room and walks out of celebrity golf match." It made the front-page splash the next day.

It turned out that Bing Crosby then had to get Burt Lancaster to play two matches. And Sean Connery and Bruce Forsyth were happy because the British team won the tournament in the end.

I never did get to meet George C. Scott, either before or after the big dinner. Which was just as well really. Because with his reputation as a tough guy, I don't think I'd have fancied tackling him on a story like that.

But again, that was all down to old mates, having contacts like Jimmy Tarbuck. I reckoned Jimmy owed me one, anyway, for all those early write-ups and publicity I gave him in his career.

CHAPTER 8: AMERICA – HERE WE COME!

America is a fascinating place. I used to love going over there, working. But I'd hate to work there permanently. Particularly in Hollywood.

When I became the Show Business Editor on the Mirror, I went to America quite a lot. They'd send me two or three times a year, to do features. And I also flew over occasionally to do special interviews, covering films and pop music, as well as television.

But the first time I went to the States, I was so naïve. The office sent me for a week or ten days to see if I could round up some big-name interviews. I thought it was going to be easy. In this country, with a paper like Daily Mirror, you only had to pick up the phone, and the stars were happy to talk to you because they all love the publicity. In the States, it's very different. They love the publicity - but only when they want it, and only with the journalists they choose.

I spent practically the whole week in my hotel room, phoning agents and PR people for all the top American stars, asking for interviews. I had a list of them - all the top TV names of the day. Jack Lemmon, Peter Falk who played Columbo. I couldn't get any of them. Starsky and Hutch was the top-rating cop show at the time, so I tried for them. I talked to the agent of Michael Glaser, who played Starsky, and he was very pleasant and said he would try to get Mr. Glaser to see me. Every day, for four days, we talked. He kept promising, but nothing definite. Then finally my patience snapped. I knew they were filming at Universal Studios, so I phoned the studios direct and asked for Michael Glaser.

Somehow, I got through to him on the set. I explained who I was, but he didn't want to know and said he was too busy to meet anyone. That's when I lost my temper. "Listen, I've been in this awful place Hollywood nearly a week now and I keep getting fobbed off by agents and PR people," I told him. "But the one guy who seemed really genuine was your agent, and I am disappointed if you are now going to put the kibosh on the interview I was half promised."

Well, I think Glaser was so surprised at all this, that he said, "Have you met my agent?" I said, "No. I've only talked to him on the phone. But he sounded like the only genuine guy in Hollywood."

Glaser then said, "Well, he is. That's why he's been my agent for ten years. Get yourself down here and let's meet. We'll go from there."

Hastily, I shot down to the studios by taxi, met Glaser, and his agent who happened to be there too. "Let's go for lunch, said Glaser, who had just finished the morning session filming.

From then on, it was all very pleasant. We got on very well and I had a terrific, very frank interview.

"I don't wanna talk about the goddam series," he said. "I've been doing the thing for so long there is nothing new I can say about the part. All I am interested in is developing as an actor and taking on new challenges in my career."

He was so bored with playing Starsky that the year before he had threatened to quit and even went to court to get out of his contract. He ended up mutually agreeing to a contract which gave him three million dollars over a three-year period. But with the new deal, he also insisted that they cut down on the violence, which they agreed to do.

"My trouble is I never know whether people see me as a commodity, as a property, or whether they really go for me for my acting talent," he told me. "I don't like playing at being a film star. I can't be doing with all that crap. Being a star is not important. But it's very easy in this business to be seduced into thinking you're special. I'm not. I know I'm not. Because the moment you think you've arrived, you're dead."

There was no pretentiousness about Glaser. Up to a year before, he drove around in a five-year-old Mazda and lived in a small rented house which he'd occupied since long before his TV success came along. "Now I've finally bought a house. And I've also bought a new car," he confessed reluctantly.

I found his candidness remarkably refreshing. "To be honest, I rarely watch the programme," he said. "But I did get stoned the other night and watched a single episode. Afterwards, I just got even more stoned."

And before we parted, he said, "I see we are No.36 in the ratings this week. If we keep this up, we could be off the air sooner than we think." And he winked mischievously.

It was his agent who also told me the secret of where I'd been going wrong. I was simply staying at the wrong hotel, he pointed out. In Hollywood, when anyone rang, agents would say "We'll get back to you." But if you weren't staying at the right hotel (five-star, or at the minimum a four-star) they wouldn't even bother returning your call. Any journalist staying at a Holiday Inn or any ordinary tourist hotel, had no chance of getting called back. It was the hotel that was important, not the name of the person. It was all showbiz snobbery and nonsense, of course. But that's the way it was in the US.

I once went to Hollywood with a team of Mirror writers. The Editor decided that a General Election was coming up, people were going to be bored silly with all the political news, so he sent half a dozen of the paper's top team to the Golden State. It was "California, Here We Come!"

It was a great trip – in 1978. They sent Marjorie Proops, Fleet Street's legendary agony aunt, our fashion editor Lesley Ebbetts, investigative reporter John Pilger, gossip columnist Paul Callan, and me, as the showbiz editor, and our chief photographer Kent Gavin.

We knew it was going to be something of a fun trip when we arrived at L A airport and had to face the usual long queue to get through Immigration. Except that this day the queue seemed to be much longer than normal.

As we patiently waited to show our passports, Paul Callan suddenly leapt into action. He went to the back of the hall, grabbed a wheelchair, came and put Marje Proops in the chair, then pushed the wheelchair through to the front of the queue.

Confronted by the uniformed Immigration officer, Callan, in his poshest English accent, announced, "This is Lady Proops from London. We are in rather a hurry."

"And who are you?" Paul was asked. "I'm her private secretary," he replied.

To our astonishment, and the rest of the people in the queue, the officer took their passports and visas, smiled and almost bowed, and waved them through. "Welcome to the United States, Lady Proops. I hope you have a very enjoyable stay."

Paul just waved at us, a big grin on his face, and wheeled Marje away through the exit doors. They were waiting outside, when we finally got through, with two taxis lined up for us.

Marje was rather tickled with the idea of being Lady Proops, and the title stuck for the rest of our trip. When we had trouble one night trying to book a particularly good restaurant for dinner, I went on the phone and said, "It's for Lady Proops, from London. We have a party of six." The manager immediately replied, "Tell Lady Proops we'll reserve the best table in the house." And they did. We really got the red-carpet treatment.

We all stayed at the same hotel in Beverley Hills, and Marje behaved like a Mother Hen to everyone. The idea was that we would all go off and organise our various features, then come together in the evening and discuss what we had got.

But Marje was a bit stumped and confided with me that she wanted to do an "interview" with Miss Piggy, because The Muppets were very big at that time. But the American producers wouldn't co-operate with her. She asked if I could help.

So I phoned Lew Grade, the boss of ATV in London, told him Marje Proops wanted to do a big feature on The Muppets, and he was delighted.

Doors were immediately opened. I was told to get Marje down to the studios next day to meet Miss Piggy in person.

All went well. She came back to the hotel, thanked me, and said she had done a splendid and very imaginative piece.

When we got back to London, however, Marje's feature appeared in the paper. And it was a huge centre-page spread. "Miss Piggy Talks to Marje Proops...about her Sex Life."

Unfortunately, all hell broke loose. My phone rang early in the morning, as soon as I was in my office. It was ATV's Chief Press Relations manager Dougie Howell, saying that Lew Grade was going up the wall because Miss Piggy was doing nothing but talk about sex. And, anyway, she hadn't said any of this stuff that was in the paper.

I said to Dougie, who was an old chum of mine, "Hang on a minute. This is a puppet we're talking about. You must know that Proops was going to have to make all this up, in her usual girl-to-girl chat style."

Dougie said, "You know that, and I know that, but Lew doesn't see it that way. I don't know what we can do to appease him."

When I told Marje of Lew Grade's reaction, she fell about laughing. "Don't worry," she said, "I'll go on and sort him out. The man must have no sense of humour." And she did sort him out.

Actually, Lew Grade did have a great sense of humour. He was a superb showman. A great self-publicist. Every Christmas, he'd throw a Press party and invite all the top showbiz writers from every paper to a marathon lunch.

We'd all get a bottle of champagne and the biggest Havana cigar you've ever seen. Even people who didn't smoke would take one home, as a Lew Grade souvenir. Those of us who did light up, would spend the rest of the day puffing on it.

I got to know Marje Proops quite well on that US trip. It's strange how you can work with colleagues for years in an office and never really get to know them. But when you spend time away with them, drinking in hotels overnight, you sometimes confide in them a lot more, and even become friends.

As for Marje, though, she had a secret life none of us knew anything about. For although she spent her working life as Britain's No.1 Agony Aunt, offering moral advice to the thousands of readers who wrote in to her, it later came out that she had been living a lie. The husband, Sydney Proops, who was marred to her for years and whom she constantly referred to in print as simply Proops, was someone she had despised and hated for most of her life. They never shared a bed, and in fact after his death she revealed she had been having an illicit affair for years with a Daily Mirror legal executive, Philip Levy, who died only about a year after her husband.

When Marje died, at the age of 78, in November 1996, I went down from Manchester to her funeral at Golders Green cemetery. Hundreds turned out for her. It was a very sad occasion and a lot of fond tributes were paid to her. She really was a Fleet Street legend and a one-off character.

CHAPTER 9: HOLLYWOOD

JANE SEYMOUR

Hollywood is a quite amazing place. It's not for real people, of course. But a kind of wondrous Fantasy Land. The top hotel there is the Beverly Hills on Sunset Blvd. - or it was when I was over there on the showbiz beat. And the place to be seen, or to do some star-spotting if you can afford it, is the famous Polo Lounge.

I remember my first time there. I was interviewing Jane Seymour, the English actress who went over there to try her luck and liked the place so much she decided to stay. She's lived there for some years, long before the Brits invaded the place and were accepted as equals to the Americans in the star system.

She asked me to meet her in the Polo lounge, and then suggested we had lunch out in the garden restaurant.

It was a beautiful, warm and sunny day, and she was very pleasant, a nice enough woman. But very affected. What I would call starry-eyed and very, very Hollywoody. But I suppose that was the way she had to play it. And for many years she was the only English rose determined to make a living on that side of the pond.

When I met her, the first thing she said was "I may have just made the most expensive mistake of my career." She was talking about the new multi-million dollar science fiction series Battlestar Galactica, with Jane in the role of a sexy news broadcaster called Serina from the planet of Caprica.

"I get killed off after only three episodes," she said. "I was quite happy about it. I didn't really want to get involved in a long-running TV saga. But this now happens to be the most successful and talked-about series on TV, so I may have made a terrible bloomer."

Jane was not really worried, though, about the cash she would lose by coming out of the series early. "I've never been desperate about money. I've been earning my living since I was 13," she told me.

"I have bought my own house in the Hollywood Hills and paid off the mortgage. I've always been very independent. I could never bring myself to ask anyone for money."

After three years there, she was now well established. "I came here originally for six weeks, without a job, an agent, or any real prospects," she said. "All I had was a lot of very good acting experience."

The first thing she tried to do was drop her English accent. "I have been in so many American films and TV shows that most people now think I am American.

"I do feel I belong here more than I do in England, although naturally I love to go home to London as often as I can."

At 28, Jane had two broken marriages – the first to Michael Attenborough (son of film maker Richard) and the second to businessman Geoffrey Planer. "I'm not particularly proud of being twice divorced before I was 27 – but that's life I suppose. I certainly don't blame show business for my marriage failures."

Jane moved to Hollywood originally, with the James Bond film Live And Let Die behind her, as well as a string of good TV credits in such shows as The Onedin Line, The Strauss Family and Our Mutual Friends.

"I've been lucky," said Jane. "But it's a jungle in Hollywood. I certainly wouldn't recommend anyone to do what I did, to come out here without a job. I'm forever taking chances in life. My philosophy is simple: Nothing is for ever. Live from day to day and stop doing it if you don't enjoy it any more. That way, nobody gets hurt."

JOAN COLLINS

Another one, of course, who made it in Hollywood was our beloved Joan Collins. I remember going out to interview Joan when she started working on Dynasty.

I'd met her before, in London, so we knew each other. But I was invited to meet her and do an interview on the set, because she'd just been signed up to do the new soap Dynasty, and she was very excited about it.

We had lunch in the studio restaurant, and I recall her telling me, "This is really going to take off, this show. And it's going to get me back at the top of the tree." She knew it was right for her. She had a gut feeling, because for years she had been pretty well ignored in Hollywood. But once she started on Dynasty, she couldn't drive around with the hood down on her car, because when she stopped at traffic lights, people yelled at her, "Hi, Alexis."

"When the public started calling me Alexis, I knew the show had taken off and I had a whole new career ahead of me," she said.

One other thing she told me was, "This is not just any ordinary TV soap. They put real flowers on the set every day. Flowers are so expensive in

Hollywood, and that's a major expenditure. If they can spend so much on the fresh flowers, they must have a huge budget to match."

Joan Collins is a great character. I invited her to an office lunch in London one day with the Editor and a couple of executives. And she was so funny, she had everyone wrapped around her little finger.

A journalist on the Sunday People, Tony Purnell, who is an old pal of mine, mischievously unearthed a copy of Joan's real birth certificate, and printed it in the paper. And it turned out she'd knocked seven or eight years off her age. Joan was furious at the time, but with the passing of the years she has relaxed a bit on that subject. In fact, she now openly boasts about her age. Why shouldn't she? For a woman in her eighties, she still looks stunning.

Although she might look affected, she's really remarkably down to earth and is nobody's fool, our Joan. And she's got a great sense of humour.

TIPPI HEDREN

One of the most amazing interviews I've ever done was with Hollywood actress Tippi Hedren. She was the star of the classic horror film The Birds, a very attractive blonde, and the woman who so fascinated the great film producer Alfred Hitchcock that he became obsessed with her after she turned down his sexual advances and refused to be one of his conquests. She's the mother of film actress Melanie Griffiths.

I was invited to go and do an exclusive interview with her at her home for a new film she was making, all about animals, and was promised it would be something really special. I flew to Los Angeles early in 1982 to meet up with her.

She lived on a ranch out in Soledad Canyon, with her film producer husband Noel Marshall and her three children.

I was with a PR woman from the film company and my American-based photographer Eddie Sanderson. We were warned of what we were going into. But even then, I couldn't have expected what happened when we got there.

Tippi was lovely, very attractive and very friendly, and welcomed us into her house. "There are some animals around. So always be ready for the unexpected and keep your wits about you. But don't be afraid of the animals," she insisted.

We were shown into the lounge and given coffee. And she then told us she shared her life with dozens of wild animals, which she had living in her kind of home zoo. She had 180 acres of land and most of the animals, including elephants, lions, tigers and cheetahs, all roamed free.

What she didn't tell us was that some of her really big cats were house trained and liked to come indoors quite a lot. I was sitting in the lounge, interviewing Tippi, when suddenly there was a terrific roar, and this giant fully grown Siberian tiger leapt through the kitchen window and ran into the room.

To my horror, it jumped over my head and leapt on top of Tippi. She then started stroking and playing with it. "Don't worry, he won't harm you," she said.

The tiger then jumped up at my photographer Eddie and had its paws around his mouth. I could see from Eddie's face, he was terrified.

Somehow, he managed to keep calm and then took some pictures of the tiger in the kitchen, with Tippi feeding him some lunch from a dinner plate.

Tippi then talked about the new film she had produced with her husband. It was called Roar! And it featured a pack of lions and tigers who take over a terrified African family's home.

The film had taken her and her husband Noel eight years to produce and had cost them £9-million to complete.

Tippi then revealed to me that she once had her head ripped open by a lion, and her daughter and two sons had all needed surgery after being mauled by animals. Husband Noel (also the producer of the film The Exorcist) had been injured too, but shrugged it off, and simply said, "I just wanted in this new film to show the world what wonderful, strong animals they are."

We then went outside and Tippi took great delight in introducing me to various lions, tigers and leopards, and insisted that I had a ride on a full-sized elephant.

The elephant I didn't mind. But she then invited me to sit down with her in the long grass, while this massive tigress came over and jumped on top of me. Tippi lay there alongside me and encouraged the animal to play with us. At first, I was petrified, especially when the tigress became a bit too friendly and reached out with one of its paws to grab my neck. Eddie then stepped in with his camera and started taking pictures of me with Tippi and the tiger and, somehow, I managed to smile. We ended up rolling around together.

I mean, a roll in the hay with the gorgeous Tippi Hedren was one thing. But with a tiger for company, well, I wasn't so sure!

Of course, it all made a smashing and very unusual feature, with some really great pictures. And we then spent the rest of the day with Tippi and her family of animals.

It was a very worthwhile trip. I've never had a day quite like that one. And it turned out to be one of the best and most memorable jobs I've ever done. Her new film was sold around the world and was released in Britain a few months later.

I made the most of that job and managed to wangle a few extra days by taking time off to fly to San Francisco and enjoy the City by the Sea. Frisco was everything I expected, and even though I stayed only one night, the place was jumping and I was in for a few surprises. I fell in love overnight and it's still my favourite resort in the States.

ALICE COOPER

People often ask me how journalists get their stories. How do we work? How do we get to interview the top show business names and the Hollywood stars?

Well, when I was operating in Fleet Street, it was all quite straightforward. There are three main avenues of operation. First, you become so well known that you make friends with the people you interview, or at least build up a trust between you so that they are always happy to meet you again and do another interview, knowing that they are not going to be misquoted or assassinated in print.

Secondly, there are people in the business who are always willing to phone a journalist up and tip us off with some bit of scandal or snippet of news, hoping to make a few pounds for themselves.

Then, of course, there are the full-time Public Relations people who are paid to get publicity for their clients. And they will come on to us, trying to set up interviews. Now the trouble with this system, is that in most cases the PR tries to insist on sitting in on the interview, and in many cases even advising their clients only to answer certain questions and not others. I hated that way of doing things, but sometimes we had to go along with it, particularly with really big stars and with top film companies. And this was always the way it worked in America. Unfortunately, it's now the same in this country.

When these PR people do set up interviews, some are on an exclusive basis, with only one paper. But mostly, they are what we used to call a "gang bang," when individual journalists would be invited in, one at a time, and each given about half an hour to chat to whoever the star was. This was quite often a waste of time, but in some cases, it was the only way we were ever going to get at these ego-inflated people.

Most of these publicity sessions would be set up in hotel suites, with the journalists being quickly ushered in and out. But the very best interviews, which I always relished doing, was when I was invited to interview someone in their own home. This, of course, was usually only after they had got to know you and trusted you.

Now maybe I was lucky, or I'd like to think that it was because of my professionalism and the way I built up trust over the years, but I did get to meet quite a few people in their homes. Funnily enough, some of them were in Hollywood, and with stars I was meeting for the first time.

One of those was the legendary Alice Cooper, the outrageous rock star. When I managed to arrange an interview with him, he suggested I go to his home. He lived high in the Hollywood Hills, not far from that big famous sign HOLLYWOOD.

To my surprise, he wasn't a bit like the awful rock character he creates on stage. He was a really nice, friendly, quiet bloke. We sat out by his swimming pool, and he had tea and cakes served and we chatted for hours.

He explained that he had two quite separate lives, one very normal and the other as the frantic, painted ogre he played on stage. Which was why his father, who was a church preacher, hadn't taken too kindly to his son changing his name and becoming an outrageous rock star.

His real name was Vincent Furnier and he liked to divorce himself completely from the outrageous character he played on stage.

When I first met him, he walked out on to the patio with his long hair tied up in a bun and his scrawny arms dangling from a black T-shirt. He smiled like a young toothy Devil and said, "Hey, is that lady Mary Whitehouse still around? Is she still trying to have me banned from Britain?"

He was referring to his previous trip to the UK when the Clean Up TV campaigners tried to deport Alice and his band because of their terrifying behaviour on stage. Well, I suppose they did make the Rolling Stones and The Who look like Boy Scouts, in comparison.

A lot had happened since his last trip, he told me. He was off the booze after voluntary psychiatric treatment when he found he was drinking two bottles of whisky plus two dozen cans of beer a day. He was also now married and a father, doting over his baby daughter Calico. He was afraid to admit he was happily married – in case his fans thought he'd "gone straight."

Nervously, he laughed and said, "Alice and I are different people, y'know. That guy Alice is a crazy loon. I wouldn't hang around with him for a minute. But me, I'm just an all-American boy."

He did acknowledge though that being Alice Cooper for 15 years had made him a multi-millionaire. "The trouble with Alice is that if someone said you can't do that, he'd say, 'Really?' and then do it. I'm 34 but Alice is going on 17. Since I gave up drink, I've had so much energy, I love it.

"I look forward to becoming Alice every night. My wife Sheryl gets scared. She says I change completely. I don't go out there with the attitude 'Gosh, I hope you like us tonight.' An audience loves to be taken apart and almost raped. If they look away, they miss something. That's the way it should be. I've got a good band behind me. Guys working with Alice need the right sense of humour, otherwise they won't last long. But on stage we are not allowed to laugh or even smile. I have a riding crop and anyone who breaks attitude, they get it right across the knees. I'm competitive. I consider myself an innovator. If I keep doing the same thing, it goes stale. There are many imitators. But only one Alice."

Vincent worried about Alice Cooper's image. He even gave up playing golf for a time because of his fans. "I love the game. I was playing real good. But I was playing with guys of 50 or more and I began talking like them. And the kids don't like Alice playing golf, so I quit the game."

He was a clever mixture of intelligent businessman, philosopher   and raving nut. "Y'know, I've never worked a day for a boss," he told me. "Once, when I was 16, I worked for fifteen minutes in a car wash. I didn't like it and decided I was destined for bigger things, so I walked out."

Alice Cooper completely changed his life. The name came out of thin air. "It could have been Betty Thompson. Now, Alice is a living legend," he said proudly. "There is nothing you can do on stage to shock any more. Alice has done it all.

"Sometimes, I say 'What's Alice so angry about?' On stage, I let all that anger out. I use it as a fuel. If everyone had an Alice, there would be no need for psychiatrists.

"We never have any fights in our audience. They are too exhausted to fight. Everything is going on up on stage. I want them exhausted at the end.

"The amazing thing is that for the ten years I drank heavily, they were my most productive years. I could never do a show without a bottle. I was sick, not eating, and throwing up blood. I couldn't walk across a room without a bottle in my hand. Finally, I said enough. It wasn't hard to stop. It was uncomfortable for seven days. Coming off alcohol is worse, they say, than coming off drugs.

"I was never involved in drugs. I've always been legal about things. I could never steal anything, for instance."

This in-built honesty, he admitted, probably went back to his upbringing. His father was a church minister, and his father-in-law was a parson too.

"I've been accused of all sorts of terrible things. I never deny any rumours about Alice. People said I bit the heads off chickens and drank their blood. I just shrugged and said, 'Really? Well that's Alice.' I can always blame him. I have done a lot of terrible things on stage. But the imagination is terrific!"

And he added. "It's going to be tough when my girl Calico grows up and asks, 'What does Daddy do?' How do I explain?"

Never have I met such a chameleon of a character. Over the years, Alice Cooper has remained one of rock's true icons. When I've seen him on TV, quite recently on chat shows, he has not changed a lot. He still comes over as a very sensible, down to earth guy. And I think he's gone back to playing golf.

ERNEST BORGNINE

Another film legend who was happy to meet me in his home surroundings was the great Ernest Borgnine. He was the star of that wonderful film Marty. But he went on to do many more films and worked well into his later years.

With that gnarled and battered old face, he could pick and choose his parts. A lovely man, and very gentle. He, too, lived up in the Hollywood Hills, in a magnificent house. And he insisted on showing me around, before sitting down and having lunch together. He was full of offbeat stories.

MARILYN MONROE

On one trip to America, I happened to be staying at a hotel in West Hollywood, which I discovered was only a short walk away from the cemetery where Marilyn Monroe was cremated.

I went around there. Her ashes had been put into a wall, with the simple inscription "In Memory of Marilyn Monroe." And I learned that, every day, a single fresh rose was put in a small vase there. It's been done for years, ever since she died such a tragic death.

No one ever knew who was responsible for paying for those daily roses. Some said it was her American husband, the playwright Arthur Miller, or Jack De Maggio, the sports star. But others thought it might have been the Kennedy family, because of her association with President Jack Kennedy and his brother Bobby.

I don't suppose we'll ever know. But I found it a very quiet and moving memorial place for such a legendary star.

LIZA MINNELLI & DUDLEY MOORE

If anyone ever asks me who was the worst or disagreeable person I have met or interviewed, then I would have no hesitation in saying that top of my list would be Liza Minnelli, without a doubt. Which is a shame really because I was a great admirer (she shares my birthday, March 12th) and I was looking forward to meeting her. But she let me down very badly.

I flew to New York to do a couple of showbiz jobs, and one was to go on location when they were making the film Arthur, and do exclusive interviews with the two stars, Dudley Moore and Liza Minnelli. It had been set up by the film company, and they were anxious for me to do it because they wanted publicity for the film when it was released in this country.

Dudley Moore was fine. I knew Dudley anyway, having interviewed him several times in this country, long before he went to settle in Hollywood where he became such a huge international star.

We had lunch together at a swish restaurant. I did the interview and it was all very pleasant. He even fooled around and played a medley of songs for me on a nearby piano, and we had a few laughs.

Next day, I was set to interview Liza. But I got a phone call at my hotel from the woman PR for the film company telling me that Liza was going to be busy, and could we leave it until the following day? I agreed. Then, the next day, another excuse and our meeting was put off again.

Finally, on the third day, a time was fixed. I went over to where they were filming in Central Park. I patiently watched the filming, and Dudley came over and said hello. But there was no sign of Miss Minnelli. I waited most of the afternoon. In the end, I began to get the feeling all was not well.

Eventually, the PR woman, who was fussing around all the time, came to me, and said Liza would see me but she didn't have much time - could I do the interview in 20 minutes?

Annoyed now at all the hanging about, I protested a bit and said I'd come all the way from London to interview her, waited three days, and 20 minutes didn't seem much of a deal.

However, I could see it was going to be that or nothing, so I eventually agreed. I was then ushered into Liza Minnelli's caravan, and there was Dudley Moore sitting with her.

Liza was very cool at first, but then relaxed a bit. I quickly proceeded to interview her, knowing that I didn't have much time.

In the end, I got about 12 minutes with her before she finally said, "Well thanks for coming. Look, I'm sorry. I'm so busy. Can we wrap it up now?"

Well, I came out of the caravan, and I wasn't very happy. The PR woman was full of apologies, and Dudley followed me out and tried to explain. It seemed that Liza didn't want to do the interview at all, and wouldn't have done it if Dudley hadn't reassured her that he knew me and that I was okay.

I told the PR woman what I thought of Miss Minnelli and that this would probably be reflected in the piece I was going to write.

When I got back to the office in London and wrote it all up, I had a smashing feature on Dudley. But I then cut Liza Minnelli down to size in a brief piece (because I hadn't got much out of her anyway) and I made sure I put over what an awful, temperamental lady she was.

As it happens, when I saw the finished film, Arthur (which also had Sir John Gielgud in it) it really was a load of rubbish, although it did very well for Dudley Moore, and helped establish him in Hollywood after his smash-hit movie 10, in which he starred with the magnificent Bo Derek and Julie Andrews.

But Dudley was quite mischievous when I met him in New York. Jill Elkenberry was playing his cool, blonde fiancée, and Liza was an Italian girl he rescued from the law. The location was a university building they'd taken over to film scenes of Arthur's family mansion, and the walls were littered with phony Rembrandts, Vermeers and Van Gogh paintings to create the atmosphere of affluence.

"Nice 'ere, innit?" said Dudley in that strange squeaky voice he used in his old Pete and Dud TV shows. "I was just explaining to my fiancee 'ere what a khazi is." He turned to Jill Elkenberry, towering above him. "It's a lav, a toilet, a bog, a John, dear. The place where you go for a slash."

Dud's conversation was constantly interrupted with a mixture of gags and funny voices. "I remember doing an Eamonn Andrews TV show in England. That's where the Cuddly Dudley image started," he said.

"Now, the film 10 has really put me in an area of straight parts and got me away from comedy. I had actually made nine films before 10," he chuckled. "But I'd never really got to grips with film-making."

How did he live up to his new image as a sex super star? I wanted to know.

"I practise every day," he grinned. "There's nothing to live up to, really – I've been one all my life. You know me, Ken."

Dud had two or three other films lined up and was then one of the hottest properties in Hollywood. But he still missed England, he confided.

Home for him then was a place in California. And his current girlfriend was the statuesque American star Susan Anton. "As soon as I finish filming on Arthur, I'm hoping to take six weeks off. I'm taking Susan to Europe for a holiday. We're going to see all the choice bits – Rome, Venice, Florence," he said.

He might even take her to see Dagenham, where he was born, I suggested.

Dud insisted that in spite of all his past insecurities, he was now happier than ever. And he claimed that years of therapy from various psychiatrists had helped him.

"I don't regret seeing all those shrinks. It's the best investment I ever made. Some people are able to achieve security and happiness without too much bother. But others, like me, find it difficult.

"Now, I'm doing exactly what I want to do. I can be depressed and still be basically happy at the same time. Does that sound daft?"

What made him depressed? I asked. "Just the fact that I can't see my bird as often as I want, when I'm working," he smiled.

Yet he had no plans to re-marry. His first marriage to actress Suzy Kendall ended in divorce. And his second wife, American Tuesday Weld, who had custody of their son Patrick, also divorced him.

With two failed marriages, maybe he was not very good at it? I queried.

He chuckled. "How dare you! I think I am very good at it...That's the bloody trouble."

RITA COOLIDGE

The dark-haired beauty in trim blue jeans looked out over the Hollywood hills through the window of what used to be Charlie Chaplin's house, turned to me and said, "It's beautiful here. But I'm learnin' to live without a man. It isn't easy. But I'm learnin'."

It was Rita Coolidge, the 35-year-old singing star with what many considered to be the sexiest voice in the world, and she was talking about life since the break-up of her marriage to Kris Kristofferson. He was the man of whom she once said, "I want to be with Kris for ever. I watch the minutes ticking by until he walks through the door."

I suspected that deep down she was still in love with the guy, even though the boozing, high-living film superstar gave her a hell of a life.

They'd been divorced six months earlier. "We did it the civilised way," she said. "Kris and I broke clean down the middle. We did all the settlement out of court, before we brought lawyers into it. So it was all very peaceful and quiet."

She said that she and Kris still met regularly for family outings with their six-year-old daughter Casey, of whom they shared joint custody. "There's no reason why people should hate each other because they don't live together any more. I talk to Kris just about every day, from wherever he is, and we both say hello."

If they were such good friends, what went wrong? I asked. "The pressures on our marriage from the music business and the film industry were just too hard," she said. "Maybe he was envious of the fact that my musical career had gone sky high, and his hadn't, although his film career certainly had.

"Kris's first love has always been music, yet he still hasn't had any real success as a recording artist. But I've no doubt he'll make it eventually."

When I suggested she had not had an easy life, living with Kris, Rita smiled and said, "Sure Kris did outrageous things. But I knew he was an outrageous person when I married him, so I didn't ever try to change him. I still care very much for him and the love story will never be over, because there's a little girl there that's never going to go away. We'll always have a good relationship. But I wouldn't turn the clock back and change anything even if I could."

She was quite modest about her role in helping Kris kick his heavy drinking habit. "Oh yes, Kris is still off the booze. I might have made him aware of the intensity of the problem. His drinking was unbelievable. He'd drink anything and everything."

Their marriage had lasted eight years, and Rita spoke with great composure about the other women in Kris's life.

Barbara Streisand, for example, was an ex-girlfriend with whom he was said to have rowed with while making the film A Star Is Born. Then there was the British star Sarah Miles, who nearly broke up Rita's marriage when she posed naked with Kris for Playboy magazine.

Rita said, "As for other women in his life, well, I hope he finds what he is looking for. There would be something wrong with him if he didn't. I mean, our marriage didn't work out, so he's got to share his life with somebody."

She said she had worked out a simple philosophy to help explain the sorrows of the past. "Some people get love for ever and some just get it for a little while," she said.

I came away from that interview with a lot of admiration for Rita. She really did live up to her name, and was a very cool, sensible lady.

DYAN CANNON

I was reporting from New York when I met her, in 1980. The vivacious little blonde with a laugh like an hysterical hyena was Dyan Cannon. "I've finally found what I'm looking for. Now I've got everything in life," she screamed.

Dyan, one-time Hollywood sex siren, had got over the disaster of her broken marriage to the great Cary Grant, and had a new man in her life as well as a new film career as a producer.

A few years earlier she had quit acting because she was bored with the Hollywood rat-race. Now, at the age of 40, she was talking to me as the co-star of a new film called Honeysuckle Rose. She was playing opposite top American country singer Willie Nelson, and at the same time she was also writing and producing two new films.

The man in her life was Jerry Schatzberg, the director of Honeysuckle Rose. Tall, bespectacled with hair like greying wire wool, he told me, "We were both pretty surprised that we've fallen in love. It was the last thing that either of us expected.

"The movie we've turned out is all about the life of a country and western singer whose marriage is threatened by a love affair he has while touring."

Willie Nelson obviously played the singer, and Dyan played his faithful and outraged wife. I saw the film and it certainly emphasised that Dyan Cannon was not just a pretty face and a beautiful body, but a very accomplished actress.

She was once described as the actress with more sex appeal than all the other Hollywood blondes put together. And while married to Cary Grant, she remained ambitious and independent and was determined to succeed in her own career.

Her marriage to Grant lasted only three years. Their daughter Jennifer, who was 14 when I met her, shared her life with mum Dyan.

After splitting with Grant, Dyan made a series of good films, including Heaven Can Wait, opposite Warren Beatty, and The Revenge of the Pink Panther, with Peter Sellers.

The woman that Cary Grant was unable to tame told me, "I've now discovered that movies are not the most important thing in my life. I discovered peace of mind in writing. There are times that are rough. But they don't make me crazy as they used to. I can deal with them now."

On her new film, she said, "I play the most beautiful and perfect wife a man could wish for. And that's what I am. I can associate myself with this role. My girlfriends have always trusted me with their husbands."

But was she always faithful? I asked. She stared at me hard. "Always. I couldn't be otherwise," she said, and broke into hysterical laughter again.

THE DAMNED

When I went over to New York, in 1977, British punk rock had just hit America and a wild band called The Damned, who had been vying with The Sex Pistols for the title of the most disgusting group in England, jetted in to see how much havoc they could cause.

The young rock fans in New York were still wondering what had hit them. The Damned played a four-night stint at the citadel of punk rock, the CB & GB Club in the downtown Bowery district. And for my sins, I went to find out what they were all about.

"For us, this is like playing the London Palladium if you're Cliff Richard," said one of The Damned, who called himself Rat Scabies.

They were the first British punk band to cross the Atlantic, and their wild reputation preceded them, resulting in all their concerts selling out because of their "freak value."

They admitted to going on stage "stoned out of our minds", and they screamed abuse and obscenities and spat all over their audiences. They had been signed up by Island Records in London and were hoping for a big-money contract with an American recording company. Their success, I was told, depended on how well – or how badly – the boys behaved.

The group was made up of Brian James, 21, a guitarist; Rat Scabies, 19, their drummer, who had been turned down at 29 previous auditions; Captain Sensible, 20, a bass guitarist who had worked alongside Scabies cleaning out lavatories in Croydon's Fairfield Hall before joining the group; and singer Dave Varian,19, a former grave digger who always dressed in black.

Their manager and mentor Jack Riviera, said, "Three record companies in America are interested in them. I decided to let them see what they are letting themselves in for. Punk rock in America is like a vicar's tea party compared with the sort of stuff British groups get up to. Our boys are quite outrageous and disgusting. Anything awful the American bands can do, we can do worse."

And Riviera, who said the boys "should be in a zoo," described them individually to me. "Captain Sensible has got no sense at all. We need a lead to put on him. He is totally nuts. I love him dearly, but he is such a pain in the arse.

"Then there's Rat Scabies. He's just a lout but he happens to be a most incredible drummer. He can pack more four-letter swear words into any minute of the day than anyone I know. And he can live on baked beans and eggs.

"Brian James is the songwriter and is good-looking. He's the most sensible of the lot, but he's still a loony.

"And Dave, well the girls go for him in a big way. His girlfriend Valentine has a weekly change of colour in her hair. Dave is very courageous. As the singer fronting the band, he has to take a lot of stick from the audiences. But he never backs off. He's a nutter of course. But then, they all are."

Riviera told me, "At the hotel, we daren't let them go near the restaurant. They're like animals. We just feed them by throwing burgers into their rooms and locking them in."

The Damned earned between £500 and £750 a night for concerts in London, he told me. But all the boys received was £30 a week each. "They smash up so much musical equipment on stage, that most of the money goes in buying new gear. Microphones cost £60 each, and they smash those up every night."

On their first night in New York, which I unhappily sat through, the lads came on and threw flowers to the hysterical audience. Then they went off for a break, came back on stage and threw hundreds of meat pies at everyone.

At the end, I still didn't know whether America was quite ready for The Damned. I certainly wasn't.

LYNDA CARTER

One of the most stunning women I have ever met was American actress Lynda Carter, who had a sexual chemistry that was almost scary.

Lynda played the incredible Wonder Woman, and I flew to Los Angeles and set up an interview with her, when she was appearing on an afternoon TV chat show in Hollywood. When I turned up at the studios and was shown into the waiting-room, there was one man sitting all on his own. It was Peter Ustinov and he was booked to be a guest on the same show. He was a brilliant raconteur.

He seemed nervous, and when I introduced myself and told him I was from London, he immediately seemed more at ease. "I don't really like doing some of these chat shows," he said. "They always expect me to be funny, and I get fed up telling the same old stories. But it's all part of the business, I'm afraid." I felt quite sorry for him, but then I got my call to go. "Best of luck on the show," I said. "Thanks. Best of luck to you with Wonder Woman," he replied.

When I was ushered into her dressing-room, I found Lynda Carter to be quite charming. We were served tea and biscuits, and she said, "I ordered tea because you're English, and I thought it would make you feel more at home." Which was nice of her. The trip turned out to be well worth while, for I got a good feature out of her. She'd started out in life as a beauty queen, winning a local contest in Arizona and going on to become Miss America, and then competing for the title of Miss World in 1972. After years of trying to make it as an actress, she landed the role of Wonder Woman, which she then did for three series, making her a worldwide star.

It was tough living up to the title of "The Most Beautiful Woman in The World," especially in Hollywood where gorgeous girls are as common as Cadillacs.

"Life is wonderful for me right now," she told me. "But I don't see my present success going on for too many years. I don't think I could live under the strain for long. I'm expected to work, work, work. I like hard work, but it has now become crazy."

She smiled when I reminded her of The Most Beautiful Woman in the World tag, "It's very flattering, but I could never think of myself like that," she said. "And I don't kid myself. Ten years from now, people will probably be saying 'She doesn't look so great.'

"When I see my name up in lights, or when I see my face on the TV screen, I somehow think of Lynda Carter as a completely different person."

She acknowledged that Wonder Woman had been good to her. "As restricted as the character might seem, I'm hoping it will give me the opportunity to get into other areas of acting. I don't want to go on playing Wonder Woman for ever. I want to do other things."

She was branching out as a recording artist and made her cabaret singing debut at Caesar's Palace, Las Vegas. "I want to expand my musical career. I don't want to be still acting when I'm 40," she said emphatically.

THE CARPENTERS & HERB ALPERT

One of my busiest periods, when I was flying over to America quite a lot, was in the early 80s, when we were publishing a lot of showbiz stuff and I was constantly on the lookout for fresh interviews and new features. One of the best captures I made was when I pinned down The Carpenters for an exclusive face-to-face session.

The meeting was set up in their recording studios at A & M in Hollywood, and I found both Richard and Karen to be remarkably friendly and nice.

At that time, the brother and sister duo was just about the biggest thing in pop music. Their string of hits established their star status for ever. And their music is still being played around the world.

Who can forget such great songs as Close To You, Yesterday Once More, Top of the World, and We've Only Just Begun? I know Richard was the song-writing genius, but I think it was Karen who made them so successful, with that beautiful singing voice which sounded so pure and angelic.

When it came to interviewing them, Richard did most of the talking, while Karen (who started out as a drummer before becoming lead vocalist) was happy to sit there, quietly agreeing with everything he said.

They had shocked the pop business by splitting up when they were the undisputed No.1 vocal duo in the world. Now they were back working together again for the first time in three years.

Ironically, the reunion came after 31-year-old Karen met and married American businessman Tom Burris. "I can't tell you how happy I am. I'm so head over heels in love, it's not true," said Karen. "Tommy asked me to marry him on June 16 last year. I only met him on April 12. Before that it was always work and sleep, nothing else. Then, all of a sudden, when we were waiting to go to the recording studio, there's Richard yelling at me, 'You wanna go out on a what? What's a date?'"

She giggled furiously. "I was having to make excuses for not working at night."

When Richard saw that Karen really was in love and determined to get married, it made their working relationship stronger than ever, she said.

Karen told me, "We'd been going for eight straight years and wanted to take a little time off. Richard simply wanted to re-charge, so I went off to pursue a solo career. I started working on a solo album, but I missed Richard terribly. When you work with someone for all those years, you get used to each other. Deep down I felt I was only doing other things until Richard got his pep back. But I'm really   glad I did that stint on my own. I proved to myself that it was possible, and it was fun to work with other people."

The Carpenters were once dubbed the Goody Two Shoes of pop music. They were criticised for being too nice and too sugary. "In most instances, we were put down for simply striving for perfection," said Karen. "A lot of the knocks we took were through jealousy."

She was attractive but was painfully thin. But she had always looked that way. What the public didn't know at the time was that Karen Carpenter was slowly dying. She had been in and out of hospital a few times, with weight losses and food disorders. But in 1983 she collapsed at her home in California, was rushed to hospital, but died. She was only 32. They said it was a mixture of anorexia and sleeping pills.

The same day I interviewed The Carpenters, I also pinned down the great Herb Alpert, the man who first discovered them and put them on record. He was the big boss at A & M, and apart from being a songwriter and record producer, he was also a top trumpeter and bandleader with his popular Tijuana Brass combo. He had his own string of hits, the most memorable I think being This Guy's In Love With You. And at one time, his albums were even out-selling the Beatles.

For a guy with so much talent and money, I found him remarkably modest.

LORNE GREEN

Lorne Green was the Big Daddy of TV's most famous Western series Bonanza, which was screened around the world for many years. But when I met him in Hollywood he was about to be launched into a new science fiction series called Battlestar Galactica. He was playing the commander of the spaceship Galactica, an inter-planetary man-of-war. A kind of cowboy boss in space.

Although a major TV series in the States, it was to be released in Britain first as a cinema feature film and was expected to do even better at the box-office than the amazing Star Wars.

For Lorne Green, the grey-haired handsome veteran, this meant TV stardom all over again. "I suppose you could call me one of Hollywood's survivors," he said. "I've been around a few years now, and it's nice to be working hard on something as big as this. The series seems to have taken off like a rocket. But I'm always cautious. Bonanza ran for 14 years. You never know in this business – anything can happen."

It was Bonanza, and Ben Cartwright, boss of the Ponderosa, which really made Green a worldwide star and earned him enough money to retire. "But I'm a worker. I'm not going to be pensioned off early," he told me.

The twice-married star lived in a handsome house in Bel Air, Los Angeles with his wife Nancy and young daughter Gillian. He also had twins, a boy and a girl, from his first marriage.

"When they offered me this TV part, I went to a bookshop and asked for the names of the ten best authors on science fiction and bought one each of their books. I wanted to immerse myself in science fiction literature," he said.

"As you can see, whether it's horses or space ships, I take my job seriously."

CHAPTER 10: THE NICE GUYS

MORECAMBE & WISE

Eric Morecambe really was a lovely man. Both Eric and his comedy partner Ernie Wise were nice guys and I got to know them, and their wives, very well over the years, and interviewed them many times.

We were away on a TV festival in Switzerland once, the Golden Rose of Montreux. They both had their wives with them, and it became very noticeable that, once all the TV viewings and the work was done, Eric and his wife Joan, and Ernie and Doreen never dined together. And Ernie explained to me that, although they were great pals, once they had both finished work they did not socialise very much together. Which was fair enough.

We'd often see Eric in the BBC bar, having a drink after they had recorded their TV shows. But not so much Ernie, who liked to go straight home to the missus.

I remember once chatting to Ernie about cars and he was going on about how wonderful his Rolls Royce was. He'd had several, and he would never change from a Rolls, he said, and asked me if I'd ever had one. I was something of a car enthusiast and always had good cars, like Rovers and Jaguars, but told him I would have loved a Rolls, but they were far too dear. "Nonsense," said Ernie. "They're not as expensive to run as people think. I get about 16 miles to the gallon from my car, and I'll bet you don't get much more from your Rover. I think you should buy a Rolls, you'd really enjoy it." Ah, if only I could have afforded it!

There was a story Eric told me once, about the time he had his first heart attack. They had been playing a theatre up in Yorkshire, and Eric was driving home after the show when he felt pains in his chest. He was alone, and he felt really ill and knew something was wrong. The only person he could see was a man on a bike. He pulled up alongside him and asked him where the nearest hospital was.

Eric eventually said, "Look, can you drive me to the hospital? I don't feel very well."

The man said," Well, what about my bike?" Eric said, "You can come back later and get the bike. Just get me to a hospital. Please."

So the man got behind the wheel of Eric's Rolls and then said, "I've never driven one of these before." Eric, now desperate, said, "It's quite easy. It's automatic. You've only got to steer it."

78

Eventually they set out and arrived at the hospital. The man ran in and said, "I've got Eric Morecambe outside. He's been taken ill."

They rushed Eric into hospital on a trolley and found he'd had a minor heart attack.

But as he was being wheeled away, this chap was still standing there. Eric leaned over and thanked him. And the bloke said, "Look, my mates will never believe this when I tell them tomorrow." Then he gave Eric a pen and a piece of paper and he actually said, "Can you give me your autograph before you go?"

Eric swore it was true. He told that story on a TV chat show later.

One of the saddest days of my life, a few years later in 1984, was having to write Eric's obituary for the paper. He died from another heart attack and he was only 58. He really was just about the funniest comedian of them all.

Another story about the much-loved Morecambe and Wise Show. When Eric and Ernie were top of the ratings, and they were getting just about every big-name to appear on their programmes, I heard from one of my pals in the BBC that they had signed up Angela Rippon, the news-reader, to go on and do a dance routine.

The BBC tried to keep it all secret and wouldn't confirm it. But I talked to Eric and he told me it was true.

In those days, I used to go regularly into the BBC, poke my head into the Press office and say hello, and then often wander around the various studios to see what was on, and sit and watch rehearsals.

And on this occasion, I also managed to get a Mirror photographer, my pal Kent Gavin, in as well. It was the dress rehearsal for the show being recorded for Christmas transmission.

Angela came on, stepped out from behind her news desk, stripped in this fantastic see-through silk gown, and did her dance routine. Kent Gavin discreetly shot a roll of film, and I wrote the story.

The Mirror came out with this big picture piece - Angela Rippon kicking up her legs and dancing on the Morecambe and Wise show. It was exclusive. The BBC went mad that we had sneaked in and taken the pictures. But Eric and Ernie were secretly quite pleased because a story like that in the Daily Mirror would guarantee them maximum publicity. And I think their Christmas Show came out with the highest audience ratings of the year.

KENNY EVERETT

It's very important, being a showbiz journalist, to make contacts and to try and make friends with people you interview. But I must admit this can sometimes have its drawbacks and you can get too close to someone, so that it may even become embarrassing.

In a way, that's what happened to me with Kenny Everett. I had been interviewing Kenny for years, often going over to his place in Notting Hill in London. He was always good for a laugh and was what we called "good copy". He woulds come up with something new to say and quite often was deliberately provocative. We would have fairly regular lunches together, and I'd inevitably get a good piece out of him. Apart from anything else, I really liked him. He was fun to be with.

I also became quite a close friend of his wife, Lee. She was a bit of an oddball character. She believed in the spirits and psychic powers and all that stuff. But I always found her friendly and funny (At one time, before Kenny came along, she had lived with pop singer Billy Fury).

However, I got a phone call from Kenny one day, and he said, "Ken, do you want a good story? Lee and I are splitting up." I couldn't believe it, because they seemed to be so happy and compatible. Then he followed up and said, "Look, come down and have lunch and we'll talk."

So I went down to their place, and Kenny and Lee were both there. They insisted we went out for lunch, so they took me to a rather trendy fish restaurant around the corner, and Kenny ordered two bottles of champagne with our fish and chips.

Between them, they then continued to tell me that they were splitting up. It was simply that Lee couldn't stand it anymore. We had always suspected that Kenny was homosexual, because he was so outrageously camp, but he had never actually admitted it, not in public anyway.

Now, for the first time, here was Lee telling me, "I've known for ages about Kenny. But he's finally fallen in love with this Spanish waiter, and it seems to be serious. I've had enough. I think Kenny loves him more than he loves me. I want out of it."

They wanted me to write the story for the Mirror. I said to Kenny, "Look, is this really what you want?" He opened the bottle of champagne, poured us all a glass, "No, it's Lee's idea. She wants to tell the world. What can I do about it?" Lee was half laughing, half crying.

We then started drinking champagne together. And Kenny got louder and louder, and ended up screaming, "Tell the world I'm gay. Ken Irwin is going to tell the world. Are you listening, World?"

Again, I asked Lee, "Is this what you really want?" She said, "Yes. We've given you the story because Kenny likes you, you're a mate. If you don't write it, I'm going to ring up the Daily Express and talk to David Wigg. Maybe he'll understand more easily." That was a tongue-in-cheek comment because David Wigg, then showbiz writer on the Express, was discreetly gay, too, and was a rival of mine although we were great friends for years.

We ran the story next day. It was a big front-page splash. They insisted I got a photographer around to the restaurant, and got a picture of Kenny and Lee ending their marriage over a bottle of champagne. It was terribly sad, of course. But that was Kenny.

He remained a good friend. We continued to meet for the occasional lunch or drink, and I wrote a few more pieces on him, before and after I packed up at the Mirror.

I was not around when he finally died of AIDS, I'd left London   and moved back up North. And I was glad about that. I know some of the papers gave him a hard time. I wouldn't have wanted to be involved in any of that.

I know he remained chirpy right up to the end. From what I read and heard, Kenny was still laughing right up to his untimely death.

He was a strange little man. But in his own way, he was something of a comic genius.

NORMAN WISDOM & BILL OWEN

When it came to being a comic genius, Norman Wisdom took some beating.

Not everyone's taste in humour, of course. But for sheer slapstick comedy, he was the natural successor to the great Charlie Chaplin.

Norman and I became great friends after I was invited by his PR man, Clifford Elson, to go down and interview him at his home.

He lived in a magnificent Spanish-style detached house with lovely gardens, not far outside London. Then twice divorced, he lived alone except for his housekeeper, who became very close to him.

Norman had a very sad life. From his very early childhood, when he was an orphan, he was conscripted into the Army as a teenager, and became a trumpeter.

At that first interview, he poured out his heart to me over lunch and a few drinks. And as I sat and listened to him for several hours, absolutely enthralled by the poignancy of his life story, I realised what a remarkable little man he was.

Absolutely self-made, he was not only a genuinely funny man, but also a very astute businessman.

At one time, Clifford Elson wanted me to help write Norman's autobiography but, somehow, we never got around to it.

Over the years, after Norman's career slackened off, he moved to the Isle of Man, which of course was a tax haven for the super-rich. And Norman was certainly that. He would fly back and forth to England whenever there was work in the offing. And he once told me, "I'll never retire. It's not just the money. You don't retire in my game."

Then one day I got a phone call - after I'd left the Mirror and was now freelancing - telling me that Norman Wisdom was going to make a guest appearance in TV's Last of the Summer Wine. I knew the cast of that show very well, and often went up to Yorkshire on location to write features on Nora Batty, Compo and Co.

I was the only journalist there to greet him when Norman reported for his first day's work. He was quite surprised when I turned up, because we hadn't seen each other for many years. But as soon as they broke for lunch, I got the chance to talk to him, and he was rather chuffed at the idea that I wanted to write a piece about his new character.

The weather was foul. Windy and wet, up on the moors, and when I suggested we had lunch, Norman said rather quickly, "Let's take some sandwiches and sit in your car and chat. I'll feel more comfortable there."

It then became obvious to me that, even in such a short space of time, there was a bit of jealousy brewing among the cast. After all, the stars of the resident cast were Bill Owen (Compo) and Peter Sallis (Norman). And although I knew Bill and Peter quite well, I also knew how they worked and how protective that whole cast were with each other. And I could see that someone like Norman Wisdom joining the show was likely to maybe put a few noses out of joint. Wisdom was, after all, a huge star, and Bill Owen and Peter Sallis were not accustomed to playing second-fiddle to anyone.

Norman took it all in his stride, however. From that original lunch-time chat in my car, he made it clear that he was a thorough professional and he was there to do a job. And as it turned out, his character became quite a popular addition to what was already a top show.

Incidentally, I sat through many happy hours, watching them film scenes for Last of the Summer Wine. And Bill Owen was always good for a story or two. I recall him once telling me, "We'll go on with this show for the rest of my life, I hope. I mean, I'm 78 this year. Where else can I get a regular job at my age?"

Not surprisingly, he felt more at home in Yorkshire than in his native London. During filming, he rented a bungalow at Holmfirth, where the series was set. "I love all the fresh air you can get only in the Northern countryside," he said.

He'd then already played Compo for 20 years and told me, "I don't have to worry any more. For years, I had to take on parts I didn't really want to play because I needed the money. Now, when a new producer comes on to me and says, 'I've got a lovely little cameo role for you,' I say, 'Do me a favour – no thanks. Sod off!' I just don't like playing small parts. I like big showing-off parts."

At the time, Bill was busy writing his autobiography. "It's a very ordinary life but I've had my moments," he chuckled. "I've had two wives – but who hasn't? I've never been arrested, and I've never been caught in somebody else's bed. I have been in people's beds that I shouldn't have been in – but again, who hasn't?

"I never took my socks off. That's my motto – never take your socks off, and always know where your shoes and trousers are." He had a wicked sense of humour.

Bill fell in love with the Yorkshire Dales and was determined to be buried there when he died.

After his death in 1999, at the age of 85, he was buried in the church graveyard at Upperthong, Kirklees in Yorkshire.

Bill's son Tom then joined Summer Wine, too, playing Tom Simmonite, the son of Compo. He looked just like a younger version of his father.

As for Norman Wisdom, he was knighted in 2000, and ended up in a nursing home on his beloved Isle of Man. He eventually suffered from dementia. But from a TV documentary I saw on him, he never lost his sense of humour and still loved to go out for a drive in his Rolls Royce. He died in 2010 at the ripe old age of 95.

A great comic. And a warm and very likeable man.

TERRY WOGAN

When it comes to nice guys in show business, well they just don't come any nicer than Terry Wogan. With Terry, what you saw, really was what you got. I've known him ever since he joined that motley crew of disc-jockeys launched by Radio 1 on the steps of Broadcasting House. What an odd assortment of characters they were!

Since then, Terry and I have had a few lunches at the George Hotel, around the corner from the BBC, and enjoyed a bottle or two of what he would call "fine wine." He invited me over to his home once, and we sat out on the lawn, having drinks, while Terry talked rapturously about his garden, and how much he loved his sit-on lawnmower.

Although his various TV programmes kept him busy (his celebrity chat show, the game shows like Blankety Blank, and his mammoth annual Children in Need spectacular) it was his long-running Radio-2 programme he loved doing best.

"You know me, Ken. I never take myself very seriously," he'd say. "People either love me or hate me – there is no in-between. The whole of my radio show is a self-mocking thing. I don't use a script or prepare the programme at all. I just say the first thing that comes into my head and hope that the audience out there appreciates my sense of humour. If they don't, it's too bad."

Most of the letters he received proved that his audience was on the same daft wavelength as he was. "They insult me something rotten," he said. "So, I have a go back at them. But I think people who listen to my show regularly know by now that it's all done tongue in cheek."

Terry had his own serious philosophy on broadcasting." It would be very easy to sit down and plan the show to make sure I never offended anybody. A lot of broadcasters make a very good living doing that and taking no risks. But I don't agree with that. I think 'live' broadcasting is all about taking risks. I would hate to just sit there, like a great blancmange."

In his earlier years, he would regularly take the mickey out of fellow disc-jockey Jimmy Young, whose programme he preceded every morning, and this would often upset Jimmy's fans. He had a running gag at one time about Jimmy's string vest and raincoat.

When I once mentioned this to him, Terry responded, "As for Jimmy Young, well, anybody who goes to Cairo on holiday and asks for two boiled eggs for breakfast, and steak and chips for dinner, deserves all he gets!"

For some time, he had a daily horse-racing tip for listeners, which he called Wogan's Winner. It was another of his jokes. "I don't know a damn thing about horses," he told me. "I did have a share in a horse called Wogan's Wager for a while. But it never won a thing for me. Jockeys kept getting off him and beating the horse to the post. I owned only a part of him – the part that went last past the post. I never won a penny, but after we sold him, the horse went on to win three races.

"And I was once praised by the Council of Churches. They said that my daily horse-racing tips on radio put people off gambling!"

For many years, I covered the Eurovision Song Contests, all over Europe, and of course Terry was always the BBC's presenter, with that wonderful tongue-in-cheek technique which he mastered so well.

I used to organise a Sweep for the Press mob. We'd each put in a pound and draw out the name of a country. And the punters would include the BBC production team, Bill Cotton, their jovial TV Controller, and Mr Wogan. Our sweep became a very popular little side event, almost as popular as the song contest itself. And it was all very scrupulously run.

Terry was always happy to say, "Count me in." Well, one year, he came up lucky. When the song contest winner was announced, I looked at my written list of punters, and it turned out that Terry had the winning ticket. The trouble was, he was so busy at the after-show party, and then flew back to London very early next morning, and I didn't get the chance to give him his winnings.

A few days later, I sent him his winnings to the BBC, with a note congratulating him.

To my surprise, next day on his radio programme, he announced, "I'm a very happy man this morning. It seems I won the British Press Sweep at the Eurovision Song Contest. And thanks to Ken Irwin of the Daily Mirror for the twenty quid. That'll buy me lunch."

That wasn't the only time, though, when Terry gave me a plug on radio. I will never forget that he did me a very special favour once which involved my lovely young sister Joan.

She lived in Upton, Wirral, but she had applied for a new job which entailed her having to go down to London on a two-week training course. She came and stayed at our house in Harrow, and I agreed to drive her over to Kenton every morning to her work, before going in to my office.

Now I knew that she'd listened to the Terry Wogan radio show every morning for years. So, without telling her, I dropped Terry a line.

Then, with the radio on as usual, I was driving Joan in the car, when Terry Wogan suddenly announced on air, "Hello, this is a special greeting for Mrs. Joan Jones. I understand you are probably on your way to Kenton right now. Probably stuck in traffic. But here's a song especially for you." He then played a record for her.

Well, I tried not to smile. But I glanced sideways, and Joan's face was a mixture of surprise and horror. For a few seconds, she didn't quite know how to react. It was as though she couldn't believe what she was hearing.

Then she turned to me, thumped my arm, and said, "This is you, isn't it? How does Terry Wogan know I'm in London?"

It was one of those magical moments that just happen in life. It not only made her day, but she talked about it for a long time afterwards. And we'd often laugh about it.

I was glad I did it. Our Joan really was the nicest, kindest, sweetest girl, woman, who ever lived. Sadly, she died only a few years later. A brain haemorrhage brought her life to a tragic end, when she was still so young. She was lying in a coma in Walton Hospital, Liverpool, and I was sitting alone at her bedside, talking aloud to her but not knowing whether she could hear me or not. And I reminded her of that moment when Terry Wogan played a special request for her. Unfortunately, she never recovered and died only a few days later.

As for Terry, although I knew him for years, I never plucked up the courage to ask him if he wore a wig. There was always much speculation about that.

A friend of mine from another paper did ask him once, and Terry said, "Look, take a good tug at it. It's not a wig." But the guy wasn't convinced and still didn't know whether it was his real hair or just a very strong adhesive he used. But it's one of those things he just wouldn't talk about. And who cares anyway?

The thing about Terry, is that he was a great survivor. He'd worn very well and was clever in the programmes he chose to do. Our Tel was a very shrewd businessman.

And particularly when you look at the tremendous work he did in raising millions for Children in Need over the years - well, was there anyone better?

When Terry died so suddenly - at the age of 77 in January 2016 - it came as a complete shock. For he had kept his battle against cancer a secret from everyone except his family. The reason for this, they said, was that "he didn't want to make a fuss." He did not want people feeling sorry for him, even though he knew he was dying and had not long to live.

BBC executives and his colleagues were expecting him to return to work. Instead of revealing the cancer diagnosis, he told even his closest friends he had a back problem.

His death caused widespread nationwide mourning. He was hailed, quite rightly, as probably Britain's greatest and most popular broadcaster.

RUSS ABBOT

Russ Abbot is a very talented performer, in my opinion. And another nice guy. Always very pleasant, easy to talk to, and with none of the pretentious behaviour often displayed by other star names.

He was living in Chester when I first got to know him, and he was successful as a drummer with the pop group the Black Abbots before turning to comedy and re-inventing himself as a stand-up comedian.

Russ was always very ambitious and was very determined to make it to the top. In the 80s, he became Britain's biggest comedy draw, vying with Cannon and Ball as the No.1 box-office star in the theatre and also on TV.

Five times he picked up an award voting him The Funniest Man on Television.

I remember interviewing him, just after he'd gone from ITV to the BBC in 1986. "The reason I've crossed channels is because the BBC has given me more scope to do a show with a completely new look," he said. And he was then joined again by his old pal Les Dennis and his faithful female stooge Bella Emberg.

Some of those characters he created in his sketch shows - like Basildon Bond, Cooperman, Jimmy the Scot, and Vince the Teddy Boy- were quite hilarious.

But I recall that he had two sons keen to follow him in the business. Gary, then 19, was with a pop group and wrote the theme music for Russ's TV show. And Richard was only 16 when he started working backstage with Russ in the theatre.

Russ was very strict however. "I have told both my sons that if they want to go into show business, I can't open doors for them. They're on their own and they have got to learn the business the hard way, the same as I did," he said.

In between topping the bill in his summer show at Blackpool's North Pier and recording his TV shows, Russ had been suffering secret heartbreak. For his mother Elizabeth, who was then 71, was in a nursing home suffering from senile dementia, which left her unable to recognise Russ.

"It's breaking my heart," he confided. "I arranged to bring her over for a night to see my show in Blackpool. I asked her afterwards if she had enjoyed it, and she just said, 'I've got to go now.'

"I send her a big bunch of flowers every week. When I last visited her and said, 'The flowers are nice,' she said, 'Yes, they're from Russ Abbot, you know.'"

It was very sad. It wasn't easy trying to make people laugh, when he was all choked up inside, he told me.

Once, when I went to see him in Blackpool, the sun was shining, and we walked together along the seemingly endless wooden North Pier to the theatre where he was topping the bill in his summer show. "There's nothing quite as long as this North Pier on a cold night," he chuckled. "And when it's raining, it's the longest walk in the world to this place. But I love it. It's my lucky theatre."

Russ loved Blackpool. He thought it was the best resort in Britain. He'd first played there with his music group The Black Abbots, doing summer seasons in 1976 and 1977 on the smaller South Pier. But when he dropped the band and turned to comedy, he topped the bill at the more commercial North Pier in 83, 86 and 88, and one of his summer shows established an outstanding record in seaside entertainment by taking more than £2 million at the box office.

"Blackpool is now the Las Vegas of Britain. It's alive, it's vibrant and it caters for everyone," he said. You would think he was doing a commercial for the place, but he insisted he really did love the resort.

Russ had a long and very successful run as a comedian. But he told me, even in his early days, that he wanted to emulate Dudley Moore and become an actor. And that's exactly what he did. He went on to become a straight actor and took on serious roles on TV and the theatre. I wasn't surprised when he went on to join those old timers and give a much-needed boost to the long-running Last of the Summer Wine, where he found new TV fame, before that show was finally wrapped up.

DES O'CONNOR

It was impossible to meet Des O'Connor without immediately breaking into a laugh. Because he has an infectious sense of humour and is one of those people who just never stops smiling. He was just born, I guess, with a face that was made to laugh.

The nice thing about Des is that he has a great sense of humour. It was just as well, because if he hadn't, he would not have been able to cope with all those insults he had to suffer at the hands of Morecambe and Wise. It was all a joke, of course. Really, Eric and Ernie were great pals with Des, and whenever they worked together Des was happy enough to let them have a go at him.

They joked about his "awful" singing. But Des actually had quite a good voice, and the fact that he produced 36 record albums and had four Top Ten singles, including a No.1 hit, I Pretend, must prove that someone liked him.

Des wasn't just a singer though. He was an all-round entertainer. But was he a comedian who could sing a bit? Or a singer who could tell jokes? I don't think even Des knew himself. He once told me, "I don't really care whether the public regard me as a comedian or a singer, as long as they like me."

He started out wanting to be a professional footballer, and he played for Northampton Town before deciding he wanted to be an entertainer.

But like most comedians starting out, he found it a struggle. And I like the story about the first time Des went to Scotland to play the Glasgow Empire, which was a theatre with audiences notorious for hating English comics and giving them a hard time if they weren't funny.

When Des, then an unknown newcomer, went on for the first time, his performance was greeted with a stony silence and then as he walked off, a chorus of booing.

He was petrified and didn't want to go on again for the second house. But he had to do it. So, as the curtain went up and they announced his name, he took the only action he could think of - he fainted. Or at least pretended to.

As he lay on the stage, apparently unconscious, the producers dragged him back behind the curtain, and the show continued without him.

They frantically tried to revive him, but Des was still flat out on the floor. Someone dialled 999 and an ambulance quickly arrived, and the medical crew brought out a stretcher to take him to hospital. Just as they were lifting Des on to the stretcher, he opened one eye. And the ambulance man spotted this, must have realised that Des was only suffering from nerves and was not seriously ill, and winked at him. They then took him away, with Des still pretending to be unconscious.

I once asked Des if this story was true, and he laughingly confirmed that it was.

The Glasgow Empire continued for some years to terrify English comedians. But no one had ever got off stage by pretending to faint, as Des did.

Years later, Eric and Ernie continued to tease him about it. "If you want to get off stage in a hurry, just do a Des O'Connor!"

Des, who started out in 1956 as a comedian, has lasted more than 60 years in the business.

After finishing with his TV variety shows, he went over to being a chat show host, and did seven series of Des O'Connor Tonight between 1977 and 2002. Personally, I thought he was at his best in those chat shows, just talking amiably. Even though he was notoriously sycophantic, he always managed to get a lot of laughs out of his guests, which was really what is was all about anyway.

Des has married four times and has five children. And he always had a reputation as a ladies' man. Once, when we were having lunch in Torquay at one of his summer seasons, he laughed loudly when I brought up the subject of women.

"I like women. But unfortunately, I also like wedding cake," he quipped.

CANNON & BALL

Tommy Cannon and Bobby Ball worked as factory mates in Rochdale for several years before they took the plunge and turned pro, as singers. They were welders by day and played the local pubs and clubs as a double act by night, working under the name of the Harper Brother. Tommy's real name was Thomas Derbyshire, and Bobby's was Robert Harper.

The odd thing was, when they first got what they thought was their big break on telly in 1969, on Hughie Green's talent show Opportunity Knocks, they upset Hughie first by appearing as singers on one of his auditions, but then changing their act completely to become comedians on the actual TV appearance. As it turned out, when the votes came in, they finished last.

It was some years later before they got another TV chance, and that was on Bruce Forsyth's Big Night Out show. Fortunately, it was Michael Grade, then a big boss at ITV, who saw something in them and decided to give Tommy and Bobby their own show.

That's when I first met them. I went up to Rochdale to interview them, and they struck me immediately as a couple who were going places.

It didn't take long for the great British public to like them, too. Cannon and Ball simply shot to stardom. In the mid-1980s they more   or less took over as top comedians from Morecambe and Wise. Their TV series topped the ratings and drew regular viewing audiences of over 18 million a week, and they went on to sell-out summer shows at Blackpool and every other big resort.

I interviewed them quite a lot, and I recall Bobby once inviting me up to his home - a lovely period house, which was a centuries-old converted coach house, high in the Lancashire hills, near Rochdale.

With their friendly banter and likeable personalities, they could do no wrong. They even moved into films with a comedy movie called The Boys In Blue. It was not a great success however, so they cleverly stuck to TV.

Between them, Tommy and Bobby had everything. The big houses, they drove around in Rolls Royce cars, and even had their own cabin cruisers. They bought holiday homes in the Canaries. Bobby invested in a nightclub in Rochdale, which he called Braces. And Tommy bought the local 4th division football club.

But then, quite suddenly it seemed, it all came crashing down around them. They were dropped from television, the TV bosses deciding the public had experienced enough of middle-aged Northern comedians. Then, one day, Tommy opened his front door, literally to find an Inland Revenue Inspector standing on the doorstep with his accountant, telling him that the Cannon and Ball company owed more than £1 million in back tax.

Overnight, their luxury lifestyle had to go. Now more or less back where they started, in the clubs, Tommy and Bobby worked their socks off and paid every penny of their tax bill.

It was then revealed that, secretly, the boys had fallen out and things became so bad that for a few years they even refused to speak to each other apart from when they went on stage.

Bobby admitted later that he went wild. Drinking, women, fighting. "I was completely lost," he said. But miraculously, he became friendly with a church priest, who talked to him about religion. And Bobby became what they call a born-again Christian. He confessed all to his lovely wife Yvonne, who forgave him everything, and he admitted to Tommy what a fool he had been, and the couple made up and became friends again.

A few years later, Tommy was so impressed by Bobby's new life of Christianity that he, too, became converted to God.

They are still working, albeit quite modestly compared with their past bill-topping days. Both now in their 70s, they insist they have no plans to retire. "We'll go on working together until one of us drops dead," said

Tommy. And Bobby, who is six years younger, and always looking for the cheap laugh, said, "That'll be me burying you, then."

From a personal point of view, I have always got on well with both of them. But it was Bobby who was the favourite with my mother. Because when she was on holiday in Blackpool, some years before she died, she went to see Cannon and Ball in their summer show, along with a group of blind friends from the hotel she was staying at. "And Bobby Ball came around and gave us all a kiss and a hug. It was lovely," she told me.

So rock on, Tommy! And Bobby, too.

LITTLE & LARGE

Another Northern double act that followed Cannon and Ball, were Little and Large. Though they were never as funny, they were still remarkably successful. They had their own TV shows and they topped the bill at theatres throughout the summer.

I was aware of them from their early days and I always found them great fun to be with.

They landed their first seven-week TV series in 1977, and when I went to interview them they were both tremendously nervous. They'd been playing pubs and clubs for about 13 years, since giving up their jobs, Syd as a painter and decorator, and Eddie as an electrician.

They were then being tipped as the next big comedy duo on TV. "The danger is that the boys are inevitably going to be compared with Morecambe and Wise, Mike and Bernie Winters and very other double act in the business," said their producer Royston Mayoh. "But they are quite different. They are unique. They are going to be really big stars."

It was Eddie Large who always did most of the talking, while Sid, the skinny one, used to be happy to sit in the corner and just chip in with the odd remark.

I felt sorry for Syd because on stage it was Eddie who got most of the laughs. He was the fat bully-boy who would chastise his gormless little mate throughout the act. And it was the very same, offstage. Poor Syd was hardly allowed to get a word in.

They based their act, of course, on the great Laurel and Hardy. But to even talk about them in the same breath would be considered sacrilege.

But I can remember Syd saying, "To me, Eddie is the funniest man in the world. I only have to look at his face, and I start laughing. I am more than happy just to be the straight man." Eddie then chipped in, "I know everyone thinks it's the funny-man who does most of the work in a double act. But this isn't so. This fellow Syd does far more work than I do. He's supersonic and he's a great guitar player. He's the best straight man in the business."

And Syd said, "When we started out playing in the pubs, we were earning £30 week between us, and we were too scared to ask for more money in case we got the sack. We were then offered £35 a week for our first big date - in Bernard Manning's nightclub in Manchester. We thought that was a fortune."

The pair had very different personalities. Syd worried about everything, while Eddie told me, "I only worry about the important things in life - like whether Manchester City win or not, and if I can get my golf handicap down from eleven."

They stayed at the top, earning big money, much longer than even they would have anticipated, I'm sure of that.

CHAPTER 11: MIKE & BERNIE WINTERS

It would be wrong to look back at comedy double acts without referring to Mike and Bernie Winters. Now they really were looked upon as the Poor Man's Morecambe and Wise. They even used the phrase themselves, and often laughed at it.

The story was told that, whenever anyone talked about the famous Glasgow Empire Theatre, the name of the Winters brothers would come up. The Glasgow Empire was notorious for years as being the worst theatre in the world for English comics. Comedians hated playing Glasgow, because the audiences were renowned for their dislike of comedians from south of the Border. They rarely applauded. And often they would pelt the performers on stage with coins, or rotten fruit, if they didn't like them.

Les Dawson once told me, "Glasgow Empire audiences were horrific. If they liked you, they let you live!"

Mike and Bernie made their debut there, as very young unknown comics. Fresh faced and fearful. And their act consisted of Mike going on stage alone for the first few minutes and playing the clarinet, and then Bernie coming on as the comic. On the first night, Mike went through his clarinet solo, to be greeted with a stony silence from the audience. Then Bernie appeared from behind the curtain, and stood there, in a silly pose, beaming with that big toothy smile on his face. And there was an immediate loud cry from a man up in the gallery, "Christ, there's two of them!" which brought the house down.

Actually, Mike and Bernie, brothers from London's East End, were really very nice guys. After struggling and treading the boards for years, they finally made it big and became major TV personalities. Their shows ran from 1965 to the late 70s. I became particularly close to them after they landed their own series, Blackpool Night Out, and I went over regularly to see their shows, which were produced from the ABC Theatre.

The shows went out, sometimes live, at 8pm on Sunday nights. And in between rehearsals, throughout the afternoon, we'd spend hours drinking in the nearby bar of a little restaurant called the Blue Parrot.

After the show, it would be more drinks with Mike and Bernie, before we'd go for a bite to eat, and then stumble back to our hotels. I spent a summer or two doing just that. My office was quite happy for me to do it because I invariably got some good stories, as well as plenty of gossip for the telly pages.

94

It's important here to stress that, being a journalist, it's part of the job to build up a friendship with the people you interview. I always thought so, anyway. And that was the way I worked. There are, of course, the straightforward one-off interviews, when you are probably not going to meet that person again. But, as far as I was concerned, I always liked to think I could go back to a showbiz star, or whoever, because I was trusted. I have never made up a story in my life. Ever. Everything I wrote was true.

A journalist learns to depend on his instinct. You have to have the ability to sniff out a story. The art is to ask the right questions, and then sit back and listen. You learn to know when someone is lying to you, and when they are being honest. It's all part of the game.

Inevitably, you get to know some people better than others. And I used to like to think that, once someone got to know me, they could forget I was a journalist, and just regard me as a friend.

Well, that's the way it became with Mike and Bernie Winters. We saw each other so often - particularly during their long stints in Blackpool - that we became great pals.

You have to learn to be discreet sometimes. If someone tells you something "off the record", then you don't report it. That doesn't mean that you don't forget it.

But even I was surprised one Sunday night, when Mike Winters came over to me after the show and said, "What are you doing tonight, Ken? Do you want to go out and have a few drinks?" As I had nothing planned, I said Yes, sure.

So off we went together. I asked where Bernie was, and he said casually, "Oh, he's busy. His wife Siggi is up here for the night. So he's got to be a good boy."

I didn't think anything more about it, until he then suggested we go over to a nearby pub, to meet a couple of people. Well, it turned out to be two girls. They were very young, maybe 18 or 19. One was a small, very ordinary looking brunette, and the other a tall, willowy attractive blonde.

He introduced me to them, and it was obvious they were old friends, or at least familiar. He then told them that Bernie was busy somewhere, but did they want to come back to his hotel. They seemed thrilled at the invitation. We took a taxi back to the Imperial Hotel, where Mike and I were both staying.

Once there, Mike took us all to his room, then phoned down for Room Service and ordered sandwiches and a couple of rounds of drinks. The two girls took their coats off and made themselves at home.

The food and drinks arrived, and we all sat around chatting. And it suddenly became pretty clear to me what the set-up was. The girls obviously knew Mike and Bernie very well and had clearly been through all this before. I was just getting a little worried about how it was all going to pan out. But it was all very friendly, and Mike was doing most of the talking, as he sat back and puffed away on his pipe, which he often smoked.

Then suddenly, the niceties came to an end and Mike got up, yawned and said something like, "Well, I don't know about you guys, but I'm ready for bed. Shall we split and say goodnight?"

Then he winked at me and to my surprise, he got up, gave the willowy blonde her coat and said, "Perhaps Ken will see you home." Then he ushered us out of the room and said goodnight. The other girl stayed with him.

It was now about one o'clock in the morning. The blonde girl and I walked down the corridor, and she said, "I usually go off with Bernie. But I always have to be home before breakfast, or my Dad will go mad." I said, "Where do you live?" She told me a couple of miles away. "Do you think you could give me a lift home? I haven't got the money for a taxi." She was a very sweet girl and I felt sorry for her.

So I agreed to take her home. We walked out of the hotel, as furtively as I could, because I was now feeling extremely embarrassed at the whole situation. I wasn't used to sneaking out of a hotel with a young girl in the early hours of the morning! My car was in the car-park, so I dropped her off home.

As I drove back along the prom to the hotel, I was mulling the whole thing over in my mind and was now quickly sobering up, when a seagull suddenly flew straight into my car and splattered itself all over the windscreen. I got back to the hotel, went to bed, and then after breakfast checked out, and had to clean all the feathers and the dead bird from my windscreen before driving to Manchester. What a strange night it had been.

I didn't see Mike until the following Sunday, when I went over to their next show. It was Bernie who came up to me, after their rehearsals, and said, "Hi, Ken. Heard you had a good time last week with Mike. Thanks for helping out." It was all quite surreal.

Funnily enough, when I went to see subsequent shows throughout the rest of that season, I would be sitting in the theatre and I would see those same two girls sitting, quite happily, in the front stall seats. They'd obviously been given tickets by Mike and Bernie. Once or twice, they would even wave to me, in a cheeky kind of way. I realised that this was my first direct experience of teenage groupies. It was usually the pop groups and singers who had girl groupies waiting outside the stage doors. But apparently, comedians had their share too.

They obviously regarded me as someone they could trust to be discreet. I mean, it wasn't the first time some star name had played away from home and cheated on their wife, I suppose. But it was the first - and the last - time I had been directly involved in any of it.

Not surprisingly perhaps, my relationship with the Winters brothers took a new turn from then on.

The next time I met Mike and Bernie was a couple of years later, when they were doing their summer stage show in Bournemouth. I went down to catch up with them, to interview them for a new feature, and they left a ticket at the box-office for me to see the show. Afterwards, I was invited by Mike to an after-show party. As we had a few drinks together, he was surrounded by half a dozen of the gorgeous dancing girls from the show. Mike certainly enjoyed having female company around.

Then in 1978, the boys were appearing on the Isle of White, and they decided it was going to be their farewell tour, because they were about to split up. I got a phone call from one of them - did I want to go and see them in their last show?

Well, I did. It was cold, miserable weather and the end of the summer season. And the show was very mediocre, very ragged, but they both tried to put on a brave face.

I was sad to be there to sit through it. But on September 16, 1978, they did their very last show together, at the Pavilion Theatre, Shanklin.

Bernie made the announcement on stage with tears in his eyes, "This is our last performance together." Then he presented Mike with a beautiful cut glass bowl bearing the inscription: "To The Best Straight Man In The World."

The audience would have been forgiven for thinking they were witnessing the break-up of a close family partnership. Though they may have noticed that Mike gave Bernie nothing in return. And after the show, he went off to a dinner party with his family and friends, to which Bernie and his wife were not invited.

They had trod the boards together for nearly 30 years. At their height, in the early 70s, only Morecambe and Wise were bigger.

After they split up and went their separate ways, Mike went off to America and tried to establish himself in various businesses, including running a theatre- club in Florida, and promoting dinner boxing matches.

Bernie meanwhile wanted to continue as a performer, but the prospect of going on stage alone for the first time in 30 years terrified him. People had been saying for a long time that he was the funny one in the act. Now he had to go out and prove it.

The chance came when Thames TV offered him a trial show of his own. It was then that Bernie hit on the idea of bringing a dog into the act. "I need someone to talk to. I just can't go out there by myself," he told Siggi. So he hired a huge St. Bernard dog, named it Schnorbitz, and introduced it on his first solo show. The four-legged stooge was an instant hit with viewers, and Bernie was soon back in the big time. The only surprising thing was that he had actually replaced his brother with a dog.

He had two TV series of his own and was then signed up by ATV to play the lead in a 90-minute special about the career of music hall star Bud Flanagan.

But a few years later I was surprised to get a phone call at the office from Bernie's wife Siggi. She wanted to know if I would do a write-up for the Mirror on her life with Bernie. "We want to tell our story, the full and frank truth. No holds barred," she said. "But I want payment for it."

Siggi, German born, very attractive and an ex dancer, was quite a tough lady but I had always got on well with her. I hesitated when she said she wanted paying, because I was never really happy getting into cheque-book journalism. I had always prided myself on being able to get the big stories without resorting to bribes and up-front payments.

But she knew value of the story, and when I told my Editor he was immediately interested and gave me the go-ahead to sign her up and pay her.

So I went over to see Siggi and Bernie at their home, in north London, and we sat for hours talking. "Look, I know what he's been getting up to when I'm not around," she said. "I've told Bernie it's time to come clean - in public."

With my tape-recorder running, they both then continued to tell me lots of stories about the disintegration of the relationship between Mike and Bernie. Some of it was quite vitriolic, which surprised me. But I went away, wrote it all up, okayed the finished articles with them because I had given them what we called "copy approval," and the Mirror ran an exclusive two-parter over the next couple of days. Siggi was so grateful that she even sent me two bottles of vintage champagne, from Harrods, which I hadn't asked for or expected.

To outsiders, Mike was the serious one, the brains, and Bernie was always introduced as the dumb-dumb. But Bernie was the shrewder of the two when it came to handling business, Siggi told me.

Apparently, they always split their money fifty-fifty. But there were times when Bernie was offered extra work - particularly lucrative TV commercials - without Mike, and that hurt the older brother. But Bernie would still give Mike half of anything he'd earned on his own.

The first real row they had, I learned, was in 1971 when they were playing a summer season in Bournemouth. Out of the blue, they were offered £20,000 to sign a contract with a new agency, MAM. Mike jumped at the chance, but Bernie wanted them to stay with their own agent, Joe Collins (father of film star Joan Collins) who they had been with for years. Bernie regarded Joe as a second father, and they had no contract with him, just a handshake.

Bernie won the day, and they never signed the new contract offer. But that's what opened up a rift between them which was to last for ten years.

It was during that same Bournemouth season that Mike walked out after the first show and didn't come back for the second house. As the theatre filled up, Bernie phoned Siggi at home and said he didn't know what to do. He was in a panic.

The theatre manager was unsympathetic. "You're a comedian, aren't you? "Can't you go on alone and tell some jokes?"

In the end, Bernie had a hurried meeting with two members of the show, dancer Lionel Blair and comedian Peter Hudson, who both knew the brothers' act very well. They agreed to share Mike's role between them, with Lionel feeding the straight-man lines to Bernie in some sketches, and Peter taking over in others. They worked like that for a week. Eventually Mike sent a doctor's note saying he was ill. Even then, on pay-day, Bernie insisted on everyone getting a share of the cash - Lionel, Peter, Bernie, and as usual Mike.

That was the beginning of the end, though. The rift between the two brothers grew worse. They started arguing more and more over the comedy material they we using. Then they started arguing over girls. And sometimes the friction would spill over into embarrassing public scenes.

The first, Siggi told me, was at Heathrow airport in 1974 when they were setting off for a short tour of Australia. The two wives were at the bookstall when suddenly a furious row erupted between Mike and Bernie.

99

Onlookers stood and watched in amazement as the two brothers yelled at each other. It ended with Bernie screaming at Mike, "I'm not going on stage with you anymore. I now give you one year's notice - then we quit."

When they arrived in Australia, they were still so steamed up that they booked into separate hotels. And they never talked to each other again, except when on stage.

Even their two wives couldn't bring themselves to be in the same room together.

But then came the big dilemma facing the Winters brothers. It was the girls and the affairs they were both having, away from their wives,

To my surprise, Siggi told me all about their womanising when we had that long session, chatting away in the lounge of her home, with Bernie sitting nearby and looking rather sheepish.

It was on an earlier tour of Australia, in 1973, when she first realised that Bernie had been cheating on her, big time. Cassie, Mike's wife, had stayed home because she was ill. And one day, Mike walked into a restaurant with a young girl on his arm. But seeing Siggi sitting there, he turned around and walked out.

"I suppose it was naïve of me. But that was the first time it really occurred to me that the boys must have had birds around when we weren't there," she told me.

She still didn't suspect anything of Bernie, even when, on the same trip he said to her, "What would you say if I told you I had a girlfriend?"

Siggi replied, "Get rid of her quick - before I find out."

The secret then lurking behind Bernie's apparently abstract remark was the presence of a beauty queen called Dinah May. Bernie had met her the previous year in a Birmingham nightclub, where he was a judge in a bathing beauty contest. Dinah won. It was her first success in a career which later saw her crowned as Miss Great Britain in 1976.

Dinah May was 18, Bernie was 40. But that meeting, apparently, was the start of a passionate affair which went on for years.

Siggi told me, "It seems that everyone knew about it but me. They say that the wife is always the last to know. They used to meet here, there and everywhere."

She remembered the time when the boys were going off to do some shows in Aden, and Bernie showed her a photograph of a young girl that they wanted to introduce into their act to do some "stooging." "She's a very good-looking bird," said Siggi. It was Dinah May.

Mike too was having his flings. His girl at the time was a dancer. But his wife Cassie wasn't aware anything was going on.

In 1975, Mike and Bernie even rented separate houses in Blackpool for the summer season. Like a Whitehall farce, their wives would arrive from time to time, and spend a night or two, but once they'd gone back home, the dancer would move in with Mike, and Dinah May would be back in with Bernie.

Siggi told me that, in 1976, she watched at home on TV a heat of the Miss Great Britain contest. She taped the programme for Bernie to watch later, and even remarked casually, "Isn't that girl pretty?" She had picked out the eventual winner - Dinah May.

Then one night as they were getting ready to go out for dinner, Bernie said to his wife, "Look, I've got something I have to tell you." That something was the bombshell that Bernie was being named by Dinah May's husband in a divorce suit.

The night ended with another public row. They went to a Greek restaurant, where Siggi tried to drown her shock in drink. She danced with every man in the room and rounded off the night in traditional Greek style by smashing hundreds of plates at Bernie's feet, making sure that a few of them hit him. Bernie just sat there, emotionally drained, not saying a word.

Over the next few weeks, Siggi and Dinah May had numerous shouting matches over the phone. Not satisfied with Bernie's confession, Siggi hired a private detective to watch him. In the process, she then found out about Mike's affair with the dancer.

Finally, Siggi decided that if anything was to be salvaged from this matrimonial mess, someone had to act decisively. She told Bernie straight, "You've got to decide - it's me or this girl Dinah May. Who do you want?"

Bernie looked at her meekly and said, "Well, put like that, I think I want her." Siggi admitted to me that she was devastated at the time.

Ironically, when Bernie walked out on his wife, he headed off to be re-united with Dinah May. But he was only away half a day. Siggi had great delight in telling me, "He drove to meet his fancy lady, and at that time she was in bed with her husband." Bernie turned around and went back home, and assured Siggi, "I don't want anything more to do with her."

Even when Dinah May phoned him at home, and pleaded with him to return to her, he remained adamant that the affair was over.

Dinah May was divorced soon afterward, though for the sake of his public image, Bernie was not named in the case. He did, however, agree to pay Dinah's legal costs. She then went on to marry again. A musician.

But after that, it was Siggi who laid down the rules as far as Bernie was concerned. And it was Siggi who was responsible for the boys finally splitting. Because she could see that the tension between the brothers was making it impossible for them to work together.

During their pantomime season at Newcastle in 1976, the mutual hostility reached the stage where they insisted on having separate dressing rooms in the theatre. And it erupted in to open warfare in a Birmingham nightclub soon after Bernie's affair with Dinah May ended. Mike walked into the club with his girlfriend, a dancer, on his arm and began to tease Bernie. "Who's been a naughty boy, then?" he taunted. "I didn't get caught with my bird, did I?" They were immediately swapping punches and had to be pulled apart.

After that they hardly spoke to each other offstage. And even on it, their act began to suffer because they wouldn't rehearse together. They performed like robots, mechanically going through their familiar old comedy routines, but both delivering their lines into space to avoid making eye contact. Pathetic, really.

In the end, it was Bernie, backed by his wife, who told Mike, "Let's call it a day. We'll finish all the engagements we've got in the diary and then split up." And that's what they did.

After going solo, Bernie's marriage was much more stable. Siggi told me herself, "I was very hurt at Bernie's unfaithfulness. For a long time afterwards our relationship was very bad. But it grew strong again. Bernie is no saint. Touring, staying in hotels, having to fill in between shows - girls are all part of the hazards of show business. But now that this has all come out into the open, we are very close, and nothing can ever touch that."

As for Mike, after the break-up, he said "Bernie and I reached stagnation in our performances. We had a hell of a good innings and we had some great times together. We made people laugh for a long, long time, and we were very successful - don't forget that."

And of course, he was right.

Sadly, Bernie was eventually forced to retire through ill health and died from stomach cancer in 1991. He was only 60.

Mike, meanwhile, went off to America and became a writer, before returning to this country with his wife, living in Gloucestershire. He wrote a few novels and another book of memoirs, nostalgically titled The Sunny Side of Winters. He died in 2013, aged 86.

CHAPTER 12: DAVID JASON

David Jason was an actor I got to know quite well. Long before he became famous as Del Boy in the brilliant Only Fools and Horses, he was doing bit parts for years in any work he could get.

But as he worked his way up to the top in a variety of good shows, it became obvious that little Mr. Jason had talent in abundance. There were long periods out of work for him, however.

I first got to know him when he used to drop in to the bar regularly at London Weekend TV on the South bank. Every Friday night, to round off the week, a gang of TV journalists would end up in the private Press bar which was organised by LWT's always friendly and generous PR guys Peter Coppock and Charlie Bain.

It would be open house for journalists. And David Jason popped in one night, and he enjoyed it so much that he often came back for more.

It was obvious that he enjoyed the Press banter, not to mention the free drink, and we more or less adopted him as a Fleet Street buddy.

We watched as Jason moved from one good show to another. And it wasn't long before he became a top-name star, with super shows like Porridge, as Pa Larkin in The Darling Buds of May, and as the detective in A Touch of Frost. None of it ever really changed him though. He was always easy to chat to and very accessible.

But I had a bit of a dilemma to face, one day early in 1989, when I received a phone call at my office from an unknown bloke in Yorkshire. He was a Daily Mirror reader, had seen my name in the paper, and said he had a good story - was I interested? I asked him what the story was. And he said, "I don't want to talk about it over the phone. But it concerns David Jason, and I can assure you it will be worth your while to come up here to see me. I will not be wasting your time. This will be front page news."

Intrigued, I set off for Yorkshire and drove to this fellow's house in Leeds. He was a 60-year-old man called Alex Camponi, who had his own sandwich-making business. And as we sat in his kitchen, he angrily spilled out his story.

He told me that his 29-year-old girlfriend Gillian Hinchcliffe, who had been his lover for ten years, had left him and was having an affair with David Jason, now the TV star Del Boy in Only Fools and Horses.

"If I ever get my hands on the little swine, I'll throttle him," he threatened. "We were perfectly happy until she met David Jason and ended up in bed with him.

"Now she's left me and my whole life has been shattered. I don't know where to turn." He was almost in tears.

Alex told me that the affair started when David was filming a new TV series in Yorkshire, called A Bit Of A Do. Gill apparently worked as an assistant on the show, which had been produced some months earlier.

"Despite the big difference in our ages, Gill has been my lover for the last ten years. But once she met David Jason, she changed," he said. "On my 60th birthday, Gill was supposed to come over for the night. She said she was working late on the TV show. That's when she stayed the night with Jason.

"I was completely shattered. I was prepared to forgive and forget. But she carried on with the affair. She couldn't stop talking about him and told me she thinks she is in love with him."

At the end-of-show party, on completion of the TV filming, Alex had apparently gone to the studios to tackle David. "I hung around all night, but I think she warned him, and he hopped out of the back door," he said.

Alex added, "Despite everything, I would have Gill back tomorrow because I still love her. You can't stop loving someone after all those years together. Everyone thinks Jason is a nice, funny little chap, but as far as I'm concerned he's a creep."

The fellow was clearly very upset and struck me as being a genuine guy. But he was having trouble facing up to what had happened. I said I'd check it all out and get back to him. I obviously had to confirm if it was all true. Or maybe the guy was some kind of nutcase.

When I tracked down Gillian Hinchcliffe at her home later that day, she said simply, "I have finished with Alex. He is a very irrational man. He is crazed with jealousy since we split up."

I then had to go and tackle David Jason, of course, which I was not looking forward to, because he was something of an old mate.

So I drove back to London, and confronted David (who was then 46, by the way) at the BBC studios where he was rehearsing for Only Fools And Horses.

David was not very happy that the story had leaked out, but said, "It's sad this bloke should be giving Gill a hard time. I don't care what he says about me."

We ran the exclusive story next day. "Del Boy Stole My Girl... Says Alex the Sandwich Maker." With accompanying pictures of Alex at home, Gill looking gorgeous in a swimsuit on the beach, and on holiday with Alex, and a head shot of David Jason.

I never heard anything more from Alex Camponi. But some years later David Jason, only 17 years her senior, married Gill. First, he became a father in 2001, at the age of 61, with the birth of a daughter, Sophie Mae.

Then in 2005, he was Knighted by the Queen at Buckingham Palace. But at the celebration party afterwards, David happily announced that they had been quietly married at the Dorchester Hotel the night before he became a Knight. And they are still happily together, I think, after more than 25 years.

I wish them well.

CHAPTER 13: DICK EMERY

There was another top-name comedian whose complicated love life I became involved with, and that was the wicked Dick Emery.

A strange man, he could be outrageously funny one minute, then become quite morose and sinister the next.

He was one of those entertainers who started out as a comedian after being de-mobbed from World War 11 as a Corporal in the RAF. But in fact, he had been in show business all his life, because his parents were a music hall double act called Callan and Emery, and he was on tour with them from a baby of three weeks old and was actually taken on stage to perform with them as an infant.

For years, he worked as a supporting actor on radio and TV for other comedians, including Tony Hancock, Michael Bentine and Charlie Drake, before finally breaking through and being given his own shows.

When he did make the big time in TV, the Dick Emery Shows ran from 1963 until 1981. And he also ventured into films, making several good-at-the-box-office movies between 1956 and 1972.

Emery certainly enjoyed the rewards of his success. He had his own plane (having acquired a pilot's licence) the Rolls Royces and a string of expensive sports cars. In fact, he used to boast "I change cars whenever the ash-trays get full."

Dick was only 5ft 8in tall, he had a very camp way of walking, and he used to like dressing up in drag a lot. He also coined the catchphrases "Hello, Honky Tonk," and "Ooh, you are awful - but I like you." All of which made a lot of people think that Emery was gay.

Far from it. He was not only heterosexual, he was outrageously randy. He was married five times and fathered four children. And goodness knows how many other women he had.

He once told me, "I love women. All women. The trouble with me is that I can't just love them - I feel I have to marry them." He reckoned later in life that he had only six long-term relationships - and he married five of them.

It was blondes he usually went for. Tall blondes, who towered above him when he was out in public. "I love women with long legs. With legs that start at the bottom in high heel shoes and go on forever," he chuckled.

I interviewed Emery many times throughout his career. But one day, in July 1980, I was on film location with the popular Dad's Army, when one of the actors I knew quite well, pulled me aside over a lunch break and said, "Have you heard about Dick Emery?" Heard what? I asked. Then he mischievously went on to tell me that Emery had walked out on his wife and left her for a young showgirl. It was one of those nudge-nudge wink-wink situations.

It was still something I felt I should check out. The next day, back in the office, I phoned Dick at home and his wife Jo answered the phone. This was Josephine Blake, and she was an actress and singer who was quite well established herself in the business before she married Emery.

There was no easy way of doing this. I said, "Is Dick working today? What time will he be back?" She cautiously said, "I don't know." So I then ventured, "Well, I've heard rumours and I wanted to talk to him."

She then said, without further hesitation, "Ken, if it's about our marriage, then it's true. He's walked out and gone off with some slag. If you come over later, I'll tell you all about it."

I went down to her house in Weybridge. I had got to know Jo fairly well over the years, and she then poured her heart out and told me everything. "I am heartbroken, absolutely shattered," she said. "Dick and I have been together for fourteen years and married for eleven, but now he's left me."

The other woman, she revealed, was an actress called Fay Hillier, a tall leggy blonde and mother of two, who had appeared in several TV shows with Dick.

"I feel very bitter about this woman mixing with a man she knows is married. As far as I'm concerned, she has broken up my marriage. Dick has known her for about a year, and I have been aware of their affair for six months

"In the years we've been together we've had our ups and downs, but basically we've had a very happy marriage. Now I only see him when he comes home at weekends. He packs a suitcase and off he goes again."

Jo, who was then 41, told me, "Dick is a very insecure man, as all comedians are. Outwardly he's full of fun. He flirts as part of his job, because he always has a lot of women around him. But he always knew he had me to come home to. I think it's over between us now. You'd better ask him."

That was my next task, of course. I learned that he was busy filming, so I phoned him at the studios. He wasn't available, but someone said they'd give him my message and he would get back to me.

Soon after, I got a phone call from Emery's PR man Clifford Elson, an old friend of mine, saying that he could confirm the marriage was over, and he had advised Dick to talk to me - and only me. He gave me a private number and said Emery would be waiting for me to contact him.

When I phoned him, Dick was almost in tears on the phone. He told me how sorry he was at leaving Jo, but he had fallen in love with this woman Fay Hillier, and he felt he couldn't give her up. He said he was relieved that it had finally come out, and he was happy for me to run the story.

Next day, I had it on the front page of the Daily Mirror. "Dick Emery leaves wife for Fay the showgirl" - with a big picture of sexy Fay, blonde, long legs, in black underwear and suspenders, grinning, with a bottle of champagne in her hand.

That same day, Dick Emery called a Press conference in London to officially announce the end of his marriage. I couldn't get to it because I was flying off to America to do a couple of other jobs. The Mirror sent my colleague Tom Merrin, who wrapped up the follow-up story, along with all the other national papers who knew they had been well and truly scooped.

Emery was a terribly nervous man. Throughout his career, he suffered dreadfully from stage fright and low self-esteem. There were long spells when he underwent psycho-analysis treatment.

"It all goes back to my childhood," Dick told me. "I was on tour with my parents at three weeks old. My mother was an actress, my father a comedian on the music halls. They split up when I was eight. You tell me a child from a marriage like that who isn't going to grow to be very mixed up. What lived with me for years afterwards was fear of my father, a man of almost Victorian views. I was petrified of him. All that was bound to manifest itself in me later. I grew up scared to death of any kind of authority.

"I still get constantly depressed. But at the same time, I know from experience that once I get out on stage, I will be all right."

After his fourth marriage ended in divorce, Dick had doubts about a fifth try. Josephine Blake was twenty years his junior. And he admitted to me, "Most of my success was due to Jo. I couldn't have gone on without her."

I talked to Jo again when I got back from the States. She was still terribly bitter but thanked me for the way I had handled the story, and even suggested she would like me to do more publicity on her because she was determined to get back into show business herself.

It never really happened though. Dick moved in and lived with Fay Hillier, who continued to work with him. But he died only a couple of years later.

In December 1982, he was rushed to hospital with severe chest pains, and after a short spell died of heart failure. He was only 67.

Ironically, although he was still with Fay Hillier, he remained married to Jo Blake.

Maybe, he felt that five marriages were enough, and he couldn't go through with a sixth.

CHAPTER 14: LES DAWSON

They just didn't come any funnier than Les Dawson. Offstage, that is.

On stage and in front of the TV cameras, he could be funny, depending on the comedy material he had to work with. But off duty, and usually in the bar, he could be hilarious with his droll, rather lugubrious ad-lib humour. I spent many a happy hour with Les, propping up the bar, mostly in Manchester, which was his home city.

He was one of those deadpan comics who also had a very serious side.

When I first got to know him, he was desperately trying to establish himself as a comedian, after years being out of work and earning a living as a door-to-door salesman.

In his early days, he went to Paris and worked as a piano player in a brothel. That's where he turned to comedy. "I'd get so bored, that I started playing the wrong notes on the piano, and it brought me a few chuckles. I then realised I could earn more money getting laughs than as a pianist," he once told me.

His big break came in 1967 on Opportunity Knocks, with Hughie Green. It wasn't instant success by any means, but Les slowly worked his way up to become a household name with his own TV shows, and later took over as presenter of game shows, including Blankety Blank which he inherited from Terry Wogan.

I always thought he was at his best when he was playing the piano and would then go off and hit all the duff notes.

He once told me, quite straight faced, "I learned to play the piano at a very early age. And I was so good at it that, whenever I was playing in our front room, the neighbours would come out and throw a brick through our window, so they could hear me better."

Away from the comedy, Les always had a serious side and he took up writing books. "I'm a wordsmith at heart," he told me. "I wanted to be a journalist at one time, but somehow I got sidetracked." He wrote three or four novels.

But I recall one occasion when I was invited by the BBC to make an appearance as a judge on the popular TV show Seaside Special, from down on the South coast. Les was the compere. And after we'd done the show, we were all tucking into sandwiches and having drinks, when a young BBC secretary came over to me and said, "Ken, do you know if Les Dawson is married?" I said yes, as far as I know. She then said, "Well, he's been trying to chat me up. He's a bit drunk and he wants me to go back to his room. But I don't fancy him anyway. He's not my type. The randy old devil!"

Next morning, at hotel breakfast, I saw her again. She laughed and said, "After all that drink last night, I had a very good sleep. How about you?" As for Les, he'd checked out early.

Les once invited me over to his house in St. Anne's, near Blackpool. It was splendidly furnished but a bit over the top for my taste. And he had lots of stone statues in the garden.

One story I like about Les Dawson, however, was told to me by a very good friend of mine, John Stevenson, a veteran scriptwriter on Coronation Street. It seems that John was once at one of those Royal occasions when the Queen and the Duke of Edinburgh were guests of honour at a Coronation Street "do".

When he was introduced to the Royals in the usual line-up, the Duke said to John, "I understand you wrote that very funny sketch tonight. It was very good. I enjoyed it."

Then he said, "Are you from the North?" John replied that he was.

"Do you happen to know the comedian Les Dawson?" asked the Duke. Yes, said John. "Then, coming from the North, how would you cook black puddings?" asked the Duke, quite seriously.

More than a little puzzled, John asked him what he meant. And the Duke said, "Well that fellow Dawson once told me that black puddings should be boiled, whereas I insist they should be fried. What do you say?"

And he then added, "Now, whenever I bump into Dawson, which is probably more often than I would wish, I just shout 'Fried' and he shouts back 'Boiled.' It's all rather amusing, really."

John swears it's a true story and he's been a fan of the Duke of Edinburgh ever since.

Les Dawson's wife Margaret died from cancer in 1986, after years of suffering. He then married again three years later - a barmaid he met in his local pub. A bubbly blonde called Tracy. Les already had two children. He then had a daughter with Tracy, called Charlotte. But the baby was only eight months old when Les, who had already suffered heart trouble, died after a heart attack. He was only 62.

CHAPTER 15: BERNARD MANNING

There was no one - and I emphasise no one - bigger and better at taking an insult than Bernard Manning. He had the skin of a rhinoceros. He once told me, "Insults just bounce off me. I've got the thickest skin in the world."

And he needed it, because throughout his long 40-odd years as a stand-up comedian, he probably took more flak than anyone else in show business.

Bernard was labelled sexist, a racist, a bigot. But he just shrugged it all off and simply got on with making people laugh and making money. That's all he really cared about.

I got to know him very well, and I suppose I would be considered a friend. He loved publicity but didn't care if the critics and newspaper columnists attacked him. "I'm only here for the punters. They're the ones that matter. As long as they keep coming through that door, I'm happy," he'd say.

The punters, as he called them, were his regular audience who paid to go into his club, the Embassy in Collyhurst, Manchester, which in later years he cheekily re-named The World Famous Embassy Club.

It was a tatty, run-down building, but Bernard employed many of the top comedians to appear there. Some were up-and-coming hopefuls keen to gain experience, but some were big-name TV performers. I remember comedian Frank Carson telling me, "When you go into Bernard's club, you don't brush your shoes on the mat when you go in, you brush them before you go back out on to the street." And fellow comedian George Roper used to say, "Manning's place is not so much a club, more a giant ashtray with music."

Bernard originally started out as a singer in local pubs. He had a very good tenor voice, and he turned pro and became resident vocalist with the Oscar Rabin band.

He then talked his father into selling his greengrocery business and buying a snooker hall which he then converted into a nightclub. He reckoned it was the best investment he ever made. It became the family goldmine. While Bernard was the resident singer, compere and comic, his wife Vera would be behind the bar, and his mother would be on the till, checking the money.

When TV came along, and Bernard was given his big break by Granada, he was signed for a trial run of The Comedians by producer Johnny Hamp.

Johnny told me later, "I knew I was taking a chance with Bernard, because he was so blue in the clubs. I had to tell him, 'You've got to cut out all the naughty stuff, Bernard. No blue gags on TV, or you're off!'"

Knowing his career depended on it, Bernard was as good as gold. "I can do clean or dirty. It depends on what audiences want," he told me more than once. "I have a rule of thumb at my club. Immediately I go on stage, I deliberately throw in a couple of real naughty gags. Then if anyone is offended, they might leave and walk out. But I then know what kind of a crowd I've got in, and just how far I can go."

On TV, he soon became the heavyweight king of the Comedians. Alongside such very funny stand-up comics as Frank Carson, George Roper, Colin Crompton, Duggie Brown, Ken Goodwin, Mike Reid and the rest, Manning more than held his own. He could compete with anyone.

Specialising in Jewish jokes, many people thought Bernard was Jewish. He wasn't. "I'm a not-very-good Roman Catholic," he said. "But travelling around with the Oscar Rabin band, I picked up a lot of Jewish jokes. One of my best mates was a Jewish salesman - I don't mean he sold Jews, he's not that good!"

In The Comedians' New Year's Eve programme, Bernard was given a song spot for the first time on TV. It resulted in him getting a recording contract as a singer. His first LP, called The Serious Side of Bernard Manning was released. And Bernie said, "It's crazy. When I was a singer, no record company wanted to know me. Then, when I turn comedian, they give me a recording contract as a singer."

Bernard could be a mischievous so-and-so. He used to infuriate some of his fellow comedians by going on TV and deliberately telling the same jokes he knew they had lined up for later in the show. He did it just to annoy them.

Little comedian Sammy Thomas once said on the show, "Bernard Manning was found lying on the floor outside his club in Manchester, bound and gagged. The police have issued a statement to the effect that it wasn't his own gag."

When Bernard heard that they were to play the London Palladium for a short season, he cheekily put a half-page advert in The Stage newspaper to say: "After 23 years of messing about, I've finally made the Grades!" I was told that Lew Grade and his brother Leslie were so amused, they phoned him up to congratulate him.

But despite all his bravado and his loud-mouthed boasting, Bernard was a very different man when he was offstage and away from the cameras.

I was invited to his home quite a few times. And there he'd be, sitting quite unashamedly on the sofa in the living room, wearing only his vest and underpants, and gazing at a giant fish tank the length of one wall. Or else, he was watching the horse racing on telly, and trying to pick the winners. That was his only real hobby. Gambling. He would think nothing of putting a bet of £5,000 on a horse. But he once told me, "I never gamble more than I can afford. I'll never lose more than I can earn working the next week."

He never ever went on a holiday. "I hate holidays. A total waste of time. I would get bored after the very first day away," he would say. His wife would go on luxury holidays though, usually expensive cruises, but she would go off with their son Bernard junior, or maybe friends.

For a few years, Bernard had a very strange lifestyle. For while his son Bernard lived at home with his mum, big Bernard lived mostly with his ageing mother Nellie, a couple of miles away. He always maintained that he could not leave his mother alone, because he couldn't bear to think of her living on her own at the age of 86 or whatever.

And when he was at home his domestic philosophy was simple. "I don't lift a finger. I don't wash the pots or even knock a nail in the wall. My job is to bring the money in. If that sounds like the old cave-man attitude, then that's the way it is."

But all that came to an end in 1986, when his wife Vera died of a heart attack at the age of 56. And I was there, at first hand, to see just how her death affected him. I have never seen a man quite so devastated.

I went to see him only two weeks after her death. And that big tough-guy character was still in tears. He opened up his heart to me in a way I would never have expected.

He had been on stage, working in clubs up and down the country. "I've been trying to keep audiences laughing - and myself from weeping," he told me.

The night Vera died, Bernard was on his way home from working in a club in Nottingham. He arrived home about 4.30am. "The nurse told me that Vera had gone about half an hour earlier. It was a bombshell," he said. "The awful thing was that I'd stopped for a meal at the service caff on the motorway. I never dreamed she'd go just like that."

They had been married for 30 years. And Bernard was suddenly talking to me about his memories of how they first met. "It was in a club. I sang the song Autumn Leaves. Vera said afterwards, 'You sang that beautifully.' I danced with her later and then I took her home. I'd just got out of the

Army, and Vera was a secretary in the office of a cotton mill. We courted for seven years.

"I used to go on singing engagements and pick up £2 a night. We stuck all our money in the bank. We were determined to have our own house before we married. I bought my first car, a little Ford Popular, and I'd go off to do nightclub bookings, and Vera would come with me." They married in 1956, their son was born four years later.

Bernard was in tears as he told me, "I don't know what I'm going to do without Vera. I loved that woman. She was just an ordinary housewife, but she kept me in check. Vera used to enjoy a good laugh. She'd look at me and say, 'You're no oil painting, but you do make me laugh.'

"Now she's gone. Born, married, and buried - all in the radius of two-and-a-half miles. Everybody knows how much I loved her. And she knew too. I've done nowt but cry for a fortnight.

"The thing I am going to miss most is not seeing her every day. Just sitting and talking things over. Having a good laugh together."

Bernard was then still very much in demand, even after the TV heydays were over. He was still earning around £7,000 a week doing his cabaret act in nightclubs all over the country.

"I have to go on working, especially at a time like this," he said. "Working is the only thing that keep me sane. I would only pull out of a show if I was too ill to walk on. The adrenalin just flows once I'm on stage. It's a mixture of the spotlight, the musicians behind me, and the audience in front of me, I can't really explain it.

"The greatest satisfaction is a standing ovation. When people come up to me after a show, shake my hand and say 'Bernard, you've given us a bloody good night out', that's what counts for me. If I gave up work, I know I'd be dead within six months."

Bernard survived in the business for 50 years. He once said, "I don't smoke, I don't drink, and I've never been a womaniser. And I've never deliberately hurt anyone."

Some people might argue with that last sentiment. Because he loved the idea of still being able to shock people.

After the death of the Queen Mother in 2002, he joked, "All the Royal corgis were happy to hear about her death, as they would no longer be blamed for urinating on the settee." Some people were outraged. Others probably thought it funny. That was our Bernard!

He died, a very rich man, in 2007 aged 76.

CHAPTER 16: PAUL DANIELS

One of the perks of being a journalist, particularly a show business reporter for a paper like the Mirror, is that you are occasionally invited on to TV shows. Judging talent shows, like New Faces, which I did for a while, or bathing beauty contests, which I did quite a lot of in the days when girls showing off their curves and boasting about their vital statistics was all part of popular television light entertainment.

Once, I was invited by magician Paul Daniels to be a guest on one of his BBC TV shows. He wanted me to do a bit of magic with him. I agreed to do it, but I had to tell him, "I don't want any tricks with cards, because I'm not very well up on cards."

He asked me what I meant. And I had to tell him the story, which was true, of the very first time I was ever invited onto a TV show was when I was a young Northern TV critic and appeared on the Chan Canasta show.

Chan Canasta was a top magician, long before Paul Daniels came on the scene, and he had a weekly TV series on BBC in the early 60s.

The show was done from their studios in Manchester. I turned up, and was shown into the make-up room. Then, literally ten minutes before the show was due to be televised live, myself and two or three other guests were introduced to Chan Canasta, and he told us briefly that he was going to do a card trick with each of us. I, maybe wrongly, said to him, "Look, I don't know much about cards. In fact, I know a Heart and a Diamond, but I don't know the other two. I can't tell a Spade from a Club." And I was being honest. Those cards always confused me. Still do.

Well, he got into a right state. Suddenly, red light - we were on air! We were all sitting in a row on stage. He introduced us. Then, one by one, Chan Canasta did a trick with each of the other guests, but he steered clear of me. I thought he was going to ignore me altogether. But he couldn't really. So eventually he came over to me, and he was sweating, looking quite terrified. And he said, "Please concentrate. This is a very simple trick. Even you can do it. We've never met before, right? There has been no collusion with us?"

I automatically said, "No. Not with me, anyway. I don't know about the others." Oh, he got all flustered again. "No, there's been collusion with anybody," he insisted, almost bellowing at me. Anyway, he did the trick with me, and it all worked out fine. And he didn't produce a single Spade or a Club." There was a huge round of applause from the audience.

117

The show ended. Afterwards, the producer Barney Colehan came over and said to me, "Thanks Ken, that was fine. You were quite funny on there, with one or two jokes. I'd like to use you again, another week, but Chan Canasta has said No. He wants nothing more to do with you - in fact he said he would never have had you on the show if he'd known you knew nothing about cards!" Barney and I had a laugh about it.

So years later, when I told Paul Daniels about my encounter with Chan Canasta, he fell about laughing and insisted I go onto his show. I've forgotten the exact details of his trick, but it involved Paul coming into my office at the Mirror, giving me a sealed box. Then a week later, I had to go onto his TV show and he performed this amazing trick. I don't know how he did it. But, of course, it worked perfectly. But that's Paul Daniels, he really was the best magician of the lot, I think.

I've been over to his house once or twice. On one occasion, I got him to do a stunt with me, which was an illusion looking like he was sawing my arm off. We ran this in the Mirror. I've still got a photograph of this at home. It's really a clever illusion picture, and it fools a lot of people. Although I do know exactly how he did this trick, I am forever sworn to secrecy.

I liked Paul Daniels. He was a very astute businessman as well as a clever performer. But he did admit to me once, after he'd revealed that he was bald, "I don't know why I wore that awful wig for so many years. I may look older now that I'm bald, but I never enjoyed that wig."

He certainly knew how to turn on the charm, too. Some years ago, I was walking down Regent Street in London, doing some Christmas shopping with my wife, and we had my sister Louise and her husband Ernie with us, when we bumped into Paul Daniels just outside of Hamley's. He stopped, met my family, and insisted on kissing the hands of my wife and my sister, and bowing courteously. It made their evening. I don't think my sister ever forgot that day she actually met Paul Daniels.

The last time I was invited to his home, in the village of Wargrave, Berkshire, we sat in the garden and he just talked. Something he was very good at. "There are few people who can out-talk me when I really get going," said Paul, who had a reputation for ad-libbing a lot on stage. "I've never been known to dry-up in my life."

Paul first became interested in magic when he was eleven. After leaving school he got a job as a junior clerk in the treasurer's office with Redcar Council, Yorkshire. "I always wanted to be a magician, but my parents thought I should have a secure job," he said. After a spell in the Army, he

118

went back into office work and started entertaining part-time in Northern working men's clubs. But after nine years working in the clubs he decided to take a chance and become a professional entertainer.

He was a perfectionist in everything he did. "I think people are very suspicious of magicians. When I do a TV show, I insist that the director takes his cameras anywhere I'm performing – so as not to conceal the tricks. It's important. I don't want viewers at home to think that any of my tricks are done with the help of trick camerawork."

Paul was married and had three sons. But his marriage broke up when he was still in his early twenties, because he admitted he was more interested in pursuing his career than in family life.

When he was 40, he attracted a lot of attention when he met a young dancer who was auditioning for his stage show, the petite blonde Debbie McGee, who was only 20. She became his assistant on stage. She then moved in to live with him, and they were married ten years later.

Throughout their lives they had to put up with nudge-nudge wink-wink sarcasm from people who said they would never last. But Paul and Debbie were an ecstatically happy couple, and she became his business manager as well as his stage assistant and wife.

Sadly, they had the shock news, early in 2016, that Paul was suffering with terminal brain cancer. He had a brain tumour, and he was given only a few months to live. Sympathy poured in from all over the world.

Paul was very dignified about the whole thing. He said that dying didn't really worry him as "it was just like going to sleep."

And that's exactly what he did. When Paul died, Debbie said they had been sitting in their garden, eating ice cream and joking. Paul was singing some Beatles songs and trying to make her laugh.

He later fell into a deep sleep and died peacefully the next day. Their marriage lasted 27 years. "We had a wonderful partnership," Debbie said. "Never a day went by without us having a laugh together."

CHAPTER 17: ROBERT POWELL

One of the most memorable foreign jobs I did was on the production of that mammoth TV series The Life of Jesus, which starred Robert Powell, and was financed by Lew Grade's ATV.

Italian director Franco Zeffirelli was responsible for producing the epic series, and they were filming the Crucifixion scenes out in Tunisia. Several English newspapers were invited out, to cover the filming, and I was sent for the Mirror, along with our photographer, Mike Maloney.

We had a tremendous trip. I think it was in February or March, but the weather was hot and lovely, so it was a brief break for us from the British winter. We were supposed to be away for about three days, but when it came to the actual Crucifixion scene, they wanted the weather to be dark and dreary. But, in fact, the sun was shining every day.

Zefirelli, being such a perfectionist, insisted on waiting for the right weather. "Go and take it easy, and relax at your hotel, and in the morning, I'll phone you if the weather is right for filming," we were told. So we all kicked our heels around the hotel, ate and drank too much, and simply waited...and waited...and waited. But after three days of doing nothing, we journalists had to go to Franco and say, "Look, this is all very well. Much as we like sitting in the sun, our editors won't let us stay here forever, they'll want us back in London in the next day or two."

Okay, said Franco. And he agreed that if the weather wasn't bad the next day, he would fake some of the scenes, put darker lights on the set, so it would look more realistic of the Biblical version. This meant that we could get the right Crucifixion pictures for the Press, regardless of the weather.

However, next day, it was dull and overcast, almost as though God had heard and granted our wishes. The phone call came through from the Zeferelli - "Okay, we're going for it!"

We all dashed down. And finally, they got the vital Crucifixion scenes under way. It really was a splendid event. They'd had castle walls specially built in the town, and they had hundreds of actors as extras, dozens of donkeys and other animals. They took all day to get the required film scenes. But it was very impressive, and the Press photographers got some great pictures.

Everyone was happy. And the day after, Zefferelli threw a big dinner party for everyone, the Press and the leading cast members. They were setting out the seating arrangements for the dinner and decided to stick all the photographers up at the far end, just to get drunk and away from the actors, so that the journalists could have chats with the stars and do interviews during the meal.

I jumped in smartly and said I would like to sit next to Anne Bancroft (who was playing Mary Magdalene). There I was, I had Anne Bancroft on one side, and Robert Powell (Jesus) on the other.

But I found Anne Bancroft a bit of a let-down. She was very nice, but very boring. She had nothing at all to say. So my image of the great sex screen siren (as seen in the film Mrs. Robinson) was shattered forever.

Which was exactly what Terry Wogan also found, some years later when she appeared on his TV chat show. I remember Terry telling me, "Anne Bancroft? Oh, she was such a let-down." And I had to agree with him.

Incidentally, there were some very amusing moments on that trip in Tunisia. Robert Powell liked his cigarettes. And, as soon as the cameras stopped rolling, he would quickly light up a fag, as a form of relaxation. But on the actual Crucifixion filming, he had to spend most of the day tied up on the cross for several hours. And he was so desperate for a fag, that he got someone to light a cigarette for him, and there he was, puffing away, while he was waiting to have the nails hammered into his hands.

My photographer Mike Maloney, who was a very sharp operator, if not a devious bloke, sneakily pointed his long-lense camera at Powell and shot some film of Jesus on the cross, with a cigarette in his mouth.

Mike came to me later and told me what he had done, but felt a bit guilty about it. Then somehow it leaked out to Zefferelli that the Mirror had got some sneak pictures of Jesus having a drag on a fag. Franco confronted Mike and pleaded with him not to use the pictures. And together we agreed, Mike and myself, that we wouldn't take the pictures back for publication. And we were as good as our word.

After we were back in London, and all the papers had printed huge picture features of the Crucifixion scenes, Mike received a lovely letter from Zefferelli, thanking us for being so discreet and keeping our promise to destroy the pictures that would have embarrassed Powell and the producers.

Robert Powell became quite chummy after that. For him, of course, it meant worldwide stardom. He was always a good working actor. Suddenly he became an internationally recognised face.

We were quite good friends for a while and met, had lunches and did many interviews after Jesus of Nazareth.

Of course, he then married that gorgeous blonde Babs, who years earlier had been one of the sexy dancers in Pan's People on Top of the Pops. I'd known Babs since she made her bow on the pop show and had interviewed her many times for the Mirror and for the Top of the Pops Annual, which I edited for several years.

I must say though that Robert and Babs made a very handsome couple and they remained inseparable for years.

CHAPTER 18: FREDDIE STARR

When it comes to comedians, Jim Davidson may have appeared a bit mad at times, but he was nothing compared to Freddie Starr.

Now Freddie was a very funny man on stage. In fact, he could be brilliant. Off stage, however, he was completely bonkers. I interviewed him many times and got to know him quite well.

There was one occasion when I went onto him and said I wanted to do a two-part feature on him, and he agreed to do an in-depth interview.

He invited me over to his home, a lovely house in Windsor. I arrived there about one o'clock, we started talking and I put my tape recorder on, as well as taking notes. This was something I always did - I use a tape recorder but always take a lot of notes as well.

Freddie poured out his heart to me. We covered everything, all about his drinking, his womanising. He even talked of having taken drugs, which was all quite new at that time.

He just went on talking and talking, pacing up and down the lounge, rather like a caged lion, getting carried away, telling me how he once thumped his producer, and all sorts of stories which made very good copy, but half of which I could never have used because it would have been libel.

Anyway, it was now about 6 o'clock, and he hadn't stopped talking. I'd run out of tapes and notebooks. In the end, I had to say, "Hold on Freddie. I can't take any more. Can we take a rest?"

"Oh, would you like a cup of tea?" he asked. Well, yes, I wouldn't mind, I said. So, and I'll never forget it, we were sitting in the lounge. He picked up the telephone and said, "Can we have some tea in here, please, for Mr. Irwin? And maybe some biscuits." And ten minutes later his pretty wife (I've forgotten which one it was now) dutifully came in with tea on a silver tray. Freddie introduced me. "This is Mr. Irwin. Ken, this is my lovely wife. Thanks darling." Then he dismissed her. I couldn't believe it, that he actually phoned through from one room to the kitchen!

That was Freddie, completely mad. Next day, I wrote all this material up and I phoned him to query one or two things with him, because I wanted to make sure it was accurate. And he immediately started adding some more stories, over the phone. No, no, I screamed. I've got enough. As it was, I had to what we call "spike" a lot of it, because I knew our lawyers would never have let me get away with it because it was too outrageous.

Although I always got on well with him, Freddie really was manic.

I recall Engelbert Humperdink telling me a story about Freddie. Engelbert was having a big dinner party at his home, and he'd invited a lot of showbiz friends, including Freddie Starr.

A lot of big-name stars were already there, enjoying cocktails. The doorbell rang. His wife opened the door, and in walked Freddie. They were all dressed up. Dinner jackets, smart suits. Engelbert went to greet him, they shook hands, and he ushered him through the lounge and out into the garden, where everyone was mingling. Then, in front of dozens of startled guests, Freddie just grabbed hold of Engelbert and pushed him into the swimming pool.

Everyone was so embarrassed. Freddie stood there, laughing. Engelbert climbed, dripping, out of the pool...and he was not amused.

Freddie was a Jekyll and Hyde character. On stage he was brash, cocky and never lacking in confidence. Offstage, he could be quiet and quite serious and would even talk about politics and trade unions.

He once talked me through all his brawls, battles and backstage punch-ups. Yes, he had grabbed a celebrity by the throat. Yes, he did blow his top with a TV director. Yes, he did throw a punch at a singer.

"I know I had a bad name, but some people think they can walk all over me," he said.

He got up to some outrageous antics, though. Once, playing in summer season at Paignton, Devon, Freddie spotted a man asleep in the third row of the front stalls. "I couldn't resist it," he told me, "I jumped down off stage, climbed over the front seats and tried to give him a kiss. I then challenged him to come on stage and put the boxing gloves on with me, if he fancied a fight. But he didn't.

"I'm not up there to be abused and insulted. People pay good money to come and see me, just like they pay to see Muhammad Ali in a boxing match.

"When I'm finished for the night, I'm whacked, tired, like the bloke who works in a factory all day. I just want to go home, sit back and have a rest."

Freddie had been in trouble ever since he was a kid in Huyton, Liverpool. "I was never a tearaway, but I was cheeky, and I got the cane a lot for pranks. I was more an exhibitionist," he said.

He came from an extremely poor background. He was the youngest of a family of five. "I can remember as a kid of eight, I knew my mum and dad had very little money, so I stole a sack full of coal from a nearby site and carried it home on an old pram," he told me.

"I used to wear wellies in winter, summer, all year round, because my mum couldn't afford to buy me shoes."

He started entertaining when he was 15, formed his own rock n roll group, calling themselves Howie Casey and the Seniors. When he turned solo comedian, he went on to win Opportunity Knocks. But the really big break came when he was given a ten-minute spot on the Royal Variety Performance at the London Palladium in 1970, and he "stole" the show. Max Bygraves, who was the compere, was forced to bring Freddie back on stage for an encore. After that, he never looked back.

CHAPTER 19: DAVID FROST

David Frost was a remarkable man. Quite uncanny in many ways. Someone in show business, I've forgotten who it was, once said that, despite any faults you may have found in him, it was impossible not to like David Frost. And I would certainly go along with that sentiment.

He could be infuriatingly clever and smug. But at the same time, he was always so delightfully charming and polite. And invariably, he was good company.

I first met him when he was quite young and about to make his bow in the BBC show That Was The Week That Was. The year was 1961 and I was a young TV writer with the Mirror, based in Manchester, but had been brought down to do a stint in London. Ambitious to a fault, I was determined to show just how good a reporter I was. So, when we had a tip-off in the office that the BBC were planning a brand- new satire comedy show, I was sent off one Sunday, to find out more about it and do a news story on it.

At the time, I thought my department boss, TV Editor Clifford Davis, was testing me out and didn't really expect me to come up with anything, because the BBC were trying to keep the new show secret, and they would not thank us for revealing their plans. I went along to their smaller studios in Lyme Grove, Shepherds Bush, mostly used for news and documentary programmes. But when I went in to the front reception area, I was quickly shown out of the door by a commissionaire, who was furious when he asked me who I was, and I said I was Press. No one was allowed in unless they had an appointment, he insisted and anyway, as it was a Sunday and there was no Publicity officer available perhaps I should try again next day.

This wasn't good enough. Our original tipster had specifically told us that the BBC were working on the new show that day. So, annoyed and extremely frustrated, I was determined to get in somehow. I walked around the block to the back of the building, climbed over a low wall and found that the rear door of the premises was not locked, and completely unmanned.

Trying not to look like a burglar, I let myself in and then wandered through a few corridors of offices, and then finally came to the studio, which was buzzing with activity.

At first, I stood at the back and tried not to be seen. But there was David Frost, striding up and down, script in hand, surrounded by various actors, and singer Millicent Martin who was warbling her way through a song, with a pianist.

Then one of the production team came over to me and asked if they could assist me in any way. I simply replied that I had come to watch the show, and he then took me over to meet Ned Sherrin.

Ned was intrigued to know who I was. And when I introduced myself and told him I was from the Daily Mirror, he smiled ruefully and simply said, "Well, now you're here, you'd better make yourself comfortable. We are just doing a final rehearsal. Come over and meet David and the team."

We then went and chatted with Frost and one or two of the others, like John Bird and John Fortune. Kenneth Cope was the only one I knew, because I had met and interviewed him a few times when he was playing Jed Stone in Coronation Street.

It was then made clear to me that this was the pilot show, but they were hoping for a full-length series if it proved successful.

I was also quite relieved, because both Frost and Sherrin seemed very happy to talk to me and said they wouldn't mind if it appeared in the Mirror, as they were fed up trying to keep it under wraps for far too long.

They ran through the whole show, and I sat at the back, making notes.

Next day, I had a very good exclusive news story in the paper, and I think my London bosses were rather impressed.

That, for me, was the start of a very long friendship with David Frost. When That Was The Week That Was eventually came to the screen, it was a huge success and Frost and his new army of pals were set up for life.

David had a unique knack of remembering everything, and after that first meeting on the pilot show, he was always happy to do stories with me. Funnily enough, we were about the same age, and had similar Methodist backgrounds. He was the son of a Methodist minister and in his early days was aiming to be a lay preacher himself, just as I was, at one time. But the joke was that, after his university days at Cambridge and his early fame on TV, David was soon doing more laying than preaching, and he became notorious for having a string of attractive girlfriend in tow.

Actually, TW3 (as the show was nicknamed) ran for only l8 months, but it became the BBC's first really dynamic weekly satirical show, and it helped launch Frost as an international TV personality.

There was no stopping him. He went on to earn a reputation as a tough TV interrogator, was signed up in America to do chat shows there, and at one time was commuting weekly between London and the USA, and became Concorde's busiest first-class passenger. The jewel in his crown was in getting the former US President Richard Nixon to break down in tears and admit his part in the notorious Watergate political scandal, an interview which earned Frost a fortune.

He then quit the BBC and was one of the famous five who launched TV AM, with Michael Parkinson, Robert Kee, Angela Rippon and Anna Ford.

As well as his serious chat shows, he also devised and produced more entertainment shows, such as Through The Keyhole, which he did for 20 years, and established his own film company, before returning to the BBC to do more years of Breakfast with Frost and then Frost on Sunday.

I got to interview him quite a lot, and one of the things I discovered was that David had an uncanny talent – he could put a name and a face to anyone he ever met. He would amaze me by walking into a room, with 50 or more people, and he would not only remember all their names but would also recall the last time he'd met them. He did it with me, many times. He'd come over and say "Hello, Ken. How are you? How's your football team Everton doing? I think they lost 2-1 last week, didn't they?" He had an uncanny gift of immediately boosting people's ego, making everyone feel important. I asked him how he did it once. He just smiled, with that toothy grin, and explained, "Call it a gift, dear boy. I'm interested in people, and once I meet someone I never forget a name or a face." I've never known anyone with such charm. Though I suppose some might have called it smarm.

But he also maintained his reputation as a notorious romantic. In 1981, he finally gave up being a man-about-town bachelor and married the lovely Lynne Frederick, daughter of a theatrical agent, who was much younger than him. But the marriage lasted only a year, and they were divorced.

Then he married again, Lady Carina Fitzalan-Howard, and they had three sons, and were together until his untimely death. But previously his name had been linked with some of the world's most beautiful women, and at one time David was engaged to the lovely black Hollywood singer and actress Diane Carrol.

He made the headlines by buying her an engagement ring with a diamond the size of an egg. And the Press were constantly urging him to name the day.

Now, I shall never forget Dianne Carrol, although I never met her. But one day, I had set up an interview with David, and he suggested I go over to his house in Fulham and we have lunch together.

It sounded like a splendid idea, and I readily accepted. I went down, and we had a long chat over a very pleasant lunch. He was great value, as usual. He was a good talker, and once he got going, it was difficult to stop him.

Then eventually, we wrapped it up and I thanked him, and left his house about 3 o'clock in the afternoon, and took a taxi back to Fleet Street.

On arriving back at the office, however, all hell broke loose. It seems that news had leaked out in Hollywood that Dianne Carrol had called off her engagement to David Frost, and it was all over the TV news in the States.

My News Editor was on my back immediately. He suddenly realised that I had been interviewing David at his home, and he wanted to know what he had to say about breaking off the engagement. Could I write a news story immediately?

Slightly embarrassed I suppose, I had to tell him that David had not said anything at all to me about Dianne. In fact, I was pretty sure that when I left his house, he was not aware of the story breaking in the States. And I stick by that. There was no way David would have continued to have lunch and chat to me as he did, if he had known that his romantic world was about to be torn apart.

Of course, I immediately phoned David at home, to try and establish what had happened. Was he still engaged to Dianne or not? But he was suddenly not answering his phone. Ominous, obviously. Persistent phone calls were not answered, and eventually we realised that David had flown his nest, left home and no one knew where he was.

Next day, we ran the story from America, along with every other newspaper, about Frost and Carroll splitting up. And I added to it, with some of the stuff he'd talked about in our interview.

For a long time afterwards, I felt slightly embarrassed, and had pangs of regret that maybe I should have pushed him more about his relationship with Dianne.

But it was later revealed that it was Dianne who had called off their marriage, because she had decided she simply couldn't go through with it.

Dianne went on to marry four times, the last of her husbands being the great American singer Vic Damone. And years later, when she was asked why she did not marry Frost, she said, "David needed to have a family, and I did not want to have children at that stage. He also lived in London, and I did not want to move there."

David went on to have a very happy marriage with Carina, and they were together for 30 years, before his death in 2013 at the age of 74.

It wasn't always sunshine and roses for him, however. Throughout his career, David had to fight attacks of jealousy and hate from some of his showbiz friends. Although David had a nice-guy image, Peter Cooke was one bloke who particularly took a dislike to him, probably I suspect through sheer jealousy. He accused the successful Frost of stealing comedy material and called him "the bubonic plagiarist."

On one occasion, in Hollywood, Cooke dived into a swimming pool and helped to save Frost, who was not a very good swimmer, from drowning. Ironically, when Peter Cooke died, their delightful old chum Alan Bennett, at the memorial service, recalled that Peter had often said that saving Frost from drowning "was his only regret in life."

David was working right up to the end, although age was beginning to show, and he was slowing down a bit. Tragically, he died on the Queen Elizabeth liner while on a Mediterranean cruise. He was booked as an after-dinner speaker but had a fatal heart attack after a few days at sea.

Journalist, comedian, writer, producer, chat-show host, presenter. David Frost was the lot, all rolled into one. After more than 40 years in the business, it was reported in 2006 that he was worth £200 million. Typically, he said this was a slight exaggeration of his wealth.

Certainly, David was a gentleman who I always regarded as something of a friend.

CHAPTER 20: BRUCE FORSYTH

My relations with Bruce Forsyth over the years have been what I would call up and down. I was interviewing Brucie from the early days when he was King of the London Palladium, and he was always happy to do stuff for the Mirror, because he knew the value of publicity. I got to know him quite well, and he was always friendly and approachable.

All that came to an end one day, when there were lots of rumours going around about Bruce. And the Editor came to me and said, "You know Bruce Forsyth very well, don't you, Ken? Well, I think you've got to tackle him and put all these rumours to him and see what he says. If we don't, then another paper will."

Rather reluctantly, I went down to see Bruce. He was doing The Generation Game at the BBC at the time, and I went to the Shepherds Bush Theatre, asked to see him, and was shown into his dressing-room.

"I've only got an hour before the show, so come in and let's have a quick chat then," he said. I hurriedly went through this bit of an interview. I was trying to play it cool, to soften him up, stay friendly, because I knew it was going to be difficult and I wasn't looking forward to it.

Eventually, I thought it was now or never. I finally said to him, "Bruce, I've got to put this to you. There are several rumours circulating around Fleet Street about you, and I must ask you if they are true. If they're not, fair enough. But if I don't put them to you and deal with them sympathetically, then another paper is going to print them, maybe without even checking."

"What rumours?" he said.

And I said, (and I now look back on it with horror) "Well, first there's the story that you are going bald and you've had a hair transplant." He looked shocked. Then I continued, "There's a rumour that your marriage has problems and you are splitting up from Anthea."

"Oh yes?" he snapped.

Then I added, "The other rumour, which I hope isn't true, is that you've got a serious drink problem and you've been receiving hospital treatment to help you dry-out."

Well, he hit the roof. "Get out," he screamed. "You, of all people. Fancy telling me all this. Get out." And he stormed out of his dressing-room.

For a while, I just stood there, not quite knowing what to do. Then in came the producer, Stewart Morris, who I knew quite well, and he said,

"Christ, Ken. I don't know what you've said to Bruce, but he's furious. He's got a show to do in an hour. I think you'd better go."

"Don't worry, I'm going," I said. "I think I just caught him at the wrong time!"

I jumped into a taxi and went back to the office and I told the Editor exactly what had happened. "I think we can say he denied it all," I said. "And I think I've probably lost a good contact, because I don't think he'll talk to me again in a hurry."

Well, it was later revealed of course that Bruce had gone bald - whether he had a transplant or not I don't know, but soon after, he bought that horrible wig, which he wore for a long time (though there have since been a few expensive replacements over the years). His marriage to Anthea Redfern did break up shortly after. And as for the drinking problem, again, we'll never know. It may have been malicious gossip. It may have been true.

Anyway, Bruce and I never talked again for quite some time.

But some years later, I was covering the Eurovision Song Contest in Dublin. And the British entry was the handsome singer Scott Fitzgerald with a song called Go. The song was written by Bruce's daughter Julie Forsyth, who was there with her husband.

Throughout rehearsals, we chatted to them, and they were both very pleasant and friendly. Then, to everyone's surprise, Bruce Forsyth suddenly turned up at the final rehearsals and stayed overnight for the actual Eurovision contest.

There were lots of Press people around, and I wondered if he'd talk to me. He grudgingly said Hello, but we didn't really talk much before the contest. And to his credit he was happy to take a backstage seat and let his daughter enjoy the spotlight.

But at the end of the contest, England finished second in the voting, and at the after-show party, Bruce got a bit, shall we say, merry. He'd had a few glasses and he started shouting his mouth off about the contest, about the judges. And when I and one or two other British Press men closed in and asked him for his views on the contest, he said very loudly, "It's all a fix. The judging is fixed. We didn't stand a chance. It wasn't our turn to win."

I remember Bill Cotton, the BBC boss, smiling when we approached him for a comment. "I think Bruce has had a little too much to drink," he said trying to be diplomatic.

Which gave us all a very good news story for the next day, of course. Bruce hit the headlines. Something like: "Bruce slams the judges. The Euro contest is all a fix!"

He may have been a little embarrassed the next day, and the BBC were quickly trying to "hush" it all up. But that's the way it works. If someone like Bruce Forsyth gets a little tipsy and says things like that, then he must expect it's going to end up as a story.

That wig of Bruce's has become something of a joke over the years. You still get people, even today, saying, "Why does he wear it?"

Everyone used to laugh at Bruce's hair-piece. Apart from that tatty dishevelled old thing worn by the late Frankie Howerd, it must be the worst wig in showbiz.

And I can recall going to a show business lunch at the Dorchester Hotel. We used to have regular monthly luncheons laid on by the Variety Club of Great Britain. All the stars would be there. And this one was attended by the Duke of Edinburgh.

The celebrities were all lined up before lunch and had to meet Prince Philip. They included Gene Kelly, the Hollywood star who was standing next to Bruce Forsyth, and the boxer Frank Bruno was on the other side of him.

I was standing close by, as part of the Press party. We were all watching the Duke of Edinburgh going along the line, shaking hands with the stars. He came to Bruce, stopped briefly, looked at his head, at this miss-shaped slightly blond wig, and said something like, "Are you comfortable? Don't you find it hot in here?" Bruce looked suitably embarrassed and made some casual joke.

Afterwards, Gene Kelly came over to me and we were chatting, killing time before lunch. He shook his head and laughed. "Couldn't he get a better hair-piece than that?" Frank Bruno just fell about laughing.

Yet, looking back at all the hundreds of showbiz people I've interviewed over 50-odd years, I can truthfully say that, apart from Ken Dodd and Bruce Forsyth (who have both since made it up with me) the only person I can't, or certainly won't, go back to, is Bill Roache!

CHAPTER 21: LENA ZAVARONI

One of the most genuinely sad and tragic people I ever became friends with was the lovely Lena Zavaroni.

I first met Lena when she was a chubby little kid who had just won on Hughie Green's Opportunity Knocks talent show. She was nine years old. But it was obvious that she had an immense talent as a singer. She had a voice way beyond her years and it didn't surprise me at all when she went on to become one of Britain's most popular young entertainers.

At 10, she was the youngest singer ever to have a a record album in the British Top 10 charts, with Ma, He's Making Eyes At Me! She went on to have her own TV show on BBC when she was 16, and then for two or three years did several series, called simply Lena.

She even went to America and sang with Frank Sinatra in a Hollywood show, and then sang at the White House for President Gerald Ford.

I interviewed her several times. But then when she was a teenager, she was haunted with that horrible Anorexia, and she was in and out of hospitals, suffering from weight loss and also depression.

After a long spell of illness, when she was out of action and had to stop working, I got a phone call from her manager and agent Dorothy Solomon, who was a close contact of mine. She said that Lena wanted to tell her life-story. Would I do it for the Mirror? I immediately said yes. She had just come out of hospital, and she was trying to make a comeback, after a long spell in the wilderness.

After interviewing her, we ran a big piece on her in the Mirror, and I then went up to Blackpool with her, to see her comeback appearance on stage. She was starting a three-month run at the Opera House Theatre, as special guest on the Cannon and Ball show, in July 1985. And she was sensational. She was singing better than ever.

At that time, the 4ft 9in star, still only 21, was a healthier six stone. She had a new hair-do and said she was feeling great.

Tucking into a big box of chocolates I'd bought her, she told me, "I've cracked it. I'm raring to go again. This is a good day for me. I've got mixed feelings. I'm excited at being back on stage, yet I'm cautious. I'm fully fit again and it's now up to me to prove I'm still a good entertainer.

"It will take time though," she said. "There were periods when I lost all my self-will. I thought I would never sing again. Now I've got to get on with my life. The next three months are going to be the testing time. I will decide after that whether my heart is still in the business."

Just listening to her was so emotional. Dorothy Solomon, who was sitting nearby, was close to tears. And I had a distinct lump in my throat.

Lena had six songs to sing a night. She had no other plans until finishing the summer season.

Her agent Dorothy said, "We are hoping Lena will be back doing more TV shows and topping the bills again very soon. But she is not being rushed into anything."

Not long afterwards though she went back into hospital. Dorothy asked me to go in and see her. She was then in a psychiatric ward, but was about to come out.

I wrote her story all over again - and it was one of the few stories I ever paid for, because Dorothy insisted that Lena was broke and needed the money. So I got the Mirror to pay her quite a bit (a few thousand pounds, anyway) and they agreed.

It was Christmas Day when she came out of hospital. And because of the financial deal she had now done with the Mirror, I had to make sure that no other paper could get to her.

This meant me having to go over and pick her up at the hospital and take her home to her little flat in London. On the Boxing Day, she was all alone. I stayed with her throughout the day, with the curtains drawn, and watching TV, and she was pretending not to be in if anyone knocked on the door.

It was a dreadful situation. But she did get better. I maintained quite a close friendship with her. I lost count of the number of times Lena told me she had got over all her health problems and she was fit again.

At one time, the Editor wanted to do a series of articles for our Women's pages on Lena. They put a woman feature writer with her, but Lena refused to talk to her, and insisted that I sit in on all the interviews, because I was the only journalist she really trusted. This was all because of Dorothy Solomon, who had become a good friend of mine, and she was like a second mother to Lena ever since signing her up as a child and managing her career.

After I left the Mirror, I lost touch with Lena. She went through a marriage which broke up, her career fizzled out, and it was reported she was living on benefits. She was seriously ill for some years. And she died rather tragically in hospital of pneumonia, at the age of 35.

She was quite the opposite of Bonny Langford. The two girls grew up together, both went to the Italia Conti stage school, and both found fame, one a singer, the other an actress.

Bonny was always very self-assured and chatty. I got to know Bonny very well. Lena had more talent. But Bonny had her head screwed on. And she handled her career much better, once she had got away from that teenage gawkiness.

She's still around, of course. Still working, in stage musicals. And now looking better than ever.

CHAPTER 22: JOHN HURT

John Hurt was a rum character. A brilliant actor, there's no doubt about that. You only have to look through the list of the hundreds of films he's made, to acknowledge that he really is one of Britain's finest. That's why he was given a knighthood, for his services to acting in 2015.

I first met John in 1980 when he made that astonishing film The Elephant Man. They allowed me to go backstage into the make-up room and watch part of the most amazing transformation scene in cinema's history. It was a make-up marathon which turned Hurt's face into that of a monster.

The movie told the touching story of Joseph Merrick, born hideously deformed, into Victorian England. Merrick became the star of a travelling freak show before meeting a young surgeon who was to change his life.

Transforming John Hurt's sensitive face into the grotesque features of the legendary Elephant Man proved a gruelling task. For each day's filming, the make-up artists gave John an entirely new head, made of latex foam, "cooked" overnight in a special oven.

This meant John spending seven hours at a stretch in the make-up studio. "It was pure agony," he told me. "I'd get up at five in the morning and not be ready to start filming until noon. It was so exhausting that we could only do it every second day. It also meant that once I had the false head on, I couldn't eat for the rest of the day."

I remember John telling me that at the end of the very first make-up session, he thought "They've finally managed to take the joy out of film-making."

At first, his own head was shaved completely. "When I looked in the mirror, all vanity went to the wind," he said. And once the false head was on, John looked forward to breakfast – which was raw eggs and orange juice sucked through a straw.

John told me, "I'd seen the cast of the real John Merrick's head at the London Hospital, so I had an idea of what I was in for. The most terrifying moment was when I walked out on to the set, that first day after being made up. If anybody had laughed or tittered at my appearance, then it would have been quite impossible for me to do the job properly. But they didn't, they all stood back in amazement.

"Wearing the huge head wasn't so much painful as increasingly uncomfortable and claustrophobic."

A couple of years later, I met up with John Hurt again when I went on a trip to Berlin in 1982, which really was a bit of an eye-opener.

The trip was for the launch of a film he'd made, called Night Crossing, which was based on a real-life story of a German and his family who had made the daring escape from East to West Germany in a hot air balloon. I was invited exclusively by the film company to interview John, and then also meet the German Peter Strelzyk, hero of the drama.

Peter Strelzyck, with his friend Gunter Wetzel, somehow successfully piloted their two wives and four children over the Wall in the balloon made from curtains and bed sheets.

The fly-away families were given a standing ovation when the film was premiered in West Germany.

We flew to Berlin and watched the completion of filming. And frankly I found it all rather scary. The dreaded Berlin Wall was still up, and as Hurt and the cameras went about their business, safely on the Western side, we were all aware that we were being watched constantly through the massive 20-feet high barbed-wire fence by the armed German guards on the Eastern side, who patrolled the perimeter border with savage dogs 24 hours a day, to prevent anyone escaping from East to West.

In fact, those guards were doing exactly the job which Hurt and the film producers were highlighting in this film. I found it all very surreal, and I was glad when we eventually retreated from the wire fence and moved back to our hotel.

Peter Strelzyck had tears in his eyes when he first met John Hurt who gave him an affectionate hug. The German was now living and working happily in West Berlin, and it was difficult to realise just how hard it must have been to be a prisoner in the East for most of your life.

John told me later, "This escape was more of a miracle than anything else. Expert balloonists say that this balloon had only a ten per-cent chance of flying. The other risk was that the wind was in the right direction. If it hadn't been, they could have been blown straight to Moscow."

At the same time, I was intrigued about the political set-up, as most first-time visitors to that city were. When I had a half day free, I decided to go and have a walk around the Eastern part of the city, which was governed by the Soviets. This meant going through the dreaded gates of what was then known as Checkpoint Charlie, the notorious passport centre, which had two booths, with sets of armed guards, one on either side of the Border Control.

Not knowing quite what to expect, I must admit to being shocked. For apart from the fact that all the buildings looked grey, drab and run-down, there were long queues of people, shabbily dressed, outside the few shops on the main street, most of them selling food and liquor. It was like stepping back in time, being suddenly faced with what life must have been like in war-time 40 years earlier. As though time had strangely stood still.

After about an hour of wondering around on my own, I turned and made my way back to the control gates of Passport Charlie. Never in my life had I ever felt such feelings of relief. I then spent some time looking around the war museum which they had erected on the Western side.

Looking at the yellowing black-and-white photographs and reports they'd amassed over the years, showing life in East Berlin, and some of the daring attempts by people who had tried to escape to the West, some of them successfully, but most of them ending up being shot and their bodies left to rot, as a warning, to deter others. It was a museum of human misery. There was no other way to view it. It was a pictorial revelation of what some of those people must have been through, and a realisation of how privileged I was in a way to actually meet, shake hands and have a drink with this German hero of the film we were there to publicise.

John Hurt was obviously as moved by the whole situation, too. He had spent several months there and admitted that he would be relieved and glad to get back home. I don't think the film was ever a big box-office success. But no one really expected it to be. It was just one of those films which was worth making.

The whole trip didn't go without a few laughs though. On our final night there, I was invited to go and have dinner with John Hurt, accompanied by the film company's young PR man. It all started off well enough, we had a nice meal, a few bottles of wine, and I soon realised what a good drinker John was.

He was in a very talkative mood. Now acknowledged as one of the world's finest actors, he had won more awards than most. They included Best TV Actor award for his unforgettable portrayal of the homosexual Quentin Crisp in The Naked Civil Servant, and Best Film Actor for his compassionate title role in The Elephant Man.

Yet he had turned down offers to move to Hollywood, and home for John was then a beautiful Queen Anne house in the Cotswolds, with Marie-Louise, the French woman who had shared his life for 15 years.

"Hollywood is very seductive," said John candidly. "I could move there tomorrow and be welcomed by the community because they're always looking for new blood, a new piece of furniture. But I prefer not to be a piece of furniture, and as the world gets smaller, with aeroplanes everywhere, I don't think it matters where you live."

The huge fees demanded by some film actors in Hollywood infuriated him. "Why does Robert Redford ask seven million dollars for a film, then accept six million?" he asked. "What can you need six million dollars for? It's crazy. You could build hospitals for that. I don't know what he does with it.

"I'm not a rich man but I can't claim to be wanting. In a world where everybody seems to be wanting, I'm doing what I want to do. It seems to me crazy to develop a greed which stops you actually working."

But he looked pale, his face tortured, almost debauched. "It's the result of a lot of travelling to promote Night Crossing, plus too many late nights in German clubs," he smiled. "I believe in working hard and playing hard. The most important thing is never to regret anything you've done in your life. Never make excuses for living."

At the end of the meal, John suggested we move on and go to a nightclub. There was one in particular which he had in mind. So, off we went, the three of us.

Now I have been to some nightclubs in my life. But nothing quite like this one. They say that Berlin has some of the best, and naughtiest, nightclubs in the world. Well, this would have come under the naughty category.

We were shown to a table, then with a few bottles of wine, we sat through what started out as a fairly routine cabaret. Nothing which you couldn't have seen in, say, Paris or even London. But then it developed gradually into a strip show, with men and women on stage, cavorting around in a very provocative way, which I can only describe as, well, rather rude It was much more than dirty dancing.

John had obviously been there before and seemed more interested in drinking than the on-stage antics, and after a while I soon became bored and started looking at my watch. It's odd how quickly tits can become tiring. It was now well after midnight. And I thought we'd all had more to drink than was good for us.

All of a sudden, John turned to us and said, "Bugger this, I've had enough. I'm going to move on somewhere else. I feel like some different company."

Then to my surprise, he looked at the PR guy who was sitting between us, and said, "Have you got any money? I'm a bit short of funds and would appreciate some cash." I was even more surprised when the young Mr. PR fetched out of his pocket a brown paper envelope, which looked like it contained a wad of money, handed it over to John, and said, "Sure. Here you are. Hope this is enough."

"Thanks," said John, rather curtly, and slipped it into his pocket. Then he quickly finished his drink, got up from the table, said "Goodnight then. See you in the morning," and walked out.

As we finished our drinks, I looked at Mr. PR, and my expression must have puzzled him. All he said, a little sarcastically I thought, and with a bemused smile, was, "It's all part of the service. It comes out of the film budget. As long as John is happy!"

We made our way back to the hotel. And I remember thinking next day that I could never, ever become a Public Relations man. Never. I would sooner stick pins in my eyes!

As for John, he wasn't around at breakfast time. I never did find out what he got up to after he left us in the nightclub. We flew back home later that afternoon.

CHAPTER 23: JAMES BOND

I've not met all the James Bonds, but I've had encounters, happily, with a few of them. Four, to be exact.

Sean Connery I met up at Gleneagles, while playing golf in the Pro-Celebrity tournament for the BBC. I found him not very sociable, with very little to say. But then, he was probably more interested in the golf than talking to a Mirror journalist.

One story concerning Sean Connery was told to me by the late Dickie Henderson, a popular comedian who graced our TV screens for many years and had his own series.

It seems that Dickie Henderson, Sean Connery and Bruce Forsyth were going to a boxing match together. They got into a taxi in central London, and said, "Wembley Stadium, please." As they drove off, the taxi driver kept turning around, looking at Bruce Forsyth.

Bruce wasn't quite the big star he is today, but he had appeared at the London Palladium and done lots of other TV shows. The cab driver said, "Don't I know you? I'm sure I recognise your face. Have you appeared on telly? No, don't tell me. It'll come to me."

This went on for some time. The driver insisted, "I'm sure I've seen you before. I just can't think of your name." In the end, Bruce got a bit irritated and said, "Oh, for goodness sake, I'm Bruce Forsyth." At which the cabbie burst out laughing and said, "Come off it, mate. If you're Bruce Forsyth, then I'm James Bond."

And Sean Connery, sitting quietly in the back, piped up, "No. I'm James Bond!" They all fell about laughing. Bruce confirmed that story was true when I asked him some years later.

Connery was the opposite from Roger Moore, who I met a few times and he was always very friendly and forthcoming with the anecdotes.

We had lunch together once at ATV's studios at Elstree, when Roger was playing The Saint and had become a TV heartthrob. At the time I met him, he was driving an Aston Martin, the same car he used to drive in The Saint.

He's got a wicked sense of humour, and I recall him telling me, "The thing I enjoy most of all is when I draw up to the traffic lights, alongside another car. When the lights are on red, if the driver looks across and recognises me, he can't wait to beat me away from the lights. So I rev up my engine and then, when the lights turn green, I deliberately stall the car or drive off very slowly, so the other car shoots ahead of me.

"It's much more fun than putting my foot down. And it probably makes their day. The day they left The Saint at the traffic lights!"

Piers Brosnan was, without doubt, the most handsome man I've ever met. Even more strikingly good looking than the giant Charlton Heston, whom I once interviewed and had a drink with at the Ritz Hotel.

I was invited over to Brosnan's London house in Chelsea, to talk about his role in the American TV series Remington Steele, screened here in the early 80s. There were constant rumours that the Bond film producers wanted him to take over as 007 from the rather disappointing Timothy Dalton. But Brosnan was tied down to a long contract with NBC to play Remington Steele and couldn't get out of it.

He did eventually step into Bond's shoes, with Golden Eye in 1995, and followed up with three more movies as the suave lady killer, which set him up for life financially.

In that first interview he did with me, he prepared lunch for us both in the kitchen and was so charming and chatty that I should have known that it was inevitable that one day he was going to take over as Bond.

Daniel Craig, who has now widely been acclaimed as the best James Bond of them all, first came to my attention long before he was cast as 007. I interviewed him when he was an up and coming actor and completely unknown.

He was lined up to appear in a brand-new TV series set in Newcastle on Tyne, called Our Friends In The North, screened by the BBC in 1996. It had a cast of four unknown actors - Geena McKay, Christopher Ecclestone, Mark Strong, and Daniel Craig - and turned out to be quite a popular drama.

Daniel, then 28, played a character called George (Geordie) Peacock, one of four friends in a saga of their various relations over a 30-year period.

I chatted to them all, quite separately, and did a big feature. I found it hard going, because none of them had had much publicity before and one or two of them seemed slightly suspicious and ill at ease talking about themselves.

They were all polite, but I found Daniel Craig to be the most striking prospect of the bunch. He was very down to earth and confident. He struck me as being a very nice guy, the sort of bloke you'd like to go to the pub with and have a pint or two. That Northern series proved good for them, for all four went on to become much more than jobbing actors, but star names (Ecclestone became a Doctor Who).

143

But, of course, it was Craig who went on to become a millionaire and a worldwide superstar. I've not met him since that very first interview. But when I see him in chat shows and from what I read about him, he seems to have remained very down to earth and has not changed a lot, despite his phenomenal success.

CHAPTER 24: FRANK SINATRA

If anyone was to ask me who I would have loved to have interviewed, but never got the chance, the answer would have to be Frank Sinatra. I've always been a mad Sinatra fan and have all his records.

We all know that Sinatra hated the Press and never, ever gave interviews. The nearest I got to him was on two separate occasions.

The first was when Sinatra was on one of his rare visits to London. Not appearing here, but just apparently in town.

I was in a pub with a couple of Press mates. One of them was Dougie Marlborough, who was the showbiz writer on the Daily Mail. And he got a phone call from his News Desk, telling him to go over to an address in Portland Place, near Broadcasting House, because Sinatra was supposed to be staying there and they wanted Dougie to interview him.

Dougie was furious. He said he'd had a row with his News Editor, told him he was now off duty, he'd done enough stories that day, and he was going to resign if they made him "doorstep" Sinatra. I told him not to be such a fool. "You can't resign over something like this," I said. "Go around and do the job."

Eventually I agreed to go with him. We took a taxi to Portland Place, and walked into this elegant terraced block. As we walked through the front door into the hallway, two huge guys, more like gorillas than humans, suddenly appeared from out of the shadows. "What do you want?" one demanded.

I took one look at them, and thought immediately, well this is the right address. Quickly I said, pointing at Duggie, "He wants to talk to Mr. Frank Sinatra."

There was no more conversation. These two gorillas just moved towards us, one picked up Duggie, the other picked me up. And we were pushed out through the front door and unceremoniously dumped onto the pavement. "Beat it," they said. "And don't come back."

We picked ourselves up. Duggie was outraged and wanted to go back in to argue. He was a little guy, smaller than me, and weighed, I guess, about nine stone, wet.

"Forget it. Now you go on to your News Desk and tell them that Mr. Sinatra does not want to talk to you," I said.

He went on the phone, but came back and said, "The office said I've got to stay here and doorstep him, because he's bound to come out sometime." Duggie was still seething and threatening to resign.

"Fine. Do as they say," I advised him. "Now let's go and have some dinner." We went to a little restaurant in Soho, where we ordered a bottle of red wine and had a nice meal. And every half hour, he kept going on to his News Desk, saying, "Sinatra has not come out yet." At about 11 o'clock, his News Editor finally relented. "Okay, you can go home now. Forget Sinatra."

We finished the wine, split the bill and both went home. Dougie was back in his office next day. He'd forgotten all about his resignation threat.

The only other time I got near Old Blue Eyes was when I flew to New York to cover a rock concert. I had to take two Mirror readers, who had won a competition, to a show at Madison Square Gardens. And my office put us up at the swish Waldorf Astoria Hotel. It was a lovely hotel and we stayed there for three nights.

On our second day there, the couple of readers, a father and daughter, came to me and said, "Do you know Frank Sinatra is staying here?" It didn't surprise me. "Oh yes, we were going out this morning to do some sightseeing, and we saw Sinatra with his wife, and an entourage of people in the foyer. We wanted to get his autograph, but one of his minders wouldn't let us."

I didn't see Sinatra at all. I knew it would be futile to even make an approach, even if he was staying in the same hotel.

As for those two Mirror readers, I think they were more thrilled at seeing Sinatra and his party than they were with the rock concert they'd come to see, when I took them backstage afterwards and they met Ozzie Osbourne and his band Black Sabbath.

CHAPTER 25: JIMMY SAVILE

Jimmy Savile is a man who has now gone down in British history, as probably the most evil pervert and paedophile in show business. And I have to confess that I knew him quite well. Or at least, I thought I did. That was before all the unbelievably nasty details came out a few years ago of his sordid and depraved life.

I wish I had a fiver for every time someone has asked me since then if I ever suspected that Savile was such a monster. But of course, I didn't.

I've got to admit, however, that there were always rumours around Fleet Street about Savile. One, that he was homosexual. Another, that he liked young girls.

The rumours persisted, even though he would strenuously deny that he was involved in any wrongdoing.

But if anyone ever dared to question Jim about allegations of having young girls backstage, he would immediately laugh it off in that smarmy way he had about him.

I can understand how people have since said they felt he was creepy. He was. But he always had a sense of fun, which in a way was quite infectious. Jim could lay on the charm and could fuss over you to such an extent that you would think that, in spite of his eccentricity, he really was a generous and caring person.

Of course, we now know it was all a façade. He was evil to the core, and just good at manipulating people. I am almost ashamed to admit it, but Jim, I thought, often regarded me as a friend. "Ah, my friend Mr. Irwin. Come in, come in," he would say putting on that cheesy smile and waving me to a chair. "Sit down and let's talk."

But, despite all that has been written about him, Savile was no fool. And the reason so many journalists - me included - continued to pursue him, and tolerate his odd whims and often nauseating behaviour, was simply because the man was "copy."

When you interviewed him, he would always come up with something new. He was adept at giving journalists what they wanted. If it was a dull day, there was not much happening, and you wanted a story, get on to Jimmy Savile – he would oblige.

He'd come up with stories about his close friendship with Prince Charles. The lovely Princess Diana and how she'd make him laugh. How he would go to Christmas dinner with Maggie Thatcher every year. How he had access to Prime Ministers and people in power. And   he would always tell you about his tremendous charity work, how many millions he had raised for good causes, and how he gave up two days a week of his life to work as a hospital porter or visit sick patients. How could anyone argue with him?

I first met Jimmy when the BBC launched Top of the Pops as a try-out show, and it was televised live on New Year's Day 1964 from their tiny studio in a converted church in Manchester. He was the presenter of the show, and the line-up on the first programme included The Beatles and the Rolling Stones, who were vying for the top spot in the pop charts.

Savile, with his long, dyed yellow hair, came over as a rather good, lively, and knowledgeable disc-jockey, which in fact he already was, from his earlier radio shows.

I reported on that first show for the Daily Mirror. But I must say that I was probably much more interested in meeting the Beatles and the outrageous Mick Jagger and the Stones than I was in worrying about the performance of Savile.

Later, over the years, I interviewed him many times. And when the show was moved to London and became a permanent fixture in the BBC schedules, it out-ran every other pop show on the box. When it was firmly at the top in the popularity stakes, I was invited by the BBC to write and edit the Top of the Pops Annual, which I happily went on to do for seven years.

As for Savile, he actually lived a very frugal life. His lifestyle was unbelievable. I visited him more than once, in his home - a flat in a beautiful Nash terrace near Broadcasting House. And the furniture in the main room would consist of a sofa, a chair, a coffee table, and a TV set. And in the kitchen, he'd have a small cooker and a fridge, but the fridge was always empty apart from a bottle of milk.

Go for a chat with him, and he'd grudgingly make you a cup of tea. I recall him once telling me that he preferred to live in his motor caravan, which he had parked in a car-park near Euston Station (now we know why, of course).

Very few journalists were ever invited back to his house, though. So I don't know whether I should have felt privileged or not. He preferred to do interviews at the BBC or wherever else he might be working.

On one occasion, after a Top of the Pops show, which I had been looking in on, Jim asked me if I was going back to Fleet Street, and if I could give him a lift back to his flat. I agreed I would, and went to get my car out of the BBC White City car park. He jumped into the front passenger seat, buckled up, and as I was driving off he noticed I had not got my seat belt on. He insisted I fasten it. When I told him that I didn't like wearing a seat belt because I found it too constricting, he threw a little fit. "Clunk Click. Every Trip," he yelled (which was the famous catchphrase he'd devised in the Safety Driving TV adverts). "If you don't fasten your seat belt, I'm getting out." And he went to open the door. Reluctantly, I buckled up, and we drove into central London.

When we reached his luxury terraced block, he jumped out and shouted, "No, you're not coming in because I've got no milk for a cup of tea. I'm going to have a cigar and go to bed. Goodnight." And he waved me goodbye.

Once, we even discussed writing a book together. It was my idea. I thought this guy was interesting enough for a book. I intended to write it as a biography. I didn't really need his permission, but I wanted Jim's approval because it would help if I needed to talk to any of his friends and associates.

At one stage, Jim was very keen to co-operate and was even quite enthusiastic about the idea. But then, I suddenly received a short, hand-written note from him, which read: "Hi Ken. Re the book, have just done a deal with Readers Digest no less. Sorry. How about an in-depth article? There's always lots of mags driving me potty for stuff. I'm off to the States in Jan for a big blast so you could sell summat out there if you have the contacts. Check with Ted Beston at B.H. when I'm there. Cheers." And he signed it with his usual extravagant signature, which was a smiley face on the Jimmy, and the S on the Savile turned into a dollar sign. And he added OBE.

I've still got that signed note in my files, along with letters from other celebrities sent to me over the years.

I wonder how much a Jimmy Savile autographed letter is worth these days?

CHAPTER 26: BENNY HILL

Benny Hill was a strange little man. He could be cheeky and full of fun, but it depended on what mood he was in.

Over the years, I interviewed him many times. But only once did he ever invite me over to his home. He lived just around the corner from the Royal Albert Hall, in a rather elegant block of flats. But I was more than a little surprised when I visited him to find that Benny lived what can only be described as a frugal life.

There was very little furniture in the lounge, and no pictures at all on the walls. In the kitchen, he had the bare essentials.

When I asked him about his lifestyle, he just laughed and said, "I'm a very simple man with very simple tastes. Why should I have a lot of furniture cluttering up the place?"

It wasn't as though he was poor. Quite the opposite. Benny was never out of work and must have had a few million in the bank, even in those days.

He wrote all his own TV shows, as well as starring in them, was consistently high in the ratings and was for years one of ITV's big guns in the popularity stakes. At his peak, his shows drew a regular audience of more than 20 million viewers a week.

While other performers enjoyed all the trappings of fame - the flashy cars, the big houses - he was content to live the quiet bachelor life.

In fact, he didn't own a car, because he couldn't even drive. He was happy to catch a bus if he wanted to go anywhere.

He lived on take-aways and would go out with a plastic bag to do his own shopping locally. So he was not a recluse by any stretch of the imagination.

He spent a lot of his time, when he was not working on TV, going off on foreign trips, particularly to Spain. "I love Spain. When I go over there, and just sit in the sun, it can be paradise," he told me.

But even then, he never really stopped working, because Benny would have a pen and a notepad constantly at reach, so that he could jot down comedy ideas that came to him.

"I'm a great observer of life," he told me. "I like just sitting out, watching people. You'd be surprised how funny people can be when they don't know you're watching them."

His only other pastime was being a boxing fan, which was rather surprising because he was a very gentle man. But he would go to watch all

CHAPTER 26: BENNY HILL

the big fights in this country and on the Continent. "And I will fly off anywhere in the world to watch a really big title fight," he'd say.

But there was one big question mark which hung over Benny's life, and which undoubtedly intrigued the Press: Was he gay? He would chuckle and say, "Oh, I'm too busy having fun with the ladies."

He did have lady-friends, as he called them. And he would often be seen out with a girl on his arm. Invariably, they were dancers or actresses who appeared on his shows. He even had one or two favourite girls who stayed close to Benny, even after they had gone off and married.

Benny's Girls, as they were called, remained remarkably faithful to him. One got the impression that some of them were happy to stay close to him socially because it was a way of staying in work. But that would be a cynical view.

I did venture the question once or twice to Benny: Why have you never married? And he'd reply with a chuckle, "That would spoil all the fun."

It was impossible not to like Benny, though. He had an infectious sense of humour and he could be fun to interview, and we enjoyed a few lunches together down at Teddington studios, where he did most of his programmes.

However, his success came to rather an abrupt and unexpected end. For some time, there had been questions raised over Benny's style of humour. And with changing public attitudes, it became clear that his saucy innuendo in most of his jokes, not to mention his well-known chasing of scantily-clad girls which was the finale in every show, was becoming unpopular. He was suddenly being labelled as sexist.

It was me who finally broke the news that he was being dropped from TV. I received a tip-off from an old mate who worked for Thames TV, telling me that Benny had been sacked. At first, I couldn't believe it, because he was still such a big star and enjoyed being top of the ratings.

But I checked it out, confirmed that it was true, and we ran the news story as an exclusive in the Daily Mirror. It made the front page - on May 31,1989. The headline: "Benny Hill in 'I quit' Shock. Fed-up star pulls out of TV." It was sensational news. And every other paper followed it up next day.

A close friend of his at the time told me, "Benny has become tired. He's in need of a long rest. He has been a top name for the last 20-odd years and he now wants to take time out to enjoy himself more."

As for Benny, you had to feel sorry for him. After Thames TV ended his contract, he never really worked again. Even then his TV shows were being sold to more than 80 countries and were still being screened around the world. It was estimated that he was worth more than £10 million when he quit.

But Benny had always insisted to me, "I am not really interested in the money. Only in doing good comedy and making people laugh."

He was forced into retirement really, after his brand of comedy came under criticism from the TV watchdogs. He was accused of being sexist and out of date.

Colin Shaw, then director of the government's new Broadcasting Standards Council said, "It's not as funny as it was to have half-naked girls chased across the screen by a dirty old man."

And Benny himself had recently revealed, "The Women's Lib brigade were forever having a go at me. I just think the time is right when perhaps one shouldn't be quite so raunchy."

After his contract came to an abrupt end at Thames TV, Benny quietly retired and became something of a recluse.

Sadly, he died only three years after finishing work. He was found dead at his home in south west London after the police were alerted by neighbours when he wasn't seen around for a few days. He was 67.

After Charlie Chaplin and Norman Wisdom, I reckon we would have to rate Benny Hill as the next most successful truly international comedy star to come from Britain.

CHAPTER 27: FRANKIE HOWERD

Frankie Howerd was a weird fellow. Neurotic by nature, he was a bag of nerves and was probably the most insecure bloke one was ever likely to meet.

Although he was, without doubt, one of the funniest comedians to emerge, first on radio, and then on TV, Howerd was never fully able to accept that he had cracked it, even though he was a household name.

By his own admission, he could never relax. And you got the feeling that he didn't even enjoy whatever success he'd achieved. He lived in constant fear that his secret homosexuality would be made public.

I first interviewed him when he was appearing in a show in the West End. I was invited to meet him in between the first and second house, and arrived at the theatre and was quickly ushered into his dressing-room.

Frankie was sprawled out on the sofa, in a dressing gown, and had a towel which he used to repeatedly mop his sweaty face. He offered me a drink and then said, "Right, let's go. Ask me anything you like. Excuse me if I seem a bit on edge, but I've got another show to do tonight. I can't really relax until I'm on my way home."

We then chatted away. But it was hard going, because he would be pacing up and down the floor one minute, and then lying down on the couch the next. I was eventually glad when it was time for him to go back on stage, and I said my farewells and left.

His career lasted more than 50 years but wavered all over the place. For years, he was a top-of- the -bill act. Then his TV shows kept him in the public eye. But there were long, lean spells when he was out of work and doing nothing. He once told me that he thought he was finished.

But then his career was miraculously revived - when he daringly did a one-off performance at Oxford University, and the students loved him. Almost overnight, he became a cult figure. The TV bosses suddenly realised just what potential he still had, and he was soon back on the box, a whole new career ahead of him.

Again though, much like Benny Hill, when his career faded out, Frankie became a recluse and shared the rest of his life with his long-lasting partner and manager, Dennis Heymer.

Frankie first met Dennis Heymer in 1958 when Dennis was a wine waiter at the Dorchester Hotel. Howerd was 40, and Dennis was 28. He became Frank's lover and his manager, and they stayed together for more than 30 years, until Frank's death in 1992. He collapsed of heart failure, aged 75.

Strangely, Frankie died just one day before fellow comedian Benny Hill. In fact, news of the two deaths broke almost simultaneously. And some newspapers ran an obituary of Howerd in which Benny was quoted as regretting Frank's passing, saying, "We were great, great friends." The quote was released to the Press by Hill's agent, who was not aware that Benny had already died, too.

Frankie's old home, in Wavering Down, Somerset, later became something of a tourist attraction, as a museum of his memorabilia and personal effects, which included Frank's false teeth and that ill-fitting wig he wore for so many years.

When Dennis Heymer died, some years after Frankie, they were buried together in an expensive replica of an Egyptian sarcophagus.

CHAPTER 28: EUROVISION SONG CONTEST

For my sins in life, I was sent by the Mirror every year to cover the Eurovision Song Contests. Not just one or two, but quite a lot of them. In fact, looking back, I covered the annual Euro event for 18 years, without a break.

I can remember, as a youngster, first listening to the song contests on radio, because the Euro event actually dates back to 1956. And I certainly remember hearing singers like Irishman Ronnie Carroll (who finished fourth in 1962 and fourth again in1963), Matt Monro (who finished second in 1964), and that great little songbird Kathy Kirby (who a year later also finished second).

The first one I was actually lined up to cover was in 1967, with the barefooted Sandie Shaw singing Puppet on a String in Vienna. But for some reason, I didn't want to go, so chickened out of it. The office sent my colleague Jack Bell, instead.

As it happened, Sandie Shaw won it. So I missed out on Britain's first-ever Euro celebrations.

The first contest I did cover was in 1968 when the lovely Spanish singer Massiel won with the song La La La. That's when our own Cliff Richard made his bow with the commercially successful song Congratulations. Many people seem to think, because that was such a big hit, that Cliff won the contest. But he didn't, he finished second.

And this was the start for me of a very long and affectionate association with Eurovision. I actually liked the idea of an international contest to find the best song, and I really enjoyed going off and reporting on them in countries all over Europe.

What probably gave me a taste for them was the splendid time we had the following year, in 1969, when the contest was staged in Spain, and I flew to Madrid with our popular little singer Lulu as Britain's entry.

The amazing thing was, instead of just going to Madrid to watch and report on the contest, all the foreign Press were invited to fly out and spend three days visiting the Spanish islands like Menorca and Majorca, as the guests of the Spanish government. We guessed later that this was the post-Franco era and the Spanish authorities' way of keeping foreign journalists occupied and not asking too many political questions. But hey, who cared?

Two or three other English journalists were with me, and we met up with all the Press from other countries taking part, so we really got to know each other. The hospitality was terrific. We were wined and dined and put up in luxury hotels. And we had a hell of a good time.

Apart from the wine, which seemed to be on tap around the clock, they took us one night to see a typical Spanish nightclub show. As well as a splendid dinner, it proved to be really top-class entertainment, ending with a display of Spanish dancing. The male dancers were all very fit, wearing tight-fitting trousers and high Cuban heel boots. And the women dancers, well, they were all about six feet tall, dressed in beautiful costumes and feathers in their hair which made them look even taller And of course all very beautiful.

Then, the dancers suddenly ended their routine, and looked out into the audience and asked for volunteers to go up on stage and dance.

Now that audience was made up of at least 150 journalists, most of them men. And when no one volunteered, the tallest and most vivacious of the Spanish dancers came down and started looking for someone to accompany her on stage. And to my utter horror, she stopped, stared at me, and picked me out as the sap of the night. To say I was horrified is an understatement. I cannot dance to save my life. But suddenly here was this six-foot-something woman dragging me up on stage, with the audience of Pressmen hooting and shouting their approval.

What could I do? I could either sit down and sulk and refuse to go, which would have made me look a silly spoilsport. Or get up and get on with it. Which is what I foolishly did.

Except that, once on stage, in the middle of all those Spanish dancers, instead of just following instructions, I suddenly went crazy. Some devilish particle inside my brain must have taken over, because as soon as the music struck up and this lovely raven-haired lady grabbed me round the waist and twisted me into her body, I threw myself into a frenzy of mad antics. I started jumping up and down, banging my heels on the floor like a Spanish dancer, and waving my arms around like a crazed whirling dervish. I had no choice. I felt I just had to go for it.

It seemed to go on for ever. But my attempts at Spanish dancing brought the house down. At the end of the show, the Press mob in the audience were all on their feet, whistling, yelling, and clapping. The applause was unbelievable. I not only amused the audience, but all the dancers too were hysterically laughing and applauding.

With a kiss from the lovely leading lady, I was eventually helped from the stage, where my colleagues immediately ordered another round of drinks to celebrate my debut as a dancer. "Here's to English Ken!" they toasted.

Funny, but that night also brought me the start of several friendships with foreign journalists which went on to last for some years. In particular, two Dutch guys and a fellow from Belgium who all became quite close mates. We used to enjoy meeting up every year for the Eurovision thrash.

But with that little three-day trip around Spain over, we then had the rest of the week in Madrid. And the well-organised events continued. One night, we were taken on a trip to Real Madrid's football ground. We were shown into the trophy room, which was the size of a ballroom, and packed with a display of silverware which must have been the envy of every soccer team in the world.

To round off the night, we were invited down on to the pitch. And I couldn't resist the chance to actually kick a ball about on that famous field. I had a few penalty shots, with some of the Press guys in goal. What a thrill that was for someone like me, brought up on watching Everton or Liverpool!

That week ended with the song contest finishing in the first-ever four-way tie, with Lulu sharing the honours with Spanish singer Salome (and her unforgettable song Vivo Cantando), and France and Holland.

But the most memorable thing of that trip occurred the day before we were due to return home. For the three or four days we were staying in Madrid, after watching rehearsals, we would return to our hotel, and I would find boxes of gifts left in my room. Every day, there was another very nicely wrapped gift. I had bottles of champagne, brandy, best Spanish port, jewellery, expensive aftershaves, cut glassware, and even porcelain ornaments.

One day I mentioned it to Bill Cotton, the BBC's head of the British delegation, and he told me that he, too, was getting all these goodies, and he thought it was very nice, and was just Spanish TV's way of being hospitable. "Just enjoy it," he said. When I mentioned to my Press colleagues about the gifts, they were puzzled, because they had not received anything.

However, on the day before the big contest, the phone went in my hotel room, at about 8 am. I was still in bed. It was the hotel manager, and he said, rather curtly, "Signor Irwin, I have two gentlemen here from Spanish TV. It seems they have been sending gifts to your room. Now they say it is a big mistake, and they would like everything back please. I am sending them up to your room now."

I was still half asleep and a little hung-over from the night before, but I quickly got out of bed and went into action, now suddenly wide awake.

Half of my room was by now stacked with boxes and bottles of free loot. I grabbed some of the boxes and stuffed as much as I could into the wardrobe and shut the doors.

A knock on the door, and I opened it to find two hefty sour-looking men who asked if they could come in. They looked like everyone's idea of Mafia heavies or spies from the KGB. They asked if I had been receiving parcels and I said I had. They then said, "Are you from the BBC?" I said No, I was a Pressman from the Daily Mirror in London.

Ah, they said, "This be big mistake. Our fault not yours. We think you work for BBC. The gifts were meant for BBC guests only. Can we have them back, please?"

We then spent the next five minutes with me trying to argue that if they were gifts, why should I hand them back. And the Spanish Mafia insisting, "Eaza mistake. You not understand?"

In the end, we agreed to what I thought was not a bad compromise. They would leave me some of the gifts, but not all of them. Which ones would I like to return to them? So we then had an amusing session, when I opened up the wardrobe, where they would grab one box and I kept possession of another. Then we played a game of alternately swapping items: You can have this, I will have that.

With great haste, they brought in a luggage trolley and piled it high with all the gifts they had now confiscated. But they insisted they were so sorry at my disappointment and that I should take home "a few souvenirs." They thanked me for my co-operation and left with a quick handshake.

When I looked at the remains of the blitz later, I was still left with some nice little freebies - including ladies and men's perfumes, a lovely porcelain doll (which I still have on my shelves somewhere) and more bottles of booze than I could possibly carry home, which I ended up sharing with my Press mates, most of which we drank before departing.

When I bumped into Bill Cotton later, I told him, "Hey, I've been raided at dawn and they've taken half the freebie stuff back. Apparently, they thought I worked for the BBC." Bill just chuckled and said, "Well, why didn't you tell them you did?"

What a wonderful trip that was. I even received a lovely letter from the woman who was Head of Press when I got home, thanking me for "having such a good time in our country - and for your Spanish dancing which we shall never forget!"

The following year, 1970, was a memorable contest, held in Amsterdam, because I sat through all the rehearsals and was immediately struck by only one song. It was a tuneful ditty called All Kinds of Everything and was sung by a sweet dark-haired little Irish schoolgirl called Dana. She was only 14, but she had a beautiful voice and all the assurance and confidence of an adult. I had a little flutter on the Irish entry, and it romped home the clear winner. I felt so pleased with myself.

That was the year when we had the lovely young Welsh singer Mary Hopkin representing Britain with Knock Knock, Who's There? a number written for her by none other than Paul McCartney, who had a bit of a fling with her at one time, it was rumoured. Pleasant singer though she was, Mary could not match Dana, and she finished only sixth in the voting.

After her win in Amsterdam, however, I became quite friendly with Dana and her manager, and wrote a few follow-up pieces on her. She was always chatty and had perfect manners and was a joy to spend time with. She went on to have a very successful career as a singer, which didn't surprise me at all, and later in life turned to politics and enjoyed a high-profile career as an ambassador for Ireland.

Dublin was always a great place to visit, and in fact the Irish have won the Euro contest more than any other country. And when they hosted the show, usually in Dublin, you always knew you were in for a good time.

Johnny Logan was their most successful singer. He was the only guy to win the contest twice - in 1980 with What's Another Year, and then again seven years later, with his own composition, Hold Me Now. A nice guy, Johnny, and a very dedicated musician.

After covering it for a few years, I used to look forward to the Eurovision gatherings. One of the most hilarious occasions was in Scotland, in 1972, when the BBC were responsible for producing the show and chose Edinburgh as the venue.

There were quite a lot of parties organised that week, and a lot of drinking was done. And I recall that at one of those late-night gatherings, my Scottish journalist colleague, a woman called Ruth Wishart who worked on the Mirror's sister paper, the Daily Record in Glasgow, suddenly came up with the suggestion that I would look good in a kilt. I don't know where the idea came from or whether it was the whisky talking, but the conversation turned to whether I had the guts or not to turn up on the big night of Eurovision in full Scottish dress, instead of the normal dinner jacket and bow tie.

Of course, I should have had the sense to say No, especially the next morning when we had all sobered up. But any suggestion that I might now bow out gracefully and forget the whole idea was quickly dashed, when Ms. Wishart was waiting for me at my hotel, after breakfast, and insisted on taking me out shopping along Princes Street to a rather distinguished gentlemen's outfitters. She pushed me through the door of the establishment and said, "My friend here wants to hire the full Scottish evening dress for tomorrow night."

The manager of the shop looked me up and down and got out his tape measure.

"And what tartan are you?" he enquired seriously.

"I don't know," I replied, "but I'd like a kilt with some blue and green in it. Not red." His face took on a horrified expression. And Ruth stepped in quickly to explain. "He's English. Take no notice of him. Just let's have any tartan, and a kilt that's a good fit."

He then proceeded to measure me, waist, length, inside leg, the lot. "And would sir require the full outfit - jacket, socks, and shoes?" "Yes," said bossy-boots Wishart. "The lot."

We eventually left the shop, with the promise that my outfit would be ready for collection next morning. Ruth made me pay a deposit. "That's it. You'll look great," she insisted.

When it came to Saturday, we collected the parcel from the outfitters, but I had serious doubts about the whole thing. A couple of hours before the actual contest was to be televised, Ruth knocked on my hotel door and said, "Right, let's see what you look like." So I went into the bathroom and changed. And when I came out, complete with kilt and all the rest of it, Ruth sat there and said, "Wow! I knew you'd have the legs for it."

But I still wasn't convinced. "I feel like that fellow Andy Stewart, when he sang Donald, Where's Your Troosers?" I said. She howled with laughter. "Never mind your trousers. What you need is a good stiff drink. Come on. Let's go to the bar. I'm buying."

It needed more than one drink before I felt confident enough to step out in public, though. But after two or three whiskies, I felt a lot better.

Ruth was so delighted with her achievement of having got me dressed up that she then said, "I'm on your arm tonight, Mr. Irwin. I'm going to get changed and put my best frock on. I'll see you at the top of the stairs of the grand ballroom, and we'll walk across to the hall together."

Well, to say I surprised a lot of people, would be an understatement. As we entered the hall, where the contest was being staged, some of my foreign Press chums looked in awe, and one of them said, "I didn't know you were a Scotsman, Ken."

"I'm not," I said, "I'm doing it as a dare."

Then as we walked up the steps, making our way through the crowd, I was suddenly aware of someone very close behind me, and I felt a hand go up my kilt. And I heard someone say, "What have you got up there?" I turned around quickly to find that it was Bill Cotton, the BBC chief. "Have you get anything on underneath?" he yelled with a laugh.

It seems that I was fair game for everyone that night. But once we were seated inside, everything was fine, and the marathon show went on as usual. And I must confess I began to feel quite at home, strutting around in my kilt.

At the end of the show, however, I was in for another surprise. When the winner was announced, it was Vicky Leandros from Luxembourg. And the dozens of photographers were falling over each other to get pictures of her.

Then we, the rest of the Press, were ushered in to meet the winning singer and ask questions. Which was fine. Vicky Leandros was very cute, though she was feeling a little stunned and overwhelmed.

As I was the only one dressed in a kilt and Scottish garb, some of the photographers grabbed me and pushed me forward, insisting that I chat to Vicky. She was delighted to do it, of course. And the camera flashes continued for what seemed like an eternity. One of the photographers then explained to me that this was just the picture they wanted - the beautiful winning singer alongside a gentleman in a kilt, because it perfectly portrayed that we were in Scotland.

It was a bit of fun really. What started out as a bar-room bet ended in those bizarre pictures being sent around the world of me in a kilt.

I never really lived that down with the rest of the Press gang. And I left Ruth to return my hired costume to the outfitters, after we'd departed by train to go back home next day. She and I had a good laugh about it all later.

Ruth Wishart was a smart, canny lady. She turned out to be a very distinguished journalist North of the Border, and some years later I watched her on TV when she was a guest celebrity, more than once, on the BBC's prestigious Any Questions? programme.

Without doubt, though, the best Euro contest for me was in Brighton in 1974, when the BBC were again responsible for producing the show. It was staged in the Palace Dome and Aussie-born Olivia Newton John was our vocal representative.

She didn't win but finished fourth. Because that night there was only one real act which stood out like a Brighton lighthouse beacon- and that was the Swedish group Abba, with the song Waterloo. I knew they would win as soon as I heard their first rehearsal.

That combination of the four Swedes - musicians Benny Andersson and Bjorn Ulvaeus, and the two girls, red-haired Anifrida Lyngstad and beautiful blonde Agnetha Faltskog - were quite sensational. It was not only their crazy colourful outfits, but the way they put over the song. I think I fell in love that night with vivacious blonde Agnetha. For me, she was pure sex on legs.

After Brighton, life would never be the same again as far as Eurovision was concerned. Abba went on to become the biggest and most successful singing group in the world. They had hit after hit, sold more records than the Beatles, and toured the world with sell-out concerts everywhere.

A few years after Brighton, I went over to Stockholm to interview Benny and Bjorn in their office, and found them both charming and really very modest, considering the huge success they were then enjoying.

In fact, in 2005, when a special Congratulations concert was staged, Abba's Waterloo was voted the most popular song of all the entries over the first 50 years of Eurovision. Some achievement, that.

The UK have won the contest five times but finished second on 15 occasions. The last time we won it was in 1997, with Kathrina & The Waves, and a song titled Love Shine The Light.

After Congratulations, Cliff Richard went on to try his luck for a second time in 1973 but only finished third, with Power To All Our Friends. But in 1975, I went over to Stockholm with The Shadows, to see if they could do any better than their old buddy Cliff. They couldn't - they finished second.

They may not have won, but I can tell you they had a lot of fun while they were there. Because we were all rather amused, the British Press corps, to see the four guys from The Shadows in action, not just on stage but in the nightclubs.

Some of those nightclub dives and strip joints in Stockholm were pretty sleazy. And we were a little surprised when two of the lads from The Shadows were openly boasting about the things they had seen and been up to the night before. Let's just say that our Cliff might not have approved.

Britain won again in 1976, when Brotherhood of Man came top of the votes with the catchy Save Your Kisses For Me, in The Netherlands. This time it was in The Hague, which is a lovely city, and I enjoyed it a lot. The Dutch people are so hospitable, and their Press and PR team were so efficient and friendly. I fell in love with The Hague. They don't like to rush things. They enjoy life at a more leisurely pace.

We were back there again four years later, when Ireland's Johnny Logan was successful all over again and ended up the winner, with What's Another Year. Going back to The Hague only emphasised for me what a beautiful place it was. And again, we were treated so well.

Paris, in 1978, was another contest which holds great memories. I love Paris, and we went on a few sightseeing tours around the city. Paris by night was always so wonderful. We had great fun there.

Bucks Fizz were our next winners, in 1981. They were in Dublin, and their winning song Making Your Mind Up was one of the slickest and certainly one of the best choreographed entries we'd ever seen. They were a very handsome foursome, and those two attractive girls ripping off their skirts in an unexpected finale was the show-stopper. They were great fun to be with, and our friendship continued for quite some years, particularly with the chatterbox of the group, Cheryl Baker, who went on to forge a whole new career for herself as a TV presenter.

Munich, in 1983, I remember mainly for the antics of old friend David Wigg, the showbiz reporter from the Daily Express. Half a dozen of our Press gang were all enjoying a night out in the historic Beer Keller, the cavernous pub which was famously known as the place where Adolf Hitler first started giving his speeches and recruiting his notorious Brown Shirts as part of the Nazi movement. The beer is served not in pint glasses but more like glass buckets. And between us, we'd supped quite a few. Everything was okay until David Wigg, or Wiggy as we called him, started singing some English war-time songs in a very loud voice. He started off with Run Rabbit, Run Rabbit, Run Run Run. We did our best to stop him, but he had consumed so much that he didn't care anymore. Eventually, we were in danger of being thrown out for unruly behaviour and upsetting the German locals. So we decided to leave, and had to drag Wiggy on to his feet and back to his hotel. It was quite a night.

The many places we went to on the great Eurovision bandwagon are good to look back on. Amsterdam, Luxembourg, Dublin, Stockholm, The

Hague, Jerusalem, Munich, even Harrogate and Brighton. They all come flooding back.

We had some great little singers over the years, too. Clodagh Rodgers, The New Seekers, Olivia Newton John, Lynsey de Paul and Mike Moran, Black Lace, Prima Donna. In later years, even Engelbert Humperdink and the great Bonnie Tyler were persuaded to have a go (he finished 25th, and she finished 19th). They may not have won but I bet they had fun trying.

The last contest I covered was in 1988, in Dublin, when the winner was an attractive, demure young singer with a very good voice who won it for Switzerland. Her name was Celine Dion. Now whatever happened to her?

But I think we enjoyed the best years of Eurovision in the 70s and 80s. It used to be a proper contest to find some good songs. And despite all the political voting that went on, most countries were happy to produce decent singers and revel in the competition.

All that has now gone. It's become more of a weird international Gayfest. And it's so gimmicky and freakish, that it's now boring and not even worth tuning into any more.

CHAPTER 29: EMMERDALE

With the success of Coronation Street, it was inevitable that other weekly or twice-weekly drama serials would follow. The BBC tried for years to come up with something to rival The Street, but it wasn't until they hit on the idea of the very same format (a group of people living in a terraced street, with a pub and local shops) but set in east London instead of the North, that they hit the jackpot with EastEnders.

We then started calling them Soap Operas, a term which came from America, where they had been producing these kind of domestic drama serials for years. And then we lazily shortened the term to simply Soaps. Since then, we have been invaded with them. Our TV screens became awash with soaps.

But one of the more successful has been Emmerdale. It started out in 1971 when Yorkshire ITV, jealous of the Granada company over in Lancashire, wanted another running weekly drama to match Coronation Street, to bring in the same kind of advertising revenue. So they set it out on the Yorkshire hills and called it Emmerdale Farm.

At first, nobody gave it any chance of ever really rivalling Coronation Street. But there it is, still running more than 40 years later. And as popular as ever, it seems.

I covered the comings and goings of Emmerdale from its very early days. Most of the action centred around the Sugden family, up to their knees in real mud in their farmhouse, brothers Jack and Joe and their widowed mother Annie.

They had the usual post office, the pub and an assortment of eccentric locals, including the Vicar, a gamekeeper called Seth Armstrong (brilliantly played by Stan Richards) and two peculiar middle-aged bachelors, Amis Brealy, (played by Ronald Magill) and Mr. Wilks (Arthur Pentilow) who never really did anything at all.

Over the years, I often went out on location with the show and got to know most of the regular cast, and they were a cheerful enough lot. Except for old Annie Sugden, who was played by Sheila Mercier, a veteran of the London theatre who was related to the king of farce Brian Rix. Sheila was forever moaning about the cold weather and hated it when they were filming out on the moors. Yet she stuck with it for more than 35 years, so I guess she liked the money.

The heart-throb of the show was handsome young farmer Joe Sugden, played by the popular Frazer Hines. It was Frazer who got most of the fan

165

mail from female viewers. Plus the occasional pair of knickers which women would post to him, along with their phone numbers, he once told me.

Then there was big brother Jack Sugden. As solid and reliable as a garden spade. Did nothing but milk the cows and work and never had much fun in life. The actor who took over playing Jack was Clive Hornby. He was a very likeable bloke and he later married the actress Helen Weir, who also played his wife Pat in the show.

Clive invited me over to his home once for lunch. They had a lovely big old farm house tucked away in the hills. It was so unfortunate that his character on screen was such a boring and tedious bloke.

The character I used to like best though was old Seth Armstrong, the poacher-turned-gamekeeper, with his deerstalker hat and plus-four tweed trousers, and the gun under his arm. I spent many a happy hour drinking in his local pub with Stan Richards, an actor who always had a few stories to tell. He liked a pint or three after work, did Stan. And he would often indiscreetly supply me with all the latest gossip from behind the scenes.

Then there was Richard Thorpe, the handsome actor who had been in the theatre and films for a long time before joining the show. He became a stalwart, playing well-to-do farmer Alan Turner. Richard was a very jolly fellow, loved his food and could be seen every day eating at his reserved table in the local pub restaurant. Not for him any of that TV location food, if he could help it! He put on a lot of weight in his later years, but his ballooned appearance was acceptable because he was always one of those farmers more interested in doing the books and counting his money than actually using much energy out on the farm.

Jean Rogers was a very fanciable actress who I got on well with. She came in and brought some much-needed glamour to the show, playing Dolly Skilbeck from 1980, and stayed more than ten years. Jean and I became quite good friends, and she invited me over to her house once or twice to do interviews, which was much more comfortable than sitting out in the farmyard.

The producers soon became aware that they needed a constant supply of young actresses, to provide some sex in the story-lines. So in came the dishy Claire King. She played the glamorous Kim Tate, married to farm owner Frank Tate (Norman Bowler) and later to turn Mrs. Nasty.

Claire was always good for a chat and was a constant publicity seeker, so we'd have lunch in the local pub quite regularly. She too stayed with the show for ten years, before moving on.

She was in the wilderness for a while. With the passing of the years, she could no longer play dolly-bird roles. Ironically, she moved into the old rival soap Coronation Street in 2015, playing the middle-aged divorcee Erica, friend of Rovers landlady Liz McDonald. She quickly had her feet under the table there and looks like being one of those intriguing characters who can come and go whenever they require a gossipy old girl still capable of showing some cleavage and flickering those long eyelashes.

But the actress who, for me, really first brought sex into Emmerdale was the lovely little blonde Malandra Burrows, who played Kathy Bates. She came in from 1985 and played the character of Kathy on and off for 20 years. Mal came from Liverpool, was a very ambitious teenager, and her divorced father with whom she lived would often come on the phone to me, offering stories of his young daughter which he would like in the Mirror.

At one time, she only had to fall over or sprain an ankle, and her dad would be on the phone to me to tell me all the details. There was nothing wrong with that, of course. He was only keen to push his ambitious daughter, who actually started out as a tap-dancer and singer and appeared on Hughie Green's talent show Opportunity Knocks at the age of twelve.

I did a lot of stories on Mal and watched her grow into a very fine actress. But one of the highlights of her time in Emmerdale was when the producers decided, in 1988, that the popular Kathy Bates should get married to her farmyard sweetheart Jackie Merrick, who was played by the very likeable young Ian Sharrock. And the story-line had the young newly-weds going off on an exotic honeymoon to Tunisia.

The good thing from my point of view was that the producers invited the Daily Mirror to go along with them, so I quickly jumped at the chance and flew over with one of our photographers, Phil Spencer, to meet up with them, staying at a luxury hotel in Hammamet.

It was a marvellous trip because it was the middle of January, and whilst it was snowy and cold here, it was 70 or 80 degrees over there, and so it was just like taking a week's holiday in the North African sunshine. What could be better? Phil and I both packed our sun tan lotion and off we went.

We then spent a week just watching them filming, then interviewing Malanda and Ian when they had finished work in front of the cameras.

They were filmed having the inevitable camel ride, lying on the beach, and jumping in and out of the hotel swimming pool. The evenings they spent dining quietly together at a candle-lit table in the corner.

Mal and Ian looked the picture of youthful happiness. They captured all the joy of a couple in love and on their honeymoon. They certainly had a magic between them in their acting. So much so that Phil Spencer and I were actually speculating one day, and he said to me, "Do you think they are just acting on this honeymoon - or is their romance for real?" Well, we were just left guessing, of course.

Mal and Ian had recently appeared in a stage pantomime together, and Mal said, "We get on very well. We're great mates." Both their characters in Emmerdale had been through other romances. "But I think Kathy and Jackie were meant for each other all the time," said Mal.

The fact was, Ian, then 28, was married and went to great lengths to tell us that his wife Pam, who worked in the Yorkshire TV Press Office back home in Leeds, was expecting their second baby in about four months' time. And he was phoning home every day to check on how she was.

As for Phil and myself, we were happy to lie back in a couple of deck chairs and sit in the sun, with a nice cold drink or two, and catch up with the young actors back at the hotel later. It really was one of the best perks I'd ever enjoyed in the job. And we ended up not just with a sun tan but with a really good two-page spread on the lovey-dovey honeymooners.

However, some years later, I read somewhere in the Sunday papers a piece about Ian and Malandra, and it was revealed that they had been more than just good friends and were actually lovers at one time.

It can be difficult sometimes to tell fact from fiction.

CHAPTER 30: EASTENDERS

LESLIE GRANTHAM

I was never really into EastEnders. Perhaps this is because I'm a Northerner at heart and have never been very fond of either cockney slang or really felt at home south of the Thames. Even when I worked in London for more than 20 years, I preferred to live north of the city, in Harrow.

Apart from that, I always felt that the BBC soap really was a desperate attempt by the Corporation to come up with something - anything - that would prove a rival to Coronation Street. For years they were intensely jealous of Granada's success with what became commonly known as Corrie. And in the end, EastEnders was simply the very same format - a terraced street, with a pub on the corner, a few shops, and a bunch of working-class residents who never really liked each other. The only difference was that it was situated in east London, with cockney accents instead of Manchester with the Lancashire dialect.

But for my money, EastEnders has never matched Coronation Street for humour. They have depended instead on more violence.

The viewing figures have of course dropped dramatically from what they used to be, and the two shows have each had turns of being top-dog, with a yo-yo situation when it comes to picking up annual awards.

However, The Street is not even half as good as it used to be. For years now, it has been looking tired and dreary, and the characters have become boring and easily forgettable.

Frankly, anyone with any sense, if they step back and take a proper, unbiased look at what is being produced on screen, would have to question why and how both Coronation Street and EastEnders are still there. After more than 50 years, The Street is well past its sell-by date. And EastEnders, too, would not be missed.

If that sounds harsh, well, too bad!

I did have one or two laughs on the odd occasion I covered news stories on EastEnders. I have to confess though that when I was show business editor of the Mirror, I did have a special inside spy within the BBC - an employee who was a snitch, if you like - who had access to EastEnders scripts, and he would often phone me with information. Mostly it was just the story-lines of what was going to happen in upcoming episodes, which I was not really interested in. But one day I did get a tip-off which I thought was worth following up.

My secret informant assured me that Dirty Den, just about the biggest and most notorious character in the programme, was going to be killed off - literally. Leslie Grantham played the vicious, nasty ex-landlord of the Queen Vic pub, who was now mixed up with gangsters. He was probably the most hated man on TV at that time.

Grantham had gone into EastEnders in 1985 with his wife Angie (played by Anita Dobson) to take over as manager of the Queen Vic. But his constant underhand dealings, bad tempered behaviour and ill treatment of his wife made him a hated character. And viewers had never forgiven him since that memorable Christmas episode in 1986, when he presented her with divorce papers and spitefully leered, "Happy Christmas, Ange!"

Right from the very start, Dennis Watts was nothing but trouble in the East End soap. In fact, he was dynamite. Because Grantham made his screen debut as Den Watts on February 19, 1985. And four days later, he was exposed on the front page of the Daily Mirror as a convicted murderer. It doesn't take long for this kind of news to leak out, and Leslie must have known that it was inevitable.

The fact was that Grantham had actually been convicted of shooting dead a German taxi driver in 1967, while attempting to rob him. He was given a life sentence but was finally released after serving only ten years.

Ironically, it was while he was in jail that Grantham started acting in prison plays and, on his release, he was encouraged to go to drama school, and then became a full-time actor. He'd done a few smaller acting gigs but going into EastEnders really did propel him into the big time.

When he was first signed up for the role, Grantham did tell the BBC about his violent past and his prison record, but they agreed to hush it up. They obviously didn't reckon on the Daily Mirror! And when the news broke, he offered to resign immediately. But the BBC decided to stick by him. Let's face it, they knew the publicity would boost the show and they had struck oil.

But after four years of hitting the headlines both on and off the screen, Grantham decided he'd had enough and wanted to leave. That's when the scriptwriters hit on the idea of bumping him off in a gangland fight.

It also led to me missing my lunch and being down on a canal bank near Wembley, on a sunny Sunday afternoon. Because that's where I'd been secretly tipped off the BBC camera unit would be - with Dirty Den getting his final come-uppance.

When I arrived, with a Mirror photographer in tow, it was quite clear my information was right. For there was a small BBC film unit, with make-up artists, and Leslie Grantham all ready to go into action. They were not very pleased to see me however, and I was politely asked to leave by one of the production team. When I refused, and pointed out that it was a public footpath, they quickly realised that there was nothing they could do about. So they continued filming, and I agreed to stand well away, behind some bushes, with my photographer all ready with his camera poised for action.

We stayed for an hour or more. Long enough to see Dirty Den stroll casually along the canal bank, suddenly to be confronted by a mysterious dark figure of a stranger carrying a big bunch of flowers. Then, without warning, we heard the gunfire shots and realised that the stranger had a gun hidden inside the bunch of flowers. And Dennis Watts slumped forward and then fell awkwardly into the canal, with a loud splash.

That was it. Dirty Den killed by an unidentified man as part of a gang warfare. There was no rescue. I seem to remember that there was a slight ripple of applause from some of the camera crew, in appreciation of Grantham's final acting scene. And that became one of the most memorable and famous death scenes ever shot on TV.

Of course, I got a wonderful exclusive front-page picture-news story for next day's Mirror. Plus a telling-off from the BBC Press Office, who were angry at my breaking their story-line. Or, at least, they went through the motions.

Well, they always pretended to be annoyed on those occasions when the Press occasionally revealed in advance what was going to happen in the TV soap stories. But they weren't really. In fact, Press Officers quite often used to leak stories to TV journalists, and then pretend to be horrified when the story appeared in print, by saying "We never discuss future story-lines because it spoils it for viewers."

It was all hypocrisy, of course. They all did it. Coronation Street, Emmerdale. And the worst of all was Brookside. They knew it was good publicity for the show.

As for Leslie Grantham, he left the show and went on to do other things. Dirty Den had been killed off for ever. Or had he? A body was later pulled out of the canal and his grief-stricken wife Angie adapted to becoming a widow and everyone in the Queen Vic happily got on with life, because Den had earlier sold the pub to Frank Butcher.

For a few years though, there was always a sinister speculation that viewers had not seen the last of Dirty Den. And I was actually at a Press conference for Leslie Grantham, who was plugging a new show he was doing, when one newspaperman asked him the direct question, "Is Dirty Den really dead? Or will you be going back to EastEnders at some time in the future?"

Grantham chuckled loudly and pointed to me, sitting near the back of the conference room, and said, "Ask Ken Irwin. He knows. He was there on the canal bank when I got shot by a bunch of daffodils."

Leslie always hated the Press, especially since that early bad publicity he'd had to endure, when his criminal past was revealed. He would never do interviews. But I must say, in my dealings with him, I found him to have a wicked sense of humour.

Grantham did lots of other work in TV and films and was much in demand for a while, mostly playing villains. But then, surprise, surprise, he was tempted back to EastEnders by an offer he couldn't refuse, 14 years after being killed off. The BBC, in a desperate effort to boost the flagging viewing figures, got out the big fat chequebook. He was reported to have agreed a British soap record fee of £500,000 a year to sign a new contract (though personally I found that hard to believe and think the figure was grossly exaggerated).

But it became another of those fatuous "Bobby Ewing returns from the dead in Dallas" situations. The EastEnders scriptwriters suddenly came up with the story that Den Watts had survived that fatal shooting, that the body pulled out of the canal had somehow been wrongly identified, and Den recovered and fled to Spain where he lived in secret for 14 years. Now, he was homesick and wanted to return to Albert Square.

They can do anything in TV soaps, of course. It isn't real. Over 17 million viewers tuned in to watch the much-awaited episode when Den walked back into the life of his busty daughter Sharon Watts, with that familiar, smarmy smile and the simple line "Hello, Princess!"

He then stayed for another 18 months with the programme and resumed where he'd left off, wheeling and dealing. But it wasn't long before he was in trouble again. For real. In 2004, Grantham made front page headlines again when he was reported to have been involved in a sordid sex scandal. A Sunday newspaper published photographs of him exposing himself and masturbating via a webcam from his dressing room to an undercover reporter named "Amanda."

He claimed he had been "set up," but went through the humiliation of issuing a public apology in a statement which read: "I am wholeheartedly ashamed of my behaviour` and feel that I have let down my colleagues, as well as my friends and family."

Shortly after, he was written out of the show again, and this time the BBC confirmed that his character would definitely be killed off - "and the coffin lid will be nailed shut."

In February 2005, viewers saw the last of Dirty Den. In a violent scene, he was killed by his second wife Chrissie, who hit him over the head with a heavy dog-shaped doorstop after he attacked her during an argument. So it was really self-defence. R.I.P. Dennis Watts!

MIKE READ

It was ironic that Mike Read, the big brash cockney who took over from Dirty Den as the Queen Vic landlord Frank Butcher, also hit the headlines, with the revelation that he too had a violent criminal past.

Read joined EastEnders in 1987, and although Frank had a dark side and an obvious dodgy background, he had a great sense of humour with the punters and proved a far more popular character than Den Watts.

It then came to light however that Mike had been more than a bad boy earlier in life. In the 1950s and 60s, he was a member of an East End gang, spending a lot of time high-jacking lorries, blowing up safes, and carrying a shotgun when going out on robberies. He ended up with a long criminal record. But then after a spell in Brixton Prison, he decided to end his criminal career for the sake of his wife and family, and turned to a more legitimate occupation, before becoming an actor.

I first met Mike Read 15 years or more before he became Frank Butcher. He had just been signed up by Granada TV to do the second series of The Comedians, and we met for lunch to discuss his career, because I was then writing a book on the show. I found him a very quick-witted and likeable character and we got on really well and remained friends for some years

When he went up to Manchester to join the show, Mike had one or two initial reservations, because the rest of the stand-up comedians were all from the North and well established, and he was the first cockney to penetrate that Northern enclave. He soon found he could more than hold his own, however.

I recall him telling me that he earned his place on the show when he phoned up the producer Johnny Hamp out of the blue and asked if he could come for an audition. Johnny said, "I haven't got time for auditions. Do something over the phone."

"Over the phone?" Mike queried. "Yes. Tell me a joke," said Johnny. Rather reluctantly, Mike reeled off the first gag he could remember. "Advert seen in the paper today: 'Woman, deaf in left ear, wearing hearing-aid, would like to meet man, deaf in right ear, wearing hearing-aid. Object - stereo!'"

"That's not bad," said John, "Let's have another."

So Mike came up with another gag. "Two geese flying high over the M1 when a jumbo jet comes screeching overhead at a helluva speed. One goose says to the other, 'Harry, I wish I could fly as fast as that.' The other goose says, 'You would, mate, if your bum was on fire."

Hamp said, "You're booked. Come up to Manchester and do a taping."

That was Mike's first time in front of the TV cameras as a comic. And from that one appearance, he was rocketed to stardom with his fiery, bash-bash, heavyweight brand of humour.

Born in Hackney, he left school and became a coal man. Then a series of jobs followed. He was a steward in the Merchant Navy, then a bricklayer's labourer, a navvy, digging roads, and a scrap metal dealer.

He first got into show business when the compere didn't turn up at his local pub. Mike got up on stage and sang a few songs, and was asked if he wanted a regular job, at 25 shilling a night. He jumped at it. He turned full-time professional, starting out as a singer, doing Frank Sinatra numbers, but then started telling gags in between the songs, and gradually the comedy took over.

For five years, he worked as a stuntman in films and TV, and then came second in a Butlin's national talent contest, finishing up with a prize of £750 at the London Palladium.

It was The Comedians that made him a national name, and one time when he invited me over for lunch at his house in Little Easton, Essex, he told me that he would be eternally grateful to John Hamp for giving him that first shot on TV. "Doing The Comedians was the happiest time of my life," he said. "Just trying to compete with those guys - particularly heavyweights like Bernard Manning and Frank Carson - gave me the valuable experience I needed. But I think I proved I was as good as any of them."

Once he was established in EastEnders, his popularity soared. He was given the opportunity to bring a lot of his natural comic humour into his antics behind the bar of the Queen Vic. And he had two wives to play off. Big Pat, played by Pam St. Clement, and Peggy, by that tough little nut

Barbara Windsor. His relationship with both women could sometimes be hysterical.

Mike left the show after a long 13-year stint, said he was suffering from exhaustion, and he'd had enough. But he was tempted back after a couple of years, and we had more laughable shenanigans from Frank Butcher before he finally bowed out and quit the show in 2005. He vowed he was going to take life easy and play more golf and went to live in Spain.

Tragically, Mike died of a heart attack only two years later, at the age of 67. And sadly, he died penniless. It was reported that he left nothing in his will, after £900,000 of debts had to be settled.

CHAPTER 31: BREAD & CARLA LANE

Carla Lane was a quite amazing woman. I first met her in 1969 when I got a phone call from a contact of mine in the BBC telling me that two "ordinary housewives from Liverpool" had been signed up to write a new TV series, to be called The Liver Birds.

After a few enquiries, I discovered who they were, and eventually managed to set up an interview with them in the BBC bar at the TV Centre in Shepherds Bush.

When I turned up, I was introduced to these two middle-aged, married ladies, both quite attractive but very different. One was quite flirty, the other plump and more down to earth. Their names were Carla Lane and Myra Taylor. And as we sat and chatted over drinks, it turned out they had been trying to write scripts together for years, but they had not done anything professionally, and they were unashamedly naïve when it came to TV production.

This first script they'd written was obviously semi-autobiographical, although they tried to deny this. But it was about two young dolly-birds sharing a flat in Liverpool. One was very tidy and practical, the other one completely scatty. And, of course, they had all the usual domestic anxieties, financial problems, romances and boyfriends coming and going.

One could have been forgiven for easily dismissing this first script as being the work of two amateurs - amusing but trite and very predictable. But there was something about it which intrigued the BBC's Head of Drama Michael Mills, who liked their script, gave it a trial in the Comedy Playhouse slot, and put producer Sidney Lotterby in charge of the production.

And I was equally intrigued. So I wrote a story for the Mirror - Liverpool housewives hit the jackpot! - with a picture of Carla and Myra enjoying a bottle of bubbly which I paid for.

The BBC cast the lovely Pauline Collins and newcomer Polly James as the two Liver birds, Dawn and Beryl. And the show took off and became a huge hit with viewers. It was the start of a long and successful writing career for one of them. And it was also the start of a very warm friendship between Carla Lane and myself.

The Liver Birds went on to run for ten years. There was a change in the leading cast after the first series, with Pauline Collins leaving and Nerys Hughes coming in as Sandra Hutchinson, the new flatmate sharing the bills and the laughs with Beryl. Mollie Sugden was also brought in to play Sandra's mother.

Sadly, the two scriptwriters later split up. Myra opted out of the TV show, and it was left to Carla to take over on her own. But the two remained friends. Myra went through a divorce. And there was no way that Carla was ever going to be called a housewife again. She now had her feet very firmly on the ladder to fame, and though she too divorced her husband (Arthur Hollins, an antique dealer) after 26 years of marriage, she never stopped working.

Carla became one of the most prolific TV writers we've ever had. She went on to produce one winning show after another. After The Liver Birds, she gave us Butterflies (with the wonderful Wendy Craig) for five years, Solo, Leaving, and The Mistress. And then came her other top-rating winner, Bread.

Over the years, Carla and I had many long chats. Many cups of tea and glasses of wine. We both came from Liverpool, so we had a lot in common. Both Scousers with very much the same sense of humour and the ability to laugh at ourselves. She was what I would call Posh Scouse, which used to amuse her, because she came from one of the more prosperous areas of the city and had a good education and a very cultured outlook on life.

After she'd moved down to London, Carla invited me over to her house in Chiswick a few times. It was set right on the banks of the Thames, and we could sit on her front door step and watch the world go by, the joggers and people strolling by the river, and Carla feeding the ducks which she loved to do.

Once when I was there, Linda McCartney, Paul's missus, suddenly dropped in for tea. She was a great friend of Carla's, they were both vegetarians and had a passionate love of animals. And I recall that as we sat in the back garden together, having tea, there was a strange hefty-looking guy who was lurking quietly in the shrubbery, among the trees. I wondered who he was. "That's Linda's bodyguard," said Carla. "He tries to be as discreet as possible. Paul feels better when he knows Linda is being protected."

I suppose I was a bit surprised, but I shouldn't have been. It was fairly obvious that someone like Mrs. McCartney could always be a target for kidnappers with a big ransom in mind.

Linda herself was lovely. Very chatty and down to earth. That was the only time I ever met her, though I think I did tell her that I knew Paul in his earlier days with the Beatles.

To say that Carla had a love of animals is a huge understatement. She was besotted with them. Her house was always full of creatures of all descriptions, cats, dogs, parrots. For years, her closest companion was a huge dog, an Irish wolfhound the size of a small donkey, who would lope around after her, all over the house.

Later, she moved down to Sussex and opened her own animal sanctuary. I visited her there, in Horsted Keynes. "I know most people think I'm a lunatic and a crank, but I don't care," said Carla. "I moved house just for the sake of my animals, and now this, to me, is sheer heaven."

The impressive 16th century manor house was set in 20 acres of beautiful garden and parkland, with four lakes. She turned it into an animal sanctuary, and when I visited her she had 18 ponies, 20 goats, 10 dogs, 15 cats, and more than 800 birds including ducks, geese, lame pigeons, gulls with their wings shattered. There was also a one-legged heron she introduced me to.

She ploughed most of her money into the sanctuary, which she called Animaline. She said, "People just turn up here with animals they can't afford to keep. They know I'll look after them. But it is an expensive business, and one day I am going to run out of money.

"A few years ago, I swore I would never move out of London. But I had too many animals to look after. Even walking my dog Egor was difficult, because people don't like dogs being walked in London. I just felt that my dog needed more space.

"I put my house in London up for sale and then when I found this place I fell in love with it. I'm not sure exactly how many rooms it has, I think it's 55 or 57. But we have 23 bathrooms, one for every bedroom. We occupy only the downstairs and a few bedrooms." She could be very scatty at times.

Carla was awarded an OBE in 1989, not only for her contribution to TV and the entertainment industry but also for her care and compassion of animals.

But some years later, she controversially returned her OBE to the government in protest at a CBE being awarded to the managing director of a firm who had a contract with animal testing laboratories.

That didn't surprise me at all. Carla was undoubtedly a woman who would stick to her principles. She then actually received a handwritten letter from Prime Minister Tony Blair, saying her OBE was fully deserved and it would be safely kept in case she ever wanted it back.

She was certainly a one-off, Carla. She was very headstrong. In fact, I would categorise her as being a wonderful eccentric. She ended up having to sell up and move on from her animal sanctuary, in 2009.

Further proof of her eccentricity came when she bought her own island - a craggy rock called St. Tudwal's just off the coast of North Wales, south of Abersoch on the Llyn Peninsula. There she tried to create a nature reserve

A few years ago, Carla sold a lot of her TV scripts for charity. Again, it didn't surprise me.

She used to write most of her scripts by hand. "I can't really type very well," she said. And she confided to me once, "I hate dusting and cleaning, that's why I don't do any housework. And I'm not a very good cook. In fact, on the domestic side, I don't think I was a very good wife. I've always been happier just writing than being a perfect home maker."

There was a lot of Carla in most of her scripts, though I'm not sure she'd like to admit it.

When she came up with the idea for Bread, however, she had the perfect vehicle in which to vent her feelings on every social ill and propaganda campaign that took her fancy.

Ostensibly a comedy show, it had huge and serious undercurrents of social morality. It had a lorra, lorra laughs, as our Cilla would say. But it also had pathos and the ability to infuriate and antagonise viewers in equal measure.

The programme was set around a working-class family called the Boswells, living in a deprived dockside area of Liverpool. Correction: They weren't working-class at all because they didn't work and were experts at skiving and "working the system".

Supposedly a devout Catholic family, the Boswells consisted of four brothers of varying intelligence trying to out-do each other, a young scatterbrain sister called Aveline, their mother Nellie, who was the matriarch of the household, and a work-shy father who had left the family to go and live with his strange girlfriend, nicknamed Lilo Lil. Plus a grandfather who lived next door but kept popping in and out and expecting a ready-made meals service to be delivered to his armchair table.

It really was a mad scenario. But it was the clever casting that made it work. The brilliant Jean Boht was the link-pin. She played the mother Nellie, though she was always referred to as Mrs. Boswell. Ronald Forfar was Dad, Freddie Boswell. And the boys were Peter Howitt, as big brother

Joey, Jonathon Morris (Adrian, the poetry-loving bookworm), Victor
McGuire (the well-intentioned Jack) and Nick Conway (Billy, the idiot).
Kenneth Waller played Granddad, the scrounger.

And an odd assortment of characters flitted in and out, including the
local priest who was always dropping in to say prayers but wouldn't go
without a glass of sherry. And later, a mysterious cousin called Shifty
moved in, fresh out of prison, and became another family sponger. He was
played by Brian Murray.

Daft as it all was, the show produced some hilarious situations. One
was when they had air-head daughter Aveline marrying Oswald Carter, a
Church of England vicar (played by Giles Watling) which caused many
religious rows.

There was cousin Shifty running a greengrocery business from the back
of a hearse. Then there was Granddad, who lived next door, but who
decided to swap houses with his daughter Nellie, so that they could then
charge each other rent and re-claim it on benefits from the DHSS.

And there was the constant charade of keeping two permanent private
parking spaces outside their front doors - by putting stolen police traffic
cones on the pavement.

The show was shot on location in Elswick Street, Dingle, which was on a
steep hill sloping down to the dock road and the River Mersey. It was a
street of unpretentious terraced houses with nothing to distinguish it from
many others in that run-down part of the city - until the BBC moved in with
Bread.

After that, life for many of the folk living behind solid doors and trim
lace curtains was never quite the same again.

The couple who actually later lived at No.30 (which was the house
supposedly occupied by the Boswell family, and where all the TV filming
was done) were Ian and Linda Griffiths. Ian was a van driver and Linda was
a packer in a departmental store. They'd been married for 18 months and
were very proud of their little two-up-and-two- down first house. "We
bought it for just £14,750," Ian happily told me when I first met him. "We
knew nothing about the TV show until after we'd signed the contract on
the house. Then we were told it was the Boswells' house in Bread on the
telly. We couldn't believe it at first. When the BBC asked us if they could
go on using our house for filming, we said yes. We thought it was great."

The BBC used only the outside of the house for filming and never really
set foot over the neatly scrubbed front doorstep. So inside No.30 was
nothing like the Boswell home which viewers saw on TV. But that didn't

stop Ian and Linda from enjoying a little glow of fame. For years, they had a constant stream of callers asking for the Boswells. "We got used to it," said Ian. "When people knocked on the door, I'd usually say, 'Joey's not in - but come in and have a look around.' People come in and want to have their pictures taken with us. They even ask for our autographs." And Ian opened the door once and a young chap asked him if Joey Boswell was in, because he wanted a few tips on the latest fiddles with the DHSS.

But it was at No.28 where grumpy Granddad was supposed to reside. And the real owners were a lovely couple of pensioners, Edith and Charlie Helm. They admitted after a couple of years that they would be lost without the BBC and Bread. Because everyone on the programme, cast and crew alike, used their place as a home from home. "They're almost like part of our family," Edith told me. "In fact, we really miss them when they're not here filming."

One of the biggest surprises came one day when Paul and Linda McCartney unexpectedly walked in on them. "I couldn't believe it when Paul arrived in our kitchen and made himself at home, and asked for a cup of tea," said Charlie, who started work at 14 and retired after 34 years as a tanker driver with a brewery. Edith was a canteen manageress at the same firm for 35 years.

The couple admitted that they enjoyed laughing at the weekly antics of the Boswell family. "But I don't like people confusing fact with fiction," insisted Charlie, who was then the owner of a little C-registered Datsun. "There are no flashy Jaguars down our street, except when Joey is here filming. Then his big black Jag is always parked outside our front door and I try to keep an eye on it."

When strangers knocked on their front door and asked for Granddad, which they did frequently, Edith would invite them in for a cup of tea. Then she would hand out signed photographs of the TV cast, so they wouldn't be disappointed. "They come from all over the world to see our street," she'd say. "We've even had people from Australia who have seen the show and come to Liverpool specially to meet the Boswells. I feel so sorry for them sometimes. They just stand there and stare at the houses."

As for Granddad himself, Ken Waller was supposed to be 75 as the bad-tempered grandfather, but he was really a very lively 60-year-old.

"What is so wonderful about this show," Ken once told me, "is that there are no prima donnas. We are not stars. The Boswell family is the real star. And we really do get on like one big family."

Ken was always a great believer in fate. Two years before the show started, he was lined up to do a film with Omar Sharif and Jewel In The Crown actor Art Malik in Spain. But Malik broke his arm a week before they were due to fly out. Shooting was postponed, and Ken couldn't do the film later because he was in a BBC play. He was so disappointed, but not for long, because the BBC were casting for a new comedy series called Bread, and he was invited to play the grandfather. "It was a gift from God," he said. "If I'd been filming in Spain, somebody else would have landed this part."

By the time real stardom arrived, Ken had spent more than 30 years in the theatre. When he moved to London, his first TV part was a walk-on in a Terry Scott comedy show. Although he had played lots of old men in Rep, the first he was asked to play on TV was in the classic Are You Being Served? He appeared as store owner Mr. Grace. But it was Bread which catapulted him to real fame.

Ken recalled for me that he once upset his mother so much when he appeared on TV in a play and had to say "Piss off". "My mother was so disgusted that I should use such language. I had to explain that it was only a joke, and no one was really offended. But she still wouldn't speak to me for a week," he said.

Funny, but that same line - Piss off! - became his familiar catchphrase as doddery Granddad in Bread.

Away from the show, Ken, who was originally from Huddersfield, lived a quiet life in a rented two-bed maisonette in North London. "I don't want life to be complicated. I don't yearn for possessions and property," he'd say. "My idea of treating myself is to buy some fresh Scotch salmon from Marks and Sparks, and half a half bottle of champagne with my supper."

He was so chuffed with his years of success in playing Granddad that he even turned down a role at the Royal Shakespeare Company at Stratford. "My agent told them I was too busy doing a new series of Bread to go into Shakespeare. It gave me a little twinge of satisfaction to turn them down. Because 30 years ago I went for an audition with the RSC and they didn't want to know me!" And as he told me that, his wrinkled old face broke into a jolly, satisfied smile. Just like Granddad.

It was Joey who stole most of the scenes, though. Peter Howitt was superb as the chief benefits scrounger, always dressed in black leather, driving around in a flash old Jaguar. He knew all the rules in the Unemployment book and some of his scenes down at the Labour Exchange or dole office became memorable classics.

PICTURES

An innocent at 5 years old.

Table Tennis. Winning team at St. Domingo, 1954.
L to R: Vic Lane, Les Davies, my sister Louise, Bill Fairhurst and
yours truly, the skinny one.

**Busy in the office. With Eric Firth (left) on the
Birkenhead News.**

Smart dresser. Reporter on Evening Express, Liverpool.

Reporter in action. On Nottingham Evening Post.

**Skating on thin ice. A lesson from world champion
Sheila Birtles.**

Boxing with world champ Hogan (Kid) Bassey.

Taking the donkeys for a run on New Brighton beach
as a young reporter.

**Judging first beauty contest. Miss New Brighton.
I'm on the left.**

Close encounter. Interviewing tigress Eartha Kitt.

A kick-about on the Anfield pitch.

A judge on the panel of ITV's New Faces. 1974.

Spelling it out – with comedian Bernard Manning.

Kenneth, where's your troosers? In full Scottish dress at Eurovision Song Contest in Edinburgh.

With international Press, attending TV festival in Belgium. I'm 1st on left. Love those flairs.

Off to America. Daily Mirror page, 1978.

**At the Checkpoint Charlie border crossing
in West Berlin in 1982.**

Meeting my boyhood football hero Dave Hickson
at Goodison Park.

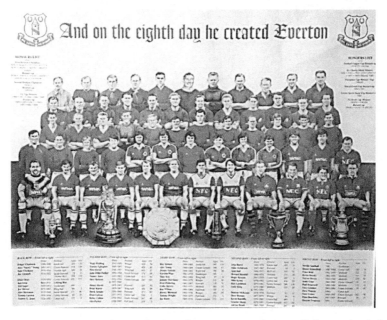

A picture to remember. Playing for Everton. I'm sixth from the left,
back row between Dixie Dean and Ted Sagar.

**Choosing an engagement ring with
Thelma Barlow (Mavis Riley).**

Selling bricks for charity on Coronation Street with Jean Alexander (Hilda Ogden).

Having a laugh with Kenny Everett.

Peter was always the actor who was going places. Self-assured, full of confidence, he was ideally cast as the big-headed Joey, as well as being a magnet for the girls.

I became quite friendly with Peter, though he once reminded me of our very first meeting, long before Bread. It was a night when I happened to be up at Yorkshire TV in Leeds in the club bar, drinking with the Press office guys. And this handsome young bloke sitting nearby came over and started chatting to me. "I know you're with the Daily Mirror," he said, "Do you happen to know Frank Howitt?"

I quickly replied, without thinking," Yes. I do. He's one of the biggest drinkers in Fleet Street." He laughed and said, "Well, he's my father. Hi, I'm Peter Howitt." and he shook hands.

When I looked suitably embarrassed at my flippant remark, he said, "No need to apologise. You're absolutely right. He is an infamous drunk." Frank Howitt was, in fact, a first-class journalist, a hard crime reporter, but he did have a reputation for propping up the bar. Like so many I knew on Fleet Street.

Peter and I laughed at it when we met up again on location for Bread. I did many write-ups on Peter and it was obvious he was very ambitious and determined to make it as a star.

The role of Joey Boswell helped establish him, but he wanted to move on after a couple of years, and was replaced by another actor, Graham Bickley, who took over as the same character but was never as good as Peter.

Hewitt, who came from Manchester but was brought up in London, went on to establish himself in the film world. And I was not surprised, some years later, when he produced the hit film Sliding Doors, starring Gwyneth Paltrow. Peter wrote the screenplay and also directed the film.

He has since settled in Canada, where he has made a name for himself as actor, film director, screenwriter, and has his own production film company.

Another role which had to be re-cast was that of Aveline. When Gilly Coman decided to leave, after five series, in came Melanie Hill. I got to know both Gilly and Melanie quite well and did various features on them. Gilly was always terrified of becoming typecast, but she left the show to have a baby. Tragically, after having four children, Gilly died of a heart condition, at the age of 54.

Melanie was much more outgoing. She was one of the few actors in the cast who wasn't a Scouser. She was born in Brighton but brought up in

Sunderland. She went on to marry tough-guy film actor Sean Bean, had two children, but was later divorced. She's always managed to keep her own career going nicely and was in the popular school drama series Waterloo Road. I was pleasantly surprised when, more recently, she moved in to Coronation Street to become a regular, as Cathy Matthews, a possible love interest for sad café owner Roy Cropper.

Melanie, when I knew her, was always good for a laugh. She has a kind of tough resilience about her.

In one series of Bread, film star Rita Tushingham suddenly came in, playing a character called Celia Higgins, a rather strange divorcee who moved in next door to the Boswells.

Rita happened to be another close friend of Carla Lane's, as well as a fellow Liverpudlian, so she was ideal. Carla often liked to write special parts into her scripts for old friends.

Rita had first fascinated me in her big-screen debut movie A Taste of Honey, in 1961. And then in that marvellous film Dr. Zhivago, a small part but with those big eyes she was captivating as the long-lost daughter of the poetry-writing doctor (Omar Sharif) and his lover Tara (Julie Christie). She also made a less-publicised film called Girl With The Green Eyes.

I met her several times, with Carla, and those eyes really were as big and strikingly penetrating as I had first remembered when seeing her on screen.

She stayed for only one series, doing 11 episodes. But she clearly loved being back home in Liverpool, where she was brought up as a child always yearning to become an actress.

The daughter of a grocer and born in Garston, she went on to work with the Royal Shakespeare Company and starred in a string of films. But Rita was always cheerful and happy to reminisce about her schooldays, and she could put on a Scouse accent to match any of us. It was good to see her receive an Honorary Fellowship from Liverpool's John Moores University in 2009, for what they called "her outstanding contribution to the performing arts."

Jean Boht was another fine actress who was proud of her Liverpool roots. I got to know Jean really well, and she did many interviews with me.

Once, at her lovely home on the high street in Barnes, she'd invited me over for lunch. And she was just like Nellie Boswell busy cooking in the kitchen. Her friends in the cast had bought her a bread-making machine as a symbolic birthday present, and she insisted on me sampling a few slices of her crusty, fresh bread.

She was married to Carl Davies, the internationally famous composer and conductor. And she insisted on him coming down from his music room upstairs and joining us for lunch.

Although she then lived in London, Jean would get back to Liverpool whenever she could. At one time, Jean went through a punishing work schedule which would have terrified most people, because she was travelling up to Liverpool to film Bread all day and was then dashing back to London each night to star in the stage play Steel Magnolias at the Lyric Theatre. I remember her telling me, "This is the first time I've ever had my name up in lights in the West End, and it's thanks to Nellie Boswell. I owe her such a lot. Fortunately, I can sleep on trains. So, on filming days, I catch the midnight sleeper to Liverpool and get made-up in front of the cameras right after breakfast. Then it's another dash back by rail to be at the theatre in the evening."

How she managed it, I don't know. But Jean had the large house in London to look after, as well as a couple of teenage daughters and a husband to feed. "I surprise myself sometimes, but I like to keep busy," she said.

She was a very homely woman, a bit of a chatterbox, and far more charming than Mrs. Boswell. "I've hardly ever been out of work so, unlike the Boswell family, I have not had to go on the dole very much. I was always a good shorthand typist and when acting jobs were scarce, I hustled an office job somewhere."

In her early days, she was a commercial traveller with her dad's confectionary firm. Then when she went into acting, she worked with Rep companies for £1 a week. It was only when she got on TV in gritty Northern dramas like Boys from The Blackstuff and Scully that she started earning decent money.

She was very practical. "I love playing Nellie Boswell, but I suppose I will be saddled with her now forever, no matter what other work I do. But I don't care. How can anyone knock a show that draws an audience of more than 21 million viewers? I love Nellie. She's the salt of the earth."

Jean also once told me, "I'm still very much a Northerner at heart, and always will be. I know the value of money. I'm amazed when I hear that people actually pay out £1,000 for a set of curtains - I make my own.

"Carl, my husband, has a very different attitude. Being American, he doesn't believe in doing jobs around the house. Get someone in to do it, that's his motto. But I won't pay out if I can do the job myself." She could sound a bit like Mrs. Boswell, sometimes!

CHAPTER 32: BROOKSIDE

Brookside, the TV soap set in Liverpool, ran for 21 years on Channel 4, ending in 2003. But I'm willing to wager that if you stopped anyone in the street and asked them what they can remember most about it, they would almost certainly come up with two memorable incidents - 1, the body buried under the patio. 2, the Lesbian kiss.

The show went through just about every story-line it was possible to dream up. Murder, mayhem, rapes, gangland feuds - it had the lot. And the programme probably brought in more complaints on a regular basis from an angry public than anything else on television. Yet the more violent and controversial it became, the more popular it proved to be in the ratings. Its audience only amounted to a few million a week, though, and never really competed with the big boys like Coronation Street and EastEnders, because it was confined to Channel 4, always very much a minority channel.

In fact, the programme was launched on the very first night that Channel 4 came on the air, November 2, 1982. And it was created especially as a brand- new soap to build up a regular audience for the new channel. The first episode drew an audience of just over 4 million viewers.

I was in on Brookside, even before it went on air. I went up to Liverpool with a photographer to see the pilot show and do a big feature for the Mirror. That's when I met this young and rather incredible man Phil Redmond for the first time, who took me around the estate and introduced me to all the leading cast members.

What Redmond did was something no one had done before. With his new company Mersey Television, he put money into buying all the houses in a cul-de-sac on a new estate being built in the West Derby district. Then he had special hidden cameras installed in every house. And once the show went on air, the actors moved in and "lived" in their natural surroundings, playing out the action and following the scripts. There were no studios like other TV companies had. The whole thing was cleverly devised to give maximum authenticity. And it certainly worked.

Only six houses were occupied by fictional families, originally. Then, one house was used as a canteen, another as a make-up department and rest-room, and a couple of houses were used by the Press department and as administrative offices. Redmond had it all planned out very carefully and economically. This was the man who had devised the popular Grange Hill school series for the BBC (which ran eventually for 30 years). But now at Brookside, he had his own company and he was the boss, and he was brimming with new ideas and big plans.

There was an infectious enthusiasm about Redmond. With his long, shoulder-length hair, a constant, leery smile on his face, and his unpretentious Scouse accent, he looked like a hippy who was determined to stand out in a crowd. Not for him the smart suits of other TV executives. Here was a man who never wore a tie and liked to be casual. A self-made rebel. Mr. Cool personified.

RICKY TOMLINSON

When I walked into Brookside Close, I was introduced to the cast - first Sue Johnston, who played Sheila Grant, and then Ricky Tomlinson, who played her husband, trade union worker Bobby Grant.

Ricky came over, gave me a fierce handshake and said, "Hello, mate. I read all your stuff in the Mirror. I know your kid brother Eric. We went to school together."

Really? I'd never met him before. But he was suddenly telling me all about his schooldays at Venice Street Secondary Modern, the same school I attended for four years. He was four or five years younger than me, so I didn't know him. But he knew my brother. "We were in the same class together," said Ricky. "Isn't he a jeweller now, in Chester? Give him my regards next time you see him." In fact, Eric was in the same class for two years. But Eric won a scholarship at the age of 13 and went on to Liverpool Art School, while Ricky stayed on at Venice Street until he was 15.

When I later told my brother about my meeting with Ricky, he just laughed and said, "Oh yes, I remember Ricky Tomlinson. He was a scruffy bugger, sat near the back of the class, and was always causing trouble."

Some years later, when I got to know Ricky well and we became quite good friends, I told him of my brother's remark, and we had a good laugh about it. "The cheeky sod. But he is absolutely right. I was a bit of a trouble-maker at school," he admitted.

Ricky was unknown when he went into Brookside. His background had been a series of jobs, mostly in the building trade, where he had become a strong trade unionist. And he was jailed in 1973 for "conspiring to intimidate" during the leading of a strike. He became one of the infamous Shrewsbury Two, released after two years, and hailed as something of a working-class hero on Merseyside. In fact, Ricky has since spent years fighting for a full pardon from that prison sentence, maintaining that he was wrongfully arrested.

He had been a pub entertainer, playing the banjo and singing songs, with some comedy thrown in, and then had a few bit parts as an actor. But it was Brookside which established him as a TV star. He stayed with the show for six years, and then went on to bigger things, starring in tough-guy parts in a few films.

His private life was a mess, however. And I had the unfortunate job of occasionally having to write about his domestic life as well as his show business success. His first marriage ended in a bitter divorce, and his business ventures came and went.

I recall once being invited to go and see him in a rather run-down afternoon drinking club which he had bought and was running in Liverpool city-centre. That was Ricky. Life was always a bit of a roller-coaster.

Then of course he found fresh TV success all over again with the comedy show The Royle Family, which became another big hit. He moved in as the layabout husband Jim Royle, with his old sparring partner Sue Johnston teaming up with him again to play his poor put-upon wife Barbara.

Like it or loathe it, The Royle Family was certainly different. Simply a working-class family who did nothing but sit around and watch TV all day. It became a classic. And it was not without laughs, producing some memorably funny scenes, as well as moments of sheer pathos.

One of the strangest occasions, however, was when I met Ricky at a Press conference for something or other in London. We were having a drink together and, as always, I was trying to get a story out of him. He suddenly said to me, "Well, the trouble is, I'm homeless at the moment. I'm living in this ice cream van."

Hang on, can I have that again? "What do you mean, you're living in an ice cream van?" I said. At first, I thought he was joking, but then realised that he was deadly serious.

He went on to explain that he had hit on hard times, and that he had bought an ice cream van as a temporary home. "It's great. I can go anywhere I want in it. And I usually park it outside my Mum's house, have a kip in it, and then go in and have a shower and some breakfast at her place."

Well this was just too good to be true. What a great story, I thought. I asked him if I could send a photographer around and take a picture of him, in the van, outside his mother's house. Ricky, always keen for a bit of publicity, happily agreed. "Let's fix a date. I'll give you a ring in a couple of days," he said.

Unfortunately, he must have changed his mind. I waited for his call. It never came. The only thing he rang was the bell on his van. For me, it was the picture-story that got away.

A few years later, I heard that Ricky and his wife had moved into one of those posh flats in a converted warehouse overlooking the River Mersey. The price was in the region of £1 million. So I assumed he'd sold the ice-cream van.

Ricky is certainly one of life's survivors. He's come a long way since his days at Venice Street school.

SUE JOHNSTON

One of our finest TV actresses, and for my money very under-rated, is Sue Johnston. I first met her when I went to Liverpool to watch them filming the new Mersey soap Brookside. "Hello, I'm Sheila Grant," she said. "Well, I'm Sue Johnston – but I'm playing Sheila Grant." And when she laughed, I knew we were going to like each other and would end up being friends.

And that's the way it's turned out. In my job, there are lots of people you meet, actors and celebrities, who you know you are only going to meet once, or maybe twice. They are quite often just putting on a front, trying to be nice, hoping for some good publicity. And then there are people you meet who you know instinctively are genuinely nice. Well, Sue was one of those.

There is no front with her. No special effort to try and impress you. Just a down-to-earth, very practical person, very warm, very caring.

We met many times during her years on Brookside, both on and off the set. And our paths have crossed on other shows since, like The Royle Family, which brought her back with Ricky Tomlinson again playing her husband, the fat and loathsome layabout Jim Royle.

Sue and I have had lunch a few times, had a few giggles, and I've been over to her house in Warrington. I have watched her pursue her career while bringing up her son Joel, as a single parent. And I would hope she now regards me as more of a friend than a newspaper reporter, someone she can talk to casually, knowing that I'm not going to dash off and put her into front page headlines.

Long before Brookside, Sue was in Coronation Street, but only in a minor role, before she became a recognisable face. I think she would have loved to have stayed longer and made a name for herself in The Street, because it is a programme close to her heart. But it's not her favourite show, though. The programme Sue loves best of all is The Archers, on radio, which she would have adored being in, even in a small part. I once happened to phone her at home on a Sunday morning, and Sue yelled at me, "Ken, I'm listening to The Archers omnibus. You should know better than to phone me during The Archers. Ring me back."

Once, over lunch, we somehow got around to the subject of football. I was surprised to find that she knew the names of every player, their positions, even the tactics of the game. Then she revealed she was a keen Liverpudlian and had a season ticket for Anfield.

Well, on that one, we just agreed to differ. "How can you be so sensible on everything else, but then support the Reds?" I asked her. She just laughed.

I mean, as everyone knows, there are two good teams in Liverpool – Everton and Everton Reserves!

Sue would reminisce about her early days and the tough times she had as an actress. After that early appearance in Coronation Street, she was disappointed that her character had not made her a star, as one of the regulars. That's why she found such satisfaction later in Brookside.

My association with the programme went on for many years. I was a regular visitor to the little cul-de-sac and did lots of news stories and features on the comings and goings, particularly after I left the Mirror and set up on my own as a freelance in the North.

There were many of the cast I got to know and like - including Dean Sullivan (Jimmy Corkhill), Michael Starke (window cleaner Sinbad) who later went on to become a regular in the ITV hospital series The Royal; Simon O'Brien (Damon Grant) who moved into property development and became a TV presenter on DIY shows; Noreen Kershaw (Kathy Roache) who gave up acting and moved into production, becoming a top director on Coronation Street; Nicola Stephenson (Margaret Clemence) who had the most gorgeous natural red hair and went on to appear in many top-rating dramas; and the sexy Polish actress Kazia Pelka (who played nanny Anna Wolska). Now Kazia really was a tease.

Then there was the very fanciable Amanda Burton, one of the original cast who played Heather Huntingdon. I loved interviewing Amanda because she was always so delightfully flirty and had an Irish charm about her. She left after four years, married big-name Fleet Street freelance photographer Sven Arnstein, and had two children before divorcing him. She went on to become a TV star in her own right.

Amanda played Beth Glover, a doctor in Peak Practice; then criminal pathologist Professor Sam Ryan in the long-running drama series Silent Witness; Clare Blake, the tough cop in The Commander; and Karen Fisher, the headmistress in the popular Waterloo Road. Three times - in 1998, 1999 and 2001 - she won the coveted National TV Award as the most popular actress on the box. Which really said it all.

ANNA FRIEL

But the girl I will remember most from the Mersey soap is the lovely Anna Friel.

I first interviewed her in 1993 when she came in as a 17-year-old, and they had a little Press party to introduce some new residents, the Jordache family. There were three new actresses, the experienced Sandra Maitland, to play wife Mandy Jordache, and her two teenage daughters, Anna Friel, as Beth, and Tiffany Chapman, as younger sister Rachel. Then there was Brian Murray, to play head of the household, Trevor Jordache. Brian was quite well known, had done a lot of TV work, and was a real charmer.

Tiffany came in straight from school and had her mother with her. But Anna, I seem to recall, joined the show after leaving college. I felt rather sorry for her because she was on her own, and she was obviously a little in awe of the surroundings and didn't have much to say for herself. I interviewed them all, in turn, but it was this girl Anna Friel I found to be quite captivating. There was something about her. Not only was she stunningly beautiful, but she had a kind of cool, quiet confidence about her.

During her long stint on the show, I got to know Anna quite well. I interviewed her a few times, and although she was always wary of the Press and reluctant to do too much, I took her to lunch once with the TV company Press woman in tow, and we got on like a house on fire. She suddenly opened up, as though she could trust me, and started talking about all sorts of things. After that, our relationship improved, and she became a lot happier about doing interviews. She made no secret of the fact that she was very ambitious and was determined to make the big time.

211

It was Anna, of course, who was involved in those two big story-lines - the body under the patio, and the Lesbian kiss.

The much talked-about kiss, which horrified the nation, came early in 1994, when Beth Jordache and the petite Margaret Clemence, a nanny living with a neighbouring family, became rather too closely attached, and it culminated in a passionate embrace and kiss. It brought a torrent of complaints from outraged viewers because it was the first lesbian kiss ever screened in a British TV soap, and it was pre-watershed. Naturally, Mr. Phil Redmond made sure his Press office did their job to leak it in advance to all newspapers!

The Jordache family highlighted the problems of domestic violence in the show, with the wife-beating father Trevor not only terrorising his wife, but also secretly abusing his daughters. It all came to a nasty end when wife Mandy and daughter Beth both stabbed and killed him in the kitchen, and were then helped by Sinbad, the window cleaner, to bury the body in the back garden, and then cover it over with a concrete patio.

The mystery of Trevor's sudden disappearance went on for months and became a cliff-hanger which viewers latched on to with a mixture of horror and outraged sympathy. But inevitably the truth had to come out, and when the patio was dug up by police and the body found, Mandy and Beth went on the run in Ireland, before eventually being captured, charged with manslaughter, and sent to jail.

That was the end for lovely young Beth. The viewers felt cheated, but she was never seen again, and the scripts had her dying from a genetic heart disease whilst still in prison. Her death was all because Anna Friel wanted to quit the role because she had her heart set on bigger things.

Anna has certainly achieved everything she must have dreamed of as a teenager. She has gone on to be the most successful actress of all to come from that Brookside housing estate. She's had her name in lights in London's West End and appeared in a string of film and TV roles.

In 1995, she won the National Television Award for Most Popular Actress for her work on Brookside. A year later, she got more exposure when she appeared in the Stephen Poliakoff film The Tribe, which included her in a nude scene in a menage a trois story-line.

She made her big-screen film debut in Land Girls, and went on to do A Midsummer Night's Dream, and Timeline. She wowed the audiences when she starred in the West End stage show Breakfast At Tiffany's at the Royal Haymarket Theatre.

She's picked up various awards, including a Royal Television Society Award in 2009. She was also given an Honorary degree by the University of Bolton.

Anna has never stopped working and is one of those actresses who is constantly in demand.

In her private life, she met popular actor David Thewlis, and they were partners for ten years, and have a daughter, born in 2005. But after they split up, she met and fell in love with Welsh actor Rhys Ifans, and they were together for some years. He was the tall skinny oddball flat-mate of Hugh Grant in the film Notting Hill. (Remembered mostly for two riotous scenes – walking in on Julia Roberts when she was in the bath, and then opening the front door to a battery of Press cameramen and posing in his skimpy underpants).

I thought it was symbolic though that when Anna had her baby daughter, with David Thewlis, she named her Grace - after the legendary Gracie Fields, the singer and film actress who came from her home town of Rochdale.

Now, Rochdale has another fine actress to boast about.

As for Phil Redmond, the man with the big ego, he was another who was proud of his roots. After Brookside, he created the spin-off soap Hollyoaks, which he set in Chester. He has happily become by now a multi-millionaire. In 2004, he was awarded the CBE and he became a cultural ambassador for his home city, with ambitions, I think, to one day move into politics.

He decided a long time ago that he was not going to join the rat race in London, where he knew he would be only a little fish in a big pool and opted instead to be a bigger fish in Liverpool.

MY "ACTING" ROLE

I still have fond memories of Brookside and the ten years or so I spent over there, picking up stories as a freelance.

And I'll never forget the time when I actually appeared in the programme. It was at the height of its popularity. I was invited by the producers to do a bit part. A walk-on, if you like. Though it was more than a walk-on. More a hanging-about-doing-very-little part.

It was for the opening of Barry Grant's restaurant, called Grants, and I was supposed to be a newspaperman, a reporter covering the grand event, which was a lavish VIP affair.

It turned out that it was also the very first debut of Lily Savage. She (or he) had been invited along to officially open the restaurant.

I must confess I'd never heard of Paul O'Grady, who played Lily, until then. When this strange creature turned up, six feet tall, a great busty blonde with hair piled high on her head, and her face layered in tons of make-up, I didn't quite know what to make of her. It was all outrageously over the top.

The scenes were shot. We all had to mill around, and I had a notebook in my hand and was supposed to interview Lily Savage, while everyone was drinking champagne and chatting.

It all went well. It was a bit of fun. We had a few laughs afterwards, and I really got to know Paul O'Grady quite well. I later did a few interviews for real with him, because after that Brookside appearance Lily Savage rapidly shot to fame and became a big-name in his (or her) own right.

What I hadn't been prepared for, however, was the reaction afterwards. A couple of days after that Brookside episode was screened, I happened to go into my local post office in Disley, Cheshire, where I lived at the time. And the woman behind the counter screamed, "Oh, I saw you on Brookside the other night, swigging champagne. But who was that awful, big blonde woman who was with you? Was it a woman or a man in drag?"

Well, the post office was crowded, and suddenly everyone started laughing and I was the focus of attention.

It was too late then. For years, I'd been going into the post office, quite anonymously. But suddenly I was a "celebrity," albeit a dubious one - and all because of a five or six-minute appearance on Brookside!

I was never really a fan of Lily Savage, or Paul O'Grady for that matter. Since he took off the frock, the false eyelashes and the make-up, and confined Lily to the drag scrapheap, Paul has completely re-invented himself.

He somehow landed his own chat show, and then moved into animal programmes. But I'm still not a fan. There's something weird about him which makes for uncomfortable viewing.

CHAPTER 33: DAD'S ARMY & ARTHUR LOWE

Dad's Army ran on the BBC for nine series from 1968. Lasting much longer than World War 11 itself, in which the programme was set.

And it's still running more than 45 years later, because they are repeating the shows in peak-time and have never stopped. All of which must prove that the show was not only funny, but it has stood the test of time.

Younger viewers must now be laughing at the antics of the British Home Guard unit from Walmington-on-Sea, even though they can't have the faintest idea what that mob was really all about.

I spent quite a lot of time on location in Thetford, Norfolk, where the shows were filmed. Interviewing the cast. Drinking and eating with them. Sometimes just lolling around, sitting in a deckchair and laughing as the old-timers stumbled amiably through their scripts, waiting for a tea-and-biscuits break. Or waiting for the day's wrap, when they could all pile on to the bus back to their hotel and take off their boots for a lie-down before dinner.

It was a jolly happy routine they had, and producer David Croft made sure that the ageing cast were afforded every possible comfort. For he was well aware, as he often told me, that his cast had a few hundred years of experience between them and were all "knocking on a bit."

Apart from young Ian Lavender, who played "stupid boy" Frank Pike, most of the cast were well past pensionable age when they first started on the show.

But they were an odd bunch of actors. I already knew Arthur Lowe (Capt. Mainwaring) very well, from his Coronation Street days, and I soon got to know the rest of them. Frankly, they were very much true to the characters they played on screen. John Le Mesurier was always very charming, though he smoked too much. John Laurie (Private Frazer) was a cantankerous old bugger and was forever complaining about something or other. Arthur Ridley, who was the oldest of them all, was happy to just be plonked in a chair, and would fall asleep until someone would prod him awake and lift him up and help him in front of the cameras whenever he was needed. Bill Pertwee was much   more pleasant than the belligerent character he played, ARP Warden Hodges, and he would quite often tip me off with snippets of gossip from the theatrical world, for the cost of a pint or two.

Clive Dunn, as the butcher Corporal Jones, was not as old as everyone thought, and had been playing old men since he was in his thirties. He was a lovely chap, and once invited me over to his home in Barnes for lunch, when he took me up into his attic to show me some of his paintings. He was quite a fine water colour artist.

But it was Arthur Lowe I was always happy to see. We had dinner together when I booked in once or twice at The Bell Hotel, where they all stayed while on location. Arthur liked to get away from the others as often as possible. "They are all nice enough, but we don't have to live in each other's pockets for 24 hours a day," he would point out. "I'm not a great socialiser and I like to choose my own company."

When the show finally came to an end, in 1977, the BBC announced that they were retiring off the old Home Guard unit for good. But they had no kind of farewell party or anything for them.

Rather surprisingly, my Editor at the Mirror, Mike Molloy, asked me to set up a dinner for the whole cast, no expense spared. So, I booked the banqueting suite at the Café Royal in Regent Street and invited them all to a slap-up dinner. The Editor and all our top executives also attended.

It turned out to be one of those rare and memorable occasions. It was a full dinner-jacket affair, and Arthur Lowe insisted "Medals will be worn." We had the sight of all these old actors, some of them proudly wearing their own wartime medals.

The champagne flowed. And at the end of the dinner, Arthur stood up (maybe with a little help from his friends) and gave a toast. He announced in his best Capt. Mainwaring voice, "Gentlemen, I want you all to rise and drink a toast to the Daily Mirror." And the whole cast stood up together and raised their glasses.

It was somehow a very touching moment. Then he went on, "I never thought I would ever say this, but it is the Daily Mirror - and Ken Irwin - we have to thank for this dinner, and not the BBC, who for all our years of service gave us bugger all!"

It brought the house down. Next day, of course, we had the whole of the double page centre-spread of the paper devoted to the show, with a huge picture of their last supper. Headline: "Fall Out, Dad's Army." It was a wonderful occasion I'll never forget.

Everyone thought Arthur was a bad-tempered old codger, but he had a wry sense of humour and could be very good company, especially after a few glasses of wine and a brandy or two.

Not long after he finished with Dad's Army, he invited me over to his house in Maida Vale, and he was happy to reminisce about his career. He even invited me onto his yacht once - a beautiful old wooden schooner which he and his son Stephen used to sail around the south coast.

Arthur Lowe will probably be best remembered for his two outstanding TV roles - as Leonard Swindley in Coronation Street (which he played for five years) and Capt. Mainwaring (for nine years). But he did much more. After The Street, he did a long comedy series, Pardon The Expression. He was superb as Doctor Louis Pasteur in Microbes and Men in 1974, then in David Copperfield, as Mr. Micawber. And he played Labour foreign secretary Herbert Morrison in the ITV play Philby, Burgess and Maclean. He took on such a wide variety of parts.

Early in 1982, Richard Burton was so determined to have Arthur play a cameo role in the TV series Wagner that he sent his private plane to pick him up and fly him to the location.

Unfortunately, in his later years Arthur suffered bad health, made worse by his heavy drinking. And appearing with his actress wife Joan, who was a tough lady, he ended up doing provincial theatre tours, and even panto, which he hated.

Sadly, the end came in April 1982 when he was on tour with his wife in the stage play Home At Seven. In Birmingham, he appeared on the BBC lunch-time chat show Pebble Mill At One, to give the play a plug, but then later that day collapsed from a stroke in his dressing room at the Alexandra Theatre, and never recovered. He was rushed to hospital but died early the next morning. He was only 66, though he had always given the impression of being much older.

Even then, when it came to his funeral, his wife Joan refused to attend to join the mourners, insisting in the tradition that the show must go on and that she could not miss a performance of the play, in Belfast.

It was gratifying to hear that, late in 2007, the people of Thetford affectionately erected a bronze statue of Capt. Mainwaring in the village square, and it was unveiled by David Croft and Jimmy Perry, the two men responsible for producing the scripts for Dad's Army. And two historic blue plaques were also unveiled, one at Maida Vale, where Arthur lived for so many years, and one at his birthplace in the little village of Hayfield, in the Derbyshire Peak district.

CHAPTER 34: THE JAILED ONES

In recent years, there have been several big-name entertainers and celebrities who have ended up behind bars for some pretty shocking sex crimes, mostly historical. And there have been a few more who were up in court, but found not guilty.

Three who were sentenced to long prison terms were Rolf Harris, Stuart Hall, and Max Clifford. And I must say that it came as something of a shock, because I knew all of them, two of them quite well.

Rolf Harris I've met a few times. In interviews at the BBC, he came across as a pretty good guy. He was always cracking gags and was extremely pleasant to meet. I loved some of those painting shows he did, and he became a very fine artist whose paintings sold for thousands. He even painted a portrait of the Queen.

Rolf, at the age of 84, was branded a paedophile when he was convicted of a string of sex attacks on young girls and was sent to prison for six years.

Stuart Hall I got to know when he was the presenter of It's A Knockout, which ran for years. Barney Colehan was the producer of the early shows, and one year he invited me to go with them to Paris to do a feature on one of the inter-nations productions.

We spent three or four days in Paris, Stuart Hall was with us, and was the life and soul of the party as we gadded around Paris and ended up eating together at night.

Stuart always had a high-octane sense of humour, sometimes a bit over the top. But he was bright and breezy and loved to show off when he was in public.

He also did regular radio commentaries on football and every week, whenever he appeared in the Press Box at Goodison Park, he would turn up in his brown fur coat, wave to the crowd, and enjoy the banter with fans. I used to have a season ticket seat just a couple of rows behind the Press box and enjoyed watching the flamboyant Stuart make his entrance every Saturday. The football fans loved him.

Stuart, who lived in Wilmslow, Cheshire, was a close friend and near neighbour of actor William Roache.

Hall was sent to prison in 2013 after being found guilty of a number of sex crimes. He admitted 14 counts of indecent assaults on girls aged nine to 17. His 15-month jail sentence was then doubled by an Appeals court, and later another two years and six months were added to his prison term for further offences. He was stripped of his OBE by the Queen.

Then there was Max Clifford. He was more of an associate than a friend, but, working in Fleet Street, I had quite a close relationship with him. Max was always exuberant and full of bright ideas. He would come on the phone, suggesting stories and trying to get publicity for his clients. And he did have some of the biggest names in show business on his books, including I think Frank Sinatra at one time.

Max had a little office in Bond Street, and journalists were always welcome to pop in. I quite liked Max, but to be honest never really trusted him. I mean, how could you take him seriously? He was the man who dreamed up the headline stories "Freddie Starr Ate My Hamster," and "Tory MP David Mellor Made Love in a Chelsea Football shirt."

Max knew it was no good coming on to me unless a story was kosher. I did not deal with make-up stories, and he knew that. He dealt more with the Sunday papers, where he knew he could make more money.

There was one particular incident that caused me to be suspicious, though, and that was when he tried to flog a story to me, and suggested that I have dinner at a nightclub with him. And, wink, wink - there might be some girls around to join us! Nothing came of it, I'm glad to say. But I have heard from other journalists that it was not unknown for Max to offer a "sweetener" to help sell a story.

My final dealing with Max was when I became involved in a blatant double cross. Among his clients, Max had the comedians Lenny Bennett and Jerry Stevens, who were very popular and had their own TV series. He came on the phone to me one day and gave me the shock news that the comics were splitting up and were quitting the show. Did I want an exclusive interview with Jerry Stevens, who was willing to talk frankly about his bust-up with his pal Lenny Bennett?

There was no money involved, but Max insisted that I meet Jerry the next day, a Friday, and that my piece for the Mirror would be in on Saturday. He wanted my guarantee on that. So, I agreed and next day I went to interview Jerry in Max's office.

It all worked out splendidly. It was a good story, it made a full-page feature, and we ran it as an exclusive in the TV page on the Saturday morning.

Next day, reading the Sunday papers, I opened The People to see a full-page interview with Lenny Bennett, telling his side of the comics' bust-up and how they hated each other. The story was written by Tony Purnell, the paper's showbiz reporter.

I couldn't help but chuckle. Because we had obviously got a scoop by announcing it all in the Mirror the day before. What I didn't know though (until Tony Purnell told me in the pub a few days later) was that Max Clifford had sold Lenny Bennett's story to The People earlier in the week, with the promise that it would be exclusive, and no other paper would have it.

Tony Purnell was livid. As I would have been, if the situation had been reversed. He felt he had been conned by Max. And he had, of course. It just looked like Max couldn't resist the temptation to secretly play one of his clients off against the other, and one journalist against another. I came out of it okay. I even bought Purnell a pint, to commiserate with him. After all, the story cost me nothing. But I'm not sure whether The People had to shell out to Max for their non-exclusive!

Max, who lived in some style, driving a Rolls Royce, with a big house in Surrey and a villa in Spain, was jailed in 2014 for eight years for a string of indecent assaults against girls and young women. It was later reported that his PR business was wound up with debts of nearly £500,000.

CHAPTER 35: CRAZY ACTS

ROD HULL

Rod Hull was an odd fellow. Certainly an eccentric. But then, who wouldn't be, spending more than half your life with a dummy like Emu stuck on your arm? And that Emu could often get up to some pretty nasty tricks. Just ask Mike Parkinson. Or even the Queen. It was as though Rod's arm had a life of its own.

But I got to know Rod quite well. We spent a week together at a TV festival in Belgium, and I don't think I've had so many laughs in such a short time.

Rod was the same age as me, born in 1935, in the south of England, and was an electrician by trade before being bitten by the bug to get into show business. After marrying and having two daughters, he moved to Australia to try for a better life. And it was in Sydney that he got his big break, working for Channel 9 TV, as a comedian in a kid's programme, calling himself Constable Clot.

After a few years, he hit on the idea of having an imaginary Emu as a "partner" and he built up his act on TV and in cabaret in Australia, before returning to England.

The big breakthrough which changed his life completely was when he was booked for a short spot in the Royal Variety Performance in 1972. He was a riot. His performance stole the show. And he then got all the headlines, because in the Royal line-up after the show, when all the artists are supposed to be on their best behaviour to meet the Royal family, Rod couldn't contain his sense of humour, and his Emu jumped up and grabbed the Queen's bouquet of flower and destroyed them. His career took off in a big way. From then on, Rod Hull and Emu were topping the bills. Or was it Emu and Rod Hull? It was a lifelong partnership Rod was later to regret.

Rod was such a wacky bloke that he just couldn't control his Emu character. When he went to America and appeared on Johnny Carson's top Tonight show, the damned Emu attacked Carson, even though Hull had been warned beforehand by the producers not to do it.

Then, of course, there was the unforgettable appearance he made on Mike Parkinson's chat show back in London in 1976, when Emu attacked a bewildered Parkinson, dragged him out of his seat and wrestled him to the ground, grabbing a mouth full of nuts on the way.

Mike was not at all amused. In fact, he admitted later to being terrified as well as sore in a delicate area.

Comedian Billy Connolly, who was a fellow guest on the show, nearly fell off his own chair, laughing, but he quickly threatened Hull, "If that bird comes anywhere near me, I'll break its neck, and your arm with it!"

My own experience of the wretched bird came that week when the BBC submitted a variety programme starring Rod Hull and other guests at a light entertainment festival in Belgium. I was invited as the only British journalist to cover it, and I flew over with producer John Ammonds and the rest of the BBC team.

I'd never met Rod Hull before, but we sat next to each other on the plane, had more than a few drinks together, and by the time we arrived on Belgian soil we were the best of pals.

When we all went to collect our baggage, however, Rod was still waiting near the airport carousel, looking a little confused. He had collected one bag, but it seemed his second suitcase had not appeared. I decided to wait with him, and when all the bags had been collected and the revolving carousel was now empty, we were advised to go and report the missing suitcase to the lost luggage office nearby.

Off we went, with Rod and I both clutching one bag each, but with him becoming increasingly desperate. Then he suddenly revealed why. "Emu is in that bloody case," he fumed. "I always put him in a separate bag. He likes to travel alone, and I don't like putting him in with all my clothes in one bag."

Explaining all this to the lost luggage staff, of course, was not easy. In fact, at one point it became quite hysterical, and I was trying not to wet myself by laughing too much.

When the duty officer asked Rod to describe the missing suitcase and its contents, he declared, mischievously, "Well, my pet Emu is in there. He always likes to travel separately."

"Emu? What is an emu?" he was asked.

"Well, it's an animal. Haven't you ever seen an emu?" said Rod.

"An animal? You have an animal in your suitcase? How big is this animal?" demanded the officer, calling for his colleague to come over and assist him.

"He's about this big. About the length of my arm," replied Rod, keeping a straight face.

Like the Germans, the Belgians are renowned for not having much of a sense of humour. And the more Rod went on talking, the more confused they became.

"Do you know you are not allowed to have animals in your luggage, travelling with you?" said one officer. "This is a very serious offence."

It didn't help when Rod chipped in by saying, "But he travels everywhere with me. I've never had any trouble before. This is the first time he's ever been lost in a suitcase. Can I sue the airline?"

Then one of the officers asked, "Have you been drinking, sir?"

"Well, yes. I've had a couple of drinks on the plane," said Rod. "But I'm not drunk. And as for Emu, he never drinks. He's teetotal."

Well, as this went on, I fell about laughing and had to move away to avoid upsetting the duty officers. The whole thing had now become a farcical situation. It was funnier than anything a comedy scriptwriter could ever have created.

But then suddenly, Rod became quite serious and confused the luggage men even more when he told them, "I need Emu. I can't work without him. I'm here to do a TV show, and I'm helpless by myself. You must find him. Urgently. Please."

Eventually, I pulled Rod aside and tried to explain the whole situation, assuring them that we were not drunk and explaining that Rod Hull was a famous entertainer from England, and that Emu was part of his comedy act. And I desperately resisted the temptation to add that "without Emu, he is armless!"

Finally, they made Rod sign an official lost luggage report, and assured us they would try and locate the missing suitcase, and hopefully it would be delivered to our hotel by the next day.

We took a taxi to the hotel, where Rod had to explain to producer John Ammonds what had happened. Everyone had a giggle about it, and fortunately they had two or three days of rehearsal before the show was to be staged. Among the dancing girls on the show were some of the old Vernons Girls group, including the beautiful long-legged and popular Maggie Stredder, always remembered by viewers as the only dancer on TV who wore glasses. I'd interviewed her a few times before, and when we met in the bar that night, she had hysterics when I told her about the antics with Rod at the airport.

Fortunately, the suitcase was delivered to our hotel the next day. It seemed it had been left at Heathrow. Rod and Emu were reunited. So all was well in the end.

I not only got a good feature out of it, but also an exclusive news story: "Emu lost in airport baggage chaos!" I also had a very pleasant week, with Rod and I enjoying late-night suppers and exchanging showbiz gossip and anecdotes. I don't think we ever met again, after that. But it was an unforgettable week.

Rod went on to have a very successful career. He married again, had a second family, and bought an enormous country house. But when the work dried up, he got into financial difficulties and was declared bankrupt in 1994.

In his later years, he became resentful about how his career had gone downhill, and he blamed Emu for his misfortune. It turned out that for years he had wanted to kill off Emu and go it alone as a comedian. But it was too late - the Emu had become so famous that no one wanted to know Rod on his own. He couldn't get work without Emu.

He settled for a more modest standard of living and bought a house in Winchelsea, near Rye. Then in March 1999, tragedy struck when Rod died in a freak accident. It was one of those things which would have been funny if it wasn't so tragic. He climbed up on to the roof of his house at night to try and adjust the TV aerial because he was watching a football match and was getting interference on his living-room set. But he slipped, fell off the roof and crashed through a greenhouse. He had a fractured skull and chest injuries. He was rushed to a hospital in Hastings but was pronounced dead on arrival. He was only 63.

Ironically, his son Toby then brought Emu out of retirement a few years later and went into the panto Cinderella at the Theatre Royal, Windsor, and later did some TV shows with the puppet.

But, do you know, without in the slightest way being disrespectful, I think the Rod Hull I got to know and like would have been more than amused, looking back, at the circumstances in which he died. Only Rod would have been so daft as to attempt a stunt like that, climbing onto the roof in order to watch a football match! He would have laughed his head off.

BERNIE CLIFTON

When it came to entertainers earning their living and depending on "animals" or puppets to support them, another zany performer in the same mould as Rod Hull was Bernie Clifton.

Remember him? Bernie's act was to get dressed up in a costume, and romp around as though he was riding on the back of an ostrich. The ostrich was called Oswald, and of course it often had tantrums and would run off in the wrong direction, with a frustrated Bernie trying desperately to control the animal by tugging violently on the set of reins he had fastened on to him from the animal's harness.

It was hysterically funny. Very much like Emu, Oswald never uttered a word. But he got most of his laughs by being physically violent. Often, he would run off into the audience, trying to scare them into a panic.

Bernie, a Lancashire lad from St. Helens, earned a very good, if slightly odd, living for over 50 years, running around on his own two legs as a frustrated ostrich.

But then in January 2016, he suddenly announced he was launching himself on a new career – as a singer, under his real name of Bernie Quinn.

He applied for an audition on the TV talent show The Voice. He was then 80. And he comically quipped, "I didn't want to peak too early in my career!"

Bernie didn't win. But he did prove that he had a fine voice. And he brought the house down when he performed in front of the TV audience.

HARRY CORBETT

Ventriloquists were ten a penny at one time. Every variety bill had a vent act on the show. Some of them good, some of them so bad, you never wanted to see them again. Probably the most famous one I can remember was Peter Brough with his schoolboy puppet Archie Andrews, who went for years on BBC radio and became a huge star in the 40s and 50s. But then when TV came in, and Brough found himself in front of the cameras, he was exposed as such a lousy ventriloquist. TV audiences were horrified at just how bad he was. You could not only see his lips move, but his whole face gave him away and there was no "voice throwing" art to his act at all. Let's face it, anyone can be a brilliant ventriloquist on sound radio!

But then along came Harry Corbett, with Sooty the bear. Now that really was a unique master stroke of audience trickery. The bald- headed Harry spent all his time talking to the bear in a one-sided conversation. But Sooty said nothing. Not a bleeding word. I know the whole thing was originally aimed at the kids. But Harry Corbett and Sooty were then promoted to prime-time TV. And the whole nation sat around and tried to laugh at the juvenile antics of an old man talking to a tiny teddy bear. Strewth!

I met Harry Corbett only once. In my early days as a TV writer, I was sent to interview him. He was a lovely man. Very friendly. Very ordinary, but a really canny Yorkshire businessman. And I got a very good feature out of him.

He created Sooty in 1948 and made his first appearance on BBC TV in 1952. He told me that the whole act was dreamed up while he was trying to keep his own kids amused whilst on holiday in Blackpool. He bought the original little bear from a seaside novelty shop for 7s 6d and called it simply Teddy. But then, when he thought of expanding it as a theatrical act, he blackened its ears and nose with soot and re-named it Sooty. Then later, he introduced another little bear to the act, a "female,", who came in as Sooty's girlfriend, Sweep.

Harry never claimed to be a clever ventriloquist, however. He considered himself a puppeteer. But he became one of the richest entertainers in the business and topped the bill in theatres and had his own TV series throughout the 1950s and 60s.

Harry suffered a heart attack in 1975, and his son Peter (adopting the stage name of Matthew) later took over the Sooty act, buying his father out for £35,000.

But somehow, it never had the same magic as when old Harry was doing the chatter.

Before he became famous, Harry Corbett played the piano and worked in a fish and chip restaurant in Guisley, Yorkshire, owned by his mother's brother, the renowned Harry Ramsden, who became a multi-millionaire and created the Harry Ramsden food empire.

The legendary Harry Corbett later continued to work as a pianist and entertainer, without Sooty. Sadly, he died in his sleep, aged 71, in August 1989, after playing to a capacity audience in a summer show at Weymouth Pavilion, in Dorset.

CHAPTER 36: HUGHIE GREEN

Hughie Green was something of a chameleon character. He could be nice, and he could be nasty, depending on which mood he was in. On the surface, he was always charming and helpful. But underneath that smooth, smarmy facade was a man who was malicious and quite ruthless. It took me some years to find this out, though.

The first time I met Hughie was when I was working for the Northern Mirror, and he was on a nationwide tour, looking for new contestants to appear on his tremendously popular show Opportunity Knocks. So when he came to Manchester, looking for new talent, I went to interview him, and I was quite flattered when he suggested I sit in with him and his team on the auditions. I had a photographer with me, and Hughie was quite happy for us to take pictures not only of him, but also any of the unknown performers, who were queueing up anxiously in a long line in a room next door.

The auditions went fine. There was not a lot of talent there, to be honest, but one or two of the acts looked quite promising and Hughie took a few of them aside and told them they might be on his shortlist to appear on a future show.

Then he turned to me and said, "What do you think, Ken? Who would you like to win from this lot?" I was not sure quite what he meant, but he then made it clear that, whichever act I chose, he would definitely agree to put them on TV, in front of the cameras. A little surprised at his audition methods, I eventually picked out an attractive young girl who was quite a good singer. "Fine, she's on the show," said Hughie, then posing for a picture with her. "If she's good enough for the Daily Mirror, then she's good enough for Opportunity Knocks!"

Then he turned to me and said, "Just make sure we get some good publicity on this, Ken."

That was it. Hughie moved on to another city, looking for more talent. We published a piece with a few pictures from the auditions. When his next series returned on screen, I tuned in once or twice, but I never spotted the young singer we'd picked out at the Manchester auditions.

Over the years, I got to know Hughie quite well. When I moved down to London, I would often cover Press conferences he held to promote various programmes. And he was always the master manipulator.

Hughie himself had been a child discovery. At the age of 14, he had his own radio programme on BBC, and toured with a children's concert party.

He went to Hollywood as an actor and appeared in Tom Brown's Schooldays. Then during World War 11, he served as a pilot with the Canadian Air Force, married a Canadian society beauty, Claire Wilson, and at the end of the war moved to London where he became a radio presenter and then devised the Opportunity Knocks talent show for radio.

At that time, however, there was another far more famous talent-spotter on radio, called Carroll Levis. When the BBC dropped Green's show, he went to court and sued both the BBC and Carroll Levis. But he lost the case, paid out huge costs, and in 1956 was made bankrupt. It was more than two years before he was discharged from bankruptcy.

But it was with Double Your Money, the quiz show originally brought from Radio Luxembourg, that Hughie became a household name, in 1955. He then revived Opportunity Knocks, transferred it to television and became one of the biggest star names on ITV throughout the 50s, 60s and 70s.

Opportunity Knocks drew regular viewing audiences of 18 million a week, and some of the stars Hughie claimed to have discovered were Frankie Vaughan, Les Dawson, Lena Zavaroni, Bonnie Langford, poet Pam Ayres, singer Mary Hopkin, and many more.

Hughie was a great self-publicist and liked to put on the style wherever he went. He once turned up at Montreux in Switzerland to attend the annual Golden Rose TV festival, when I was there, and he had two beautiful young women in tow. They were identical twin sisters, and he told us they were singers, and a double act, and he was going to make them stars. But we never heard them sing. They spent most of the week simply looking glamorous and accompanying Hughie and his producer, wherever they went. And posing for pictures with the Press, of course.

Hughie had been divorced for some years, but he invariably had a woman friend to escort in public.

It all came to a dramatic and tearful end for Hughie in 1978 when he was finally axed by Thames TV. This followed a period when the TV bosses thought Hughie had lost it and gone slightly bonkers. He had become very Right Wing in his politics, and on one of his shows, in 1976, he suddenly went into a mad, political and moral rant, on air, urging viewers to "Stand up and be counted." It shocked everyone.

After that, he was finished. Hughie became very bitter and morose, and retired, hitting the bottle heavily.

Hughie lived for many years in an expensive fifth-floor flat in a period building in Baker Street, just above the Tube station, and had a Rolls Royce down in the car-park. A couple of times he invited me over. He would phone to say he had a good story to tell, but then when I went to see him, he would just sit around for a couple of hours, offering drinks, and engaging in small talk.

He became unbelievably bitter in his old age, and for some apparent reason – which was not very clear at the time – he developed a feud with Jess Yates, a well-known TV personality who was very popular with ITV viewers as the presenter of a long-running religious programme Stars on Sunday. Hughie made no secret of his dislike for Yates and seemed determined to destroy his career.

About this time, Hughie had been confronted himself by a tough investigative journalist from the News of the World, Noel Botham, threatening to expose him for something or other. Instead, they ended up as very good friends.

But then, Hughie got his revenge. He leaked a story to Botham revealing that Jess Yates, Mr. Nice Guy of religious TV, was having a secret affair with an attractive singer, Anita Kay, and this was splashed all over the News of the World.

Jess Yates was devastated at being exposed as a hypocrite, though I couldn't help feeling at the time that this was one of those "who is the kettle, and who is the pot?" situations. Yates was dropped by Yorkshire TV and his life was in tatters.

Having ruined Yates' career, that still wasn't the end, however. Hughie Green's last act of malice came from beyond the grave. For after Hughie died from lung cancer in 1997, aged 77, his old pal Noel Botham came out with the astonishing front-page story that Hughie was the real biological father of Paula Yates, and not Jess Yates, the father she had lived and grown up with.

It was a real stunner. And Paula, then a TV celebrity in her own right, and the wife of Bob Geldof, only found out about her parentage when she read it in the tabloids. Apparently, Noel Botham had been sworn to secrecy until after Hughie's death.

One couldn't help but have sympathy for Paula, of course. Her whole life was suddenly turned upside down and she discovered that, as Hughie's daughter, she had a whole new family on the Green side. A DNA test proved that Green was, in fact, her father.

As it was, Paula had a tragically short life herself. In her marriage to Bob Geldof, she had three children – Fifi, Peaches and Pixie – but then had an affair with wild Australian rock star Michael Hutchence and had a child with him, Tiger Lily.

She was shattered when Hutchence died, under suspicious circumstances, when he was found hanged at his home in Australia.

Paula then died, reportedly from accidental heroin overdose, only three years after Hughie Green's death. She was only 41.

Then, another tragedy in the family which Bob Geldof had to deal with, was in 2014 when Paula's daughter Peaches also died, from a massive drugs overdose, at the age of 25. It really did look like the Paula Yates/Green/Geldof family were plagued with repeated disasters and tragic life-ruining events.

When Hughie Green died, his estate was bequeathed to his live-in lover, Christina Sharples, who was the widow of Bob Sharples, for many years the musical director on most of Hughie's shows.

He was cremated at Golders Green Cemetery, and a memorial plaque there reads: "You were the star that made Opportunity Knocks. You will Never Be Forgotten. Christina."

CHAPTER 37: CORONATION STREET

SOME WHO DIDN'T SURVIVE...

MARK EDEN

Actor Mark Eden was a nice guy. I always got on well with him. I met and got to know him long before he joined Coronation Street and took on the role of Alan Bradley, in 1986.

He's what I call a man's man. Always liked a drink or two at the bar, and would regale you with amusing stories from his theatrical past.

But he was also considered quite a ladies' man, too. Strikingly handsome, he was married and divorced twice (to Joan Malin in 1953, and Diana Smith in 1974) and had three children, before meeting and falling in love with Sue Nicholls, and setting up home together. They were eventually married in 1993.

Sue has played Street hairdresser Audrey Roberts now for more than 30 years. She came in originally as the sex-mad Audrey Potter and was popping in and out of the Northern serial for six years before they gave her a permanent contract in 1985, when she married grocer Alf Roberts (played by Brian Mosley).

I recall Sue telling me at the time, "I'm looking forward to being in the programme for a long run. Audrey Potter has had so many men, I reckon she must eat them for breakfast. But it now looks like she's going to have to settle down."

So, when Mark was signed up a year later for the soap on a long-term contract, it meant they could be together all week, instead of just at weekends, although they kept their London base, as well as Sue's flat in Manchester.

Sue actually came from a very privileged and wealthy background. Her father was Lord Harmer-Nicholls, at one-time Conservative MP for Peterborough and later made a Peer. She at first found it hard to acquire a Lancashire accent for Audrey. But with years of practice, she's now become as eeh-bah-gum as any of them.

For Mark, however, the end came when the scriptwriters turned him into a real baddie, and Alan Bradley became one of the Street's notorious villains, as the wife- beating boyfriend of shopkeeper Rita Fairclough.

He had to go, of course. And the producers were annoyed with me (or at least pretended to be) when I broke the news that they had plans to bump him off. One of my Granada TV insiders tipped me off that they were going to dramatically kill Alan Bradley in the most bizarre road accident.

It was no ordinary road accident, though. Bradley finally died after chasing a distraught Rita across the road on Blackpool's Golden Mile promenade. Rita was running away from him, and as Alan tried to grab her he was knocked down by a tramcar, and ended up in a pool of blood.

On the day they filmed the big scene, I had a photographer discreetly placed behind a nearby lamp post, and he caught the whole thing on camera. Although officially Granada TV refused to confirm the tragic death, they didn't have to – we already had it on camera. I wrote a news story to tie up with the picture and the Daily Mirror ran an exclusive on the front page. (Another Irwin Coronation Street scoop!)

The funny thing was, that particular TV death scene has become something of a famous landmark. Because a plaque was later erected at the nearest tram stop on the Prom to recall the event, and tourists and holidaymakers now still visit the scene in ghoulish interest.

PETER ADAMSON

The trouble with Peter Adamson, a lot of people thought, was that he too often liked to play Len Fairclough off the screen as well as on it. What they didn't know was that the basic cause of the problem was his drinking. He was an alcoholic.

His fits of temper, his public rows, his verbal punch-ups with civic leaders, Mayors and their wives, his behaviour with the police when he was picked up for drunken driving, all hit the newspaper headlines.

It all sounded too much like Len, Coronation Street's notorious tough guy, taking over the personality of the man who created him. This wasn't strictly true. Peter was usually well aware of what he was doing. He made a habit of switching Len Fairclough on and off whenever it suited him.

What the viewers at home did not know was that for four years Peter Adamson was working under the most awful strain of being an alcoholic.

On screen, he tried to keep up pleasant appearances as Len, the jovial beer-swilling character who held up the bar at the Rovers Return, but who was also a socially-conscious local Councillor. A man, too, who had a roving eye for the ladies, and for next-door neighbour Elsie Tanner in particular.

232

Off-screen and away from the studios, he was in and out of hospital, undergoing treatment to cure him of the booze.

I was the first journalist Peter confided in about his problems. I went along to the studios to do what I thought was a straightforward one-to-one interview, but then as we sat in the Green Room together and started talking, he suddenly opened up and poured his heart out to me.

"I'm finished as an actor unless I lay off the booze," he said. "I've been warned so many times by the producers that this was my last chance. They even banned me for a month and told me to stay away from the studios."

The company had even suspended him, without pay. "Granada have bent over backwards to help me. They've now told me that the next time, I'm for the bloody high jump and they will get rid of me."

So, Peter was written out of the show, he joined Alcoholics Anonymous and even underwent psychiatric treatment. His wife stuck by him. "Without Jean, I would be either in jail or in a psychiatric ward for a very long time," he said. He was almost in tears as he talked to me.

His first meeting of Alcoholics Anonymous was frightening, he told me. He realised that he was mixing with all members of society, company bosses and down-and-outs. Many of them had been in prison. Some had lost their families through drink. In one branch meeting of the AA he attended, they had lost three members. Two had died through alcohol, and one had been murdered by his wife. Peter was clearly shocked by his new surroundings.

When we finished that meeting (it wasn't so much an interview, I felt more like a psychiatrist and Peter was sitting on the couch pouring out his troubles) I told him, "Look, this is a hell of a story. Do you want me to print it all?"

"Why not?" he said, "I've got to tell someone."

Even then, I gave him a chance to change his mind. I drove back to London and next day wrote up his story from my notes and tape-recording. But I phoned him first and asked him if this was really what he wanted. "What have you written? Can you read it out to me?" he said. I then read him the whole thing, over the phone.

"What do you think?" I asked. Without hesitation, he said, "Fine. Go ahead. Print it."

So we did. It was the Mirror's exclusive front-page splash next day. There was no payment involved. Peter phoned to thank me. The truth was finally out. Granada were not too happy at the whole exposure because they thought it might reflect on the programme. But they also realised, I think, that this was the only way Peter was ever going to get over his problem – by finally admitting it in public.

Eventually, he recovered and returned to work to tell his colleagues just how close he'd come to ending his life. And he told me, "If I had not joined the AA, I would probably have carried on drinking. I would be out of the show. I'd get national publicity for three days, then the public would merely forget. Then perhaps in ten years' time, someone might stop me in the street and say, 'Didn't you used to be Len Fairclough?'"

Peter was as good as his word. He didn't drink again for 14 years. But then his whole world came crashing down in 1983, when he was dramatically arrested by the police and charged with sex offences involving little girls.

It was alleged that he had indecently assaulted two schoolgirls, aged eight, in a public swimming baths near his home in Bury, Lancashire. He was immediately dropped from Coronation Street, and then hired the best lawyer in the business, George Carman, QC, to act as his counsel in court.

Peter then had to sit through a seven-day trial before being cleared of the two offences and found not guilty. It took a jury of eight men and four women exactly 36 minutes to reach their unanimous verdict. The 53-year-old actor simply shook hands with George Carman and said, "Thank you."

His wife Jean, who sat in the front row of the public gallery with their two sons Michael and Greig, broke down and wept. Jean, who suffered badly for years from severe arthritis, was now disabled and in a wheelchair.

Outside the court, there was a stampede of journalists and members of the public, some of them cheering him with shouts of "Good luck, Len." And Peter was smuggled out and bundled into a car by two heavies trying to protect him, because he had done a deal to sell his story to The Sun.

I wrote the front-page story for the Daily Mirror that day – 27 July 1983 – and the headline was: "Cleared! But will Len go back to the Street?"

Well, he didn't. For a short while, no one knew what was happening. It was generally felt that Peter could not be sacked from his job because he had been found not guilty of the sex offences. But Granada were determined to get rid of him and decided that Peter was in breach of his contract by selling his story to a national paper without their permission. So he had to go.

A month later, I revealed exclusively that he would be killed off ("Len must die! 'Blow me up' says TV star" was the headline). The scriptwriters had to write him out.

Peter himself, now knowing he was not going back, even suggested his own dramatic end. "If I've got to go, I want to leave The Street with a bang, not a whimper," he said. "The script could see me off with a petrol tank explosion or a shotgun blast."

In the end, they decided that Len would be killed in a motorway crash. But there were no dramatic scenes. The TV bosses decided on a low-key funeral for Len because they didn't want a lot of sympathy from viewers. It was all done with a make-shift cemetery behind high walls and locked doors at Granada's studios.

There was only a handful of mourners to pay their last respects. Len's widow Rita was grieving in black, alongside his old flame Elsie Tanner. Also there, was young actress Tracie Bennett, who played the Fairclough's daughter Sharon. Tracie was brought back briefly into the programme just for Len's death.

Peter had been in Coronation Street for 23 years. After his sacking, there was not much of a life for him. He went off and did a few minor acting parts and tried to revive his career in panto. But he ended up broke and living in a caravan, something of a hermit.

Then, rather shockingly, it was reported that Peter, when talking about his trial and the sex offences with little girls, actually confessed that he was really guilty. He died a few years later.

JENNIFER MOSS

Jennifer Moss was the little girl who grew up too quickly. She was a schoolgirl in Wigan when Coronation Street first went on the air, and she cheekily wrote a letter to Granada asking for an audition. To her surprise, she was invited to the studios, and came away having landed the part of Lucille Hewitt, daughter of bus driver Harry Hewitt.

She was 16 at the time, and her parents decided she could leave school and pursue an acting career. Lucille was supposed to be only ten, but Jenny was only four feet eleven inches tall, a slip of a girl, and so skinny that she didn't look her real age, so she could get away with it. But when she started developing physically, the producers instructed her to bind part of her body with bandages to hide her breasts and lose her maturing figure in front of the cameras. She heaved a great sigh of relief, literally, when the bandages came off, when Lucille was approaching her 14th birthday.

As a TV character, Lucille Hewitt was a precocious little madam. And away from the studios, the young Jenny Moss earned a reputation as a bit of a swinger. It wasn't easy for her. She was plagued with a double identity. Most of the time she had to act like a naughty schoolgirl, six years her junior. Yet quite naturally, she hated people treating her as a child once she was out of her TV gymslip.

Consequently, she went to the other extreme to prove she was an adult. She was the only youngster in a cast full of hardened and experienced actors. And she tried to keep up with them. Very soon, she was driving her own car, smoking, drinking in pubs, and invariably had boy friends around her.

Within three years of joining the TV soap, she had left her parents' house in Wigan and moved into her own flat in Manchester. "It is important for a girl to be independent while she is still young," I recall her telling me. "I had very understanding parents." By the time she was 20, she had moved out of her flat, and had her own house.

She suddenly revealed to her employers and friends that she had been secretly engaged for two months - to Peter Hampson, a gangling youth of 19 who was six feet tall. Jenny, now 23, was still only 4ft.11ins. They were married the following month, quietly at a register office in Stockport on a Saturday morning, with Peter Adamson the only actor present at the wedding.

A few months later, the production team was thrown into consternation when Jenny announced that she was expecting a baby. They were plotting how they should write her out when the time came, but only a few weeks later Jenny was rushed to hospital. She had a miscarriage and lost the baby. Lucille was out of the programme until Jenny recovered.

She returned to the show for a while, but then became pregnant again, and left to have a baby, which although premature, was born on New Year's Day 1970. She called her daughter Naomi Ruth. A few weeks after the christening, however, Jenny sadly told newspapermen that her marriage of less than two years was over.

After leaving Coronation Street, after 13 years, Jenny's life collapsed, and she spiralled into poverty. She found herself with three broken marriages, her two daughters were in council care, she was an epileptic and an alcoholic, struggling to even pay her rent.

I went to see her once when she had moved to Liverpool. She was 38, and living on her own in a slum, a house provided by the Merseyside

Housing Improvement Trust. Most of the houses in the street were boarded up, their doorsteps piled high with rubbish.

Jenny was a recovering alcoholic. She had changed her surname from her third husband's name to Davies. "I chose the name Davies because it's Welsh and I was living in Wales at the time, no other reason," she said. But she had moved to Liverpool because the city had 28 Alcoholics Anonymous meetings every week.

She was living on Social Services benefits. "I've lived like a Nun," she said. "No man has ever come up to the flat alone. I don't have a boyfriend, and I am in no rush to have one."

It was really quite heart-breaking to see her like that. Yet despite everything, she always tried to put on a brave face.

Five years later, though still on her uppers, she was out of work and trying to find a job. She was now a 42-year-old grandmother with four broken marriages behind her. One of my contacts told me that she had applied for a job at Granada TV - as a tourist guide, showing people around the studios, including the mock-up replica of Coronation Street which was being opened as a new tourist attraction. The job paid £2.85 an hour.

When I contacted Jenny to ask if it was true, she said, "Yes. When you have been out of work as long as I have, and been through all that I've been through, you are happy to take any job offered to you. I'm not embarrassed at the thought of showing visitors around. With my knowledge of Coronation Street, and I am still quite friendly with a lot of the cast, I think I would be ideal to show people around and chat about the programme. I am now fit and well and I just want to get back to work."

She was quite upbeat and very hopeful about her prospects. She had applied as soon as she heard that the TV company wanted 70 guides for their new three-acre site.

When I went on to Granada and asked whether Jenny would be taken on, their spokesman said, rather stiffly, "Jennifer has been in for a chat. We have a lot of people still to interview, so we cannot confirm at this stage whether she will be taken on or not."

Later, I was told that they had turned her application down. I couldn't believe it. They were advertising for 70 people, at £2.85 an hour. I think it was pretty heartless of them to turn her away, knowing her background.

Jenny, despite everything, was always quite cheerful. Even when she was in the depths of despair, she would still look back on the happy times. I remember her joking with me once over her reputation as a teenager.

It had been reported that William Roach, in his younger years as Ken Barlow, had a reputation as a great womaniser, even though he was married. In fact, he later claimed himself to have had affairs with some of the women in the cast, including Pat Phoenix. And Jenny recalled that on one occasion, when she was very young, she had been seduced by Roach and had a one-night stand after a drunken night out. The story went that they finished up in bed together. But Jenny said, "It all ended in disaster. We started having sex. But I fell asleep, and when I woke up it was all over." Jenny confirmed to me that the story was true, and I have it on a tape recording.

But she also told me that some years later, when she attended a memorial service in Manchester Cathedral for one of The Street cast, she bumped into Bill Roach, who was with his wife. Jenny tried to talk to him, but he pulled a funny face and ignored her, she said.

Jenny Moss died in 2006. She was 61.

FRANK PEMBERTON

Without doubt the most tragic character to stumble from Coronation Street was Frank Pemberton. The Oldies will remember Frank. He played Frank Barlow, the father of Ken and David, the genial postman who became widowed when his wife Ida was killed in a bus accident not long after the programme started.

It seemed that tragedy was to follow Frank around, not just in the fictitious TV street but also in real life.

Frank, who came from Manchester, served three years in the Royal Navy during World War 11, and on demob decided to become an actor. He worked with various repertory theatre companies and then got one or two parts on TV, including some shows alongside the great comedian Tony Hancock.

Completely out of the blue came the chance to audition for a new Granada TV series to be called Florizel Street. His agent told him they were looking for a "middle-aged Dad with a genuine Lancashire accent" on a five-week trial period, paying £40 a week. He went for the audition like a shot.

It was the most exciting day of his life when he landed the part. He went into what was re-named Coronation Street, for the very first programme as the head of the Barlow family, living at No.3.

Strangely, his son Ken, now an old-age pensioner, is still living there more than 50 years later.

Frank's very first line was a row with his son Kenneth, who went to university and was complaining that his dad never wore a collar and tie around the house. And Frank replied, "Can't a feller eat a meal in his own house without a flamin' collar and tie on?" (Sounds like the pretentious Ken hasn't changed much, has he?). It was the first of many such family rows in the Barlow household.

But once the show became established and ran on beyond its original five weeks, the TV role brought security for Frank for the first time in his life. He bought his first car, and he also bought his first house, an attractive home only a stone's throw from Richmond Park in East Sheen, Surrey.

In private life, Frank was married to actress Jean Marlow and they had a daughter called Penny. During the week, Frank lived in "digs" in Manchester, and every week-end would drive home to London to be with his wife and daughter.

Frank went on to appear in nearly 400 episodes. But he became one of the victims of what was known as the Great Purge of 1964, when he was dropped from the show, along with several others, at the whim of a new producer.

Leaving The Street after four years, he was back on the boards and did a 13-week theatre tour with a comedy play. But that was the last work Frank ever did, became he found himself on the dole.

The shock of suddenly being axed from Coronation Street after four years of security was too much for him to take. One day, on his way to the Labour Exchange on a quiet afternoon in February 1965, he had a stroke and collapsed on the pavement. He was immediately surrounded by a number of passers-by, and in his physical struggling and agony, he later recalled someone looking down at him and saying, quite clearly, "Oh, look, it's Mr. Barlow from Coronation Street!" He was rushed to hospital in Richmond.

Frank was then 50, an awful age to be struck down physically. He spent months in hospital and when he returned home, he had lost the use of his left arm completely and found that he could not walk without the aid of crutches or a stick. Mentally, he grew depressed and spent time in different hospitals.

The news of Frank's personal tragedy got back to Coronation Street, and they decided to invite him back, just for one episode, to see if he was fit for work. Frank was delighted at the chance of making a "come back" as an actor.

Unfortunately, this was not to be. He travelled to Manchester, in 1967, and was given a few lines to speak. Bill Roache, who was in a scene with him, later recalled, "It wasn't easy for him. We all admired Frank tremendously. But he could hardly walk."

Then came more heartache for Frank. When he returned home from Manchester after playing that one scene, he was told that his wife wanted a divorce. He was returned to hospital and put in public care. His divorce went through, and his wife sold up their house and moved away to another part of London, taking their daughter with her.

Disabled and all alone, Frank came close to suicide. And then miraculously, he found something to live for again. He fell in love with Sheila Cook, a nursing sister who was one of the people who had desperately tried to nurse him back to health. And Frank and Sheila were married in June 1968.

Now, when I was doing research for the book I was writing, The Real Coronation Street, I located Frank and he invited me down to his home to interview him. He was then living in a small bungalow on a site near the Cheshire Homes in Copthorne, Essex. The bungalow was specially fitted out for invalids, with sliding doors, no stairs or steps. He was living on a disability pension.

It was several years since we had last met, but I found him reasonably cheerful and he was obviously very pleased to see and talk to me. "If only I could get a part where I could sit down all the time, and not have to move about, it would be fine," he said.

Obviously, I felt very sorry for him, because Frank had always been a nice bloke. So, when I got home, I phoned Bill Podmore, who was then the current producer of Coronation Street, and told him I had been to see Frank Pemberton. And I suggested, "Why couldn't you have him return, as Frank Barlow, and let him sit in his wheelchair? He doesn't have to walk around. You could easily write a good story-line for him, that old man Barlow had returned to see his family, or even live with them."

Bill was very appreciative and said he would think about it. And later Frank was, in fact, invited back to the studios to meet some of his old Street neighbours. He was pushed into the Rovers in his wheelchair, and just sat quietly having a pint, with very little to say.

The producers decided however that he simply wasn't up to it and there was no way he could go back to work full time.

Frank went back to his little bungalow, with wife Sheila as his carer. He died a few years later.

LYNNE CAROL

Lynne Carol spent nearly four years in The Street, as busybody Martha Longhurst, one of the three old-age pensioners – Ena Sharples, Minnie Caldwell, and Martha – who sat every day in the Snug of the Rovers, constantly sipping their drinks and gossiping.

And when they killed her off in 1964, it was one of the greatest mistakes the producers ever made. In fact, Violet Carson, who played the hair-netted battleaxe Ena Sharples, was so annoyed, she marched upstairs at the studios and told Granada boss Sidney Bernstein they would regret it, splitting up the trio.

They got rid of Martha when she had a heart attack and died over her glass of stout in the Rovers, her spectacles falling onto the table.

The shows were then recorded and screened a fortnight later. The night she was due to die on screen, Lynne was determined to watch her fatal last scene. I suggested that I should actually sit in with her and that we could watch the last episode together. At first, she thought it was a good idea, but then changed her mind and told me, "No, I think I am going to be too upset. I'll just watch it quietly at home with Bert. But if you want to talk to me afterwards, just give me ten minutes to recover and then give me a phone call."

She was married to Bert Palmer, a lovable old actor who had appeared in hundreds of TV roles and films. So they switched on the telly and watched Martha's very moving death scene together at their home in Blackpool, with a stiff drink to help them. I phoned her afterwards. Bert answered and said, "Here she is, Ken. But don't keep her too long. She's really very upset." Lynne was then close to tears as she talked to me.

A few weeks later she admitted, "I cried when I watched my own funeral scenes." She never quite forgave the producers for killing her off. She did a few theatre tours and appeared in the odd TV play, but people still remembered her as Martha Longhurst and would stop her in the street for a chat.

"Working on The Street was such a happy time. I was absolutely heartbroken when they sacked me," she said, some years later. "I'm still accosted by people who recognise me as Martha. A few months ago, I was waiting for a train in London when a woman came up to me and said, 'I know your face. How long have you been dead now?'

"Some people have even suggested to me that, if they can't bring Martha back, they should bring in a new character – maybe Martha's twin sister, which I could play."

She would have jumped at the chance. But Granada weren't interested.

STEPHEN HANCOCK

Stephen Hancock played Ernie Bishop, loving and faithful husband of the popular Emily, for seven years. But in 1978 he was involved in a contract dispute with the producers, and shortly after Ernie was brutally shot dead in a wages snatch at Mike Baldwin's factory.

Hancock was a classic example of what can happen to an actor if he isn't a good boy. Stephen was a very fine actor, but he was quickly out on his ear as soon as he started causing trouble.

The scene in which Ernie Bishop lost his life, trying to fight off an armed burglar, is still remembered as one of the most dramatic moments in the programme's long history. It left Emily as a weeping widow. And the old dear has never got over it. More than 40 years on, she still refers occasionally to her beloved Ernie.

Some years later, Stephen told me, "I have no real regrets. I left on a matter of principle. Some of the actors were on one contract, and the rest of us were on second-grade contracts. It was all most unfair. I told them I wasn't going to sign a new contract.

"Perhaps it was silly of me. And I admit I was a bit surprised when none of my fellow actors stood by me. They watched me go."

Although he managed to get a few TV parts, he spent long period out of work, and back on the dole.

It's of little consolation, I suppose, that Emily Bishop is still going strong. And still has that old framed photo of husband Ernie on the mantelpiece.

ALAN ROTHWELL

Alan Rothwell played David Barlow, younger brother of Ken, on and off for about ten years. But when they finally wrote him out in 1970, he heaved a hefty sigh of relief.

"To me, acting is all about playing different parts," Alan told me. "Playing the same role, week in and week out, eventually drove me potty.

"Of course, you enjoy the money. But you're finally stuck with the same boring part on TV. I felt I was going backwards. The trouble with being in a long-running series is that you become cocooned. It's like doing a nine-to-five job. Eventually I decided to get out."

He was written out when viewers were told that David Barlow had died in a car crash in Australia. "When they finally killed me off, it was conclusive. I knew I could never go back to it," he said.

Alan went through some lean years when he might have regretted leaving. He had long periods unemployed, and at one time worked as a part-time taxi driver to help pay the rent.

I caught up with him some years later when he was signed up to join Brookside, and we had a cup of tea and a chat on the set. They wrote him a very good part, playing a nasty philanderer and wife-beating husband of the lovely housewife Heather Black (Amanda Burton).

He's been in and out of work since. Alan is one of those good jobbing actors. And you just can't keep a good man down.

DORIS SPEED & ARTHUR LESLIE

Mrs. Ada Speed sat through half-an-hour of Coronation Street one night. Then when the programme faded out she turned to her daughter Doris and said, "I'm 87 years of age, but thank God I never looked as old as you looked on TV tonight."

Doris refused to talk to her mother for four days after that remark.

It was nothing really new to her, for Doris looked after her ageing mother for many years in their little semi-detached house in Chorlton-cum-Hardy, Manchester. She was accustomed to such barbed insults because her mother was her sternest critic, although Doris knew that secretly the old lady really adored the programme.

Doris played Rovers Return landlady Annie Walker from the very first episode, with Arthur Leslie as husband Jack. They were both veteran actors when they joined the show and came from similar theatrical backgrounds. Doris made her stage debut at the age of three, in panto with her parents, who were struggling music hall artists.

At 14 she became the breadwinner of the family. Her father was out of work more than he was on stage, and Doris took a shorthand-and-typing course and got a job in an office to help pay the rent.

Later she turned to acting and did quite a lot of radio work before landing the part of Annie Walker, The Street's outrageous snob. She once described to me her version of her TV character. "She is really horrid. She is a silly, pretentious woman, but her silliness is amusing. Her judgement is wrong on almost everything, but she is not an unkind person."

Doris never married. "Not because I haven't wanted to, but perhaps I set too high a standard on the man I would like," she once told me. "There have been plenty of nice, pleasant men around, but the one who would make me give up everything just hasn't turned up." Besides, she was always busy looking after her parents.

In many ways, Doris lived a frugal kind of existence. One of her few luxuries was the first fur coat she bought herself, after establishing herself in the Coronation Street role. She called it "My Tony" - after Tony Warren. And she lived in the same unpretentious little semi for most of her life.

"When you have been poor all your life, you don't suddenly change and live like a Queen," she told me, over a cup of tea in her dressing-room. "I was taught as a child not to spend, so I've been conditioned to poverty most of my life. I'm not mean, but I find it very difficult to spend a lot of cash, even when I've got it."

One of her great joys in life was going to the sales and taking part in the mad scramble for marked-down items of clothing on the bargain counters. "It is a long time since I needed to buy anything that was marked-down, but my feet automatically take me there. It's awful, I know – but it's too late for me to change now," she said.

In later years, she was very deaf. "Come over and sit on this side of me, darling, so I can hear you better," she'd say. I loved Doris. She was a delight to meet.

Arthur Leslie had never met Doris before they teamed up together behind the bar at the Rovers. He came from a family with three generations of actors, and on his wife Betty's side there were five generations. And Arthur was more or less preparing for retirement after a lifetime of theatre in the provinces, when the role of Jack Walker came along.

He had no idea how long the show would run when Granada gave him his first five-week contract. Only when they extended it to a six-month contract, and then one for two years, did he fully realise that, whether he liked it or not, he was going to have to get used to being called Jack Walker for the rest of his life.

He and his wife Betty moved into a comfortable semi-detached near the sea front at Blackpool, and this was regarded as his one big extravagance. Arthur travelled from Blackpool to Manchester by train every day for rehearsals. The only sign he displayed of added prosperity was that he travelled first-class on the train, instead of sitting in second-class which he'd done for most of his life.

"I still don't honestly know whether I have become Jack, or Jack has become me, but the two are very close," he once told me with a chuckle.

Arthur died quite suddenly, while on a summer holiday in 1969. After pulling pints in the Rovers for nearly ten years.

Doris Speed went on working, long after Arthur had died. Annie took over the pub single-handed and ruled in female splendour for many years.

No one knew exactly how old Doris was. She would never disclose her age to anyone, though everyone knew that she was obviously much older than she looked.

It all came to a sad end when the truth finally came out. In 1983, the Daily Mirror somehow checked out her birth certificate and revealed with big headlines that Doris was really much older than everyone thought. She was 84. (I must point out and emphasise that I had absolutely nothing at all to do with this story).

Doris was heartbroken and quite devastated by the newspaper revelation. She collapsed and was taken home. A few weeks later, her house was burgled overnight while she was asleep. The stress of everything caused a minor breakdown, and she later moved into a nursing home and became a recluse.

She made one final appearance however. In 1990, she was invited as a guest to Coronation Street's 30th birthday party and received a standing ovation from her old colleagues. Doris herself had been happily in the show for 23 of those years.

She died in 1994, aged 95.

PHILIP LOWRIE

Philip Lowrie was one of the original cast of Coronation Street, on a starting salary of 50 guineas a week, which was a lot of money in those days and a small fortune to a young man who was only a couple of years out of RADA and with practically no TV experience at all.

When he travelled from London to Manchester for an audition (they paid him a £10 fee for his trouble) they told him the part of Dennis Tanner was between him and another actor. The other fellow turned out to be Kenneth Farrington. Philip eventually got the part of Dennis, and Ken was given the role of Billy Walker, son of Jack and Annie in the Rovers Return.

He then spent the next six or seven years, playing Elsie Tanner's wayward son Dennis, but hating it most of the time because he knew it was going to type-cast him for life.

Although he enjoyed playing Dennis on screen, he disliked all the business of being regarded as a celebrity when he was out in public. And he tried to get away as often as he could, to do stage plays in his holiday breaks.

Philip soon grew tired of his TV role. Unfortunately, Dennis Tanner was quietly helping Philip to become quite a rich young man and he found himself depending on the programme more and more for financial security.

He bought his mum and dad a lovely bungalow in Northampton. Then he splashed out more money and bought himself a magnificent country house only eight miles away from his parents, with a swimming pool and two acres of garden. He called it North House, and at weekend away from the grind of the TV programme, he lived the life of a country squire.

Philip invited me down to his house once, and proudly showed me around. He was a completely different person when he was away from the studios, far more relaxed and friendly.

He tried more than once to break with the programme, but found it wasn't easy. Finally, he signed on for a three-year contract, and made up his mind that during those three years he was working solely for the security. The money was then carefully invested so that it would keep him in out-of-work periods after he quit The Street for good. He made sure he would have no financial problems for, apart from his own house and the one he'd bought for his parents, he also acquired a big house in the Islington district of London, which was fully paid for and had been converted into four flats. Philip used one of them as his London base and the other three brought him in a steady income.

Eventually, he managed to escape from the cobbled Northern street, which was the way he put it to me. "I had to get away before I went mad," he said. "I was always running and hiding when I was in Coronation Street. I felt like a little mouse on a large wheel. I was a well-fed mouse on a well-padded wheel, but I was in one hell of a rut."

So he dropped to a tenth of his TV salary and went back to the theatre. And he swore that he would never go back. Dennis Tanner was dead as far as he was concerned.

And he was as good as his word. I met him a few times after he'd left and he was always cheerful and optimistic. Like most working actors, he was in and out of employment over the years. But I found it interesting, because there were many other actors who swore they'd never go back after leaving Coronation Street, but as soon as the chips were down, and work became scarce, they were happy to scuttle back to Manchester and climb back on to the lucrative gravy-train.

Philip Lowrie never did that. He was the only actor who stuck to his promise never to return, despite being out of work and back on the dole for long periods.

But then, a couple of years ago, even Philip finally relented. I don't know what his circumstances were, but after turning down several offers to return, he gave in and went back to playing Dennis Tanner. I must say I was very surprised.

He returned, still looking remarkably good for his years, and still with a full head of hair, even though it was now turning grey.

Older viewers were probably glad to see Dennis back. And the scriptwriters wasted no time in marrying him off to old widow Rita, who of course was one of his neighbours all those years ago.

The marriage didn't last long. Dennis was soon on his way out again. Rita's still there, now a divorcee as well as well as a widow.

Whether we'll ever see Dennis again, who knows?

JACK HOWARTH

Apart from the fact that he paid a hell of a lot more Income Tax than he used to, Jack Howarth always maintained that playing Albert Tatlock had not changed him at all over all the years he was in the role. "We were never on hard times, even before I started in The Street," he said. And that was true. He was always in steady work.

In fact, for many years he only played two regular roles. For before Albert Tatlock came along, he played Mr. Maggs in Mrs. Dale's Diary, the popular BBC daily radio serial for 14 years. He was already a pensioner when he gave up radio and became a TV star in The Street.

He had been acting since he was 12, and met his wife Betty Murgatroyd, an actress, in a stage play at Llandudno. After they married, they made a vow they would always work together, and if this was not possible, then one of them would give it all up and travel around with whoever had the more successful career. It turned out to be Jack.

After becoming established in Coronation Street, Jack and his wife lived in a nice bungalow in Deganwy, North Wales at week-ends. But for five days of the week, when Jack was working, they stayed at the plushy 4-star Midland Hotel, only a short walk away from the studios. The Howarths had their own apartment, though Jack told me once that they preferred to use a bathroom across the corridor, rather than have their own private en-suite, because this cut the cost of their weekly bill.

Jack was a jolly old soul, but he did watch the pennies. "I'm not mean, just thrifty," he'd boast.

He would always take a holiday break to coincide with the Golden Rose TV festival in Montreux, and he and Betty would fly out to Switzerland and be treated for a week as TV celebrities. He liked to mix a lot with the Press guys and would buy his round if he had to.

What amused me, though, was that even if the weather was lovely and sunny, instead of sitting outside and enjoying it, Jack and Betty would insist on going inside and watching every single TV programme screened, in the dark viewing rooms, all day long.

Jack loved to reminisce about his old theatre days. But he once told me an amusing story. Their only son John was educated for a time at Rydal, a public school in North Wales. And Jack recalled the time he and Betty visited the school, and came across a little red-haired lad, crying noisily in the junior playground.

"What's your name?" said Jack, trying to console the boy. Back came the sniffy reply, "Billy Roache."

"And where do you live?" "England," said the boy, "And I don't like Wales."

Jack still teased the red-haired fellow over that incident many years later, for Billy Roache, the Englishman, became Ken Barlow. And Jack, as Albert, became his uncle.

VIOLET CARSON

When Violet Carson received an important-looking envelope bearing the Royal crest through the post at her home in Blackpool, one morning in the autumn of 1965, she had absolutely no idea what it could be. With trembling fingers, she opened it – and it was the official notification she was to be awarded the OBE.

She was stunned and immensely pleased, but puzzled as to why she should get the award. "I would like to think that it was some sort of recognition for the whole of my career. People tell me I have managed to make a lot of folk happy. I hope I have," she said.

Only when she went to Buckingham Palace to meet the Queen, did she fully realise the impact of it all, she told me later. It was the crowning point to a long and successful career in show business. For Violet had been a big-name on the radio as a pianist and singer, long before Coronation Street came along.

Actually, she had her first piano lesson when she was three years old and made her professional debut at the of 15 when she played the piano at a silent-movie cinema in Manchester. She then played in various picture-houses, and did a song and dance act with her sister Nellie, before eventually being "discovered" and going into radio, where she became known as Auntie Vi in the BBC's Children's Hour. She was then pianist for many years with Wilfred Pickles' popular Have A Go programme.

Then along came Ena Sharples - and Violet's BBC days were over. Her whole life changed. One Italian newspaper, Il Giorno, wrote: "Ena Sharples is better known in Britain than the Prime Minister." And only a year after The Street was launched, Blackpool Corporation paid Violet the greatest compliment ever bestowed on one of its own residents when she was invited to switch on the resort's massive illuminations.

Her famous face went into Madame Tussaud's waxworks, and she had a rose named after her by a leading rose-grower. She insisted on only one thing, that the rose be called the "Violet Carson" and not Ena Sharples.

Vi didn't suffer fools gladly. She could be more than a battle-axe when she wanted to. But for some reason, I got on well with her. She normally hated publicity and didn't make a habit of talking to the Press. But from my very first interview with her, we seemed to hit it off, and I never had any problems in arranging to chat to her in her studio dressing-room.

In fact, she once invited me over to her house in Blackpool, where she lived with her sister Nellie, in the bungalow left to them both when their mother died at the age of 90. Nellie served us tea and scrumptious home-made scones, and we chatted all afternoon.

Violet was nothing like Ena, of course. Once she had taken off the three hairnets (yes, she wore three at a time) Vi was a different person. She was absolutely charming and could be very funny as well.

She had a strict routine when she was working. Vi travelled every day from Blackpool to Manchester by train, catching the 8.35 in the morning and returning on the 5.50.

On Thursdays, she stayed overnight in a small hotel in Manchester, in order to be in the studios early on Friday, when two programmes were recorded. She stayed at the same hotel for years. "I wanted a small place, just for one night a week, because I had no intention of ever moving to Manchester to live," she said. On Friday nights, after recording the shows, she treated herself to a hired car all the way to Blackpool, which she regarded as a real luxury.

Railway officials and porters knew her well, and for good reason. At one time, the Manchester-to-Blackpool train service earned a bad reputation for being late. Violet was among the regular passengers who complained. Next day, British Rail officials promised: "The train will be more punctual in future."

"Now, they have only to see me coming down the platform, and things start moving. Once I'm in my seat, whistles are blown, flags are waved, and the train leaves dead on time," she told me, chuckling.

When Violet Carson died - on Boxing Day, 1983, at the age of 85 – the whole nation mourned her passing.

About three weeks after the funeral, her sister Nellie invited me over to her house for a chat. She was very lonely, but she wanted to talk about the sister she had grown up with, and of their 80 years together.

Over tea, Nellie told me, "Vi never regretted getting the part of Ena Sharples, but she did regret it going on for so long. It was something that was eating up her life. If she had known she was going to spend the rest of her life playing Ena, she would never have taken the job."

And she told me a surprising thing. "Vi could not bear to watch herself on TV. I don't think she ever watched a single episode of Coronation Street that she appeared in. If the programme came on when she was at home, she would walk out of the room and stay out until it had finished."

So how did Ena Sharples change Vi as a person? I wanted to know. "She went more into herself," said Nellie. "As the years went by, she completely forgot how to enjoy herself. She respected Ena Sharples as a character, but she didn't know what to do with her.

"Even when she took time off from the TV show, Violet didn't want to go away very much. Then when she became ill and had an operation in 1980, she became very depressed. It was sad to see her over the last few years. She became very ill with pernicious anaemia.

"We tried to play down her illness, but we knew she was not going to get better."

It was sad to meet Nel on that occasion. She was suddenly a woman on her own, with only memories to cherish.

GEOFFREY HUGHES

Geoffrey Hughes was a nice guy. He played Eddie Yeats, the big, fat likeable window-cleaner who was a lodger with the Stan and Hilda Ogden, and became one of the most popular characters ever to waddle down the cobblestones of Coronation Street.

Everyone loved Eddie. It was impossible not to. He always had a smile on his face and was ready to pull a prank, just to get a laugh. Like an overgrown, roly-poly schoolboy. I think he regarded the lovely Hilda as his adopted mum.

Geoff, who came from Liverpool, was with the programme for ten years and attracted a lot of fan mail, believe it or not. He was not so much a sex symbol as the kind of bloke people would like to have living next door.

One day in May 1983, I got a phone call from Norman Frisby, Granada's chief Press officer, telling me that Geoffrey Hughes was to leave The Street. This was most unusual, because the TV company never announced when actors were leaving, and in fact fiercely protected their privacy, and were always annoyed when newspapers "blew" their story-lines in advance of transmission.

However, Norman said to me, "Geoffrey has decided to leave when his contract comes to an end in six months' time. We know this will leak out before then, but Geoffrey wants it made public. And the only person he wants to talk to is you. Will you come into the office and meet him?"

So I went down to the studios, met Geoff in the Press office, and over a cup of tea he poured out his story to me. He'd had enough of playing Eddie Yeats. It was all quite amicable. He was not being sacked, it was entirely his decision to go. He was very chirpy and told me how happy he'd been in The Street, but he simply wanted to go off and do other things. Away from the studios, Geoff lived the life of a working farmer in Peterborough, Northants, while his wife Susan ran a craft centre at a local country estate.

I realised then that Geoff was playing things straight down the line. He knew that Granada had a very strict policy of not letting actors talk to the Press without their permission. But by talking to me, through the Press office, he had played it strictly by the book. After all, some actors had been fired in the past for talking to the Press (eg, Peter Adamson!).

Norman Frisby, who ran the Press office for years and years, was a stickler for abiding by the rules. A hardened journalist, he had worked on the Northern Daily Express and then TV Times before becoming poacher-turned-gamekeeper and joining Granada as a PR. He was also a JP and sat on the magistrate's bench occasionally.

Norman and I had a somewhat ambivalent relationship, and the occasional bust-up over the years. But we had a mutual respect for each other. He was so devoted to the job, and a real company man, that when it came to retirement age and he had to quit his executive role in the Press office, Norman kept his shoes polished every day and took a job as a Granada tourist guide, showing visitors around the studios.

As for Geoff Hughes, he was just as happy as Eddie Yeats had ever been. After leaving The Street, he was barely out of work. He cornered the market in playing overweight and idle characters and became the best slob in the business.

"I'd like to think it's my acting as well as my appearance that gets me so much work," said the 16-stone Geoff. "The way you look tends to predestine some of the things you do. I can't remember ever being thin. I've always been chubby."

When I met Geoff eight years after he'd left The Street, he had landed the role of Onslow, the layabout brother-in-law of Hyacinth Bucket in the BBC sitcom Keeping Up Appearances. There he was, back in his string vest, lying on the sofa, swilling beer and watching telly. It was a part created in heaven for him. Geoff was like a pig in mud.

The BBC series really took off and Geoff found fame all over again. "Onslow is not a stupid person but he has decided not to join the rest of the human race," Geoff told me with a chuckle. "He's happy the way he is, and   doesn't want to play the silly game of life. He sits in front of the telly with his six-pack of beer and every time he is moved and has to do something, it's another intrusion into his life. I suppose everyone must admire the freedom to do exactly as you please in life. There are few of us who can do that. I certainly can't."

And Geoff said, "I'm much too busy to be a layabout. I would never dream of watching TV during the day and don't even watch much in the evening. I do like my beer though, so long as it's real ale and not that horrible fizzy stuff." He then went on to join the cast of The Royle Family, ideally cast again as the beer-swilling pal of superslob Jim Royle (Ricky Tomlinson). They both spent their life sitting on the sofa, watching telly. On reflection, only Ricky could outdo Geoff when it came to being a couch potato.

Geoff still lived in the little Northamptonshire village, and kept a couple of goats and hens. "I love the country life. After a run in a West End play or a long spell in the TV studios, living in the country helps me re-charge my batteries and brings me back down to earth."

He hasn't changed. Still a lovely bloke.

JEAN ALEXANDER & BERNARD YOUENS

"Before joining Coronation Street, I never had more than £15 in the Post Office Savings Bank in my life." That's one of the things Jean Alexander said to me when I interviewed her for the very first time. Which must be about 50 years ago.

When she finally left The Street, after 23 years playing Hilda Ogden, her bank account was much healthier. And most of the money she'd made over those years was still intact, safely deposited in building society accounts, paying a decent interest. For Jean was quite canny when it came to money.

We became quite good friends, and even today still exchange Christmas cards and try to keep in touch.

When she took the train journey from her home in Southport to Manchester on her very last day as Hilda, I had a photographer with her on the train, and I was waiting on the steps of the Granada studio to give her a farewell bouquet and a bottle of champagne.

But our association didn't end there. I followed her ensuing career with great interest. Because when Jean declared that she'd had enough of Hilda, and was determined to find other acting parts, I knew she meant every word of it.

It didn't take her long to prove that she was capable of more than one TV role. Because within a year Jean had forgotten all about Hilda and had several other jobs lined up. I was invited to her home for tea, and we discussed the various things she had in the pipeline.

First, she was busy filming a Christmas edition of Last of the Summer Wine, playing the dotty old eccentric running an antique shop. Then she was appearing on Les Dawson's quiz show Blankety Blank. She'd also recorded an episode of Boon, playing a busybody journalist. And she had also sneaked off and played her first full-length film role in years, as prostitute Christine Keeler's mother in a new movie called Scandal.

She was also very enthusiastic about a new character they'd created for her in a six-part serial called Rich Tea & Sympathy on ITV, in which played a glamorous granny who shared her house with her divorced daughter (played by Patricia Hodges).

It was very funny when I met her on that occasion. Although I'd interviewed her many times at the studios, this was the first time I'd ever been to her house. And when she popped her head round the corner of the kitchen and said, "Let's have some tea, shall we? Earl Grey or ordinary?" I couldn't help but smile.

Earl Grey? Hilda Ogden offering me a cup of Earl Grey — has the world gone mad? I thought. But, of course, this wasn't Hilda. The cheery little Mrs. Ogden had been consigned to the dustbin forever, Jean assured me

There were no flying ducks on the wall. No celebrity photographs around, as there are in most stars' homes. And when she brought in a silver tray (with a plate of sliced cake and home-made brandy snaps) she poured the tea into beautiful bone-china cups, and said, "I'll fill the cups up. What really annoys me on TV is when characters pretend to drink tea, and there's obviously nothing in the cup. That infuriates viewers. When I was in The Street, I always insisted on having enough tea in the cups so that you could see it." Funny, but true.

"I've had a smashing year. I've done exactly what I said I'd do," she told me. "I wanted a rest, and I've had it. Now it's time to get back to work, and happily the jobs are coming in. I've been working hard all my life, since 1945, and I've got everything I need. But I like to keep busy."

There were no tears when she left The Street. She always said she didn't want to go on playing Hilda when she was drawing her old-age pension. "I grew tired of Hilda. I wanted to give the old dear a rest," she said. I haven't missed Coronation Street at all. Once I walked down the studio steps on my way home, Hilda was forgotten. I never let her interfere with my private life."

But she did tell me, "I don't mind admitting that before I went into Coronation Street, I was almost broke. I've been through the bad times, and sometimes I was down to my last sixpence in my purse."

Jean moved into her nicely-furnished but unpretentious semi-detached house with her mother in 1970, not long after her father died. She looked after her mother for many years, and when she died Jean was left alone, because she had never married. "I enjoy my own company, and I've got lovely neighbours and lots of good friends," she said.

A couple of years later, I caught up with Jean in Yorkshire when she joined the cast of Last of the Summer Wine on a regular basis, playing Auntie Wainwright. In a way, I had been responsible for helping her get that role. In an interview I'd done for the Mirror, she mentioned that her favourite TV programme was Last of the Summer Wine. I received a phone call from Alan Bell, the producer of Summer Wine, asking me if this was true, and did I think Jean would be interested in joining his programme.

"Why don't you ask her?" I said. "She might jump at the chance."

And that's exactly what happened. She was 65 when she decided to cross the Pennines and join that bunch of pensioners led by Bill Owen, Peter Sallis and Brian Wilde.

When I went to interview her on location in beautiful Holmfirth countryside, she was giggling like a schoolgirl. She'd just been signed up for a new series of eight programmes. "I can't believe I've been lucky enough to join this gang," she said.

"Auntie Wainwright is one of those rare TV characters, a real eccentric. I suppose you could call Hilda Ogden an eccentric. But this one is even dafter. She's a real money-grabbing crusty old faggot. But I love her."

Although a lot of filming was done in Yorkshire, the shows were actually produced and edited in London. And going down to London regularly brought back a lot of unhappy memories for Jean, because it reminded her of the bad old days when she tramped the streets looking for work, she told me.

"I spent three years in London trying to break into TV and no-one wanted to know me. I used to walk everywhere because I had no money. I remember hiking miles from my lodgings in Cromwell Road to the BBC TV Centre in Shepherd's Bush for an audition. I was only in there ten minutes, and I didn't get the part. I couldn't afford to eat, and just used to smooch around the streets, looking at the historical buildings."

But she added, "Last week, I didn't have to walk to the studios. I can afford a taxi now. But I still don't like London. I don't stay any longer than I have to. As soon as I get off the train at Euston Station, I want to get back on again and go home."

She went on to play Auntie Wainwright for several years until the BBC decided to wrap up the programme, which was then the longest-running comedy series on TV.

"I've spent all my life looking forward to the time when I could afford not to work if I don't want to," she would tell me. "But I want to go on acting so long as I can remember my lines and stand on my feet."

But she hated the celebrity side of her job. She didn't go to showbiz parties. And she was annoyed when she suddenly found out that she was something of a tourist attraction in Southport. One day there was a knock on her front door, Jean told me, and a group of women were standing on the doorstep.

"Yes?" said Jean. One of the women said simply, "We've just come to look at you. To see what Hilda Ogden really looks like."

"How did you know where I live?" asked Jean.

"We're staying in Southport on holiday and the manager of our hotel told us," said the woman.

"Which hotel? I'll have his guts for garters!"

Jean explained, "There am I, trying to forget all about Hilda Ogden, and folk come to my doorstep and just want to stare at me, as though I'm a local monument."

When the offer of an audition for The Street came up for Bernard Youens, in the autumn of 1960, he was frank and very definite about it. No, thank-you-very-much, he said. Bernard was a staff announcer with Granada TV, and it was the first steady job he'd had for many years.

There was a lot to be said for a regular weekly pay packet and a retirement pension to go with it. And Bernard had seen other TV shows come and go.

A year later he was kicking himself, for the show had caught on, and whereas everyone in The Street was drinking shorts, he was still on the old pints of bitter.

He thought the chance had gone. Then in1963, Jose Scott phoned him from casting department and said, "There's a new family coming into The Street. Are you interested?" "By God I am," said Bernard. He had now been doing the announcer's job for four years and he was itching to get back into acting.

They asked him to read for the Stan Ogden character. The description of Oggie: Big, fat, boozy, devil-may-care bloke who likes his beer. Ex-lorry driver, Lancashire accent.

Bernard chuckled. It was right up his street, he thought. After an audition, they phoned him back a week later. "Will you come in and discuss a contract?"

Another lucky day for Bernard was when they picked Jean Alexander to play his wife. They had never met before, but when Bernard and Jean did a dry-run together, within a few minutes of reading the script he knew he had found a partner. They clicked into place like a human jigsaw puzzle.

Bernard played Stan Ogden for twenty years. But he died in 1984, after years of illness. His real wife Edna contacted me a few years after his death because she had found an old box in the attic containing not only his medals but all his old war-time diaries and poetry, and I negotiated with her for us to print them in the Daily Mirror.

Edna and Bernard were married for 49 years. He called her Teddy and she called him Bunny. "I worshipped the ground he walked on. I was more in love with him the day he died than the day I met him," she told me.

And Edna said, "I don't mind admitting that I cried when I heard that Jean Alexander had decided to leave the show. I used to watch the programme to see my lovely Bernard and Jean appearing together as Stan and Hilda. They were a wonderful partnership. And I don't think they had a cross word in all the years they worked together. After Bernard died, then I just watched it for Hilda."

There were some memorable times when Bernard and Jean met the Queen and other members of the Royal family. But Edna told me she was really worried when the Queen visited the Coronation Street set in 1982. "Bernard and Jean had been invited to meet her, and Bernard told me he was going to think up something funny to ask the Queen. I told him not to be such a fool. But he'd do anything for a laugh. Then to my horror, I saw them on TV, and there was Bernard chatting to the Queen. He told me later that he said, 'Excuse me, Ma'am, but my wife Hilda here would like to know if I could have the contract to clean all the windows at Buckingham Palace?'

"The Queen apparently smiled and told him she thought he might be taking on too much."

Jean always told me that Bernard was an absolute joy to work with. "When we first came together, we found an instant rapport," she said. "It was a marvellous partnership right from the start. It was like telepathy. When we rehearsed together we would go through our scripts and play Scrabble at the same time. We'd say our lines, and then add up our Scrabble scores.

"After about eight years, we'd got so used to each other's game that we couldn't play any more – because after four moves the board would be blocked."

But Jean never cried over Bernard, not even when he died. In fact, she told me very frankly, "I find it impossible to cry. I'm a fairly calm person, and I'm a fatalist. All the weeping and wailing is not going to change anything. I simply cannot shed tears.

"I feel very sad and very miserable, but nothing comes out. I just go very quiet. It probably makes me sound callous. I'm not really. At Bernard's funeral, some newspaper reports said that I was crying. But I wasn't. I wish I could have."

In later life, Jean spent a lot of time going on exotic holiday cruises. A couple of years ago she had a health scare when she had a stroke and was rushed to hospital. But she was soon back home, and joking, "Don't write me off. There's still life in the old dog yet." Since then, she's had to take things easy. God bless her.

NIGEL PIVARO

Mancunian Nigel Pivaro played tearaway Terry Duckworth, the jail-bird son of Vera and Jack Duckworth and all-round bad-egg, and he certainly livened things up in The Street. He was in and out of the programme for years, depending on whether it was convenient for Nigel or whenever the producers decided to bring him back for a spell of hatred and nastiness.

Nigel was thoroughly at home playing the bad boy, because before he became a serious actor, he was in trouble himself. He had a criminal record and was jailed as a teenager for burglary. But he reckoned that this made him a better actor, because of his early experience.

I became quite friendly with Nigel. He was a very straight bloke and spoke his mind. And I remember that when I was in a spot of bother myself, and was being sued for libel by William Roache, Nigel was one of two or three of The Street actors who phoned me sympathetically and offered support, even though I couldn't get them into court on my side because they were contracted to Granada. I was always grateful for that.

Once, I recall meeting Nigel when he had just come out of The Street after a three-year stint because he was going to do a stage play. And he'd just had another brush with the law. He had narrowly escaped another prison term when he was caught behind the wheel of his car with eleven days of a driving ban left. He escaped with a £275 fine and a suspended six-week jail sentence.

Ironically, the stage play that he was in was called No Further Cause For Concern and he was playing a convict. But Nigel told me, "I realise only too well what an idiot I've been. I'm sometimes very stupid and hot-headed. All my plans would have gone out of the window if I'd gone back to prison. But I still can't believe they gave me a suspended jail sentence. The magistrates were trying to make an example of me. Until I got breathalised and banned from driving last year, I had not been in trouble for seven years. Now it looks like I'm going to be branded for ever."

Nigel was successful, in fact, in living down his bad-boy image.

When he first quit The Street, he was written out under a cloud. The wayward Terry, who had been in so many scrapes over the years, ran off with his best pal Peter Jackson's wife Linda.

And as their screen romance hotted up, Nigel fell in love with actress Kazia Pelka, who played the frustrated Linda.

Nigel told me, "It was one of the most enjoyable periods of my career. I had only six weeks on screen to meet Linda Jackson, fall in love with her, seduce her, and then take her away from her husband. But I really fell for Kazia and we are still very much together."

When I asked him if he had any plans for marriage, Nigel looked at me as though I was crazy. "I'm not the marrying kind," he said with a wicked grin.

I've not seen Nigel for a while. He returned to The Street several times, and his character Terry Duckworth became nastier than ever. He broke his mother Vera's heart and even blackmailed his father and conned him out of huge sums of money, before Jack died.

Some years later I went over to Brookside in Liverpool, and the lovely Kazia Pelka had joined the Mersey soap, playing a nanny to one of the residents. When I met her for an interview, she lay at my feet, provocatively teasing me. I asked her if she was still with Nigel Pivaro. She giggled and said, "You know Nigel. He's a great guy and I love him dearly. But we are both free spirits." So, I took that as a No!

LIZ DAWN & BILL TARMEY

Liz Dawn and Bill Tarmey were almost inseparable. Once they had been cast as Vera and Jack Duckworth, and signed on long-term contracts, they hung out a lot together both on set and in the bar after work. In fact, Liz and Bill probably saw more of each other than they did of their own partners at home. But then, the Duckworth partnership was a marriage made in heaven, as far as the The Street producers were concerned.

The scriptwriters loved them. Idle Jack was always up to mischief and with an eye for the women when the wife was not looking. And Vera was the loud-mouthed fish wife who could hold her own against anyone when it came to a slanging match. Together, they provided some of the greatest comedy scenes the programme ever produced. And a lot of them were written by my old mate John Stevenson, who was for my money the best scriptwriter The Street ever had. (He actually wrote 447 episodes over a period of 30 years).

Liz Dawn was born Sylvia Butterfield in Leeds, in 1939, and was a factory worker before taking the plunge and trying her luck as a singer in local pubs and nightclubs. She was a pretty good vocalist, too. I saw her in action a few times.

She then turned to acting, landed a few small parts in Northern films, and ended up in Coronation Street in 1974, playing a factory worker.

A few years later, Bill Tarmey joined The Street, first as an extra, just downing pints and playing darts in The Rovers, and then on a more permanent basis.

Bill, from Manchester and with a very similar background to Liz, started working life as a builder's labourer and then turned to singing in nightclubs as a full-time pro.

It was as though they were made for each other. The producers spotted the potential and put Liz and Bill together, creating the warring Duckworth couple. And they knew almost immediately they'd hit the jackpot. Vera and Jack became the natural successors to the great Hilda and Stan Ogden.

It wasn't all plain sailing though. For a few years, after playing Vera and becoming a star, Liz went through a rather wild patch. She was drinking a lot, still doing her cabaret act in nightclubs, and hit the headlines when she was involved in drunken brawls. In one, it was alleged that she turned up to do a singing spot in a Yorkshire club and ended up throwing a punch at the manager.

She then left her husband Don Ibbetson, who was also her manager, and was suing for divorce, after wife-beating allegations. Liz arrived at the TV studios one day with two black eyes. Which prompted her best pal Lynne Perry, who played little Ivy Tilsley, to say, "Blimey, Liz. You look like a bloody panda." Lynne told me that story herself.

But it was no joke. Her bosses at Granada were furious and in 1984 they threatened to drop Liz from the show to teach her a lesson. They were concerned about the constant headlines concerning her domestic life, and felt she had brought the TV show into disrepute with a series of newspaper articles revealing sordid details of her private life and also criticising others in the cast. The TV bosses did not like this kind of behaviour from their stars.

However, Liz managed to ride that particular storm. She patched up her married life, cut down on her drinking, and promised more or less to be a good girl.

With Bill Tarmey, it wasn't so much the drinking (although he did like a pint or three) but his health which was the big worry.

He was plagued with heart trouble. He suffered his first heart attack in 1976 and then had a stroke the following year, all before going into Coronation Street.

But then, eight years after playing Jack D, he suffered another heart attack and underwent quadruple bypass surgery.

After a four-month lay-off, Bill returned to the show. And he agreed to do a one-off exclusive interview with me for the Mirror. There was no money involved. (I always dealt in words, not in cash, and most of them were happy with that).

When I met Bill for lunch, he sat at the bar, a glass of cold lager in his hand, and said, "I could kill right now for a fag." Then he shrugged and added, "But I know it wouldn't do me any good. In fact, the doctor told me if I go back to smoking, I'll be signing my own death warrant."

He had to give up smoking 50 cigarettes a day. But he talked for the first time about his health problems. "A few months ago, I thought I was a goner. The doctors told me I had to go into hospital immediately for a bypass operation. I said I couldn't because I had the very important TV scripts to do, and I just couldn't get out of Coronation Street at the drop of a hat.

"The doctor said, 'Okay, we may – and he emphasised the word may – see you then. But it might be too late. Our advice is to do it now.'

"So I took their advice and went into hospital immediately. The scriptwriters didn't even have time to write me out of the show properly. I just vanished 18 weeks ago. But I'm convinced now that if I hadn't had this operation, I would be dead within six months. For me, this was the final warning, because I'd had heart trouble a long time, long before I took on Jack Duckworth. It took me a couple of years to get back on my feet. But I've always been a grafter and was never happy unless I was working."

Bill admitted to me that he was terrified before having the operation. He prepared his wife Alma and his children, Carl and Sarah, for the worst. "I put my house in order, I made out a will and all that sort of thing, just in case something went wrong, and I didn't pull through. It may sound macabre, but you've got to face facts in this situation."

Bill was looking much fitter. He had slimmed down from nearly 15st to 13st 4lbs and was told to take long walks.

He was also trying to catch up on what had happened in The Street while he had been away. His tearaway son Terry had quit the show. But before Nigel Pivaro left, he got together with Bill and Liz for a farewell dinner in Manchester.

As for Bill, he was just glad to be alive. "I'll be more than delighted if I am still playing Jack when I'm an old age pensioner walking in on sticks," he said. "I just can't wait to get to grips with Vera again and have a few slanging matches."

Once back in The Street, Bill was happy again playing Jack. He also cashed in on his singing again and had several record albums released. Unfortunately, he had a bit of a relapse and after another heart attack had a pacemaker fitted, in 2002, but continued to work.

In 2001, Liz and Bill won a British Soap Award for Best On-Screen Partnership, which they thoroughly deserved. But then Liz was diagnosed with the incurable lung disease emphysema, and although she struggled on, she was eventually written out of the show at her own request.

Vera died peacefully in her sleep, in January 2008, with Liz having completed 34 years in The Street. She later picked up a Best Soap Award for Lifetime Achievement. Which was something she was proud to look back on.

A couple of years later, Liz returned for one brief scene – a poignant dream sequence with Jack falling asleep and having a final dance with Vera. It was schmaltzy, but beautifully done.

Bill struggled on, playing Jack as the lonely widower. But then sadly, Bill died quite suddenly while on holiday with his real wife Alma in the Canary Islands, in 2012.

The scriptwriters then had dear old Jack dying at home – in his favourite armchair.

SARAH LANCASHIRE

Sarah Lancashire is now one of the most popular actresses on the small screen. No matter what kind of role she takes on, whether it's light comedy or heavy drama, she always guarantees to give 100 per-cent and comes out smelling of roses.

But it hasn't always been like that. At 18, she was diagnosed with clinical depression. For years, Sarah suffered from nervous attacks, bouts of depression, and even contemplated suicide. There were times when she found it hard to work, and even came close to packing it in altogether. Thank God she didn't.

Sarah, who comes from Oldham, was more interested after leaving school in working in theatre production, or something behind the scenes, because she did not have the confidence to get up and perform on stage.

Her father was Geoffrey Lancashire, a journalist who became a regular scriptwriter on Coronation Street. I knew Geoff very well and we used to have the occasional drink and bump into each other around Granada studios. He was a really nice bloke and a very witty character. Sadly, he'd split up from Sarah's mother, and then died at rather a young age.

When she eventually decided to become an actress, Sarah was still so insecure that, in between acting parts, she worked for five years as a drama teacher at Salford University.

Not surprisingly, it was in Coronation Street that Sarah really became established. She landed the role of Racquel Wolstenhulme, the dizzy barmaid in the Rovers Return, and brought a bit of glamour to the dreary Street. Viewers loved her, especially when the scriptwriters teed it up for her to have a romance with the popular binman Curly Watts (Kevin Kennedy). But it had a bitter-sweet ending, and Sarah left the Street in 1996 after five years, because she'd had enough and wanted to see if she could fly off to bigger things.

Sarah has certainly done that over the last 20 years and is now one of the most in-demand actors around. She has managed to come up with two very successful TV dramas, both compelling in their own way - Last Tango in Halifax, playing the mixed-up daughter of Anne Reid, alongside Derek Jacobi; and Happy Valley, playing the tough police sergeant, Catherine Cawood. Both earned her rave write-ups.

And it was one show which led to the other. Last Tango In Halifax won a BAFTA award as Best Drama Series and Sarah was nominated for Best Actress, as the lesbian headmistress. The scriptwriter Sally Wainwright was so impressed with her performance that she went away and created the new series Happy Valley specifically for Sarah.

Despite the success she has had, Sarah is still reluctant to talk about her work. "I don't watch anything I am in. I'm too critical," she says. "It's something I learned early on. It's best for me not to look at my own work. I dissect what I do in an unhealthy way. When I'm working in the theatre, I never go to the bar with the others. I go home and think about what I did wrong.

"I never feel proud about anything I do. All the fuss and all the plaudits are uncomfortable. It's fleeting, and then you have to go out and prove it all over again. Sometimes you get it right and other times you don't. It feels like a constant battle. It's tortuous."

In her private life, Sarah married musician Gary Hargreaves and had two sons in her ten-year marriage (which she later described as lasting ten years too long). She then married a second time, and has another son with Peter Salmon, who is a high-powered executive with the BBC. She now lives in London, and says she is only really happy when she is not working and just being a wife and mum at home.

She has cheered up a bit though. "I'm really very lucky to have been involved in two of the most beautifully created and written series," she said recently. "But I'm still happiest when I'm at home. The older I get, the harder it is to be away from home. I love having nothing on the diary."

Somehow, I think her dad Geoffrey would have been proud of her.

JOHNNY BRIGGS

Johnny Briggs played Mike Baldwin, the cockney owner of The Street's factory, for more years than he probably cares to remember. And that's exactly what Johnny was in real life – a cocky cockney.

Born with an in-built smile on his face, he went through life with that devil-may-care attitude and always liked to give the impression he was the big man, the boss, totally in control.

Mike Baldwin was a flash character who drove around in a Jaguar, liked a drink or two with the lads, and always had an eye for the ladies. Johnny, too, was flash and stylish, drove a Jaguar, and also liked to think of himself as a ladies' man.

In the end, it was difficult to tell the difference between Mike Baldwin and Johnny Briggs. Which was the actor and which the fictional character?

He wasn't the only one of course. Most of the long-running actors in The Street take on that risk.

Johnny was a child actor in films and theatre long before he went into The Street, and was one of those blokes always in demand. Taking on the role of Mike Baldwin really elevated him to star status.

And he certainly had some fun over the years. Baldwin got into some nasty scrapes and the scriptwriters devised some sensational audience-pulling story-lines for him. The most memorable was the infamous punch-up between Baldwin and Ken Barlow in the Rovers when Mike tried to steal Ken's wife Deirdre. And Baldwin himself went through almost as many wives as Barlow, including the controversial period when he even married Ken's daughter Susan, which he did out of spite.

I used to drink with Johnny quite regularly. If he wasn't in the Granada bar, he'd be in the pub over the road, after work, holding forth and regaling us with showbiz stories. I think he quite liked the company of journalists and realised the value of good publicity.

One story he didn't like, however, was in December 1986 when the scriptwriters had Mike Baldwin mixed up in some domestic trouble. His marriage to the lovely young Susan was on the rocks after she found out that he had an illegitimate son by an old flame, and the "other woman" turned up in Coronation Street as shapely Maggie Redman.

Unfortunately, at the same time, Johnny Briggs, who was then 50, hit the newspaper headlines himself when it was reported that he had secretly flown off to Barbados on holiday with a 21-year-old barmaid, Hilary McMillan.

The story broke while Johnny was still away, and it was reported that his wife Christine, at home with their three children in Stourbridge, West Midlands, was furious and was waiting for her husband to come home from the Caribbean to face the music.

The whole thing was dynamite. Granada TV bosses were embarrassed that Baldwin's love life on screen seemed to be following a similar pattern off screen.

A company spokesman said, "Johnny Briggs is away on holiday and his personal life has nothing at all to do with us. Obviously, the TV scripts involving Mike Baldwin were written months ago. And we cannot comment on Mr. Briggs' private life."

The story provided plenty of nudge-nudge wink-wink moments around the studios, and there was much anticipation in the Press when Johnny finally arrived back home.

But he managed to keep that permanent smile on his face and rode out that particular spot of domestic trouble. As far as I know he patched things up with his wife, went back home, and returned to Coronation Street to fight another day. But his second marriage also later ended in divorce.

When he finally left The Street, in 2006, he'd served 30 years. And he was still smiling, of course.

JULIE GOODYEAR

Julie Goodyear was the girl who first went into Coronation Street as a 24-year old inexperienced hopeful, all long legs, short skirts, peroxide hair and a gleaming smile. And came out of it some 37 years later, still with the peroxide blonde hair, but a hardened, experienced old diva who saw herself as the Queen Bee.

When she made her bow in 1966 with a few walk-on parts, she had in mind only one thing – she wanted to be The Street's No.1 sex symbol, emulating her idol, Pat Phoenix. But the first thing Pat advised her to do was to go away and get some acting experience.

When she returned, four years later, Julie was determined to be around for a long time. And she did eventually take over from Pat, who was old enough to be her mother, as the Street's sex tease Bet Lynch.

She ended up playing the Rovers barmaid-to-licensee for 25 years, and then went back for further stints before admitting she wasn't up to it any more.

Julie was a strange woman. To say she was mischievous is an understatement. I've had some laughs with her. But oh, how she loved to lead the Press a merry dance!

She was in and out of scrapes with the producers for years. She enjoyed telling you one thing, then doing the opposite.

Julie was married four times, with a few affairs in between. She had a son, Gary, when she was only 17. Then she married Ray Sutcliffe when she was 18, but was divorced shortly after. She then married Tony Rudman, but actually parted from him at the wedding reception, and that was annulled very quickly.

Her third husband was Richard Scrob, in 1985, but that didn't last long. He died two years later.

Then came a strange, much-publicised affair she had with well-known professional footballer John Fashanu, twenty years her junior, who was said to be gay. He later committed suicide.

After years of denying rumours of being lesbian and/or transsexual, Julie married husband No.4 – Scott Brand, a handsome hunk much younger than she was.

She revelled in all the publicity her love life attracted, and she began to think that anything Hollywood could do, she could do better, right there in Manchester on her own doorstep.

Once or twice, I inadvertently got caught up in Julie's romantic adventures.

In 1983, she revealed that she was madly in love with Bill Gilmour, one of the Coronation Street directors. And they announced their engagement. Julie, then 40, even told her colleagues, "For the first time in my life, I know what true love is."

At the same time, she admitted that she had jilted an American boy-friend, rich airline executive Richard Scrob.

Her marriage to Gilmour in Manchester was all set. The wedding date was fixed, Julie had Anne Kirkbride (Deirdre Barlow) as her chief bridesmaid. They'd booked the wedding reception and planned a honeymoon in Greece.

But then three weeks later, we found out it was all off. Julie had changed her mind.

She broke down in tears in the studio while recording scenes for The Street.

One of the actors told me, "Julie was distraught. She was so upset she could hardly act in the scenes." And a member of the production team said, "We have all been told quietly that the wedding is off."

When I phoned the Manchester hotel where they were having the wedding reception, they confirmed that it had been cancelled.

I knew Bill Gilmour very well. But I had the unenviable job of having to phone him to ask if it was true – was the wedding on or off? He was pretty broken up, but he said that he didn't know what was happening. He was still trying to sort things out himself.

In the end, it was called off. Julie went back to playing Bet Lynch. And Bill resumed his job as a director.

Now, fast forward a year. Everything was back to normal, when I suddenly received a phone call from one of my contacts on Coronation Street, telling me that Julie Goodyear was buying champagne for her fellow actors at lunch-time because she'd just been married.

When I checked this out, it seemed that during a lunch break in mid rehearsals, Julie announced to her colleagues, "I've got something special to tell you all. I'm now Mrs. Richard Scrob."

It came as a complete surprise to everyone. Julie had recently gone off on a Caribbean holiday. And, apparently, she had married her old flame Richard Scrob, who was 47, and lived in Los Angeles.

During the celebrations, she assured the producers she would not be leaving the show.

But the TV company would not confirm anything, except to say, "Julie seems to be amazingly happy. But she is not wearing a wedding ring. If she has got married in secret, then we must congratulate her and wish her well. We are obviously pleased that she is not leaving us. As far as we know, Mr. Scrob is not with her in Manchester. He is back in America."

Later that night, it was confirmed in Barbados that Julie was married there, earlier in the month. And actor John Cleese, star of Fawlty Towers, and an unknown woman were said to have been the only witnesses.

Julie signed a new contract, as Bet Lynch was about to take over as the manager of the Rovers Return.

Sometime after all the fuss over Julie's wedding, we still hadn't seen this mysterious Mr. Scrob. Then, quite suddenly, Julie announced that her son Gary was to marry. And then, even more intriguingly, that she was expecting her husband Richard Scrob, who still lived in the States, to come over and accompany her at the wedding.

The wedding was on a Saturday, and the Press had a real field day. Although I was off that day, I went over to Yorkshire, mostly out of curiosity, but also to keep an eye on it for the Sunday Mirror, and to add my two-penny-worth if I wanted to.

It was a mad scramble. The church was invaded by dozens of Press photographers, all fighting to get the best pictures. Then the mysterious Richard Scrob turned up and climbed out of the wedding car with our beloved Julie on his arm. They stood and posed for pictures. I felt quite sorry not so much for Gary Goodyear, but for his lovely young bride. This was supposed to be her wedding day. But it was her new mother-in-law who took most of the limelight.

At the wedding reception, they had a team of heavies to keep the Press out and make sure no one got in without an invitation. But I couldn't resist it. I went quietly and knocked on the door and asked if there was any chance of a few words with the bride and groom, pointing out that I was an old friend of Mrs. Scrob. As I expected, I was politely but firmly told that the married couple did not want to give any interviews. Fair enough, I thought. And went home.

A couple of days later, on the Monday, I just happened to be around the Granada studios. As I was walking down a corridor, I heard a yell, turned around, and it was none other than Julie herself. "Hello, Mr. Irwin," she said, a little sarcastically. "I'll tell you something. We were having a look at the video film of the wedding last night, and it was a scream. I've never seen such a Press scramble in all my life. And you were there, right in the middle. I spotted you, jumping over the church gravestones to avoid the crush. I was howling. I must show you them some time." She never did. But we had a good laugh together.

When it came to weddings, Julie may have been an old hand at matrimony, but Bet Lynch wasn't. She had dozens of affairs and one-night stands, but she was always the tart left on the shelf.

Then in 1987, the producers decided it was time that Bet should get hitched. After 17 years of serving pints behind the bar, she went off to marry Alec Gilroy, the dodgy club owner played by roly-poly actor Roy Barraclough. And they did it in some style.

They filmed the wedding at a church in Bolton and tried to keep it secret. But the news leaked out, and when I turned up as an uninvited wedding guest, with a photographer, there were 30 or more members of the public hanging around the church anxious to catch a glimpse of the not-so-blushing bride.

Joking with me later, Roy Barraclough swore that he heard a woman spectator comment after the ceremony, "Bet's too good for that horrible little weasel."

Alec's best man was played by Tony Booth, making his debut in the show and tackling his first acting job since the death of his wife Pat Phoenix. Tony told me, "I'm hoping my character might spin off into more than just two episodes. The last year has been an absolute nightmare for me. This will help to lift me out of it."

The marriage, in fact, was all a bit of a joke for the producers, because Julie herself was single again after three divorces. While Alec, who was then 51 and a lovely quiet man, was very definitely what they called a confirmed bachelor.

Julie left the show in 1995 after 25 years, but then returned seven or eight years later to make a comeback. By then, the show had changed, they were doing more episodes each week, and it was far more frantic. She couldn't cut it anymore, so reluctantly retired.

Julie always lived up to her wild, outrageous image. At the height of her fame, when Bet Lynch ruled the roost, she had a series of Granada Press officers at her beck and call. There was one particular bloke from the Press office who used to indiscreetly tell some pretty outlandish stories, particularly about Madam Goodyear's antics. He was expected, he said, to be on call for her day and night. And one night, quite late, having received a phone call from her saying she wanted to see him urgently, he turned up at her house, and she was in the bath.

Feeling a bit awkward and a little embarrassed, he hovered outside the bathroom door. But to his surprise, she then said, "Why don't you come in and join me?"

So what happened? I wanted to know. "Well, what do you think? We had a hell of a night," he boasted.

I was never quite sure whether that story was true or not. He was a boastful little sod. And I wondered exactly what he told his wife when he got back home that night.

On the other hand, nothing would surprise me about Julie.

PAT PHOENIX

When Pat Phoenix finally decided to leave Coronation Street she did it, as she did everything in life, with a gesture of high drama. She dropped her "I quit" bombshell in a one-page letter to Bill Podmore, the show's executive producer, after storming into his office, knowing that it was going to cause the maximum impact.

She had been there, as the Street's middle-aged sex symbol Elsie Tanner, from Day 1 for 22 years. Now at the age of 59, she'd had enough. Her contract was due for renewal in two months' time, but she had already been offered a new 12-month deal along with other members of the cast.

When one of my spies inside Granada tipped me off, I went on the phone immediately to Pat. "Yes, I have resigned. That is definite," she told me. "Beyond that, I can't say anything, Ken, until after my present contract expires. I can't go further into the reasons why I'm quitting. I will be in breach of my contract if I say any more."

I made one or two quick phone calls and was told by one of her closest actress friends that she was simply fed up with playing the same character, she thought the programme was on the decline, and she didn't want to stay there for ever until she dropped dead. "I've told her she would be crazy to leave. She may not be the glamour puss any more. But The Street is safe, the money is realistic, and she can make a lot more with personal appearances."

Even Tony Booth, her long-time boyfriend, tried to persuade her not to leave. But she was determined to go.

When I went on to Bill Podmore, he was clearly shocked by events. "All I can say is that Pat has been in to see me," he said, before dashing off to the pub to drown his sorrows.

It was obviously a big news story, and I had it to myself as an exclusive. But before going into print, I made a call to Granada's Chief Press Officer Norman Frisby at home to get the company's response.

First, he wanted to know how I had got the story. When I told him I had talked to Pat and also to Bill Podmore, he said, "Well, I've heard nothing of this. I will check and phone you back." Ten minutes later, he phoned and confirmed my story was true.

Fine. I immediately filed my story through to the office, stressing that it was exclusive. It was then about 8 pm.

Later, I was at home, after dinner, and I got a call from the News Editor, saying "Ken, I thought this story on Pat Phoenix was an exclusive?" "It is," I said. "Why?"

"Well, Granada have put out a statement to the Press Association confirming the whole thing." He then read out to me the news story which PA had put out.

I couldn't believe it. This meant that every newspaper would now have the same story, courtesy of Press Association.

Immediately, I called Norman Frisby to find out how the Press Association had become involved, and he said, "I gave them Granada's statement."

I was furious. "Why?" I asked. "You know I had that story exclusively. Why did you give it to PA?"

His answer amazed me. He said quite simply, "Because if you run it on your own in the Mirror, I will have all the other papers on the phone to me later tonight, chasing it up and asking me to confirm it."

"So?" I said.

"Well, I want an early night. And I don't want phone calls from the rest of Fleet Street," he said. His excuse was so incredible, it was hard for me to take in. I was livid. I had known Norman a long time, both as a journalist friend and in dealing with him as a Press officer, but I took this is a stab in the back, and a really spiteful bit of work.

As far as I was concerned, he had been totally unprofessional. Giving my story to PA just so that he could have an early night...well, it was beyond comprehension. I told him what I thought of him in no uncertain terms and slammed down the phone. When I told my News Editor later of Frisby's excuse for involving PA, his language was worse than mine. "Tell him next time you see him that he is a c+++ with a capital C!" he said.

Next day, we had the whole of the front page: "TV star's bombshell. Elsie To Quit The Street" (with a picture of Pat and Tony Booth, at home). Unfortunately, all the other papers had the story, too. Thanks to Mr. Frisby and the Press Association.

When Pat finally left The Street, there were many critics who said she would never work again, that she was too type-cast as Elsie Tanner. But she proved them all wrong. In fact, she used her fame and celebrity status as Elsie Tanner to get her fresh work as an actress.

She went back into the theatre with a long stage tour with Tony Booth as her partner. Tony was the reformed hell-raiser with a lot under his belt – one marriage, one common-law wife, four daughters, many love affairs, a lot of drinking, two bankruptcies and a horrific fire accent which nearly killed him – and he had moved back in to live with Pat.

Two years after leaving The Street, Pat was back on TV with a brand new six-week sitcom specially written for her – Constant Hot Water, in which she played a landlady at a seaside boarding house. And Tony, who had then given up the demon drink, was also back on TV ten years after finishing as Alf Garnett's layabout son-in-law, Mike the Scouse git, in Till Death Us Do Part. He had landed a role as a publican in the ITV soap Albion Market. So they both had cause for celebration.

Pat's new series was being filmed in Bridlington, and I went up to interview them both, and the three of us had dinner together. I'd never seen them quite so happy before.

"I'm as nervous as a ten-year-old," said Pat. "I was stuck in a rut in Coronation Street. And it wasn't until I was 60 that I plucked up the courage to wave goodbye to Elsie Tanner.

"Meeting up with Tony again changed my whole life. I became as free as a bird. I started living again. I'm really thrilled for Tony. He's a very talented actor and he deserves this break. We've appeared together in stage plays over the last couple of years. Now it's wonderful for us both to be back on TV, even in different shows."

She was now 62, and Tony 54. "As for our home life, we're more in love than ever," she told me. "We're like a couple of daft kids. But I'll tell you this, Ken, we are not going to get married unless I'm pregnant!"

And of her new TV role, she said, "Phyllis Nugent is very different from Elsie Tanner. Elsie was all heart and legs. But Phyllis is very prim and proper. A bit of a Mary Whitehouse character. There's no hanky-panky going on in her guest house. She likes to think she is very refined. She's a very bossy, domineering character. I would hate to live next door to her. If people compare the character of Phyllis with Elsie, I don't care. And if people in the street start calling me Phyllis, instead of Elsie, that's all right by me."

She was so happy that night, and we finished dinner with a bottle of bubbly.

After she completed that six-week series, the shows were screened on ITV. They were funny enough and quite entertaining, but they didn't cause any stir in the ratings. But at least Pat had created another character.

Sadly, that dinner I think was the last time I had a giggle with Pat. For later that year her health went rapidly downhill, and she went into hospital suffering from cancer.

Pat and Tony lived in a lovely rambling old 16th century cottage in the Derbyshire village of Mottram, which they shared with a housekeeper, and an assortment of five dogs and several birds including a talkative parrot.

When Pat was admitted to hospital, they knew it was cancer but didn't know just how serious it was. I went to her cottage and left a bouquet of flowers with Tony to take in to hospital.

I was away for a couple of weeks on holiday in St. Ives, Cornwall, when the news broke that Pat Phoenix had taken a turn for the worse and her condition was so serious, she had only a few days to live.

In those last days, Tony and Pat dramatically decided to get married, while she was on her deathbed in hospital, and they called in a priest.

My office phoned me the day she died, and the Editor wanted me to quickly up-date Pat's obituary and also write a personal tribute to her.

I recall having to phone over my last story on her from a public call-box in St. Ives. It was one of the saddest jobs I ever had to do.

However, not long after Pat died, I had a phone call from Nell Hayward, who had been Pat's faithful live-in friend and housekeeper for many years. She wanted me to go over and see her. Just to talk about Pat, she said.

Pat regarded Nell as her "Big sister." They met just after the war and Nell became Pat's dresser. When Nell's mother died, Pat took her into her own home and Nell shared Pat's cottage for the last 15 years, right up to the star's death. Whether it was to sew a button, pop a champagne cork, or provide a shoulder to cry on, Nell was always there to help. She knew Pat's innermost secrets as well as the men in her life.

Nell herself never married. "The man I loved got killed in the war, and I never met anybody else. But I've had a few boyfriends, and so did Pat. We both had affairs, and shared some secrets, the way women do about men," she told me.

Over the years, she knew most of Pat's boyfriends, as well as her husbands. Taxi-driver Bill Nadin was Pat's childhood sweetheart and her first love – in fact, she lost her virginity to him. But they drifted apart and lost touch.

Pat married a young actor called Peter Marsh in 1953, but the marriage lasted only a year. Then Bill Nadin came back into her life quite by accident, when Pat hailed a taxi in Manchester – and Bill was the driver.

With Pat now established as the star of Coronation Street, Nadin became her manager, chauffeur and live-in lover. "Bill did absolutely everything for her, but they never got around to marrying," said Nell.

Then Pat met actor Alan Browning, who was playing her husband in The Street. "Suddenly one day she told me she was giving up Bill to marry Alan. I wondered why at the time, but I think she liked that little piece of paper, the marriage certificate," said Nell.

Bill Nadin and Pat remained friends and both had a share in a country pub in Derbyshire. But Browning completely swept Pat off her feet, and they married in 1972. "She was crazy about him. He was a lovely fellow and could be very charming. But we didn't know about his terrible drink problem," recalled Nell.

"In the end, there was nothing Pat could do for him. He was an alcoholic. He'd go into hospital, she'd have him home, and we'd look after him. But just when we thought he was all right, he'd start drinking again."

Eventually, the booze killed him. Pat couldn't even bring herself to go to his funeral. Their marriage had been over for three years.

Then Tony Booth came back into Pat's life. They'd known each other as young actors and appeared on stage together. It wasn't until years later when Tony was terribly burned in a fire accident that nearly killed him, that Pat confessed to Nell that they'd had an affair.

When Pat met Tony after his accident, she got a terrible shock. He was as thin as a rake, was badly scarred and his hair had turned grey. "But Pat liked challenges," said Nell, "and she helped Tony get his life back together. The first time Tony visited the cottage, I saw Pat coming down the stairs to greet him. If you could have seen the joy in her face. She was just like someone in her twenties. I knew immediately 'Oh yes, this is it.' From that moment on nobody was going to be able to do anything about this affair, although lots of people tried. I knew this romance was for real. Tony moved in to the cottage with us shortly after."

But Nell lived for two years with the dreadful knowledge that Pat was dying of cancer. "When she first heard of the cancer, she told me but swore me to secrecy not to tell Tony or anyone of her illness," she said. "It was awful having to keep that secret for so long."

As we talked, Nell broke down in tears. She'd been Pat's friend for 40 years, and for the last 15 years she was Pat's handywoman, secretary, cook, and closest confidante. Yet only a week after Pat's funeral, Tony Booth brought in a married couple to keep the house for him, and Nell, in her late sixties, had to move out.

She now lived on her own in a little terraced house in Leeds, which was where I met her. She admitted that she was hurt when Tony told her she would have to move but accepted his decision.

"Tony and I haven't had a row. I must face the fact that I'm not wanted any more. I just have to try and make a new life for myself," she said, fighting back the tears.

After Nell's mother died in 1972, Pat had invited her to move in with her and Kitty Smith, Pat's old housekeeper.

Nell first met Pat through an actress friend, Jean Kitson, for whom she made costumes. "I went into Jean's dressing room in a Bradford theatre and the first thing I saw was a pair of long legs up against the wall in cami-knickers. It was Pat and she was doing her exercises. She said 'Hello, you must be Nell. Jean's told me you are a dressmaker – can you finish this waistcoat for me?' She made me laugh and we became friends immediately."

But there was not much laughter about when Pat told Nell the grim news that she had cancer. "We were at Eastbourne and she and Tony were in a show. Pat came in from a shopping trip and said, 'I've got cancer, but I'll never speak to you again if Tony or anyone else finds out.

"She said the cancer wasn't terminal at that stage, but she was coughing up blood and the hospital had found a shadow on her lung. But Pat came home one day and said, 'Nell, I'm clear. Get the champagne out.'"

But the moment of hope was short-lived. "We all knew she was dying," said Nell, "And when Tony eventually broke the news to me, I said 'I know – she told me she had cancer two years ago, in Eastbourne, but begged me not to tell you.'

"Tony just said, 'I don't know whether to admire you or not.'"

The final months of Pat's life brought such sadness, Nell told me. "The doctor was giving her tablets, but she was eating them as though they were dolly mixtures. I knew she wasn't going to recover. I have never seen anyone change so much within a couple of weeks."

Nell's only regret was that she was not at Pat's wedding when she married Tony in a moving deathbed ceremony with only a few close friends present. "I hadn't a clue they were getting married. I don't think Tony knew himself until that morning. So who actually suggested marriage, Pat or Tony, I still don't know. I never asked him.

"Tony phoned me from the hospital and said, 'Nell, get a taxi over here as quickly as possible and I'll pay for it.' My heart sank – I feared the worst.

"When I finally arrived at the hospital, they were married. They'd done her room up lovely. Pat looked at me and simply said, 'Come here and give me a hug. I'm Mrs. Booth – but not for long.' Then she said, 'Have a piece of cake, have some champagne.' Instead I had a cup of tea."

Nell saw Pat for the last time two days before she died. "I was in her room at the hospital. There was me, Tony, and her very old friend Ernst Waldner. Pat made us all sing hymns. She made us all kneel on the floor and say the Lord's Prayer.

"Pat was saying 'Kneel, Nell. Kneel.' Pat had an oxygen mask on. She then touched us all, and said, 'That's it – goodbye!' Then she slipped into unconsciousness. The men were so upset, they left. I stayed alone with her. My mother had died in my arms, so I was used to death. I tried to tidy her hair, and I was holding back the tears. I kissed her gently goodbye.

"Then I had the awful job of getting Pat's clothes out of the wardrobe and taking them back home.

"The day she actually died, I had to go into hospital myself for treatment to my hands. It was in the ambulance on the way back home when the driver said, 'Pat died earlier this morning.'

Nell knew that it was going to take a long time for her to get over Pat's death. "I still hear her voice, and I can see her lovely face," she said. "We had some really wonderful times together. I've been through the bad times and the good times with her. She was a lovely person.

"Pat could have been a very, very rich lady. But she spent it as fast as she earned it – particularly over the last couple of years. A lot went on having the cottage improved."

It was clear that Pat's death had created a huge hole in her life. But Tony Booth had to move on, whether Nell liked it or not.

I must say that I always got on well with Tony. He wasn't everyone's cup of tea, but there was a lot more to him than the randy Scouse git which he played so convincingly alongside Warren Mitchell. In fact, Tony once told me that he was sorry he had ever taken on that part, because he knew he was never going to get away from it for the rest of his life. And how right he was.

TONY WARREN

By his own admission, Tony Warren had always been a conceited chap. Starting out as a child actor, he retained that theatrical arrogance and egotistical grandeur throughout his life, even after becoming a writer.

He was not the easiest fellow in the world to work with in his days at Granada TV.

Long before Coronation Street went on the air, his colleagues were accustomed to Warren's tantrums and tears. He was a promotions script writer and after working on the People and Places programme, he was moved in to work with producer Harry Elton, who put him in with a team of writers, adapting for TV the stories of Capt. W.E. Johns and his famous war-time hero Biggles.

Unfortunately, Tony didn't take too well to the new job. He later told me, "I was going slowly mad. I felt I wanted to throw the typewriter through the window. Asking me to write scripts for 'Biggles' was like asking Charles Atlas to do a fan dance. It was something totally alien they were expecting me to do."

One day, he flipped. He clambered on top of a filing cabinet in the office and started to scream. He was told to come down, but he refused. "I hate writing Biggles," he yelled. "I don't even know anything about bloody aeroplanes. I'm not coming down until I can write something I know about."

There must have been something about the sight of a six-feet-plus man of 22, doing his nut on top of a filing cabinet, which fed some grain of sympathy into Harry Elton, for he kept his patience remarkably well.

"What do you know about?" said Elton. "Get down from there and bugger off out of my sight for 24 hours. But I shall want to see you back in front of my desk with a real, original idea for a show by tomorrow."

Warren relented. He climbed down, left the office and went home. He stayed up all night, and then walked back into Elton's office exactly 24 hours later, almost to the minute, with a complete 30-minute script. It was titled 'Florizel Street' and was based on an assortment of neighbours living in a cobbled street, with back yards and outside lavatories, just like he remembered from his grandmother's house so many years ago.

Harry Elton liked the script but wasn't sure how to sell it to the powers-that- be on the top floor. "Write a memo about it for Upstairs," he told Tony. "And make it snappy but literate."

The memo he came up with took Warren two days to write: "A fascinating freemasonry, a volume of unwritten rules. These are the driving forces behind life in a working-class street in the North of England. The purpose of Florizel Street is to examine a community of this nature and, in so doing, to entertain."

It was, he admitted later, quite the most pompous thing he had ever set down on paper. But miraculously it did the trick. The Granada bosses liked the idea of the new drama series. And the day that Harry Elton burst into the office and screamed at Warren, "We're all but on the air, son," there was nothing the tall, gangling youth could do but break down in tears.

The rest is history. Tony wrote the 'pilot' show for The Street and the first batch of scripts while still on the company payroll as a £30-a-week continuity writer. For a long time, this was a distinct source of embarrassment to him. Granada later offered him an exclusive seven-year contract, but he turned it down. He was afraid of "selling" away the next seven years of his life. But he was getting bored with The Street and when the producers brought in a well-organised team of scriptwriters, he found himself a very small cog in a giant machine, and he strongly resented this.

Instead, he settled for a 12-month contract, where he was paid for the scripts he wrote, plus a very small payment for each programme as a credit for the original idea. He also collected one or two bonuses in the form of cheques from Granada. One was for £500. Even then, Tony told me later, "I would much rather have had a crate of champagne and a note signed 'With love' from somebody. Anybody would have done."

At one time, Tony was living at Hayfield, a little village in the Peak District about 15 miles from the studios. I got a phone call one day from a local store manager, a greengrocer or butcher, who asked if I was interested in what he thought was a good news story on Tony Warren. "What is it?" I asked. "Well, he has run up quite a big bill with me, and I'm having trouble getting paid," he said. "Mr. Warren is always making excuses. But I've warned him if I don't get paid, I am going to sue him. Do you want to print the story?" I told him I'd look into it.

When I phoned Tony at home, I told him of this chap's complaint, and asked him if it was true and if he had any comment to make. To my surprise, he let out a mighty scream and went off the line, leaving me hanging on the phone. Then someone, a young man, picked up the phone and yelled at me, "I don't know what you've said to my friend Tony, but he's just ran out of the house into the road. If any harm comes to him, I will hold you personally responsible," and he slammed the phone down. I honestly can't remember whether I wrote a news story or not, because it was all so trivial and melodramatic. But if I did, I may well have said simply that Mr. Warren declined to comment.

Eventually, Tony grew tired of working at Granada and stormed off and left Coronation Street because he felt they didn't want him anymore. He wrote his first play for the theatre and called it Strumpet's Daughter. It was all about a female impersonator. The play flopped. It went on tour but failed to reach London, folding prematurely in Sheffield.

Warren then turned his attention to films, and Brian Epstein, manager of The Beatles and several other pop groups, approached him to write a screen play for Gerry and the Pacemakers. They decided on the title – Ferry Across The Mersey. But after two or three months, Tony collapsed from sheer nerves and tension, and said he couldn't do it, so they agreed to part amicably, and Epstein had to bring in another writer to take over the script.

Tony went to pieces, and for a time thought he would never write another word again. One day, in a fit of depression, he burnt all the copies of his original Coronation Street scripts. He explained this to me, "I did it out of sheer frustration, annoyance and bitter disappointment. I was very resentful."

He also publicly disowned the TV show which had given him virtual overnight fame, if not the fortune that sometimes goes with it.

After Granada removed his name from the list of credits on the programme, he went on record as saying, "I'm only too happy not to have my name associated with the programme as it is today. I did not go to its 500th birthday party, but I wouldn't mind attending its funeral."

Warren found himself broke, and he was being chased by the Inland Revenue tax man, so he took off for the Continent and earned a meagre living doing a drag act on stage. He wrote himself a cabaret act when he was in Austria, in which he sang saucy songs in German and also did impressions of some of the Coronation Street characters.

"I was just running away. I felt that Coronation Street had ruined my life," he told me. But he couldn't go on running forever, and he eventually returned to Manchester. And when Granada sent him an invitation to the 6th birthday party, he went back and ended up crying on the shoulder of Harry Kershaw, who was then the producer. "Harry, can I come back, please?" he begged. Kershaw said, "Let's go and have a drink and talk about it."

But it wasn't as simple as that. The programme had moved on. Next day, Kershaw brutally told him, "Write one script for us – we'll commission that. Then let's see." It was a nasty taste of reality for Tony. He did write a few more scripts, but it didn't work out.

Instead, he went away and wrote something completely different. The War of Darkie Pilbeam was a three-part drama series (again, a case of harking back to his childhood days of the 1940s).

When I went to his home in Hampstead to interview him once, we carried a feature in the Mirror, asking why the man who created Coronation Street was not earning a penny from it any more. Sidney Bernstein, boss of Granada, saw this and immediately put him back on the payroll. I received a phone call from Tony's agent, saying, "Thanks for your article. They have now agreed to put his name back on the screen credits, and he will receive a small payment for every programme."

When he wrote his first autobiography, titled I Was Ena Sharples Father, he gave me a copy, and signed it: "For Ken. Having got page 74 out of my system here is the author's first book and his home telephone number." Page 74 was having a go at me and reminding me of my first Coronation Street crit in the Mirror.

Tony went on to write more books and gave up on television.

There was another amusing incident between Tony and myself. Some years ago, when I was with the Mirror in London, I received a phone call. It was Tony Warren, whom I hadn't seen or heard from for some time. He said he had a wonderful idea he'd like to kick around with me and asked if he could see me. He suggested we meet at the BBC's Broadcasting House. I agreed a time, and we got together, late afternoon, for some tea.

Tony was bubbling over with enthusiasm. He had this marvellous idea for a new drama series, he said. He was going to call it The Seven Deadly Sins and it would run to seven scripts, each one based on a different sin. He asked what I thought of the idea. I said, "Well, it sounds original. I don't think it's been done before. Yes, I think it might work."

He was like an enthusiastic schoolboy, and so grateful for my approval. "Right, you've helped me make up my mind," he said. "That's my next new project. I'm going to start researching it straight away."

Then he suddenly said, "Can you lend me some money?" I looked at him, puzzled. "The banks are closed now, and I've not got much money on me. But I want to go off and commit my first sin," he said.

"What do you mean?" I asked. "I want to go and see if I can commit adultery. Can you lend me, say, £30?" And he explained that before he could start writing, he would have to experience each of the seven deadly sins, to make the scripts more authentic. He assured me that this was the way he worked, and it was essential he did some research by experiencing everything for himself.

I gave him £30 on the understanding that it was strictly a loan. He said, "Right, I'm off to Soho. I can't wait to get started."

His agent eventually sent me a cheque. I didn't see or hear any more about The Seven Deadly Sins. To my knowledge, it never made it onto the TV screen.

A lot of water has flowed under the Manchester Ship Canal bridges since then. Tony, after a lot of tears and heartbreak, was very much back in the Coronation Street fold. In recent years, he was always first up on stage at any awards ceremony.

He was so proud of the fact that Coronation Street was his original baby, even though it did grow completely out of his control.

When Tony died early in 2016, there was a lot of sycophantic fawning that went on. He was hailed, in death, as some kind of literary Messiah who revolutionised TV drama in the 1960s, which was nonsense of course. Most of it was way over the top and came from people too young to know all the facts, but just happy to jump on the bandwagon and be in the limelight for a day or two.

Tony and I had a very ambivalent relationship over the years. But there is no doubt at all that he had a unique talent for getting underneath the skin of the characters he wrote about.

And there are a lot of people who should be eternally grateful to Warren for their careers. Not only the actors who are still making a living from Coronation Street, but the Granada company itself for the millions they have made out of producing the programme for more than 55 years.

SOME WHO SURVIVED...

WILLIAM ROACHE

As the only member of the original cast to have survived, Bill Roache went into the Guinness Book of Records as the longest-serving soap actor in the world.

He's still there, well into his 80s, after more than 55 years in the same boring role. But he's certainly had his ups and downs over the years.

In 1991, he sued The Sun, its editor Kelvin McKenzie, as well as me, for libel. Although he won the case, he then had to pay out a fortune in legal fees, after losing an appeal and being told by a Judge that he was a "very greedy man." Then he decided to sue his own lawyers for wrongful advice, lost the case, and later was declared bankrupt.

When he devised a board game called Libel, which he thought might make him a fortune, it flopped.

Then, much more serious, he was arrested in 2013 on suspicion of raping a 15-year-old girl, which he strenuously denied. But then he appeared at Preston Crown Court, when he was charged with a further five counts of alleged indecent assault against girls aged between 12 and 14.

He was eventually found not guilty and cleared of all charges, in February 2014, but Roache had to suffer the indignity of being suspended from the programme during the months leading up to the trial (they wrote him out by suggesting that Ken Barlow had gone off to Canada).

On his acquittal, after three weeks in court, Roache gave a brief statement saying that there had been "no winners" and he was simply anxious to get back to work.

Meanwhile, an image of Ken Barlow was removed from Madame Tussaud's waxworks in Blackpool due to fears it might be vandalised. It was later returned to the exhibition. And Roache went back to work on The Street shortly after.

But he hit the headlines again when he appeared on a TV chat show and he was reported to have admitted sleeping with up to 1,000 women during his earlier years as a so-called sex stud. The Guardian referred to "Corrie's unstoppable sex machine" and brought up again his old nickname of Cock Roache.

He admitted, "I didn't have any control over my own sex drive. But what I did find is that it does not bring you happiness and is not the way to be. I had the opportunity, I indulged, and I can tell you this: it's not worth it."

He also talked about his brief affair and one-night stand with fellow star Pat Phoenix, by saying, "At that time, she had a reputation and I had a reputation, and she just felt we should meet, as it were."

Frankly, I don't think that kind of revelation did him any favours.

Then, early in 2016, Roache brought upon himself a whole load of bad publicity when he suddenly, for no apparent reason, disclosed that actress Anne Kirkbride, who died a year earlier, had been an alcoholic who was battling depression.

It was reported that at the Royal Television Society Awards, he said, "She had been an alcoholic but was off the drink. She was on anti-depressant drugs all her life and then she just started crying a lot. I spent half my life sort of comforting her and trying to get her back on track. We were holding up scenes because she was being weepy." He revealed that

282

Anne had been given three months to pull herself together by the TV bosses. But she succumbed to cancer before she returned. He even added that she had "a right lung full of cancer and a brain tumour."

Anne, who was 60, was suffering from breast cancer, and had died after a stroke.

His badly-timed comments upset a lot of people. This was the actress who had appeared so closely alongside him in the programme for over 35 years and played his wife Deirdre. And his revelations brought him a torrent of abuse on the social network from people who thought he was being nasty and unkind and should have kept these things to himself.

He was criticised in some parts of the Press. One columnist, Jan Moir of the Daily Mail, said this was "One soap storyline we didn't need to know, Bill."

One way and another, I think there are one or two things Mr. Roache has certainly lived to regret.

MICHAEL LE VELL & JANETTE BEVERLEY

Michael Le Vell was a young man I first met when he joined the cast of Coronation Street as trainee garage mechanic Kevin Webster. He was still in his teens, had not done any acting apart from in local drama school, and had gone straight from working in a vinegar factory.

His girlfriend was Janette Beverley, a year younger than him but way ahead of him as a professional actress, because at 19, having had a run in Coronation Street in a smaller role, she was already a TV star, playing Sharon in the popular BBC comedy series Sharon and Elsie, alongside Brigit Forsyth.

She was a lovely girl, Janette, a very attractive blonde with a lot of talent way beyond her years.

After she married Michael (he was 21, she only 20) they bought their first house together, and she invited me over one day to do an interview. As we sat having tea in the kitchen, she fussed around delightfully as the house-proud young newly-wed.

I thought Janette might have gone on to become a really big star. But when Sharon and Elsie finished, she did a few more years of acting, but settled for being the housewife, and then started a family.

Michael of course went on to really establish himself in The Street, and Kevin Webster became a popular character, particularly after he married Sally.

Even with all their ups and downs, the Websters are still there, divorced and separated, but still part of The Street fabric.

Michael has had his problems though, away from the programme. His personal life was fiercely laid open to public scrutiny when his marriage broke up and he was in court, on serious charges of child sex abuse.

He was eventually found not guilty, but the trial at Manchester Crown Court went on for seven days, during which he confessed that his heavy drinking had ruined their 25-year marriage, and that he had been unfaithful. He told the court that he had several one-night stands throughout his marriage, and had never been man enough to confess all to his wife and his affairs were his "dark secret."

His own barrister described him as a "weak, stupid drunk", a "bad husband," and an "inadequate father."

Janette then shockingly revealed that she was actually suffering from cancer when Michael cheated on her with another woman. And in newspaper headlines, she threatened to reveal more about his dreadful behaviour, and said she was determined to keep her children away from him.

After being cleared of all charges in court, Michael then volunteered to undergo treatment to fight his alcoholism.

Janette was given custody of their two children and was trying to make a new life for herself.

Michael was also trying to get his life back together again and returned to work at the Granada studios. He has been playing the same character for so long now that I doubt he will have the guts or the confidence to ever leave and find other acting roles. Like the other old-timers on the programme, he will be happy to stay on that cobbled back street for the rest of his life. Or for as long as the producers want to keep him.

Well, I suppose it's better than working all your life in a vinegar factory.

EILEEN DERBYSHIRE

Alongside Ken Barlow, Eileen Derbyshire has now become the other ancient monument in The Street. Another great survivor. She is also well into her middle 80s and still going strong. Well, maybe not strong, but still doing a gentle breast stroke while swimming in the shallow end of television.

Eileen, who comes from Urmston, Manchester, started out as an extra in four episodes in 1961, after working in the theatre and travelling around with various Repertory companies. She then took on the role of Emily Nugent on a permanent basis.

She's been playing Emily so long now that she is the longest-serving female cast member in a British soap.

Apart from being jilted at the altar by Leonard Swindley in the early days, (or did they jilt each other?), the only really memorable thing that has ever happened to Emily in 50 years or more, was the famous scene when her husband Ernest Bishop was shot dead in a dramatic wage-snatch in the local factory.

It really has been a pretty uneventful life for Emily Bishop, and why Eileen, once a very fine actress, has stuck it out all these years is very hard to understand.

Or maybe it isn't. As an actor, you choose which path to take. Either you play it safe and stay in a comfortable job in a TV soap with reasonably good pay for the rest of your life, or you take a chance and prove how good an actor you are by taking on different roles. Eileen quite clearly settled for comfort and security.

She always shied away from publicity, anyway. I did a few interviews with her in her early days, but she was never one to enjoy talking about herself and had little of interest to say except for her love of classical music.

A very private person, she hasn't changed much over the years. Eileen was married only once – to Thomas Holt. Her only son, Oliver Holt, is now a sports journalist on a Sunday newspaper, and she has three grandchildren. She was awarded the MBE in 2010 and lives a quiet life in a lovely part of Cheshire.

Eileen gave up on any acting ambition a long time ago. Longevity is the name of the game. She has now settled for keeping her nose clean, being able to remember her lines and not tripping over the studio furniture.

BARBARA KNOX

There is now a trio of Octogenarians on The Street payroll.

Barbara Knox is another who fell too easily into the trap of financial security which Coronation Street undoubtedly gives to any actor. She went into the programme for a single episode in 1964, as a friend of the young Dennis Tanner, and ended up staying for the rest of her life.

After that first episode, as Rita Sullivan, she returned and became a regular member of the cast in 1972.

Barbara, born in Oldham, left school at 15. Her mother worked in a mill, her father in a foundry. Her first job was as a telegraphist in the Post Office, before she made her stage debut at Oldham Coliseum Theatre and became a dancer and singer. After turning to acting, she had small parts in TV shows like George and the Dragon, A Family at War, Never Mind The Quality, Feel the Width, and Emergency Ward 10, and even did a few sketches in Ken Dodd shows.

But once she had her feet under the table in Coronation Street, it was obvious that Barbara Knox was there to stay.

As the popular Rita, she was married three times – to Len Fairclough, then Ted Sullivan, and eventually to Dennis Tanner. In between the husbands, there were lots of boyfriends, the most notorious being Alan Bradley, who tried to kill her before being hit by a Blackpool tram and ending up in the graveyard.

In real life, Barbara has been married and divorced twice, and has three children. Along with her good friend Eileen Derbyshire, she likes to keep her life private and has never courted publicity.

The only blemish the ageing Barbara had on her character was when she hit the headlines in 2014 by being arrested and charged with drink-driving in her home town of Knutsford, Cheshire.

She later pleaded guilty and was banned from driving for a year and fined £3,000, with £1,750 costs.

As Rita, she continues to knock the gin-and-tonics back in the Rovers Return, though. In fact, these days, she does very little else but run her little general store and spend the rest of the time supping with Norris and Emily.

I suspect, at her age, she'd be scared to death if they came up with any bigger scenes to do.

HELEN WORTH

What can we say about Helen Worth? Now one of the stalwarts of The Street, she came in as a teenager in 1974 and has been with the programme for more than 42 years. Unbelievable.

She still plays the mercurial Gail. But over the years she has had so many marriages and so many changes of surname. She was originally Gail Potter. Then Tilsley, Platt, Hillman, McIntyre, and Rodwell.

Her mother is hairdresser Audrey Roberts, and Gail now has three children, Nick Tilsley (Ben Price), Sarah-Louise Platt (Tina O'Brien) and David Platt (Jack Shepherd). Plus grandchildren.

I interviewed Helen several times in her early years, and always found her to be charming. But her TV character has changed so much and so drastically, that she has become a joke.

These days, with a face like a cheeky chipmunk, Gail changes her personality almost as often as she changes her cardigans. She has become everything from a precocious teenager to a nutty mum, a crackpot granny, and it wouldn't surprise me if she ends up as an axe murderer.

Gail has been around for so long that the producers now know they can pull any crazy stunt and she will happily go along with it. So much for integrity.

CHAPTER 38: JUST MEMORIES

SOME FUNNY, SOME SAD, SOME EMBARRASSING...

There was a time at the Mirror, when I was the Show Business Editor, when the paper's Editor liked to have weekly lunches on the premises, and we invited big-name VIPs, like top politicians, businessmen, and celebrities to meet the Editor and top staff. Once a month, it was a showbiz lunch, and I was responsible for inviting TV stars or people from the entertainment world to come in and amuse the Editor and the hierarchy.

They were often really jolly occasion, and I quite enjoyed them. But it was sometimes a bit of a headache getting big names to come along who I thought the Editor would get along with.

Once, I recall, we had Angela Rippon with us, and she was terrific because it turned out that when she was first trained as a journalist, she had been on provincial papers in the West country but had never worked on a national. And she said, "It was always my ambition to work on the Daily Mirror, but I've never been in this office before. You would never give me a job here, but here I am having lunch with the Editor - and all because I read the News on the BBC!"

Angela was great company, and for a while we became quite good friends.

But it was always a problem trying to get the right "mix" of guests for those Mirror lunches. One of the jolliest lunches I ever organised was when I invited Joan Collins, and she jumped at the chance. But who could we get to join her? Then I also invited John Mortimer, the barrister and writer and author of that wonderful TV series Rumpole of the Bailey, and with him Leo McKern, the actor who played old Rumpole.

It turned out to be a very long, but wonderful lunch. Joan Collins, looking as glamorous as ever, is a witty, intelligent woman and she got on well with Mortimer, McKern, and everyone else.

They all told some very funny stories, and the wine flowed. The Editor then thanked everyone for coming and said it was the best and most enjoyable lunch we'd ever had in the office.

There was only downside to it, and that concerned Leo McKern. He was a very funny man, but he did like a few glasses of red wine. And after the brandy, he was ready for his favourite party trick, which was rather revolting.

Leo had one false eye (from an accident earlier in life). And when he was drunk, he liked to shock people. He took out his false eye and put it on the table and would then pretend it was something he'd found in his dinner.

It was thoroughly disgusting of course, but it was also quite hilarious, some of the things he did with that false eye. Joan Collins was under the table with laughter.

Never to be forgotten.

TELLY SAVALAS

Telly Savalas, the tough-guy actor who played Kojak, was a larger-than-life character. I once had to interview him. He was staying at London's Savoy Hotel, and we had a few drinks together, over a chat.

He was a really big international star. He'd played baddies and goodies in film Westerns, long before he landed the role as the New York detective chief Kojak.

I found him to be a really intelligent, very articulate man. I got a lot of good stuff out of him.

"Wherever I go, people seem afraid of me. I'm really a big pussycat," he said. And at the end of our interview, he reached over to a box and produced half a dozen lolly-pops.

"Here, take some of these," he said. "I hate the damn things. But because Kojak is always sucking a lolly-pop, the TV people give me these by the bagful and insist I should always suck them in photographs or when I'm in public. To be honest, I hate the taste of them."

I went back to the office with a pocket full of Kojak lolly-pops and gave them to colleagues.

JOHN CLEESE & GARY GLITTER

One of the strangest interviews I ever did was when I went to see John Cleese when he was making a film at Elstree studios. I was shown into his dressing room and he said, "You don't mind if I lie on the floor, do you? Only I've got a bad back."

So we did the whole interview, for an hour or more, with Cleese lying on his back on the floor.

Another strange and rather similar interview I did was with Gary Glitter, when he was at the height of his fame and in big demand as a performer. I went to the Westbury Hotel in London to meet him, was ushered into his room. And there was Glitter, wearing a sparkly gold suit which was probably one of his stage outfits. He lay stretched out on a long couch and had a bowl of grapes on his lap which he fed to himself throughout the whole interview. It was as though he thought of himself as a modern-day Emperor Nero.

EARTHA KITT

Eartha Kitt was probably the sexiest and also the scariest woman I ever interviewed.

We were in Blackpool, and as I was sitting in the room waiting for her, she walked in, dressed in a white tight-fitting trouser suit, climbed on top of a grand piano and said, "Come over here, darling, and talk to me." I then moved my chair closer to her, and she lay stretched out on the piano throughout our chat. She kept leaning over to me, so that sometimes our faces were only inches apart.

She wasn't so much talking, as purring. Her dark, sparkling eyes were constantly focussed on my face. And there was the slightest of smiles playing around her lips throughout our whole time together. It was as though she was deliberately acting out a private seduction scene, to see how I would react. She really did try to live up to her reputation as a man-eater.

Yet she was quite charming when you got to know her. Because I met her for a second time, when she was appearing in a London West End show some years later. We were in her dressing room and she insisted on making tea for us both.

We chatted for a long time and she discussed everything from politics, religion and race relations to the London weather. She then threw in the snippet that her favourite hobby was embroidery, which surprised me a little.

She was an absolutely fascinating woman. And it was hard to believe it when she told me that her grandparents had actually been slaves in America.

SHIRLEY McLAINE

The most fascinating woman I ever met was Shirley McLaine. She really is very intelligent, very witty. She can talk about any subject under the sun.

And for me, she's still got the best pair of legs in the business. But strangely, I observed, she had the oldest hands I've ever seen on a woman, even of her age.

We met in London at a publishing party for one of her books. And she was seriously delightful. She knows how to tease, too. Because one of the bits of gossip she let drop was that she once had a fling with a top British politician, but she wouldn't reveal who he was. It got the Press gang guessing, and the intrigue went on for some time.

The book she was trying to promote was titled "Don't Fall off the Mountain", and it was her first attempt at writing her memoirs. She had written it completely unaided.

She simply cancelled all film plans for a year, had a few typing lessons, took off her shoes, and wrote it, she told me.

Shirley signed a book specially for me - "To Ken. Always Love." - which I still have on my shelves. I also have somewhere an old video cassette in my collection, of her appearing in a TV musical documentary in which she went to Paris and performed on stage with the scantily-clad fabulous Moulin Rouge dancers, as well as with guest star Tom Jones. She was sensational. And, oh, those legs!

DAVE ALLEN

Irishman Dave Allen was one of the most brilliant stand-up comedians I've ever met. Except that he didn't stand up. He sat down on a stool for most of his act, with a cigarette in one hand and a large glass of whisky in the other. And he had the driest sense of humour imaginable.

I once had the temerity to ask him if it was real Scotch whisky he drank, or was it watered down just for his stage act? He was quite horrified. "Of course it's real. Not always Scotch though. Sometimes it's Irish."

Dave was married at one time to Judith, the sister of Mirror Editor Richard Stott, but there was never any pressure put upon any of us to write about him, either in good terms or bad.

Over the years, I interviewed him many times, and he was always very astute and careful with his comments, which I put down to his background, because he started out as a journalist in Dublin and came from a newspaper family.

He was hugely successful as a comedian and had his own series of shows on TV which ran for years. He came under a lot of criticism for telling anti-religious jokes, particularly against the Catholic church. The fact was that Dave made no secret of being an agnostic and I liked the way he used to invariably end his TV programmes by signing off: "Goodnight. And may your God go with you."

One of the strangest and most comical occasions when we got together however was when he was recording one of his TV series, Dave Allen At Large, and I was invited to join him on location in Bournemouth. I was told to bring a photographer and make sure we both had a pair of wellies with us.

I went down to Bournemouth, very curious, accompanied by the BBC's Gay Robertson, who was their light entertainment Publicity officer, and we checked into a hotel for dinner and an overnight stay, because we were required for an early morning photo shoot. Gay, who was on top form, kept assuring me that I would not be disappointed because Dave Allen had something really unusual planned for next day. I was up a lot in the night, and didn't sleep much, due to sheer curiosity of what was in store.

After an early breakfast, Gay had a cab waiting for us, and in five minutes we were down on the seafront at Studland Bay.

There, on a deserted beach, we met up with the BBC production team, and a Dave Allen I would never have recognised. Because he was wearing a flowing gown, a pair of sandals, and beard and a long heavy grey wig, topped by a crown. He was made up to look like King Canute.

"Now, let's see if I can make the sea obey me," said Dave, chuckling away.

A huge throne was placed on the sand, near the water's edge, and Dave was plonked down on it. "Action. Take One."

He then went through this very funny charade of re-enacting one of the most famous scenes in British history - as King Canute commanding the waves to recede.

It was a freezing cold morning, and the tide was coming in quite fast - in spite of Dave bellowing continuously, "Go back. I command the waves to go back."

This must have gone on for an hour or more, and after four or five "takes", Dave was still sitting there on his throne, now smoking a cigarette, with the water coming up almost to his waist.

In the end, he just jumped up. "Stuff this for a lark. I'm bloody freezing. My feet are turning blue. Get me a stiff drink - and I don't mean coffee."

The whole thing turned out to be quite hilarious. And after completing the rest of the morning's filming, he ripped off his whiskers, and we went off and had a pleasant location lunch and a long chat.

My photographer, who had been snapping away during the filming, said later, "Just as well I brought my wellies, Ken. It was really quite cold out there in the sea."

Of course, we ended up with a very unusual and exclusive picture-feature, which made the trip very worthwhile. And Gay Robertson admitted later that she was more than satisfied with the outcome. When I saw the finished King Canute sketch on TV some months later, it made me smile.

Dave was one of the most genuinely inventive of our funny men. He normally shunned publicity and interviews. "I don't like talking about my family, what kind of clothes I wear, what I eat, and all that crap It's of no interest to anyone but me," he said.

As well as being a comedian, he made his bow as an actor on the West End stage in Edna O'Brien's play A Pagan Place and received rave reviews. "I don't see why I shouldn't be accepted as an actor in the theatre and a comedian on TV," he said. "I hate being categorised. Why shouldn't I try my hand at everything?"

But he was happiest doing comedy, even though he was often in trouble for some of his anti-Catholic jokes. He believed that no subject was sacred. His philosophy was simple. "We laugh at the Japanese, we laugh at the Scots, we laugh at the Jews, and we piss ourselves laughing at the Irish. So why shouldn't we laugh at the Pope - providing the joke is funny?" said Dave.

"I'll do a joke or a sketch on any subject – but it's got to be funny. And I would find it difficult to get into the spirit of telling a gag if I didn't enjoy the gag myself."

THE ROLLING STONES

The Rolling Stones were always in trouble with the Press, particularly in their earlier days when they drew a lot of bad publicity for outrageous behaviour in their well-publicised drug-taking periods.

I first met them when they made their bow on the original Top of the Pops show in Manchester, alongside the Beatles and other groups in the Top Ten charts, and I interviewed Mick Jagger and the band from time to time. And I must say that whenever I talked to Jagger, I found him very polite and attentive.

But there was one occasion I can recall when things got a little out of hand. It was when I was still working in Manchester, as the Mirror's

Northern TV Critic, and I had a little office tucked away at the end of the News Room, with a TV set, a desk and chair, and one spare chair which was there for the use of anyone who wanted to pop in to see me. Quite often, a chap called Norman, who was the senior adult messenger, and a very friendly fellow, would come in during his dinner break in the evening and ask if he could watch TV with me for half an hour. I was okay about this, as long as he was quiet and didn't disturb my viewing.

But as well as Norman, we had one or two younger lads employed as messengers, usually there as copy boys (to run around collecting reporters' stories and deliver their copy to the sub-editors).

One day, Norman came in to see me at about 3 o'clock and said one of the younger lads had gone off for lunch and had not returned - did I know where he was? I said I had no idea. Then, about half an hour later I got a phone call. "Hello, Mr. Irwin," said the voice on the other end. "This is Tony."

"Tony who?" I asked. "Tony, the Mirror messenger," he replied. "You'll never guess where I am?" "Okay, where are you?" I asked.

"I'm with Mick Jagger and the Rolling Stones in their hotel. Honestly. I've just left Mick's room now. He's terrific. We've had a few drinks and we've had a smoke. And he's happy chatting to me."

I suddenly realised that the Stones were in Manchester that day, doing a stage gig in the evening.

"What are you doing?" I queried. "Aren't you supposed to be here in the office?"

"Yeah, but I thought it would be good to meet up with the Stones, so I came over to try and chat to them," said the lad.

"And how did you get in to meet them?" I asked. "It was easy. I just said I was from the Daily Mirror, and they sent me up to their room."

I couldn't believe it. I just said to him, "Look, you'd better get back here. Now. Your boss Norman has been wondering where you have been since lunch-time. Tell Mick Jagger we want you back at the office urgently. Get a taxi if you have to."

Half an hour later, a staggering Tony sneaked into my office and fell into the chair. He was smelling of booze. "Hey, it's been great. We've been drinking whisky all afternoon and we've been smoking," he boasted.

Slowly, I managed to get the whole story out of him. It seems he had found out which hotel the Stones were staying at, had gone there and told them he was from the Mirror and wanted an interview with Jagger.

"Didn't they ask for any identification? To see your Press pass?" I asked. No, he said. "Mick just said I looked very young. Then one of them offered me a drink, and it just went on from there."

"How long have you been there?" "Oh, about three hours," he said.

The outcome, of course, was that he was now pretty legless. I didn't even ask him what kind of cigarettes he'd been smoking, and how many drinks he'd had. I asked him what time his shift ended, and he said in about two hours.

There was no way he could have gone back to the News Room and resumed working. He was well and truly smashed.

I said, "Look, you will be sacked if the office Manager finds out about this. You'd better get out of the office and go home. And I mean straight home. Take a taxi. You are in no fit state to get on a bus." And I gave him a couple of quid for his fare.

After seeing him safely off the premises, I went back into the News Room, found his boss Norman and told him that Tony had been taken ill, nothing serious, but I had advised him to go home. So he wouldn't be finishing his shift.

Norman was puzzled why the lad had come to me, and not him, to tell us he was unwell, but didn't make any big deal of it.

Next day however, when I went into the office, I noticed that Tony was back, and busy running around doing his usual job. Rather sheepishly, he knocked on the door and came into my office. He apologised and thanked me for not telling the office manager what had happened.

"Forget it," I said. "But in future, don't go posing as a Mirror reporter - not until you've started shaving anyway!"

That night, his boss Norman came in as usual to watch TV during his break. "That lad Tony is a right little liar," he said. "I asked him why he'd suddenly gone off sick yesterday, and he came up with some excuse about having a few drinks at lunch-time. The cheek of the lad. He's only sixteen. He shouldn't have even been allowed into a pub."

I often wonder what happened to that messenger kid. Although I couldn't approve of his behaviour, I couldn't help having a quiet chuckle.

As for Mick Jagger, he must have thought the Mirror were taking on kids straight from school as reporters. But then, maybe he was too stoned himself to really care.

The PS to this little story was that, come the following Christmas, Norman came into my office and gave me a little wrapped Xmas gift. It was a pair of cufflinks and a tie pin. "Just to say thanks for letting me pop in and watch telly during my dinner break," he said.

ELTON JOHN

Elton John is a strange fellow. Always has been. He's a talented musician, there's no doubt about that, but his ego is bigger than that of anyone I have ever met.

In his teenage days, he started out doing gigs as a piano player in his local pub at Pinner, which was only a mile or so away from where we lived in Harrow.

But the first contact I had with him was when he signed a recording contract with the Dick James office, and they were pushing him very hard for publicity.

He was on Top of the Pops a few times when I was there in the studio. But his gradual rise to super stardom saw him change dramatically.

At the height of his success, I think he began to believe he could walk on water.

I remember once, for one of his birthdays, Elton threw a lavish party and somehow managed to acquire the banqueting hall in the Houses of Parliament for his celebrations.

A section of the Press were invited, and I was one who managed to be on the guest list, and I was quite looking forward to it because I had never been inside the Palace of Westminster before. Everyone was there. A host of stars who were close friends of Elton turned up for the occasion. The drinks flowed and the guests were mingling not only inside the great hall but also outside on the terrace overlooking the river.

The most amazing thing about the evening, though, was the amount of jewellery Elton decided to wear. He had diamond studded ear rings, gold rings on every finger, and a diamond encrusted gold chain dangling around his neck. He posed incessantly for pictures. And a publicist was on hand to point out that we would not be far out if we estimated that the cost of Elton's jewellery for the night was over £500,000.

After I had filed a brief news story about the event, there was little to do except drink the champagne and wander around trying to make conversation with any of the star names who weren't too busy fawning and brown-nosing over Elton.

Comedian Billy Connolly was strolling around, trying to make people laugh and constantly replenishing his glass. And the more he drank, the louder he became.

He suddenly came over to me, stared at me close up, and said, "Why do you keep looking at me?" I mumbled something about not being really interested. But he persisted, "Oh yes, you've been following me around. Are you checking up on how much I'm drinking or something?"

He began to bore me, so I just said, "I don't really care how much you've had to drink," and turned my back on him. And I then decided it was probably time to go home, anyway.

As I left, I turned to look at Elton. He was still the centre of attention, and happy to be toasted over and over again by an enthusiastic coterie of friends. He was just another year older.

The next time I saw Elton was a few years later, in Montreux, Switzerland. I was there with the usual Press pack covering the annual Golden Rose light entertainment festival. We usually went for the full week, watching the so-called best TV entries from around the world, and finishing with a lavish dinner and awards ceremony on the Saturday night.

This particular week, however, Elton John suddenly flew in and was booked into the same hotel most of us were staying at, the lovely old Montreux Palace, overlooking beautiful Lake Geneva. He was there for a mammoth pop music festival, which was to feature just about every top singer and band around at the time.

But then, only a day later, we heard that Elton was checking out because he'd been involved in some sort of row with the producers about who was getting top billing on the show.

The trouble was, Elton was not answering his phone in the hotel suite, the hotel management were refusing to say whether he was still booked in or not, and it quickly developed into a frenzied search to pin down the British singer.

All the Press guys were now congregated in the hotel bar area. It was mid-morning, and the usual serene schedule of watching TV programmes in the Golden Rose contest was interrupted, and in fact ditched altogether. Because we all knew that if we didn't get to Elton, our News desks back in Fleet Street would go ape and would give us no peace until they had some answers.

Then, out of nowhere, a helicopter suddenly appeared above us, zoomed down and landed right in the middle of the manicured lawn of the

Palace hotel gardens. Everyone was puzzled - what the hell was happening? "It's for Elton," shouted one reporter. "He must be leaving."

Fortunately, there was only one main entrance and exit door that led to the gardens "He's got to come through here. There's no other way he can get out," We all agreed. It was a matter of simply waiting to see what happened.

We didn't have to wait long. For without any kind of warning, Elton appeared in the reception area, accompanied by a couple of heavies, and they realised that the only way they could get out to the waiting helicopter, was by going through the Press pack in the bar area.

Suddenly it was a scrum. Everyone was shouting questions as Elton made a run for it. He refused to say nothing, but just turned on his heels and ran for the main door, reporters chasing after him, and the bodyguards pushing people aside.

Once he was through the mob, he simply sprinted as fast as his little legs could take him and was determined to get into the copter without talking to anyone. As he fled off into the sunshine, most of us just stood back and realised it was futile trying to stop him.

But my everlasting memory of that whole silly episode was the sight of one of our colleagues, a skinny young Rick Sky, who was a showbiz reporter for The Sun, chasing after Elton across the lawn, and shouting. "Stop. Come back, you fat little bastard!"

We all burst out laughing, as Elton scampered up the steps of the helicopter, and the plane took off within a few minutes. A bemused Rick Sky (what a name for a pop writer, eh?) strolled back into the bar, wiping the perspiration from his forehead, and said, "God, I need a drink. Who's buying?"

Then it was back to watching the rest of that day's programme entries for the Golden Rose. Hopefully, breaking for a nice leisurely open-air lunch at one of our favourite lakeside restaurants, the Joli Site, with a few glasses of chilled white. And then maybe later a game of crazy golf, before making plans for dinner. Who cares about Elton Whatsisname ?

ROBERT MAXWELL

The ogre Robert Maxwell was to crop up a few times in my life. Apart from my dealings with him at the Mirror (see Foreword), he mysteriously went overboard from his yacht on the very same day that my libel trial with William Roache came to an end. After five days of headlining the news on TV and in the papers with the trial, the verdict and judgement were announced, and we were cleared off the front pages in the later editions by Robert Maxwell's death. That was November 5, 1991.

When he went overboard and drowned (whether he committed suicide or not has still never been proved) he had already raided the Mirror pension funds. He had stolen more than £400 million pounds from the funds, and thousands of Mirror employees thought their pensions had gone forever. Mine included. Some pensioners even committed suicide.

Eventually it was sorted out. The government came to the rescue and became involved. But most of the money was never recovered, it was salted away in foreign banks, and of course his two sons later faced trial for fraud, but somehow managed to get away with it.

However, the PS to my dealings with Maxwell ended when I was on holiday later, with my wife, and we went to Israel. We were staying in Jerusalem, and I decided to go and find Maxwell's grave, because he had been buried on the Mount of Olives, with full Jewish ceremony - that was before they discovered he was a villain and a thieving rogue.

But I took a taxi with my wife up to the Mount of Olives. It was a very hot day. I didn't know exactly where the grave was, so I asked a man who was hanging around the gates of the graveyard. After I refused to buy some ancient foreign coins he tried to sell me, I asked where Maxwell's grave was, and he just waved me in the general direction.

Leaving my wife in the taxi, I clambered over all these gravestones and eventually found the biggest grave of the lot, which I figured would be Maxwell's. It was piled high with stones - which is a Jewish tradition. I couldn't help myself. I decided to take a few stones off the pile. They were quite pretty actually. I bunged them into my pockets and quickly returned to the waiting taxi, where my wife was waiting anxiously. The stones went into my baggage when we returned home.

Some months later, I saw Maxwell's grave on a TV newsreel, so I was convinced it was the right one I'd visited.

I now had these stones, so I used one or two as paperweights on my desk. And the others I put on a water fountain in the back garden.

Well, I thought, now I've got some of Maxwell's old stones. So, in a way, Maxwell is still working for me. And those stones look quite nice as paperweights!

MAGNUS MAGNUSSON

I will never forget the day I spent on Mastermind, when I had to sit in that famous not-very-comfortable steel and black leather chair and face the great Magnus Magnusson. No, it wasn't me facing the tough interrogation under that sinister spotlight, but Magnus. It was his idea, not mine. When the BBC went to Beverley in Yorkshire to record a programme, I decided to go up to the venue and quiz the quiz master. Magnus was in a genial mood and decided that I should sit in the black contestants' chair and ask any questions I wanted, and he would do his best to answer them.

It was a reversal of roles. But he knew what he was doing, for Magnus was an experienced journalist long before he became a TV presenter and quiz master. And he had a great sense of fun, which most viewers never realised because he was usually so stern-faced and serious.

After a bit of lunch, we sat down, and I did an interview with him, before the studio audience came in and the terrified real contestants were ushered in one by one to see if they could prove they were as clever as they thought they were.

Personally, I would never dream of applying to appear on the show. My general knowledge wouldn't be so bad, I hope, but I don't know what my specialist subject would be! Everton football club, maybe? The boring characters of Coronation Street over 50 years, perhaps?

Interviewing journalists is never very easy, because they know most of the tricks of the trade and are not going to be cajoled into giving indiscreet answers (as I found out also with people like Michael Parkinson and Alan Whicker). But Magnus was a canny old so-and-so and we got on very well and he phoned me up after my piece on him appeared in the Mirror, to thank me for being both courteous and accurate, and we became rather chummy.

In fact, so chummy that not long after our Mastermind meeting, he phoned me at the office and said, "Do you want a good story?" I said yes, of course. And he then revealed that his daughter Sally Magnusson was expecting a baby shortly and would be leaving her job at the BBC. "But don't tell her I told you," he said.

"I just thought you might be interested in running a piece in the Daily Mirror." And he gave me her home phone number.

So I then phoned Sally and asked her if it was true she was going on maternity leave and when was the baby due? She said, "Who told you that?"

"Oh, come on, you know as a journalist that I cannot reveal my sources," I said, trying to stifle a chuckle.

"I know who it was," she replied. "It was my father, wasn't it? He's such a blabbermouth. And he's so delighted to be a grandfather." We just laughed together. But she confirmed everything and was happy for me to run the story but emphasised that she was not giving up her TV career for good.

Both Sally's parents were journalists. Magnus, who was born in Reykjavic, Iceland, went to Oxford, and worked in newspapers in Scotland before going to the BBC as a reporter. And her mother, Mamie Bird, was a journalist from the age of 17 and worked for the Express in Glasgow, before marrying and bringing up a family of five children.

Magnus went on to present his beloved Mastermind for 25 years. He became famous for his chirpy catchphrase "I've started, so I'll finish", which he once told me he'd never be able to shake off. "Taxi drivers and people in the street now shout it at me," he chuckled.

Sadly, he died of pancreatic cancer in 2007, aged 78. Sally's mother died five years later, and Sally wrote very movingly about Mamie's dementia.

Sally, with those lovely sparkling blue eyes and the Scottish lilt in her voice, married film director Norman Stone, and has brought up a family of five children as well. She has tackled a variety of programmes with the BBC, including being one of the most popular presenters of the long-running Songs of Praise.

ENGELBERT HUMPERDINK

Engelbert Humperdink was an interesting guy. A suave customer with an air of mystery about him. I once went to see him in concert in Germany. I flew over with Engelbert's PR agent Clifford Elson and we went to his show in Munich. He was on a European tour and it was an open-air stadium. Eight thousand people, a sell-out. And it was a fabulous show.

Afterwards, we went back to Engelbert's hotel and I was invited to join him for dinner, to do an interview with him. We got on very well and had a very enjoyable meal. He was surrounded by his entourage.

But after dinner, I was about to make my way back to my hotel, along with Clifford, who was staying at the same place. As we came out of the restaurant, we bumped into a middle-aged, quite attractive German lady who was waiting in the foyer. As Engelbert came out with us, the woman pounced on him, tried to kiss him, and made a big fuss of him. She then introduced a much younger woman, a tall very attractive redhead, to Engelbert, and said, "This is my daughter. She is a big fan of yours, as I am. Would you like to have a drink with us?" She then quite openly made a play for the singer. "My daughter and I are staying in Munich. Can we join you?"

Engelbert put his arms around the two women and said, "I'm feeling rather tired. I was actually ready for bed."

He just stood there, grinning. Then his PR man Clifford, who was quite a good friend of mine, said diplomatically, "Come on, Ken, I think it's time for us to go. We'll see you in the morning, Engel." So we said goodnight.

Engelbert, this smile on his face, and a woman on each arm as he walked back into his hotel, said, "Yeah, see you in the morning, Clifford. But don't make it too early though, will you?"

CILLA BLACK

Cilla Black was always good for a laugh. But she could be pretty bolshy sometimes if you got on the wrong side of her. As I found out once, myself.

For years, I'd been interviewing her - more or less since her emergence with Brian Epstein and the Beatles - and she loved to talk about her Liverpudlian roots.

But on one occasion, when she was just about at the height of her career and had her own weekly TV series, I arranged with her publicist to do a one-to-one interview with her, and I booked a table for two at a posh West End restaurant.

Everything went well, we had a pleasant meal, and Cilla was happy to chatter away for a couple of hours.

She said Tara, which was her favourite word, gave me a peck on the cheek, and I put her in a taxi in Regent Street.

A couple of days later, my piece on her appeared in the paper – a full page interview, with a nice picture of her. Then came a phone call from her publicist. "Ken, thanks for the piece in the Mirror this morning. I thought it was great. But I've got to tell you – I've had a call from Cilla and she's not very happy. She insists that I pass on a complaint to you."

"What's that?" I asked. "Well, to quote her exactly, she came on and said she'd had a lovely lunch with you but was annoyed because you said in your article that her Scouse accent wasn't as pronounced in real life as it was when she appeared on TV, and you were therefore suggesting that she was exaggerating her accent."

I couldn't believe it. I said, "Well, unless she was putting on a posh accent for me, which I doubt, she certainly does exaggerate the Scouse bit when she's chatting on TV. You know that, and I know that."

He just laughed and said, "Ken, don't worry about it. I thought it was a smashing piece. And I told her if that was the only thing she could find to complain about, then it was fine."

We had many laughs after that, though. I recall Cilla telling me stories of her early life, living in Scotland Road, then working in the Cavern Club cloakroom, before being discovered by Brian Epstein. And she loved talking about her Mum.

When Cilla started earning big money and became a star, she offered to buy her Mum a new house. "She always insisted she wanted a nice house on a main road in a decent district," said Cilla.   She bought a lovely house in Woolton, which is considered quite a posh area. But although she was grateful, after a short while her Mum told Cilla the house was not quite right for her. What she really wanted, she said, was a house with a bus stop outside. "I couldn't believe it," said Cilla. "She actually wanted a bus stop right outside her front garden gate, so she wouldn't have to walk 50 yards to get on a bus." And, of course, Cilla duly obliged. Mum got a new house with a bus stop right outside. "She's really happy now. She can watch people getting on and off the bus, and she has her own door-to-door bus service whenever she needs it," she said.

Cilla could be a tough woman when the mood took her, however. Ask Gordon Burns.

Gordon was the Northern news man who presented The Krypton Factor on ITV for many years and went on to be anchor-man on the BBC's early-evening news magazine programme from Manchester. He was signed up for Cilla's hit show Surprise Surprise, as her sidekick and straight man. They were such close pals that he was with the show for five years.

Then, completely out of the blue in 1992, Burns was dropped for no apparent reason, except that Cilla felt like a change. He was dumped and replaced by comedian Bob Carolgees.

For Burns, it really was a case of Surprise Surprise – you're sacked!

Over the years, we became quite friendly. But I think Cilla always had at the back of her mind, the fact that she had left Merseyside and moved South to live in luxury in leafy Denham, Buckinghamshire, with the big house in acres of ground. And this had to a certain extent alienated her

CHAPTER 38: JUST MEMORIES

from a large section of Liverpool fans. Just the same as with the four Beatles, and Jimmy Tarbuck. She was a born-and-bred Scouser, but she had chosen to leave Liverpool because it wasn't good enough for her anymore!

That's the tough, uncompromising attitude those dyed-in-the-wool Scousers have in life, believe me. That's why they still adore Ken Dodd. Because he became a big star and made a fortune – but he never left. It can be a pretty unforgiving city, Liverpool. Well, they may forgive – but they never forget!

In fact, when Cilla died in 2015, in such tragic circumstances (she had a nasty fall at her home in Spain and was found by son Robert, who had been out for a couple of hours, shopping) and her body was returned to Liverpool to be buried, the public lined the streets and turned out in their thousands to mourn. Our Cilla was back home again! One of them!

She left £15 million in her will, divided equally to her three sons, Robert, Ben and Jack. But she also left property in Spain, a holiday home in Barbados and her house in England. Cilla also left a sum of £20,000 to her housekeeper of 30 years, Penny Walker.

GLENDA JACKSON

One of the most intriguing women I've ever met was Glenda Jackson, the actress turned politician. Not remarkably beautiful by Hollywood standards, particularly in her later years as an MP when she didn't wear any make-up. But I found her remarkably sexy and she had an aura of authority about her which is hard to describe.

Born in a working-class area of Birkenhead, her father was a builder and Glenda worked for two years behind the counter of Boots the chemist before winning a scholarship to RADA at the age of 18 and becoming an actress.

She went on to work with the Royal Shakespeare Company for four years, before breaking into films and becoming one of Britain's most successful truly international stars.

She won an Academy Award for Best Actress in the film Women in Love, in 1969. And I first met her in 1971 when she starred as Queen Elizabeth 1st in the prestigious TV drama Elizabeth R. I managed to get a one-to-one interview with her at the BBC studios, and was shown into her dressing-room, to wait for her to have a break in filming.

When she walked in, fully dressed in period costume, I was immediately shocked because not only did she not look anything like the Glenda Jackson we were used to seeing, but her face was gaunt and white, and she had no hair, with her forehead having been shaved right back, to resemble the old queen. She then revealed to me that she had agreed to have her head shaved completely, to accommodate the wig which she had to have fitted.

It was a strange interview. She was very polite, answered all my questions, and came over as a very intelligent woman. But she was most unlike any other actress I'd ever met. She had a no-nonsense attitude about her, and I remember thinking at the time that this was one tough cookie and I would not like to get on the wrong side of her.

That TV series was a resounding success and she later won an Emmy award for her performance. When we'd first met, she had laughed at my suggestion that she had a sexy image. But when she made the film A Touch of Class, only two years later, there was no way she could ever deny that she was one of the sexiest women around. I loved that film. She was so deliciously sparky and at her brilliant best, and it won her a second Academy Award.

It turned out that despite her Shakespearean background and her rather serious image, Glenda had a great sense of humour. This was displayed in the appearances she made on the Morecambe and Wise TV shows, which earned her a whole new army of fans. The one which stands out, which I saw her do in the studio, was when she played Cleopatra in a sketch with Eric and Ernie, and she completely stole the show from them, getting the biggest laughs and the loudest applause.

They had all the big-names as guest artists – but none better than Ms Jackson!

When she suddenly gave up acting for a career in politics, she became an MP in 1992 and won the seat for Labour in Hampstead and Highgate. Her constituency later became Hampstead and Kilburn.

I wrote to her congratulating her on her new career, and she wrote back to thank me and sent a signed photograph, which I still have.

Always a fierce critic of PM Maggie Thatcher, after falling out with PM Tony Blair, she became a backbencher with a fiery reputation. But after being re-elected, she announced in 2011 that she would be standing down and not seeking re-election at the end of that parliament. Characteristically, she declared, "I will be almost 80 by then and it will be time for someone else to have a turn." True to her word, when the next election came along in 2015, she gracefully retired, just two days before her 79th birthday.

A woman with a lot of spunk. I found myself a great admirer of Glenda Jackson. Both the actress and the politician.

WENDY RICHARD

Wendy Richard was another fiery lady I got to know quite well. She had a sad life, with lots of traumas and heartaches, although she always liked to put on a brave face.

She was a very attractive actress in her early days, so it wasn't surprising that she landed parts in some of those zany Carry On films. But it was her role as Miss Brahms in the BBC comedy series Are You Being Served? which really established her as a TV star in the 1970s. As the daffy assistant to Mrs. Slowcombe in the women's lingerie department, she played her way through some hilarious scenes, and won a whole army of male fans over to the programme.

The trouble was, Wendy was always aware that she was there to provide the glamour. "I'm fed up just playing a glamour girl," she told me. "Because I've got long legs and a nice pair of tits, producers think that's all I am."

A lot of people thought that Wendy was a Londoner, a cockney. But she actually came from Middlesbrough, and moved to London with her parents, who ran a pub.

The best thing that ever happened to her was when the BBC launched EastEnders, in 1985, as their answer to Coronation Street, and she landed the part of Pauline Fowler. She stayed with the show for over 20 years and made Pauline an iconic figure, proving that she really was a fine actress and not just a glamour girl. In 2007, she received a British Soap Award for Lifetime Achievement for her role in EastEnders.

But Wendy's private life was tragic. I interviewed her many times, and she poured her heart out to me. We used to meet for a drink in her local pub on the corner of Baker Street and Marylebone Road, where she could be found most evenings, enjoying her favourite tipple, always champagne.

She would talk about her sad life, about the husbands who had abandoned her.

Wendy's father committed suicide when she was just eleven, and she discovered his body. It was something she never really got over. Then she was married and divorced three times. One husband used to beat her up, she admitted. Another walked out on her after only a few weeks. He said he was going out to buy some cigarettes but never came back, she told me. She even made it sound funny.

She was also diagnosed with breast cancer, had an operation, and was given a clean bill of health, but the cancer returned a few years later.

After leaving EastEnders, Wendy asked David Croft, top producer and an old friend, to write something for her, and he came up with a show called Here Comes The Queen, in 2007. I was invited to go on location with them when they were filming, and she laughed as she told me over tea and cakes, "This part is like an older version of Miss Brahms. But not as glamorous." Sadly, it was one of the last things she did.

Her fourth husband was John Burns, who was a painter and decorator 20 years her junior, with whom she finally found love. They were married in 2008.

But then the cancer returned, and Wendy died in a Harley Street clinic, in 2009. She was 65. Later that year, David Croft unveiled a Heritage Foundation plaque at The Shepherds Tavern in London, the pub which Wendy's parents had once run.

Wendy was the kind of person you just don't forget!

AMANDA BARRIE

Actress Amanda Barrie was what most red-blooded men would consider a really gorgeous looking woman. She was the kind of good-looking girl who would attract wolf whistles when she walked down the street. And she certainly got plenty of male attention, particularly after appearing in the title role of Carry On Cleo, playing the sexy Cleopatra, alongside Sid James and company in the film released in 1964.

She was a Lancashire girl (born Shirley Anne Broadbent) and came from unglamorous Ashton-under-Lyne, before going to acting school in London and training as a dancer. And she was a dancer in the chorus and appeared in nightclubs and West End musicals. But it was the Carry On films which launched her career and made her name. She lived in a flat right in the heart of London's theatre land.

Amanda married a theatre director, Robin Hunter, when she was 32, and continued in stage shows until breaking into TV in the 80s. Then, after several short appearances in the show, she was offered a long-term contract in Coronation Street in 1988, playing Alma Sedgewick, later changing her name to Baldwin when she married factory boss Mike Baldwin (Johnny Briggs).

Playing Alma really established her as a popular TV character and she stayed with The Street for 13 years, until finally being written out when her character died of cancer.

After Coronation Street, she appeared in various TV productions, but it was mostly back to pantomimes.

Then, somewhat surprisingly, Amanda shocked the public by suddenly revealing a well-kept secret. In her autobiography, It's Not A Rehearsal, published in 2002, she announced that she was bisexual.

Although she had been separated from her husband for years, they had never actually divorced. And he died in 2004.

Long before this however, I got a phone call from one of my old Daily Mirror colleagues, saying, "Hey, have you heard the latest gossip?" "What?" I asked. "Hilary Bonner has moved in with Amanda Barrie and they've now set up home together."

I was not entirely surprised. Hilary Bonner was an old colleague of mine and worked with me on the Mirror. She had got into journalism with the Mirror group training scheme in Plymouth, and I first met her when she landed a job with the Sun, as a showbiz reporter.

We would often meet up, along with the rest of the Fleet Street showbiz pack, on routine Press conferences and TV company bashes. And I must say that I always considered Hilary to be a very average reporter, though she was always amiable and friendly.

After a few years on the Sun, Hilary moved to the Mail on Sunday, and was then taken on by Richard Stott, editor of the Sunday paper, the People.

Richard, a brusque little bully of a man, had worked his way up on the Daily Mirror and came through the reporting ranks to be promoted to Features Editor, which meant I worked very closely with him when I was Show Business Editor. He was what we called super ambitious and once revealed that he was determined to be Editor of the Mirror before he was 40.

He was then given his first Editor's job – as boss of the People, one of our sister papers, along with the Sunday Mirror. And as things turned out, Hilary Bonner did well and seemed to forge a good working relationship with Stott.

So much so, that after I left the Mirror in London and asked for a move back to Manchester, Stott was then promoted by owner Robert Maxwell and given the prestigious job of editor of the Mirror. And Stotty then brought in Hilary Bonner from the People and gave her my old job as show business editor.

It wasn't exactly a popular move, and I know that some of the reporters and writers in the showbiz department resented the situation. My old pal Tony Purnell, a good solid investigative reporter, had moved from the People to the Daily Mirror and was then showbiz editor, but was bluntly told by Stott that Bonner was replacing him. And Tony and veteran writers like Jack Bell, Patricia Smyllie, and Tony Pratt suddenly found they were working under a much younger woman who didn't have half the experience they had.

She was quite bossy, re-vamped the department, and even brought in her own male secretary, who was openly gay, was at her constant beck and call, and flounced around the office, not only making the coffee but more or less running the department when Hilary wasn't there. The male secretary bit became something of an office joke. But Hilary didn't give a damn and seemed to enjoy the idea of having a cute, flamboyant little chappie running around at her command.

At one time, Hilary let it be known that she was married. I never met her husband, who was Clive Gunnell, a TV documentary maker well known in Devon and the West country, and he was much older than her. Frankly, I always thought Hilary was a bit butch. She was six-feet-something tall and powerfully built.

The last time I saw Hilary, I think, was when I decided to branch out as a freelance writer, and finally left the Mirror at the end of 1989. She helped them throw a farewell party for me in the London showbiz office, and presented me with a few gifts, including a framed picture by Mirror cartoonist Griffin, of me standing at the bar of the Rovers Return, with busty Coronation Street barmaid Julie Goodyear (or Bet Lynch) serving me a pint.

A few years after I'd gone, Hilary Bonner also left the Mirror and started writing crime books. It was then that she moved in with Amanda Barrie and they became Lesbian partners. Amanda is my age, and Hilary is 13 years younger.

It was reported that they were together for ten years or so when they decided to tie the knot, if that is the right phrase. And they were legally wed, under the new same-sex marriage law in 2014. Hilary's husband Clive had died in 2006, at the age of 80.

It's a strange world, isn't it? Nothing ever surprises me anymore.

CAROL VORDERMAN

I first met the dishy Carol Vorderman when she was an absolute beginner, making her TV debut on the first edition of Countdown, which was to launch the new Channel 4 in 1982. I went up to Yorkshire TV in Leeds for the opening day, to see how the programme was produced. And Carol was teamed up as a presenter to partner Richard Whiteley, who was already well known in Yorkshire from his appearances on local regional programmes.

They made an excellent team, Richard as the pleasant enough question master, and Carol picking out the letters and numbers for the contestants and also demonstrating her brilliant mathematical skills. She was there too of course to provide the glamour, and she was fully aware of that.

When she made her bow at the age of 21, she was an attractive lass, though slightly gawky. But I found her very pleasant to talk to and a bit of a chatterbox. She soon learned the tricks of the TV trade, though, and worked on her image by becoming more glamorous. It then became obvious that Carol was going to attract her own regular army of male fans, which of course the producers encouraged.

Only three years after doing Countdown, Carol was married – to a chap called Chris Mather. But the marriage didn't last long, because about a year later I had the unfortunate job of having to tackle her about a break-up.

Somehow, I got an inside tip-off that all was not well, and when I tracked down Mr. Mather, he was very frank in telling me over the phone that Carol had left him, and he seemed pretty upset at the prospects.

When I went on to Carol, to ask for her side of things, she confirmed that they had split up, and said she was relieved that the news was now out, and I would be doing her a favour by reporting that her marriage was over. She was determined there would be no reconciliation. We duly printed the story. And she was divorced within a year.

Strangely, after that she became quite friendly, and I did one or two features on her, and whenever I was up at Yorkshire TV on other jobs, I would occasionally pop into the canteen and meet her for a cup of tea in the afternoon.

She then stayed with Countdown for 26 years and, appearing fives time a week, became a household name.

It was ironic really, because after leaving university Carol had her mind set on becoming a civil engineer and had a degree in engineering to back it up. But it was her mother Edwina who was responsible for her TV success.

She spotted a newspaper advert, seeking a young woman with good mathematical skills to appear on a quiz show, and she secretly sent in an application form on behalf of her daughter. It came as quite a surprise when Carol was offered an audition, and then given the job.

The only previous experience of any kind of public entertainment Carol had was back in her university days when she appeared as a backing singer in a pop group called Dawn Chorus and the Blue Tits, which was fronted by lead singer Liz Kershaw, later to make a name for herself as a radio DJ.

Carol was married for a second time, in 1990, to Patrick King, and had two children. But she divorced again after ten years.

Professionally, she became a human dynamo. As well as her Countdown job, she branched out into writing books on Maths and produced audio games and websites, as well as appearing in TV commercials, which made her a fortune. At one time, she was said to be the highest-paid woman on TV, earning more than a million pounds a year.

When her TV partner Richard Whitely (or Twice Nightly, as he liked to call himself) died in 2005, it was the end of a 23-year working friendship for Carol, and she began to tire of the show. She received an MBE in 2000, and was voted Rear of the Year in 2011, after undoubtedly helping to bring bums back into fashion. It was something she was quite proud of.

Finally bowing out of Countdown in 2008, she was replaced by the younger and very attractive Rachel Riley, who soon tried to prove she could out-do Carol by wearing even shorter skirts. But she was never really able to match her for personality or her mathematical genius.

Carol then threw herself into a flurry of other activities, mixing her penchant for making money in her various business enterprises with taking on new TV shows, joining ITV lunch-time show Loose Women, and then presenting the Daily Mirror's annual Pride of Britain awards.

The last time I bumped into her, a few years ago, she told me, "You know me, Ken, I'm only happy when I'm working. I enjoy being a workaholic."

She has had a few well-publicised romantic partners and continues to change her image on a regular basis. But now well in her late 50s, she is looking much more glamorous than she ever did in her younger days.

Our Carol is living proof that women can improve with age. Or is that just the view from an older man's outlook?

THE GOONS

Without doubt, one of the most amusing and enjoyable jobs I ever did was when I took The Goons out "busking" for the day. I've forgotten whose idea it was, either Spike Milligan or Harry Secombe, because I knew them both quite well. But one of them suggested, "Why don't we go busking down Oxford Street?"

Wow! What fun this could be. So I arranged it. There was Spike, Harry, and they roped in Peter Sellers. Spike was on trumpet, Sellers had a drum, and Harry had a penny whistle. It was a very odd musical combo.

They all dressed in old clothes, like tramps. And they sat outside Selfridge's store in Oxford Street. I had a photographer, shooting them with a long lens, from across the road, and I was inside Selfridge's doorway, watching it all.

Buskers are ten a penny around there, until the police move them on. They started playing some tunes, and Spike was even adding the occasional vocals. No one recognised them at all. A few people dropped money into the cap they had on the pavement.

After about an hour, Peter Sellers said, "Come on, I've had enough of this. Let's go and have some coffee."

We all went over the road to the Kardomah café, and we counted up the takings in the cap. I remember Harry counting up the coppers and silver and announcing in a loud voice, "We've got £1.58. We're rich!" It wasn't until they started fooling around in the café that people then recognised them.

They were great. I got a very good offbeat picture-story out of it.

Spike, in particular, would do absolutely anything for a laugh. Once, he told me, he and Eric Sykes were returning back to their joint office after one of their regular long drinking lunches, when they were passing the window of an Undertaking firm. They stopped, Spike got Eric to lie down on the pavement outside, pretending to be dead, then Spike knocked on the Undertakers door and shouted, "Shop!"

There was also the story, which Spike told me, of Peter Sellers buying himself a new Rolls Royce. One night, Sellers phoned Spike and said, "I'm coming over to see you. It's very urgent."

It was two o'clock in the morning and Spike got out of bed. When Peter arrived, he told Spike he had a problem. At first, Spike thought he was ill. But no, he told Spike he had a mysterious squeak in his car, and he wanted Spike to help him find where the squeak was coming from.

So they went outside and Sellers persuaded Spike, who was still in his pyjamas, to climb into the boot of the Rolls. "I'll drive around slowly, and you see if you can detect exactly where the bloody squeak is coming from," said Peter.

Reluctantly Spike agreed to do it. So off they went. Unfortunately, they were stopped by a police car, who observed this Rolls Royce being driven very slowly round and round the block. They stopped the car, saw Sellers driving it, and asked him what he was up to at that time in the morning, thinking he was drunk or something. Sellers explained, then opened the boot, to reveal Spike lying there, giggling like a lunatic.

The policeman took one look at him, returned to the police car and told his fellow officer, "Oh, it's those two. They're both mad. Let's go."

On one occasion, I went down to South Wales to interview Harry Secombe, and see him on stage during a nationwide tour. He put on a great show, in front of a packed theatre. We agreed to meet next day for a chat. But Harry surprised me by turning up at my hotel in his Rolls Royce. "Come on," he said, "Let's go for a ride. I'll show you where I was born, before we have lunch."

We then drove around Mumbles, with Harry pointing out the various places he remembered from his childhood. And we ended up having fish and chips for lunch sitting in his Roller.

"Smashing this, Ken. We must do it more often," he giggled.

RICHARD BURTON

When Prince Charles married the young and beautiful Diana Spencer on July 29, 1981, it was all set to be biggest and most colourful Royal wedding in history, certainly as far as television was concerned.

Every member of staff on every newspaper was busily engaged on some aspect of the wedding. On the Mirror, they didn't quite know what to do with me, so I was finally dispatched to report on how the wedding was being covered on radio. It was one of the lesser tasks, but I was more than happy to do it because it meant me simply going over to the BBC's Broadcasting House in London and listening to the radio all day. And somehow, I managed to wangle things with the BBC so that I could sit in the studio, alongside the great Richard Burton, who had been signed up to assist with the commentary.

No one had a voice as good as Richard Burton, and the BBC considered it quite a coup to tempt him into sitting throughout the whole day's ceremony, to add his own personal comments in that rich baritone voice which had made female hearts flutter for years in his string of big-screen movies.

They were not expecting a huge radio audience. Everyone would be in front of their TV sets to watch the events. But I didn't care about that. I was just happy to be sitting alongside the great Hollywood actor, though initially a little worried, I must admit, as to how he would accept me.

As it turned out, he was great. After being introduced to him, I was just told to sit down and keep quiet during the actual broadcast.

Burton was an acting legend, and fully lived up to the image wherever he went. He was outstandingly handsome, and even that deeply-pocked skin gave his face a rugged, brutal charm. I was not surprised that this fellow was considered one of the world's most attractive men and had women like Elizabeth Taylor happy to be seduced by him. In their case, they'd been married not once, but twice, then divorced again.

At this time, of course, he was considered a little past his best. His wild drinking days were behind him, he had overcome being an alcoholic, and he had settled down and was married again – to his third wife, Suzy Miller.

In the studio, they had drinks on hand, to be replenished regularly throughout the afternoon. "What would you like to drink?" Burton asked me politely. "We've got coffee, tea, or water. Nothing stronger, I'm afraid," He smiled, as though anticipating my question. "Me? I've been on the wagon for years. Don't touch a drop these days. I'm a good boy now. Well, it depends on how you interpret the word good!"

Some years before this, I had been with Peter O'Toole and he had told me of the wild nights of drinking he had shared with Burton, Richard Harris and others in the film rat pack.

But the man I sat with throughout the Royal wedding was quiet, polite, and surprisingly courteous. "Diana really is a beautiful young woman," he kept saying as we watched the ceremony on the studio monitors.

At the end of his stint on radio, when the microphones were switched off, he turned to me and said, "Well, I've really enjoyed my day." We chatted for a short while, before he finally looked at his watch, and put on his coat, declining the offer of a drink down in the BBC bar.

"I must be going," he said, "The little lady will be waiting for me." And he smiled enigmatically.

And it was funny. It sounded just like any other working man, tired after a day's work and simply wanting to get home.

As for me, I'd enjoyed the day, too. After all, it was hardly hard work. And I'd spent the day with a true movie legend.

Three years later, Burton died, at his home in Switzerland – with a new wife, Sally Hay. He was only 58.

DUDLEY MOORE & PETER COOKE

Peter Cooke could be a nasty piece of work. Brilliant though he was as a comedian, I always got the impression when I met him that he resented the success that others had, not only his old adversary David Frost, but also his working partner for so many years, Dudley Moore.

Watching him on so many TV chat shows, he came across as someone who was immensely funny, yet he had an in-built spitefulness which meant that he was never really happy unless he was putting someone down or scoring points off them.

A pity really, because he had a good brain, a talent for coming up with witty ad-libs, and there was no doubt that he could have been one of our finest British comedians, had it not been for his personality shortcomings. I think Peter envied the fact that Dudley had made a big name for himself in the States, while he hadn't.

He also had a drink problem, too, of course, which helped to shorten his career.

Yet when he teamed up with Dudley Moore, some of those Pete and Dud shows, Not Only...But Also in the 60s, were the best thing he ever did. The way they worked together was uncanny. They'd start out with a script, and then deliberately forget half of it, preferring to ad-lib their way through, each trying to make the other fold up with laughter. Some of those sketches remain classics.

It was only when Dudley moved to America and made a name for himself in Hollywood, that the obvious friction set in between the couple.

At one time, Peter Cook said, "There is a whole generation now who can only identify me with the foul-mouthed Derek and Clive records I made with Dudley. I want to put that right by doing lots of stuff on my own."

Peter, the son of an ex Colonial office bigwig, was ear-marked for a diplomatic career. "But it didn't happen that way," he said. "I simply walked from stardom in university revue to stardom in the outside world."

With his tiny friend now making more than a million dollars a movie in Hollywood, wasn't Peter thirsting after the same superstar scene? "Not really. Dud always wanted to be an enormous star. I don't," he said. "At one time, I had ideas of doing romantic leads and I did a film which had me running around with a gun in my hand. But I looked such a berk, I couldn't carry on."

Nevertheless, Peter did have Hollywood offers of massive amounts of money and he kept pushing up the price to see how far the US moguls would go.

Asked near the end if he was happy with his life, he replied, "I'm content for a large part of my life, which I think is par for the course. It's an unreasonable expectation to be happy all the time."

I loved Dudley Moore, though. He was a smashing bloke, and I got to know him quite well and interviewed him several times. He was the same age as me – well a month younger, actually.

He was only five-feet-two-and-a-half tall ("Don't forget that half inch. Size does matter," he would joke) and was born with a club foot, with his left leg shorter than his right. It meant he had to have a built-up boot to help overcome a distinct limp.

But he would never let this get him down. Not in public anyway. And he was always tremendously bubbly and full of fun. You couldn't be in his company long without having a laugh.

Women adored him, which was something he liked to reciprocate. He got all sorts of nicknames – from Cuddly Dudley to The Sex Thimble. The film 10, opposite that sex goddess Bo Derek, really turned him from a little funny man into an international superstar. He was married and divorced four times.

Having got to know him well in London, when I went to New York to meet him - when he was filming the movie Arthur in 1981, with Liza Minnelli and Sir John Gielgud – I noticed he had changed. Oh, he was still the mischievous old Dudley, the Brit who wanted to talk about life back in England, but it was inevitable I suppose that his huge film success in the States had given him a new air of confidence.

We had lunch together, and he immediately sat down at a nearby piano and started to run through his repertoire for me. He really was a very fine pianist and could play anything from jazz to classical. I could have listened to him playing jazz all day.

Sadly, when Peter Cooke died in 1995, at the age of 57, it affected Dudley very badly. It was reported that for weeks after Peter's death, Dudley would ring him on the phone at home, just to listen to his voice on the answerphone.

Dudley's career then came to an abrupt end, with his failing health. He suffered a degenerative brain disorder, couldn't function properly, and ended up in a wheelchair. He died in New Jersey in 2002, only a month before his 67th birthday, from an attack of pneumonia.

DIANA DORS

Diana Dors was a really fun character, in every sense of the word. She was this country's answer to the great Marilyn Monroe, and without doubt became Britain's No.1 sex symbol throughout the 50s, 60s and 70s. And it wasn't all down to her acting either.

She was born in unglamorous Swindon in 1931, and her name was actually Diana Mary Fluck, but when she was 14, she lied about her age, got herself a place in drama school, and at 16 was signed up by the Rank Film organisation as a starlet.

Inevitably, she had to change her name – to Diana Dors. And she later explained, "They asked me to change my name from Fluck. I suppose they were afraid that if my real name was up in lights and one of the lights blew a fuse...well!"

After a few early films, mostly sex romps showing off Diana's obvious physical talents, she became a half-decent actress, went to Hollywood, appeared with some big- name stars, and even turned to singing and played the cabaret circuit in Las Vegas, before coming back to settle in England.

She had a tempestuous private life. She was married three times. Her first husband, Canadian Dennis Hamilton, whom she married when she was 20, helped make her a star but then unashamedly exploited her until he died eight years later. Her second, Richard Dawson, she divorced after seven years. And her third husband was Alan Lake, an actor from Liverpool with a wild streak who was much younger than Diana, and also cashed in on her fame. I interviewed Lake a couple of times, and I must admit I didn't particularly like, or trust him. He was far too flash for my liking.

The thing about Diana was that we all had her home phone number, and on quiet days when there was not much news around, I would ring her up, and she would always come up with a story or two. She was such a gossip, and she loved publicity. She would do anything to get her name in the papers.

When the films began to dry up, however, Diana started making the headlines in a different way. Having gone through twenty years or so as a

317

vamp and something of a sex goddess, she became quite famous for organising naughty celebrity parties at her home, rambling Orchard House in Sunningdale, Berkshire. She liked to call them adult parties rather than orgies, and she would invite big-name stars and friends as well as an assortment of pretty young starlets. She didn't care about the bad publicity this generated. In fact, she thrived on it. It was even reported at the time that Diana would have video cameras strategically placed throughout the house, particularly in bedrooms, to record all the activity. And she would then enjoy watching the video film footage next day with her husband. She really did believe in living life to the full.

She was reputed to have had several lovers, starting in Hollywood with her first big co-star Rod Steiger. One of her later lovers was comedian Bob Monkhouse.

When her looks faded, Diana put on a lot of weight, and found herself fighting a battle against cancer. Even then, she refused to let it bring her down, and she moved into television, with her bubbly personality, and became popular as a celebrity co- presenter on the TV-AM breakfast show. She also put her name to several autobiographical books, outlining some of the naughty things she'd got up to.

Sadly, Diana died in 1984 at the age of 52. She had two sons with second husband Richard Dawson, and one boy with Alan Lake, Jason, who was barely a teenager when she died.

The tragedy that followed was quite unbelievable. After giving away all Diana's clothes and belongings to charity shops, Alan Lake then dramatically gave a last interview over the phone to Jean Rook, a columnist on the Daily Express, then went into a bedroom at home, put a shotgun into his mouth and pulled the trigger. He was 43, it was only five months after Diana's death, and he chose the date of exactly 16 years to the day since they had first met, to kill himself.

The mystery that followed Diana's death, and that of her husband, was even more weird, though. Before she died, Diana claimed to have left a large fortune – something like two million pounds – to her son Jason in her will. But the money was hidden away in foreign banks, and it could only be accessed via a secret code, which was in the possession of Alan Lake.

After Lake's suicide, the code was never found and the exact whereabouts of the huge sum of money remained a mystery. Bizarre? It was a tragedy which, knowing Diana and her strange sense of humour, one could be forgiven for thinking that she was secretly having the last laugh.

Whatever her faults and frailties, she was certainly an unforgettable woman.

BARRY HUMPHRIES

Barry Humphries was a rum character. I first met him long before he started getting dressed up in a frock, a wig and those eye-catching glasses to become Dame Edna Everage.

The Australian funny man came to Britain in 1959 to try and make a name for himself as a comedian. He became friendly with Peter Cooke, Dudley Moore, Alan Bennett and Spike Milligan, and teamed up with them to play The Establishment and other trendy nightclubs in London in the early 60s.

When the BBC decided to take a chance by giving him his own TV series, I was the first TV reporter to interview him. I'd never heard of him, when I was invited by the BBC to meet him, and I went to the TV Centre in White City where he was waiting for me in the Reception area and we then went to the canteen to have a chat.

He was a wild, talkative man, very physical, and spilling out with zany thoughts and ideas. And I must confess I didn't quite know what to make of him. But I came away, wrote a piece for the Mirror TV page, and waited to see how he progressed.

The TV series was called The Barry Humphries Scandals, and it didn't exactly set the world alight, but in a way became the forerunner of Monty Python's Flying Circus and other crackpot shows.

A few years later, however, Humpries completely transformed himself into a drag act, with Dame Edna, and then that awful slobbering character, Aussie ambassador Sir Les Patterson. He shot to fame and has been playing the exuberant Dame Edna ever since, and now into his old age.

When he first started out with his strange drag act, I suspect a lot of people thought he may have been gay. In fact, Barry turned out to be a randy old sod. He was married and divorced three times, before marrying for a fourth time. He married Lizzie Spender in 1990, and they've been together ever since.

He must like wedding cake, as they say!

OZZY OSBOURNE

The first time I met Ozzy Osbourne, they gave me a set of ear-plugs to drown out his music. It was in New York, and the office had sent me to cover one of his concerts at Madison Square Garden.

I was in for a shock. I must have been to dozens of music shows over the years, but never one quite like that. This was the frienzied Ozzy fronting Black Sabbath, the first of the really wild heavy-metal bands, at the height of their fame. It wasn't my kind of music at all, and I was grateful for those ear plugs which someone gave me on the way in. But it was a night never to be forgotten.

The ridiculous thing was, I was not on my own, but had as my companions two readers who had won a Daily Mirror competition. The prize was a three-night stay at the famous Waldorf Astoria Hotel, plus two seats at the Black Sabbath concert.

I still don't know which they enjoyed most - the luxury hotel, or the concert.

The winners turned out to be a very friendly middle-aged father and his teenage daughter, and they admitted when I first met them at Heathrow airport, to escort them on the trip, that they were not really heavy-metal fans, and had just entered the competition in the hope of winning a free holiday to the US.

Now that was fine as far as I was concerned, but I wasn't sure what the reaction would be by Ozzy and his mates when I took the couple back-stage to meet the band after the show.

As it turned out, Ozzy didn't give a damn. I don't think he even knew we were there half the time. He was well away with the fairies. Oh, he was polite and quite friendly with us. But it was clear that after a gig like that, with twenty thousand screaming fans going wild in appreciation, and Ozzy trying to unwind in his dressing-room, he was not in the mood to really entertain a Daily Mirror writer and two unknown prize winners with any great enthusiasm.

Chubby Ozzy was dripping with sweat as he flopped into a dressing-room chair. Outside the fans were still screaming for more. They had lit thousands of tiny candles to illuminate the arena, and many of them held up wooden crosses, the symbol of Black Sabbath.

"Just listen to them. They were fantastic tonight," said Ozzy. "I'm a wreck, but that reaction makes it all worthwhile. I come alive only when I'm out on stage. It takes me several hours to wind down afterwards.

"Tonight's show was a big one. We've played Madison Square Garden before, but it's always like climbing Everest."

Black Sabbath were a much bigger draw in America than they were in Britain. They were on a hectic world tour, playing 30 concerts before getting home for Christmas, with further tours of Japan and Australia lined up.

Ozzy found time, though, to talk to me about his early life before he joined up with his Brummie pals to form Black Sabbath. "As a kid, I was a ruffian, a real tearaway," he said. "I tried all kinds of jobs but ended up as a professional burglar. But one day I got caught breaking into a house, and I ended up getting three months in prison.

"It was a real lesson for me. That's when I got together with the other lads to form a band. It was music that saved me from becoming a hardened criminal."

As this wild man and the rest of the band showered and got changed, it gave me a brief insight into just what kind of life these top rock n roll stars lead.

Tables were laid out, full of food and various drinks. And we were invited to help ourselves to anything we wanted. Then, when Ozzy re-emerged, freshly dressed, he joined us, a bottle of beer in hand, and tucked into some food.

We were there for about an hour, and he was warned by his back-room staff that a lot of the fans were still hanging around outside, waiting for him to leave.

To my surprise, we were invited to leave with them. "Come on. Be a rock star for a night. Come and see what it's like," screamed Ozzy, making it sound like a dare.

We piled into one of those great long black limos, with Ozzy sitting next to me. I think there were three cars in the convoy. Then, with a roar of "Okay, let's get outta here!" from Ozzy himself, the cars shot out of the back doors of the building at a hell of a speed, avoiding hordes of screaming fans who were trying to bang on the windows in a mixture of happiness and frustration. As I looked back through the rear window of the car, I remember feeling quite sorry for all the kids still waving and shouting, in the early hours of the morning. But hey, that's rock n roll!

Ozzy, of course, went on to become one of the greatest rock legends of all time. Not so much for his singing, maybe, but more for his antics both on and off stage. He admitted to 40 years of alcohol and drug abuse.

But he finally sobered up a lot, and in early 2000 he became a star all over again when he and wife Sharon agreed to do what turned out to be an outrageous reality TV series with their family, inviting cameras into their Hollywood home to see just how they lived. To say it was an eye-opener would be an understatement.

Sadly, though, the Brummie wild man was diagnosed with a condition which is an early form of the dreadful Parkinson's disease. And was told he must be on medication for the rest of his life.

BARCLAY JAMES HARVEST

Another rock band I went abroad to cover was Barclay James Harvest, made up of three rockers from Oldham, in Lancashire. I flew out to Berlin to cover a concert they did in 1980, which was unique in that they were doing it for nothing.

The band – John Lees, Les Holroyd and Mel Pritchard – had been playing together for about 14 years, when they decided to do this one-off concert in Berlin.

It was the time when the dreadful Berlin Wall still separated the East from the West. But they insisted it was not a political demonstration, and simply because they had missed out the city on a big European tour they had done earlier that year. I was invited to join them, to do a report. And I can honestly say that it turned out to be one of the saddest and most depressing experiences of my life.

The decision for the band going there was for purely nostalgic reasons. And John Lees told me, "As a band, we got to the stage where we knew we weren't going to advance any further in Britain.   Then we decided to try our luck in Germany – and wham! It all started happening for us. We love the people of Berlin. Despite the Cold War, the people are always nice and friendly – on both sides of the Wall.

We hope they will be listening to us on the East side as well. They can't help it really – we've got the loudest sound system it's possible to have."

On the Continent, their record sales were phenomenal, and they were soon headlining sell-out concerts. But the sad fact was that, because of the political set-up, they were not allowed to perform in Eastern Europe.

That night, however, they staged their concert right up against the Western wall of the famous Brandenburg Gates. And when they hammered out their thunderous music for two hours or more, with an audience of ten thousand fans cheering them on, it was estimated that at least the same number were gathered simply to listen on the other side of the wall. It was heartbreaking to think that those poor unfortunate people in East Berlin were still trapped, and in poverty, all those years after the end of World War 11.

The Mirror headline in our pop music page after that show, was: "Rock against the Wall - Ken Irwin reports from Berlin."

That's why I, and millions of others around the world, cheered and cried tears of happiness when that awful wall was finally knocked down in 1989 and the divided city of Berlin became united again.

NEIL DIAMOND

Singer Neil Diamond had a kind of magical charm about him. I first met him when he came to London to do a show for ATV, and Lord Lew Grade held a Press conference to launch him and insisted in his usual flamboyant manner of handing out giant Havana cigars to everyone as a bribe in return for some publicity.

I've always liked Diamond. He's got a great voice and a really nice personality to go with it. I was up there in front, asking some of the questions, because although Neil Diamond was big as a recording artist, he had not done much television, certainly not in this country.

After the Press conference, he hung around and chatted happily for quite a long time. And when his first show for ITV came out later, it proved a big hit. Everyone was happy. Particularly Lew Grade.

Fast forward some 35 years or so, and I spot an advert that Neil Diamond is on a British tour and is doing one night in Manchester at the Evening News Arena. I happened to mention this to my daughter Susan, and she said "Oh, I'd love to see him. I've always been a fan of his."

This came as a complete surprise to me, because I had always associated her more with Michael Jackson, the Osmonds and other artists I'd got tickets for her to see on Top of the Pops when she was a teenager. So I bought two tickets to see Neil Diamond in action. And it turned out to be a great show. Even if most of the audience was made up of blue-rinse old ladies, some of them in wheelchairs.

But then, complete humiliation. I found myself the only one still sitting down, listening to the ageing Mr. Diamond go through his routine. Everyone around me in the stalls was up and dancing, waving their arms around. Including my energetic, almost ecstatic daughter. I'll never take her to a pop concert again.

323

GERRY AND THE PACEMAKERS

Whenever I go on one of my favourite little jaunts and take a trip on the Mersey Ferry (which isn't so often these days, but I enjoy it when I do) I find that I can't get away from Gerry Marsden.

Remember Gerry? The little guy who shot to fame in the 60s, alongside the Beatles, as frontman with the group Gerry And The Pacemakers.

Although the Beatles became worldwide stars, Gerry had his fair share of hit records. One of them, of course, was Ferry Cross The Mersey. It wasn't a bad song, a catchy tune with some soulful lyrics, particularly if you were a Liverpudlian and in need of some nostalgia. The first time I heard it, I liked it. But then, hearing it time and time again over the years, it could become a little tedious.

Now, I positively hate it. Because, for some strange reason, that record Ferry Cross The Mersey is still played at the start of every journey the ships make, from Liverpool, from Birkenhead, and from Wallasey. And whereas it might provide the odd bit of entertainment and a smile from tourists taking their first trip across the river, it has become a bloody bore to those who travel that route more often.

So, please, can I appeal to the Mersey Ferry Services, to toss that scratchy old record into the river, and find another more up-to-date song to play, or else sail off in silence!

Another of Gerry's songs which also became a big hit is You'll Never Walk Alone. This is still played at Liverpool football ground before kick-off at every match and has become something of a supporters' anthem to the Anfield faithful.

Now a lot of people – football supporters included – think that this was an original Gerry Marsden song. Wrong!

That song was from the 1945 Rodgers and Hammerstein musical Carousel, and was recorded by a number of great artists, including Frank Sinatra, Judy Garland, Andy Williams, Doris Day, and even Elvis Presley, long before Gerry and the Pacemakers decided to record it, when it became a No.1 hit for them and stayed top of the British pop charts for four weeks.

I haven't met Gerry since I last interviewed him, over tea and biscuits at his manager Brian Epstein's house in Woolton, fifty-odd years ago. Gerry, a true Scouser, still lives in Wirral, regarded as the posh side of the river.

It's not that I begrudge him all those record royalties he must have earned over the years. Just that he supports the club on the wrong side of Stanley Park.

As for that song, I heard one comedian recently joke, "They only play You'll Never Walk Alone as a warning to visitors - nobody in their right mind would go out alone at night in Liverpool!" Cheers, Gerry!

MOIRA STEWART

Moira Stewart was one of the most intriguing and tantalising women I ever met. And with the dirtiest laugh imaginable. She was the dark lady with the deep velvety voice who read the news on TV for so many years. In fact, she was the first black woman to be appointed by the BBC, in 1981, as a regular newscaster.

We first met when I found myself sitting next to her at an awards dinner in London, organised by the TV and Radio Industries Club in 1988, when Moira was named TV Newsreader of the Year. But she was so shy and withdrawn, she gave the impression that she was embarrassed to receive the award.

Once we got chatting, however, she loosened up a bit, the wine helped, and it turned out to be a very enjoyable evening. I even got one or two tit-bits out of her that I thought would make our TV pages, and she ended up by thanking me, and saying, "I've had a lovely evening. I hate these ceremonies and dinners, but you really made me laugh."

Next day, my Editor Richard Stott happened to hear that I'd sat next to Moira at the dinner, and he dashed down to see me. "I want a full-page feature on her – now," he demanded. "This woman never talks to anyone. She's a recluse. I want her in tonight's paper."

Well, I hadn't got enough from the dinner to write a big feature on her, so I then phoned Moira at the BBC, and she surprisingly agreed to see me in her BBC office that afternoon.

We then spent an hour or so in a face-to-face interview, which she admitted she had never done before, because she hated publicity and never talked about her private life. "I'm only doing this because you made me laugh so much last night," she said.

It turned out fine. She was full of fun. And I felt afterwards that I had at last unveiled something of this reclusive woman.

She told me, "I've worked hard at keeping a low profile, and here I am throwing it away. News-reading fascinates me, but my heroes are the reporters who are out there, chasing around and ducking the bullets. My job is just the front woman. I really am a tiny cog in a very large wheel. I don't regard it as a glamorous job. All I am is a talking newspaper."

She got into news-reading by accident. She graduated in economics, did a secretarial course, and applied for a job at the BBC, joining them as a production assistant on radio programmes like Farming Today. After four years she was encouraged to apply for a job as a news-reader. To her astonishment, she got it.

"I had to think long and hard before I moved over to TV, because I enjoyed the anonymity of radio," she said. "Being black has its problems," she told me candidly. "But other minority groups are the same. I love problems, I really do. I can't change now. With Moira Stewart, what you see is what you get."

Her background was one of hardship. Her mother was a nurse from Bermuda, and her father, a solicitor from Barbados, but Moira was born in London. "We lived in the east end, Hackney, then Golders Green, but my father left when I was ten months old.," she told me.

"When I was 16, I tried to find him. I went to Somerset House, and I uncovered his death certificate. It turned out he was killed in a car crash, and had lived not far from us. So I might well have passed him on the street without knowing it." Her mother married again. "We had a very tough life, but my mother was a marvellous, fantastic woman."

Moira herself has never married. She was 38 when we first talked, and lived alone.

She's had to put up with rumours that she might be gay. But she told me very firmly, "I think men are gorgeous. It's just finding the right one that is so difficult. You can't just go out there and grab one," she laughed.

Moira had a very mischievous sense of humour. After we printed a picture of her, full-length, which she posed for, showing her legs, I happened to bump into her a few months later, going into the BBC Centre. And she flounced into the Reception area, cheekily pulled her skirt up, and shouted, "Hi, Ken. See, I really have got legs!"

She eventually quit news-reading, after more than 25 years in the job, and moved back into radio, doing a variety of shows as a freelance.

But I still think the funniest story which Moira recalled from her days in the news-room was the night she was sharing the TV news-reading stint with John Humphrys. At the end of the bulletin, John turned to her, knowing the microphones were switched off, and said, "You're the most sensationally sexy lady I know. I suggest the best thing we can do for the next few hours is to make mad, passionate love down in the basement."

What he'd forgotten was that it was a summary of the news for the deaf. And most of the viewers could lip read. "I had hysterics," said Moira. That really summed up this woman for me.

PICTURES

A letter from Jimmy Savile, 1975.

**Cartoon by Griffin. A farewell gesture when I left the
Daily Mirror in 1990.**

A cartoon by JAK in the London Evening Standard, 1991.

A hairy moment. In Hollywood with actress Tippi Hedren – and an over friendly big cat.

Backstage with Perry Como at Southport.

Riding an elephant in the Hollywood hills.

How does he do it? Up to tricks with magician Paul Daniels.

Having a friendly lunch with Pat Phoenix (Elsie Tanner).

**Larking about with Liz Dawn (Vera Duckworth)
and comedian Dustin Gee.**

Cheers! Enjoying a glass of something fizzy
with Terry Wogan.

**Aye, Aye, Captain! Taking the wheel of Jim Davidson's speedboat.
Taking a backseat (below).**

**Nice work if you can get it. Judging a beauty contest on TV with
Hollywood actor David Tomlinson.**

**With Dave Allen as King Canute, making the
waves go back.**

**Taking a ride with Eamonn Andrews
in his limo in Ireland.**

**With singing duo Peters and Lee and Judy Simons
of Daily Express.**

The heavy mob. Daily Mirror show business team at the London
Palladium. I'm second from right.

Getting serious. With Alan Whicker.

Getting my hands on the FA Cup.
Not at Wembley but for charity at Sainsbury's.

With Angela Rippon. General Election night, BBC studios.

MAUREEN LIPMAN

Maureen Lipman is just about the funniest woman I ever met. Not particularly beautiful, but very sexy in an odd sort of way, and with a gorgeous pair of legs.

We became quite good friends after she married an old journalist mate of mine, Jack Rosenthal, who worked as a scriptwriter with Granada TV in Manchester.

Jack wrote for Coronation Street, before branching out and writing some superb TV comedy plays.

They married in 1974. Maureen, who came from Hull, was always proud of her very Jewish background (her father Maurice was a tailor and had his own shop) and she would create her own brand of comedy by often gently mimicking her mother Zelma, and telling Jewish jokes at her expense.

She started out acting and singing at school, imitating that great singer of the time Alma Cogan ("Alma was a nice Jewish girl who was big in our house," she quipped). She then won a scholarship to the London Academy of Music and Dramatic Art, having decided that the only thing she wanted to do in life was be an actress.

She was so talented that it wasn't long before Maureen was doing steady work in the theatre, then TV and films.

After a few very successful TV shows, she landed her own sitcom series, called Agony, in which she played a Jewish Agony Aunt with lots of domestic problems of her own. (I couldn't help feeling that this was based on Marje Proops, my colleague on the Mirror).

Then Maureen landed the role which was to earn her a lot of money but from which she found it hard to escape - playing Beatrice Bellman, the talkative Jewish grandmother in the long-running series of adverts for BT. She soon found she couldn't go anywhere without being recognised, and had people calling out to her in the street, "What's new, Beattie?"

With Jack now a successful writer, churning out a stream of award-winning TV plays (the best, for me, being The Evacuees), Maureen also turned her hand to scribbling, and alongside her acting, wrote some very funny columns for various magazines and newspapers. She received the CBE in 1999.

Whenever I was short of a story, I would only have to ring up Maureen and she would come up with some funny anecdotes, which I would pinch for my column.

She had a biting, sarcastic wit, which I always found extremely funny. I recall once phoning her when she was staying at a hotel in Hollywood, and she screamed at me, "Hang on, we've just had an earthquake here, and I've been tossed out of bed."

Sadly, she was widowed in 2004 when Jack died from cancer after a long illness. Maureen dutifully completed his half-written autobiography, titled By Jack Rosenthal, and then played herself in her daughter Amy's adaptation of the book on Radio 4 in 2006, which they called Jack Rosenthal's Last Act.

Typically, Maureen has proved she is not a woman to be taken too lightly.

She tells the story against herself. When the well-known TV critic A.A. Gill wrote a scathing review about a programme called Best of British, which featured Maureen, he compared her "to a piece of ---- that won't go down the toilet even though you flush three times,"

She took her revenge. When she found herself at a party, with Gill also as one of the guests, she walked up to him and said loudly, "I just want you to know that I hate you, that I will always hate you, and nothing you can ever write will stop me hating you." And then walked off, leaving him completely lost for words.

She was only sorry, she said later, that she didn't throw a glass of wine over his head.

That's our Maureen. A trouper to the last!

JUDI DENCH

I must confess I love Judi Dench. I have secretly been in love with her ever since I attended the BAFTA Awards dinner in 1968, and this beautiful young thing picked up the coveted award as Most Promising Newcomer.

And if there is one woman who has certainly fulfilled that early promise, it's got to be Judi. Or Dame Judi, as we must now call her.

Over the years, I got to know her quite well, and we used to often meet for tea and cakes when she did those wonderful TV series for the BBC, first A Fine Romance, with her husband Michael Williams, and then As Time Goes By, with Geoffrey Palmer.

Our get-togethers were invariably organised by the BBC Light Entertainment Publicity Officer Jenny Secombe (daughter of comedian Harry) who knew that both Judi and I had the same sense of humour which led to good teatime chemistry.

She has a really wicked sense of fun which is quite infectious. She quite easily breaks out into a fit of the giggles.

Although she started out in her career as a serious actress, making her debut at the Old Vic in 1957 and then doing Shakespeare for years, she became a much more all-round actress when she moved into light comedy.

She married fellow actor Michael Williams in 1971 and they appeared together in many productions, the best being their partnership in A Fine Romance, from 1981 until 1984. They were a couple made for each other. Judi often told me that she was madly in love with Michael, and he in turn confided to me that he wouldn't know what he would do without her.

They had a daughter, Finty, who looks remarkably like Judi, and followed her parents into the business.

Judi made some great films. I particularly liked A Room With A View, which they did in Italy. She won her first Oscar in 1997 for her role as Queen Victoria in the film Mrs. Brown, but has been nominated seven times for the Oscars. When she was cast as the mysterious spy leader M in the film Golden Eye in 1995, she continued the role in all the Bond films until Spectre in 2015. I loved her though in that nostalgic film for the oldies, The Best Exotic Marigold Hotel, set in India, and its follow-up, The Second Best Exotic Marigold Hotel.

Her beloved Michael died from cancer in 2001, ending a blissful 30 - year marriage, and for some years Judi insisted that she could never find anyone to replace him.

Happily, she found love again ten years later when she revealed that she had met and was going out with a handsome old fellow, David Mills, a wildlife park owner who lived "only a few fields away."

The one thing which Judi says annoys her most in life is when people ask her why she doesn't put her feet up and retire. She is never going to retire, she insists.

And why should she?

ANGELA RIPPON

Angela Rippon was a journalist and worked on local papers in the West country before joining the BBC. And, of course, she went on to become oe of the most popular news readers on the box.

Her big breakthrough from being not just a newscaster but a celebrity came when she stepped out from behind the desk and cheekily danced her way onto the Morecambe and Wise Show, in those very brief sexy knickers, in 1976.

I had a tip-off from one of my mates in the publicity department that Angela was to be a surprise guest on Eric and Ernie's Christmas show. So I managed to get in to the run-through of the final rehearsal at the TV Centre. And sure enough, there she was. Angela looked stunningly sexy when she stepped out from behind her news-reading desk and ripped off her business-like top to reveal a flimsy see-through silk dress split to the top of her thighs. She then went into a smart high-kicking dance routine, as good as any of the old Tiller Girls.

So I had a terrific exclusive story which we carried in the Mirror next day. But the BBC kicked up an almighty row when they decided to put a ban on the pictures of Angela being published. In the end it became a bit of a farce because when the show was recorded, all the other guests – Elton John, actress Kate O'Mara, and John Thaw and Dennis Waterman from The Sweeney – posed for photographers.

The show's producer Ernest Maxin was all set to let Angela be photographed – legs and all. But BBC publicity chiefs suddenly insisted on vetting all the pictures before they were published. Then the Head of News, Andrew Todd, pompously declared, "Angela must not show her legs at all." He thought it was bad for her image as a serious newsreader.

Angela herself was ordered not to get involved in the row, and to say nothing at all to the Press. But she told her close colleagues, "The whole thing has got beyond a joke."

When the show was finally screened at Christmas, it drew a record viewing audience of more than 25 million.

After that, things were never the same for Angela. Because after giving up her news-reading job, a few years later she landed the role as presenter of Come Dancing.

I was in Blackpool with her in 1987 when Angela put on her dancing shoes again and took over the helm of Come Dancing, which even then was the longest running TV show in history, dating back to the 50s.

She replaced the veteran disc-jockey and presenter David Jacobs, who had become rather pompous and old-fashioned, and the BBC wanted to give the programme a new sexy image which would appeal to younger viewers.

That's what really set Angela off on a new dancing career. As I watched her in her first Come Dancing show, I recall the producer Simon Betts telling me, "She has got a warmth which viewers like, and is also a very fine and enthusiastic dancer, so she will be taking to the floor to demonstrate a few steps herself."

And she's been doing well for herself ever since. Angela has certainly proved that you can't put a good dame down. She's still out there working, well into her free bus-pass days.

LIZ HURLEY

When I first met Liz Hurley, she was completely unknown. But the first thing that struck me about her was her pure beauty. She was so attractive and demure. She was just stunning. The only word to describe her.

It was in the late 80s, and she was filming on location for her first leading role in a five-part mini-series called Christabel.

Talking to her was hard going, because she was quite shy and had very little to say. The only thing she had done before this, was a small role in an episode of Morse. But the producers, desperate for publicity, were insisting to the Press boys that this girl was going places, and she was going to be a great actress.

Well, a great actress? No! But she did go on to become a top model and the face of Estee Lauder. Not to mention the girl-friend of actor Hugh Grant and others.

And even at 50-plus, she is still looking great. Not so shy any more, though. She was quoted as saying she loved meeting new people, and "I flirt with anyone – man, woman, animal, inanimate objects."

Then, the woman who can count not only Hugh Grant, but Aussie cricketer Shane Warne, and tycoon Steve Bing among her many suitors, cheekily announced that she was looking for a new boyfriend, saying she was "single" for the first time in more than 30 years. "Since I was 17, I have always been with someone," she said.

And then added mischievously, "Look at Joan Collins – she is married to a   fabulous man 32 years younger than her. In which case, I can now date an 18-year-old. Anything goes!" And this, from a woman who has a teenage son.

Oh yes, Ms. Hurley has certainly changed from the shy young thing I first met as an ambitious little starlet.

PIERS MORGAN

Piers Morgan was a young man I first met when he worked on the Sun, as a fresh-faced showbiz columnist. I was old enough to be his father, and was still working on the Mirror, so probably regarded him as a young upstart.

The Sun and the Mirror were great rival newspapers then (still are, I suppose) and when this fellow Morgan landed his own full-page daily column, mostly filled with pop music snippets and showbiz gossip, I must confess I regarded it as a load of, well, you know what! It was pure trivia.

What really amused me, however, was the style in which he wrote it. Whatever pop group he interviewed, he always insisted on being pictured in the photograph with them. It got to the stage where Morgan just had to get in on the act. It was obviously an ego thing. In the end, the whole thing developed into a kind of "I'm Piers Morgan – I'm more important than any of the people I am writing about" column. Nevertheless, I'm sure his editors were happy with him. But as more of an old, traditional journalist, I was not really a fan of such blatant self-publicity.

However, we finally met when I went along to a BBC Press launch for something or other, in a back street off Tottenham Court Road. This well dressed young man came up to me and said, "Hello, may I introduce myself? I'm Piers Morgan from the Sun." And he put out his hand to shake mine. "Oh, hello, I'm Ken Irwin, from the Mirror," I replied.

"I know who you are. So you're THE Ken Irwin. You're almost a legend. We meet at last. A pleasure to meet you," he said. The guy was so polite and so nice, and so gushing with his compliments, that I was quite taken aback.

What a charming young man, I thought. Not a bit like the Piers Morgan whose columns I had glanced through in the Sun. He was so smooth and patronising that I couldn't help thinking at the time that here was a young fellow smart enough to go places.

He went on of course to become Editor of the Sun. Then, a few years after I left to set up my own business as a freelance, Piers moved over and became Editor of the Daily Mirror. I'm told that he wasn't a bad guy to work for, before he got the sack. Although I would consider him very lightweight compared to what I like to call the real editors who used to run Fleet Street.

It doesn't surprise me at all that Piers moved into television and soon got his own shows. He has a lot going for him. Good looks, a sharp brain, and a good solid training as a journalist. But I was a bit surprised, I've got to admit, to see him reach such heights of fame and become such a big name in America.

When you see him now, back here, doing some of those celebrity interview shows for ITV, they make me cringe. He has a self-confessed ego as big as a house, a personality which is to cheesy, and a style of questioning which is so sychophantic that it makes you want to reach for the sick bucket.

He knows how to wind people up, though, and I think if I was one of those co-presenters working alongside him, when he is deliberately trying to up-stage and embarrass you, I would pick up the nearest microphone and hit him with it.

In spite of all that, you've got to admit – the boy done good, as the Sun would say!

TOM JONES

The first time I met Tom Jones was when he was brought to London by his young manager Gordon Mills, who had discovered him singing in pubs and clubs in South Wales, as Tommy Woodward. He was a tough looking hunk of a fellow, with a mass of black curly hair, and he wore drainpipe trousers like a Teddy boy and high-heeled winkle-picker boots.

The thing I noticed most about him was that he had an enormous nose. It was very pointy and seemed to stick out from his face, like a bulbous lump. But he had a great toothy smile which immediately gave him a very friendly look.

Mills was a very enterprising guy and although he couldn't really compete with the big agencies, he was anxious to build up a team of singers he could manage and promote. He then brought in Engelbert Humperdink, who had previously sung under the name of Gerry Dorsey, and then a strange little fellow who was not in the same mould at all, called Gilbert O'Sullivan.

Under Mills' astute management, all three of them soon shot to stardom. But there was always a rivalry between Tom and Engelbert, even a deep- down jealousy. Engelbert was more handsome and had a more melodious voice, while Tom was simply rugged and raw. They both appealed to female fans but in different ways.

As they progressed however, the rivalry became more intense. If one had a Rolls Royce car, or a Bentley, the other would want a newer, and better one. And when it came to women, well, they reputedly constantly competed in the number of groupies they could go through in a year.

But then, very noticeably Tom Jones was visibly re-invented by manager Mills.

Originally quite fat and hefty, Tom was put on a fast-acting diet and a rigid fitness routine which brought his weight down from 15 stone to 11 st.6 lbs. Then he secretly underwent surgery to have his double chin taken away and his giant nose re-shaped.

They tried to keep it under wraps from the Press, but it was obvious just by looking at Tom that something drastic had happened. We discovered later that he actually went into hospital to have the "nose job" late in 1967. Suddenly, he appeared in public with this brand-new face. The Concorde-like conk was now more like a ski slope, similar to that of Hollywood star Bob Hope.

It was all cleverly explained away by Mills' chatty little publicity man Chris Hutchins, who later put out a statement saying that Tom had not had cosmetic surgery but, because he had broken his nose as a lad, he had now had an operation to unblock a nasal passage, to help with his singing.

Whatever he'd had done, it worked. After the success of his first No.1 hit, It's Not Unusual, he moved to America, started playing Las Vegas on a regular basis alongside Elvis Presley and the Frank Sinatra ratpack, and bought a house and settled in Los Angeles.

A string of record hits followed – What's New Pussycat?, Delilah, Green Green Grass of Home, and many more. When women in the audiences started throwing their knickers at him, he played it for laughs but became a sex idol.

His manager Gordon Mills died, and Tom fell out with Engelbert, and it was over a woman apparently.

A lot had happened to the lad from Pontypridd, who in his early days told me that he spent two years of his life in a sickbed with TB from the age of twelve, and then wooed his school sweetheart Linda Trenchard and married her in 1957 when they were both 16, after getting her pregnant. The miracle was that they are still married. Some years ago, Tom heard from relatives back in Wales that the old phone box that used to stand at the end of Linda's street was to be removed and scrapped. He immediately bought it, had it shipped to the States and put it up at the side of their Hollywood swimming pool, with a working phone installed. "I couldn't let it go. That's where Linda and I did all our teenage kissing," he said.

The last time I saw Tom was when he was back in Britain doing the BBC talent show The Voice, as one of the judges. It was a role he was more than qualified to do, and I enjoyed his performances. I could well understand his shock and anger when the BBC dropped him, in 2016. Particularly when he was replaced by such a lightweight character as Boy George. Ah well, that's show business!

PAT O'HARE

Pat O'Hare is a very good friend of mine. And one of the best singers around. I first met him in the early 1960s when I was in Manchester, working as the Mirror's TV Critic, and he was singing in cabaret around Northern clubs.

Someone at the BBC spotted him and he was booked to do some radio shows with the Northern Dance Orchestra, and then did so well that he was given guest spots on North regional TV shows starring the popular Sheila Buxton.

When I first saw him on stage, there was something about him I immediately liked. He had a wonderful tenor voice, a warmth that could captivate audiences, and a mischievous and pleasant personality. So I lost no time in interviewing him and writing a piece for the Mirror, more or less saying that here was a star in the making and he was going to be big one day.

Pat was very appreciative, and he then landed his own radio series titled So Nice To Come Home To.

I watched his progress with a keen interest, and then one day suddenly decided that all he needed was some good publicity and he could be a big star. We got together over a drink and clinched a deal that I should be his Publicity Manager. This was something I had been vaguely thinking about for some time. Having become fascinated with the inside workings of show business, I now decided that maybe this was something I could develop as a sideline to journalism.

The next step was to take on more artists. This developed further when Ronnie Taylor, who was the BBC's Head of Light Entertainment in the North, quit his job and set up his own management agency, with his assistant Margaret Bottomley, which they called Taylor-Vision. They had on their books a lovely young singer from Liverpool called Julie Jones, who was a rival to Sheila Buxton, and a very clever young comic and impressionist from Cheshire called Peter Goodwright.

Ronnie, knowing of my little ambition to get in on the showbiz scene, then came to me and asked if I would join him, in helping to promote all his artists. So this was something I agreed to do, but on a part-time basis.

Consequently, I drew up contracts with Julie and Peter, and they both agreed to pay me a small percentage fee on a monthly basis. It was hardly big money, but it did give me some experience of the business. After a while, I found myself busier than ever. And one of Ronnie Taylor's associates then brought me in to do publicity for a number of up and coming pop groups who were emerging in the wake of the Beatles.

With a lot of publicity which I managed to get them, Julie Jones and Peter Goodwright both quickly became star names. Julie got her own radio series, Have You Heard Miss Jones? in which she was backed by the best band in the country, the NDO. And Peter did guest spots on various TV shows.

Meanwhile I still had Pat O'Hare to promote. And although he was doing okay and getting regular work, we decided that we should re-launch him under a new name. The name we came up with was Guy Stevens. I then had the tough job of starting from scratch with this great new singer Guy Stevens.

I got him a lot of publicity and we put him with a new London agent. But sad to say, things didn't work out as well as we hoped, and the TV work dried up. Pat came on to me and said he had decided to go back to his real name of Pat O'Hare. He was still doing quite well in the clubs, but wherever he appeared, as Guy Stevens, people were coming up to him and saying, 'Aren't you Pat O'Hare, who used to be on TV?"

Another young singer I added to the "bunch of stars" I handled was Alberta Laine, or Abby, as she was known, a tall, dark, really attractive vocalist from Manchester with a very distinctive and seductive voice. She had a marvellous vocal range and could sing everything from classical to jazz.

She was first spotted by TV producer John Hamp, who signed her up and put her on Granada's Scene at 6.30 show, and then People and Places, as a resident vocalist. I handled all Abby's publicity for some time, and she went on to become a sensational performer, working in TV, cabaret, nightclubs and panto.

Julie Jones then left Ronnie Taylor's office, and I took over her management for a short time before helping to get her signed up to a big London agent, Dave Forrester, who was Ken Dodd's lifelong agent.

Julie joined the popular mid-day programme Lunch Box, from ATV in Birmingham, teaming up with the great Matt Monro as one of the show's resident singers. She also toured extensively as resident vocalist with the Eric Winstone Orchestra. She then got married, gave up the business and returned to Liverpool.

Peter Goodwright went on for many years, doing TV, radio and stage shows.

When I moved down to London in 1966, I had to give up all my ambitions about going into show business management. It was never really on. I guess I wasn't cut out to be a showbiz mogul. I was never going to be another Lew Grade, that's for sure.

Working in London, I lost touch with most of them, but tried to keep track of their progress.

Pat O'Hare, who had now settled down in Manchester, continued to earn a good living as a singer in cabaret and nightclubs.

But then in 1974, I was signed up to become one of the regular judges on ITV's top talent show New Faces. And when I went to Birmingham to do a show one week, I was surprised to find that one of the hopeful contestants was none other than a handsome Irishman called Pat O'Hare.

It was an uncanny coincidence that Pat should be on the show, and I was one of the judges. Of course, I had to declare my interests. Pat came on stage, looking very trendy in a white suit, and he was singing as well as ever. When it came to me to give my judgement, I said immediately, "I have to confess that I know Pat O'Hare. More than ten years ago, I wrote a piece in the Daily Mirror, predicting that he would become a star. Well, he never quite made it. But I'd like to think that tonight, he could finally do it." It earned great applause from an ecstatic studio audience.

Sitting on the panel with me were top band leader Jack Parnell, nightclub owner John Smith, and TV celebrity Shaw Taylor. Fortunately, they were all full of praise for Pat, with Jack Parnell saying, "This young man is a superb singer. I've never seen a vocalist with so much talent. He has a great voice; his diction is perfect. Everything about him is great." More wild applause.

When it came to the scores, he got nothing but 9's and 10's. And I wrapped it up by saying, "Can I give him another ten?"

The result was that Pat won that show overwhelmingly. We had a drink together afterwards, and I felt so pleased for him. He went on to appear in the All Winners Show, a few months later. I wasn't a judge that particular week. But Terry Wogan, the BBC's top deejay who was on the panel, said, "If there is a better ballad singer in the country, then I have yet to hear him."

Pat didn't win the Final but came third or fourth in the overall voting. But merely by appearing on the show, it helped to revive his career and set him up again for another chance of stardom.

Pat and I remained friends and kept in touch only by exchanging Christmas cards once a year. But then, last year, I suddenly decided it was time we met up again, so I phoned him, we met for lunch in Manchester and I found that, apart from playing golf and enjoying life, he was still singing and doing the occasional gig.

He invited me to go and see him perform, so I drove up to Batley in Yorkshire, to see him action. It wasn't the big Batley Variety Club, once so famous in the 60s and 70s which attracted world-class stars, but a more modest working-men's club which puts on cabaret shows every Sunday afternoon, to cater for local drinkers.

I wasn't quite sure what to expect. And when I saw they had installed a chair-left at the bottom of the stairs inside the front door, I feared the worst.

Once inside and upstairs (on my own two feet, I must add) I found it had quite a cosy atmosphere. The natives were friendly, and when my old chum Patrick appeared and bounded on stage, backed by a rather good musical trio, it was almost like old times. Well, not quite. The glamour of TV had gone. But Pat warbled his way through a routine for an hour or more, and I was pleased to see that he still had it. He was still singing like an old trouper. Not a bum note, and he could still hit those high notes with effortless ease. Not bad for an old 'n of 82. The audience, numbering only 40 or 50, applauded in appreciation.

For me, watching Patrick in action again brought back nostalgic memories. It was just as though he was still singing in the Wilton Club in Manchester 50 years ago, with him smiling and cheekily dedicating his next song, That's Why The Lady Is A Tramp, to an admirer in the audience, TV's Elsie Tanner, star Pat Phoenix.

We had a laugh, when I told him this over a drink at the end of his show. "Oh, yeah!" he said. "I think she used to fancy me, y'know. Pat

Phoenix came in regularly and had a front row seat. I had to fight her off some nights."

I looked at him, quizzically. Did you ever ...? I started. "No, I didn't. Behave yourself," said Pat.

I think we'll probably remain mates until one of us kicks the bucket!

ANNE ROBINSON

When it comes to tough characters, how about that red-haired she-cat, Annie Robinson?

Anne, who became the most hated woman on television as the caustic presenter of The Weakest Link, was an old colleague of mine and we became quite good friends.

The first time I met Anne was when she joined the Daily Mirror staff in 1980. She came from Liverpool - albeit the posh part, Crosby - so we had that in common. But I would never have looked upon her as a fellow Scouser, although she did have that wonderful sense of Merseyside humour we Liverpudlians like to boast about.

She came up through provincial papers, as I did, which is the only real way to learn our trade, working on the Liverpool Echo before going on to Fleet Street and, I think, the Daily Mail and The Times, before joining us at the Mirror, as a women's columnist.

It was obvious that she was very ambitious and determined to get to the top, and it wasn't long before she had taken over from Marje Proops, who was then ailing a bit and showing her age. She not only took Marje's job, but also her large office, which was right next door to mine.

As the newly promoted Show Business Editor, I thought it would be a nice gesture to take Anne to lunch and get to know her a little better. I booked my favourite little restaurant - El Paradiso on The Strand - and off we went.

As we were looking through the menu and choosing what we were going to eat, I automatically picked out and ordered a good bottle of wine.

It wasn't until the waiter came and delivered the wine and poured me a taster, that Anne looked at me and said, "I hope you're going to drink all that - because I don't drink."

She then ordered a soft drink, an orange juice or something, and we had a very pleasant meal, but she remained sober, while I had to drink the whole bottle of wine. We chatted a lot, had a few laughs, and I knew from then on I was going to like her. And I think it was mutual.

It wasn't until we got back to the office, however, and I mentioned to someone about our lunch, that they told me, "She's an alcoholic - didn't you know?"

I didn't know anything of her history at that time. But years later she revealed in her splendidly frank autobiography the truth about her drink problem, and how she lost custody of her young daughter because of her wretched alcoholism.

Anne's second husband was John Penrose, a reporter on the Mirror who was later promoted to an executive position, and he was a great pal of mine. Now, going to lunch with him was very different. John was a good drinker and one of the lads, and always great company.

Anne rose to the dizzy heights of assistant editor when I was still on the Mirror, and outranked her husband. But she had bigger ambitions - to get into television. And it didn't surprise me at all when she left newspapers and took over at the BBC as presenter of Watchdog, and then went on to create that wicked witch image as the front woman on The Weakest Link, which brought her international fame and a fortune to match.

Penrose - as she always called him, not John - also quit journalism and became her manager and much valued private estate agent, before they decided to divorce and go their separate ways.

It pays, though, to have friends in high places. As I found out myself some years ago when I was buying an expensive hand-made French bed, which was being advertised in the Press. I ordered it through mail order. But the bed never came.

Then I read a report that these beds were not all they were cracked up to be. I went on to the firm in London and cancelled it.

They kept fobbing me off and said they were sending me the bed. The reason for the delay was that they'd had an inferior batch sent to them from abroad. I told them I wanted to cancel it, but they insisted, "No - you can't cancel. We will deliver."

Eventually I threatened that if they didn't cancel it and send me my money back, I was going on to Anne Robinson's Watchdog programme to complain.

"Ah, that's what they all say," said the manager, laughing. "But I mean it. I know Anne Robinson, and I will," I said.

So, I went on to Annie's office at the BBC. She got one of her team to take up my case. Apparently, there had been a lot more disgruntled customers complaining about the inferior quality of these beds and they wanted their money back.

The programme confronted the bed company and did a damning story which was broadcast on the Watchdog show. I got my bed cancelled immediately and received my cheque back within a few days. No more arguments.

It's amazing what the power of TV can do. It used to be the power of the Press. Now, I think TV is an even stronger weapon.

JOHN THAW

John Thaw was one of our finest actors, in my view. Very down to earth, he came from a poor background and was brought up in Manchester by his father, a lorry driver, after losing his mother when he was only a kid. After an assortment of odd jobs, he won a place at RADA which set him on the road to acting.

He picked up many awards, and it was a toss-up whether his detective role in The Sweeney was better than the long-running Morse, or if his wig and gown role as a defence barrister in the title role of Cavanagh QC was classier than both of them.

I got to know him quite well. Thames TV used to hold an annual summer event, with an open-air party in the gardens behind the Inns of Court, just off Fleet Street, attended by every one of the stars from all their programmes. The Press would turn out in force, because it was a good opportunity to meet the celebrities and get some stories.

On one of these Sunday-afternoon parties, John Thaw sauntered over to me for a chat, a drink in one hand, a plate of sandwiches in the other. After the usual pleasantries, he turned to me and said, "Ken, who is this fellow Tony Pratt you have working on the Mirror?" I explained that he was one of the TV writers who worked in my department. Why?

"Well, I'd like to meet him some time because he wrote a really nasty piece about me a few months ago," said John. "If I ever catch up with him, I'll thump him."

"Well, here's here today, somewhere," I told him. I looked around, spotted Tony Pratt chatting to some people about 30 yards away, and pointed him out to John.

"There he is, over there. Would you like me to introduce you to him?" I said.

John, who was about my size, stood back, eyed up Tony, who was about 6ft 2ins tall and very stocky, and said quietly, "Oh, I don't think I'll bother. Just tell Mr. Pratt that he's very aptly named."

RICHARD & JUDY

Before they became famous as Richard and Judy, TV's long-running day-time chat show hosts, Richard Madeley and Judy Finnegan worked together as co-presenters on Granada's regional evening news programme in Manchester.

One day, I received a phone call from Judy's husband David Henshaw, who was a producer at the BBC's Manchester HQ. He told me he was upset because he knew his wife was having an affair with Richard Madeley and suggested I should make some enquiries and do a news story for the Mirror.

It wasn't a very pleasant job, but I first went on to Judy, and then Richard at Granada, and told them of the accusation, and asked if it was true. Neither would say much, but then they both suggested that I should join them next day and have lunch together. So we did.

At first, it was a little awkward, but then they both confirmed that, yes, they were having an affair. They were very much in love and Judy had left her husband and had now moved in with Richard. The only difficulty they had was that Judy had two young children, Dan and Tom. But she was adamant that her marriage was over, she was taking the children with her, and she would not be going back to husband David.

They knew I would have to write the story and encouraged me to do so. In fact, Richard said he was relieved that the rumours would finally be made public.

Not long after I broke the story, Judy went through a divorce and then married Richard. It turned out that Richard had also been divorced (he had got married, very young, as a journalist in Yorkshire).

Richard and Judy then had two more children to add to their family. They also went on to become something of a national institution as a TV team, before Judy decided that her looks had faded, and she didn't want to continue as a double act any more, turning her time to writing books instead.

DENNIS WATERMAN & RULA LENSKA

Dennis Waterman liked to think of himself as one of the lads. He was always good for a pint and a laugh, whether it was with John Thaw on The Sweeney or George Cole on Minder. But he also had women trouble. He went through several marriages and hit the headlines with his womanising behaviour.

One of the most unusual romances he went through was with that fiery redhead Rula Lenska I first got to know Rula when she was one of the trio Little Ladies, the sexy girl band in the hit show Rock Follies. She was pretty hot stuff. I interviewed her and then she came over to see me at the office, and I took her into the office pub, The Stab, in Fetter Lane.

The pub was usually occupied mostly by journalists, but suddenly it became much more crowded because Rula proved to be something of an attraction, and we were invaded by dozens of printers and others, all anxious to get a close-up look at "that tall redhead from off the telly." Rula loved it, of course, and enjoyed playing up to an adoring gallery.

Some years later, she hooked up with Dennis Waterman, and the Press were desperately intrigued because they met when Rula appeared in an episode of Minder, the series which starred Dennis alongside George Cole.

The next thing we knew was that Rula and Dennis were married. It was a strange partnership. Rula had an aristocratic background, the daughter of a Polish Countess who had come to Britain to escape the Nazis in World War 11. Rula had just divorced, ending a ten-year marriage with Brian Deacon, and had a young daughter.

Dennis, on the other hand, was a rough and tumble cockney character who had been acting since his schooldays and liked to spend most of his spare time with his mates down at the pub. He already had two broken marriages behind him.

For some years, they both got on with their careers and seemed happy enough. Dennis was one of those actors never out of work and he became a big star.

However, the big Rula-Dennis romance came crashing to an inevitable end when they split up and he walked out on her, with Rula later alleging that the marriage had become violent and that she was the victim of assault.

After their split, Waterman went back to his wild days. And I remember one occasion when he hit the headlines again by being seen out with an attractive and very young blonde on his arm. This led to a frantic Press hunt to find Waterman and reveal his mystery new girlfriend.

Now a freelance, I was commissioned to go and interview Dennis for one of the top women's magazines. I flew to Ireland where he was on location, filming a new series called Stay Lucky, on the wet and windy coast of County Mayo. I wasn't alone. There were other journalists all anxious to talk to him.

Dennis was pretty cool about the sudden Press attention. And there with him was his new mysterious girlfriend, attractive blonde 28-year-old Fiona Black. It turned out she worked as a locations manager, and he had first met her on the set of Stay Lucky.

Dennis made no attempt to hide their friendship, and they canoodled and fooled around together in between him working in front of the cameras. But he did insist that Fiona would not be interviewed and had nothing to say to the Press. She just stayed pleasantly in the background, after agreeing to one photo of them together, strolling casually arm in arm, both in jeans and Dennis wearing dark sunglasses.

Having travelled all that way, I was determined to get something out of Dennis, and eventually he agreed to talk exclusively to me after he had finished filming for the day. We had a few pints and he seemed to be back to his old self.

You could be forgiven for thinking, however, that his laughter was a bit forced. Although he was filming a new series of Stay Lucky, life for the then 43-year-old Dennis had been anything but lucky recently.

In the past year, he had split up from wife Rula after nine years together, he had narrowly escaped a jail sentence when he was convicted of drink-driving for the second time in five years. His attempt to become a Hollywood movie star failed after Cold Justice, a feature film he made with Roger Daltrey, flopped at the box-office, and he lost a personal fortune because of the film disaster. He nearly had to give up his mansion in Buckinghamshire – which he'd shared with Rula – because he'd mortgaged it to finance the film.

"Yeah, I got the Full House last year," Dennis quipped, taking another swig of beer. The failure of Cold Justice, in which he played a hard-drinking priest, was a big blow for someone who had never really had a flop before.

"The plan was simple. I thought making a film would be a good career move. But this one failed on two counts - we didn't get paid and nobody saw it because of distribution problems," said Dennis.

"I've learnt my lesson from this venture. I hope to make more films once I'm back on my feet, financially. But in future I'll make sure the money is up front first."

After his Hollywood disaster, Dennis had gone back to television with Stay Lucky on ITV and also on BBC-1 in the chirpy sitcom called On The Up.

Given his current misfortune, the irony of the titles of those two shows made Dennis smile ruefully. "Sure, I'm lucky. I've always been lucky. I'm fortunate in the stuff I've done and the fact that I've always been surrounded by nice people," he said. "But I wish the two series weren't on TV at the same time – it will look like I'm always on the box, and some viewers get fed up seeing your face."

He admitted that it hadn't been easy carrying on with his career while his personal life was in such a mess. "There would have been a lot more pressure on me if I hadn't been working so hard. If you're under contract, you can't say, 'My life's in tatters, I can't work today,' and go home crying."

Whatever impression his boozy behaviour created, there was never any doubt just how seriously he took his job. "Some people may think I'm not really a good actor, because it doesn't look like I'm acting. That's lunacy. Acting comes easy to me because I've done it all my life," he said.

He gave up his lucrative role as Terry McCann, Arthur Daley's Minder, after Dennis decided to leave actor George Cole because he thought he was getting too old to play the "heavy" after ten years.

"There was no big row when I finished with Minder. They asked me if I would like to do more, and I said no."

Being "one of the lads" was always very important to Dennis, whose pastimes were drinking, playing football, and watching sport on telly. "I admit I'm not very good on my own. I hate it. I won't even go into a pub and drink alone. That's no fun.

"People think it's rather funny, I suppose. They probably look at me and think I earn all that money and all I do is work and laugh all day. Well, I'm afraid that's exactly what happens!

Drinking with his pals was one of the reasons why his wife Rula branded him a "male chauvinist pig." Dennis, the son of a railway porter, didn't disagree with her.

"My behaviour wouldn't upset a lot of women as much as it did Rula. But her background was very different from mine. There's every reason why she should be upset, she's a Polish countess," he pointed out.

He refused to go into details of why the marriage failed. "I'm not very good at relationship-type conversations," he said. "I find this whole thing of 'we must talk about this' doesn't help very much. It wastes time and it is often destructive.

"I'm a bit of a coward and I don't like talking terribly personally. I keep things to myself. If I've got a problem, it's mine. I don't want to change that.

"People can speculate as much as they like. I don't want to talk about Rula or anyone else. Whatever Rula has said is up to her. But what we've been through is personal. Nobody else needs to know."

The situation then was that Rula lived in their Buckinghamshire house, with her daughter Lara from her first marriage. And Dennis continued to see his two daughters, Hannah and Julie, from his marriage to actress Pat Maynard.

"I wouldn't discourage either of my daughters from going into acting or show business, but I do insist they finish their schooling," he said. "If they've got a good education behind them, then they've got a chance if things get rough."

Dennis was one of those actors never out of work for long and has gone on to do lots of things including the popular BBC police series New Tricks, as the veteran detective.

Rula went on to further her career with various film and TV roles, including To The Manor Born, Casualty, Doctor Who, and Footballers Wives. She also had a spell in EastEnders, as girl friend of Frank Butcher. And then in 2009 she joined Coronation Street, as Claudia Colby, an old friend of hairdresser Audrey Roberts. The last I heard of Rula was that she was now a grandmother.

It's hard to believe that the sexy redhead from Rock Follies who wowed 'em in my office pub is now a granny.

JENNY AGUTTER

When I was show business editor of the Mirror, I had a drinks cabinet in my office, which I'd inherited from my predecessor, Alan Garratt. It was well stocked on a regular basis and was regarded as one of the perks of the job, although I only used to open it on special occasions or when we had visiting celebrities coming in to see us.

I remember one time setting up an interview with Jenny Augutter (once the childhood star of that great film The Railway Children) and she said she'd happily come into my office, rather than me go to her home.

When she came in, middle of the afternoon, I asked her if she'd like a drink. She said, "You mean tea or coffee?" I said, "Something stronger, if you like. Do you fancy a glass of champagne?" She looked at me, in a disbelieving way, and said yes, she loved champagne. I nodded to my secretary, who opened up the cabinet, quickly put a bottle in an ice bucket, and Jenny and I got down to our little chat.

As she left, she said, "I could get used to this. I must do it more often."

Then, looking very demure and pretty, she had to suffer a couple of wolf whistles from cheeky sub-editors, as we went through the News Room on our way out to the front door.

JOHN INMAN

John Inman was another who used to occasionally pop into our office pub to have a drink with me. A lovely fellow, John. Always so quiet and polite. He was well aware of what a fuss his presence would cause whenever he appeared in public, particularly after the huge success of that TV show Are You Being Served?

He could hardly go anywhere without someone shouting at him, "I'm free!" But he didn't care. "I just smile and let it wash over me," he'd say. "I don't deliberately camp it up. I can't do anything about it, anyway. Most people are quite nice to me. I'm harmless, after all."

WARREN MITCHELL & DANDY NICHOLS

When Johnny Speight's hit show Till Death Us Do Part was at the height of its success on BBC, I went to interview Dandy Nichols, who for years played bigot Alf Garnett's poor abused wife, Elsie. But I found that she was a much tougher character than I expected. For when we came to discuss Alf Garnett, her dreadful husband, Dandy looked at me and said, "Do you really want to know what I think of him? He's a real nasty bastard."

When I said, "You mean Alf Garnett, of course?" she replied, "No, I mean both of them. They're both awful men. Warren Mitchell as well. I don't like either of them."

Some time later, when I was interviewing Warren Mitchell, I asked him what he thought of Dandy Nicholls. And he replied, "She really is not just a silly moo, but a nasty old cow."

HYLDA BAKER & JIMMY JEWEL

Hylda Baker and Jimmy Jewel were both big stars, though fading a little and had seen better days when they teamed up in the ITV comedy Nearest And Dearest. Hylda had been a top-of -the- bill comedienne on her own for years. And Jimmy was in the double act Jewel and Warris, with his cousin Ben, before they split up and he turned to acting.

Nearest and Dearest ran for seven series, from 1968 to 1973, with Hylda playing Nellie Pledge, and Jimmy as her brother Eli, running a Northern pickle factory they'd inherited. Most of the comedy came from their continual bickering and squabbling.

The fact was that they were like that in real life, too. They hated each other and made no secret of it.

Hylda, a very jealous and mean-spirited woman, turned quite nasty in her old age. And Jimmy once told me, when I went to interview him at home, "She's an absolute nightmare to work with. We just don't talk to each other, unless we're working."

One year, in between doing the TV series, they were both signed up to star in a stage show for a summer season at Blackpool.

A few weeks before they were due to open, I heard on the grapevine that Hylda had gone to the theatre and was horrified when she saw the posters plastered up outside She went inside, sought out the wardrobe mistress, and borrowed a tape measure from her. She then went outside and measured the size of her name on the posters and compared it with the size of Jimmy Jewel's.

She angrily went back in and told the theatre manager that she was the star of the show, not Jewel, and her name had to be made much bigger on the posters than his. When he pointed out that it was too late, that thousands of posters had been printed, and were on billboards throughout the town, Hylda went berserk. She threatened to pull out of the show and cancel the whole thing unless they agreed to tear down all the posters and put up new ones with her name in much bigger type. In the end, they relented.

I later asked Jimmy Jewel if this story was true, and he confirmed that it was.

"I'll never work with her again," he said. "She's a monster."

WOODY ALLEN, ALFRED HITCHCOCK & LAURENCE OLIVIER

One or two big names I was rather disappointed with when I met them were Woody Allen and Alfred Hitchcock. And then even the great Laurence Olivier.

I met all three of them on separate occasions at Granada's studios in Manchester. Woody Allen was a guest on an early evening show, and he was introduced to me by producer John Hamp. Although he had this tremendous reputation in the States, he was fairly unknown here. He had very little to say, and his performance in front of the cameras was pretty dismal. But he did give me one of his LP records (an album as it was later called) and when I took it home and played it, I found it hilariously funny. Only then did I fully appreciate just what a tremendous stand-up comedian he really was.

Alfred Hitchcock came in as a special guest of Granada owner Sidney Bernstein, and he walked into the studio as though he owned the place. I didn't like him at all. To be honest, I found him to be a bit of a wet fish.

As for Laurence Olivier, he was appearing in a prestigious TV drama, and I met him having a cup of tea in the studio canteen. To everyone's surprise, all he wanted to talk about was Coronation Street, which I think he had seen in rehearsals. He even hinted that he might like a walk-on part in it one day, though I don't think anyone took him seriously.

JOAN BAKEWELL

Although I'd watched her plenty of times on the box, the first time I actually met Joan Bakewell was when I was invited on to the BBC-2 chat show Late Night Line-Up as a guest in a discussion on current TV programmes. I was grilled by Joan, who always wore extremely short skirts, revealing long legs which everyone knew was the programme's best attraction and helped add numbers to the meagre viewing figures. I think it was about the same time that veteran scriptwriter Frank Muir gave Joan that tongue-in-cheek but very sexist compliment, describing her as The Thinking Man's Crumpet. It was a tag that stuck, although she always insisted she resented it. But it certainly didn't do her career any harm.

On one occasion, I was invited by Joan over to her house to do an interview with her, and she was remarkably friendly.

It was later of course that Joan became involved with the playwright Harold Pinter and they had a secret love affair, while he was married to actress Vivien Merchant, which Joan later revealed went on for some eight years, before he married Lady Antonia Fraser.

There's no doubt though that Joan, like a fine wine, has matured with age. She was made a Dame in 2008, and was given a life peerage, joining the Labour benches in the House of Lords in 2011 as Baroness Bakewell of Stockport.

Now in her 80s, she not only still looks remarkably sprightly, but comes over as a woman who talks a lot of sense and will not be compromised.

Only recently, she announced rather boldly that she intended to spend her wealth before she dies, rather than leave it to her two children. She announced, "I've told the children that my interest is in spending as much as I can before I go. I intend to spend their inheritance, and they are perfectly happy about that. I don't mind admitting that as I grow older, I've grown fond of posh restaurants, nice clothes, and good handbags. I don't go mad and buy designer wear. If I spend £100 on a handbag, that's a bit of an event. But I feel I've earned the right to indulge myself. It's important at my age to look after oneself."

She also revealed that the house she bought in London's smart Primrose Hill area had cost only £12,000 when she moved in, 52 years ago. And it was now valued at five million pounds. "But I'm not moving out in a hurry. I will only downsize if I really feel forced into it because it's no longer practical," she said.

Good for her, I thought. And I felt like giving three cheers for good old common sense.

She's come a long way from being Joan Rowlands, the head girl at Stockport grammar school who won a scholarship to Cambridge.

SIR DAVID ATTENBOROUGH

David Attenborough is always good company. I got to know him quite well when he was Director of BBC-2 and responsible for the second, more cultural channel. His Press conferences were invariably lively affairs, and David fully appreciated the value of publicity.

It wasn't until he quit his executive job and moved over into programme making that he really realised his ambition. Some of his wildlife programmes have been out of this world and he has fully deserved all the awards and compliments he's received over the last 30 years.

He would always come up with something new, whenever we'd meet. But, after watching him being mauled by those giant orang utans in the jungle, and all the other fierce creatures he'd handled, I remember being quite surprised when I once asked him what was the most frightening animal he had ever had to face. "Rats," he said. Rats? I queried. "Yes, Rats. I hate them. They scare me to death. I would handle anything rather than deal with a rat."

Funny old life, isn't it?

MICHAEL ASPEL

Michael Aspel, I always thought, was one of the best of the BBC's news-readers. He always looked smart, he was quiet, authoritative, and super cool.

It was not surprising, after he gave up news-reading and landed his own chat show, that he became something of a heart-throb with women viewers.

He knew and acknowledged that he was never going to be a tough, investigative inquisitor, like David Frost in his heyday. But Michael had a nice light touch to his questioning, and he made his studio guests feel comfortable and at ease. It was pure charm that did it.

He once invited me over to his house in south London, and we spent a pleasant afternoon, chatting over a few beers. We somehow got onto the subject of gardening, and when I told them I had quite a nice sized garden in Harrow, his wife Lizzie, who was the one with green fingers in their household, gave me a little parcel before I left. It was, she pointed out, a small plant - a gift from their garden to mine. It was a lovely surprise, and much appreciated.

EAMONN ANDREWS

Talk about the charm of the Irish, Eamonn Andrews had it by the bucket load. He had almost as much blarney about him as Terry Wogan but was probably more astute and business-like than his fellow Irishman.

As a youth, I used to listen to Eamonn Andrews as a boxing commentator on radio. He covered all the big fights and had a great voice. But it was when he transferred over to TV that he really became a success. First as the question master in the popular What's My Line? Then his chat shows, and his long-running This Is Your Life programmes made him a household name.

But regardless of how successful he was in Britain, Eamonn never forgot his roots and retained his many business ventures in Ireland.

He once invited me to go and join him on a whirlwind trip to Dublin and we spent two days, with Eamonn chairing various business meetings and popping in to keep up with things at his TV commercial company. It was a real eye-opener for me. It wasn't often one would get the chance of watching not just a TV star but a businessman in action.

370

When I flew back and wrote a full-page feature for the Mirror, he phoned me up the next day and said, "I liked your piece. Thanks. There's only one thing you've got wrong. When you printed how much money I make, well, I only wish I did. It was a slight exaggeration – but I'll forgive you this once!"

ESTHER RANTZEN

Esther Rantzen was someone I got to know when she was working as a researcher at the BBC, and then became on-screen assistant to Bernard Braden in his popular weekly TV show Braden's Week. She was very attractive, very bright, and clearly very ambitious.

A Canadian, Braden was a big-name broadcaster who had been around for years and was very popular with the viewing public. Bernard made his name on ITV fronting his consumer programme The Braden Beat, but then moved over to BBC with a similar show, which they called Braden's Week.

He was married to the lovely Barbara Kelly, also a performer, who shot to fame as one of the TV panellists on the long-running quiz show What's My Line? sitting alongside that great veteran grouch Gilbert Harding, Lady Isobel Barnett and magician David Nixon.

However, whilst Bernard Braden was quite happy to work with Esther Rantzen, and regarded her as an asset to his show, it became obvious after a while that she was becoming more popular around the BBC than he was. And when Bernie took an unfortunate break to present a similar show back in his native Canada, the lively Esther lost no time in replacing him in London.

In fact, she then took over the show completely, becoming the star and presenting the re-vamped programme, which they called That's Life! Braden's BBC contract was then not renewed, and he was gradually forced into retirement, which he took quite badly.

Bernard and wife Barbara were very resentful at the time. I knew them both quite well, and Barbara once invited me over to their house in Regent's Park, then drove me to lunch in her very trendy white Mercedes two-seater sports car. And I recall her telling me at the time, "I shall never forgive Easther Rantzen for the way she took over Bernie's show."

Bernie died in 1993. Barbara, who had such a wonderful personality and a quick-fire wit, later gave up acting and became a theatrical agent. She died, aged 83, in 2007.

Esther, meanwhile, became more popular than ever, though she was known around the Beeb as The Teeth. Viewers liked her sparky wit and the way in which she went out on the streets with a camera team to round up passers-by and involve them in crazy stunts. Her show That's Life! ran for more than 20 years.

In her personal life, however, she created something of a scandal when she fell in love with Desmond Wilcox, who was her boss at the BBC, and then moved in to live with him when he left his wife, Patsy, who also worked in the same department.

The whole situation became an embarrassment to the BBC, especially when Patsy refused to divorce Desmond. She finally only agreed to divorce him when Esther became pregnant, and Des and Esther were eventually married in 1977.

Des then quit his executive job at the BBC, turned freelance, and went on to win awards as a fine documentary producer and presenter. Des worked for years as a reporter with the Daily Mirror before going to the BBC, and he was a very likeable bloke. He died from cancer, leaving Esther a widow with three children, in 2000.

Since then, Esther has forged a whole new career for herself. She launched the charity organisation Child Line, trying to protect children from abuse, and followed up with The Silver Line, aimed at combating old age and loneliness. And she is still active with various TV programmes, after more than 40 years.

More recently, she came out with the controversial suggestion that the BBC and other broadcasting organisations should set up dedicated phone line centres where staff can report any celebrities they suspect of sexual abuse. This was following the Jimmy Savile scandal, when Esther and others (including me) were asked why no one had ever "shopped" Savile and brought him to justice for his crimes. It's an interesting idea.

One of Esther's daughters, Rebecca Wilcox, has now followed her into television. It must be something in the genes, I guess.

I've always liked Esther. She's never lost her sense of humour, and she's proved that age is no barrier when it comes to working hard.

TOM BAKER

For me, Tom Baker was definitely the best Dr. Who of them all. With that colourful knee-length scarf, the trilby hat and that toothy mischievous grin, he won a whole army of young fans - and never scared a single one.

Baker was a one-off. He was marvellous company. He came from Liverpool, so we had a lot in common. He was working as a bricklayer when he first won the role of the Time Lord, for he had long periods when he was out of work as an actor.

From a devoutly Catholic family, he actually spent six years, after leaving school, as a monk on the island of Jersey, before deciding that the monastic life was not for him. He lost his faith, he said, after suddenly realising that he wanted to break every one of the Ten Commandments in strict Biblical order, so decided to forsake the Church before he did something he'd regret.

We once had lunch together while he was on film location, and he spent most of the afternoon regaling me with anecdotes about his crazy life style, and exchanging jokes.

A few days later I received a postcard from him, saying "I enjoyed our lunch. And I'm still laughing at the joke you told me, which I had never heard before. I'm going to have some fun re-telling it."

Tom was a true eccentric, but also a great storyteller. He once told an anecdote of how he was walking into a recording studio in Wales, when he was accosted by a man he'd never seen before, who shouted at him, "I will never forgive you, nor will my wife, for what you did to our grammar schools." Tom replied bluntly, "What are you talking about, you daft bugger?" The stranger then replied, "Oh, I'm so sorry. For a moment, I thought you were Shirley Williams."

He could also be very serious and melancholy, though. He discussed how he would like to die and told me he had already picked out the spot for his burial and even ordered the gravestone.

Having not seen him for some years, I wonder if he has ever changed his mind.

MICHAEL CRAWFORD

Another guy always good for a laugh was Michael Crawford. Actor, singer, comedian – he had the lot.

He shot to TV stardom as the unbelievably daft young newly-wed husband Frank Spencer in Some Mothers Do 'Ave 'Em, with Michelle Dotrice as his frustrated wife Betty.

Michael insisted on doing all his own stunts, and some of the things he got up to were really quite dangerous. But he loved it, and before long he couldn't walk out in the street without being ridiculed in a friendly way by strangers. "Ooh, Betty!" they'd shout, in that mincing voice which Michael had very carefully cultivated as his own comedy tool.

He was quite a lad with the girls, and at one time he became very friendly with one of the secretaries in the BBC Press Office at the TV Centre. He would come into the bar to pick her up, and she enjoyed a spell of telling everyone, "I'm dating Michael Crawford."

To bump into big-name stars around the corridors of the BBC was not unusual. But for one of them to be dating a girl from the Press office, well, that was something different. Some of the Publicity officers and their secretaries would often meet up in the bar, after finishing work. And Michael became quite a familiar character, joining us in the club bar, and buying his round, like the rest of us.

The greatest night for Michael, as far as I'm concerned, was when he opened in the musical Barnum at the London Palladium in 1981. I was at the first night, reviewing the show, and I think it was the most exciting and exhilarating performance I have ever seen from any actor. He was simply stupendous as the circus artist who did everything – singing, dancing, clowning, and finishing the night on a breath-taking tightrope walk on a very high wire above the heads of the theatre audience. To say that he brought the house down would be an understatement. He earned rave reviews, including one from me, and the show went on to have a record box-office run.

The only show ever to match that was, of course, Phantom of the Opera. Again, Michael was superb. And he took the show to the States and wowed them all over again on Broadway. Among the many awards he won, were two Laurence Olivier Theatre Awards, one for Barnum in 1981, the other for Phantom in 1987.

He really is an exceptionally talented star. It's strange to think that the Michael we used to drink with is now a grandfather.

JERRY HALL

Jerry Hall is usually quite a spectacular sight. I met her in London when she was trying to establish herself as an actress, after giving up modelling. She was wheeled out by her publicity people to talk about a new TV game show she was taking part in. It turned out to be nothing special.

The most obvious thing about Jerry is all that blonde hair. And those teeth. Yet she had sex appeal in abundance.

After years of making the headlines mostly as the ex-wife of Mick Jagger, it came as a big surprise to everyone in 2016, when the statuesque Jerry found herself an even richer man, in the unlikely form of ageing newspaper tycoon Rupert Murdoch, who was old enough to be her father, but wasted no time in announcing their engagement. And they married a few months later.

TOMMY STEELE

No one was more of a perfectionist than Tommy Steele. I first met and interviewed him at the Liverpool Empire when he was a cocky kid topping the bill as an up and coming rock n roller, aged about 21. And 50 years later, nothing had changed, except that Tommy had become not only an international superstar but even more of a man who wouldn't compromise and was determined to do things his way. A total professional.

I interviewed him several times, and he was always adamant. "I won't do any show at all unless I get my own way. I must be in full control and have people around me who know what they are doing."

Once, in 1977, I went down to see him in summer concert in Paignton, Devon. When I arrived at his hotel in Torquay, to have lunch with him, I found him slumped in a chair, in a sweat-soaked tracksuit. "Gawd, I'm really whacked," he said. "But I feel as fit as a fiddle."

He had just finished his daily two-hour session on the squash court, before going off to have what he called his "keep fit cocktail." The cocktail consisted of two raw eggs, a pint of iced milk, two scoops of chocolate ice cream, and five spoon-fulls of Horlicks. That was his recipe for fitness.

Later, he would grab an hour's sleep in the afternoon, before going on stage. This was his first summer season run for seven years "It's bloody hard work, doing two shows a night," he pointed out.

Tommy, then 40, had taken on the summer production to celebrate 21 years in show business. He'd matured from the shock-haired rock n roll Cockney kid I'd first met in Liverpool into one of the world's most respected and popular entertainers.

He had acquired a reputation of being difficult to work with, but he denied this to me. He simply knew what he wanted, and he expected people around him to match up to his standards.

With his stage shows, and in TV, he always had full control. In films, it was different. "The directors and the men who cut the films have all the control," he said. "I've not always been happy with that."

375

At that time, he had made eleven films. "But to be honest, there were only three of them I was really happy with and would ever want to watch again." Which films were they? "The Happiest Millionaire, Half A Sixpence, and The Tommy Steele Story," he told me.

The nice thing about Tommy was that, even though he became a millionaire and a superstar, once he got back home he was still the boy from Bermondsey. "My favourite nosh is still jellied eels and pie and mash," he always insisted.

TONY HANCOCK

Tony Hancock was a brilliant, one-off comic genius. There's no doubt about that.

There are some who would argue that he was the best comedian not only of his generation but of the last century.

First through radio, then after transferring to TV, Hancock became the best-known funny-man in Britain. Everyone knew his face - with that sad, droopy, depressed look. But his voice was even more recognisable. And his perpetual moaning became all part and parcel of the man himself. Hardly ever known to laugh, he might well have justified the tag of Mr. Misery.

But despite his immense talent, Hancock was flawed throughout his life. He had a constant battle with two things – bouts of acute depression and alcohol.

Having been brought up as a kid listening to radio, I used to love Hancock's Half Hour, with his assortment of BBC pals. Who could ever forget those classic shows, like The Blood Donor ("What do you mean, a pint? That's almost an armful.").

Then, when he came to TV and we could put faces to those wonderful voices we'd grown up with, it was all too good to believe. Watching a Tony Hancock TV show was like being in Heaven.

Over the years, however, Hancock's health began to suffer. And he lost a lot of friends through his drinking and bouts of depression.

I got to know Tony quite well in his later years, and knew his wife Freddie even better because she was his agent and handled all his business affairs and publicity, before they eventually got married.

Unfortunately, their marriage became a volatile, violent and abusive affair, and ended with Freddie trying to commit suicide.

Tony's career went through various phases. He did films, stand-up comedy tours and TV sitcoms, but he was so insecure that he was never really happy with anything he did, even though he was the top earner in his field.

It was when he signed up with ABC TV to do a series of weekly variety shows from Blackpool that I really got to know him and saw something of the real Hancock in action. He kept assuring everyone, "I'm more mature. I've stopped worrying. I did too much intellectualising. I now just want to make people laugh. That's what it's all about."

He did bring a refreshing new approach to the business of being a compere. Instead of the usual whipping up of synthetic enthusiasm for the feast of entertainment about to be brought to the viewers, Hancock would face the camera with a jaundiced eye and say, "Well, we've got a right load of old rubbish for you tonight." The viewers loved him.

Tony would travel up to Blackpool at weekends to do the show, and back home he shared a flat with Freddie in Knightsbridge.

He was still drinking quite heavily however. In July 1966, after a drunken row with Freddie at home, he left for Blackpool, and did the show next day. But the news leaked out that Freddie had been rushed to the Middlesex Hospital after an attempted suicide.

The next week, Tony returned home, and Freddie was moved into a nursing home, to help her recover. Tony then gave an interview in which he said their marriage was finished

Later, Freddie said, "I believe now that Tony was very angry and had convinced himself that I had phoned up all the newspapers to tell them I had taken an overdose in order to hurt his career. The last thing I wanted to do was to harm his career."

The following Sunday, 25 July 1966, Hancock ducked out of doing the TV show, claiming to be ill, and the producers hastily brought someone in to replace him.

Tony went into a nursing home to be 'dried out'.

The big question was being asked: Is Tony Hancock finished?

Then, out of the blue, I got a tip-off that he was out of hospital and was rehearsing for next week's TV show. I hurried down to the rehearsal rooms in central London, and found Tony, alone with one of the producers reading through a script. Although they seemed surprised to see me, Tony invited me to sit down and have a cup of tea with them.

He was quite cheerful, cracking jokes, and he assured me that he was fully fit and rearing to go. And yes, I could tell all Daily Mirror readers that he would definitely be back on TV next Sunday. In the end, he thanked me for tracking him down, rather as though he was relieved to get it all out into the open.

Next weekend, I drove up to Blackpool to watch the show 'live' from the ABC Theatre. There was a pack of newspapermen backstage, all anxious to witness Hancock's come-back.

But the remarkable thing was that everyone wanted him to succeed. And when the producer came out and talked to the Press, he asked if we could respect Tony's wishes. He was requesting that if we let him do the show first, he would be available to talk to us all immediately afterwards. And to a man, we all agreed.

When the show went on the air, he bounced on stage, and his first line was, "Sorry about last week. I had a touch of sunstroke or something."

After the show, which went remarkably well, he was as good as his word. We were all ushered into a Press conference, and while we were given drinks, a very subdued Tony walked in, a cup and saucer in hand, and said, "Thanks for coming. Cheers! You don't mind if I stick to tea, do you?" This immediately met with a ripple of applause from the Press mob, which I thought was a nice touch.

He went on to assure us he was fit again and looking forward to doing the rest of the shows in the series.

His private life was still a mess, however. Hancock told his wife Freddie that he had found someone younger as his mistress, and they announced plans to divorce.

Later, Tony went to Australia, where he still had a big following of fans, and signed to do a series of 13 programmes for Sydney's Channel 7. The trouble was, Hancock was back on the booze and the producers more than once threatened to axe the whole series unless he sobered up and worked properly.

He was staying at a motel. One morning, there was no answer from his room. When a friend finally got in, the lights and heaters were on, and Tony was lying on the bed in just his underpants and socks. He was dead. There was a pen in his hand and two notes written on the back of his scripts. There was an empty vodka bottle and a scattering of pills.

One note was for his mother, who lived in Bournemouth. "Please send my mother this. I am sorry to cause her any more grief as she has already had enough. But please pass on this message to her – that the soul is indestructible." And in the second note, he'd written, "This is quite rational. Please give my love to my mother but there was nothing left to do. Things seemed to go wrong too many times."

The post mortem showed that Hancock had died as the result of taking a large number of tablets and an excessive amount of alcohol. The coroner's verdict was suicide.

On 18 July 1968, there was a memorial service at St. Martin-in-the-Fields, London, and six months later the BBC screened six of Hancock's old TV shows. They included The Blood Donor and The Radio Ham.

For those who still remember him, they talk about him only as the funniest comedian of his time.

JASPER CARROT

Jasper Carrot has always been an odd bloke. But although he looks a little crazy and behaves in a pretty weird way, he is actually a very ordinary and down-to-earth chap.

The first time I met him, in Birmingham, I didn't quite know what to make of him. He behaved like a young eccentric. But when I got to know him better, he became more normal, while at the same time being hysterically funny.

I first bumped into him in 1978 when London Weekend TV launched him as the greatest new find of the year. The trouble was, ITV was then fragmented and only a small part of the country could watch his shows.

Programme chief Michael Grade started the ball rolling, after seeing him in a one-man show at the Royal Shakespeare Theatre, Stratford. Grade wrote to every ITV company programme boss, urging them: "Give this boy Carrot a chance to prove himself. He's the funniest man we've found in a long time."

Michael told me at the time, "I heard a lot about this bright new comic with a big following in the Midlands, so I went to see him. His TV shows are going to be great. He breaks down all the old comedy barriers. He's going to become a big name, believe me."

When I went to meet Carrot, I could see exactly what Michael Grade was raving about. This guy was just so different from all the other comedians around. He didn't tell jokes, but simply stood on stage and talked to the audience, relating the amusing things that had happened to him.

And Jasper told me, "I find that too many stand-up comics all delve into the same pool of old jokes. I think it's pathetic. Most of them earn a living telling jokes about their mother-in-law's drawers, Pakistanis and thick Irishmen. But I see comedy as something different."

He drifted into show business by accident, after leaving grammar school and doing an assortment of dead-end jobs. Then he learned to play the guitar, opened a folk music club in Birmingham and slowly built up a name for himself around the Midlands.

His real name was Bob Davis. "I've had the nickname Jasper since I was a kid. When I was 17 someone asked me what my surname was. Just for a joke, I said the first word I could think of – Carrot. And the name stuck."

Jasper was 32 when he got his big break. Married with three children, he moved into a beautiful country home in Warwickshire, which he once invited me to.

At first, he was branded a regional entertainer – like Scot Billy Connolly and Welshman Max Boyce. But Jasper insisted, "My humour is completely English. I don't know why I've been pigeon-holed as a Brummie comic."

It didn't take long for him to establish himself nationally once his TV shows shot up the ratings, and he was at the top for quite a few years.

The last time we chatted was some years ago in London, when he suggested we meet at his hotel near Lord's cricket ground. When I turned up, expecting to have just a few drinks, Jasper said, "I'm starving. Let's go and have dinner. Do you fancy a Chinese?" I didn't really because I'm not a great Chinese food person. But I didn't like saying no because I could see how enthusiastic and hungry he was. So off we went. And any reservations I may have had about noodles and chop suey were quickly outweighed by the hysterical stories from Mr. Carrot.

KEITH BARRON

With some actors, you meet them once and never see them again. With others, you may interview them so often that you eventually become quite firm friends.

That's the way it was with Keith Barron. I've lost count of the number of times I've interviewed him because, over the years, he did so much splendid work. Like most actors, he appreciated the publicity.

He's a really likeable bloke, and always good company. At one time, when we used to go down to St. Ives in Cornwall at least once a year for holidays, I remember walking into a little restaurant in the main street with my wife for dinner, only to be greeted by Keith Barron. As he showed us to a table, he explained that he had bought the place and was determined to make a go of it. He wanted to ensure that he had some financial security, outside of show business.

Keith kept the restaurant for a few years, before selling it on. But as an actor, he was constantly in demand for a long time.

As well as working in films and the theatre, he's done so many good TV show that it's hard to keep track of them. Some of the best were the comedy series Duty Free, The Good Guys with Nigel Havers, Room At The Bottom, and Haggard.

If you see the name of Keith Barron on the cast list of any show, you know you are in for a good performance.

BOBBY DAVRO

When he was 16 years old, Bobby Davro wrote a letter to Mike Yarwood, asking for advice on how to get into show business. Mike, who was then the top comedy impressionist around, replied simply: "Be as original as you can."

Davro took the advice, worked hard on his comedy routines, and after ten years on the night club circuit eventually broke into the big time at the age of 28 with his own TV show.

Ironically, he later took over from Yarwood as the No.1 impressionist. His ITV shows, Bobby Davro On The Box, drew 11 million viewers on Saturday nights between 1987 and 1989, before his popularity spiralled and he found himself back on the night club circuit.

Bobby had a theory about this. The evolution of comedy is one of his pet themes, even today. "Look at the 70s when Mike Yarwood was drawing 24 million viewers. Then he was out, and it was my turn for a few years," he once said. "Then I was out, and comedy was all about harder humour, satire, with Ben Elton, Harry Enfield and Rik Mayall. They had a licence to be edgy, which my generation didn't."

Then of course along came new impressionists like Rory Bremner, and Davro realised his days at the top were over. "There's a perception that I'm old-fashioned. It's not true, but unless you can get on TV with the right format and prove yourself, it's very frustrating," he said.

I interviewed Bobby a few times. When he was at the height of his career, I went to see him in Blackpool, and he was hooked on the ancient Oriental martial art known as Wing Chun and was taking lessons from a Chinese guru. For although he had his own show on BBC (Bobby Davro - Public Enemy Number One!) and he was also topping the bill in summer theatre, he admitted to feeling insecure. "I've grown very grumpy and dissatisfied. I don't know why, because I have nothing to be insecure about. I have a terrific career," he told me.

Davro always gave the impression of being a flash, fun-loving extrovert, but admitted to me that deep down he was a great worrier. That's why he was learning Kung Fu. "Although it's a form of self-defence, it teaches you how to totally relax."

Some years later, Bobby's dedication to work contributed to the breakdown of his ten-year marriage. His wife had an affair with a builder, which led to the couple's divorce. Bobby admitted, "I was always worried, and I brought that unhappiness home and it made my wife feel insecure. Those years were very cruel to both of us, we should never have got divorced. It was a devastating blow for me. If I had my own way, we would still be married."

His marriage split came at a time he was earning over £500,000 a year. But the divorce cost him a small fortune, and the cost of maintaining a big house in the Home Counties and privately educating his three daughters, while trying to build a new life for himself narrowed his career choices.

Bobby took a straight acting job as Vinnie Monks in Eastenders in 2007, and then starred as a disillusioned family man in the critically acclaimed London stage play Not A Game For Boys. None of this paid as well as comedy, so he signed up for the kind of reality TV he used to fret about, appearing in Celebrity Come Dine With Me in 2009, Dancing On Ice a year later, and Celebrity Big Brother in 2015.

It was all a bit of a comedown from his days as a top-of-the-bill act. But Bobby cheerfully carries on, determined to continue working as a stand-up comedian and mimic. He still hopes he can appeal to younger comedy fans, as well as the more mature middle-agers.

"I love what I do, and I would do it for nothing," he said enthusiastically. "I want people to come and see me because I am a funny man. I will never, ever give up."

He's lost none of that enthusiasm he had when we first met, more than 25 years ago.

And the funny thing is, Bobby is still a great mate of Mike Yarwood, his first comedy hero. They keep in touch and get together for a curry a couple of times a year, I'm told.

LULU

Lulu, the little girl from Glasgow with the big voice, was always great fun to be with. In Madrid, in 1969, she was Britain's contestant for the Eurovision Song Contest with the catchy number Boom Bang-a Bang. And we had a lot of laughs with her, hanging out in Spain, before she eventually tied with three other countries for first place. A lot of champagne was drunk that night.

But once, when she invited me over to her house to do an interview, she suddenly said, "Ken, you don't half remind me of my Maurice. You could almost be his double."

Maurice was her first husband, one of the Gibb brothers who shot to fame as the Bee Gees. They married following a whirlwind romance after meeting backstage on Top of the Pops, when she was 20 and he was 19. The marriage lasted only four years when they split up because Lulu couldn't take his drinking any more, and Maurice was battling alcoholism. He died in 2003, at the age of 53.

At first, when she compared me with Maurice, I thought it was a funny thing to say to me. But then, looking in the mirror, I could well see what she meant. It was at the time when I had grown a beard, and had long, almost shoulder-length hair. And I did have a toothy grin, just like Maurice.

I remember Lulu once talking about the halcyon days when the Bee Gees used to hang out with the Beatles and other rock stars. Lulu herself never, ever took drugs, she said, but she told me that whenever they had overnight parties, she was the one who would be busy in the kitchen, making breakfast for the rest of the hung-over guests. "And with some of them, they were taking cocaine together with their eggs and bacon and coffee."

Lulu later admitted in a TV interview that she should never have married Gibb, because they were too young. She also confessed to having a love affair with English actor Davy Jones, one of The Monkees, before ditching him when she discovered he was cheating on her with another woman he was about to marry.

TOMMY COOPER

Comedian Tommy Cooper was as mad as a hatter. I don't think I ever met him when he wasn't drunk.

A journalist chum of mine, Douglas Marlborough - who was a show business reporter on the Daily Mail, and could drink a bit himself – once went to interview Tommy and met him in a pub. After a few drinks, Tommy suggested they continue their chat at Euston Station, where he was due to catch a train to Cardiff.

Then, after a couple more drinks at the station, Tommy said, "Have you ever been to Cardiff? Why don't you come with me?" And Dougie foolishly agreed and got on the train with him.

Later that week, I got a phone call from the News Editor of the Daily Mail, in a bit of a panic, asking me if I had any seen Dougie Marlborough or had any idea where he might be, because they hadn't heard from him for three days.

When Dougie eventually sobered up and returned to London, he told me that he couldn't remember much about the trip, he didn't know where he had stayed, and he wasn't very impressed with what he had seen of Wales, but he thought that Tommy Cooper was a really funny man.

Well, we all knew that, didn't we?

There was the famous occasion when Cooper appeared on the Royal Variety Show at the London Palladium, and the Queen and Duke of Edinburgh were walking down the line, meeting the artists afterwards. Tommy shook hands with the Queen, then in his booming voice, asked her, "Do you like football, M'am?" When she looked at him, a little nonplussed, and politely muttered something, Tommy said, "Because if you don't like football, I was wondering if I could have your tickets for the next Cup Final?"

Les Dawson, who was standing next to Cooper in the line-up, burst out laughing. But as the Duke of Edinburgh walked away, apparently not amused by Tommy's flippant remark, Les mumbled, "What a miserable bastard!"

Jimmy Tarbuck, who was standing on the other side of Cooper, told me the story and swore that it was true.

LEONARD ROSSITER

Leonard Rossiter, who was a brilliant actor, was another of those strange blokes who, after his death, it was revealed he was a philandering husband and a cheat.

He was always a bit creepy and gave the impression that he might suffer from constant bad breath. But you tended to put that down to the odd assortment of weird characters he played, rather than it being the actor himself.

Born on Merseyside, he was a clever chap who always resented the fact that he missed out on a place at Liverpool University because his father had died in World War 11 and Leonard had to help support his mother. He worked as an insurance clerk for seven years, before taking the plunge and becoming an actor at the relatively late age of 27. But when he got into his acting stride, by hell did he show 'em!

He was in a string of films and stage plays. But it was the role of Rigsby, the sneering, lecherous landlord, renting out seedy bedsits in Rising Damp that really shot him to fame. The TV show became an enormous hit with viewers and ran for more than six years. And they are still showing repeats today.

Then came The Fall and Rise of Reginald Perrin, a cleverly concocted comedy which had Rossiter at his brilliant best in the title role. And cashing in on his popularity, he then earned a fortune, making the long-running series of very funny TV adverts for Zinzano, with Joan Collins playing his wife.

I interviewed Leonard several times and found him an odd fellow. He was always polite and did his best to come up with stories that would be interesting for me to write. But he could be short tempered, and he told me the first time I met him, "I don't buy the Daily Mirror, and I don't suffer fools gladly - so this had better be good!"

It was something I never forgot whenever we met.

But despite his hang-dog look (he always gave the impression he was suffering from a hangover and was in need of sleep) Leonard was a keep-fit fanatic. He played squash and hated to lose. Even later in life, he was sometimes having up to three squash sessions daily.

One day, when I went to meet him, he had just finished a squash game on court.

"I'm pretty good. There are not many people who can beat me," he boasted.

When I told him that my son-in-law was a professional squash coach and had once been ranked No.14 in the world, Leonard looked suitably impressed and asked me more. I told him that my daughter Susan was married to Moussa Helal, an Egyptian who was still in the world rankings, had won many trophies, and now played for England.

Leonard immediately knew his name, and said, "Listen, is there any chance of me having a game with him sometime?" I promised that I'd try and fix it for them to meet. Unfortunately, we never got around to it.

Super fit though he was, Leonard died of a heart attack in 1984. He was waiting to go onstage at the Lyric Theatre in London's West End, appearing in the Joe Orton play Loot, when he collapsed and never recovered. He was 57.

Leonard was married twice. His first wife was actress Josephine Tewson, but they divorced after two years. He then married actress Gillian Raine after a long relationship, in 1972, and they were together until he died.

But after Leonard's death, some skeletons emerged from the Rossiter cupboard. It was revealed that he had enjoyed a secret five-year love affair with BBC broadcaster Sue McGregor. His wife Gillian knew nothing about it until she received a letter from Ms. McGregor, telling her that she was writing her memoirs, and intended to break the news of their illicit affair, and she wanted to warn Gillian about the publicity this would receive.

It really is a cruel world, isn't it?

FRANKIE VAUGHAN

Frankie Vaughan was a great singer. One of Britain's finest crooners. And he had the good looks and the personality to match the voice. He became a huge star in the 1950s and then stayed around for 30 years or more. He was a smashing guy. Always friendly to talk to, and never made any enemies, as far as I know.

He was born in a tough district of Liverpool (it's strange, isn't it, just how much talent that city of mine has produced over the years?) and served in the Army at the end of World War II. But as a kid, he wanted to be a boxer, before he started singing with local bands, and then decided his future lay in show business.

Frankie liked to dress up on stage, and started wearing a top hat and tails, and carrying a cane. It became his trademark. And when he signed a recording contract, it wasn't long before he was producing a string of hits. He tried to copy the style of Perry Como. And did it very successfully.

His first biggie was Give Me The Moonlight, in 1955. Then came Kewpie Doll, Kisses Sweeter Than Wine, The Garden of Eden, and the song he was always remembered best for, The Green Door.

Having made it as a singer, he then turned to acting, did a few films, and was taken by his manager Paul Cave to America to try his luck in Hollywood. To everyone's amazement, the Yanks loved him.

Frankie was lined up to star opposite the great sex-bomb Marilyn Monroe in the film Let's Make Love. The film wasn't bad, and he could have had a good career in Tinseltown. But there was just one big snag – Marilyn had taken a fancy to him.

She had a habit of falling for her leading men, and it looked like Frankie was going to be the next fly in her trap.

With headline publicity, Frankie quickly jumped on a plane and flew back home to London. He admitted he was too scared to stay there. His wife Stella was also furious with the publicity.

And I recall Frankie telling me himself, when I interviewed him at his home shortly afterwards, "Ken, that Marilyn is quite something. It was flattering, but it became quite frightening. There was no doubt at all that Marilyn wanted to take the title of that film literally and play it for real."

And laughing, he added, "There's no way I want to go back to Hollywood. Stella won't let me, for a start. You've met Stella, she's a very determined woman. She would hate the idea of us living in Hollywood."

He was right. I had met Stella, and she was a lovely lady. She was a good Jewish girl from Leeds, and was the devoted wife and home maker, and there was no way she was ever going to lose her husband - to Marilyn Monroe or anyone else.

Frank and Stella had three children, and stayed together until he died, from heart failure in 1999, at the age of 71.

You could say it was one of the best marriages made outside of Hollywood.

TWIGGY

Before I got to know Twiggy, it was her Mum I became more familiar with. I never actually met her, but it was her voice which I used to look forward to hearing, because she was regularly on the phone to my office. Let me explain.

When Lesley Hornby, a tall, leggy but very skinny teenage schoolgirl, got her first chance as a model, it was her Mum who was her best publicist. For whenever Lesley landed a job which meant her appearing on TV, her Mum would phone us up trying to get publicity for her in our TV pages.

She worked as a factory machinist and lived in Neasden, North London, but she would unashamedly boast that "my girl is going to be famous one day." And she was right of course, because Lesley became Twiggy, super model and pin-up, and when she was only 17 she was given the title "The Face of 1966."

She was discovered when she was 16, when the hairdresser at her local salon thought she had the looks to make a model, submitted some pictures of her to a modelling agency, and – whoosh! the girl became a worldwide sensation within a couple of years.

Her hairdresser boyfriend Nigel Williams became her manager, changed his name to Justin De Villeneuve, and then changed Lesley's name to Twiggy. He took her to America, where they loved her, and it didn't take long for Twiggy to follow in the steps of the lovely Jean Shrimpton, as one of the world's most photographed models.

Then, when she grew tired of modelling, Twiggy branched out as a singer and actress. In 1971, she made the film The Boy Friend, and won two Golden Globe awards for her performance. From then on, there was no stopping her. Her Mum didn't need to phone us anymore. Her girl was now a star.

She went on to be fine singer, had her own TV series, and became a recording artist.

Twiggy was married twice. Her first husband Michael Whitney died after they'd been married only six years. She then married actor Leigh Lawson in 1988, and they're still together, as far as I know.

I've met Leigh Lawson. I interviewed him a couple of times, on location filming, and found him to be very pleasant and easy-going.

The nice thing about Twiggy is that she has not only grown better looking with age, but she has also revived her career and become a glamour model all over again, as the more mature face and figure of Marks and Sparks. She's still working, and whenever I see her on the box, she hasn't changed a lot and has retained her happy personality.

It's just difficult to realise she's a pensioner, that's all.

JILL DANDO

Jill Dando was a lovely girl. Oh, I know everyone says that about people when they are dead – but Jill really was a very likeable person. And her sudden death shocked the whole nation.

388

Over a few years, I got to know Jill quite well. She'd worked as a journalist before going to the BBC and becoming a TV personality, and she would remind me of this whenever we met.

She was always happy to do interviews with me. In fact, she told me once that she looked forward to them - "because you always take me for a nice lunch, and I know the Daily Mirror is picking up the tab."

Jill was not only a good looker, but she was smart, witty and very professional. She had everything going for her, and as well as being at the top of her particular tree at the BBC, she was engaged and looking forward to getting married to her partner Alan Farthing. That's what made her murder even more of a tragedy.

But as far as I was concerned, it was one of the strangest experiences I have ever encountered. It must have been a couple of years or more since I had last seen Jill Dando for lunch, when I found myself in London, for personal reasons not professionally. The date was April 26, 1999.

My son Mark, who is a sports writer on The Sun, was in hospital, having a hip replacement operation, and I went in to visit him, with the customary bag of grapes, to see how he was. I was then living in Wallasey, and I drove down to London, a day or two after he'd had the operation. I went to visit him around lunch-time, and spent about an hour, chatting and trying to cheer him up.

Trying to cheer up my son Mark is not easy at the best of times. But attempting to do it when he was still suffering from post-operation stress was even more difficult. However, having done my duty, I then drove back home, and this meant me driving through part of Fulham to eventually get on to the M1.

Oh, that wonderful feeling, once you're out of London and on the way North. Back to sanity!

The journey usually took me about four hours, door to door, depending on the traffic. But I was quite happy, listening to the radio. And then the News came on – and the headline announcement was: "BBC news reader Jill Dando has been shot dead." I couldn't quite take it in. I turned up the radio, and the news bulletin went on to report in some detail how Jill Dando had been attacked and shot dead. And it was on the front door step of her home in Fulham.

Dead? Jill Dando? In Fulham? I was so shocked, I pulled over in the car and stopped for a while. And then, it suddenly hit me – I had actually been driving through Fulham earlier that day.

389

When I eventually arrived home, my wife had already heard the awful news and watched the reports on TV. "Didn't you know Jill Dando? Wasn't she a friend of yours?" she asked.

When I heard the report in more detail, it became even more weird. Because Jill was actually killed at 11.47 am. She was on the doorstep, fiddling with the front door key to let herself in, when she was attacked and shot through the head with a single bullet. The killer escaped. Jill was rushed to hospital but was declared dead on arrival.

As I went through it all, very slowly, it dawned on me that this was a very odd coincidence. I hadn't been to London for months, and the very day I was there, I was in Fulham, and must have driven along the main road, passing the actual street where Jill lived, and within only an hour or so of her murder. It was uncanny.

Jill was only 37 when she was gunned down. Although the police arrested a local man, and he was convicted of her murder and jailed, he was later released after an appeal. And after a second trial, he was acquitted.

So the murder, and why Jill was killed at the peak of her career, remains a mystery.

SUE LAWLEY

Sue Lawley was another rather dishy reporter and news-reader who was high in the popularity stakes at the BBC over many years.

She started out working on local newspapers, before joining the BBC in Plymouth. But there's an interesting story about Sue. Born in Sedgley, Staffordshire, at school she always dreamed of becoming an actress and wanted to go to RADA. But her mother talked her out of it. And instead, she went to Bristol University, and then spent three years training as a newspaper reporter.

Because of her background, she had quite a pronounced West Midlands accent which sometimes embarrassed her. When she applied to join the BBC, she was desperate to improve her accent, so she frantically took elocution lessons to iron out those Dudley vowels. She admitted later that she never wanted to "talk posh", but just wanted to "talk proper."

With the right accent, she became one of the best news-readers on the box and was then the first woman presenter of the BBC's Tonight programme, and later took over on the prestigious Nationwide.

I first met Sue in between her switching jobs from Tonight and Nationwide, when she took time off to have a baby. She invited me over to her house, and we took some pictures of her with baby son Tom in the garden. "Isn't he adorable?" she cooed. "But the fact is, I now can't wait to get back to work. I've got over the thrill of having a baby. I breast-fed Tom until he was four months old. But I had to stop because I wanted to get back to work, and you simply can't take a baby with you to the studio and then break off whatever you're doing, to feed him.

"Although I will miss Tom, it will be refreshing to get back into the outside world. A woman can easily become cocooned in motherhood."

And then she added, "Besides, we need the money. All our friends think we are stinking rich. But we're not."

Sue married David Ashby, who was a solicitor, only five months after he had negotiated the sale of a house for her.

She always played down her own sexiness on the screen. "I'm no great brain, I'm just normally intelligent," she told me. "Viewers just want intelligent questions, and straight answers. I honestly don't think the sex of an interviewer matters any more, at the BBC or anywhere else."

I liked Sue. She was very down to earth, but also had a sense of fun. Once, we were both at a BBC reception for something or other, and she came over to join me and a couple of Press pals. As we downed a few glasses of wine, she suddenly took off her shoes, and kicked them under a chair. "My feet are killing me," she said. "But please, if I have too much to drink and get giggly, keep an eye on my shoes. I don't want to lose them."

Sue later married for a second time. Her husband was Hugh Williams, who was a TV executive.

She also went on to present one of my favourite programmes on radio, Desert Island Discs. And I must say that she was much better at it than her successor, the pretentious Kirsty Young who always sounds as if she's got a plum stuck in her mouth.

VERA LYNN

The great Vera Lynn became a legend in her own lifetime. She was the singer the troops loved the most during World War 11. She was the smiling angel who not only went out to entertain the troops but was also the songbird who kept us cheerful back home in Blighty when the bombs were falling. Just listening to her voice over the radio could help brighten up your day. My mother adored her and knew every word of all her songs.

"The White Cliffs of Dover" and "We'll Meet Again" will stay with me for ever.

It was a privilege to get to know Vera. I interviewed her a few times, and I was invited once down to her home in Sussex, where I had tea with Vera and her husband Harry. He was a clarinet player in the band she sang with, and they married in 1941, two years after they met, when the war was at its worst and we were being bombarded nightly by the Luftwaffe.

She really was a lovely woman. With Vera, what you saw was what you got. She had no airs and graces, even though she was a huge star.

Known as the Forces' Sweetheart, it was a tag which stuck for the rest of her life, and she enjoyed it enormously. "It sounds awful, but the war was good to me. It helped launch my career. But I'll never forget those thousands of brave men who died fighting for us," she told me.

She began singing as a kid, on stage at the age of seven, and made her first broadcast with the famous Joe Loss Orchestra in 1935, before joining ENSA and touring the trouble spots to entertain the troops.

After the war, she became one of our most popular singers, first on radio and then on TV, when she hosted her own musical shows. She starred in four Royal Variety Shows, was given the OBE in 1969, and then made a Dame Commander by the Queen in 1975.

Her husband Harry died in 1998. But Vera continued with her singing career. The public simply wouldn't let her retire. At the age of 92, she became the oldest living artist to top the British album charts. Miraculously, she was still singing like a woman half her age. And in 2014, she had an album released, titled Vera Lynn, National Treasure: The Ultimate Collection. She was then 97.

What a woman! What a star!

GRACIE FIELDS

There was one other legendary star, even older than Vera, who came through the war, became one of Britain's most popular entertainers, and went on to become a Dame. Her name was Gracie Fields. She was born in 1898 and brought up above her grandmother's fish and chip shop in Oldham. And although she became a world star, she never forgot her roots and remained as down to earth as a pair of Lancashire clogs.

I only met her once – with the Queen Mother. Well, that's not quite right. When I met Gracie, it was for only a brief chat. Then she told me, rather curtly, "You'll have to excuse me, love. But I've got to change into a new frock, to meet the Queen Mother."

The occasion was the Royal Variety Performance at the London Palladium in 1978. With the rest of the Press, I enjoyed sitting in the theatre stalls, watching the final rehearsals for the show. There was the usual line-up of variety acts. But on this occasion, the producers had insisted on keeping the top-of-the-bill star under wraps. All they would tell us was, "We have a really big surprise in store, and we don't want to announce the name until they walk out on stage. We want it to be a surprise, even for the Royal family."

Well, we were all intrigued. And then, only an hour or so before the show was to be televised, the stage curtains were lifted, and out walked Gracie Fields. She looked amazing. She was then 80 years old. The stage hands, and even the smattering of Press guys broke out into spontaneous applause. This was to be her tenth Royal Variety show, dating back to her first in 1928.

She went through the rehearsal of her one song – it was Sally. She didn't need any rehearsal, of course, because this was a song she had sung a thousand times. But it was all quite magical, just listening to her. She still had a splendid voice.

They then gave us a brief Press conference with her, the chance to ask some questions. She obviously enjoyed it all and was brimming with pride and appreciation. But eventually it came to an abrupt end when Gracie decided it was time she changed her frock.

Later, I sat through the whole show, and then we were allowed backstage, to watch close by as the Queen Mother and the Royal party met Gracie and the rest of the artists. It was a night I shall never forget.

The following year, Gracie was made Dame by the Queen. But when she was first told of the honour, she said, "Oh yes, I'll accept. Yes, I can kneel – but I might need some help getting back up again!"

When the investiture ceremony came, she sailed happily through it. But she died only seven months later, at the age of 81.

Gracie was buried on her beloved Isle of Capri, the Italian resort where she had lived for more than 30 years.

Just below her beautiful hillside villa, which she shared with her last two husbands, there is a very smart restaurant complex, which she owned.

On holiday with my wife once, we spent a few days in Capri, and we had lunch at the restaurant. It's become a tourist attraction, surrounded by souvenir shops. But it was still a pleasant experience. Having lunch in the sunshine, overlooking the lovely harbour. And thinking of Gracie – and Sally from our Alley!

ANTHONY HOPKINS

Anthony Hopkins is one of those guys who will not stand any nonsense from anybody. Not exactly rude. But he can be rather brusque when the mood takes him. And he has not got a lot of patience. I found this out the first time I met him, which was at a Press conference in London at a West End hotel.

He went through the usual question-and-answer session, smiling politely, but not in any way making much effort to impress anyone or make the next day's headlines.

When it came to an end, and drinks and sandwiches were served, his PR people tried to get him to mingle and chat with journalists. But he was clearly not in the mood for any of it. I was standing near a window, and Hopkins made a bee-line towards me, and said quietly, "How do I get out of here? I need a cigarette."

I steered him towards the nearest exit door, at the back of the room, and he seemed grateful. As he walked out on to a balcony, he lit a cigarette, and said, "Do you smoke?" and offered me his packet. I told him I didn't, but we clinked our glasses and stood together. I have never seen a man look so relieved.

"I hate these occasions," he said. "I suppose you must be used to them. Which paper do you work for?" When I introduced myself, he suddenly seemed more relaxed, and we chatted together for a while. "I just don't like Press conferences. I get fed up being asked the same old questions," he said. I began to feel some sympathy and quickly warmed to him.

He wasn't at all starstruck, more like the kind of bloke you could enjoy taking down to the pub for a pie and a pint.

I have never met him since. But I've enjoyed some of his films and he has become one of our finest Hollywood actors, better even than Richard Burton, the star he followed from the Welsh valleys and who he was always determined to emulate.

In recent years, Tony Hopkins has mellowed, given up his hell-raising days, and developed more of a sense of humour.

I was amused to see him come out and voice his opinion on the public outcry when the BBC released a new bank-busting TV version of War and Peace in 2016. Critics condemned the BBC for re-writing the book, introducing incest into the story-line, and flaunting the nudity and erotic scenes. But Hopkins, who had appeared in the original War and Peace series over 40 years earlier, came out fighting and was full of praise for the newest production.

"Writers of screenplays have every freedom to write in what they want," he said. "The same with Shakespeare productions – they are open to interpretation." And he praised Paul Dano, the young actor who played the hapless hero Pierre Bezukhov – which was the character Hopkins had played in 1972, when the story was stretched to 20 episodes.

He said the newest TV series was wonderful. "It's beautifully filmed, a lot is packed into each episode, the battle scenes are excellent, and none of the essential story is lost. I don't bother myself with all that huffing and puffing protest. It's so unimportant. Everyone gets their knickers in a twist, but life goes on."

He even went so far as to criticise his own performance in the original version, although the critics at the time raved about him. "I didn't have much to say in those days – I just learned the lines, I suppose, and hoped it would turn out okay. I thought I was a bit all over the place. I was in my early 30s and as an actor I was enjoying myself too much," he said.

Now, even approaching 80, he has said he will never want to retire from acting because he enjoys it too much. But he doesn't like watching his own films any more. "I rarely look back and never see anything I've been involved in. It seems pointless, something like trying to remember dreams. It's an exercise in futility," he said.

Oh, I do wish I could have taken that guy for a pint.

CLIFF RICHARD

The first time I met Cliff Richard was on his 21st birthday. I was on the Mirror in Manchester and my Northern Editor suggested it would be good if we could do some kind of birthday story on the young rock n roll star who was then topping the bills and beginning to make a name for himself.

It proved easier than I thought. I managed to get Cliff, who was appearing in Blackpool, and he was happy to do it. With a photographer, I met Cliff on the Golden Mile and we went down on to the vast stretch of sand to do some pictures. For some reason, he had brought his guitar with him. It was mid-morning and too early for holidaymakers. We ended up, with Cliff on a completely deserted beach, serenading us on his guitar.

It made a great picture. Just Cliff with his guitar - with the waves crashing in the background. And as it was the Editor's own idea in the first place, we ended up with a full centre-page spread.

I got to know Cliff pretty well over the years. He's never really changed. Always friendly. For a long time, though, the Press were deviously trying to find out if Cliff was gay or not. He was seen out with girl-friends like tennis player Sue Barker and singer Olivia Newton John, but they always denied real romances. And Cliff would never talk about. Then, with the passing of the years, he revealed that he was happy living and sharing his life with his manager.

The fact is that Cliff has become one of the most successful pop stars in history and is the only artist I think to have consistent Top Five hit records in the charts in every decade over 50 years.

THORA HIRD

Thora Hird was a lovely woman. Probably the nicest person I ever met in the whole mad, egotistical world of show business. I once told her that she always reminded me of my mother, and she said, "I'll take that as a compliment, then."

But she was like my mother, in so many ways. She not only looked like her, but she was patient, kind, would sit for hours just chatting. And she would come out with the oddest, funniest phrases and memories – just like my lovely old Mum.

Born in Morecambe, Thora first appeared on stage when she was two months old - carried on by her mother, who was an actress, in a play produced by her father, who ran the local theatre and managed several entertainment venues in Morecambe.

Thora worked behind the counter at the local Co Op store for ten years, before taking the plunge and becoming an actress. And that's where she spotted so many of the quaint characters, as customers who came into the shop, and she later adapted them for some of her finest roles.

She started acting professionally in the 1940s, and from the theatre soon got into films. We tend to remember Thora mostly for her varied TV roles, but she was a big name in films before moving over to TV.

She became one of our best loved stars in comedy series like Meet The Wife, In Loving Memory, Hallelujah! and then as a presenter of Songs of Praise.

396

She was a committed Christian and told me once that she enjoyed doing Songs of Praise more than anything, perhaps with the exception of appearing in something written by Alan Bennett.

She loved Alan Bennett (don't we all?) and he wrote some of his most brilliant plays specially for Thora. Who can ever forget that wonderful tear-jerker A Cracker Under The Settee, which won her a BAFTA award in 1988?

She married Jimmy Scott in 1937. He was a drummer in a band, and he wooed her for two years. Scotty, she called him. He gave up his career and became her manager. "He's everything to me. He's my housekeeper, chauffeur, head cook, and bottle-washer," she told me. They were a devoted couple and went everywhere together.

Their only daughter followed Thora in the business, and Janette Scott, who was a strikingly beautiful young actress, became a top film star. She went on to marry Jackie Rae, a popular game show host, but they were divorced after six years. She then married Mel Torme, who was a top American singer and something of a rival to Frank Sinatra.

Thora thought Janette had found happiness, and she had two children with the Hollywood singer. More than once, Thora joyfully boasted to me, "Our Jan is married to Mel Torme, you know. He's one of the best singers in the world." She loved him, too. Unfortunately, it all turned sour and ended in an acrimonious divorce. Janette then married for a third time.

Thora once invited me over to her house - a lovely little place they had in Leinster Mews, Bayswater. And as she served me tea, she couldn't stop talking about Janette. "I love that girl so much. But she's gone through agony and unhappiness in her marriages," But later Thora became a doting grandmother.

We met quite a few times, and Thora often talked about her own childhood. I recall her telling me that her father was wonderful, but he was always her sternest critic.

The night before her father died, he told her, "You're a wonderful artist. I'm glad to have lived to see you perform like you did tonight."

"I was in tears," said Thora. "It was beautiful to finally hear that he thought I was good as an actress. Because he had never told me that before. I'm sure he loved me very much, but he was the kind of man who never actually told me he loved me, and I found that hard to accept."

I remembered that conversation much later, when Thora died. She ended up in a wheelchair, suffering badly from osteoarthritis. And she had repeated hip replacements and also underwent a heart bypass operation.

"But God has been good to me. I can't blame him for my aches and pains," she said.

In one play she did, in 1999, called Lost For Words, she played an old woman who was dying. One classic line in it, was when her son asked her, "Do you want to be buried, mum, or cremated?" and she thought for a few second before replying, "Oh, surprise me!"

When Thora Hird died in 2003, at the age of 91, they had a memorial service for her in Westminster Abbey. It was attended by more than 2,000 mourners.

I hate it when people use the phrase "National Treasure," especially when they are referring to people still alive and in most cases with a modicum of talent. Why don't they just say "well loved"? But with Thora Hird, it was different. Now she really was a National Treasure!

VICTORIA WOOD

One of the most talented women around, in my opinion, is Victoria Wood, a great bundle of energy and unbelievably creative as a pianist, comedienne, actress and scriptwriter.

She first came to light when she won the ITV talent show New Faces in 1974. Although I wasn't on the judging panel when she won in her first heat, I came across her at The Stables, a theatre company set up by Granada TV in Manchester to develop talent in the North.

She started out as a piano player who sang funny songs, but her brand of self-deprecating comedy soon developed, and it wasn't long before she was churning out her own sketch shows, as a scriptwriter.

Vicky, who came from Prestwich, Manchester (just down the road from where I now live) went to Birmingham University and studied drama but didn't really know what she wanted to do until she decided the best thing was to laugh at herself, and then found she could make a lucrative career out of it.

When she met and teamed up with actress Julie Walters, they went on to become one of the funniest comedy couples around. Apart from Vicky's one-woman shows and her sell-out stage tours, some of the TV shows she has produced have now gone down as classics.

Acorn Antiques, The Dinnerladies, not to mention her costume drama comedies like Lark Rise To Candleford, and her stage musicals. It's hard to pick out the best of her work. She's won so many awards, we've lost count.

One of the best things she produced was the TV film Pat and Margaret in 1994, in which she played the awkward fat Northern girl who was reunited with her sister, a horrible Hollywood film star, played by Julie Walters.

I went to the Press screening and reception for that, and recall afterwards, over drinks and nibbles, meeting up with Vicky and Thora Hird who were chatting together. Wow, I thought, two of my favourite comedy woman - who should I talk to first?

But Thora took the decision out of my hands. "Go on, Ken, you talk to Vicky. She's the one with all the talent. Not me," she said. "Besides, you can talk to me any time."

Vicky just laughed and gave Thora a hug. "Isn't she lovely?" she said.

IAN LAVENDER

He was the youngest, by far, in the cast of Dad's Army. And Ian, playing "Stupid boy" Frank Pike, was always aware of the wealth of experience in the veteran actors around him. As a young actor, he quickly learned to know his place.

But years later, when I was invited down to his house, I found that Ian now had white hair. We reminisced about those happy days spent filming in Thetford. And he admitted that he would always be grateful to Dad's Army for making him a star, even if it had typecast him for life.

Of course, Ian always insisted he was nothing like young Pike in real life. "I don't think anyone could ever say I was stupid," he said. "For a start, at school, I got 12 0-levels and four A-levels. And the only reason I don't have a university degree is that I went to drama school, instead."

I think one of the funniest moments came, a few years ago, when Ian appeared on a celebrity version of Mastermind. When quiz master John Humphreys asked him his name, one of his fellow contestants shouted out, "Don't tell him Pike!" (That's now become a classic line from Capt. Mainwaring in one of the original shows).

GEORGE COLE

George Cole was quite a gentle and very pleasant man. I used to listen to him on the radio, when I was a kid. And as an actor he never seemed to be out of work. But when he landed the role of Arthur Daley, alongside Dennis Waterman, in TV's Minder, he was suddenly elevated to the status of a legend. I was a little surprised though that when George agreed to meet me for a lunch-time drink and chat, one day when he was not working on the TV series, he turned up as Arthur Daley. Wearing that smart brown velvet-collared overcoat, and even smoking a cigar, he looked and behaved exactly like Arfur, the spiv and second -hand car dealer.

MERYL STREEP

I was in for a surprise one year, attending the BAFTA awards ceremony in London, because when I was shown to my seat, I found that sitting in the seat right behind me was Hollywood actress Meryl Streep. She did nothing but giggle and gossip with her partner throughout the whole evening.

If it had been a normal night out, in the cinema, I would have been tempted to turn around and ask her to be quiet. But no, I didn't.

PETER BOWLES

Actor Peter Bowles really was as pompous and arrogant as the character he played so successfully in To The Manor Born, opposite Penelope Keith. Doing any interview with him soon became pretty tedious. It was almost like being granted an audience with the Pope!

NORA BATTY

I once had lunch with Nora Batty. Well, not Nora exactly, but I took Kathy Staff, the actress who played her in Last of the Summer Wine, and her husband John for lunch in Manchester. He was a schoolteacher and was a very nice chap. But it was Kathy who did most of the talking. Her husband could hardly get a word in.

But I got the impression he was used to it.

At one stage, John joked, "When she's got her Nora Batty face on, I would never dare interrupt her."

ICE SKATING

Only once have I ever been ice skating. And once was enough, thank you very much. But then, my only skating experience was in the arms of a beautiful world champion.

It was in Liverpool, at the Stanley ice rink in West Derby. I was on the Evening Express and enjoyed doing a regular feature which took me somewhere different each week. When I chose to learn to ice skate, who better to teach me than the really glamorous Barbara Birtles, who was the World Ice Dancing Champion.

She happily agreed to do it, and when I arrived at the rink, I put my skates on and made my way to the edge of the ice. Barbara grabbed my hand and said, "Let's go."

She went, I didn't. I took a couple of steps forward and then slipped over, falling on my backside. As Barbara skated around, showing me how easy it was, I got up and was determined to do it.

A few more steps. Over I went. I was slipping and sliding all over the place. I was lucky, I suppose, that I didn't break a leg or an arm, because I was desperately grabbing at anything to hang on to.

Trying not to laugh, Barbara suggested, "Come on, put your arm around my waist and cling on close to me." Now normally, an invitation like that would have been every young man's dream, for the 19-year-old Barbara was a lovely young thing with long gorgeous legs. But after a couple more attempts, I gave up. I was useless. I watched, as young kids sailed past me, gracefully doing spins and somersaults and all kinds of fancy tricks. I wasn't frightened. It was simply that I couldn't keep my balance.

So I staggered off, took off the skates, and we went for a cup of tea. We both decided there was no way I was ever going to become an ice star.

In fact, Barbara's real partner in their ice dancing duo was Leonard Williams, who was a pal of mine and lived around the corner from us. His parents had a wool shop in Breckfield Road North, next door to the chippy.

Leonard used to occasionally come around and play football with us. He was a nice bloke. But funny enough, he was never good enough to get into our street team.

He may have been better than me at ice-skating. But I was better than him at footy.

SIR CYRIL SMITH

Although I never actually met Cyril Smith, the big, fat, odious MP for Rochdale, I came close enough on one occasion. And it was not a pretty sight. I walked into Granada TV studios in Manchester. And in the Reception area, there was the enormous Mr. Smith, obviously waiting for someone. As I sat down nearby, he smiled at me and fidgeted around trying desperately to get his huge frame from three seats into two. Then I noticed how untidy and unkempt he was. He was dressed in a suit, but he was so fat that he couldn't fasten the buttons on the jacket. And he had horrible food stains and dribble down the front of his waistcoat.

I remember thinking what an awful man he was. And I felt uncomfortable sitting even close to him.

All the stuff that came out later - about his despicable behaviour as a paedophile and how the Liberal Party covered it up and the police failed to arrest and charge him for child abuse - somehow did not surprise me at all.

DAVID TOMLINSON

When it came to those bathing beauty contests, which became so popular in the 60s and 70s, I was asked several times to appear as a judge. Organisers, for some reason, always like to have celebrities, sprinkled with a few journalists on the judging panels.

The first one I did was at New Brighton, when I was a columnist on the Liverpool Evening Express. It was held in the open-air swimming pool, and huge audiences used to turn out for the weekly events. My fellow judges were two actors appearing in summer season show at the Floral Hall Theatre.

Others I did later were at Southport and Blackpool. The bathing beauty contests became very lucrative. Every big city and seaside resort had a glamour competition, and many of the same girls used to travel around the country, competing on the circuit for top money as well as the titles. Miss England, Miss UK, and Miss World were the ultimate ambitions for the girls, of course. And for many of them, it led to modelling careers, and even the big break into show business.

A lot of the contests were on TV. And I was invited onto one big show, to be televised from Blackpool. When I arrived there, I found that my fellow judges were David Tomlinson, the British actor who was a big Hollywood name (star of Mary Poppins, and Bedknobs and Broomstick) and a woman journalist from a national magazine in London.

Before the show, David Tomlinson seemed quite keen to see something of Blackpool, so I took my fellow judges off and we shared a horse-and-carriage ride along the length of the Golden Mile prom and had an ice cream on the way back.

We did the show, live on TV, and at the party afterwards we had a few drinks.

David Tomlinson was pleasant enough, though rather aloof I thought. But our fellow judge, an attractive, middle-aged woman, was quite smitten with him, even a bit star-struck in her behaviour.

As the evening wore on, Tomlinson more or less ignored me and eventually, as bedtime approached, he took hold of our lady journalist, and they walked off together, arm in arm, without even saying goodnight.

I never saw either of them again. They were not around for breakfast and were both returning to London.

Another bathing beauty contest I did was at Southport, with ABC televising it. I travelled over to Southport the night before, accompanied by TV Press Officer Mal Griffiths and my good friend John Stevenson, a reporter on the Daily Mail. The three of us had dinner at a very good restaurant and then sauntered off and ended up in a rather dubious drinking club.

It was quite crowded, and long after normal pub hours, the doors were locked, and everyone went on drinking. We three were obviously the only strangers there, and we were happy talking to the locals and enjoying a few pints. All was fine at first, but it then became very boisterous, people were getting drunk, and one middle-aged woman came over and sat down at our table. She was looking a little the worse for wear, and offered her empty glass up, expecting a re-fill, rather too frequently. It was quite clear that she was trying to get off with one of us, and her friends at the bar seemed to be riotously encouraging her.

Things got out of hand, and when she tried to sit on my knee, I decided it was time to go, so I made a bee-line for the Gent's toilet. I was only in there a couple of minutes, when there was someone banging on the door. When I came out, it was Mal Griffiths, saying "I think it's time we got out of here, Ken. Come on, let's make a run for it." The three of us then made our excuses and left in a hurry, returning to our hotel.

Next day, we had to do the TV show. I was one of the judges, and John and Mal were both sitting in the audience. As the band struck up, and the show went on the air, I walked on stage to join the panel of judges, as the presenter McDonald Hobley announced our names. He did his opening speech, then welcomed the local Mayor and Mayoress of Southport, and one camera moved in to show them in close-up, in their regal finery, with the Mayoral chains around their necks, sitting on the front row. And to my horror, the Lady Mayoress was the woman we had to escape from in the club the night before. She sat there, demurely, smiling at the cameras. With not a trace of a hangover.

ROD STEWART

They've always said that Rod Stewart was one of those millionaires notorious for having short arms and long pockets. In other words, he never liked buying a drink. I don't really know whether this was true or not. Maybe it was just a myth he liked to perpetuate, like the great American comedian Jack Benny.

What I do know is that Rod likes to live up to his image as a super-cool rock star, and age has not really deterred that aim in life. He is certainly a lot more fun than his ageing rival-pal Elton John.

I recall having both of them staying at the same hotel in Montreux, Switzerland, in 1984, and the whole week developed into a bit of a riot.

The rather sedate Swiss lakeside town, which stages the annual Golden Rose TV festival, was suddenly invaded by rock music's biggest stars. The BBC and Swiss TV had combined to produce the most ambitious pop concert ever broadcast.

Michael Hurll, executive producer of Top of the Pops, was handling things for the BBC, and even he was surprised by the amount of talent they had rounded up. "We'll never get such a collection of big names together again," he told me, as they went through rehearsals.

The stars who flew in to take part in the show included Rod Stewart, Duran Duran, Cliff Richard, Madness, Gloria Gaynor, Bucks Fizz, Shakin' Stevens, Bonnie Tyler, Robin Gibb, UB 40, Adam Ant, Status Quo, Ultravox, Roger Daltrey, The Pretenders, Spandau Ballet, Slade, Bananarama, Tracy Ullman, and many more European and American performers.

Elton John was to have appeared, but embarrassed BBC producers by pulling out after a row over the billing. Apparently, he insisted on being top of the bill, but the organisers had ruled that the star line-up should appear in alphabetical order.

Artists would do two or three songs each, but these would be edited down to a single number. The programme was being shot over four nights, with four separate concerts. And the finished programme would be edited into a 100-minute spectacular to be screened on BBC-1 on a Bank Holiday Monday.

But the stars were not getting a massive fee for the show. They were all told, "If you want to be in the show, that's fine. But if you ask too much money, then you're out!"

Michael Hurll told me that even Rod Stewart was receiving around the same fee as the smaller artists. The extravaganza had already been sold to

32 countries, including USA, Australia, Japan and China, and some Iron Curtain regions including Russia and East Germany.

Well, we certainly had a rave-up that week. And even the gravelly-voice Rod Stewart was happy for once to cut his fee and be leader of the pack. And nobody really missed Elton John.

STEWART GRANGER

I was in Curzon Street in the West End of London one night. It was about 9 pm, it was raining heavily, and I was trying to find a taxi to take me to Baker Street tube station, to get home. After waiting for about ten minutes or so, desperately sticking my arm out in futile fashion at every approaching vehicle, I finally saw a cab with its light on. I ran to the edge of the kerb, put out my arm, and the driver stopped.

"To Baker Street, please," I said.

As I was about to climb in, a shadow came across my shoulder and out of the dark came this tall, well-dressed man. He jumped in front of me, got into the back of the cab, and said, "Thanks." Then he shut the door and sat down. I looked at the guy. It was Hollywood actor Stewart Granger.

When I started to protest, he said curtly. "There'll be another cab along soon," and turned to the driver to give him instructions. I looked at the driver. He just shrugged and pulled a funny face and drove off.

A few months later, I happened to switch on TV and saw Stewart Granger in a chat show with someone, Mike Parkinson or Terry Wogan, I've forgotten. And he spent most of the interview slagging off his fellow Hollywood actors and telling really nasty stories about them. What an awful, arrogant man, I thought.

DEMIS ROUSSOS

We were treated to dinner once by the Greek singer Demis Roussos. He was the giant of a singer with the strange high-pitched voice, and always dressed in exotic colourful kaftan gowns. He was enormously popular and had several hit records.

He took half a dozen Press guys to a Greek restaurant, just off Tottenham Court Road, and we had a hell of a good night. Wonderful food (delicious Kleftikon, I seem to remember, which melted in the mouth) and plenty of red wine.

405

Afterwards, of course, came the traditional Greek dancing and the smashing of crockery. The waiters brought dozens of plates and distributed them around the huge table we were sharing. Then we were encouraged to get up and smash the plates, to the accompaniment of the music.

It all went fine until we ran out of plates, and my mate Dougie Marlborough, from the Daily Mail, decided to go berserk. He gathered up not only the plates, but the expensive cups and saucers and every piece of crockery he could lay hands on, and hurled them wildly around the restaurant, smashing them up into tiny pieces.

The head waiter was furious and tried to restrain Dougie, pointing out that the plates they provided for smashing-up were all cheap ones, and they did not appreciate him destroying the rest of the more expensive crockery.

The party came to an abrupt end. Demis Roussos quickly jumped to his feet and demanded to pay the bill. Broken crockery included.

BRIAN BLESSED

Brian Blessed was an actor I first met when he was in Z-Cars, the police series set on Merseyside in the 1950s and 60s, and I was the first reporter to write about it.

PC Fancy Smith was always the bossy one, but he didn't have that big, booming voice we now associate with Brian Blessed. The voice is something Brian has developed over the years, and it increases in decibels every time you meet him.

In fact, it's become his trademark. Blessed The Voice.

It's amazing though, to see just what Brian has achieved since those early days in Z-Cars. He's done everything from comedy to heavy drama, films to pantomime. And even climbed Mount Everest. He's a giant of a man.

Are there any peaks still left for him to achieve?

THELMA BARLOW

I remember going shopping for an engagement ring with Thelma Barlow, the actress who played the dithering Mavis Riley in Coronation Street for so many years.

Thelma was all set to become engaged to the equally dithery Derek Wilton.

One of my spies tipped me off that she would be taking the morning off to go and choose a ring at Kendall's store in Manchester, so I grabbed a photographer and set off to join her. No one was more surprised than Thelma when I turned up at the store on Deansgate to catch up with her.

"What are you doing here?" she said, a little startled. "Just making sure you choose a nice ring," I said. She giggled nervously. But then I produced a bottle of champagne and said, "I thought we'd help you celebrate."

She went into a fit of laughter, and she knew there was no way out of it. I bought a couple of glasses from Kendall's, and she posed for a picture with me outside the store, showing off her sparkling new ring at the same time.

We used the exclusive picture with a story in next day's paper.

DUSTIN GEE

Liz Dawn, better known as Vera Duckworth in Coronation Street, was always good for a laugh. She was so popular and so funny at times, that she became an ideal target for comedy impressionists keen to get a cheap laugh. And when it came to impersonating Vera, one of the best at it was Dustin Gee.

Dustin and his comedy partner Les Dennis would team up, one playing Vera Duckworth, the other playing dizzy Mavis Riley.

One day, I was talking to Liz and she happened to mention that she thought that Dustin's wicked impersonation of her was very funny, and she would love to meet him.

So I set it up with Dustin and Liz, and the three of us teamed up at Manchester's Midlands Hotel one evening. We met in the bar, had a few drinks and were enjoying the chat.

I had a photographer on hand to take some pictures of them. Dustin had donned a curly wig, identical to Vera's, so they would look alike, in a close-up picture.

Unfortunately, it all got out of hand. One drink led to another, and we all got a bit squiffy, Liz in particular. We were sitting on stools at the bar, and suddenly Liz decided to take off her wig and plonk it on my head. "Go on, take a picture of you two," she screamed, nearly toppling over off her high stool. In the end, the photographer took snaps of all three of us. It was a quite hysterical evening.

Sadly, Dustin Gee died not long after. He suffered a severe heart attack at a Southport theatre, while playing one of the Ugly Sisters with Les Dennis in Cinderella. He was only 43.

He was buried in York, his home town, and Liz Dawn was among the mourners at his funeral. She said, "I was honoured that he chose to impersonate Vera. I once told him he was so good, he could do my job for me."

JONATHAN ROUTH

There was never a better practical joker than Jonathan Routh. He was a weird man, though. He could be friendly and amenable, but he had one of those sad, forlorn faces and, somehow, he turned being miserable into an art form.

Routh was the prankster who gave us Candid Camera, the original show which specialised in getting laughs out of people simply by recording them on hidden cameras. It sounds simple enough, and there have been many similar versions of it since. But none to match it. He first launched Candid Camera in 1960, and it then ran on ITV for seven years, with Bob Monkhouse becoming the presenter.

Some of the tricks Routh pulled off caused chaos. But it was all so cleverly contrived, that no matter how much sympathy you might have had for the innocent victims, it was impossible to watch that show without laughing. His hidden cameras captured some unbelievable TV moments.

The classic trick, which I'm sure anyone old enough to have seen it will never forget, was the car-without-the-engine. Routh took the engine out of a car and then somehow managed to drive it gently down a sloping road and onto the forecourt of a garage. He then got out and requested a routine oil change. When the garage mechanic opened the bonnet, there was no engine. Puzzled, he then went and looked in the boot, and ended up even underneath the car, looking for the engine. He just couldn't believe what had happened. And of course, Jonathan, playing the innocent driver, said he knew nothing about cars, and just wanted an oil change. Eventually, they had to put the poor mechanic out of his misery, and tell him he'd been fooled, before the chap thought he was ready for a trip to the nearest lunatic asylum.

Jonathan, I discovered, had a really strange sense of humour. I once got involved with him close up when Ronnie Taylor, the freelance TV producer, signed up Jonathan to headline his first stage show, and booked a big concert hall in Blackburn as the venue for the one-night production. And Ronnie asked me if I would handle the job of promoting the publicity for the show.

It was a variety show – with comedy impressionist Peter Goodwright, and singer Julie Jones in support – with Jonathan as top of the bill.

The trouble was, we didn't know exactly what Jonathan could do. He was a star name on TV, but he'd never done anything on a stage before. When I asked him what he was planning to do - apart from show some film clips of the funniest moments from Candid Camera - he wasn't quite sure, and said he would probably try some magic. Wonderful, I thought. What sort of tricks would he do? How about cutting a woman in half? Could he do that? "Oh yes, I'll do that," said Jonathan. "It's not a very difficult trick."

Fine, we agreed that this was going to be his big trick of the night. I then set about getting maximum publicity in the local Blackburn papers and on radio. One of the first things was to find a woman willing to be sawn in half. I set up an audition, and we ended up with a long queue of women all wanting the job. We picked out the most attractive girl, and we then had her picture on the front page in a story I'd promoted. I really did pull out all the stops, and I surprised myself at the amount of publicity I managed to get for the show. Surely this would sell tickets and maybe even guarantee getting a packed house. Ronnie Taylor was delighted.

Come the night of the show however, I walked into the theatre, and found the vast hall was not even half full. We were all disappointed at the attendance, but the show must go on, as they say.

Curtain up. Julie Jones was superb. Everyone loved her singing. Peter Goodwright was even better. His comedy impressions drew huge applause. Well, considering the size of the audience, it was hardly going to be thunderous!

Then came the interval. And it was curtain up on the second half. Time for the great Jonathan Routh to show us what he could do. Unfortunately, it wasn't very much.

Because the first thing he did was to apologise that he would not be attempting to cut a lady in half, as everyone was expecting, as he had not been able to perfect the trick and his equipment had let him down.

Instead, Jonathan quickly reeled off the TV film clips, and then proceeded to perform a series of very ordinary card tricks, sprinkling his patter with jokes which weren't very funny. I was horrified. I just couldn't believe it. The audience - or what was left of it - sat through it all in stony silence.

It was all so brutally awful that, if I'd been Jonathan I would have wanted a huge hole to appear in the stage and swallow me up.

When the end finally came, I quickly adjourned to the nearest pub, joining Ronnie Taylor, Julie and Peter, to try and drown our sorrows. It was like sitting in a morgue. Nobody wanted to say anything. Jonathan didn't join us. He had apparently decided to drive straight home.

In between drinks, Ronnie tried to lighten the mood when he said with a smile, "Well, now we know that Jonathan Routh is not going to be a big stage star. He'd better stick to television."

A few days later, the show was hammered in the local press. "Routh fails to deliver," was the headline. And the poor girl who wanted to be sawn in half ended up in tears.

It was a nightmare of an evening. But it didn't really do Jonathan any harm. He continued to pull in record viewing figures with Candid Camera.

Later, after retiring from TV, he became a painter and earned a good living as an artist. He died in 2008, aged 80.

FRANK FINLAY

The most boring actor I've ever met? No doubts about that at all. It was Frank Finlay. He was quite a big star over a number of years.

He played Casanova on TV in 1971, starred alongside Oliver Reed and Richard Chamberlain in The Three Musketeers a couple of years later, and really shot to fame in the controversial sex serial Bouquet and Barbed Wire, one of the most outrageous dramas of its era. And Roger Moore later described him as "a great co-star" in the 1978 film The Wild Geese.

I set up an interview with Finlay once, and took him to lunch in a West End restaurant. But he just sat there, eating and sipping his wine, with nothing at all to say. It was really hard work, even worse than trying to get blood out of a stone. And when I did manage to get him to answer a question or two, he was so conceited, I couldn't believe it.

Never have I been more relieved than when we finally wrapped up the lunch, and I grabbed the bill and escaped from him.

LYNNE REDGRAVE

I flew to New York once to interview actress Lynne Redgrave, and she suggested we meet in the afternoon at the Russian Tea Room. It's a very trendy place in the heart of Manhattan, not cheap, and I'd never been there before.

When I turned up, ten minutes early for our appointment, I was surprised to find her already there. Looking at my watch, I said, "I'm not late, am I?" She said, "No, but I'm one of those people who always gets there early. I can't stand unpunctuality." A woman after my own heart.

She then prattled on happily and was a joy to meet. But although she was confident and happy with her own career, I think she was always aware that she came from that great Redgrave dynasty (father Michael Redgrave, mother Rachel Kempson) and she was going to have to live in the shadow of her big sister, the more famous and by far the more vociferous Vanessa.

But I still liked Lynne. I can't forget that wonderfully silly film she did, in the title role of Georgy Girl, as the dolly bird on the loose and looking for fun in Soho in the Swinging Sixties. That film won her a New York Film Critics' Award, and nominations for an Academy Award and also a Golden Globe Award.

DAVID BOWIE

When David Bowie died from cancer early in 2016, it was amazing how the news sent shock waves right around the world. It was almost mass hysteria.

I met Bowie more than once on Top of the Pops, and at an awards show he attended for the Daily Mirror, and he was certainly a charismatic character.

But I was still surprised at the reaction to his death. The public mourning seemed to go on for weeks, and the newspaper coverage was something we'd never seen before.

There was no doubt that he had such a colourful life - from Ziggy Stardust, through so many musical changes and re-inventions of himself - that he made all the other rock stars like Elton John, Bob Dylan and Rod Stewart look like pygmies.

The saddest and yet greatest thing about the Bowie departure was the way he went. He released an album only a few days before he died, obviously knowing his end was near. And his final song, I'm In Heaven, said it all. He died with dignity. And with class.

Wouldn't we all like to go like that?

411

CROWN COURT

One of the most successful day-time drama series ever to come from TV was Crown Court, and it was quite unique in the way it was produced. Set entirely in a court room, it was supposed to be a factual reproduction of the criminal Assize system. The gimmick was that they had real actors, taking on the roles of judges, lawyers, and people on trial. But the jury was made up of ordinary members of the public.

It was devised by Granada from their Manchester studios and it became so popular with viewers that it ran for eleven series, and 879 episodes, from 1972 to 1984.

Each court case would run for three episodes, spread over a week. The intriguing point about each case was that, although the evidence was all scripted, nobody knew how it would end until the "amateur" jury came in with their verdict.

People used to write in, asking to be on the juries, and there was a long waiting list before they were selected.

By pulling a few strings, I managed to wangle a place on the jury, myself. And I sat there, with the other punters, over three episodes, with the chance of briefly being a TV star. I must say it was fascinating and I really enjoyed it, even though the hard, wooden benches were tough on the old bum after a whole day in court.

The hundreds of actors who took part in the series over the years read like a Who's Who of Show Business. Some of them were struggling actors, keen to get on the first rung of the TV ladder. Many of them went on to become established big names. They included Brian Cox, Colin Firth, Judy Parfitt, Keith Barron, Maureen Lipman, Peter Capaldi, T.P. McKenna, Juliet Stevenson, Patrick Troughton, Nigel Havers, Robert Powell, Bernard Hill, Peter Sallis, Warren Clarke, Eleanor Bron, Michael Elphick, Tom Conti, Jenny Seagrove, Richard Wilson, Ben Kingsley, Rodney Bewes, Jim Broadbent, Patricia Routledge, Honor Blackburn, Geoffrey Palmer, Cherie Lunghi, Annette Crosbie, and Stephanie Cole. They were all grateful to be on Crown Court.

As for me, although I enjoyed my brief stint on the TV jury, it didn't work out quite the same when it came to real life.

The first time I was called up for real jury duty in London, my boss, TV editor Clifford Davis, put his foot down and insisted that I couldn't go. "We can't spare you away from the office for three or four weeks," he ranted. "You'll have to make an excuse and get out of it."

So I then had to attend court on the first day of the Assizes session, and go before a Judge and try to explain why I wasn't able to do it. They don't take too kindly to people who try to get out of jury service, and this judge looked particularly fearsome.

He asked me for my reasons, and I went through some feeble explanation - that as a newspaper reporter, I might find it difficult to remain unbiased in some cases, particularly with someone who might have had prior publicity or been in the headlines. He was not impressed and asked me which newspaper I worked for.

When I told him, the Daily Mirror, he looked scornfully at me and said, "I cannot believe that a smart, young, upstanding, intelligent journalist should want to get out of doing his public duty. I'm sure the Mirror's Marjorie Proops would not approve or condone such behaviour. However, I will release you on this occasion. But you are not discharged completely. You can go about your business, but your name will remain on the court's reserve jury list for this Session, so it is possible that you may still be called on to attend as a juror at some time."

So I got away with it. Clifford Davies was delighted. So was Marje Proops when I told her about the Judge's comments.

Some years later, however, when I was living in Disley, I received an official brown envelope, demanding me to do jury service. This time, it was for the Cheshire Sessions, and I was quite looking forward to it, even though it meant I would be losing out financially for a few weeks. But when I turned up at Macclesfield Crown Court on the first day, I was surprised to find the court sessions had been cancelled.

When I complained, they said I should have received a letter, informing me of the cancelled dates. However, they would be prepared to pay me expenses for my journey, as well as one day's jury allowance.

They eventually sent me a cheque for mileage allowance for my car, plus £30 or something for the day. It hardly compensated for what I could have earned in a day as a freelance. But it was take it or leave it.

Consequently, I never did get to sit on the real jury benches, which is something I regret. It's too late now. I'm too old.

My younger son Paul did get called up for jury service, though. It was at the Old Bailey in London, and he ended up on a very high- profile court case involving an IRA terrorist. The case went on for some weeks, and Paul was elected as the jury foreman. I think he had some reservations about the whole thing, fearing he might be in danger of possible reprisals if the IRA gang leaders were convicted. The case was reported on TV, and I think we felt a tinge of pride but also relief when Paul stood up and announced a "Not Guilty" verdict.

PAUL NICHOLAS

Paul Nicholas is a nice guy. Easy going and not at all big-headed, considering the success he had both as an actor and singer.

He first found fame in that delightful TV sitcom Just Good Friends, starring as the likeable rogue Vince, opposite the lovely Jan Francis. The show was a big hit and ran for three series from 1983, elevating both Paul and Jan to star status.

Paul then went into musical theatre and was the star of Jesus Christ Superstar, and also landed the lead role of Claude in Hair, the controversial musical which had everyone stripping off naked on stage.

With his good looks and a fine singing voice, he made the switch to pop music and became a bit of a heart-throb as a singing star, with three Top 20 hits in the charts.

Paul and I became quite chummy at one stage. He used to drop into our office pub occasionally for a drink and a laugh (and certainly had the girls flocking around), and once invited me over to his home, where I met his wife and family.

Paul's father was a high- profile lawyer who acted for a number of showbiz stars. I remember (just after my own appearance in the High Court when I was accused of libel by Coronation Street actor William Roache) Paul telling me that both he and his father had followed the court case with great interest. And he joked, "Perhaps you should have had my Dad on your side. Maybe I could have got him to do you a cheap deal!"

FRENCH & SAUNDERS

I met Dawn French and Jennifer Saunders when they were starting out on their very first TV series. They were fairly unknown and looked a slightly odd couple, with the very attractive Jennifer, who was quiet, almost shy, and Dawn, the plump one with the big smiling face, who did most of the talking.

There were no other girl comedy duos around. They had come up via The Comic Strip club in Soho, and then teamed up to form a double act. Their first telly series was an assortment of sketches, some of them quite

414

rude. And it became clear that these two girls had a mischievous streak, and both shared a vulgar sense of humour.

Over the years, of course, they developed into two of our finest comediennes, both turning to acting, and then both ending up as writers.

Jennifer was the scriptwriter responsible for Absolutely Fabulous, in which she also starred alongside Joanna Lumley. The show got huge critical acclaim, and drew a cult following of viewers. I'm afraid I was never really a fan. It was too over-the-top for my taste.

Dawn, I always thought, had much more talent than Jennifer as an actress. But whenever I met them, they were both very pleasant.

They both married funny men, too. Dawn married Lenny Henry, who I have enjoyed watching since he was a gawky teenager on our New Faces show. He went on to become a Shakespearean actor as well as popular comedian.

Jennifer married the wacky Ade Edmondson, who was a completely wild and freakish punk comic when I first met him, as one of that mad lot in The Young Ones. He's mellowed considerably in old age and, now balding, has become a half decent actor and TV presenter.

RICK MAYALL, ALEXEI SAYLE & BEN ELTON

Interviewing The Young Ones for the first time, when they came to TV in a mad frenzy of post-punk comedy, was not easy. It reminded me of the first time I met the Beatles – here were four very different personalities, and all determined to try and outrage you. The only difference was that this bunch were all quite loony.

It was as though someone had opened the gates and let loose a juvenile gang of morons.

They called it Alternative Comedy. But I was never quite sure what that meant. Alternative to what? Sanity?

The Young Ones, which was written by Ben Elton, did have a tremendous following of young viewers, and the BBC allowed them full scope to continue with their TV madness.

Nigel Planer was the quiet one. I interviewed him two or three times, and always found him extremely dull and with little to say.

Adrien Edmondson was also a little withdrawn when you got him away from his manic behaviour in front of the cameras. You always felt he was just out to shock.

But Alexei Sayle, Ric Mayall and Ben Elton were different. They were very individual characters, each with something to say.

After The Young Ones came to an end and they all went their separate ways, I followed their careers with interest. Ric Mayall always struck me as the brightest and most inventive. Once you got him away from the cameras, he was quite a different bloke.

He met me once for a chat in the pub at Acton, just around the corner from the BBC's rehearsal studios, and he was surprisingly normal. He was clearly ambitious and he was buzzing with new ideas. We struck up a kind of friendship and it continued well after the brilliant comedy series he did as The New Statesman, playing the rogue Tory MP Alan B'Stard. That series ran from 1987 to 1994 and was probably the best thing Ric ever did.

When we met for lunch once, Ric told me, "I want to get rid of John Major and this Tory government as soon as possible – but not until we've finished our next series."

Maggie Thatcher had pulled the rug from under Ric's feet when she resigned, and he didn't want the same thing to happen again.

"Maggie quit at the wrong time and we had to hastily re-write some of our scripts," he said. "The same thing could happen to Major. He's under the cosh. Who knows how long he is going to stay in power? That's why we are recording the shows so closely to the broadcasting dates – so they will be bang up to date."

Ric was remarkably cynical about the character he played. "Alan B'Stard is a deeply evil person," he grinned. "He just gets worse. He is happy to represent anyone, anywhere, so long as he's on the make. Alan would even join the Labour Party if there were a few quid in it for him. Now he's jumped on the European gravy train."

In real life, however, Ric said he would hate to be a politician. "It would be far too boring," he said. "Even if you try and have some fun in a Chelsea football strip, you get found out. Just ask that Tory MP – whatsisname? I can see no pleasure at all in being an MP.

"Even though Alan B'Stard is such a conniving little git, I'm told that there are at least half a dozen real Tory MPs who are happy to claim he is based on them, which is quite frightening really."

It was such a tragedy when Ric died, after a heart attack in 2014. He was only 56.

Alexei Sayle really was a one-off. He took manic comedy to a whole new level. You either hated him or loved him. Some of his ideas in his TV sketch shows were quite brilliant. But he could then throw in a stick of dynamite or a filthy or obscene gag which would disgust his audience.

Alexei once invited me to join him for a day's filming on location for one of his shows, and over lunch I found him to be an erudite and intelligent conversationalist.

Both coming from Liverpool helped (it's surprising how Scousers get on with each other, even when away from that wonderful salt-sea air) and he told me about his early days, being brought up as a Communist.

Alexei had Communism bred into him from a very early age, and it never really left him, I suspect, even though his Left-wing politics may have softened considerably with the passing of the years. As a youngster, the only holidays he ever knew were when his father and mother took him on trips to Russia. "It was great. Nobody in our street had ever been to Russia, but we went there regularly on holiday," he grinned.

With age, Alexei has become a fine serious actor, and he has starred in some notable films in straight roles.

Ben Elton met Ric Mayall when they were both at Manchester University. They struck up an immediate friendship, and it wasn't so surprising that they should both go into comedy and end up working together.

Elton wrote the scripts for The Young Ones and also appeared in some of the frenzied shows. Politically very Left Wing, he went on to do his own series as a stand-up comedian, with a belligerent, no-nonsense style which young audiences loved but probably alienated him from the older generation.

There was no stopping him though. As a serious writer, he has churned out several novels, and well as writing stage musicals which have proved box-office hits.

MOUNT EVEREST

One of the most memorable moments, away from the mad world of show business, was when I met the great British mountaineer Edmund Hillary, when he returned home after conquering Mount Everest.

It was 1953, and Hillary had just achieved what no other man had ever done. With Sherpa Tenzing Norgay, Hillary reached the top of the highest mountain in the world, which was 29,020 ft. It was hailed as the greatest thing in mountaineering history.

After the great event Hillary returned to England, sailing into Liverpool on a cruise liner. I was a young reporter on the Birkenhead News at the time and was sent to cover the hero's arrival.

The odd thing is, he was a very humble man. He gave a bit of a speech but had little to say otherwise. I wouldn't say I was let down, but considering the enormity of this historical event, it didn't feel in any way special. Maybe I was too young to appreciate it.

Later in life, I was much more impressed by meeting one of the first astronauts to actually walk on the moon.

PAMELA STEPHENSON & ROWAN ATKINSON

Meeting Pamela Stephenson for the first time was an eye-opening experience. Because she was stunningly beautiful, but then turned out to be an hysterically funny woman. It didn't seem natural. In those days, attractive women were not supposed to be funny. And female comics had to be fat or ugly, or both, to really be appreciated. But here was a woman who defied the odds and turned stereotyping upside down.

Pam was teamed up with Rowan Atkinson, Mel Smith and Griff Rhys Jones in a series called Not The Nine O'clock News. They were all unknown and the show, produced by John Lloyd, was an experimental try-out. But it was an immediate hit.

They all went on to do their own things. Mel and Griff became a double act and did several series of sketch shows as Smith and Jones.

Rowan Atkinson created Black Adder with writer Richard Curtis, and then became a star in one comedy show after another, including The Thin Blue Lines, before ending up as a worldwide cult figure, and earning a fortune as Mr. Bean. When he decided to retire Mr. Bean, in 2012, Rowan said, "I think someone in their 50s being childlike becomes a little sad." It was estimated not long ago that he was worth £85 million.

Pamela opted out of comedy, married the hairy Scotsman Billy Connolly, and decided to become serious by writing books and earning a living as a psychologist and sex therapist, opening her own clinic in Hollywood's Beverley Hills (where else?).

But she didn't lose her sense of humour completely. Back in the UK, in the 1987 General Election, Pam put up as a candidate in Windsor for The Blancmange Throwers Party. She finished sixth in the polls, with 300 or more votes.

TWO RONNIES

Who was the funnier? And who had the most talent? For my money, it was no contest. Ronnie Corbett was a likeable enough chap and made a little talent go a long way. But Ronnie Barker was the heavyweight in this partnership.

I met and interviewed them many times, separately and together. And, believe it or not, but they were poles apart in personality, and behaved quite differently when not in each other's company.

Ronnie Corbett was always jokey. He couldn't resist the chance to come out with something funny. But Ronnie Barker was a very serious bloke, and it took a lot to make him laugh.

They first met in 1966. It was David Frost who brought them together, when he rounded up Barker, Corbett and John Cleese, all budding comedians, in his TV production of The Frost Report.

Until then Barker had been doing mostly radio, and Corbett was happily doing a cabaret act in Danny La Rue's West End nightclub, which was where he met his wife Anne Hart, who was a dancer and eight inches taller than him. Cleese had done stuff at The Comedy Club but was still pretty unknown.

What Barker and Corbett had in common was that they were both grammar school boys who didn't go to university but chose show business instead.

Once when I interviewed wee Ronnie, he talked about his early days in Edinburgh and regretted never having furthered his education.

When they finally came together as The Two Ronnies, they hit on just the right formula. Their sketch shows became classics and ran on TV for 16 years.

But what was good for them both was that they managed to keep their individuality and work quite separately on other shows. Corbett did the sitcoms Sorry, and No - That's Me Over Here!

And Barker hit the jackpot when he landed the role of Fletcher in Porridge, before Going Straight, and then Open All Hours. Porridge was by far the best thing he ever did, in my opinion, although The Two Ronnies did have its moments (I can still chuckle at their four candles/fork handles sketch).

They didn't mix much when they were not working together. "People expect to see us together all the time," said Corbett. "They are even disappointed when one of us appears in public without the other."

And Barker told me, "I've always known I haven't got a very good personality of my own. I never open fetes or do after-dinner speeches and that sort of thing. Because I'm afraid the public will be disappointed when they meet me."

He was also terrified at the thought of ever walking out on to a stage without a script. "I'm an actor, not a stand-up comedian," he said.

I recall once spending a day with them, filming on location for The Two Ronnies. We were at a deserted railway station in Kent. And little Ronnie grabbed his hefty chum and pulled him on to a huge weighing machine. "Come on," he said, "I know how to work a dodge on this machine. We can both get weighed for only one tuppence."

In went a single coin. "Twenty-two stone 6lbs," said Barker, as they stepped off the scales. "Now, half of 22 stone 6lbs is 11 stone 3lbs," said Corbett.

Looking up at Barker's puzzled face, little Ron explained, "Blimey, you used to be 15 stone. Have you been on a diet? And I'll have to watch it, as well. I must have been putting on a bit of weight lately."

"Cut," shouted director Peter Whitmore. And both Corbett and Barker broke into fits of laughter. "Let's break for tea."

When Ronnie Barker retired in 1987, he gave his little chum six months' notice, telling him he'd had enough and wanted to pack it in. He then went off and opened an antique shop with his wife.

Big Ron, always overweight and he knew it, died from heart failure in 2005, at the age of 76.

Little Ronnie was still going strong, still working and playing golf well into his mid-80s. But he died in March 2016.

OLIVER REED

As actors go, some of them can drink a lot, others choose not to. The days of heavy drinking and hell-raising are mostly over, I think. Even in Hollywood. But Oliver Reed could out-drink anybody. In fact, Ollie could drink for Ireland!

He was a brilliant actor. One of the best, there's no doubt about that. But his career, and in fact his life, was cut short by alcohol. He died in 1999 from a heart attack at the age of 61.

Who can ever forget his dreadful appearance on the Michael Parkinson chat show, when Ollie appeared in a drunken stupor and embarrassingly tried to take his trousers off to show his manhood?

On the other hand, who could ever forget the terrific performance he gave in the award-winning film Women In Love, with Alan Bates and Glenda Jackson? The man was an enigma. I met Ollie a few times. And he was never sober.

But one incident I can recall, I must admit with some humour, was when I was show business editor of the Daily Mirror, and I teed up an interview with Reed for one of our top writers, Bill Marshall.

Bill himself was no mean drinker. In fact, he had battled alcoholism in his early days, beaten it and come out the other side. And when I suggested he tackle Mr. Reed, he jumped at the chance.

The deal was that Bill Marshall should fly to Ireland and interview Oliver Reed at his home, in County Cork. So off he went.

When Bill returned, three days later, he couldn't wait to tell me what had happened. Oh, he had a good interview all right – and it made us a splendid centre-spread feature. But Bill said to me, "I never want to meet that man again. He's an idiot and a clown." Why? I asked. When he told me, I couldn't help having some sympathy for Bill, but at the same time I was trying to contain myself from laughing out loud.

It turned out that when Bill first went to his house, Ollie was fine. He talked a lot, they had a pleasant meal, spent the whole day together. And then Ollie suggested that Bill should stay over, and next day he would take him out for a ride to see the local countryside. Bill unfortunately agreed.

Next day, it was pouring with rain, but Ollie insisted they still go out for lunch. He got the Rolls Royce out and they drove to a pub about 30 miles away. Lunch was consumed, as well as unlimited amounts of alcohol (Guinness, whisky, brandy, the lot, Bill vaguely recalled) and when they were both paralytic, they set off back home, with Ollie reassuring Bill that he was perfectly okay to drive.

Then halfway home, Ollie stopped the car and said he needed to have a pee, and he invited Bill to join him. Much relieved, Ollie climbed back behind the steering wheel, but just as Bill was about to get back in the passenger seat, Ollie lunged at him, pushed him out of the car, pulled the door shut, and drove off at high speed, roaring with laughter and leaving Bill helplessly standing at the roadside. It was still raining heavily, and Bill didn't know where he was, except that it was somewhere out in remote countryside.

He started walking. Ollie never went back to pick him up. He left him stranded, about 17 miles from anywhere.

"He's a bastard." said Bill. "A raving lunatic."

"Just write it, Bill," I said. "Just write it."

ANNE REID

Anne Reid is an actress I've known ever since the early days of Coronation Street. Younger viewers probably don't know this, but older fans of the soap may remember that Anne was one of the early casualties of the cobbled back street. She played Valerie Barlow, the wife of Ken Barlow (the first of his three) who came to a nasty end when she was electrocuted whilst using a hair dryer with a dodgy plug.

It was a fatuous story line when you think about it, but it was good enough to get Anne out of The Street and far enough away to make a new career for herself.

Actually, Anne asked to be written out because she was pregnant. But after she had her baby, she couldn't get away from Coronation Street quick enough. "I want to do other things. I don't want to be stuck with Valerie Barlow for ever," she said.

After all, if she'd not been killed off by that faulty hair dryer, she might still be there, 50 years or more with the boring Ken. Instead, she chose to do other things. To prove she was a proper actress.

Well, that's what acting is supposed to be about, isn't it – playing different parts? Playing one TV role for life is not really an acting challenge, is it? If you play only one character throughout most of your life, you end up just playing yourself. That's pretty obvious. You either choose to remain safe, take the money and ensure the mortgage, or you go out and take on different roles – that's an actor's choice. And that's why, sadly, a lot of the Coronation Street characters - like Ken Barlow, Rita, Emily Nugent, Gail, Kevin Webster, Audrey - have now finished up merely playing themselves. The actors have been there so long, they're too scared to get out and attempt anything new.

I got to know Anne quite well over the years. She came from a journalistic family. Her father was a travelling correspondent with the Daily Telegraph, her brother Colin was a reporter on the Daily Mail, and she married a journalist, Peter Eckersley, who was a friend of mine. After starting out as a scriptwriter, Peter went on to become Head of Comedy with Granada TV, and helped find and develop comedy talent in the North, including working with the brilliant Victoria Wood.

Later Anne became one of that little "repertory group" used by Victoria Wood, and appeared in many of her series, including the smashing Dinnerladies.

But she also did a lot of quite separate plays and films. With age, Anne has become much in demand. She played opposite a young Daniel Craig in the controversial film The Mother, in which she surprisingly stripped naked for explicit sex scenes. She was also in the popular drama series Last Tango In Halifax, with Derek Jacobi and Sarah Lancashire.

The amazing thing is that Anne seems to get better with age. Now in her 80s, she shows no signs of slowing down or reaching for those slippers.

How glad she must be that she escaped from being Mrs. Barlow for life!

CHARLOTTE RAMPLING

Charlotte Rampling is another actress who seems to get better with age. I first interviewed her more than 30 years ago, when she invited me to her house in London. She didn't have anything particularly striking to say, but she was polite and intelligent. The thing that struck me was how amazingly beautiful she was. She had those high cheek bones which usually guarantee lasting beauty.

After being a big-name actress, she opted out of the limelight for some years and went into semi-retirement. Now she is very much back in business.

She played the magistrate in the TV series The Probation Officer, and at the age of 70 celebrated her latest role in the film 45 Years, for which she was nominated for an Oscar.

What I like about her is her frankness. There was a lot of controversy about there being no black actors nominated for the prestigious Hollywood film awards in 2016 and racism raised its ugly head, with some black actors even suggesting they were being discriminated against. One or two even boycotted the ceremony.

It was Charlotte Rampling who was brave enough to come out with the obvious observation that maybe it was simply a case of there not being any performances good enough by black actor this year to justify them being chosen.

Then, I loved it when she hit out at all those women, mostly actors and models, who go in for face-lifts and such. She spoke of her disdain for plastic surgery. Then talking about the ageing process, she said simply, "We can't stop it. We certainly can't stop it through plastic surgery. We can't stop it through anything. We are always changing from the moment we're born till the moment we die, and we might as well get used to that. I've always thought that if I can show the change in myself through cinema - not just by showing myself ageing physically, but also developing what I have to give as a human being - that would be quite interesting."

In other words, she prefers to grow old gracefully.

TIMOTHY WEST & PRUNELLA SCALES

The first time I met Timothy West was in 1982 when he landed the leading role in Brass, which was a marvellous satirical comedy series written by my good friend John Stevenson and his script partner Julian Roache. Tim played the dastardly mill owner Bradley Hardacre, hated by his under-paid workers who had to doff their caps as he drove through the gates in his Rolls Royce. It was so successful, it ran for three series from 1982 to 1990.

But I found West a bit intimidating. A little like the character he was playing, perhaps. He softened up as I got to know him, though. And years later, when I went to watch him filming for some drama, high up in an office block at Salford Quays, he had changed completely. He was affable and happy to talk. Almost friendly.

Timothy has done everything, of course. Shakespeare, heavy dramas, light comedies. He even had spells in Coronation Street and EastEnders. A working actor who has never stopped.

His wife, the delightful Prunella Scales, has tied to match him, and had her own quite separate career. She never did anything though to top her brilliant performances as Sybil, the wife of the lunatic Basil, with John Cleese in Fawlty Towers. A masterpiece of a show which will last the test of time.

Tim once recalled for me how he first met Prunella. "We were both cast in a rather bad BBC play that was not actually filmed because of an electricians' strike," he said. "After we'd finished the rehearsals, we were suddenly told on the night of the recording that it was all off. We were feeling a bit flat. I turned to the person next to me, Pru, and said, 'Do you want to go to the pictures?' She said yes, so off we went."

He even remembered the film they saw. "It was The Grass Is Greener, starring Cary Grant." Their romance blossomed from there. "It took a bit of time because I was already married, but my marriage was sort of on the way out," he said.

Tim had a daughter from that first marriage, and she had made him a grandfather.

He and Pru then had two sons, Joe and Sam.

"There was a time when Pru and I were so busy working separately, that we had to make appointments to meet. I'd be in a show in the evening, and Pru was filming. Or maybe the other way around. One of us would be up at 6 am, the other working at night. And whoever was last home at night just flopped into bed exhausted."

But I was delighted when Timothy and Prunella came together and returned to TV with their wonderful real-life excursions down the canals on a narrow boat. Their antics together, and their love for each other, was so overwhelming that it made this a most remarkable TV adventure. I never missed a single episode. I loved it. In fact, they were even given the Bargees of the Year award by the satirical magazine The Oldie.

The sad thing is that Prunella has now been diagnosed with early dementia. But the way she has accepted the illness is so touching. At 83, Pru vowed that the dementia would not stop her working, and that she could cope with it. "It just means I take a little longer to do things," she said.

The nicest thing about this couple is that, whenever we see them, Prunella never stops smiling. I find that lovely.

ROBERT LINDSAY

One of the best days I ever spent out on location filming (which can be tedious and monotonous at times) was back in 1977 when I went to interview a young actor called Robert Lindsay, who was making his bow as the star of a new comedy show, Citizen Smith. We were in South London, and the show featured Lindsay as "Wolfie" Smith, a layabout Cockney geezer who had ambitions to become the Che Guevera of London, a working-class revolutionary who wanted to change the world.

Wolfie was a guitar-strumming Marxist who went around wearing a "Freedom For Tooting" T-shirt and a "Legalise Cannabis" badge pinned on his black beret. He was only happy when he was preaching political claptrap to his pals. He saw himself as Britain's saviour from Toryism. It was all nonsense, but the show was a big hit, and Wolfie Smith became a cult hero.

The series ran from 1977 to 1980 and made Lindsay a star. It helped launch his career, and the young man from Ilkeston in Derbyshire became

CHAPTER 38: JUST MEMORIES

a straight actor who went on to do everything from Shakespeare to stage musicals. The long-running TV sitcom My Family, in which he starred alongside Zoe Wanamaker, really established him as one of TV's most popular characters.

Robert was good company. Full of confidence, never short of something to say. And with his good looks and charm, he always had an eye for the ladies. He married Cheryl Hall, a pretty and popular young actress who did a lot of telly. But it didn't last and they divorced after six years.

Then, after a long relationship with someone else, he went off and married Rosemary Ford, in 2006. Rosemary was the vivacious actress who shot to fame as one of Bruce Forsyth's assistants on the game show The Generation Game.

I interviewed Rosemary down in Torquay once when she was appearing in a summer show, and she was great company.

Rosemary and Robert now have a family and, as far as I know, are still happily together.

ALAN BATES

One of our finest film actors over 30 or 40 years was Alan Bates. Dark, brooding devilishly handsome, he liked to think of himself as a ladies' man. Women swooned over him. But, in fact, he was a very complex character, and admitted having several homosexual affairs throughout his career.

He made some stunning films (remember his nude wrestling scene with Oliver Reed in Women In Love?) but I think one of the best was Far From The Madding Crowd, opposite Julie Christie in 1967.

I was invited once to a Press reception to have lunch with Bates, to promote one of his films, in the trendy West End restaurant The Ivy. We were sitting on a long table, about eight of us, with Alan in the centre, and I was right opposite him. The rest of the journalists were mostly women, and it was obvious that some of the younger scribblers were a little star-struck and in awe of him.

He was well aware of the attraction and sexual aura he created. In fact, he revelled in it. He had deep penetrating eyes and when he stared at you, it became a little scary. I found him very sinister, although he was very polite and answered all our questions without taking himself too seriously.

Away from his work though, he had a very tortured life. Although he was married to Victoria Ward from 1970, they split up and had long periods apart but he remained married until she died in 1992.

Bates enjoyed various homosexual relationships, including affairs with actor Peter Wyngarde and Olympic skating champion John Curry, who died from AIDS in 1994. It was reported that Curry died in Alan's arms.

Bates himself died in 2003 at the age of 69. He had cancer and then suffered a fatal stroke.

MARIANNE FAITHFULL

Marianne Faithfull was one of the most naturally beautiful girls when I met her backstage on the very first Top of the Pops show, which was televised from Manchester in 1964. On the bill were the Beatles and the Rolling Stones, both vying for top spot in the charts. The demure teenager Marianne, who was Mick Jagger's girlfriend, sang the haunting song As Tears Go By. And she jumped off Jagger's lap and came over to talk to me, as I was dashing around the dressing rooms trying to grab as many of the pop stars as I could.

It was ironic that her first big hit song should have such a title. Because Marianne certainly has had a lot of tears in her life.

After the high-living days of the drug-fuelled 1960s, and after splitting up with Jagger, she has gone through the highs and the lows of life for 50 years. She has battled cancer, suffered various other health scares, depression, and re-invented herself and made more come-backs than anyone in the business.

I went to meet her several years ago, when she was staging another return to show business after batting alcoholism. I was quite shocked when I saw her. Although the traces of beauty were still there, she had the face of an old woman.

She chain-smoked continuously as she told me that she was determined to get her life back on track. This was it, she insisted, the comeback that would prove she still had talent as a singer.

Marianne probably had lots of regrets in her life, but she told me of the two biggest and most important. "One was mucking up my life to the point where I lost my son Nicholas," she said. He had been brought up by his father, he ex-husband John Dunbar, an artist, after she went through her drug problems.

"The other big regret was letting my mother down. It wasn't necessary to get into drugs. And hard drugs are Hell. It was just infantile curiosity and was never good anyway.

"Getting into drugs was selfish. You only think of yourself, never how it is going to hurt those near to you. My mother was an absolute gem. She took a lot of strain."

Her singing voice had become quite husky. "My voice used to have no soul to it, but it's deeper now, probably through too much smoking and whisky. I like my voice now. I never used to." she said.

There have been long gaps of obscurity. But the woman has got guts. She has re-invented herself once again. Only recently, in 2016, she was back on a stage tour, selling tickets for concerts, desperately trying to prove it's not yet all over.

Unfortunately, she had to admit that old age had caught up on her. She was 69 but told her audience at London's Roundhouse Theatre that she was a cripple. She needed a walking stick and had to sit down on stage because she couldn't stand any more. Then she struggled because she had forgotten her glasses and couldn't read her notes on the music stand.

She was on stage for an hour and 40 minutes but had to apologise for going off early. "It's been very, very hard with all these terrible injuries and Le Faithfull has actually ended up disabled," she announced. "I'm getting very tired now. I really am. I'm not so young anymore." It all sounded very desperate.

It really is sad to see something like that. I feel far better when people, whoever they are, accept the situation they are in and decide to retire gracefully, without trying to prove they can carry on working until they drop dead.

WENDY CRAIG

Wendy Craig was a fine actress, and lovable with it. She was in a string of TV comedies in the 60s and 70s, including Not In Front of the Children, Butterflies, and Mother Makes Three. Then from 2003 to 2011 she was a matron in the hospital series The Royal.

She had a light touch and was ideal for sitcoms. At one time, she struck up a friendship with the prolific scriptwriter Carla Lane, who wrote some of her best shows specially for Wendy.

The only trouble with Wendy, as far as I was concerned, was that she was married to Jack Bentley, who was a show business columnist on the

Sunday Mirror. He was a musician - I think a trombone player - who had given up playing in a band and gone into journalism quite late in life.

There was always a friendly rivalry between the Daily Mirror and our Sunday paper, and we had quite separate editorial staff. But whenever I went to interview Wendy, Jack would always pop in to our office to say, "I hope you're going to give Wendy a good write-up." Sometimes he would often be on the phone, suggesting we do pictures or a bigger feature on her.

To be honest, I didn't particularly like him. And I really didn't appreciate him trying to tell me what to do. One day, when I was talking to Wendy, I told her of Jack's consistent badgering. She burst out laughing and said, "Take no notice of him, Ken. He fusses over me too much. Next time he comes to you, just tell him to sod off. I do - all the time."

Jack died some years ago. Wendy has had a long career, and she's still working.

She's now in her 80s, but the other day I see she was back on our screens again in an episode of Death In Paradise. She certainly wears well.

ROY HUDD

Roy Hudd could be a lot of fun. He's a great lover of the old Music Hall entertainment and is steeped in its history.

I went to interview him once, and he arrived a bit late and apologised because he'd missed his bus. He must have caught my quizzical look, because he said, "Oh, I take buses everywhere. I can't drive. Never learned to drive a car. Never want to.

"I've got a bike somewhere. But if I can't get a bus or the Tube, I walk. It keeps me fit."

He was very thin in his early days. But he's put on weight with age. Last time I saw him, he was enjoying a long run in Coronation Street, playing a jolly funeral director. And he had ballooned enormously in size. Nice chap though, Roy.

DONALD CHURCHILL & PAULINE YATES + KENNETH COPE & RENNY LISTER

There are quite a few married couples in the acting profession. I don't know why, but actors seem to attract other actors when it comes to matrimony. I've heard it said that one actor in a house is enough - unless there is room for two egos. Also, that it depends on how many mirrors you can hang up.

There are exceptions of course. Two acting couples I got to know quite well, and in fact would regard as casual friends for some time, were Donald Churchill and his wife Pauline Yates, and Ken Cope and his missus Renny Lister.

Donald Churchill really was a lovely man. He had such a subtle and gentle sense of humour. He first met Pauline when they were both at Liverpool Playhouse, one of the best repertory companies in the country at that time.

We used to go regularly to the Playhouse Theatre – my wife, me, and a small group of friends from our church who were interested in amateur dramatics. It was the trendy thing to do in Liverpool in the 1950s. And the Rep company had a reputation for producing top-rate actors.

At the time we used to enthusiastically buy Saturday night tickets, the leading actors in Liverpool were Robert Bruce, Helen Lindsay and the really beautiful young starlet Pauline Yates. Donald Churchill joined them later. Not surprisingly they all went on to London and became big names in the theatre, and then in films and TV.

It wasn't until I moved to London that I got to know Donald and Pauline. I interviewed them both a few times for the Mirror, and I was invited over to their house occasionally. When Donald, who had appeared in The Saint and scores of other things, started writing plays, he enhanced his career more as a writer than an actor. We would chat about each other's work, and he even tried to encourage me when I started showing some interest in writing scripts.

Pauline probably had a bigger profile. Although she did lots of TV and film work, she is probably best remembered for playing Leonard Rossiter's frustrated wife in the popular The Fall and Rise of Reginald Perrin.

I first met Ken Cope and Renny Lister when they both joined the cast in the early days of Coronation Street. Ken, a Liverpudlian, played the likeable villain Jed Stone, run-around pal of Dennis Tanner. And Renny played Jean Stark, one of the flirty girls who worked in the factory. They were married in 1961.

Ken hit the big time when he joined David Frost and his company of comics in That Was The Week That Was. Then he shot to stardom as Marty Hopkirk in Randall and Hopkirk (Deceased), which became a cult TV series.

He did lots of other things. The last time I saw him was when he did a stint in Brookside, and he played a not-very-nice character called Ray Hilton. I recall that when I went to interview him, the Brookside Press officer started to introduce me to him, and Ken said, "No need for introductions, love. I've known this bloke since before you were born!"

The last I heard, Ken and Renny were still together, and happily living in Southport.

PHYLIS LOGAN & KEVIN MCNALLY

I've never really been a fan of Downton Abbey, though I did watch most of the period dramas. I still can't understand why it became such a massive worldwide hit, or why so many people regarded it as a not-to-be-missed programme. For me, it was way over-the-top, far too melodramatic, and the scripts were naff. It was never as good as the original Upstairs Downstairs, with Nyree Dawn Porter and Eric Porter.

Even so, there were some fine acting performances in Downton, and one or two of the leading ladies went on to try their luck in Hollywood.

Down below stairs though, was an actress I've long admired, Phyllis Logan (who played Mrs. Hughes and later Mrs. Carter). She has done lots of things over the last 30 years, and I've never seen her turn in a bad performance.

I interviewed her some years ago, and she invited me over to her house for lunch. I found her so friendly and nice, and I ended up feeling quite sorry for her because she lived on her own but obviously enjoyed having company.

Some years later however she married actor Kevin McNally, and they seem ideally suited. I've also interviewed Kevin once or twice, and he has a great sense of humour.

BILLY FURY

One of the early interviews I did, even before the Beatles, was with Billy Fury.

He was a very good-looking lad and was one of the pack of young rock n rollers managed by impresario and agent Larry Parnes, who insisted on giving all his singers new names with a zing to them. Others he handled were Marty Wilde and Rory Storm.

Billy's real name was Ronald Wycherley, which admittedly was a bit of a mouthful and wouldn't look right on the showbiz posters. When he became Billy Fury, she shot to overnight stardom. A string of hit records, and he was probably the biggest name on Parnes' books.

At the height of his fame, Billy invited me over to the new house which he had bought for his mum, in a posh residential district of Liverpool. That was what successful singers and showbiz people did in those days. As soon as they became famous and earned enough money, they were expected to buy their parents a bigger and better house.

I remember Billy proudly showing me around the house, meeting his mum, and having tea in the front parlour. He actually had a name for the house, and a big sign on the gate. It was called Wondrous Place. Sounds pretentious now, doesn't it? But it was a little palace to his mum.

When Billy moved to the big time in London, his live-in partner for eight years was Lee Middleton, who later was to marry Kenny Everett.

Sadly, Billy suffered years of ill health, and died at the age of 43. He collapsed at his home, was rushed to hospital but died the same day. His fans around the world were grief-stricken.

LITA ROZA

What was my most embarrassing interview? That's an easy one to recall. Although when I even think about it, all these years later, I cringe within myself and still can't fully appreciate my own youthful stupidity.

It was in my early days as a reporter and I was working on the Liverpool Evening Express. Apart from doing straight news reporting, I was trying to make a name for myself by writing bigger features. The editor gave me the chance by offering me a weekly page to go out and interview a big-name show business star.

Bearing in mind that my confines were within the area of Merseyside, this inevitably meant that the only stars around were the top-of-the-bill acts at the Liverpool Empire Theatre. No problem there, because the theatre manager was only too happy to have the local newspaper devote a whole page to their star of the week.

One of the first stars I met was Ronnie Carroll. He was fine. Then came Lee Lawrence, a lovely man and a fine singer I thought, and very chatty. My features on them were quite good and I was given big headlines, and even had my own picture in the paper.

But then came Lita Roza. She was not only top-of-the-bill but a huge national radio and recording star.

Lita was very glamorous and Britain's undisputed No.1 female singer. When I went to meet her, I was probably more than a little star-struck. I was invited into her dressing room and we started talking. She was pretty relaxed and pleasant enough. But after a short while, I began to splutter, and got very nervous. Then I ran out of questions. I tried desperately to think of something new to ask her, but it was hopeless. I just dried up.

She was very nice about it, and just sat there, smiling and waiting for me to continue with the interview. After what seemed like an eternity, I decided that it was time to go, that I should wrap it up. I had enough stuff from her anyway to write my feature. But now, I didn't know how to get out of it. I should, of course, have just said, "Well, thank you and goodnight." But I couldn't even say that, I was too nervous. I just sat there like a muppet.

Even now, I don't know how I got away with it. I think Lita was aware of my naivety, and she probably felt sorry for me but didn't want to embarrass me by showing it.

In the end, I somehow escaped from my own nightmare. Next day, back in the office, I wrote up the interview, and managed to fill the whole page. It looked quite good, actually, and I was pleased with the way it came out in print. It would look okay on my CV.

I don't know what Lita Roza thought of it, presuming she read it. I never met her again. But I learned one thing from that whole dreadful experience - to do my research in future, and always have a list of questions written down in my notebook. Just to save awkward silences and embarrassment.

JOHN STRIDE

John Stride always made a good interview. He was not only pleasant to talk to, but he knew what we wanted and never got upset at difficult or embarrassing questions.

He was a handsome brute, and he became a heart-throb with female viewers when he played David Main in the popular ITV series The Main Chance. After a lot of light comedy parts, he then showed just how good an actor he was when he played Henry XIII in the BBC's prestigious production of the Shakespeare classic, in 1979.

I remember going to interview him. And he boasted of having grown a beard specially for the role. "I can't stand all those glued-on whiskers, so I grew a full beard in three weeks. It made me feel very virile," he said.

John earned a reputation of being a ladies' man, but he smiled mischievously when he told me, "It's really David Main who is a great bird-puller, not me. I don't deny I like women. I enjoy flirting with them. My wife doesn't mind at all. She knows and trusts me, because she knows that when I flirt with a woman it's not going to be the start of a great passion. Thank God my wife is not consumed with jealousy."

Actually, John was married twice. He had two daughters with his first wife, beautiful actress Virginia Stride. Then he started another family with his second wife, April Wilding. She was the stepdaughter of Lord Pilkington, the glass millionaire.

"It wasn't a matter of me marrying into money," John told me "I just happened to fall in love with a woman who came from a rich family."

The funny thing was that when John got married, he flew off to Paris on honeymoon. And he sent me an amusing postcard while he was on honeymoon. Odd, I thought. I've never had a postcard from someone on honeymoon before. You'd think he'd have better things to do.

CHERYL LADD

Charlie's Angels was a huge international hit show from America in the 1980s, a glamorous and expensive series about a trio of beautiful girls who went around fighting crime and showing a lot of cleavage in the process.

One of them was Cheryl Ladd, and I met her a few years later when she came over to make a TV film, Romance on the Orient Express. She was a stunner when it came to looks. But she was trying to get away from her sexy image which had followed her throughout her career.

"I fell in love with this part as soon as I read the script," she told me. "There are no muggings, no shootings, killings or stabbings, and no car chases. I've had enough of all that in Hollywood."

Although she'd been filming in Venice and Paris, she never actually travelled on the Orient Express. The only train she saw was a clever mock-up of the classic luxury locomotive in the Yorkshire TV's studios in Leeds.

Not much expense was spared on this production though. In one scene, she wore a silk dress which cost £2,500, had £10,000 spent on the rest of her wardrobe, and she wore £30,000 worth of jewellery.

Cheryl, who was then 34, said, "I just want to leave that action-girl image of Charlie's Angels behind me. I won't ever do another long-running TV series. I want to stretch myself as an actress by doing different parts."

Cheryl's marriage to David Ladd (who was the son of Alan Ladd, the great Hollywood cowboy star) broke up soon after she made a name for herself in Charlie's Angels. She then married a Scots-born producer and writer, Brian Russell.

DEBBIE GREENWOOD

One of the most attractive of all the TV presenters I had dealings with was Debbie Greenwood. She was quite tall, had a beautiful face with a permanent smile, and she had great legs. But then, she was Miss Great Britain after all.

Debbie went into television after winning various beauty contests, when it was still a popular and lucrative pastime for girls to show off their curves. And she won 15 beauty titles, before being crowned Miss Great Britain in 1984.

But she was no blonde bimbo. In fact, the girl from Liverpool was a brunette and she had a first-class honours degree in French and German, after picking up nine O-levels and three A-levels at school. It was only because she didn't know what to do as a career that she started entering the beauty contests. At 20, her boyfriend Phil Eccles dared her to enter the Miss Liverpool contest as a bet. She won it - and that set her off with ambitions to do more.

She took a job with a Preston radio station, but found herself looking after the reception desk, so left after five months. Then she found a job selling advertising space in a giveaway newspaper.

Her whole life however changed when she won the Miss GB title, because when she appeared on the BBC's Breakfast Time programme, to be interviewed by Frank Bough, he and the producers were so impressed with her charm and natural wit, that she was later asked if she was interested in a job with the BBC.

She was, of course. But the BBC were too slow. Granada TV jumped in first and offered her a job on the northern programme, Weekend, with a 12-month contract. She jumped at the chance.

That's when I first met her. It was obvious Debbie was being groomed as a TV star. And when I interviewed her and wrote a big two-page double spread for the Mirror, the BBC immediately became interested in her again. They then offered her a contract to join Breakast Time in London, alongside Frank Bough and Selina Scott.

I went down to the studios with her on her first day, and we had breakfast together with Frank Bough.

Debbie was terribly nervous, but Frank kept reassuring her that she would be allright. "Just be yourself. The viewers will love you," he told her.

The only thing she was worried about was her Liverpool accent. "I think people like regional accents, so long as it's not too strong," she said. The other thing she had to worry about of course was Selina Scott.

Selina was very much the queen bee at the BBC, and she suddenly had a new rival. And a beautiful one, too. As it turned out, they got on fine together. Frank Bough was a very happy man. He now had two dishy presenters with him, instead of one, on the breakfast sofa. Frank was full of praise for his new recruit. "All that Debbie lacks is experience. And that will come. She has brought a remarkable freshness to the programme," he said.

About 18 months later, I went to see Debbie again. She was now 26, married, and had decided to sell her house in Liverpool and move to London, to set up home there. "For a year, I've had two homes, and I'm fed up with all the travelling," she said. "I think I have developed a lot in front of the cameras. I've spent a year on Breakfast Time and that's been very good experience."

But she admitted that getting up at 3.45am and starting work at 4.30 was no joke and was starting to take its toll. Well, it wasn't good for the beauty sleep!

Debbie proved she was more than just a pretty face. After leaving the breakfast programme, she went on to do lots of other shows - most of them in the more relaxed afternoon slots.

CHARLTON HESTON

When I first saw the Hollywood classic film The Ten Commandments, Charlton Heston's performance as the mighty Moses was the most memorable piece of screen acting. The film, which dated back to 1956, was produced by the great Cecil B. DeMille. And it was said that he chose Heston for the role because he thought he bore an uncanny resemblance to Michelangelo's statue of Moses.

He then went on to star in that other epic Hollywood movie Ben-Hur, for which he won the Academy Award for Best Actor.

I once got the chance to meet Heston when he was in London. He was staying at the Ritz Hotel on the Strand, and I was invited to a Press reception for the big man. The first thing that struck me was what a massive giant of a man he really was. He was about 6ft 6 ins tall and built like a buffalo.

He had such a superb baritone voice, but I was struck by his amazing steely eyes which seemed to penetrate right through you. I felt dwarfed alongside him, and his handshake was like wrestling with a small rock.

He surprised me however, when he wasn't really interested in talking about himself or the films he'd been in, but wanted to talk about British politics. And he appeared to be remarkably well informed.

When I asked him if he had ever seriously thought of going into politics himself, he just smiled and said, "I have been approached a few times to run for election. No, it's not for me. And if I did, I would only want the top job, as President. That's not likely."

But, in fact, Heston was very much into politics. He started out supporting the Democratic Party but then switched to the Republicans. With other top-name actors, he opposed the Vietnam war, and in 1963 he supported Martin Luther King, marched with the Civil Rights campaigners, and even went on record once as saying he had supported the Civil Rights cause "long before Hollywood found it fashionable."

He then campaigned for fellow actor Ronald Reagan in 1987 and helped him become President. In his later years, Chuck Heston as he was called, was diagnosed with Alzheimer's disease. And in 2003 he made his final appearance in public, when he went to The White House and received the Presidential Medal of Freedom from President George W. Bush. He died in 2008, aged 84.

PETER O'TOOLE

Peter O'Toole was another Hollywood star who certainly lived up to his reputation. As a showbiz writer, you never quite know what mood they are going to be in when you interview a top actor or celebrity. Mostly, they are on their best behaviour because they want to get good publicity. Sometimes they couldn't care less and simply tend to be rude or dismissive.

With O'Toole, I didn't know what to expect because he had a reputation for being a rather fiery character.

In fact, he turned out to be a real charmer. I met him when he was on location, filming in Robin Hood's Bay on the East Coast of Yorkshire. I'd never been there before, and it's a very beautiful little spot. It was a warm sunny day and I found him, during a break in filming, high on the hillside, sitting in a lounger. He pointed me towards a deckchair, "Take a seat. What do you want do drink?" he said. Before I could answer, he said, "I recommend this iced lemonade. It's very cooling." And he reached over to a small table, poured me a tall glass of lemonade, and said, "This is about my limit these days. My boozing days are over."

Once one of Hollywood's most notorious hell-raisers, along with Richard Burton, Peter had long since given up his hard-drinking habits. "I've seen too many of my good chums go early," he said. "I'm getting tired of going to funerals to say farewell to friends. There's only a few of us left."

Then, sitting bolt upright, he said, "Enough of that. What shall we talk about?"

Well, I was there to talk about the film he was making. But he said, "Oh forget all that bloody stuff. Let's talk about cricket. Are you into cricket?"

Actually, I hate cricket. Can't stand the game. But when I told him gently that I wasn't really a cricket fan, he yelled, "Shame on you, man. Are you English? How can you be an Englishman and not like cricket?"

Realising that I was not going to win this one, I just sat back and let him talk cricket all afternoon.

O'Toole, 6ft 2in tall and with the bluest and most sparkling eyes I think I've ever seen, holds the record for receiving more Academy Award nominations than any other actor, yet he never won one. He should have won an Oscar for Laurence of Arabia in 1962, but he didn't. That remains one of my all-time favourite films. Overall, he was nominated eight times, without success - for Lawrence of Arabia, Becket, The Lion In Winter, Goodbye Mr. Chips, The Ruling Class, The Stunt Man, My Favourite Year, and Venus.

He did however finally receive an Honorary Academy Award in 2002, which he thoroughly deserved.

It would have been a crying shame if he had not been honoured in some way by his peers. Peter died in 2013, aged 81.

CHRISTOPHER TIMOTHY & CAROL DRINKWATER

One of the most popular series ever devised for TV was the BBC's long-running All Creatures Great And Small, the story of the veterinary surgeon set in Yorkshire's lovely countryside.

Robert Hardy played the senior vet Siegfried Farnon, and Christopher Timothy was his young assistant James Herriot. Timothy was really a big favourite with the millions of viewers the show attracted over twelve years. He became something of a heart-throb. And actress Carol Drinkwater was also extremely popular as the young vet's attractive wife.

But the snag came when the two actors fell in love with each other. It wasn't the first time and it certainly wouldn't be the last. In fact, they used to say in Hollywood that it was half expected for the leading actors to have an affair during the period of the film, and then go back to their respective spouses when it was all over. Or not, in some cases. There are lots of examples of actors swapping wives after appearing on stage or film and falling for their screen lovers.

With Timothy and Carol, it was much the same old story. Along with other journalists, I had the tough job of breaking the news of their real-life romance.

The Mirror front-page headline on 28 December 1978, was: "TV Vet's Secret Love. Actor Chris jets off with his co-star Carol." And my story revealed that Christopher had fallen for his screen wife Carol and had left his real wife Susan earlier in the year. The TV stars flew off to Miami together on holiday.

Inevitably it meant talking to Mrs. Timothy. But instead of the usual "No comment. I have nothing to say," Susan seemed quite happy to talk about the affair. "I realised some time ago that they were going out together, but I don't know how long it has been going on. Three weeks ago, Chris told me he would be going on holiday. I asked, 'With Carol?' and he said yes. Then he told me about their relationship."

Previously, Chris had always denied any off-screen romance with the 30-year-old Carol.

With his 13-year marriage in tatters, the actor only returned to his home in Godalming, Surrey to see his six children, two of whom were adopted.

Susan Timothy sadly told me, "We've both been keeping this quiet. We didn't want people to think he'd left me for her. Their relationship developed after Chris left me and has nothing to do with our split up."

Only days before flying off with Carol on holiday, Chris had returned home to spend Christmas with his family and had even taken them all to a West End show.

But Susan said, "It was really for the kids. We had a nice time. But there's no chance of a reconciliation."

When Chris and Carol arrived in Miami, he said simply, "We are just on holiday together and plan to sit in the sun." And Carol added, "I simply can't understand what all the fuss is about. Chris even told his wife about it before we came on holiday, and she said she hoped he had a good time."

Chris was later divorced and was with Carol for a while. But eventually, I think, they split up and went their separate ways.

As I say, those kind of news stories are never easy to write.

MOLLIE SUGDEN

When I was interviewing Mollie Sugden once, having lunch, an impudent young man at the next table in the restaurant leaned forward and rather rudely told Mollie to stop smoking. I immediately thought he was in for a real verbal roasting.

The least I hoped for was a blast from Mrs. Slocombe of Are You Being Served? Or a curt word or two from the snooty Mrs. Hutchinson of The Liver Birds.

But no. Mollie said politely, "I'm sorry," and put out her half-smoked cigarette.

Later however, she told me, "Oh, I could have strangled that cheeky young man. Now if I'd been Mrs. Hutchinson, I'd have given him a right good telling-off. I'm afraid to admit it, but I'm really terribly shy."

It didn't seem right, somehow. Here was the woman who had earned the reputation on TV of being a tough old dragon.

"The truth is," admitted Mollie, "everyone expects me to be the same battle-axe they see on screen. And I'm not a bit like any of the women I play."

At that time, the BBC were screening repeats of The Liver Birds, and a new series was planned for later in the year, and a new batch of Are You Being Served? was ready to go into production as well. Meanwhile, after being a supporting actress for many years, Mollie was being promoted to star status with her own comedy series called Come Back, Mrs. Noah.

"I play a daft middle-aged housewife in the year 2050 who accidentally goes up in space without a pilot, and can't get back to earth," she chortled.

Mollie was a remarkably versatile actress and was always fun to interview. She lived in the stockbroker belt of Surrey, though she was born in Keighley, Yorkshire. She was married to actor William Moore, whom she met when they were both at Swansea Rep company. They had twin boys, Robin and Simon. And Mollie once told me, "I'm usually so busy at home, with my husband and the boys to look after, that I regard going to the TV studios to work as a rest."

She confessed that she loved working in Are You Being Served? But she feared she would never ever escape from playing the fussy Mrs. Slowcombe. And there was one catchphrase she could never get away from, which embarrassed her. That was when people in the street would recognize her and yell, "Where's your pussy?" Or "How's your pussy feeling?"

Fortunately, Mollie did have a good sense of humour.

FRED DIBNAH

There was never anyone I met quite as blunt and as likeable as Fred Dibnah. He was the eccentric little roly-poly steeplejack from Bolton who cared more about steam engines, pistons and blowing up factory chimneys than anything else in life.

Fred always wore the same grubby cap and dirty overalls and seemed to be genuinely surprised when TV made him into a star. He once caused a storm of protests with his constant swearing. But Fred maintained defiantly, "There's no way I can bloody stop swearing, even when the cameras are on me. I can't believe people get upset about my language. After all, when you switch on TV these days, everyone is jumping into bed with each other and people are using four-letter language, much stronger than the stuff I bloody well use."

Fred was first discovered on a Northern news programme, knocking down factory chimneys and messing about with his treasured collection of old-fashioned steam engines. But when the BBC gave him his own series, A Year With Fred, viewers actually saw the break-up of his 18-year long marriage. In the early stages, Fred was seen with his wife Alison and family. But in later programmes Alison walked out on him, taking their three daughters, Jayne, Lorna, and Caroline, with her.

So, in one programme, Fred agreed to explain the absence of his family. In a chat straight to camera, he announced, "They've left me."

Then a few years later, they had him back with a new series, which they called Dibnah and Sons - because he'd been divorced and married again. He and new wife Susan had two sons, Jack and Roger.

Fred was very philosophical about it all. "I've never let this TV lark go to my head," he told me, over a pint. "A lot of people have a taste of notoriety and try to become TV stars. Well, that's never been one of my goals.

"If people are interested in my lifestyle, so be it. I don't mind them watching what I do and how I go about my job. But it hasn't really changed my life at all. I still like my two pints of Guinness every night. But as fast as the money comes in, it goes out to Bradford and Bingley to pay off my mortgage."

When he was not working restoring church and factory roofs or pulling down disused chimney stacks, he had enough after-dinner speaking engagements to keep him in beer money for a long time.

And it looked like his young son Jack was following in Fred's footsteps, because he was filmed climbing up the side of a chimney with his dad. "I was right behind him, making sure he didn't fall. But he wasn't a bit worried by the 60 feet climb," said Fred.

"People might think I'm daft for letting him do it, but there was no risk. And to be honest, I were right proud of the lad."

DAVID ESSEX

David Essex was a surprisingly nice guy. Considering that he was so devastatingly good looking as a youth, and had such a lot going for him, one could have been excused for expecting a touch of the big-star treatment. But not a bit of it.

The first time we met was when he was performing on Top of the Pops, and I was at the BBC Centre to watch a run-through.

After rehearsal, he came into the canteen, introduced himself, and said, "I'm starving. I must eat something before we do the show." We then queued up together and ended up sharing a plateful of fried sausages.

He really was a very down to earth young man and had a lot of talent as a singer. The girls loved him.

I met him again some years later when he had turned to acting. He was playing a character sailing his boat down the canals, and it turned out to be a very pleasant comedy series.

David has managed to successfully mix singing with acting. He still does concert tours and, now grey and with a beard, is old enough to take on character parts as an actor. A few years ago, he did a stint in EastEnders, as Eddie Moon, which revived his career.

He may look older, but the handsome features are still there. And so is the talent.

ALAN WHICKER

Alan Whicker really was as cool, sophisticated, and debonair as you would expect when you saw him on TV. He was a remarkable man. I got to know him quite well, we met at lots of Press conferences, and I never grew bored listening to him.

The great thing about Alan was that he loved to listen to other people. And that, after all, is the real art of interviewing. Just ask a question, then listen to the answer. Whicker is the master at that. There is no one better. Too many chat- show hosts these days spend all their time talking gibberish, and are not interested in what their guests have to say.

Some of Whicker's early reports, when he was a news reporter on the BBC's Tonight programme, remain as classic pieces of television. While his celebrity interview series, Whicker's World, which he did all around the globe for years with Yorkshire TV, proved to be a masterclass in communication and technique.

He had his own fan club, organised by dedicated followers. They even had an annual convention, at which everyone dressed up as Whicker, with false moustaches and thick horn-rimmed spectacles. Alan loved attending the bizarre events. He lived in some style in the Channel Isles and drove a lovely Bentley around Jersey.

He once gave me a fan club tie, which I still have somewhere in the wardrobe, and he signed a copy of his splendid autobiography for me.

What I liked about meeting Alan was that it wasn't all about him. He was more interested in what was happening at the Daily Mirror and the latest Fleet Street gossip than he was in talking about his own adventures. Which I found refreshing for a man of his standing.

LADY JANE WELLESLEY

There was quite a buzz around the BBC when they recruited a new Press Officer in 1978. No one knew much about her, except that she had a title and she was also one of the favourite girl friends of Prince Charles.

When Lady Jane Wellesley walked in and took her seat behind her desk, everyone was pleasantly surprised because she was a very chatty, amenable young woman with no airs or graces about her.

Jane, who was 27, was a very attractive brunette, and joined the BBC staff as a publicity officer responsible for news and current affairs programmes.

She was the daughter of the Duke of Wellington and had for some time been a very close friend of the bachelor Prince Charles, so she was no ordinary Plain Jane.

She had no experience of publicity work, but she learned quickly, fitted in with the rest of the press office staff, and soon proved she was very capable of doing the job.

I got to know her quite well, because we used to attend a lot of press conferences at the White City TV Centre, and I would pop into the publicity office to talk to the PR guys or have a lunch-time drink with them in the BBC club. Jane soon became part of the team and regularly joined us in the bar.

One day I arranged to have lunch with her at a restaurant in the West End, simply to get to know her better and to discuss the programmes she was responsible for, hoping to pick up some stories. This was the way I worked with all the publicity people.

However, on the very day I was due to have lunch with her, a news story broke about Prince Charles, and there was immediate widespread speculation that he was about to marry. The names of various girl friends were inevitably mentioned, and high on the list was Lady Jane Wellesley.

When the News Desk realised that I was meeting Jane for lunch, they were on my back immediately. "Find out if she's going to be the next Queen. Is she still dating Charles?" I was instructed.

First, I had to phone her to confirm our lunch date was still on, because I feared she might want to cancel it in view of the Press speculation about the Royal romance.

But no, she was fine. When we met at the restaurant, she had a big grin on her face. "I have a feeling I'll need a large gin and tonic before this lunch," she said. "Am I in for a grilling?"

Over lunch, she was fun. She knew the name of the game. She knew I had to ask her the obvious questions. And I knew she was going to have to be discreet. In the end, she said she trusted me not make anything up, but assured me that she was not about to become engaged to Prince Charles or anybody else. She had not even thought about marriage and she certainly had no long-term plans to become the future Queen. "Now let's have another gin and tonic," she giggled.

Jane didn't stay in the Press office for long. Later that year, I ran a story which had her picture on the front page of the Mirror, with the news that Lady Jane had surprised her publicity colleagues by suddenly landing a new job in front of the cameras. She was to be one of the presenters of a BBC-I arts programme called Mainstream, even though she had no broadcasting experience.

Jane told me, "Someone mentioned my name to the producers, and I had to undergo one of those awful auditions." And the producer Tony Palmer said, "She is absolutely wonderful. We're very excited about her prospects."

As for Jane, she preferred to talk about her new career, rather than the fact that her marriage to Prince Charles had once been a "strong possibility."

Later, fed up with being asked about her relationship with Prince Charles, I heard that she rounded on the Press and screamed, "Do you honestly believe I want to be Queen?"

Ironically, she has never married at all. Despite some romances (one rumoured to be with Melvyn Bragg) she stayed single and forged a career for herself as a film maker and biographer.

Now in her mid-60s, she lives in Notting Hill, London.

BOB MONKHOUSE

There was nobody - and I mean nobody - quicker, sharper, smarter or funnier when it came to comedy than Bob Monkhouse. He could hold his own with any of the top comics and had a razor-sharp wit which put him head and shoulders above most of them.

The only trouble with Monkhouse was that he was too smart for his own good. He knew the problems he faced. More than once, he admitted to me, "I know I come over as a smarmy git. I'm too enthusiastic, too smug, I smile too much, I make people feel inferior, and some people hate me because they think I'm big-headed and conceited. But what can I do about it? I've tried changing my style, but it doesn't work."

Everyone knew that Monkhouse was something of a comic genius. What he lacked was the likeability factor. And he spent most of his life trying to fight his personality disorder.

Bob really was a nice guy. Funny, charming, and generous. As an ad-libber, he was up there with Eric Morecambe.

Born into a wealthy family (his grandfather was a prosperous businessman who co-founded the giant Monk & Glass company which made custard powder and jellies) Bob started off writing comedy snippets and drawing cartoons for The Beano and The Dandy comics when he was still a schoolboy. And after National Service in the RAF, gate-crashed radio and teamed up with Dennis Goodwin to form a comedy partnership in shows with Arthur Askey, Jimmy Edwards, Ted Ray and Max Miller.

When he split up from Goodwin and went into television, Bob was soon topping the bills as a stand-up comedian and starring in a variety of popular shows.

Over the years, he was never out of work, and took over hosting various game shows and quizzes as a slick presenter. These included The Golden Shot, Candid Camera, Family Fortunes, Celebrity Squares, Bob's Full House, and Wipeout.

He was also an expert on the silent cinema and had a collection of old black-and-white movies which was priceless.

Bob invited me over to his home once or twice - a lovely old house called Claridges in the village of Eggington, Bedfordshire, where he even had his own cinema. There was nothing he liked more than to invite visitors to sit down and watch a classic silent film with him, with a stiff drink to hand.

He was also a great collector of jokes, old and new. He had a classified filing system and albums full of gags. In fact, in 1995 a couple of his precious joke books were stolen from his car, and Bob offered a £15,000 reward for their recovery. The books were returned safely to him 18 months later, but the thief, although arrested by the police, was never charged.

Bob, who was married twice, had three children (one adopted) from his first marriage. One of his sons, Gary, suffered from cerebral palsy. But it was wonderful to see Bob and Gary together, playing games and being affectionate at home, and Bob was very proud of his disabled son. Gary died at the age of 40.

Monkhouse was awarded an OBE in 1993 and won a Lifetime Achievement Award for Comedy a couple of years later.

But in his earlier years, Bob had a reputation for being something of a philanderer. In his autobiography, he admitted to having hundreds of sexual affairs, including one with film star Diana Dors.

And, typically Monkhouse, he even wrote sarcastically in his memoirs, "The awkward part about an orgy is that afterwards, you're not too sure who to thank!"

MICHAEL BENTINE

After selling him a comedy script which I sent him anonymously under another name, I got to know the great Michael Bentine quite well. My first encounter with the ex-Goon was when he was at the height of his career and writing and starring in his wonderfully wacky BBC series Square World. When I wrote a sketch for him, completely out of the blue, he came on the phone to me at home and liked it so much that he bought it and used it in his next week's show. And then sent me a handsome cheque for my trouble.

Later, over the years, I interviewed him for the Mirror, and he was such a wonderful talker that he was a joy to meet. Michael had the gift of the gab.

Once, he invited me down to his home in Surrey. He made us some lunch and we spent all afternoon chatting. He poured me a large brandy and opened a box of expensive Havana cigars.

After a couple of hours, however, he suddenly became quite agitated. The living-room was now full of cigar smoke and his wife was out for the day, shopping. "Quick, the wife will be home soon and she'll go mad," he said. He opened all the windows and started wafting the curtains around. "She hates me smoking and she doesn't like the smell of cigars getting into the curtains," he screamed.

That was it. He wanted me to go immediately. He was suddenly like a naughty schoolboy, frightened of being caught smoking.

Next day, he phoned to say how much he had enjoyed my visit, and apologised for the abrupt and hasty end to our afternoon. "I do hope the curtains don't still smell," I said.

447

DANNY LA RUE

I've never really been a fan of drag acts. Female impersonators are not my cup of tea when it comes to entertainment. And with the changing of sex laws in recent years, there is far too much emphasis on gay liberation for my liking.

As they used to say, I've nothing against homosexuality, so long as they don't make it compulsory!

And when it comes to gay entertainment, there are far too many clubs and theatres now taking over from what I regard as traditional Variety. Blackpool is a perfect example of what I mean.

However, when you look at some of the outrageous, over-the-top antics of today's gay entertainers, it is easy to see and understand why Danny La Rue stood out as Britain's No.1 drag act. He was head and boobs ahead of the rest of them, even allowing for the change in attitudes and public taste.

Danny La Rue was a smashing bloke. Always friendly and cheerful. Never short of a story to tell. And with the longest and best legs I've ever seen on a man.

Born in Cork, Ireland, he moved with his family to London when he was six years old and they lived in Soho until their home was destroyed in the bombing in World War II.

After serving in the Royal Navy, Danny went into show business and became a female impersonator. Or "a comic in a frock" as he preferred to call it. And it wasn't long, with his tall and handsome good looks, before he took over as the most popular drag artist around. In the 1960s, he opened his own West End nightclub in Hanover Street, and it became the celebrity hang-out for the rich and famous.

One of his regular visitors was Princess Margaret, who liked to get away from Buckingham Palace and live it up with late-night parties with her trendy friends.

In the West End, Danny proved a sensational success in the musical Hello Dolly, and he went on to top the bills and produce his own shows around the country before breaking into television.

I recall going to see him in Hello Dolly, and he invited me backstage to his dressing room and raved about the number of gorgeous dresses he had in his wardrobe and how much they cost.

He was, without doubt, a terrific entertainer. And when he finished his act, with the rendition of his signature tune On Mother Kelly's Doorstep, he had audiences jumping to their feet in rapturous applause.

One of the richest men in showbiz, in 1970 he owned The Swan, an inn at Streatley on the River Thames, which became a 4-star hotel. He then bought and spent millions on the restoration of Walton Hall, a palace in Warwickshire, but eventually had to sell it when he lost most of his money in bad business deals.

Privately, Danny lived with his manager and life partner Jack Hanson for 40 years, until Jack's death in 1984. Though he never really talked about his homosexuality until his later years.

When he was made an OBE in 2002, he described his visit to Buckingham Palace to meet the Queen as "The proudest day of my life." As an artist, he did several Royal Variety Performances. And he was generally considered to be the Grand Dame of Drag.

He suffered ill health for quite a few years. He had a mild stroke while on holiday in Spain in 2006, went through the agony of prostate cancer, and had several more strokes before he died at his home in 2009. He was 81. And he was finally laid to rest alongside his partner Jack Hanson in St. Mary's cemetery, Kensal Green.

BILL MAYNARD

On screen, no matter what part he played, Bill Maynard revelled in being a grumpy old sod. Off screen, he didn't change much. He enjoyed being a pessimistic grumbler. But occasionally, if you got him in the right mood, he could be hilariously funny and damn good company. This was usually helped along by several pints of bitter, followed by a few shorts in his local pub.

Bill started out as a comedian, working in Butlin's holiday camps, before getting into variety in the 1950s. His first TV series was in partnership with Terry Scott in a series called Great Scott, It's Maynard! But Bill then went solo as a stand-up comic and became a star in his own right.

His real name was Walter Frederick George Williams, and when it was suggested he change his name for showbiz, he spotted an advert for Maynard's wine gums. "That will do me. Maynard will fit the bill," he said. And he became Bill Maynard overnight.

He later gave up comedy and went into acting, and reckoned it was the best thing he ever did. After appearing in some of the Carry On films, Bill starred in several top TV series.

For Yorkshire TV, he did Oh No, It's Selwyn Froggitt! He played Fred Moffatt in The Gaffer. And in the long-running and very popular Heartbeat he played the lovable rogue Claud Greengrass. Then he went on to appear in the hospital series The Royal.

I recall when he was playing The Gaffer in 1983, and he was going through agony because his wife Muriel was seriously ill at home, and Bill was finding it hard to work. I went to see him on location, and he poured out his heart to me. Although he was working in Yorkshire, he drove back home every night to Leicester to look after his wife who had cancer.

"All I'm longing and praying for is one day when Muriel gets out of bed and can walk across the room," he told me. "Before she became ill, our life was idyllic. Muriel actually said to me 'I knew something would go wrong, because no one is allowed to be as happy as I am.'

"Our two kids have been bloody marvellous," said Bill. "My daughter, who is married, stays at our place and looks after her mum during the day when I'm out working. And my son, who is a record producer, jumps in his car after work at night and drives all the way from London to the Midlands to see her.

"Muriel wants to stay at home. She pleaded with me not to be put in a hospital."

Because of his wife's illness, Bill arranged to work for only seven weeks a year on the TV series. "I love playing The Gaffer. The trouble with me, though, is that I am a naturally loud-mouthed, uncouth yobbo. I suppose I tend to frighten people at times." He finished the series. But his wife Muriel died later that year.

Bill suffered a series of strokes and became disabled himself. He still struggles but tries to put on a brave face. He also re-married. His wife was Tonya Bern, who was the widow of the great speed king Donald Campbell.

MARC BOLAN

Marc Bolan was one of the most talented young rock stars of the 70s. A charismatic figure loved and adored by fans of both sexes.

But tragically he was killed at the tender age of 20 in a car crash at Barnes Common in 1977. His death was mourned all over the world.

Four years after his death, I was contacted by Simon Napier-Bell, who had first managed the unknown Bolan in 1966, before they split up and Marc went on to create a cult following with his particular brand of glam rock and psychedelic music. He bands T. Rex, and Tyrannosaurus Rex became world famous.

Simon was very excited when we met and wanted to talk not so much about how he had discovered the young singer, but of some old tapes he had found.

It seems that Simon met the young musician after Marc phoned him to say he wanted Simon to hear some tapes he'd made.

"There was this little man with a guitar," said Simon. "He admitted he had no tapes but wanted to sing for me. He said he had chosen me to be his manager and make him a star.

"He sat in an armchair and sang a lot of songs. His intensity really grabbed me. And he had such a strange voice. There was something quite fascinating about him. I booked a recording studio, and within hours we were recording all his songs."

Simon managed Marc for a year in a group called John's Children. But it didn't work out. "Marc was going through a wispy, mystic period. He used to sit on a rug with a joss stick burning. Though he was writing good lyrics, his songs were waffling a bit and very weird.," he said.

"There was no hassle. We parted good friends. We met many times after he became a big star and we talked about the old days."

Simon then made his fortune as a songwriter and manager, moved to Spain, then to Paris, but retained his company in London and was managing other bands including the top music group Japan.

But quite by accident, Simon found a batch of early Marc Bolan tapes in the cellar of his house. He told me, "I was fascinated by them. They are the best songs he ever wrote."

He immediately hit on the idea of bringing Marc Bolan back to life on record.

It wasn't easy. "I was limited to the tapes of Marc's voice and an acoustic guitar," said Simon. He brought in new musicians, and then added vocal backing.

It took him a week to produce a twelve-track album. "We chose Scare Me To Death as a single because that was the best track."

The first reaction from the Bolan fan club was one of great enthusiasm. "One music critic said it could be the best rock album of the year, but let's wait and see," enthused Simon.

451

He realised of course that he was open to accusations of trying to cash in on the memory of Marc Bolan. But Simon denied this and said if he had wanted to cash in, he could have done so much earlier after the singer's death.

What did matter, however, to thousands of Bolan fans was that their hero had got a new lease of life - on record.

Marc Bolan has now gone down in the annals of rock music as one of the most innovative performers of his generation.

MATT MONRO

One of the most popular singers to come our way in the last 50 years or so was Matt Monro. At one time, he was hailed as "Britain's Frank Sinatra," which was just about the best compliment anyone could hope to be given.

Matt (real name Terence Edward Parsons) came from Shoreditch, and among other jobs he became a London bus driver. He had a great voice but unfortunately never quite looked the part, because he was only about 5ft 8ins tall and was rather plump.

Despite this, he shot to fame as a more than pleasant crooner in the 60s and 70s, starting out as vocalist with one or two show bands and ending up as our No. 1 recording star.

He invited me over to his house in Ealing once, and we had lunch and talked about his ambitions. Matt first came to the public's notice when he landed a recording contract and released songs like My Kind of Girl and Walk Away, which both became big hits.

He was then chosen to represent Britain in the Eurovision Song Contest in 1964, when he finished second with the song I Love The Little Things.

Then came the haunting Portrait of my Love, and the Oscar-winning song Born Free, which later became his signature tune. He also had a hit with the James Bond film theme From Russia With Love.

For some years, Matt was resident singer on the popular mid-day ITV show Lunch Box, produced from Birmingham, with my former protegee Julie Jones as his fellow vocalist.

Sadly, Matt died of liver cancer in 1985, leaving a widow, Mickie, and three children. He was only 54.

One of his sons, Matthew, later revived memories of some of his greatest hits when he went on the road and re-invented a career for himself as Matt Monro Jnr.

But for my money, there could only ever be one Matt Monro.

RADIO MERSEYSIDE

The BBC's Radio Merseyside is one of my favourite regional stations. It's very parochial of course, which it is meant to be. But unlike all the other radio stations you hear when you travel the country, Merseyside has a character and humour all its own.

I really began to appreciate this when I lived in Wirral, at New Brighton, for nearly ten years, and it gave me an opportunity to tune in virtually every day, not only to keep up with local news but also to laugh at some of the things they got up to at that little station in the heart of Liverpool.

For a start, one of the brightest and most amusing broadcasters on the airwaves is comedian Sean Styles, a real Scouser and proud of it. I used to enjoy his shows when he was a double act on Sunday mornings with Willie Miller. But then Sean went solo and got his own morning show five days a week.

Having now moved away, I don't get the chance to tune in so often. But when I hear him on the car radio, he's a laugh a minute.

There are two other regular presenters who have been going for years, Roger Phillips and the legendary Billy Butler.

Roger, who I believe was a taxi driver before landing his job as a radio presenter, runs a daily phone-in programme and plays Devil's Advocate to anyone who comes up with a controversial argument.

Some years ago, Roger phoned me at home when he realised that I had been to school with Frank Smith, who was a bit of a celebrity locally as the owner of Frank's Caff, a popular dock road eating place frequented by lorry drivers and renowned for its wonderful fried breakfasts.

He asked me if I would agree to go and meet Frank in his cafe to talk about our schooldays together at Venice Street Secondary, some 30 years after we'd left. And when I agreed to do it, Roger set up his programme as a live outside broadcast, and we did the whole show, chatting over mugs of tea and bacon butties. It was a hoot, and I think they got a very good reaction from the listeners.

I always enjoy Roger's programme. It is a little gem in an ocean of mediocrity.

When it comes to Billy Butler, he really is a legend in that part of the world. He goes back to the days of the Beatles when he was a disc-jockey in local night clubs. And since becoming a radio deejay, he has been the rock of local broadcasting, swapping jobs between the commercial City station and the BBC's Radio Merseyside.

Billy's afternoon programme is a mixture of music and chat, with the accent on nostalgia.

One of the old long-running features of his show was a crazy quiz game which attracted nutters from all walks of local life. Billy would ask daft and quite easy questions over the phone, and then get laughs out of the punters' silly answers. The game was played by listeners invariably begging him to "Give us a clue, Billy."

They have had such fun with this quiz over the years that they even produced commercial discs which have sold out overnight.

The most famous one of all, which has now gone down in the annals of broadcasting stupidity, was the time they had on a woman contestant who was asked, "What was Hitler's first name?" She thought about it for a few seconds and said, "I don't know, Billy. Can you give me a clue?"

"Oh, come on, love. Hitler's first name. You must know that," said Billy.

After a long pause, she came back, "No, I can't think. Come on Billy, give us a clue."

In desperation, Billy said, "I don't know what kind of clue I can give you. Except that he was German. It's a pretty easy question. What was Hitler's first name?"

Then the woman suddenly blurted out, "Oh, I've got it, Billy. Was it Heil?"

That has now become a classic.   Cilla Black heard it and told the story to get a huge laugh when she was a guest on the Mike Parkinson chat show.

Billy Butler really is a one-off. But let's face it, with so much natural and moronic comedy material out there in his audiences, he can't go wrong, can he?

RAY MOORE

One of the saddest stories I ever had to write was when BBC disc-jockey Ray Moore died in 1989. Ray was one of the BBC's most popular presenters on Radio-2. But then, quite suddenly, he stunned the nation one day by calmly announcing that he had throat cancer, and he told his radio audience, "They have told me it is incurable. The horse has bolted."

Within a day or two, he received more than 4,000 cards and letters, flowers and other gifts from a stunned public who loved him. "I didn't know I had so many friends out there," he said.

On air, Ray was truly a one-off, a great and under-rated broadcaster. He was almost as popular as his Radio-2 mate Terry Wogan, but he was on earlier in the morning.

For 20 years, he dominated the air waves from 5.30am to 7.30am with a kind of Old Moore's Almanac of dry Liverpudlian humour, interspersed with records.

I actually sat in with him in the studio on one of his early-morning shows, just two months before he signed off for good. It was a rare privilege, because he never liked anyone in the studio with him when he was broadcasting

"It's a very personal two-way thing between me and the audience out there, and I don't want any distractions," he told me. "It may be egomania, but I still get a kick out of broadcasting. When the show goes well, there is no high on earth like it."

The show did go well that day when I sat quietly in the corner, just watching a master at work. His comic song Bog-Eyed Jog - linked to a series of early-morning jogs around the country - had raised more than £100,000 for the Children In Need fund, and also given him a hit record. He had already made one record - My Father Had A Rabbit, which went to No.24 in the pop charts a year earlier.

Ray's daily routine never varied. He was up at 3.30am every morning. Right away he would have a cup of tea and his first cigarette of the day. At the studio, after coffee and more fags, he'd splutter his way in front of the microphone. That familiar asthmatic chuckle, the smoker's cough and the gravelly voice which often broke into a guttural Liverpudlian Scouse twang, were all part of the Ray Moore charm.

"I only come in to the BBC to have a smoke, because my wife Alma won't let me smoke at home." he joked.

It was a joke which was to turn tragically sour. Even when he knew that cigarettes were shortening his life, he couldn't give them up. As the cancer took a grip, he suffered in silent agony.

Sadly, I shall always remember joking with him about his awful scruffy new beard.

"It's dreadful, I know. Nobody likes it," he said. "I grew it to look more sophisticated, but it turned out white, and I look like Father Christmas."

455

What he didn't tell me - and what he kept secret from even his closest colleagues - was that the beard was there to hide the ugly, painful lump growing even bigger in his neck every day.

He was suffering from cancer of the throat, but he was determined it would not stop him working. Eventually, of course, it did.

But looking back on his early life, Ray fell in love with radio at a very young age. It was hard to believe that he was once a docker. "I humped bags of cotton from ships for six weeks, while I was waiting for my A-level results at school. I saved up enough money to buy my first motor bike."

Then he worked in a shipping office. "I was in the Mersey Docks and Harbour Board building on the waterfront. It was the most tedious six months of my whole life," he told me.

"In desperation, one day I went out to look at the ships on the river and I suddenly thought 'This is ridiculous. I'm 18. I have no ties. I can go anywhere and do anything I want.' So I went back into the office and resigned. My Dad went potty. I'd given up a steady job with a pension."

Ray desperately wanted to be a broadcaster, but when he went to the BBC they wouldn't even let him in the front door. "So when they weren't looking, I slipped into the tradesman's entrance," he said. He got a job with the BBC in Manchester.

"Then when Radio1 and 2 started, I moved to London in 1967 to do the early-morning show. The fact that I was still doing the same job 20 years later, shows just how much progress I made in life," he joked.

"I suppose people must have thought I was mad to do a show like this every morning. It's a ridiculous time of the day to be on the air, and it's obviously a constant strain getting up at 3.30 and going to work. But the compensations are enormous. The reaction of the audience is tremendous, and that kept me going. We get more of a mixture of audience than any other radio show. Over that two-hour period, the listening audience changes so much. It's a great mixture of all ages and all classes. There is an addiction about broadcasting. I always get a kick out of it. I was never bored."

With the silly records he made, he sparked off so many other fund-raising stunts that in two years he collected more than £250,000 for Children In Need.

Ray, who had no children of his own, said, "For me ever to make records as a singer was laughable. I've got the most tuneless voice in the world. The first record was made purely as a joke. I thought it would probably make threepence, so I donated the royalties to a children's charity. If I'd kept them, it would have brought me in a small fortune. I could have had a new kitchen! I didn't make a penny out of the records. In fact, I was out of pocket, because it cost me 35p to get a bus to the recording studio!" That was Ray. He could never resist a joke.

Right to the end, when his condition was worsening, he insisted he was not being brave. He was just determined to die as he had lived - with dignity.

He was 47 when he died. Ken Bruce, who is happily still going strong on Radio-2, summed up the nation's feelings, when he said, "We have lost a great broadcaster, a wonderful man and a lovely friend to those who knew him."

CHAPTER 39: SPORTING MOMENTS

Sport has played a big part in my life. In fact, I think without sport, life would be very dull indeed. From my early years as a kid, when we kicked a ball around in the street and played cricket in the summer, sport became a passion.

Looking back at those years when we lived in Loraine Street, Everton, brings many happy memories. We had a street football team. Loraine United we called ourselves, and we played friendly matches against other local streets. Except that sometimes they were not so friendly, and the odd game would occasionally erupt into a fight, with someone throwing a punch, and then everyone piling in. Because we didn't have any referees. The only form of refereeing was which team had the biggest, strongest and toughest lads.

It's laughable now, but our little team of Loraine United was very highly organised. Every lad in the street was expected to play, and George Stirrup, who lived next door but one to me at No.13 (and ended up being my brother-in-law after marrying my wife's sister Irene) was the goalkeeper and captain. He was the best goalkeeper around, no doubt about that, but the only reason he was captain was because he owned the ball. Without George and his ball, we wouldn't have been able to play at all.

But every week - usually on a Thursday, around tea-time - George would announce the team for the game on Saturday. And this became quite a ritual because he would pin a sheet of paper up on the notice-board of Loraine Street school, opposite our house, with all the names of the players he'd chosen. But it was no ordinary sheet of paper. It was a highly decorated masterpiece of art, painted in different colours, with his name - G. Stirrup, Capt. - in goal, highlighted by a tiny drawing of goal posts and a net. And we would all gather round to see who else had been chosen for the team, and which positions we were playing in. Which was ridiculous really, because the names never changed from one week to the next, as we only had eleven lads in the street, and on the odd occasion when we might be short, we'd have to go and recruit a pal from another street, maybe Salisbury Road, or Granton Road.

But George was a great organiser. He was also the captain of the street cricket team - again, because he was the only one who owned a bat and a set of stumps and a cricket ball. A real cricket ball. Not a soft tennis ball, but a real red cork ball. And later, George even became the proud owner of a pair of cricket pads, which he insisted on wearing when he went in to bat - which was No.1, opening batsman, of course. And which he also wore throughout the rest of the match, because he was the wicket keeper. Nobody else ever got to wear those pads.

The trouble with playing cricket was that Loraine Street was hardly a level playing field, and in fact was cobbled. So the ball was likely to fly up in any direction, and when struck fiercely with a bat it was anybody's guess where it would end up. With luck, we would hit the ball in a straight line, down the sloping street, and score six runs. But quite often, I'm afraid, the ball ended up crashing through one of the nearby windows, and we would then have a ranting neighbour to contend with. Mrs. Plum, at No.11, and Mr. and Mrs. Gibbs at No.7 were both particularly vulnerable residents, I seem to recall. And once, Mrs. Bainbridge, at No.5, came out and confiscated the ball because she was so distraught at having her front window smashed and her afternoon nap disturbed.

Normally when we smashed a window, there would be no problem. We knew it would cost three shillings to have the glass pane replaced, and we would all contribute from our pocket money to pay for it. Most of the residents were happy with that arrangement, though the odd grump would chastise us with a few words of unnecessary advice: "Why don't you go down and play in Stanley Park, instead of breaking my windows?" The trouble was, Stanley Park was a mile away.

However, it got to the stage at one time that we were breaking so many windows, that someone (and it was probably George again) decided that we should change the cricket pitch and play inside the school playground, which had a smooth concreted surface and would obviously be easier and safer to play on. As the school gates were always locked outside of school hours, this meant us all having to climb over the 8ft high railings to get inside. It did make for a better game of cricket though. The only trouble being that, strictly speaking, the school yard was legally out of bounds. And if a passing policeman came by and spotted us - which they frequently did - we would all be in trouble. Consequently, it was essential that the outfielders on the boundary had to be constantly alert, keeping one eye on the match and the other eye looking out for coppers.

On such occasions, the mere shout of a warning, "Here comes a scuffer," would send us all into action, grabbing the stumps and everyone running to hide behind the other side of the school wall. Once the policeman had walked by, glanced through the railings, and peacefully gone on his way, we would all re-emerge and re-start the game where we had left off.

That all worked out well for a while, but then one day it happened. Disaster. Someone bowled a full toss, the batsman hit the ball a mighty wallop, and it flew straight through the school window, completely smashing the full plate glass window, with the ball ending up inside the classroom. And who was the culprit? It was George Stirrup, our beloved captain. He may have scored a six, but he'd lost the ball. And the game came to an abrupt end.

For some minutes, we all discussed what we should do. Should someone climb through the broken window and retrieve the ball? Or should we just leave it and scarper? I think in the end we decided that secrecy was our best option. So we all climbed over the railings and went home. It was dinner time anyway. And there was no doubt in our minds that this massive window was going to cost a lot more than the usual three shillings to repair. We left it with the headmaster and the school authorities to sort out. I suppose eventually it must have come out of the school's budget. We never found out. Not even George admitted to that one. All we knew was that we'd lost a ball, and we'd have to wait for George's dad to buy a new one.

Oh, happy days!

Away from Loraine United and our cricketing antics on the cobbled street, my footballing skills improved rapidly. I eventually got my first pair of leather football boots (with six lethal studs on each boot, and a tin of Dubbin which was used to clean and polish them each week). Then my dad bought me a real leather case ball. The proper thing. Not even George Stirrup had one of those. As the proud owner of a full-size casey, it immediately gave me new status. The only trouble was, with a big ball like that, it really was too dangerous to play in the street any more. And we did have to go down to Stanley Park for our kick-around after that.

When I moved to senior school, Venice Street Secondary, I played for my house team, Livingstone, and became quite a good player. Well, I thought so anyway. I played inside right, No.8, or outside right, No.7, as a fast, tricky winger. Only once can I recall scoring a goal, though. But it was a cracker. I received the ball just over the halfway line, and ran with it like a demon, with two or three defenders frantically chasing me. Just as one lad was about to catch me, I let fly with my right foot, and the ball went like a rocket into the top corner of the net, with the goalkeeper flailing away helplessly. I don't remember whether we won the match or not. I didn't care. All I could remember was everyone slapping me on the back and congratulating me. It was a great feeling. Unfortunately, it never happened again.

Although I played in the House team, I never quite made the school first X1, although I was chosen as a regular reserve, and travelled with the team to all away games and to our home ground, which was in Townsend Lane, Walton, every Saturday morning. Sadly, I stood around for a whole season, shivering and waiting hopefully for someone to get injured, so that I could get a game. But it never happened. And I was particularly upset, one Saturday, when some little twerp watching on the touchline, came over and said to me, "You'll never be in the team. You're only chosen as first reserve because you've got your own footy boots!" How hurtful kids can be. It may have been true. But I didn't want to hear it.

As kids, we would be off to see a real game every Saturday afternoon. The professional stuff. One week at Goodison Park, the next at Anfield. But we couldn't afford the full entrance fee every week, so a gang of us would go for a kick-around in Stanley Park and then, when the gates opened at three-quarter time, we would run in and push our way through the crowd of spectators to the front, and ask, "Who's winning, Mister?" Then, knowing the score, we would watch the game for the last 20 minutes or so. It became a weekly ritual for us.

A few years later, when we could afford to pay at the turnstiles, we'd go in the Boys Pen and enjoy watching the whole match, imprisoned in a caged section at the back of the ground.

The first full-length professional football match I ever went to was when I was ten and I was taken by Uncle Billy to Goodison. It was 1945, the full leagues hadn't been re-organised after the war, and Everton played a friendly game against Fulham. The Blues won 10-1.

I couldn't quite believe it. Harry Catterick, the centre forward, scored five and all the other forwards were on the score sheet. Joe Mercer, playing in defence, came up with a magnificent overhead kick to save a goal. It was just incredible. After that, I knew what team I wanted to support for the rest of my life. How could I be anything but an Evertonian after watching a match like that?

Moving on a few years, after leaving school I joined the club at St. Domingo Methodist Church, and became a regular player in the soccer team. It was a tough league we were in, but we had a very good side. George (Stirrup) was goalkeeper, my Uncle Billy (McNichol) was centre-forward, and Victor Lane was centre-half. Vic, in particular, was a great player. As steady-as-a-rock defender, with immaculate ball control and a relaxed coolness about him. He was two years older than me, but I knew I could never be as good as him. We became best mates, on and off the field. And we are still in touch.

And this was, of course, the same St. Domingo from where Everton football club was originally formed - in 1888. That's why we were all Evertonians. We were following in the footsteps of the great pros.

Later, Vic Lane, Les Davies and I became best mates. We went everywhere together. To church, to the youth club, and we went to football matches. We were at Goodison Park for a memorable derby game against Liverpool which attracted the biggest-ever crowd - 78,299. It was a hot sunny Bank Holiday, and we were packed together like sardines. Every few minutes, someone fainted, and the bodies were rolled down above the heads of the crowd, being pushed on to the side of the pitch, to be taken away on stretchers and attended to by St. John's Ambulance Brigade, who attended every match.

Billy Liddell was my favourite Liverpool player. He was a fast, tricky left winger, played for Scotland, and was also a lay preacher who once came to give a talk at St. Domingo club. A really pleasant, modest man.

Of all the wonderful footballers I watched over the years, I had to rate Stanley Matthews as the greatest. He was a right winger, known as the Master of Dribble, who would beat a man and then stand back and wait for him so he could beat him again. Matthews (from Blackpool and Stoke City) was just superb when he was in the England team. And with Tom Finney, (from Preston North End) an equally clever winger over on the left, Tommy Lawton (from Everton) as the free-scoring centre-forward, and Wilf Mannion (Middlesbrough) inside left, wow, that was some England side!

The only time England won the World Cup, of course, was in 1966. They've never done it since, and I doubt if they'll ever win it again.

I regard 1966 as my favourite year. It really was. That was the year when I finally made the move to work in London with the Mirror. Everton won the FA Cup, and England won the World Cup.

Staying at The White House, near Regents Park, I watched Everton in the Wembley final on TV in my room. And when they came from 2-0 down to beat Sheffield Wednesday 3-2, with Mike Trebilcock scoring two goals, and Derek Temple the winner, I went crazy. I jumped up and down on the bed and banged on the wall in sheer delight. It was just pure joy. I celebrated by going down to the bar, buying a bottle of champagne and taking it up to my room. What a great afternoon!

Then, when it came to the World Cup final at Wembley, I actually watched it from the lounge bar of The Phoenix, the pub just around the corner from the BBC Press office in Cavendish Place.

A gang of us were in the bar all afternoon, drinking lager and watching the game on TV. When Geoff Hurst ran free and scored that incredible last-minute goal to complete his hat-trick and beat West Germany 4-2, well, I've never seen a place erupt like The Phoenix at that moment. Everyone went berserk. There was a group of Aussies who were drinking with us and one of the girls, a skinny but gorgeous blonde, just flung her arms around me and screamed, "Wow, we love you guys. Hi, I'm Judy!"

Oh yes, 1966 was a never-to-be-forgotten year. Alan Ball, the little red-haired terrier of a midfielder, was the youngest player in the England team. He went on to sign for Everton and for years it was Bally who became the maestro of the Blues' team. Later came Howard Kendall and Colin Harvey.

When Ball eventually left Everton, I had a bit of bother at home. My son Mark, who was a mad-keen Everton fan, hero-worshipped Alan Ball and had his bedroom wall decorated with football posters and pictures of him. The day Everton announced Ball was leaving to join Arsenal was sad enough, but when I was about to leave for work in the morning, my wife said, "You'd better have a word with Mark. He's very upset and is refusing to go to school."

When I went up to see him, he was sulking in his bedroom. He had torn down all his pictures of Alan Ball and put them in the bin. "I hate him. How could he leave Everton to go to Arsenal?" he screamed. He was almost in tears. I did my best to pacify him, and I think we eventually talked some sense into him and packed him off to school.

Many years later, I happened to be attending a sports awards dinner in a London hotel. And sitting at the next table to me was Alan Ball, now retired as an England player and doing his best as a football manager. There was an interval during the proceedings and I couldn't resist it, so I went over to Alan Ball's table and introduced myself. I then told him this pitiful story of how he had upset my son's day when he signed for Arsenal.

But he then surprised me by saying, in that squeaky little voice he had, "Well tell your son it wasn't my idea. I didn't want to leave Everton and go to bloody Arsenal. They did the whole deal very quickly and I was just told I was on my way."

We shook hands and had a laugh about it. I went back to my table, happy that I'd met one of my true soccer heroes.

There was a sad occasion, though, when I decided to go down to the funeral of the great Tommy Lawton. I'd never done that kind of thing before, but he was such an iconic figure that I felt the journey might be worthwhile and that I should pay my respects to one of Everton's greatest. There was a big turn-out of fans at the church, including a lot of veteran footballers. Among them was Lawton's old England team mate, the one and only Stanley Matthews, in a black leather overcoat and dark glasses. After the funeral, I introduced myself and shook the great man's hand. He smiled and we exchanged a few words.

One of the most memorable free trips I ever went on was a World Cup jaunt in 1974. The ITV sports unit, who were televising full coverage of the month-long soccer event, came up with a very generous invitation to take a small group of TV journalists over to Germany to watch some of the World Cup games.

England had not qualified for the final stages, but Scotland had. And Peter Coppock, the ITV sports press officer, picked out four of us who he knew were football-mad to join him, all expenses paid. It was a chance not to be missed.

As well as me, there was Martin Jackson from the Daily Express, Sean Day-Lewis from the Daily Telegraph, and Peter Fiddick from The Guardian. We flew to Munich, watched the opening ceremony and had VIP seats in the first match which featured the great Brazil. Then for the first week of the tournament we were driven to different cities to watch a game at every venue.

Scotland's opening game was a fantastic occasion. The Scots were not going to win the tournament, we all knew that. But they had more than 10,000 marauding Scots fans supporting them at every match. And if it had been alcoholic consumption they were competing for, the Scots would have won the World Cup without a doubt.

It was reported later that hundreds of Scots fans enjoyed the soccer festivities so much, they spent all their money, never bothered to return home, and went AWOL somewhere in Germany.

For us, it was an enjoyable action-packed week. We stayed at the best hotels, Peter Coppock was a splendid host, and everything was so magnificently well organised.

We also had the company of the great Jimmy Hill and his TV crew, which was good fun.

When we finally returned home and staggered through Heathrow, we were all hung over from the night before. A noisy Martin Jackson was wearing a green and gold Brazil cap and waving a large Brazilian flag. The Customs officers took one look at us, laughed, and waved us through.

When it came to meeting other national football heroes, I once stopped Stan Mortenson, who played alongside Matthews in the Blackpool and England teams. He was walking along the Blackpool prom, and I couldn't resist just saying hello to him. A few years later, I did the same with Peter Beardsley, the England and Newcastle star. I saw him standing all alone, a forlorn figure in a grubby mac, outside a souvenir shop on Blackpool's North Pier. He seemed quite chuffed that someone had recognised him, and was happy to chat to me while his wife was inside the shop.

On another occasion, I went to one of the cup finals at Wembley with my son Paul, and when we took our seats we found Paul was sitting next to Peter Shilton, probably the best ever England goalie. I prompted Paul to ask him for his autograph, but he was too shy.

The funniest incident I can recall about a Wembley game was when Liverpool played Everton in the first all-Merseyside FA Cup final, in 1986. Again, I was with Paul, and we were queueing before the match at one of the stadium's bars. The fans wore a mixture of red and blue scarves and hats, and it was later described as the friendliest-ever final with two sets of fans happy to mingle together without any trouble. We both had blue scarves on.

It was a long queue, moving very slowly, and we seemed to be waiting an eternity for drinks. Getting impatient, I blurted out, "Oh for God's sake, hurry up."

At which, I felt a hand on my shoulder, turned around and a big bloke, with two or three pals all in red scarves, said, "Hang on, mate. You Evertonians just have to learn to wait. It's always like this. And we come EVERY year!" It was a real put-down, and a reminder of the Scouse sense of humour. Paul couldn't stop laughing.

Wembley holds some happy memories, especially from the 1980s when Everton ruled the roost in the top division, and there was no team to match them.

Paul was with me again in 1984, when Everton beat Watford 2-0 to win the FA Cup. Paul lived in Wembley then - he had a little maisonette only a few roads away from the stadium, his first step on the property ladder. We both ended up walking back to his place after the match, and he was waving an Everton flag around like a maniac.

The Blues were back at Wembley for the FA Cup final the next two years, in 1985 and 1986 but, unfortunately, we lost on both occasions, one of them to Liverpool.

Everton had some great teams over the years. When I first started following them, week in week out in the 50s, they had players like Peter Farrell, the Irish captain, Tommy Eglington, Eddie Wainwright, Wally Fielding, centre-half T.G. Jones, and the best England goalkeeper of his generation, Ted Sagar.

Then there was the era when we had truly superb players like midfielder Bobby Collins and centre-forward Alex Young, dubbed the Golden Vision for his silky ball-playing skills. Then came centre forwards like bustling Dave Hickson, Fred Pickering, Andy Grey and Graeme Sharp. My favourite centre-forward of them all was Duncan Ferguson.

Big, strong, 6ft 4ins of sheer muscle. He took no prisoners, big Dunc. Happily, he's still with the club today. Now a coach with the reserves.

When I returned North after leaving London, I bought myself a season ticket in the main stand, just a couple of rows behind the Press box. And the guy who sat next to me, who I quickly made friends with, turned out to be a Labour MP and a great pal of Tony Blair's publicity spin doctor Alistair Campbell, who used to work on the Mirror as a reporter. So we had a lot in common, and he used to bring me up to date every week with what had been happening in the corridors of power.

As soon as they were old enough, my two granddaughters Amina and Jessica started going to Goodison with me. Amina in particular became a true Blue, and so I ended up buying two season tickets instead of one, which we kept for several years.

During that time, I had two special treats with the girls. The first was when we booked a half-day tour around Goodison Park, and arrived to find that our tour guide was the veteran footballer Dave Hickson, my hero from the 1950s and 60s.

He was so delighted at the behaviour of my granddaughters that he posed for pictures with us, and we became friends. (Sadly, Dave died only a few years ago).

Then I also got back in touch with Bill Kenwright, who had taken over as the big boss, chairman of Everton. Bill was an actor and I first got to know him when he joined the cast of Coronation Street, playing Gordon Clegg.

When he heard I was now a season ticket holder, he invited me (and granddaughter Amina) to go to one match as his special guests. When we turned up, he gave us a personal tour of the trophy room, pointing out all the pictures on the wall and telling Amina, "These were the footballing heroes when Ken and I used to come here as kids." He then reserved two VIP seats for us, with dinner laid on. It was a really great day and Amina was more than impressed.

Another particularly memorable day at Goodison was when I was 60. Without telling me, Amina secretly booked three pitch-side seats and also arranged for my name to be flashed across the score-board in lights before the game: "Congratulations to Ken – 60 today!" My son Paul came up from London to join us at the match. We beat Newcastle United 2-0, so it ended a perfect day (not to mention Paul taking his mother on a quick spin around the block on the back seat of his motor-bike).

When my first grandson Edmund (son of our Mark and Karen) was born - on 17 January 1991 - I couldn't wait to register him as an Evertonian. I was determined that he was going to follow his grandfather and his father as a lifelong Blue, even though he lived in Wimbledon. I went on to Goodison and signed him up for the fan club at one day old. I even received a document, declaring him to be the youngest fan. Some years later, the club's official magazine carried a double page feature showing pictures of some of their youngest fans. And I made sure that Edmund was in there, pointing out that he held the record as the youngest-ever fan, at one day old! I even sent a copy of the programme to Mark, to show Eddie, thinking how proud he would be.

Imagine my horror when I went on the phone, a few years later, and I talked to Eddie and reminded him that he was still Everton's youngest-ever fan. I couldn't believe it when he said to me, "I'm not really interested in football. And if I was, I think I'd support Manchester United."

What? Not interested in football? Support Man Utd.? He's got to be joking! How can a grandson of mine not be interested in football?

To say I was disappointed is an understatement. We laugh about it now. Ed is 25 or more, and 6ft. 2in. tall. He's grown into a fine young man and I'm very proud of him. But I still can't understand why he doesn't like football.

I have one other grandson, Tommy (Paul's son) and he's quite the opposite to Ed. He lives for football. I knew he was going to be a good player when I first saw him, kicking a ball around in the garden when he was a two-year-old. He had a lethal left foot, and could kick with both feet.

He's now 14, and he plays not only for his local team in Milton Keynes, and for the school, but was also spotted by a soccer scout and plays for the junior academy with MK Dons, the First Division team.

Whether he is good enough to sign up for them, or be a professional, we shall have to wait and see. A lot of young lads are taken on by professional clubs these days, but then kicked out if they don't make the grade by the time they are 16 or 17.

We can only hope, though I still joke with Tommy that he might end up playing in a blue shirt for Everton one day. He comes up to watch the occasional game at Goodison with Paul. And Tommy is now a walking encyclopaedia of football knowledge.

Treading the turf of Goodison was a really thrilling moment for me, even though it was only on the perimeter of the pitch. I also went down to Anfield a couple of times and had a kick-around with veteran centre-forward Ian St. John, and then a few years later with Kenny Dalglish. Even more thrilling was when I was in Madrid, for a Eurovision Song Contest, and I got the chance to visit Real Madrid's ground, walk through their magnificent trophy room, and even go down on the pitch and have a few penalty shots into one of the goals.

I also once managed to get my hands on the FA Cup. Yes, the real thing. But no, I wasn't at Wembley, as the winning captain. It was in Sainsbury's store in Upton, Wirral, doing the "weekly shop" with my wife, and they had the cup on display. For a £5 donation to a local charity, you could be photographed holding up the Cup. It was a chance not to be missed.

One of the proudest moments from the past, though, was when my young brother Eric actually played at Goodison Park in a Liverpool schoolboys' cup final. He was only 12 and he was in the Venice Street team that won 2-0. I was there as a young reporter and covered the match in my sports column in The Liverpolitan.

We always joked with each other. As a teenager, I was a pretty good table tennis player (in fact with my sister Louise, we were mixed doubles champions of Liverpool one year) and Eric would often remind me, "You may have been good at table tennis, but I was better at football." He was too.

The greatest young player I have ever seen at Goodison was, without a doubt, Wayne Rooney. Anyone who knows anything about football could have spotted it. Here was a young kid with exceptional talent. The first time I saw him play, I just knew that this was a player who was not just good, but he was going to be great. He had all the skill and ability to be the best player of his generation. As good as Stanley Matthews or Tom Finney, even.

When he made his debut for Everton at 16 years old, in a match against Arsenal, and he scored that wonderful goal, you just knew that here was a real-life Roy of the Rovers. A future England player. A future England captain. He was all of these things. And more.

When Rooney played for Everton, I knew he was going to be one of our greatest ever players. When he signed for Manchester United, some fans at Everton hated him and poured scorn on him. Why? You can't hold back talent. You can't blame a kid for being ambitious. There is no way he was ever going to stay at Everton for the rest of his life. He was, and I hate to admit this, too big for Everton.

That's the way football is today. It's a business, not a sport any more. It was inevitable that he was going to end up at a bigger club. He's proved over the last ten years to be as good as I always knew he was. Both for Manchester United and for England.

But he's still a Scouser, and we discovered him. Still an Evertonian at heart. And it wouldn't surprise me one little bit if Wayne doesn't end up back at Goodison one day. Maybe as manager? Now there's a suggestion - maybe Wayne Rooney and Duncan Ferguson together as a managing duo at Everton? Nothing is impossible.

I have a huge picture on the wall of my study at home. It's a specially framed montage of all Everton's great players, past and present, dating from 1888 up to 1994 when Duncan Ferguson was still playing. And sitting among them, is me (or at least my head, cleverly superimposed) on the back row, with goalkeeper Ted Sagar on one side of me and Dixie Dean (the legendary all-time record goal scorer) on the other.

The picture, which I treasure, was given to me by my mother as a birthday gift some years ago.

The bold title at the top of the picture is: "And On The Eighth Day He Created Everton." It includes the names and faces of most of the greatest players to put on an Everton blue shirt. They include Tommy Lawton, Joe Mercer, Gordon West, Ray Wilson, Joe Royle, Kevin Ratcliffe, Duncan McKenzie, Neville Southall, Tony Cottee, Peter Reid, Dave Watson and Gary Lineker.

Away from football, squash has been the dominant sport in our family. My daughter Susan, when she was still at university, met and married a top international squash player, Moussa Helal. He played for Egypt, travelled around the globe competing in international events, and at one time was ranked No.14 in the world. He has dozens of cups and medals, has won various national titles, and was a member of the British team for some years. He then became one of Britain's top coaches.

My two granddaughters, Amina and Jessica, playing squash from a very early age, both played for Lancashire, and Amina went on to play for England, before winning a sporting scholarship to America, where she played for Trinity College at Hartford University. During her first year there, she captained the team that won the US national college championship.

My proudest moment though was probably when Amina, then playing for England, competed in the World junior women's championships in Belgium, and was only narrowly beaten in the final, but won the silver medal. The girl who beat her, from Malaysia, went on to become No.1 in the world and she is still one of the top international professionals.

Amina, choosing not to go professional, is still playing for fun and has qualified as a national coach.

Jessica, meanwhile, moved to America and lives in Huntington Beach, California, where she too is now one of the top professional coaches in the US. In a recent magazine poll, she was voted No. 10 in a list of the Top 50 most influential players in US squash.

Quite a sporting family, eh?

There was a time in my own career when I thought I might become a sports writer.

In my early days in Liverpool, I covered football and boxing for a number of local papers. Then when I moved to Manchester, I worked for BBC radio and did football reports and also presented a Saturday-afternoon sports programme as anchor man for a while. I really enjoyed it and I could have done more, but eventually had to decide what I wanted to do, so I gave up broadcasting and chose journalism.

Strangely, my son Mark, following in my path as a journalist, chose sport. After starting work with a Fleet Street sports agency, he went on to become Editor of Shoot, the football magazine, and then joined the Daily Mirror as a sports writer, before moving to The Sun, where he still works as one of their top sports reporters.

My other son Paul, on the other hand, has never really been the sporting type. He likes watching sport, rather than participating. Just like me these days. Paul is an air traffic controller, originally working and trained at Heathrow, but now happy at Luton airport. He's got what we call a proper job.

CHAPTER 40: THE HACKS

Journalism is something of a mad world. You've got to be very dedicated if you want to succeed. They say that good journalists are born, not made. And I believe that. You don't go into journalism to make big money. There are very few journalists I know who ended up rich, although you can make a very comfortable living if you get the right jobs.

Over the years, I have worked with some very smart, intelligent, well educated people. As well as a lot of pretty averagely talented colleagues who were just content to eke out a decent living.

But I've also had to work alongside some odd screwball characters and a few crazy eccentrics. Let me tell you about some of them ...

I was grateful to many of them, particularly in my early days when I was a rooky trying to learn the trade. People like Peter Graham, editor of The Liverpolitan, who came from a wealthy family in Wirral, took a chance and gave me a break as a complete novice. Hugh Hyland, a tough, experienced middle-aged reporter, was my senior on the Bebington News, and taught me a lot before he left for pastures new. Eric Firth, who took over from Hyland as my boss, was everyone's idea of what a reporter should look like - slightly scruffy, he wore a dirty mac, trilby, and rolled his own cigarettes. He'd travelled around a lot as a journalist but was always going on about Derbyshire being the most beautiful county in England. He was a lovely fellow and we got on very well.

George Rowlands was an odd old sod. He was the Editor of the whole Birkenhead News group of papers, who first took me on as a junior reporter. He was also a distinguished JP who regularly sat on the bench at the magistrates Courts in Birkenhead and Bebington. Which meant that whenever we were on court duty, reporting in the courts, and Mr. Rowlands was on the magistrates' bench, we had to make sure we reported every single case and dare not miss one out, even if it might be an ordinary drunk-and-disorderly or a speeding fine.

After I'd been on the paper more than two years, I went to the Editor and told him that I'd just become engaged, and as I wanted to get married, I'd like a pay rise. And I more or less hinted that if I didn't get more money, I'd have to look for another job. He looked at me dismissively, shrugged his shoulders, and said, "Sorry, there's nothing I can do."

In those days, there was a weekly magazine called The World's Press News, which was usually delivered to all newspapers offices. This became essential reading for all journalists, because the two back pages were full of classified adverts for jobs available throughout the country. If you wanted a new job, The World's Press News became your best friend. In fact, in most offices, there would be a mad but discreet scramble every Friday morning by journalists to get their hands on the WPN. And after a rapid scan of the Jobs Available page, it would be passed on to the next bloke.

So I looked through the WPN, and found two jobs I thought might be worth applying for. One was in Newcastle upon Tyne, looking for a sub editor, and the other was in Nuneaton, seeking a news reporter. I quickly wrote off letters to both, and received replies inviting me to interviews.

Taking a day off, I took the train to Nuneaton and went through an interview with the Editor. I was feeling quite pleased when he offered me the job and said, "When can you start?" The only fly in the ointment was when he told me that I would be expected to take up lodgings with the chief printer and his wife, for about £5 a week, because that was the usual arrangement with new reporters.

I went back home to think about it, and also the other job in Newcastle. I was in something of a dilemma and couldn't decide what to do. I went to see my Editor George Rowlands again, knocked on his door, and asked for his advice. I told him about the two jobs I had applied for, but was worried about the one in Newcastle because I hadn't done any sub-editing before. Would it be a good idea for me to go to Newcastle and get experience as a sub editor, or should I stick to reporting and go to Nuneaton? I asked.

For a minute or two, he just looked at me. Then he got up from behind his huge desk and said, without a glimmer of a smile, "I don't quite know what to say to you, Irwin. You came to me a fortnight ago and said that if you didn't get a pay rise, you would be looking for another job. Now you tell me that you have the offer of not one, but two jobs, and you are asking for my advice. Well, all I can say is that jobs must be bloody easy to come by. It's up to you. Close the door on your way out."

Well, I felt so embarrassed. But that confrontation with Rowlands had now made up my mind. I was determined to leave. I didn't take up the job in Nuneaton (I was put off by the suggestion of lodging with the chief printer) but landed a much better job (thanks to the good old back page of the World's Press News) with the Nottingham Evening Post.

Nottingham as a city was much nicer than Nuneaton. It was a bigger paper with tradition and a good reputation. And I ended up lodging with the Methodist minister, the Rev Walter Joyce and his family at the manse in Ruddington (but that was my idea, not the Editor's).

472

When I eventually left the Birkenhead News, Mr. Rowlands was pleasant enough. He said he was sorry to lose me, shook hands, and wished me well for the future. When I asked him if he would be kind enough to give me a reference, he said of course, he would forward this on to me.

But there was also a question of some money. The News, which was published twice weekly, had what was called a shared Lineage system. This was an arrangement that Rowlands had with the bigger evening papers, the Liverpool Echo and the Evening Express, that we would provide certain news stories from our area and send them over to them on a daily basis. It meant a bit of extra work for us, and whenever we phoned over stories to them, we would just say, "From Rowlands, Birkenhead." Then at the end of the month, they would calculate how many stories they had published, and pay Mr. Rowlands accordingly. He, in turn, would then work out how much he'd received, and would divide the pot and pay out each journalist for whatever stories they had written. Usually, this worked out fine. It meant we could pick up some extra cash each month. Sometimes it could be only a couple of quid, or it could be as much as nine or ten pounds, depending on how many stories you'd chalked up. The only trouble was that Mr. Rowlands had a habit of often delaying the pay-out. Sometimes it could even roll over into a second month. But unless you were desperate, no one really cared because you knew you would get paid eventually.

On my leaving, Rowlands assured me he would send me a reference, as requested. Oh, and there was the question of the Lineage pot. He would work it out, do his calculations, and send me a cheque for whatever I was due. Fine. A week or so later, I received the reference, and it was a surprisingly pleasant one. Good, that will add to my CV nicely, I thought. But there was no cheque, no final payment from the lineage pot. It didn't worry me. I was too busy trying to establish myself in my new job in Nottingham.

The story of George Rowlands did not end there, however. Some years later, after I had left Nottingham, moved to Liverpool and worked on the Evening Express, I then joined the Daily Mirror in Manchester. And after a few years there, I started working for the BBC, doing football reports on radio, which took me all over the North region every week.

It just so happened that one Saturday the BBC booked me to report on a match involving Tranmere Rovers, in Birkenhead. So I went to Prenton Park, took my seat in the Press box and did my report over the radio line. At the end of the game, the Press boys are usually invited to have some tea and sandwiches, so I walked into the back room, to grab a cuppa, and the first person I saw was George Rowlands. And I suddenly realised that George, among his many distinguished jobs, as newspaper editor and magistrate, was also a director of Tranmere Rovers.

He was standing at the back of the room, cup of tea in hand, talking to somebody. He was looking a little older, his hair and even his military moustache had turned grey, and he had put on a bit of weight. But he was still very dapper, in an expensive suit and a gold watch and chain straddled across his bulging waistcoat.

It must have been nine or ten years since I had last seen him. I couldn't resist it. I walked over to him and introduced myself. "I don't know whether you remember me, Mr. Rowlands," I said. He shook hands and said, "Of course I do. How are you? Nice to see you. What are you doing here?" I explained I was there as a BBC radio reporter. He wasn't exactly surprised. In fact, he said, "Oh yes, I think I've heard you on the radio a few times."

We chatted for a while, and then I finally came out with it. "Do you know what," I said, "When I left the Birkenhead News, do you remember me coming to ask for a pay rise?" He looked bemused. "Well, I think that if you had only offered me a rise - even another pound a week - I would have stayed," I said.

He then grinned and said something that I could never, ever forget. "Don't you think I knew that," he said. "You might have stayed, but for how long? I knew when you first came to join us as a junior reporter that you were something special. You had a lot of talent. And I knew you were destined for Fleet Street and bigger things. I didn't want to hold you back."

Well, I didn't know whether to laugh or cry. Was this a wonderful compliment he was paying me? Or just a load of bullshit? Anyway, I thanked him. He congratulated me on having joined the Daily Mirror, and we said goodbye.

Now some years later, I was walking down the Mirror News room, and about to get into the lift, when one of the reporters, John Jackson, stopped me for a chat. John had been a reporter on the rival Birkenhead Advertiser, and we did courts and councils and the fire-stations run together. He suddenly said, "By the way, do you know George Rowlands is dead? Died last week."

I don't know why I said it, but I just replied, "Well, he died owing me money." John looked at me, puzzled. "Really! How come?" "Lineage," I said. "He still owed me from the lineage pot."

He burst out laughing and held the lift door open for me.

One eccentric reporter we had in the Daily Mirror's Northern office in Manchester was a guy called Ian Skidmore. A portly little fellow who wore tweeds and three-piece suits with a gold watch and chain dangling over his waistcoat. He was a good journalist and a great raconteur, especially when he'd had a few sherberts.

A lot of drinking was done even during the lunch break in those days. And Ted Fenna, the Northern Editor (the man who gave me my job on the Mirror) had a reputation for regularly going out for a two-hour liquid lunch.

One lunch-time, Ian Skidmore, who had had a skinful, returned to the office, sat back in his chair in the news room, put his feet up on the desk, and promptly fell asleep. About 20 minutes later, the Editor staggered back from the pub, weaved his way through the news room, and stopped when he saw Skidmore, who was fast asleep in his chair.

Ted shook him on the shoulder to wake him up and said, "Pissed again, Skidmore!"

To which, Ian, trying to sit up straight, replied, "Don't worry, Ted. So am I."

Douglas Marlborough was a brilliant journalist, one of the best, but he did have one failing – he got drunk too easily and too often. Dougie worked for the Daily Mail, as their show business and TV reporter, and I first met him when I moved to London from the Mirror's Manchester office. I'd heard a lot about him but found him a strange fish at first.

The BBC at that time had a Press Office based in Cavendish Place, London, with a room set aside for journalists to work in. And all the daily papers had their own reporter who would hang out there every day, to pick up and file stories.

When I first went in, as the new recruit from the Mirror, everyone introduced themselves and they were all very friendly. Except one, Dougie Marlborough. Each day, we would go around covering various Press conferences at the ITV companies, and return in the afternoon to the BBC Press room, to file our stories. Often, we would share cabs, going from one event to another.

After three or four days of working perfectly amicably with everyone, I was puzzled, and a little worried that Marlborough had not said a single word to me, even though we were all typing away furiously only a few yards from each other. So I eventually went over to him and introduced myself. "I'm Ken Irwin from the Mirror. We've never really met," I started. And he replied, quite viciously, "I know who you are. You're from Manchester. And the sooner you go back there, the better!"

I was really quite shocked. And he was quickly chided by one or two of the others who had heard our exchange. One of them said to me later, "Take no notice. It's Dougie, he's had too much to drink."

We let it go. But the next day, I was determined to sort things out with him, so at the first opportunity, when we had a quiet moment, I pulled him aside and asked him if there was a problem. He then came out with a little speech. "I'm sorry for being so bad tempered with you yesterday. I do apologise. But I'll tell you what the problem is. Two or three weeks ago, I got a late-night phone call from my office over a story in the Daily Mirror, which you had written. The story about Z-Cars which was on your front page, marked as an exclusive. I then had to start checking it out and re-writing it for my paper. Now I'm not used to getting late-night calls from the News Desk, so you had better beware."

Still a little puzzled, I pointed out that the story he was talking about was something I'd picked up and filed in Manchester. What did he expect me to do?

"You're now in London, not Manchester," he said. "You'd better learn the rules. We all work together here. We share stories. If you want to continue getting exclusives, then that's up to you. But for every story you get, you'll have six of us up against you, so we'll get a lot more. And you will be getting more calls dragging you out of bed than we do. It's up to you."

The message was there, loud and clear. The TV correspondents worked as a pack, and all pooled their stories. And they obviously expected me to comply, otherwise I'd be in trouble.

In a way, it made a lot of sense. Most days, we were filing five or six news stories. It was hard work. But Marlborough's system made things easier. When reporters got back to the BBC every afternoon, they would agree which stories to share, and everyone would write a different story, and hand a carbon copy around to the others. Everyone would then simply re-write each story to suit their particular paper's style. It just meant that no one got an exclusive.

The practise in Fleet Street was that after the first editions came out, around 10 pm every night, every News Desk would quickly check out what the rival papers had in, and if there were any stories they'd missed, there would be hasty phone calls to their specialist reporters to "match" the story from other papers. This could sometimes be a nightmare for reporters, trying to confirm and catch up on a story we didn't have. But that's the way it was.

So I went away and thought about Dougie's proposal. Well, not so much a proposal, more a threat. And I figured I had no alternative but to "join the club." I had plenty of confidence in my own ability. But working on my own and taking on the rest of the Press lads was something else. There would be six of them working against me. I knew I was good. But not that good. When I went back to my office, I had a word with my boss, TV editor Clifford Davis, and my colleague Jack Bell. They told me, "That's the way it works down here. You'd better get used to it."

The next time I saw Dougie Marlborough, I agreed to be pals. We had a drink, we shook hands, and he said, "Welcome to the club." It did make life easier.

The astonishing thing was that, within a few months, Dougie and I became really close friends. We both operated in the same way. He had not only an enthusiasm for the job, but a canny knack of uncovering stories, an in-built news sense, and I liked to think I had it, too.

In fact, one day when we were in the pub together, and Dougie was on his seventh or eighth glass of red (he never drank beer) he actually turned to me and said, "It's great working with you. We both think alike." I knew then the rift was healed. We'd be friends for life.

Dougie really was a one-off. He got up to so many escapades. I once saved him his job when he resigned in a fit of rage after being thrown out by Frank Sinatra's heavies. (See chapter on Sinatra). The Daily Mail news desk once phoned me to ask where Dougie was when he went missing with comedian Tommy Cooper in Wales for three days (See chapter on Cooper). And he got drunk so often that he'd miss the last train home, and end up staying in London, kipping on someone's sofa.

Once, there was an altercation between Dougie and Martin Jackson, of the Daily Express. When Martin, in a mischievous mood, jokingly asked him, "Are you queer, Dougie? Are you homosexual?" Dougie (who was very thin and weighed about nine stone) just punched him.

Dougie was actually happily married, but how his wife Pam put up with his awful behaviour was beyond me. Pam was a part-time football referee and a lovely woman.

Every day, we would be attending four or five Press receptions, some of them ending up as late-night parties. Dougie was notorious for asking awkward questions at Press conferences, and he would often become belligerent and rude. At one stage, he was getting drunk so often, that he told me he had a special arrangement with his office secretary. She had his diary, and she would phone every place he'd been the day before, to check on how he had behaved. If he'd been extremely rude with someone, she would send them a bouquet of a dozen roses as an apology. If he'd been really badly behaved or obnoxious, it would be a bottle of champagne she'd send. Then at the end of the week, she would tot up how much she had spent out on apologising for Dougie's misdemeanours, give him the bill and he would pay her. Dougie would often joke with me, "I must have been a good boy last week. It only cost me twenty quid!"

Hughie Green once told me a funny story about Dougie. I was at Hughie's apartment in Baker Street, having a drink, and Hughie said, "You know, I love Douglas Marlborough, I really do. He's a damn good journalist. But when he's had too much to drink, he's a pain in the arse." And he told me how, a few months earlier, Dougie had sat exactly where I was sitting, on the sofa. They were drinking all evening, and eventually Hughie yawned and said it was time for Dougie to go home. He looked at his watch, it was past midnight, and Dougie said he'd missed his last train home. Hughie suggested he take a taxi, but Dougie said it would cost too much. He lived out in Sutton. He then asked Hughie if he would mind giving him a lift home.

"Well, I wasn't too happy, because I'd now had a lot to drink myself. But I felt sorry for him, and I certainly didn't want him staying the night, so I got the Roller out and we set off to take him home," said Hughie.

When they got to Sutton, Hughie turned to Dougie, who was slumped in the front passenger seat, and asked him exactly where he lived. Dougie replied that this would be fine. "Just drop me off here, I can walk the rest of the way." No, insisted Hughie, now determined to take him all the way home. So Dougie directed him to his road. "What number?" demanded Hughie. "No.136," said Dougie. Hughie drove his Rolls Royce up to the house, on to the drive, and opened the door for Duggie to get out right on his front doorstep. He then turned around, did a U-turn on the lawn, before waving to Dougie and driving off.

"I realised I'd probably ruined his lawn, with the weight of the car, but at least I got him home,"said Hughie, with a chuckle.

Peter Black was a strange fellow. He was the distinguished TV critic with the Daily Mail for years, and worked from home, so the only times we saw him was when he turned up at some of the TV festivals abroad. He didn't take part in any of the hurly-burley of Fleet Street and admitted to me that he had never been "a proper reporter," and didn't get into journalism until he was thirty. In fact, he told me once, when we were having a quiet drink, "I envy you because you can sit down and write a news story and phone it over to the office in ten minutes. I can't do that. It would take me hours to do what you can do. I simply haven't got a news sense."

Peter had only one arm, but it didn't seem to handicap him at all. And he was quite a keen golfer.

We became quite good friends and had a mutual respect for each other. But I remember the first time I went to cover the Prix Italia festival, and I met him at Heathrow airport. The Prix Italia was a prestigious and very serious documentary festival which Peter used to go to every year. He was horrified when he saw me. When I told him that this was the first time the Daily Mirror had decided to cover the festival, he looked very worried. "Oh no, I suppose this means you are going to be doing news stories every day, and scooping me," he moaned. "I've been doing this festival for ten years, and I've been the only British journalist invited there. I regard it as a week's holiday, just watching TV programmes. Now you are going to spoil everything. Anyway, it's all far too highbrow for the Daily Mirror."

We laughed about it, but he was deadly serious. He was terrified that if any stories appeared in the Mirror, then he would get phone calls from his news desk, asking him to file some copy. To put his mind at rest, I had to assure him that any stories I did, I would tell him about them, so that he could file them as well. It was then that I realised Peter couldn't write a news story. He was brilliant as a TV critic (in fact probably the No.1 in Fleet Street and certainly the most respected). But he would agonise for hours over what was a very short and simple news story. I ended up, later in the week, actually writing a couple of stories for him, re-jigging them to suit the Daily Mail. I've never seen a man so grateful in all my life.

However, when we were seated on the plane - bound for the beautiful little city of Mantua - there was an announcement that the plane had developed a fault, and all passengers would have to disembark. For an hour or more we waited back in the lounge, and Peter and I were standing together at the back of the hall when we were suddenly joined by an airline captain, our pilot for the flight, who started chatting to us. He asked where we were going and what our business was, and when Peter introduced himself, the captain told us he was a regular Daily Mail reader and was delighted to actually meet the distinguished TV critic in person.

Eventually, we got back on the plane, and as soon as we took off and were in the air, a stewardess came to our seats and served us a bottle of champagne and a bucket of ice. "With the compliments of the captain," she said. It was a delightful surprise. Thanks to Peter Black, it was a very enjoyable trip.

Martin Jackson was the TV reporter with the Daily Express for many years and became a great friend. He was one of the TV Press pack and we all worked closely together. Martin was a good-looking bloke, and a happy-go-lucky bachelor who didn't get married until he was well into his mid-thirties. When he did finally tie the knot, it was with Maureen, divorced first wife of Lonnie Donegan.

Lonnie was the big-name entertainer who had scores of hit records ("My Old Man's A Dustman" etc.) and became an international star with his special brand of Skiffle music, which he introduced to get away from hard rock n roll, in the 50s and 60s.

Maureen was a very attractive woman, with a young family. And Martin quickly settled down to married life, although I did find it odd that whenever he talked about his wife, he would always add that she was Lonnie Donegan's ex. It was almost as though she was some kind of status trophy.

Still, she was always very friendly, and we had a few laughs together. One year, Martin took Maureen with him to the Golden Rose festival in Montreux, and she was a lot of fun, like one of the lads. But she did have a hard side, and Martin would often joke that Maureen was the boss and wore the trousers at home.

Another year, however, when Mrs. Jackson did not come to Montreux, we were pleasantly surprised to be blessed with the presence of the vivacious Sandra Gough, from Coronation Street.

Sandra was the leggy and very attractive young actress who played Irma Ogden, wayward daughter of Stan and Hilda Ogden in the Northern soap opera. I knew Sandra very well, from previous experience. She claimed to be a strict Catholic and was always banging on about religion, and she also had a mischievous streak which had upset some of her fellow actors.

We were not quite sure why Sandra was in Montreux. She wasn't there officially. But she certainly put herself about and seemed determined to have a good time.

After a few days, it became pretty obvious that she had taken a fancy to Martin Jackson, who I think was quite flattered by her attention. We were all staying at the same hotel, and we became rather amused as the week went on and it developed into a kind of nudge-nudge situation. Martin would disappear for long periods, and so would Sandra.

Then Martin came down to breakfast one day, beaming all over his face, and told us he'd had a great night. I knew he was playing with fire, but I said nothing. After all, he was a big boy.

The frolics continued, but on the final day of the festival, the day before we were due to fly back home, Martin looked very concerned, and he opened up to me and said, "I'm a bit worried about going home." Why? I asked. "Because it's been very frantic. And my back is torn to shreds. I daren't take my shirt off in front of Maureen. She'll know what I've been up to. She'll go mad."

Without going into graphic detail, he gave a few of us some idea of what he'd been up to for most of the week. He was half boasting, half complaining. There was little any of us could say.

Clifford Davis was my boss when I moved to the London office from Manchester.

He was the TV Editor, old enough to be my father, who had been doing the job since joining the Mirror not long after the end of World War 11. In fact he claimed to have been the world's first TV reporter. When I joined his department, there were three of us - Clifford, Jack Bell, and me, plus a TV critic (first Kenneth Eastough, later Mary Malone), and we shared one big office. It worked pretty well. Clifford marked the diary each day, and assigned us all to different jobs.

Apart from his TV job, Clifford was also a part-time magician, and was a proud member of the elite Magic Circle. During the war, he was a second lieutenant in the army who had ended up running the unit responsible for the forces' entertainment, which produced people like Harry Secombe, Spike Milligan, Dick Emery and others who turned professional after being demobbed.

In many ways, Clifford was a pretty smart operator. Always immaculately dressed, he had a lot of style. He also had his fingers in a lot of pies. Every morning, he would spend the first half hour on the telephone, talking to business associates and financial advisers, buying and selling shares. He was constantly wheeling and dealing and quite often, it was almost a case of Clifford fitting his Mirror job in between his many business interests.

When it came to his holidays, he would get his agent to book him a couple of weeks at some venue or seaside resort, doing his magic act.

I got on very well with Clifford. He liked me, I think, because I was a grafter. And we'd have lunch together at least once a week - always the same table at The Nosherie, a little Jewish restaurant and sandwich bar in a back street of the Hatton Garden jewellery district, and listed in the London Good Food Guide. (I invariably had the same every day - chicken soup with dumplings, a plate of salt beef with cucumber and a lutka, followed by fruit pie with ice cream. Oh, I can still taste that delicious salt beef!).

When New Faces was first launched on ITV in 1973 Clifford, because of his background as a magician and entertainer, was booked to be on the regular panel, alongside professionals like Arthur Askey, Ted Ray and Mickey Most. And as the show grew in popularity, so did Clifford's reputation - as a judge who didn't take any prisoners!

He revelled in being dubbed Mr. Nasty. Of course Clifford always maintained that he was not putting on an act and being deliberately nasty to build up his reputation, but simply that he was being honest and telling contestants what he really thought of them.

Whatever the truth, he certainly encouraged a lot of hate mail. It came to the stage where the producers thought Clifford was being too vicious and asked him to tone down his comments because it was unfair on the contestants. He refused, so they sacked him. He was then re-instated, but Clifford was determined not to be dictated to, and returned to the show with even stronger fangs. He was fired again. But the producers were well aware that Clifford was a personal friend of ATV boss Lew Grade, and could pick up the phone to Lew at any time if he had a grievance. Which he did. So after a few phone calls, he returned to the judging panel for a third time.

New Faces was now drawing a weekly audience of 18 million viewers. The trouble was that Clifford was beginning to think that he was bigger than the show, and when he continued to live up to his Mr. Nasty image, the producers finally decided they'd had enough, and he was dropped. This time for good. He was not very happy. Calls to Lew Grade and others at ATV met with no response.

Then the producers decided to have a shake-up on the TV judging panel. Having got rid of Clifford and all the old entertainers like Arthur

Askey, Ted Ray and Noelle Gordon, they kept only two - record producers Mickey Most and Tony Hatch - and held auditions to find showbiz journalists who would make good judges.

That's when I found myself invited onto the show. After auditions in Birmingham, I was offered a contract for the next series, along with one or two journalists from other papers. I must admit I was rather pleased with myself, and I enjoyed sitting on the TV panel every two or three weeks, on a rota basis. I was determined not to be particularly nasty or especially nice, but simply to give my honest opinion of each act as they came on stage. It must have worked, because after a few weeks the producers told me they were very happy and that I was doing a good job.

At first, of course, it was a little embarrassing. Clifford had been fired, and in a way I had replaced him from the Daily Mirror. But if he was annoyed with the situation, I must say he didn't show it. He simply wished me well, and once or twice was even complimentary about my appearances.

There was no doubt at all, however, that Clifford was furious with the producers and ATV. And he then had a major row with Lew Grade, and their friendship of many years came to an abrupt end. The result of this was that Clifford showed just how really nasty he could be, because he wrote a paperback book, with the title "How I Made Lew Grade A Millionaire...and other fables". It was sold as what he called "almost an autobiography by Clifford Davis (TV's 'Mr. Nasty')"

He mentioned me in the book, several times. And on publication, he gave me a copy, with a written front-page inscription "For Ken - who knows most of it anyway."

We were friends as well as colleagues (I learned a lot about journalism and some of the tricks of the trade from Clifford) and we also worked together on one or two freelance ventures. One of them turned out to be the most hilarious, yet saddest jobs we ever undertook.

It concerned a character called Bobbie Kimber, who was an old friend of Clifford's.

He was a ventriloquist, who always dressed up as a woman, and had a dummy called Augustus Peabody, and was a top-of-the-bill entertainer in the 1950s. He had his own children's TV series on BBC, had starred in a Royal Variety show, his agent was Leslie Grade, and when the great Danny Kaye was at the London Palladium for seven weeks in 1950, Bobbie was on the bill with him. I must confess though, that I'd never heard of him.

However, the phone rang in our office one day in 1971, and our secretary Jill Ross told Clifford there was someone down in reception who wanted to meet him. The name was Bobbie Kimber. "Tell him to come up," said Clifford, so Jill went to meet him at the lift, and when she returned, trying not to giggle, she was accompanied by a rather large woman. A matronly figure with a large bust, a skirt above her knees and high heeled shoes.

Clifford shook hands with her, sat her down, offered her a cup of coffee, and asked what he could do for her. Bobbie explained that she was working in a pub at King's Cross as a barmaid, but wanted to get back into show business with her ventriloquist act. Could he give her any sort of publicity?

"Do you mean you're working as a barmaid, dressed like that?" said Clifford. She nodded. "Do they know you're a man?"

"I'm a very good barmaid. And I'm not a man. Not anymore," said Bobbie.

"But what about your wife? And your daughter?" Clifford asked.

"Oh, we're still all living together, except that Jan, my wife, doesn't like going out with me dressed like this. I have to wear men's clothes at weekends, when I'm not working," she replied.

We were all listening to this strange conversation in the office, Jack Bell, secretary Jill, and me. "Then you must have had an operation?" queried Clifford.

"Oh yes, there's nothing there," said Bobbie and then without hesitation jumped up from her chair, faced Clifford, with her back to the rest of us, lifted up her frock, and said, "Look. See for yourself."

A startled Clifford took a quick glance at what was on display and simply said, "Okay, I'm convinced. Put it away." Clifford then looked over at me, trying to get my reaction. I apparently nodded.

Clifford then said, "Well, we can certainly make some money for you. But are you prepared to tell your story? I could probably get one of our Sunday papers interested."

"That would be fine. The only problem is that I haven't told my wife about my operation. I've just told her that the only job I can get is as a barmaid, and that's why I go to work dressed like this."

Clifford told her that she should go away and think about it, but that she would have to tell the wife Jan before we embarked on any kind of publicity.

In the end, Bobbie agreed that was what we should do. Clifford then made arrangements to sell Bobbie's story to the Sunday Mirror, and asked me if I would assist him in writing it, splitting the writing fee between us.

We then spent several weeks, taping interviews with Bobbie, his wife Jan and his beautiful daughter Christine, who was about 21.

It was a really bizarre situation, because although he was still married and cared very much for his wife, Bobbie had also been going out on dates with a man, a lorry driver living in Blackpool, who knew nothing of his sex change and had even proposed marriage to Bobbie, believing she was a perfectly normal woman.

We finally pieced it all together and the Sunday Mirror ran it very big as a three-week series.

Before we went into print, though, Clifford went to Hughie Green and asked if he could introduce Bobbie Kimber on Opportunity Knocks, then one of the top talent shows on TV. He didn't tell Hughie of the sex-change operation but suggested that Kimber deserved the chance to make a comeback in show business, after working as a London bus driver for four years for £20 a week.

Hughie agreed, and in January 1972 Bobbie appeared on the show, with Clifford introducing her, and letters poured in from old fans who remembered Bobbie's regular appearances on BBC TV some 20 years earlier.

She didn't win on the show, but her appearance, with faithful puppet Augustus Peabody, sparked enough interest for Bobbie to get some bookings in clubs and pubs.

But even with the publicity of the Sunday Mirror articles, Bobbie's showbiz return was short lived. Her ventriloquist act had become old fashioned, the jokes dated.

Bobbie tried to get back to a normal life. She lived quietly with Jan, the woman he married when he was a man. Jan accepted the situation, and they lived not as an odd couple but as two old ladies, who both shared a daughter.

The Sunday Mirror bought the British rights, and the material was serialised with photographs in many overseas papers and magazines. Clifford later told me that Bobbie's share earned her over £3,000, which was a lot of money in those days, and that she gave half of the money to Jan.

It was a sad story, but at least it had a happy-ever-after ending.

Another memorable stunt which I agreed to do with Clifford is worth recording. He was booked for a week to do late-night cabaret shows at the famous Quaglino's, in the West End. I suggested I might go down on opening night and see the show, because I had never actually seen Clifford's act, although we had been hearing about it for years. But he said, "No, don't come to the show. I want you to stay at home and help me with the act."

He then explained what he wanted me to do. "Just stay by your telephone and wait for a call from my wife Pearl. She will ask you some questions and give you the answers. Just follow her instructions. And for God's sake don't let me down."

On the Monday night, I waited by the phone. It was about 10.30pm when the phone rang, and it was Pearl. "Right, she said, I am going to ring you back in a couple of minutes. The answers to the questions are - the colour Blue, the number is going to be nine, and the line from the book is 27. Can you remember that? It's very important to get it right, Ken." And off she went.

Although I didn't know exactly what tricks Clifford was up to, I followed the plan carefully. The phone rang again, I picked it up and there was a man's voice. He said something like, "Look, I'm sorry to bother you so late at night. I just happen to be in the audience of a nightclub in London and I have been brought up on stage by this magician. He is doing a trick, and I have picked your phone number at random from the London Telephone Directory. Do you mind answering a few questions?"

Well, I tried to sound surprised, and then mumbled something about having been woken up in bed. He apologised, but then asked me three questions. "What colour have I chosen?" he asked. "Blue," I replied. "What number have I got in my mind?" he asked. "Oh, is it nine?" I said. Finally, he asked me what line on the page of a book had he chosen, and I replied, "Was it 27?"

I could hear a loud round of applause from the audience, and this chap said, "Thank you very much. You are absolutely right. I don't know how this fellow Clifford Davis does it, but he's proved he is a great mind reader." And he put the phone down.

Half an hour later, I had Pearl Davis back on the phone. "Thanks, Ken. You were great. Clifford said he'll explain it all to you tomorrow. Goodnight."

When I arrived at the office next morning, Clifford was already at his desk. He was ecstatic. "You were great last night," he said, and went on to explain how the audience at Quaglino's were terrific, and that when he brought that young man up on stage and performed his trick over the phone with me, the applause was deafening. He then explained that everyone in the room thought the man had dialled a random number from the telephone directory, but in fact it was my number, and Pearl was apparently hiding underneath a table just off stage with a telephone through to me, to give me the answers.

"You were so good, especially when you pretended to be woken up from bed," said Clifford. "No one suspected a thing. They think they witnessed the work of a great mind reader." He then asked me if I would be "on call" every night for the rest of the week. When I hesitated, he said "Don't worry, I've got several other people on my list to help out with the trick. But I know now that none of them are going to be as funny as you were."

Clifford eventually got fed up with writing about television, so one day came in and told us he was going to see the Editor, Mike Molloy, with a new idea. A few days later, he was beaming all over his face when he announced he was leaving us and going to run a new department called the Daily Mirror Pop Club.

He had apparently convinced the Editor that TV was old-fashioned and out of date and the way to attract new and younger readers was with a Pop club, offering prizes and cut-price deals to members. At the age of 58, Clifford suddenly found a new lease of life.

To his credit, the Pop Club proved to be an enormous success, and did add to the Mirror's circulation for a while. Even then, though, in a friendly way, Clifford couldn't do without me. He asked me to write and edit the Pop Club Annual, which I did for a number of years.

The TV department meanwhile was completely re-organised. Bill Hagerty, a guy I liked a lot, came in for a short while to replace Clifford, before going off to become an Assistant Editor, and then Editor of one of our Sunday papers. And I eventually was promoted to TV Editor, and then merged two departments into one and became TV and Show Business Editor, with a staff of 14 writers, two secretaries, a big budget, and my own drinks cabinet. For a while, I was as happy as Larry, whoever Larry was. I had finally got the top job. And I knew that was as far as I wanted to go.

Clifford, through his various ventures, was quite a wealthy man. He lived in a beautiful large detached house with manicured gardens in Blackheath. He and Pearl had one son, who went off to work in America.

But I was very surprised when Clifford came in one day and told us he was selling his house in Blackheath and moving into a flat by the river. I couldn't believe he would even contemplate moving from such a lovely house into a flat in a converted warehouse block.

When they moved, I was invited over to dinner one night, and found it really was quite luxurious. It was in a trendy area with people like Michael Owen, ex-Foreign Secretary and the Labour-turned-Liberal MP as a close neighbour. Clifford's apartment was on the second floor, and the dining room led out on to a terrace which literally overlooked the river wall, giving great views of Tower Bridge and the river traffic.

For years, however, Clifford had kept a secret from his wife. He had a mistress. In fact, more than one.

Every year, when we covered the foreign TV festivals, Clifford would always insist that he went to the Cannes festival and any others in the South of France. Then, when he was away for a week or so, he would take a lady friend who lived in Paris and drive her down to Cannes, or wherever, to stay with him. It became an annual ritual, and he was quite open about it. Both Jack Bell and I knew about his long-running French affair.

But then he found a new lady friend closer to home. He became involved with one of the Press Officers at Thames TV. She was a very nice and very efficient PR, at least 20 years his junior. And they became an item. Suddenly Clifford was like a new man. For a few years he openly escorted her to events around London, and then ended his friendship with his French lady and started taking his London girl friend to the Cannes festival and other foreign jaunts.

Clifford didn't try to hide it. Everyone in the Thames TV Press office knew that, shall we call her Rosie (that's not her real name) was Clifford's regular girlfriend. So did our little rat-pack of TV journalists.

But then there was a tragedy. We were given the news one day that Clifford's wife Pearl had died. She had apparently committed suicide by falling from their balcony into the river.

A short time later, Clifford married his Thames TV girlfriend, and she added the surname Davis to her own name and continued with her PR work.

Clifford died in 1989. He was 72.

James Thomas was a really odd bloke. He was the senior show business reporter on the Daily Express for years and had led a very colourful life. I only really got to know him later in his career when, in truth, he was well past his best. But I liked him, and we became great friends.

Jimmy, I learned, had been in the army during World War 11, and was captured and held as a war prisoner. But he escaped, somehow fled into Italy and was befriended by the locals in a tiny village, where he stayed, was fed and protected, until the end of the war. During his time in hiding, he learned to speak fluent Italian, and at the end of the war came back to Britain and became a journalist.

Jimmy was a great character, but he had only two failings - drink and women. If you can call them failings. He could drink for England and it was very rare to ever find him sober. And he couldn't resist women. Though I must admit I found it hard to find what his sexual attraction could be to any woman, because he was a small, skinny chap, with bad teeth, always shabbily dressed and dishevelled, and as a chain smoker stank of cigarettes.

At one time - and he told me this himself - he had Charlie Drake as a neighbour. Now Charlie Drake was a really top comedian. Only five-feet tall, with a shock of curly red hair, he was a really funny man. He topped the bill at the London Palladium, and had his own TV series for years in the 60s and 70s.

Somehow, Jimmy became over friendly with Charlie Drake's wife, and it developed into an affair. When Charlie found out about it, he had a word with Jim and told him to lay off, even though Charlie was having an extra marital affair himself.

So Jimmy went back to his wife for a while, but things became so intolerable that she decided they should both go to see a Marriage Guidance Councillor.

Reluctantly Jimmy agreed, and for a few weeks he and his wife went together for weekly meetings, getting advice on how to patch up their marriage.

Unfortunately, Jimmy took a fancy to the marriage guidance councillor, who was an attractive middle-aged woman, and the feeling turned out to be mutual because they ended up having an affair. When he told me this, I couldn't help laughing.

But then came an occasion when I was covering a TV festival in Italy. Jimmy was there for the Daily Express, and he came to me and said, "Have you ever been to Portofino?" When I told him I hadn't, he said, "It's a really lovely little place, on the coast. We are not working over the weekend, so why don't you and I take a train and go and stay overnight in Portofino?"

Thinking it might be a pleasant little trip, and a diversion from work, I agreed to join him. When we arrived in Portofino, he suggested a certain hotel, so we went to book in. They had only two single rooms, one large and one much smaller. We tossed a coin and I won the bigger room.

Later we were having dinner in the lovely open-air restaurant, and Jimmy suddenly blurted out, "I love this place. My wife and I came here on our honeymoon. I haven't been back here for 30 years. Just thought I'd like to see what the old place looked like."

I had to laugh. Only Jimmy Thomas could invite me back to his honeymoon hotel to reminisce about his marriage night!

There was another crazy occasion I had with Jimmy. We were in Montruex, in Switzerland, for the annual Golden Rose TV festival, with the usual gang of British journalists, when Jimmy Thomas arrived to cover the event for the Daily Express. He was a couple of days late because he had come straight from the south of France, after reporting another festival in Cannes.

He had checked into the Eurotel Hotel for the week, where I happened to be staying that year. On his first day there, he joined the rest of the British Press gang for lunch. There were about six of us sharing a table, all enjoying the sunshine. But as Jimmy sat down, he said, "Be careful. With the dog."

What dog? I asked. "This dog," he said. "She's under the table now." And he turned to Maggie Forwood, who was sitting next to him, and said, "Could you move your feet up. Mind you don't tread on the dog."

Maggie and I both took a look under the table. "Where's the dog, Jim? I can't see a dog," I said. "Of course she's there," he insisted. "It's a stray dog I picked up in France. She's been following me around ever since. I can't get rid of her."

Maggie Forwood, a TV writer with The Sun, said to him, quite sharply, "There's no dog there, you silly old fool. You're imagining it." Jimmy looked quite pained and looked over at me for some sympathy.

As the week went on, Jimmy came up to me and said, "You're staying at the Eurotel, aren't you, Ken?" I said Yes. "Have you got a bed in your room?" he asked.

"Of course I've got a bed. Why do you ask?" I said.

"Because I haven't got one in my room. I was thinking of asking for another room, but I couldn't be bothered," he said.

490

It then struck me. The rooms were quite small, and the beds were cleverly tucked away inside a wall panel. I explained to Jim, "You have to push a button and the bed comes down out of the wall."

"Is your room like that?" he asked. "Yes, they all are. Actually, the beds are quite comfy," I assured him.

"Bloody hell," said Jim. "I've been sleeping on the floor for three nights." I felt like asking him where the dog was sleeping, but I resisted.

The final laugh of that particular week came when Bill Cotton, then Programme Controller of BBC-1, came to me and said quietly, "I'm a bit worried about Jimmy Thomas. Is he all right, Ken?" How do you mean? I asked. "Well, he's drinking a lot, isn't he?" said Bill. "And he came to see me earlier to do a special interview, and he was taking a lot of notes, but he seemed a bit shaky. Just make sure he's okay and keep an eye on him, will you?"

It was good of him to care, but Bill was that kind of bloke. He loved mixing with the Press and it would be open house in his suite, when he would open up the drinks cabinet and invite all the journalists for a late-night tipple. I've often sat up, well into the night and reminisced with Bill Cotton, a lot of it off the record.

"Listen," I said to him, "Don't worry about Jimmy. I've been to enough of these events to see him in action. He's got an excellent shorthand note, and he's much sharper than you think." He thanked me for the reassurance.

Next day however, during a coffee break in the TV programme screenings, Bill came up to me, smiling, and said. "What was that you were telling me yesterday about Jimmy having excellent shorthand? Well, he's been on the phone to me this morning, saying he's lost his notebook. And can he do another interview all over again with me this afternoon?"

THAT'S   LIFE

CHAPTER 41: THE WAR

When I heard the first bomb, there was a high-pitched whistling sound, and then a loud thunderous banging noise as though a giant earthquake had hit our little house. The walls shook, and the windows did more than rattle, they just splintered into thousands of tiny pieces and came pouring into the front room, even though we had brown sticky tape criss-crossed in a pattern on every window to save the glass from breaking.

We were sitting under the stairs, a cramped and airless cupboard, but our only futile oasis in a war that was not going to go away. We had a couple of kitchen chairs in there, and I was being cuddled by my big overpowering grandma, with her huge arms wrapped tightly around me, while my mother sat nearby cuddling the other kids in our family and trying not to cry.

I don't know whether I cried or not. I probably did, but we had been in this situation before. It wasn't the first time we had heard bombs dropping, but this one was different. We could tell from the impact and the way the house had been shaken from its foundations that this was very close.

How long the air raid went on for I had no idea. It was probably the usual, an hour or two, before the German planes, having released all their nasty, deadly bombs, turned tail and flew back over the Channel, in the hope of not being shot down on the way.

Eventually there was the blissful sound of the All Clear. That serene long droning noise that signalled that it was all over. For now, anyway. There would be no more bombs falling on us, not until the next night. We were still alive for another 24 hours.

Somehow, we managed to get some sleep for a few hours. We crawled out from under the stairs and were put back into our beds upstairs by my mother, with a "Goodnight now, go to sleep. And no bad dreams!"

It wasn't until the next morning, when we opened the front door and stepped outside, that we realised with horror what had happened. In the air was a lingering fog and a stench which was almost overwhelming. There was rubble everywhere, bricks and shattered timber strewn across the narrow, cobbled street. And the house next door but one to us had gone. Our house, No.28 Rutland Street, which was the end of the terrace, and the adjoining No.26 stood alone. Then there was a gap. No.24 had been completely flattened into a mound of ten-feet high rubble. The rest of the houses, from No.22 to the other end of the street, were still intact.

Just the one house had been flattened. Blown to smithereens by a direct hit of a heavy bomb. And in it, we learned later, the family of two boys and their mother and father had been killed instantly.

These were our neighbours. And this was war. I can remember my mother crying, sobbing throughout the day. And my grandma, or Ma as we affectionately called her, said in her wise old way, "That could have been us. Twenty yards this way, and that bomb would have fallen on our house, not No.24."

My father was away in the war at the time. He was in the Merchant Navy, and we would see him only every few weeks, when he had a couple of days on leave.

That bomb, the one that destroyed our neighbour's house, wasn't the only time we felt in imminent danger, though.

On another occasion my father was home on leave, and it was just as well he was, because during one overnight raid, we heard a whistling noise, and there was a loud bang in our backyard. My dad rushed out and found that an incendiary bomb had come down and landed in our bin but had not exploded. Fortunately, it landed in a bin full of cold ashes.

I remember that he dashed into the yard, grabbed the bin and ran with it through the front door and out into the street. He alerted an ARP warden, and between them they took the bin away. I don't know whether my dad was being a hero or a damned fool for even going near it. But I do recall him coming back later and telling us, "It's all right. No panic. The bomb didn't go off."

We were lucky. I don't know how big the bomb was, or whether it would have blown our house up if it had detonated. We thought no more about it at the time. But we never forgot it. Years later, my mother would re-tell the story of having a bomb drop directly into our backyard bin.

You simply got accustomed to bombs during the war in those days from 1939 to 1942. The devastation caused was all around us. Every night there was a raid. And every morning-after we discovered just what damage had been done.

Once, we woke up to find the whole area half a mile away was flattened.

My mother was in a panic. "We'll have to go and find out if Auntie Ruth is all right. Her street has gone," she said desperately.

Auntie Ruth lived up near Hamilton Road, only about 500 yards away. I was never quite sure who Auntie Ruth was. An aunt of my mother's, I think. But we went to try and find her. We walked through several streets of flattened houses, climbing over the debris of bricks and mortar and broken windows. We never did find her, though my mother was relieved to hear later that day from someone that Auntie Ruth had survived and was now lodging with a neighbour.

I was four years old when World War II broke out. And by the time I started school at the age of five, we'd grown accustomed to the sound of the wailing sirens, when an air-raid attack was imminent. And then the relief of the drone of the all-clear – which meant we could go and open the front door and go out into the street to see what new devastation had been caused.

Next to London, Liverpool took the biggest pounding from the Luftwaffe during the early years of the blitz.

"It's because we're near the docks. It's the docks they want to destroy."

That's what we were repeatedly told by my father. It didn't make sense to me at the time. But if he said it, and my mother said it, and then my grandma said it, then it must have been true.

A lot of families were evacuated during the war, to get them out of danger from the big cities and into quieter countryside areas. From what I understood, all families were given the option. They could send their children away on their own - to a safer environment - or the parents could pack up and go off with them, moving lock, stock and barrel.

My mother and grandma decided we weren't going anywhere. We were staying in 28 Rutland Street, and that was it, Germans or no bloody Germans! Bombs or no bombs!

Of course, the air raids continued every night. ARP Wardens would patrol the streets after dark. "Close those black-out curtains," they'd yell if they spotted a house with any kind of light coming from it.

Overnight, when everyone knew the raids were inevitable, we had one of two alternatives. Some nights, we would stay at home – and all huddle together under the staircase (although now, thinking about it, how we all managed to fit into such a small space, I just don't know. I mean, my grandma was a hefty woman, so there couldn't have been much room for the rest of us).

But some nights, my mother would decide we would go to the public air raid shelters instead. The nearest communal shelter to us was a long brick building situated behind the advertising hoardings in Breckfield Road North, only a couple of hundred yards away.

This would mean the whole family, taking blankets and pillows and traipsing over to the shelter as early as possible, before dark, hopefully to get a space on the wooden benches. Once in there, it was a case of bedding down for the night. Trying to get as comfortable as possible, with my mum or grandma encouraging us constantly to go to sleep.

The shelters would soon be crowded with other families and screaming children. And mothers who couldn't sleep would simply exchange gossip throughout the night.

Next morning, families would trundle back to their homes, having not had much sleep but, fit or not, would be expected to be ready for a new day's hard labour.

When I started school at the age of five, St. Saviour's Church of England Junior School was only two streets away, in Downing Street. My sister Louise, two years older than me, was already a pupil there, so she knew all the ropes and the rules. All I had to do was take her hand and be delivered to my place in the playground with pupils from each class lining up in straight lines before being ushered inside.

But once we were seated in class, the war imposed another very important practice into our lives. Gas masks. Every house in the country was issued with enough gas masks to go around the family. So everyone had their own gas mask fitted away neatly in a square brown box, on which you had to print your name. This was fitted with a strap which made it easy to carry over your shoulder, or even around your neck. And it was essential that you carried your gas mask around at all times. In fact, woe betide you if you forgot to take it to school. You'd be in big trouble.

Immediately following assembly, with the hymn and the prayer out of the way, we would sit down at our desks and the first lesson was gas-mask inspection. On instructions from the teacher, everyone would have to open their brown box and put on their mask. It wasn't easy. There was a knack to fitting it on properly, making sure it covered the whole of your face.

Once inside, it was an exercise in deep breathing. It smelt of new rubber and was very claustrophobic (though we wouldn't know what that word meant, and much less be able to spell it). But we would be compelled to sit there for five minutes, all staring out at 40 or more fellow classmates looking equally ridiculous and vaguely resembling aliens from another planet.

What exactly these gas masks were supposed to do, we were never quite sure. Except they would save our lives if ever the enemy decided to invade us with widespread gas attacks. That's what we were told anyway.

496

Although the likelihood of this ever happening would be minimal, I would have thought.

Another thing we had to contend with during the war was much more fun – it was called shrapnel. The very word still brings on a tingle of excitement even after all these years. Shrapnel. Such a strong word. Like British Steel.

Shrapnel, to us schoolkids, became the spoils of war. According to the English dictionary, the word shrapnel is defined as "shell filled with pellets which scatter on bursting; shell splinters." But our interpretation was much broader. Anything from empty shells, dead bullets, bits of bombs that had exploded, and even scraps and pieces of aeroplanes which had fallen from the sky or been shot down. They all weighed in as genuine shrapnel.

We used to collect it and made a game out of swapping bits and pieces of shrapnel. It could be valued either on sheer weight, or maybe more on curiosity value or the scarcity of the piece in question. ("I'll swap you a bullet for a piece of German aeroplane wing").

Some kids would even join in by introducing bits of tanks and scraps of heavy artillery gun metal which they swore their fathers had brought back from active war duty in their kit bags.

Anything was more or less legitimate. It was just like swapping marbles, which was another lucrative pastime, except that shrapnel was a much more serious business.

Once the bombing raids over Britain stopped and the Germans retreated to fighting out the war on the Continent, this signalled the end of course to our shrapnel collecting days. Our collection of twisted metal and deadly war-time bullets was put in a cardboard box and probably dumped in a wardrobe cupboard until another day. And listed as war memorabilia.

There was one other, much bigger weapon to keep us occupied, however, long after shrapnel had become a thing of the past. And that was Big Bertha.

We only came across this mighty symbol of war when we went "over the water" as we called it, to visit Auntie Grace and her family at weekends.

Big Bertha was the name given to a gun - a full-sized anti-aircraft gun which was mounted on huge wheels in the middle of Cox's field in Upton, Wirral, which was where my Auntie Grace and Uncle Frank lived, in a tiny asbestos and tin-roofed bungalow in the quiet and sedate Elm Avenue.

The gun was there for several years. It stood, like a menacing giant of war, ready to shoot down any German planes that dared to fly over that green haven of peace and tranquillity which was Upton.

It was manned by a soldier or two. But it was all very casual, and they would often wander off somewhere during the day, leaving the gun alone and unwanted. That's when we got the chance, my cousin Frankie and myself, to go over and actually touch, if not stroke, the deadly weapon.

Oh, how we wished for the day when a German plane would have the temerity to try it on with us. Sadly, it never happened.

To my knowledge, Big Bertha was never ever known to fire a single shot in anger during the whole of the six years' duration of the war. But it stood there proudly as Upton's personal answer to Adolf Hitler and the dreaded vendetta with the Luftwaffe. A symbol of British stoicism.

It remained in the middle of the field, long after the war was over. Rusting away, neglected and forgotten, like some macabre military scarecrow. Until one day, Frankie told me, they came with a huge lorry and towed it away somewhere. Probably sold for scrap, I presume. And the silent Big Bertha became nothing more than a schoolboy memory.

The end of the war was something to be celebrated, of course. We were all still alive. We'd survived. More importantly, we'd won. God knows what would have happened if the Germans had defeated us. It doesn't bear thinking about.

When peace was finally declared, we were smothered in joy. The flags were flying. Men and women were kissing each other in public and goodness knows what they were getting up to in private. People were singing. Everyone was deliriously happy.

For us, it meant street parties. Wonderful parties, with trestles and tables and long wooden benches put out in the middle of every street, with kids treated to tea and lemonade and sandwiches and cakes. And all the mothers, wearing paper hats, waiting on us and serving up goodies like jelly and fizzy pop.

We'd moved from bomb-blasted Rutland Street, only about 500 yards away, and then lived in Loraine Street. And the tables were set up inside the railings of the girls' school playground. It was all such sheer joy. With plenty of room to run around and enjoy playing games after finishing off all the grub. But there were no men around, that I can recall. They were either still away, waiting to be demobbed from the war, before returning home. Or maybe they were all in the pub down the road, which come to think of it was much more likely.

Anyway, the war was over. We were still alive. Now we could get on with life.

CHAPTER 42: SCHOOL DAYS

Miss Cray was a formidable figure. She was the first teacher I had when I started out at St. Saviour's Church of England Junior School at the age of five. My first impression of her was that she was big and fat. (But that could simply be because I was little and thin). And she had a loud voice.

Looking back all these years later, you have to accept that the memory can sometimes be deceptive of course. But I can quite clearly remember one or two things about Miss Cray and Class 1 which remain intact.

She always wore what appeared to be knitted dresses. Great woollen garments often with peepholes in the stitching, like a kind of croqueted affair, which showed through into her underwear. The idea now seems a little ludicrous, but the vision remains with me no matter how much I try to reject it. She had an enormous, flabby chest which wobbled furiously. And when she wanted to make a fuss of someone, she would grab a pupil and pull him or her onto her lap, with the invitation to "Come and snuggle." Then she'd bury their head into her ample bosom, almost smothering the poor mite.

Exactly how long you would expect to remain there was anybody's guess. It was purely down to the discretion of Miss Cray herself. And on reflection I am still not sure whether this show of affection was meant as a special treat or a punishment. All I knew, at that tender age, was that it wasn't an experience I ever looked forward to. And I was glad when it happened to others, and not me.

Only once, I think, did it ever happen to me. And I did not particularly enjoy it. Being pulled into Miss Cray's bosom could be daunting. I'm not suggesting it was a life- threatening thing, but it could certainly leave you struggling for fresh air, and it was a relief when you were finally released and told to go back and sit down.

The other eccentricity about Class 1 was being told to "Go and stand up the chimney." This was done pretty frequently at the whim of Miss Cray, and it was very clearly defined as an act of punishment for some misdemeanour or other.

The old Victorian built chimney place was a huge structure which pretty well dominated the room. And when a pupil was to be mildly chastised, it meant standing in the hearth with your head directly looking up the chimney. Again, the length of the punishment could vary. It could be five minutes, or even ten or fifteen minutes, depending on the mood of Miss Cray and how benevolent she was feeling.

It wasn't a particularly painful punishment, more a form of humiliation. Those unfortunates with their head up the chimney had to stand there and suffer while everyone in the class sniggered or laughed at them.

Whatever I say about Miss Cray, however, she must have been a darned good teacher because after exactly 12 months in Class 1, when the rest of my tiny chums and I were moved up into Class 2, I was able to read and write.

The reason I know I must have been reading and writing at the age of six was because I can definitely recall that on my first day in Class 2, we were all told to make-up and write a story in our exercise books. And our new teacher, Mrs. Telford, was so pleased with my work that she made me stand up in front of the class and read my story out aloud, and then told me, "Go and show Miss Cray what you have written."

When I timidly went into Class 1 and showed Miss Cray what I guess must have been my first composition or essay, she was so delighted that she gave me a pat on the head and then grabbed her purse and spontaneously gave me a penny as a reward. A whole penny. I couldn't believe it. When I went home later and told my mum, she was so proud.

That penny meant more to me than either Miss Cray or Mrs. Telford could ever have imagined. And I suppose now, in view of my later career, it meant that being paid a penny for my very first essay meant I could claim to be a professional writer - at the age of six!

There was no doubt then that I must have been quite bright as a child. Unfortunately, my scholastic achievements did not continue very far in the rest of my schooldays. At some stage I developed asthma. I don't know at what age. Even my mother, later in life could not recall exactly how old I was when I first started getting symptoms of the dreaded illness. It was at first merely put down to growing up in a polluted atmosphere. Liverpool was always shrouded in fog. We had some pea-soupers, as they called them, when you couldn't see further than ten yards ahead. And often when it was really foggy, we could even hear the ships sounding their fog horns on the river, which was more than a couple of miles away.

At some stage though, the doctors told my mother that I definitely had asthma, and later I was given an inhaler to use whenever I had an attack. And pills, one to be taken every night.

This meant me missing a lot of my schooling. I would stay at home sometimes for a day or two at a time and my mother would send a note with my sister Louise to give to my particular teacher, saying "Kenneth is too poorly to attend school today." This became a regular occurrence.

Some weeks, I was at home more than I was in school. Though I must confess now that maybe I did cheat occasionally and pretend to be more ill than I really was. When I was at home, I spent most of my time playing the game of Shoot with tiddly-winks on the kitchen table, with my own imaginary teams and different sets of players.

The result of all those days off school must have affected my education, though. I still have two rather tattered old school reports which I can now reflect on.

One was dated midsummer 1944, when I was in Class 3, aged nine. The roll call for the class was 55 (yes, that's right, 55 pupils in one class) and my Place in Class was 1st.

The report reads: Attendance – Fair (underlined in red ink). Conduct – Very good. Reading – Very good. Writing – Good. Spelling – Very good. Composition – Good. History – Good. Geography – Good. Arithmetic – Exam result fair. Drawing – Good. Physical Exercise – Very good.

It was signed by my class teacher, D.E. Morgan. Counter-signed by headmaster J.H. Thorpe.

The second annual report was Summer of 1946, in Class 4B. The roll call was only 32. And again, my place in class was 1st.

Conduct was Good. But Attendance was crossed out, and written in, instead, was Times Absent – 117.

On the various subjects, Reading – V. Good. Writing – good. Spelling – V. Good. Composition – V. Good. History – Good. Geography – Good. Arithmetic – Fairly Good. Drawing – Good. Handwork – Good.

But in the Remarks section, my teacher, Mr. F. Bolt wrote: "I hope his health will improve, and in a year or two he will make up the lost ground, for he has real ability."

So there I have two reports, finishing top of the class in both years. But I must mention here that I showed my wife Betty these reports recently, and I said, "Absent 117 times in the year but I still came top of the class." Her only comment was, "God know what the rest of the kids must have been like, then."

St. Saviour's was a tough school though. The headmaster was very strict on discipline. It may have been a church school, but the staff fell short when it came to Christian forgiveness. Pupils would occasionally get a smack around the head from the teacher if they misbehaved in the slightest way. But the cane was the ultimate punishment.

I can vividly remember getting the cane three times during my years in junior school. And, of course, the crimes I committed to justify such punishment.

Once, I was caned for being ten minutes late for school in the morning. (Anyone being late was automatically sent to the headmaster's office). I received two strokes, one on either hand. As I lived only five minutes away, I didn't have much excuse I suppose.

The second time was during an arithmetic lesson, when the teacher asked me, "Irwin, what's 9 multiplied by 9?" I hesitated and tried to think. It was silly really because we were so accustomed to practising our times tables, as we called them, every day. We would reel off all the mathematical tables in sing-song fashion. But on this occasion, I was suddenly stumped.

"Stand up," I was ordered. "Now what is 9 multiplied by 9?" I fumbled mentally for the answer, but couldn't get it out.

Even as I stood there, desperately thinking for the right answer, I could hear one or two of my class mates muttering quietly, "Eighty-one. Eighty-one." But instead of just responding to the helpful promptings, I stood quietly, rooted to the spot with nerves, saying nothing.

"Right, go the headmaster's office and tell him I sent you because you do not know your nine-times table," the teacher commanded.

As I walked slowly from the room, I could feel the eyes of all my class mates penetrating through my back, all sympathising with me for being such a chump.

When I saw the headmaster, it was the usual two whacks of the cane.

It was a painful lesson. But one I never forgot. Nine nines are eighty-one. And always will be.

At home, at teatime, when I told my mother I had been caned for not knowing my nine times table, she was so furious that she threatened to take me to school next day so she could see the headmaster to complain. I begged her not to, in case it resulted in further punishment. So the whole thing was dropped.

And the third time I received the cane was for climbing over the church wall to get our ball back. Ernie Ingham was really to blame. The two of us were having a kick-around at football in the playground an hour or so after school in the evening. And Ernie accidentally kicked the ball high over the wall and into the church grounds. There was a long ladder, which we presumed had been left by window cleaners or workmen, conveniently abandoned in the school yard.

Ernie suggested we borrow the ladder, and then asked me to hold on to it while he proceeded to climb over the wall to retrieve our ball. Unfortunately, just as Ernie re- appeared over the 15ft high wall, clutching the precious ball, one of the teachers who must have been working late came out of the school building and caught us.

"What are you two doing with that ladder?" he asked. "Just getting our ball back, sir," replied Ernie.

"Report to the headmaster's office tomorrow morning. Without fail," we were told.

So next day, we sat nervously outside Mr. Thorpe's office for ten minutes, awaiting our punishment. "Okay. Inside. Hold your hands out," he demanded. And out came the cane. Whack. Two strokes each. We returned to our classroom, our hands stinging with pain and red with the imminent swelling. The only thing you could do was to sit on your hands and grimace and wait for the pain to subside before summoning up the effort to try and grip a pencil ready for lessons. It wasn't a pleasant experience.

Yet, when I recalled my three caning ordeals to my brother Eric recently, he laughed and said, "Oh, I was caned so often, I've forgotten how many times."

It wasn't all pain and misery though. There were some good times at that school. When I was in the top class I was one of those chosen to be a milk monitor. It was a very responsible job. We had to collect all the crates of milk in the school yard and then distribute them to each classroom, handing out a small bottle of milk to every pupil. It was a government incentive to try and keep schoolkids healthy and make sure they had sufficient daily nourishment. Being a milk monitor was considered something of a perk, because if there were any left-over bottles of milk, they would be quickly snaffled up and drunk. The only trouble was I didn't like milk. In fact, as a child, I hated the stuff. So I would cheerfully give my free bottle of milk to anyone who wanted it.

The one special treat we all enjoyed however was having a sneaky rota system of lads nipping out of school at playtime and running down to the baker's shop on the opposite corner of Breckfield Road and buying buns or rock cakes. Everything was freshly made on the premises. The currant buns were a penny each. But for tuppence the rock cakes were better, because they were bigger and not only had currants in but also a big blob of strawberry jam on the top. A rock cake was almost a meal in itself. Certainly, it kept you going until you went home at lunch time.

On the educational side, of course, there were far more serious things to confront us. Like the 11-plus. This was the dreaded exam every child had to go through to determine just how clever you were and what your future schooling would be.

The exams covered all the main subjects and every child coming up to the age of eleven was expected to sit the various tests, spread out over several days or weeks.

The results of these exams were vitally important. If you passed the 11-plus, you went on to a grammar school. If you failed, then you went to a secondary school. The whole thing seemed such a cruel exercise. It picked out the bright and more intelligent kids from the duffers and the idiots of course. But what about kids who might have been quite intelligent but were just not very good at sitting exams? And what about late developers – those who were not quite ready for such a vital decision at the age of eleven?

If I'd been successful, I would have been bound for the Liverpool Collegiate Grammar School in Shaw Street city centre.

As it turned out, I was absent so much due to my blessed asthma that I never even took all the necessary exams.

When I had to go home and break the news to my Mum that I had not passed the 11-plus, it caused such consternation that the very next day my Auntie Dorothy angrily marched around to the school to confront the headmaster Mr. Thorpe and gave him a verbal roasting. I don't know exactly what she said, but she pointed out that I had been off sick so much and this should have been taken into consideration, and despite my illness I had still come top of the class on occasions.

Eventually I was told when I was eleven that I was to attend Breckfield Secondary Modern School in Venice Street, which was only a stone's throw from the Anfield football ground and about a ten-minute walk from home.

Venice Street was a whole new experience. For a start, it separated the sexes. This was an all-boys school. Full of tough lads. Some of them too tough, for my liking. And in the very first few months we quickly learned that secondary education came with an element of gang warfare, whether you liked it or not.

There were two gangs who were quickly formed in the first year – one was the Kingshot gang, the other a group run by a mobster called Wally something, whose name I have thankfully forgotten. Leslie Kingshot was a tall, hefty, dark-haired guy with a lot to say for himself. The opposing gang leader Wally was a fat guy, a massive brute built like a brick Anderson air-raid shelter. It was no good protesting that you just wanted a quiet life, to get on with your school work. You had to belong to one gang or the other. That was made very clear to everyone. There were strictly no pacifists, either inside school or out in the playground.

I was not sure why, but when confronted and forced to make a choice of whose gang I wanted to be in, I opted for Leslie Kingshot. He was the lesser of the two evils. There was something about him I almost liked - I think it was fear. Kingshot was as thick as four or five short planks, but for some reason he took a shine to me and became my kind of personal minder.

His friendliness could be put down to the simple fact that he started sitting next to me at the same desk. And, depending on which lesson we were having, if he was struggling he would expect me to leave my exercise book open quite wide and at an angle, so that he could blatantly copy anything he needed to from my work. This was something I was quite happy to put up with, so long as I could keep chummy with him.

It also gave me the confidence, if ever I was confronted by a member of rival Wally's bully-boy gang, to be able to say, "You touch me, and I'll tell Kingshot." It always worked a treat. On the whole, over the next four years of my school life, I found it a distinct advantage to be a friend of the fearsome, almost legendary Leslie Kingshot.

My asthma attacks continued however, and although I was not absent quite so often as I had been in junior school, my mother still had concerns about my health. I started attending regular sessions at a children's hospital in Myrtle Street, which meant me taking Friday afternoons off school to go for special "asthma treatment." This involved a regular injection in my arm, followed by rigorous exercises including deep-breathing sessions, and then stripping off my top to lie on a bed under a warm lamp for sun-ray treatment for half-an-hour.

I was never sure whether this treatment did me any good or not, but the weekly visits to the hospital with my mother meant me taking more time off from school, which couldn't have done my education any good.

Always in the A stream, my exam results for the first year were pretty encouraging. My report from Class 1A, in July 1947, read: Roll call – 41. Place in class – 5th. Times late – 0. Times Absent – 60. Conduct – Excellent.

In Dictation, I got 30 out of 30, did well in History, Geography and Drawing. And the teacher, Mr. R. W. Dorkins wrote: "Arithmetic and English books are very satisfactory. Has worked well, made progress and should win a Technical."

A Technical, I should explain, was another exam which pupils who were considered good enough had the chance to sit at the age of 13. Then, if successful, they would go on to a Technical school or college.

As it turned out, my second- year end-of-term report, in 1948, wasn't so brilliant. In 2A, in a class of 40, I finished 16th. Conduct – Good. Times late – 0. But Times Absent – 151.

In the various subjects, I was top of the class in Reading, Writing, Composition, and Drawing. My class teacher, Mr. A. W. Burnett wrote: "English excellent. Must work at Arithmetic!"

But the headmaster, Mr. David Snowdon wrote: "It's up to you, Ken. I fear Arithmetic let you down with the Tech."

So there it was in black and white. I'd missed the chance to exchange Secondary school for a technical college – because my Arithmetic wasn't good enough and I was absent 151 times over the year due to my miserable asthmatic condition.

Exactly what I would have done at a technical college I'll never know. But now at least I knew there was no escape from the Alcatraz which was Venice Street. Not until I was 15 anyway.

Happily, my health seemed to improve as I grew older, and in my last two years at school I knuckled down to things and actually began to enjoy myself more than ever before.

In sport, I was good at most games. I preferred baseball to cricket and was the pitcher for the school team. In football, we played in sports lessons with games in nearby Stanley Park. And I was a regular reserve for the school team in Saturday morning games against other schools.

It was in my final year, however, that I really began to appreciate my education. Everything seemed to come together for me. Particularly in 4A when we had a form master who turned out, as far as I was concerned, to be an absolutely inspirational teacher called Mr. Gardiner.

He was a tall, well-built man who had a slight vocal lisp, and smoked a pipe. But he gave the impression of being interested in every one of his 40 pupils and I found him spell-binding as a tutor. He took us out of the classroom, got us interested in a variety of different subjects, away from the text books.

One of the memorable outings he took us on was enrolling the whole class of boys as coal miners for the day. We all trudged off to the Cronton Colliery, near Warrington, were kitted out with overalls and helmets, and did a whole day's shift underground, to experience what it was like at the coal face. It was hard work, crawling on hands and knees in 5ft high

507

tunnels, watching the miners shovelling the coal out, and having our lunch down there, before coming back up in the huge iron cage to re-surface, going into the showers and getting dressed. One thing it did teach us was just how tough a life it was being a coal miner. No, I definitely wouldn't be doing this for a living, thank you very much!

We had four Houses in the school – all named after great adventurers. Livingstone, Nelson, Scott and Gordon. I was made a school Prefect and was then voted in as Vice-Captain of Livingstone House.

But the greatest incentive of all was when Mr. Gardiner urged us to start our own school magazine, and he appointed me as the first editor.

Having spotted that I was keen on English literature and composition, he went out of his way to encourage me to read and write as much as possible.

School life wasn't dull any more. Some of the lads in our class were tough guys, as tall as the teacher, and a few of them had even started shaving.

I recall one particular altercation between a pupil and Mr. Gardiner. For some reason, they got involved in an argument. And when the teacher told him to go and stand outside the classroom, the lad refused and let out a few expletives. Mr. Gardiner, who was a big bloke and pretty powerfully built, insisted on making his point. The lad suddenly swung a wild punch and landed more or less flush on the teacher's jaw.

Without flinching, Mr. Gardiner then grabbed his assailant and bundled him out of the room and marched him straight to the headmaster's office. From memory, the antagonist was a very bright and good- looking bloke who was a pretty popular pupil and had been with us for the past four years.

But we never saw him again. He didn't turn up for school next day. And we were eventually told that he had been expelled from school. He went three months before he was officially due to leave in the summer term.

It may have been a tough school. But punching a teacher was a step too far. That kind of thing would clearly not be tolerated.

When I finally left school, in the Spring term of 1950, I came top of the class in all my favourite subjects. And I received a personal gift of a book from Mr. Gardiner, the cost of which came out of his own pocket, not from school funds.

In my last term, I was one of several pupils who had a composition entered into an annual Essay Competition open to schools all over Liverpool. To my surprise, I was told I had won a prize for the best essay in my age group. This turned out to be a book (Mr. Midshipman Easy by Captain Marryat) which should have been presented to me by the Lady Mayoress of Liverpool (Mrs. J. J. Cleary) at St. George's Hall in May 1950. But I was by then either working in my first job, or too shy to go, so it was sent to me in the post instead. I still have the book.

On leaving and going out into the big cold world to find employment, I had no special qualifications. The only thing I had was a Scholars Reference Card, written by the headmaster David Snowdon.

Dated 3l March 1950, it read: "No. of years at this school – 4.

Class on leaving – 4A. Special Aptitude – English.

"Kenneth Irwin has attended this school since August 1946, with an excellent record of punctuality and conduct. He is a very cheerful boy, with ability above the average of his class, and an unusual command of written English. His work reflects a thoughtful and tidy character.

"A School Prefect, he has shown that he can be trusted, and he is the Vice-Captain of his House. He is a member of a Church and Club and is noteworthy in the way he occupies himself both in and out of school.

"He can be thoroughly recommended as an honest and loyal worker."

That was a good enough reference and something I was quite proud of. And I'm sure that it helped when I went for my very first interview for a job in a shipping office in the famous Royal Liver Building on Liverpool's waterfront. I was given the job as a junior clerk with Houlder Brothers & Co. Ltd., a well-established and renowned ship owning company. Finally, my school days were over.

However, my dealings with Mr. Gardiner didn't end there. Although I was quite happy working as a shipping clerk, I couldn't see myself staying there for 50 years and making a career of it. I desperately wanted to become a newspaper reporter. So I wrote a letter to Mr. Gardiner, nearly a year after leaving school, just hoping to keep in touch, telling him of my ambitions, and at the same time asking him for further advice on how he thought I could get into journalism.

It took a few weeks before I got a reply, but he wrote a letter to me, dated February 6, 1951, typed over five pages, which I still have and treasure greatly.

It read: "Dear Kenneth. Thank you for your note. I wrote to you in December, just before Xmas. When I received your second letter on the 22nd January, I felt from the way you wrote that you hadn't received my own, and I asked John Kurs to get in touch with you. He seems to have had difficulty in doing so, because it has taken a fortnight.

"It is always a great pleasure to hear from boys like yourself, who have made their mark in School and then gone into the much wider world. I make it a point always to attend to such things. I must, therefore, apologise most sincerely for any neglect of which you may have suspected me due to your not having received my letter.

"Now to some points at issue. First, the School Magazine, which you yourself had the distinction of starting. After you left, Edward Seddon became the Editor, and under him we produced a Special Camp Supplement (4d) and a full Summer Issue. The Camp Supplement was sold out completely; the Summer Issue did not do so well, but we did not make a loss.

"Now about your job and writing ambitions. If you are so keen on writing, you could, and should, have another go at getting on the staff of the Post & Echo. I have spoken to Mr. Snowdon about this, and he suggests that you should apply again. It doesn't follow that because you were unsuccessful last Easter the door is shut and bolted. Actually, the circumstances at that time were rather unusual. If you do decide to try again, it would be best to write a letter saying how keen you are on writing and asking if your name might be noted for consideration when any vacancies arise. If you express your keenness for writing with sincerity as you did in your letter to me, I think it will be noted.

"In the meantime, you are keen on freelance work for the papers. What can you do? What a complicated problem for me to tackle! I say 'complicated' because I remember well that I felt exactly the same as you. I can see that you would like to get down to a solid piece of work such as a play, or even a book, but I think you would be best advised first to write for the papers.

"Probably the first thing is to get the 'feel' of the job. This is not so easy, because the big mistake that most of us make is that we write the things that we like to write, but really we should write the things that other people want to read. It needs a tremendous wrench on our part to own up to the fact that the things which we like, which are nearest to our own hearts, are not necessarily so dear to other people. The newspaper has to print the things that most people like, and if you want to get into print, you've got to write something that the Editor thinks lots of his readers will want to read. It depends, of course, on the particular paper. An article which would suit the Daily Worker is not likely to appeal to readers of, say, the Daily Telegraph. You can only get to know the kinds of article a paper wants by studying the paper to see what kind of things they print, what particular interests, subjects, and people they seem to cater for.

"That's the theory of it. Study the paper regularly to see what particular kind of articles they seem to print. But I expect you are impatient. You want to get started. Well, why not? The more you can make yourself known, the more likely it is that you will get in eventually, provided of course that the stuff you are writing is reasonable and readable. You might write ten, twenty, yes or even a hundred or a thousand contributions without success. But the odds are that the more you write, the more known your work will become to the Editor, until at last he gives you a break. Always provided that what you write is reasonable. Better to get in a little every day, rather than a lengthy piece every few months.

"For the sake of expressing yourself and improving your style, it's a good idea to write something every day. And why not send it in? Yes, every day, if you can manage the postage. If you give up after the first few dozen attempts, you are not a writer. Keep at it, again and again – and again. And again!

"Quite a good idea is to start with Letters to the Editor. Every day, many thousands of people write to the Editor, to grumble, to criticise, comment on an article, make suggestions. It's one way of getting known to the Editor, and to the public. Some papers, such as John Bull, pay for readers' letters.

"With regard to straightforward articles, you have to consider more the subjects in which people are interested. Do you remember my efforts to get you interested in the street names in this district? And have you noticed that, recently, 'Rambler' in the Echo made up two articles on exactly the same subject? He wrote about things that you yourself could have written about a year earlier. It was quite clear that people were very interested by the number of Letters to the Editor which followed the articles.

"Of course, I could go on, but I'm afraid of preaching to you. Besides, it's now 3am and I must finish. Really, the thing to do is to write often, well, and on as many different and interesting topics as possible. I'm sure you can do it.

"One last point, for the time being. Make your work attractive and easy to read. Type it – without mistakes. (I see you're making good progress!). Use double or treble spacing, and one side of the paper only. Number your sheets and make all continuation from sheet to sheet quite clear.

"As I said in the beginning, I was very happy to hear from you, and shall be at your service, if you're not already fed up with 5 pages. Go to it! Good wishes!

Yours sincerely, S.R. Gardiner."

When I read this letter today, it still brings a lump to my throat. How many teachers do you know, today or at any time in the past, who would sit up until 3 o'clock in the morning writing to a former pupil with such heart-felt advice?

I took all his advice to heart. I followed it through to the letter. And eventually I made it into journalism and went on to Fleet Street.

The only one big regret I have is that I left it too late to thank Mr. Gardiner (I still didn't know that his Christian name was Stanley) for that inspirational letter.

When I did eventually try and track him down, to thank him, I got a phone call from his nephew telling me that he had died some years earlier.

They just don't make teachers like Mr. Gardiner any more. Or do they?

CHAPTER 43: MY CAREER – IN BRIEF

When the Careers Officer asks you, when you're 14 or 15, what you want to do in life, it's very difficult, isn't it?   I left school at 15. Venice Street Secondary Modern, in Everton.

In my last year at school, when I started the school magazine and was made the first editor, I can vividly remember reading a story in one of the comics I bought, The Hotspur, about a newspaper reporter. And I remember seeing Humphrey Bogart in some black-and-white film, playing a reporter. And I thought "That's for me."

But when the Careers Officer came around, about six months before I was due to leave school, and asked what I wanted to do as a job, I can remember telling him, "I'd like to be a reporter." He just laughed and said, "Oh, I don't think so, lad." He then added quite simply, "It's either office or factory, make your choice." Disappointed, I replied, "Office."

On leaving school, I actually started work as a junior clerk in a shipping office in the Royal Liver Buildings, with Houlder Brothers. My first wage was 12s 6d a week, plus luncheon vouchers. I was there for nearly two years and I quite enjoyed it and did well.

But I still yearned to be a reporter. I wrote to the Liverpool Echo, and went into their office. There were no vacancies. I then must have written to every newspaper I could think of - first the locals, then the nationals. Dozens of application letters, asking for a job. Back came the same replies. Sorry - no job without experience.

So, I then started writing articles on a freelance basis. The first article I ever had published was for the shipping company's house magazine. Then I wrote sports pieces and sent them off to a local magazine.

Eventually, I got my foot in the door with a magazine called The Liverpolitan. After writing the sports column for them, the Editor, Peter Graham, suddenly offered me a full-time job, as one of his staff, Richard Whittington-Egan, had gone down sick with TB. I went for an interview, was given the staff job, but then had to give in my notice at the shipping office.

My boss there, Mr Ted Brown, head of the Outward Freight department was a little taken aback when I walked into his office and said I wanted to leave. He asked me why. "Because I want to be a journalist", I said rather pompously.

He said, "Is it the money? You can have a ten bob rise if you stay. We like you. You could do well here." No, it wasn't the money. I was actually taking less money than I was already earning to go and be a journalist.

So that was the end of my shipping career. The end of running up and down Water Street, Chapel Street and Old Hall Street every day, delivering shipping notes to various offices, as well as the Cunard Building and the Mersey Docks and Harbour Board building on the famous waterfront. The end of sitting on a high stool and writing out and checking Bills of Lading on distinctive smelling parchment. The end, as junior office boy, of making the tea, and being responsible for putting up the Union Jack flag on the front of the Liver Building every St. George's Day and King's Birthday (a task that particularly scared me, because I was always afraid the flag was going to be swept away by the wind and blown in to the nearby River Mersey before I could rig it up properly).

The Liverpolitan was a glossy, rather posh magazine published monthly but with a not-very-big circulation and had an office in Old Swan. A couple of rooms above a Post Office. We had an editorial staff of only four - the Editor, Peter Graham, his girlfriend Ann Dutton, who was his assistant and woman's editor, a circulation manager, who was an Irishman with bad teeth who rolled his own cigarettes and chain-smoked all day. And me. I wrote the sports page and everything else they threw at me. A gossip column, news and society events. Anything new we could think of. But I loved it. I was with the magazine for nearly two years, before I started getting itchy feet and ambitions for something bigger.

Luck always has a lot to do with things, I suppose. After sending off applications to newspapers again, one paper, The Journal of Commerce, told me they had a vacancy for a shipping reporter. I jumped at it.

This meant going around all the docks, every day, on the then dilapidated overhead railway, and reporting on ships' movements.

It was quite boring after a while. But it was a job. Quite well paid, good experience, and I became fascinated with shipping. And still am.

After that, it was all systems go. I went on to be a reporter on the Birkenhead News. I was there for about two years, and then moved to Nottingham, worked for the Evening Post and the daily Guardian Journal. They had a split shift system, which meant working four hours on the evening paper, four hours off, then another four hours back on for the daily paper. It made it a very long working day.

Nottingham was my first job away from home, and I found lodgings with the local Methodist minister, the Rev. Walter Joyce and his family in

Ruddington. But I was then engaged to be married, and moved back to Liverpool, got a job as a reporter on the Evening Express, got married and was happy being back on Merseyside with the family.

Then disaster. The paper closed. It was taken over and amalgamated with the Liverpool Echo. We were all made redundant. I was 23, married, one child and another on the way. And out of work. Most of the editorial staff of the Express scurried off to Manchester and London, all desperately looking for jobs.

Again, I suppose I was lucky. I had become quite well known on the Evening Express and I was doing some good stuff. As well as news reporting, I had done a lot of feature writing, and one day a week was writing the popular Over The Mersey Wall gossip column. I got a phone call from the Daily Mirror in Manchester, offering me an interview for a job as Northern TV Critic.

I went for the interview with the Northern Editor Ted Fenna and was given the job. The pay was £19 a week, which was double what I was getting on the now defunct Evening Express, but it was on a three-month trial.

So I moved to Manchester, with the family. And for my sins, I was then with the Daily Mirror for 31 years. They never did tell me if I'd passed the three-month trial!

After about seven years in Manchester, they offered me a job in the London office and I eventually moved. That was every journalist's dream of success - Fleet Street! The Street of Ink! There is no place quite like it. It was everything I'd expected it to be. The Street of a Thousand Dreams. Full of eccentric characters. And adventure.

When I quit the shipping office and got into journalism, my first job was on The Liverpolitan, writing a sports column. This meant covering every kind of sport, and not just football, tennis and cricket. One of the most popular sports of that time was speedway racing, and my free Press pass would get me access to all the regular weekly race meetings at Liverpool Stanley track. I loved it. Watching those four motor bikes tearing around the track, spitting up clouds of dust was quite exhilarating. A rider called Peter Craven, I recall, was one of the most popular riders around, and he became world champion.

It was boxing however which for some strange reason took over as my No.1 sport. The Liverpool Stadium, in Pudsey Street, in the city centre, became world famous for putting on regular weekly fight tournaments.

And every Thursday evening, I got in the habit of going there to watch the blood-bath of bouts.

It meant me having to nervously go in, knock on the office door of the Stadium promoter Johnny Best, show my credentials, before being given a Press pass to get in. Once inside, I'd take my seat on the Press bench, right underneath the ropes of the ring, and wait for the brutal action to begin.

There were usually six or seven fights a night, with the headline top-of-the-bill being a top-rating or international fighter.

I quickly became an addict. Somehow, I got completely hooked on the sport. I studied the fight game, read up on it history, and after a year or two considered myself to be quite an expert.

Sitting watching those fights every Thursday night, making notes on every bout - not to mention sometimes getting splattered with blood as two boxers stood toe to toe in physical combat above me - I soon discovered it could also be quite lucrative for me.

Apart from getting stories out of it for my monthly sports column in The Liverpolitan, I quickly realised that I could earn extra money by reporting these fights for all the various local weekly papers.

Most of the boxers in the supporting bouts were local, so I simply found out where they came from. I would rush home afterwards, write up reports on each fight, and next day go on the phone to reel off a report to each fighter's local paper.

My reports were sold on a penny-a-line basis, which surprisingly built up when I sent in a monthly invoice to each paper.

The result was, before long, I was spending most Friday mornings dashing into the local public telephone box,in Old Swan, hogging the phone, and sending reports to all the local papers, including the St. Helens Reporter, the Southport Visiter, the Wigan News, Warrington News, Birkenhead News. To avoid writing under my own name, I used the pen-name Ringsider, and most papers were happy to give me a by-line under that pseudonym.

For me, it became a great source of extra income. It was never going to make me rich, but as far as I was concerned, every pound added up. And I became quite well known by the sports editors on all the Merseyside papers for my boxing know-how.

The important thing was that I was also accepted by the boxers themselves and their managers.

In the 1950s, Liverpool was the biggest boxing centre outside of London, and attracted fighters from all over the world.

One of the local favourites was Billy Ellaway, a tough Liverpool heavyweight who built up an impressive record over a few years by bowling over opponents like ninepins, even though he never became a champion. Then there was Eric Marsden, a tall, lean looking lad who weighed in as a lightweight, from St. Helens. A really classy boxer.

Wally Thom was a southpaw welterweight from Birkenhead who went on to win British and European titles and reigned supreme in that division for several years.

Birkenhead became quite a breeding ground for fighters. Johnny Campbell was a manager who had his own gymnasium and club and signed up most of the up-and coming fighters. Many of them fell by the wayside, but there were others he helped build into champions.

One of the best, and certainly the most handsome fighter I ever saw, was Pat McAteer, from Birkenhead. He was a middleweight who started his career at Liverpool Stadium and went on to become British and British Empire middleweight champion. I became quite friendly with Pat and when he eventually quit boxing, he married an American girl, and they went to live in the States. He later wrote me letters telling me of his life out there and how he had settled down in America.

There were two other heavyweights around at the time. Joe Bygraves, a big Jamaican from Birkenhead, who was one of the most popular. And then came Dick Tiger, a tough-as-oak scrapper from Nigeria who went on to become world cruiser weight champion.

Then along came Hogan (Kid) Bassey from Nigeria, who settled in Liverpool and won the world featherweight championship.

I got to know them all quite well, and became particularly friendly with McAteer and then Hogan Bassey, who married here, had a family, and became a member of the Methodist Church in South Liverpool, with the Rev. Cyril Cornah as his minister. Later, after retiring from the ring, Bassey returned to Nigeria and became a sporting ambassador for his country.

But my biggest coup of all was when I signed up the great Nel Tarleton to write his life story.

Tarleton was one of the greatest featherweight and lightweight boxers of all time. I never saw him fight. He made his living in the 1930s and 40s and became the British and European champion, but never won a world title. He was reckoned to be one of the finest boxers the ring had ever produced. Not a great puncher or a knock-out king, but a very clever tactician, who could out-box most of his opponents over 12 or 15 rounds.

517

When I look back now, I don't know how I had the nerve. But I must have been 17 when I approached Tarleton and asked if I could write his life story.

We met, he must have liked me, because he agreed to team up and do his story together. But first I was advised by someone that I should take out a legal contract with him, to make sure everything was fair and above board.

My father suggested I go to Liverpool's best- known solicitor, Rex Makin, and have a proper contract drawn up. So that's what I did. I still have it, signed by Tarleton over a sixpenny stamp, on October 16, 1952, and witnessed by Mr. Makin.

It read: "An Agreement made between Kenneth Irwin of 9 Loraine Street in the city of Liverpool, of one part and Nelson Tarleton of 15 Rossett Road, Liverpool of the other part. Whereas Mr. Irwin and Mr. Tarleton have agreed jointly to write and publish in serial form a work to be entitled 'My Fighting Days' being the life story of Mr. Tarleton written by Mr. Irwin,

"Mr. Irwin and Mr. Tarleton shall jointly write the said work in the form of 20 instalments to be published in the Liverpool Echo as hereinafter mentioned and/or in such other newspapers or periodicals as shall be agreed upon.

"The writing of the said work as aforesaid shall be done by Mr. Irwin with the assistance of Mr. Tarleton and based upon information supplied by Mr. Tarleton. Mr. Tarleton shall be entitled to revise any portion of the work written by Mr. Irwin and nothing shall be contained in the said work or published to which Mr. Tarleton shall object."

And on and on it went. All legal jargon. But the important point it made was that we had joint copyright of the material, that both our names would appear as authors, and that I was put in the position of negotiating all deals for newspapers and a book. The most vital thing was that we agreed that all payments and profits would be shared equally, 50-50, by Tarleton and myself.

After we'd signed the agreement, I set to work immediately, secretly thrilled that I'd pulled this off. It was my first real journalistic scoop in life. I went to see Nel Tarleton at his home in Crosby, interviewed him, and he gave me a pile of scrap books with newspaper cuttings, reporting on all his fights over the years

As planned, I produced twenty articles, each one of which filled a whole page in the Liverpool Echo every Saturday night for five months. The Echo seemed delighted with the series, and so did Nel Tarleton.

In fact, I then realised that Tarleton, the greatest boxer to ever come out of Liverpool, was more desperately in need of the money than I was.

After an initial up-front payment, the Echo paid me out a cheque on a monthly basis, as the serial was being published. I then had to split it and give half to Nel Tarleton. The problem was, I had Mr. Tarleton on to me every week, asking me for money, sometimes before I had even received it from the Echo. It became pretty obvious that he was desperate for cash, which I found very sad in a way.

The series eventually came to an end. It didn't lead to a book. But Nel Tarleton seemed happy enough and we parted as good friends. The real point was that it helped me make my name. The sports editor of the Liverpool Echo was soon on to me, asking me to do other jobs on a freelance basis. And I later sold another series on Nel Tarleton to Boxing News, the "Bible" of the British fight game, which added to my reputation as a boxing writer and did me no harm at all.

That first serial with Nel Tarleton proved to be a kind of turning point in my young life. Flushed with success, I suppose, I suddenly got ideas about turning freelance. So I actually put in my resignation at The Liverpolitan and set out to work on my own as a freelance writer. I must have had a few bob in the bank, but it didn't last long, and I soon found that I simply wasn't getting enough work. I became desperate. I had obviously not worked things out properly. Maybe I was trying to run before I had learned to jog properly. Or maybe it was pure conceit.

Anyway, I found myself broke. And the only thing I could do was to sign on at the Labour Exchange.

I shall never forget it as long as I live. It was the most humiliating experience of my life. I went in and sat in a queue, was asked to fill in forms and then interviewed and asked what kind of job I thought I could do. When I told them I was a journalist, they more or less laughed at me, made me sign a document, and told me to come back on Thursday when I would receive whatever unemployment benefit I was entitled to.

When I returned on the Thursday, there was a queue almost to the door. Big burly men patiently waiting to be paid out their dole money. They all knew each other. They were obviously going there every week. I couldn't face it. The humiliation of it all. I just couldn't go through with it. I turned around and came out. I was 19 and was as near to tears as I'd ever been.

I went home and scoured the Liverpool Echo classified columns looking for a job. One I spotted was for a rent collector, no experience necessary. I applied for the job and received a reply telling me to start the following week. In trepidation, I accepted. I wasn't sure I'd like it of course, but it was a job. It would at least give me a wage so that I could pay something to my Mum for my keep.

Although I'm a firm believer in fate, I still find it hard to realise it happened, but only a few days later I received completely out of the blue a letter from the Editor of the Journal of Commerce, pointing out that they had on file a letter from me applying some time ago for a job with them. It seemed they now had a vacancy for a shipping reporter - was I interested?

Well, that truly was a life-saver. I was on the phone to them immediately, I went for an interview next day with the Editor, and was given the job of shipping correspondent, starting a week later. It was also at a very reasonable salary. And, of course, it meant I was back in journalism.

The one dubious thing I had to do was now tell the company who had hired me as a potential Rent Man that I was no longer interested - thank you very much! They were not too happy with me. I received a rather terse letter from them saying that I'd let them down.

Too bad, I thought. That's life. I don't want to be a Rent Collector. I prefer to be a journalist. And so I took up the job with the Journal of Commerce, which meant travelling on the old Overhead Railway along the dock road, every day, stopping off at each dock, either North or South side, checking in at the harbour master's office, and making a note of all the sailings and ship arrivals. Then the last couple of hours of each day would be spent back in the office in James Street, reporting all the ships' movements for the next day's paper.

The Journal of Commerce was a very important and valuable paper in all shipping offices and was circulated around the world.

Unfortunately, I found it rather boring. In fact, I stayed only about four months. It was time to move on. But one very important lesson I'd learned - never give up one job until you've got a contract for another.

CHAPTER 44: GROWING UP IN LORAINE STREET

Loraine Street wasn't very long. Two hundred yards at the most. It ran from the busy Breckfield Road North up to quiet Monk Street and was a winding Victorian terrace with only 22 houses on one side, and a massive red-brick girls school with two large separate playgrounds on the opposite side. With a little church building called Bethesda Hall tucked on the end, on the corner of Breckfield Road.

The roadway itself was cobbled and the houses ran only in odd numbers from Number 1 to 43. Curious, that.

Although all the houses were identical from the front, some of them were different inside. Most had two rooms downstairs, a living-room and a front parlour, and a kitchen which led out onto a small backyard. Upstairs, most had three bedrooms, but some tenants had converted the back bedroom into a bathroom. This was considered real luxury.

All the outside lavatories were single brick-built affairs at the end of a small back yard, with a door in the rear brick wall which led out to an entry running down the length of the terrace. That's where the bin men came once a week, to empty each metal bin which was neatly built into the wall and could be accessed from the outside without them having to come into your back yard.

At the front, each house had a tiny walled garden. Some were bigger than others. Our house, at No.9, had a much bigger front garden than the others, because of its structure and situation. We had attractive wrought iron railings around the garden – until workmen came one day with a big lorry and took away all the railings as essential metal which they said was needed to help the war effort. My dad then replaced them with a neat little wooden picket fence, which we had to diligently paint once a year.

The only tree in the street was next door, at No.7, where my Auntie Dorothy and Uncle Joe lived. They had a really tiny, awkward-shaped front garden, but it had a tree about 12ft tall, which sprouted new leaves every Spring.

What kind of tree? None of us knew. It was just a tree. The only greenery in the street. But the poor thing had to withstand a daily battle not with the wind but with the milkman's horse, which came plodding around pulling the cart every day. While the milkman was scuttling about putting one bottle of milk on each step, the shaggy, tired old horse would reach up and tear down any overhanging branches, gobbling up the leaves or spitting them out with disgust. With this daily tug-of-war between horse and tree, it was a marvel that the tree survived at all. But it did. After moving into No.9, we were happy in Loraine Street for many years.

With the odd exception, we knew every one of our neighbours from the top of the street to the bottom. Most of them were friendly. Some kept themselves to themselves and didn't say much. One or two women were in and out of each other's houses, either gossiping and drinking tea, or borrowing a cup of sugar or something when they'd run short. There would be the odd row or falling out, but nothing too serious.

In 1950, the year I left school, the city polling records showed that at No.1 lived Robert Jones, occupation: glazier. No.3 – Mrs. Annie Parry. No.5 – Leslie Bainbridge, a plasterer. No.7 – Joseph Gibbs, labourer. No.9 – William and Mary Irwin. No.11 – Arnold Plum. No. 13 – George Stirrup, grocer's assistant, and wife Sarah. No.15 – Henry Hayworth, labourer. No.17 – John Sankey. No.19 – Mrs. Elsie Sutton. No.21 – Mrs. Flynn. No.23 - Frederick Swindells, a painter. No.25 -George Jones. No.27 – George Woods. No.29 – Thomas Redmond. No.31 -John Appleton, a commissionaire. No. 33 – Mrs. Sarah Dodd. No.35 – John Kurs. No. 37 – Mrs. Elizabeth Caton. No.39 – Mrs. Elizabeth Skelly. No.41 – John Newton, a labourer. No.43 -Thomas Brimage, a steward.

There were certain households who were much more lively and involved than others. The Appleton family, at 31, and the Newtons, at 41, were the largest, seemingly trying to outnumber each other. The Newton's had, I think, ten children, and the Appleton's about seven or eight.

The Sankey's, at No.17, were a very popular family, with Mrs. Sankey and daughters Betty and Margaret, always out in the street, gabbing. And the eldest son was called Sonny, for some strange reason. He was a very tall, good looking bloke, and went on to be a policeman.

But it was at our house where all the kids would congregate. My mother made No.9 a kind of Open House. Everyone would come and go. Kids would gather on the front doorstep and play in the hallway. My mother wouldn't mind at all if they came in and asked for a glass of water, or even a biscuit. She loved having children around. She loved the sound of happy voices.

There were four of us. My sister Louise was two years older than me. Then there was Eric, five years younger than me. And then came Joan, four years younger than Eric. Joan was actually born at home in Loraine Street. I remember our lovely new baby screaming her head off and everyone fussing over her.

Our grandmother, my mum's mother, known to everyone as simply Ma, lived sometimes with us, but sometimes she lived next door with her daughter Dorothy. My auntie had two children, Donald, who was a year younger than our Eric, and Yvonne, a few years younger. We were constantly in and out of each other's houses. That was until my mother had a row with Dorothy. I didn't know what it was about, but it must have been serious because, even though we lived next door, they never spoke to each other. This went on for some years. The kids still played together. Eric and cousin Donald were best mates, went everywhere together and were always up to mischief. And Yvonne was always friendly with us.

It was just strange that our mothers never actually talked to each other. Then, one day, the feud, if you could call it that, came to an end. Mum and Auntie Dorothy mysteriously made up and became friends again. Peace was restored in the Irwin and Gibbs households. And we thankfully all went back to playing happy families again.

The kids who frequently hung about the front of our house were mainly the Appleton's, Norman, Lesley and Teddy. Lesley was about my age and a bit of a cheeky rascal, but friendly enough. Norman was a couple of years older, and I think more interested in catching sight of my sister Lou in the hope of copping off some time.

Then there was Leslie Newton, from No. 41. He became my best pal for a while. The Newtons had a huge family. Where they all slept in that little house I'd hate to imagine. Leslie's big claim, which came at the end of the war, was that one of his older brothers was a paratrooper and he'd been the second or third para to actually land on the ground when our Allied troops were involved in the battle of Arnhem. I was never sure how he could be quite so certain of that particular statistic (I mean, who was actually counting as the parachutes came down on the enemy beaches?) but no one ever dared contradict his brother's act of bravery.

Apart from all the kids in the street, our front doorstep and hall, or lobby as we called it, was the regular rendezvous for young friends of ours who lived nearby. Like Les Davies, from Queens Road, and Victor Lane, from St. Domingo Vale. And our Louie's close school friends were Pat Atkinson and Chris Orr, who lived in Salisbury Road.

In fact, Pat and Chris were such good friends that they became almost part of our family. They even came away with us on holiday to Peel on the Isle of Man one year. Pat, in particular, regarded my mother as her second Mum.

We got on very well with most of our neighbours. The only woman my mum didn't have much time for was Mrs. Bainbridge, who lived two doors away at No.5.

Mrs. B, or Rose, was a strange gazelle-like creature with stick-insect thin legs hardly strong enough to support her body. And she liked to think she was very refined and a cut above the rest of us. Everyone regarded her as a bit of a snob.

She had three boys – Leslie, who for some reason we always called Buddy, and younger twins, James and David. I can never recall seeing very much of Mr. Bainbridge though.

The other family, from the bottom end of the street, were the Kurs, generally considered to be a bit dirty. The mother and father were often drunk and would come staggering home, leaning on each other for support. But one of the lads, Richie, played with us a lot. And he had a very pretty elder sister, Sally, who I often thought looked too good and was too polite to be a Kurs.

There was always something happening in our little community. Hardly a week went by when there wasn't some bit of gossip to spread, or even a full-on scandal.

Everyone was outraged when Betty Mooney became pregnant and had a baby, and she wasn't married. We never knew who the father was, but Betty lived happily with her grandmother at No. 39. And if she ever had any shame she certainly never let it show. In fact, she would wheel her infant up and down in a cheap pram and be out on the street having fun and watching the rest of us playing rounders or cricket and all the other street games.

Another bit of excitement came one day when my cousin Donald, who was a chubby little lad, managed somehow to get his head stuck in the railings of the school playground. Someone rushed over to tell his Dad, and Uncle Joe came dashing out of their house and frantically tried to release him by attempting to bend the iron bars, as though he was some kind of strong-man act. No matter how much he pulled, Donald's head remained firmly stuck.   In the end they had to send for the fire brigade, who came storming in to the rescue. They finally managed to release Donald, who was taken into his house sobbing and whimpering. He never tried squeezing through the railings again.

Another rather odd incident I can recall was when I was a keen member of the Cubs in Hamilton Road Church. We used to go out on parade once a month, but twice a week we attended Cub meetings and I earned quite a

524

few badges for passing various exams. These had to be sewn on to your green jersey to show just what a clever so-and-so you were. Our Cub Master was a man called Ernest Jones. He was middle-aged but a bachelor as far as we knew. But he was always very friendly and helpful and really seemed to care for all the lads in the Cub pack. My Dad, for some reason, became quite friendly with him, and used to meet him in the pub for a drink. I was told very strictly never to mention this, because Mr. Jones did not want his junior Cubs to know that he frequented public houses.

One day, however, we were suddenly told that Mr. Jones was giving up his Cub Master activities because he had to go away for a while, and that someone else would be taking over his duties. We were all puzzled at his sudden departure, until my father came back from the pub one night and told my mum that Mr. Jones had been sent away at His Majesty's pleasure and wasn't expected to be back for at least six months. I don't think I ever saw him again. He never returned, and we understood he had voluntarily retired from the Cub pack. I left soon after anyway.

Another strange little occupation we had for a while was when my sister Louie and myself were befriended by a very nice man who lived just around the corner from us, in Monk Street. This middle-aged chap lived all alone, but on one night every week he would invite us, together with one or two other local children, to go to his house to watch his home movies. He had what was called a magic lantern set, and the kids would all sit down while he stood at the back of his living room operating the camera which beamed wonderful black-and-white films onto a big white bed sheet which he'd pinned up on the wall.

Going to this house for a home-made film show became a regular pastime. He would hand around sweets and lemonade drinks in the interval, while he was changing films on the projector.

It might have been considered a little sinister, I suppose. But nothing untoward ever happened. He was a very nice man. Though I think my mother did warn me at one time, "You sit next to Louie. And don't let anyone touch you."

Fun though they were, the films were never as good as our weekly visits to the real cinemas. The Mere Lane cinema was just around the corner, and The Royal cinema was a ten-minute walk to Breck Road. Saturday was the day for special children's performances. We'd go to one in the morning, and the other for the matinee performance in the afternoon. My Auntie Alice worked as an usherette in the Royal, along with her friend Peggy Nurse. So Louie and I would get not only free seats

525

every week, but a complimentary ice-cream or lolly-ice at the interval. Oh, what ecstasy that was!

At the Mere Lane, they always showed cowboy films on Saturday afternoons. Either Gene Autrey or Roy Rogers. It was hard to choose which was better. But we'd come galloping out of the cinema at the end, on our imaginary horses, slapping our backsides with one hand and shooting down imaginary Indians with our two-fingered guns in the other hand.

Our entertainment during the week, after school hours, was provided by the radio. Out playing in the street most of the time, we'd be stopped in our tracks at exactly 6.45pm every evening with my mother coming to the front door and yelling, "Dick Barton's coming on!"

Everything stopped for Dick Barton - Special Agent. A quick dash back into the house to listen to the quarter-of-an-hour episode every night. Life wouldn't have been the same if we ever missed the adventures of Dick Barton and his faithful accomplices Jock and Snowy.

Apart from the adventures of Dick Barton, we used to listen to the radio a lot with my mother in the evenings. All the variety shows and comedy half-hour programmes such as ITMA with Tommy Handley and his gang. Then on Sunday, at lunch-time, it was always the riotous Billy Cotton Band Show, keeping everybody happy by playing all the most popular hit songs of the day. And he had a resident female vocalist who I remember my mother quietly telling us was the band leader's girl friend or bit on the side. Though how my mum knew this was a bit of a mystery to me, because she was hardly privy to show business gossip.

On Saturday nights, it was boxing matches we listened to. All the title fights from around the world, but particularly those staged in London. Over a few years, we tuned in to all the bloody battles. Somehow, just listening to the commentator's live reports made it more vivid than if we'd been watching in our actual sitting room. That's where I first developed my enthusiasm for boxing. My Mum was as keen as I was, too.

Bruce Woodcock, British heavyweight champion. Freddie Mills, light heavyweight. Jack Gardiner, heavyweight champ. We followed all their fights. Cheered aloud when they won, sat in silence and waited for our cup of cocoa before bed when they lost.

Some of those fighters were magical to me. When British hope Randolph Turpin beat the great Sugar Ray Robinson for the world middleweight title it was the ultimate in sound entertainment to us. Unfortunately, they had a return fight within a few months and Robinson won to take the title back to America, but even that didn't deter us from regarding Randy as our world hero for the rest of his short life.

Of course, one of the down sides to listening to the radio morning, noon and most nights, was that after a while the sound would eventually come to an abrupt end. This was simply because the battery had gone flat. There was no electricity in the house in those early days, (we had only gas, with little fragile gas mantles to bring light to the rooms). So we relied on electric batteries to keep the radio going. These were huge heavy things the shape and size of a brick. And once a week, usually on Saturdays, we would take the worn-out battery to a shop up near Hamilton Road to be re-charged. There, we would exchange it for a newly charged one, which cost a shilling or so, and then hurry home to let my mother re-fit it behind the radio set, to joyously bring the sound of the wireless back into our lives.

Sport has always played a big part in my life. In fact, I think without sport, life would be very dull indeed. From my early years as a kid, when we kicked a ball around in the street and played cricket in the summer, sport became a passion.

Looking back at those years when we lived in Loraine Street brings back so many happy memories. We had a street football team. Loraine United we called ourselves, and we played friendly matches against other local street teams. Except that sometimes they were not so friendly, because we didn't have any referees. The best form of refereeing was which team had the biggest, strongest and toughest lads.

It's laughable now, but our little team of Loraine United was very highly organised. Every lad in the street was expected to play, and George Stirrup, who lived next door but one to me at No.13 (and ended up being my brother-in-law) was the goalkeeper and captain. He was the best goalkeeper around, no doubt about that, but the only reason he was captain was because he owned the ball. Without George and his ball, we wouldn't have been able to play at all.

But every week – usually on a Thursday, around tea-time – George would announce the team for the game on Saturday. And this became quite an important ritual because he would pin a sheet of paper up on the notice-board of Loraine Street school, opposite our house, with all the names of the players he'd chosen. But it was no ordinary sheet of paper. It was a highly decorated masterpiece of art, painted in different colours, with his name - G. Stirrup, Capt. - in goal, highlighted by a tiny drawing of goal posts and a net. And we would all gather round to see who else had been chosen for the team, and which positions we were playing in. Which was ridiculous really, because the names never changed from one week to the next, as we only had eleven lads in the street, and on the odd occasion when we might be short, we'd have to go and recruit a pal from another street, maybe Salisbury Road, or Granton Road.

But George was a great organiser. He was also the captain of the street cricket team – again, because he was the only one who owned a bat and a set of stumps and a cricket ball. A real cricket ball. Not a soft tennis ball, but a real red cork ball. And later, George even became the proud owner of a pair of cricket pads, which he insisted on wearing when he went in to bat – which was No.1, opening batsman, of course. And which he also wore throughout the rest of the match, because he was the wicket keeper. Nobody else ever got to wear those pads.

The trouble with playing cricket was that Loraine Street was hardly a level playing field, and in fact was cobbled. So the ball was likely to fly up in any direction, and when struck fiercely with a bat, it was anybody's guess where it would end up. With luck, we would hit the ball in a straight line, down the sloping street, and score six runs. But quite often, the ball ended up crashing through one of the nearby windows, and we would then have a ranting neighbour to contend with. Mrs. Plum, at No.11, and my Auntie Dorothy and Uncle Joe at No.7 were both particularly vulnerable houses, I seem to recall. And once, Mrs. Bainbridge came out and confiscated the ball because she was so distraught at having her front window smashed and her afternoon nap disturbed.

Normally, when we smashed a window, there would be no problem. We knew it would cost three shillings to have the glass pane replaced, and we would all contribute from our pocket money to pay for it. Most of the residents were happy with that arrangement, though the odd grump would chastise us with a few words of unnecessary advice: "Why don't you go down and play in Stanley Park, instead of breaking my windows?" The trouble was, Stanley Park was a mile away.

It got to the stage at one time that we were breaking so many windows, that someone (and it was probably George again) decided that we should change the cricket pitch and play inside the school playground, which had a smooth concreted surface and would obviously be easier, and safer, to play on. As the school gates were always locked outside of school hours, this meant us all having to climb over the 8ft high railings to get inside. It did make for a better game of cricket though. The only trouble being that, strictly speaking, the school yard was legally out of bounds.

And if a passing policeman came by and spotted us - which they frequently did - we would all be in trouble. Consequently, it was essential that the outfielders on the boundary had to be constantly alert, keeping one eye on the match and the other eye looking out for casual coppers.

On such occasions, the mere shout of a warning, "Here comes a scuffer," would send us all into action, grabbing the stumps and everyone running to hide behind the other side of the school wall. Once the policeman had walked by, glanced through the railing, and peacefully gone on his way, we would all reassemble and re-start the game where we had left off.

That all worked out well for a while, but then one day it happened. Disaster. Someone bowled a full toss, the batsman hit the ball a mighty wallop, and it flew straight through the school window, completely smashing the full plate glass window, with the ball ending up inside the classroom. And who was the culprit? It was George Stirrup, our beloved captain. He may have scored a six, but he'd lost the ball and the game came to an abrupt end. For some minutes we all discussed what we should do. Should someone climb through the broken window and retrieve the ball? Or should we just leave it and scarper? I think in the end we decided that secrecy was our best option. We all climbed over the railings and went home. It was dinner time anyway. And there was no doubt in our minds that this massive window was going to cost a lot more than the usual three shillings to repair. So we left it with the headmaster and the school authorities to sort out. I suppose eventually it must have come out of the school's budget. We never found out. Not even George admitted to that one. All we knew was that we'd lost a ball, and we'd have to wait for George's dad to buy him a new one. Oh, happy days!

Away from Loraine United and our cricketing antics on the cobbled street, my footballing skills improved rapidly. I eventually got my first pair of leather football boots (with six lethal studs on each boot, and a tin of Dubbin which was used to clean and polish them each week). Then my dad bought me a real leather case ball.   The proper thing. Not even George Stirrup had one of those. As the proud owner of a full-size casey, it immediately gave me new status. The only trouble was, with a big ball like that, it really was too dangerous to play in the street any more. And we did have to go down to Stanley Park for our kick-a bouts after that.

When I moved to senior school, Venice Street Secondary, I played for my house team, Livingstone, and became quite a good player. Well, I thought so anyway. I played inside right, No.8, or outside right, No.7, as a fast, tricky winger. Only once can I recall scoring a goal, though. And it was a cracker. I received the ball just over the halfway line, and ran with it like a demon, with two or three defenders frantically chasing me. Just as one lad was about to catch me, I let fly with my right foot, and the ball went like a rocket into the top corner of the net, with the goalkeeper flailing away helplessly. I don't remember whether we won the match or not. I didn't care. All I could remember was everyone slapping me on the back and congratulating me. It was a great feeling.   Unfortunately, it never happened again.

Although I played in the House team, I never quite made the school first X1. although I was chosen as a regular reserve and travelled with the team to all away games and to our home ground, which was in Townsend Lane, Walton, every Saturday morning. Sadly, I stood around for a whole season, shivering and waiting hopefully for someone to get injured, so that I could get a game. But it never happened. And I was particularly upset, one Saturday, when some little twerp watching on the touchline, came over and said to me, "You'll never be in the team. You're only chosen as first reserve because you've got your own footy boots!" How hurtful kids can be. It may have been true. But I didn't want to hear it.

As kids, we would be off to see a real game every Saturday afternoon. But we couldn't afford the full entrance fee every week, so a gang of us would go for a kick-around in Stanley Park and then, when the gates opened at three-quarter time, we would run in and push our way through the crowd of spectators, to the front, and ask, "Who's winning, Mister?" Then, knowing the score, we would watch the game for the last 20 minutes or so. It became a weekly ritual for us. Goodison Park one week, Anfield the next.

A few years later, when we could afford to pay at the turnstiles, we'd go in the Boys Pen and enjoy watching the whole match, imprisoned in a caged section at the back of the ground.

The first full-length professional football match I ever went to was when I was ten and I was taken by Uncle Billy to Goodison. It was 1945, the full leagues hadn't been reorganised after the war, and Everton played a friendly game against Fulham. The Blues won 10-1.

I couldn't quite believe it. It was just incredible. After that, I knew what team I wanted to support for the rest of my life. How could I be anything but an Evertonian after watching a match like that?

CHAPTER 45: RELIGION AND ST. DOMINGO CHURCH

Moving on a few years, after leaving school I joined the club at St. Domingo Methodist Church and became a regular player in the soccer team. It was a tough league we were in, but we had a very good team. George (Stirrup) was goalkeeper, my Uncle Billy (McNichol) was centre-forward, and Victor Lane was centre-half. Vic, in particular, was a great player. As steady-as-a-rock defender, with immaculate ball control and a relaxed coolness about him. He was two years older than me, but I knew I could never be as good as him. We became best mates, on and off the field. And we are still in touch and talk quite regularly on the phone, some 60 years later.

And this was, of course, the same St. Domingo from where Everton football club was originally founded in 1878 and was elected to the Football League in 1888. That's why most of us were Evertonians. We were following in the footsteps of the great pros.

Later, Vic Lane, Les Davies and I became really close pals. We went everywhere together. To church, to the youth club, and we went to football matches.

Billy Liddell was my favourite Liverpool player. He was a fast, tricky left winger, played for Scotland, and was also a lay preacher who once came to give a talk at St. Domingo club. A really nice, modest man.

But apart from the football team, the church had a very lively youth club, open every Friday, from 7 to 10 pm, which was run by Mr. Eddie Taylor.

There, we played everything. Darts, table tennis, snooker. Fuelled by huge mugs of hot tea which cost tuppence a time with a couple of biscuits.

And that's where I learned to play proper table tennis. At first, it was just ping pong. But it soon became a serious game for me. I was on that table, practising, practising, practising, at every available moment, until I became quite a good player. And when we formed a new team and joined the Liverpool Sunday School League, it wasn't long before we were beating most of the other church teams around the city.

In fact, we liked to think of ourselves as the young invincible team, made up of Vic Lane at No.1, me at No.2, Les Davies at 3, our Lou at 4, and Bill Fairhurst at 5.

We travelled around all over Liverpool, with weekly matches. And there was only one team better than us - Great Homer Street. No matter how we juggled our playing order, we never quite managed to beat them. They were our bogey team. But it was all great fun. And when it came to the annual championships, our Lou and I won the mixed doubles title one year.

It was in my teenage years, too, that I began to develop a really serious interest in religion. Not highly organised religion, but after being made by my mum to go to Sunday School every week, our Louie as well, we both became Sunday School teachers, and Lou became a regular member of the choir. I started reading the Bible every day, avidly questioning its teachings. And for a short time, I even enrolled as a potential lay preacher, but never followed it through.

We had a period in our lives when it meant going to church three times every Sunday. Eleven o'clock for morning church service, then home for lunch. Back for Sunday School at 3pm, home for dinner. Then back to church for 7pm, evening service. It became a ritual which went on for some years. We really enjoyed it. Later, our younger Eric and Joan followed the trend and became church members too. My mother didn't go regularly every week, but only on special occasions like Easter and Christmas. But she was really proud to send all her children off to keep in touch with God every Sabbath. I think, too that she was inwardly pleased that we all chose to go, and enjoyed it, and were not being forced into it in any way. As for my father, he didn't mind at all. In the years he was at home, he would be out, probably in the pub from opening time. And we wouldn't see him until 3 or 4 o'clock, after the pubs had closed. If he came home at all.

Our religious fervour after a while extended beyond Sunday. We had two or three different resident ministers at St. Domingo. First there was the Rev. David Raymont, who came from the Hamilton Road church. Then there was Rev. R.A. Rees. But then he was replaced by the Rev. Donald Tanner, a very pleasant and down to earth Welshman who had a nice wife and a rather precocious daughter called Pamela, who was 14 but liked to think she was an adult and was spoilt rotten by her parents.

As Methodists, one of the long-standing teachings of the church was that alcoholic was banned. Strong drink was the food of the Devil!

But Mr. and Mrs. Tanner both considered themselves very modern thinkers. Mr. Tanner smoked a lot of cigarettes and I seem to remember that he and his wife even indulged in the odd glass of sherry. Even little daughter Pamela started smoking when she was still at school, just to prove a point that a clergyman's daughter had a mind of her own.

For a period, after church on Sunday nights, Mr. Tanner started organising small discussion groups back at his house and encouraged the younger members of the church to go to the Manse for tea and biscuits after taking part in what quite often turned into fierce but friendly verbal discussions about God and what He had in store for us.

I was one of the regulars at the Tanner talk-ins, along with my chums Les Davis and Vic Lane. And I grew to quite like Mr. Tanner. He was not only very sociable but always ready to help with any problems anyone might have. In fact, although he wore a dog collar, he wasn't really like any other clergyman I'd ever met.

On one night a week, there was also a Prayer Meeting we'd attend. This was more serious stuff which only attracted a small group, mostly oldies, the more devout worshippers. Mrs. Bagot and Mrs. Hughes, who always seemed to be joined at the hip, were both members. And Mrs. Hughes, a very tiny woman, would spend half the evening yelling out "Hallelujah" or "Praise the Lord," much to the silent amusement of the rest of us, including Mr. Tanner who was not really a Hallelujah-type parson.

The Sunday School Superintendent was David Phillips, a pleasant enough little man who always encouraged pupils but without the God-fearing fervour of the George and John Stirrup brothers

Mrs. Lillian Swain was in charge of the Sunday School annual scripture exams, and she encouraged everybody to attend a mid-week evening class for extra tuition. When the annual exams came around, the best and most knowledgeable pupils would receive much-valued book prizes.

Meanwhile, her husband Fred Swain played the piano, and their only son Norman was a rather jolly lad who joined in all the church activities and became popular as one of our gang.

The other thing that occupied our time a lot was the drama society which they formed at St. Domingo. We were all in it. Those who didn't feel confident enough to get up on stage and act would be enrolled to work behind the scenes, in props, wardrobe or assisting in make-up or catering.

We took it all very seriously and put on some pretty good plays over the years. Sometimes, a production would run for three separate nights and we would fill the church hall, with audiences of up to 250, all very appreciative and vociferous with their applause.

I can still recall some of the plays we put on. In fact, I still have the books we worked from, with all the text from my parts carefully underlined, to help me rehearse and learn my lines.

The first thing we ever put on was a production called "Michael," a one-act play written by Miles Malleson (and adapted from the translation of Tolstoy's story What Men Live By). Pretty serious stuff, eh?

The fee for each and every presentation of the play by amateurs was 15 shillings, which was payable in advance to Samuel French Ltd., of London, or their agents, who upon payment of the fee, would issue a licence for the performance to take place. No public performance was allowed until we had obtained that licence. These were the rules of international copyright.

It's interesting to look back at the cast we had for that play. Dave Phillips played a character called Simon, Mary Fairhurst was Matryona, and Pauline Hughes (daughter of Betty's sister Nancy, and now our niece) was the young and beautiful Aniuska. I played a Russian nobleman, Les Davies played my servant, and Mrs. Lily Swain played "a Woman." All great fun.

Looking back though, some of the casting now seems very weird and wonderful.

One play we did was "Golden Rain," a three-act comedy by R. F. Delderfield. We presented that on stage on November 30, 1957. Curtain up at 7.30pm. Admission was by programme only and cost two shillings. Ice cream was also available.

The cast list for that play (in order of appearance) read as follows:

Mrs. Tuckett, housekeeper at the Rectory – played by Flo Irving.
Sydney Palk, a young parishioner -   Ken Irwin.
Marlene Cheetah, his fiancee -   Edna Thomas.
Archdeacon Shearing – Dave Phillips.
The Rev. Roger Strawbridge, Rector of Tidingforde - Vic Lane.
Catherine Strawbridge, his wife -   Nance Hughes.
Mrs. Stukeley-Mosher, an American -   Dorothy Needham.
Mervyn Grudge, a village boy - Norman Swain.
Mr. Williams, of the County Advertiser - Harold Nelson.
Produced by Frank Barton.

I can't believe it. Nancy playing Vic's wife. She was almost old enough to be his mother! But I'm sure the play was a sell-out. I don't know how the ice cream sales went - on a night in late November!

Then there was another one-act play called "Five Birds in a Cage," written by Gertrude Jennings. It was all about five people who were stuck in a lift.

Our cast list for that was:

Susan (the Duchess of Wiltshire) -   Flo Irving.

Leonard (Lord Porth) -   Frank Barton.

Nelly (a Milliner's assistant) -   Mary Fairhurst.

Bert (a workman) -   Harold Nelson.

Horace (the lift man) - Ken Irwin.

The copyright fee on that one meant all amateur groups had to pay one guinea for a licence for each performance.

Then we did a three-act Easter play called "The Cup." The casting for that was:

John, disciple of Jesus -   played by Dave Phillips.

Peter, disciple of Jesus -   Vic Lane.

An Inn Keeper in Jerusalem -   Ken Irwin.

His daughter Elizabeth -   Muriel Jost.

His son Mark -   David Phillips Junior.

Another play we put on, which was quite a well-known comedy, was "Quiet Week-End," by Esther McCracken. I haven't got the full cast list for that, but I played a character called Jim Brent (Marcia's husband), which was quite a sizeable part. The fee to perform this one in public was five guineas a time, so it wasn't cheap.

Looking through the book I had, when we produced it at St. Domingo, it was quite impressive to read that when the play was originally produced by professionals at the Theatre Royal, Newcastle on July 7, 1941, it then had a long run at Wyndham's Theatre, London, and the cast included such film star names as Glynis Johns and Michael Wilding. And my character, Jim Brent, was played by Geoffrey Denys, quite a stalwart of the English theatre.

It was all good fun while it lasted. I don't think any of us ever even vaguely contemplated making a living on the stage. Which was just as well, really. We'd have only added to the Dole queues.

It wasn't long before I was bold enough to suggest that we start our own church magazine, and Mr. Tanner thought it a splendid idea and quickly encouraged me to launch it. It became a monthly publication. We printed it ourselves, and called it The Evangelist. It became so popular that it even earned a congratulatory write-up in the columns of the Liverpool

Evening Express, which suggested that The Evangelist was one of the best church magazines on Merseyside.

I was the Editor, but I invited contributions from anyone and commissioned certain people to write regular columns, updating us with all the latest church activities. I was determined it was to be more than a Births, Marriages and Deaths sheet. So as well as a regular page-long message from the Minister, which was in a preachy style, I made sure that, as the Editor, I had the freedom to air my own views. This meant a regular monthly rant from the Irwin pen.

Unfortunately, one month I went too far and unintentionally upset quite a few of the older church members by writing an article which clearly gave away my political leanings by declaring: "Nobody can be a true Christian if they are a Conservative."

This immediately caused quite a storm. Mr. Eddie Taylor, a stalwart of St. Domingo for many years (and I suspect a lifelong Conservative as well) protested in no uncertain terms that I had gone too far and should not be in charge of the magazine any more. He even called me a young Communist and told the Minister that my wings should be clipped and in future I should be stopped from using the church magazine to air my own personal views.

He wasn't the only one who complained. He had elders like the hen-pecked Tom Irving and his gossipy wife Florrie to back him up.

When I heard of their complaints, I told the Minister I was entitled to free speech. After all the hoo-hah, Mr. Tanner just smiled nonchalantly and told me to carry on regardless. And lit another cigarette.

But after that, I always felt my days as Editor of The Evangelist were numbered. And I think they all breathed a sigh of relief and were glad when I later moved to Manchester to work, and Frank Barton took over to replace me as Editor.

Going back to my teenage years, it was table tennis which occupied most of my spare time. I was absolutely fanatical about it. The team we had at St. Domingo church played matches all over Liverpool in the Sunday School league. With Vic Lane, Les Davies, our Lou, Bill Fairhurst, and me, we had a pretty good set of players, and we enjoyed the weekly competition from other church clubs.

But I also decided to join a proper table tennis club, on my own. I signed up for membership of The Linnets, a club in Linnet Lane, Aigburth. They had five teams playing in various leagues around Merseyside, and the club was open six nights a week.

Although I thought I was pretty good, I couldn't make the first team when I initially joined. I was deemed good enough to be in the second team, playing at No.1 or No.2. After a while I improved enough to occasionally make the first team, at No.5. But they had some really hot-shot players in that club, most of them much older than me.

To get to Aigburth wasn't easy. It meant getting two buses and then a long walk down Ullett Road. But I loved it so much I used to go about four nights a week, practising and always trying to improve my game.

When it came to the St. Domingo team, Vic, Les and I took it all very seriously. One year, I recall, we went to watch an exhibition match by British and world champion Johnny Leach and one-time world champion Victor Barna, at the Liverpool Philharmonic Hall. It was absolutely enthralling stuff. I ended up buying a Johnny Leach bat. He was my hero. All attack, attack. I would pour with sweat, dashing around the table like a whirling dervish, smashing the ball around as hard as I could.

Vic on the other hand played with a Victor Barna bat. He was much more controlled, a solid defensive player who was cool under pressure, and very hard to beat.

PICTURES

An end-of-war street party in Loraine Street
school yard. 1945. L to R: Me (in shadow), Eric, cousin Frank Jones,
Leslie Bainbridge, Leslie Appleton. My mother is among the Mums
in the background, wearing a paper hat.

St. Saviour's and Breckfield Road North.

With my chums on a ferry boat ride. L to R. Me, Les Davies,
George Stirrup, Peter Taylor.

Digging in the back yard after taking up some paving stones to make a garden.

Posing on wicker fence in front garden.

Our sad old house (on left). Boarded up and now a slum.

Vic Lane and me at New Brighton. 1953.

Me with Les Davies. 1953.

Betty (left) with St. Domingo pals Edna Thomas, Joan Orr and
Margaret Taylor.

Betty as a baby on big sister Nancy's knee.

Betty as a young girl in artistic mood.

Betty (centre) with her mother and father and little sister Irene.

At Barmouth, North Wales, 1955. Betty (left) and George
Stirrup playing on the sand.

Betty. 1955.

Betty when we became engaged.

Betty with Ken and Pauline Hughes in Nancy's back yard.

Betty in the garden of the Manse.

On our wedding day. September 1956.

On honeymoon. Betty at Old Colwyn.

Proud parents. With Betty and baby Susan.

My Mother, Molly Irwin.

My mother, with Louise, Joan, me and Eric.

Me and my mum.

Mum with Lou and Joan, in her garden in Upton.

Mum and Dad with Betty outside our house in Harrow.

Susan. On Graduation day, Liverpool University.

Paul with his dog Spot in our garden at Disley.

With Mark and Paul.

**With Betty taking a helicopter over the
Grand Canyon. 1991.**

Betty and I having dinner in Turkey.

My mother with Amina and Jessica on a visit to
Coronation Street.

THE SEVEN AGES OF MAN

(Centre) A plaster cast of me made by Amina at junior school when the teacher asked pupils to paint a picture of their grandfather.

CHAPTER 46: DISCOVERING GIRLS – AND SOMETHING CALLED SEX

Why is it that most boys absolutely hate girls – until they're 14 or 15? Then it all changes.

The first girl I can remember being interested in was Jean Moore. She went to our Sunday School and she lived in Orient Street. She had dark hair, was attractive and very neatly turned out. But although she was always very pleasant when we saw her coming and going on a Sunday, she never said anything more than Hello, as far as I can recall. And although I began to fancy her in a strange kind of way, I was far too shy to do anything about it. So she probably didn't have the slightest idea of my interest in her.

The first real encounter I had with a girl was as a young teenager, I'm not sure exactly how old I was, but I was with my cousin Frankie (Jones) who lived over in Upton, and I had my friend Vic Lane with us. We were wandering around the fields near Elm Avenue, one weekend, just going for a casual stroll, and there was a local girl who knew Frankie, and she somehow latched on and asked if she could join us. Well, nobody objected, so we all continued our walk. We were chatting and this girl was giggling a lot and was very friendly.

Then, quite suddenly and without warning, Vic, who was the eldest in our group, grabbed hold of the girl, pulled her closely into him and kissed her. She responded by holding on to him, as though she was really enjoying it.

When they parted, nothing was said, but the giggling continued as we all walked on. Vic merely appeared quite pleased with himself.

Ah, I thought, that's how it's done! So, without really thinking, I stepped forward and grabbed the girl and tried to copy Vic's impressive style of action. It was more of a fumble than a full-scale show of affection, but I put my face to hers and tried to kiss her. To my astonishment, she pulled back her head and pushed me away. She said nothing. The only thing I felt was an awkward embarrassment. Clearly I had done it wrong, I thought. Or maybe it was only Vic she fancied.

We all strolled on and eventually returned to Frankie's house, with the girl waving goodbye and going off home. I never saw her again. I don't know whether Frankie did or not. We never talked about it. But the whole incident put me off girls for quite a while.

When I started working in the shipping office, I was 15. By the time I was 16 the first pangs of sexual sensibility were aroused. We had two girls - or women really - working as typists in the outward freight department. One was a very attractive brunette called Thelma who I guess was about 24 and she became engaged to a huge brute of a fellow who worked in Inward Freight but spent far too much of his time making excuses to come and chat to his fiancée at every opportunity, which I found quite annoying.

The other typist who sat next to her was called Joy Sharpe. She was a pretty girl, with alabaster white skin, gorgeous red hair and was a very cheerful and chatty type, and I fell for her in a big way.

The trouble was, I was only 16 and she was 21, I think. So I was never sure if she took my feelings for her seriously. It wasn't for the lack of effort on my part, because this mad teenage crush I had on her developed rapidly in to my own in-built love affair.

She lived in the posh area of Crosby, and I managed to get her home phone number and then, at least two or three times a week I would phone her from my local public phone box in the evening, after work, to have conversations with her. I can't remember how long this went on for, or what we talked about, but I was happy just to know that this lovely creature was even willing to share telephone air time with me. I never did find out if she had any feelings for me at all, whether she was just flattered to be the centre of my boyhood infatuation, or if in fact she was merely too kind a person to want to hurt my feelings by discouraging me.

It was all a bit silly really, because I probably did more talking to her on the phone at her home than I did during office hours in work. But she certainly did nothing to discourage me, and for that I was grateful.

How it all ended I can't remember. Probably when I left Houlder Brothers and went off to be a journalist. There was no big farewell scene, or even a kiss or a peck on the cheek from Joy when I departed. But I kept her phone number in my book for years, and often wondered what happened to the lovely red-haired Joy Sharpe. She probably went off and got married to some handsome chap nearer her own age, had red-haired babies, and lived happily ever after in Crosby, or wherever. I hope so anyway.

A few years later, when Vic, Les Davies and I were hanging out together, we'd spend most of our leisure hours going to the pictures a couple of times a week – either the Mere Lane cinema or the Gaumont, at the bottom of Salisbury Road. And afterwards it was invariably a visit to a funny little drinks shop in Anfield Road which sold nothing stronger than lemonade and fizzy drinks. A sparkling Vimto was then the favourite drink of the day. Sometimes we'd go mad and have two.

But we also got to know a couple of girls along the way. One was Sally (Sarah) O'Brien, who lived in Venice Street, and the other was her friend, a chatty little minx with jet black hair called, I think, Yvonne who lived down in Scotland Road.

I soon fell madly in love with Sally. We used to hang around at the bottom of Venice Street nearly every night, in the hope of bumping into the girls, who would be coming and going from Sally's house at No.71.

If they were around, we would stand and chat to them - until Yvonne's bus would come and she'd jump on it and go home alone to Scotland Road, and we three would walk Sally back to her house, before we all went home and called it a night.

These Venice Street corner chat-ups went on for months. It was only me who was interested in Sally, and why Vic and Les put up with my romantic yearnings I'll never know. Except they had nothing else to do anyway, and I think they quite enjoyed the female banter as much as I did.

Eventually, I could stand it no longer. I finally asked Sally O'Brien out on a date. Thankfully she said Yes, and I bought two tickets and took her to the Empire Theatre. I'd never been on a date before, but just tried to behave as normally as possible. I think I even splashed out on a box of chocolates as well.

The evening went surprisingly well. We both enjoyed the show and afterwards we caught the No.19 tram back to Venice Street. I remember as we walked down her street, how happy I felt inside. Here was the girl I had fancied for so long, actually out with me for the night, on our own, away from Vic, Les and that corner shop doorway. And throughout the evening she had been everything I had expected, attractive, chatty, giggly.

When we got to her front door, we stopped, and she thanked me for a lovely evening. I couldn't resist it. I bent over and kissed her full on the mouth.

And then I came crashing down to reality. Sally looked slightly embarrassed. "Listen, Ken," she said quietly, "I like you. I really do. But I regard you more as a brother than anything else."

I can't remember how I responded. But when we said goodnight and she'd gone in, I walked home feeling totally deflated. Any dreams I might have had about her were now shattered.

Clearly there was no future in that relationship. We may have seen each other again, I can't remember. We may have bumped into the girls,

Vic, Les and I, at some time. But our regular door-shop meetings and all the hanging around at the bus stop came to an end. I just had to put it all down to experience.

Strangely however, a few years later, when I was working as a reporter on the Evening Express, I happened to bump into Sally's elder sister and her boyfriend, who recognised me and stopped to talk in the city centre. And they told me all about Sally. "We were sorry when she split up from you," said her sister. "Not long after that, Sally went off and got married – and he turned out to be a bad 'un. She's just gone through a divorce." And her boyfriend Roy said quite gratuitously, "She should have stuck with you, mate. But Sally is a lovely girl, y'know. We know where she lives if you ever want to get in touch with her."

I still wonder occasionally whatever happened to Sarah O'Brien. The beautiful young Sally, as I knew her. Where did she end up? Is she still alive?

Who knows what would have happened if we'd gone beyond that kiss on our first and only date. Our relationship might have developed into something serious. Maybe we'd have ended up married. And that would have been awkward, because I'd have had to tell my mother I'd fallen for a Catholic girl. Roman Catholics and mixed marriages were still frowned upon in our family. Especially by my bigoted Aunt Grace. She, I know, would never have forgiven me.

As it was, the next girl I fell in love with ended up being my wife. But that's another story.

When I was 15, my mum and dad bought me a bike for my birthday. It was my first bike and it was such a wonderful gift. A brand-new bright red Rudge sports bike with drop handlebars. It cost £20 from a bicycle shop at the end of Robson Street, and although I wondered how they could have afforded such a gift, it became my pride and joy.

Overnight, I developed a new passion in life – cycling. From then on, I cycled everywhere. At weekends I would take the bike over to Upton to meet up with cousin Frankie and we'd cycle off together all over Wirral. To really posh places in the country I'd never seen before, like Thornton Hough and Port Sunlight.

Having a bike gave me a tremendous sense of freedom. Cycling offered me a new interest, away from girls. A bike was much more reliable, I decided. A girl could let you down so easily. A bike wouldn't. Well, not unless you were unlucky enough to have a flat tyre. And even then, I had a puncture outfit in my saddle bag, so it could be fixed very easily. Forget girls and all that messing about trying to get a kiss. Who needed them?

CHAPTER 47: GETTING MARRIED

I was 20 when I fell in love. Really in love, I mean. Proper love. Something that was tangible and hopefully forever. I met and got to know Betty Bagot.

She wasn't a complete stranger. Betty had been around a few years and was the elder sister of Irene Bagot, who I knew quite well because she became the girlfriend of my pal George Stirrup who was crazy about her. The Bagot family lived in Orient Street. Their widowed mother Mrs. Ellen Bagot went to Hamilton Road church, along with her constant companion, the diminutive Mrs. Sarah Hughes. But when that church closed down, both families moved and became members of St. Domingo.

George Stirrup was still at St. Domingo, where his father George and his uncle, John Stirrup, were both very active. Brothers big John (6ft plus) was superintendent of the Sunday School, and little George (who was about 5' 5") was a Sunder School teacher and they were both lay preachers.

Curiously, bother John and George worked as managers in separate grocery stores for the popular firm of Irwin's, who had shops all over the North. (I spent a lot of my early life being asked if I was from the wealthy Irwin grocery family. No, I wasn't unfortunately).

When Irene came to St. Domingo, young George took off after her like a rabbit and was determined not to lose her, even though she openly shunned his advances at first and at one time told me quite clearly that she couldn't stand him and thought he was a jerk. True love will conquer all, however. George pursued Irene until she gave in and eventually married him. He went to a theologian college, became a Baptist parson, and they had four children and lots of happy grandchildren. Praise the Lord!

Betty, meanwhile, really turned to religion in a big way, joining up with a wildly fervent Welsh evangelist called Pastor Ball (Yes, really, that was his name). He ran a happy-clappy church of devout born-again Christians who travelled around in a God-mobile van and set up gospel tents around the North trying to bring more people to Jesus. They were great supporters of the charismatic evangelist Dr. Billy Graham, whose wealthy organisation in America set up multi-million pound religious campaigns to convert the heathen Britons and save us from our sins.

I never found out why, but Betty's religious fervour cooled down considerably and she left Pastor Ball's lot and joined her mother and sisters Nancy and Irene at St. Domingo.

That's when we first met up. Betty was much quieter than the younger, very talkative Irene. She went to church regularly every Sunday, and then started coming to the discussion groups at Mr. Tanner's manse with the rest of us.

The momentous and life-changing moment came for me - and for Betty - when the church organised a summer coach trip to North Wales. We all piled onto the coach and went to Barmouth for the day, via the lovely Lake Bala, most of us taking a picnic lunch. I'd never been to Barmouth before. It was quite a long run but it turned out to be a lovely, warm day.

We strolled through the small village of shops and finished up spending most of the day on the beach – a long beautiful, unspoilt stretch of golden sand, with nothing more than an ice-cream kiosk in sight.

It was a wonderful day out, and I think everyone was a bit reluctant when the time came for us all to get back on the coach to go home.

But on the return journey, I found myself sitting next to Betty in a double seat. She was very quiet at first, but then as everyone started to chatter enthusiastically about the day's events, she cheered up. And it was then that it happened. I plucked up the courage to touch her hand and clenched it in mine. I wasn't sure how she would react. Magically, there was an immediate response. She held on to my hand and tightened her grip. This was no accident. She was clearly happy to hold my hand.

This might sound ridiculous, but the mere holding of hands, flesh on flesh, gave me a strange tingle inside. I'd never experienced this feeling before. Never had the chance, or the courage, to hold a girl's hand for so long.

As I looked at her, she turned to me and smiled. And for the rest of the journey, we never let go of each other. The trip took a couple of hours. It was like riding on a dream. Total ecstasy.

I don't know whether that was the moment when I fell in love with her. But one thing I knew was that I didn't want to let it go. I was determined it wasn't going to end there. And as we got off the coach, and everyone started to make their way home, I followed up by shyly asking her if I could see her again. I asked her if she would like to go out with me on a date. She smiled and said yes. And wasting no time I immediately said, "What about Monday?" Again, she nodded. "I'd love to." We left it there, and both went off home.

Next day was Sunday. I couldn't wait to see her again at church. I was just hoping that she wouldn't change her mind. She didn't and we both confirmed that the date was still on for Monday. Would she like to go to the pictures? I asked. Yes, that would be nice. So I arranged to pick her up at 7 pm at her house.

Betty then lived with her mother and Irene in Newcombe Street, Anfield, at No.4. Next door, at No.2, her sister Nancy, who had married Reg Hughes, lived with Reg's mother.

When I arrived promptly on the Monday, dressed quite smartly, I was in for something of a surprise. As she was not quite ready, Betty invited me into the house, and into the back living room while I waited as she rushed around trying to get ready. Her mother was in the kitchen, cleaning or something, because she had a full bucket of water standing in the middle of the kitchen floor. Then it happened. Betty, in a flap to get ready, accidentally kicked the bucket over, and the full contents poured out all over the lino floor.

Mrs. Bagot made some kind of agonised protest and tried to suggest that Betty help her clean it up. But Betty was having none of it. She brushed her mother's protests aside, hurriedly put on her coat and said something like, "I can't. I'm in a hurry." Then she grabbed me and pushed me out towards the front door. It was all terribly embarrassing. Mrs. Bagot was not best pleased. When I hesitated and suggested we should try and help mop up the water, Betty simply marched me out of the front door and said, "Don't worry. She'll be all right."

It wasn't exactly the best way to start off our very first date, and I was a little surprised at Betty's callousness. Maybe she's not quite as nice as she looks, I thought. But whatever doubts I had about her soon went as we tripped off and made our way to the Astoria cinema in Walton Road. And the rest of the evening was bliss. I'd never taken a girl to the pictures before. It was a completely new experience for me.   And as I bought her a box of chocolates and we sat and enjoyed the film, I began to think I could quite get used to this.

After that, we started going out together regularly. Not just meeting in church and after-service discussion groups, but two or three times a week going to the pictures, or just off on walks around the park. There may have been a few nudge-nudge comments made about us, but it soon became known around church circles that Ken Irwin and Betty Bagot were now an item, and most people were quite pleased for us.

I wasn't quite sure at first what the reaction would be at home. I was only 20, and Betty was a more mature 26. My mum and dad seemed to accept the situation quite comfortably. They didn't offer me any particular advice, and as they didn't complain I assumed they approved, and were happy for me. The only one thing that came up initially was the difference in our ages. In those days, girls were more or less expected to get married soon after they were 22 or 23. And a woman who was not married by the age of 30 or so was generally considered a "spinster." (what an awful word that is). The worst phrase some women had to face was the dreaded "She's been left on the shelf."

None of this ever bothered me however. All I knew was that I was growing more and more in love with Betty, and I was pretty sure that this feeling was mutual.

Betty was a studious, quiet type. She was always extremely tidy and neatly dressed. She was very intelligent and an avid book reader. She had been a pupil at Loraine Street Girls School from the age of five and was Head Girl when she left at 14.

Her final school Reference Card on leaving, dated June 1943, read: Number of years in school - 6. Special Aptitude - "Good School Captain." And the General Remarks from the Head Teacher, A.I. Dougherty: "Elizabeth Bagot has been a most regular and punctual pupil. She possesses good ability and shows a keen interest in her school work. She is steady, earnest and painstaking. She has made an excellent School Captain, having at times been in control of the entire department. She has a delightful disposition, and is a most reliable, sensible, helpful girl. I have every confidence in recommending her to an employer."

Like most families, the Bagots were brought up in near poverty. Good, solid working-class stock, but if not actually living on the bread line, then not far off it. I learned later from Betty that her father Alfred was illiterate. He was a tiny man, apparently, not much more than five feet tall. He smoked like a chimney and couldn't read or write. He worked most of his life as a labourer in Bibby's cattle-feed warehouse near the docks.

He suffered badly from chronic asthma, and Betty recalled in horror how he once fell on to the fire at their home. He died in 1948 at the age of 58.

Mrs. Bagot, born Ellen Taylor but called Nellie most of her life, left school and worked in a German-owned shop in Great Homer Street, making hand-made chocolates. But when the First World War broke out, customers revolted against the Germans, and the shop was closed down. She then worked as a bookbinder, before marrying in 1916.

They had four children. Arnold, Annie (who preferred to be called Nancy), Elizabeth and Irene. The family moved from Orient Street to Newcombe Street, Anfield, in 1945, at the end of World War 11.

But on the outbreak of war, and the threat of the dreadful years of the blitz, Betty and Irene were actually sent away as evacuees with their school chums. They went to a place called Borth, in Lancashire, living in a large house with other schoolchildren, with their mother helping out with the supervision. This lasted only a few months before they returned to Liverpool.

Then, however, their mother decided they really would be safer living in the country, so the two young girls were packed off in 1941 to live with a distant relative in a place called Church, near Accrington. They didn't enjoy it. Not only because it meant being away from their mother, but also because the woman who took them into her home out of so-called kindness turned out to be nasty piece of work and was quite cruel to them. And when it looked like she was going to lose the few pounds a week which she got for their food and lodgings, she complained that Betty was a troublemaker and needed proper discipline.

After 18 months or so, the girls were so unhappy that one day they decided to run away and go home. But they didn't know how far it was to Liverpool or how they would get there. So Betty suggested they went to the nearest railway station and walk alongside the railway tracks and it was bound to lead to somewhere. Fortunately, they scrapped that escape route.

Eventually, when their mother heard how unhappy they were, she sent elder daughter Nancy to go and bring the girls home.

When I first met Betty, in 1955, they had no bathroom in their house in Newcombe Street. In fact, they had no hot water. To have a bath, they had to go to the Donaldson Street public wash-house once or twice a week. When they were younger, bath night was usually on a Friday, with a large tin bath brought in from the backyard and filled up with water boiled in the kettle. When the water went cold, it was time to get out of the bath. The lavatory of course was in a brick out-house at the end of the backyard. With no lighting and usually a nail on the wall with neatly torn-up pages of the Liverpool Echo as bum tissue.

It sounds primitive, but that's the way it was with most of the terraced houses in those streets. And strangely enough, nobody ever thought of themselves as being deprived. It was just life. Everyone got on with it.

Betty herself left school at 14 and her first job was working in the office of Old Mother Noblet's, a sweet shop in the city which among other things was famous for producing Everton toffees, always associated with Everton football club. (Hence their nickname The Toffees!). She then worked in the offices of the well-known Princes Salmon food company.

When we started dating, she was working in an office in Tower Buildings on the dock road, as a typist. But she moved soon after and became a telephone operator with the General Post Office, a job she really liked, mainly because with an American air force base at nearby Burtonwood, the operators got to unashamedly listen in to the amorous chat-up lines of the Yanky servicemen phoning their English girl-friends, and promising them silk stockings and other goodies in exchange for you-know-what. It worked of course because many of the girls ended up as GI brides and went off to America after the war to start completely new lives.

Betty had no discernible accent and sounded quite posh when she put on her telephone voice. It was probably due to the demands of her job.

She told me right from the start that she had not had any serious previous boyfriends. And in those days, any respectable girl remained a virgin until she got married. Those who were promiscuous were frowned upon or considered "women of the streets."

In fact, the awful truth was that if you wanted sex, you had to get married. It was as simple as that. It may have been painful for young men to accept this, but that's the way it was. Virginity was a very important thing. No man would like to think that his girl-friend or potential wife had already been sleeping around.

Eventually, Betty and I both decided that we wanted a future together. And that meant an engagement. It was only a matter of a few months before I proposed to her and she accepted. We went out and bought the best engagement ring I could afford. It was 18ct. gold with a large green emerald, and it cost me about £150, I think, which was quite a lot of money.

Still living in Loraine Street, I was then working on the Birkenhead News as a reporter, and travelling over on the ferry boat every day.

When we announced our engagement, we agreed that we would wait about nine months before getting married, and a date was set for the following September. This gave us time to discuss our finances and save up some money.

I'd been on the Birkenhead News for about two years, and I then decided it was time to try and get more money. So I went to see the Editor, a large rather pompous man called George Rowlands, who was also a respected JP who sat on the bench as a magistrate in court a couple of days a week.

When I knocked on the door and walked into his office, I told him I had just become engaged and would be getting married shortly, so was there any chance of a pay rise? And I more or less hinted that if I didn't get a rise, I would be looking elsewhere for a job.

He looked at me and said, "You're a good reporter, Irwin. But you're still a junior and you've got a lot to learn. I'm afraid a rise is out of the question at the moment."

Immediately, I then set about getting another job. In those days, there was a weekly magazine called World's Press News, distributed to every newspaper office and avidly read by journalists everywhere. Particularly because it had two pages at the back which advertised jobs and journalistic vacancies up and down the country.

After browsing through WPN, there were two jobs advertised which caught my eye. One was for a sub editor in Newcastle upon Tyne, the other for a news reporter in Nuneaton. I immediately wrote off applications to both, and received letters to go for interviews.

Taking a day off, I went on the train to Nuneaton where I met the Editor of the local paper.   At the end of the interview, he seemed quite impressed and offered me the job. When could I start?

He then told me, "You can live with our head printer and his wife. They charge a very reasonable rent for board and lodgings. It's a regular arrangement we make with all our junior reporters." I told him I'd go away and think about it.

When I got back home, I was in something of a dilemma and didn't know what to do. So I went in to see Mr. Rowlands again to seek his advice. I told him I had the offer of the reporter's job in Nuneaton, but there was also the job in Newcastle. As I had never done any subbing, would he advise me to take that job and get experience as a sub editor?

For a minute or two, he just stared at me. Then he got up from behind his huge desk and said, "I don't quite know what to say, Irwin. You came in here a fortnight ago and asked for a rise, and said that if you didn't get one you would be leaving. Now you come in and tell me that you have the offer of not one but two jobs, and you want my advice. Well, all I can say is that jobs must be bloody easy to come by. It's up to you. Close the door on your way out."

Well, I'd never felt so embarrassed in all my life. But I went away now more determined than ever to leave Birkenhead.

I turned down the job in Nuneaton, but thanks to good old World's Press News I spotted another vacancy, went for an interview and landed a job as a reporter on the Nottingham Evening Post and Guardian Journal. A much better, more prestigious and traditional paper with a great history.

It meant leaving home for the first time and working away. I found digs with the local Methodist Minister, the Rev. Walter Joyce and his family, in Ruddington. (But that was my choice, and it meant I wasn't living with the head printer and his wife).

I enjoyed working in Nottingham. It gave me lots of good experience, but it also meant me being away, and only getting back home every fortnight for a weekend.

But then after four months or so I applied for a job on the Liverpool Evening Express, was successful, and so moved back to Merseyside, where Betty and I could continue our courting. And we could count the days on the calendar to our wedding.

Meanwhile, of course we had a considerable time to get to know each other. The courting game became a whole new experience. We were both very naïve when it came to sexual matters. So much so that one day, without telling me, Betty returned from work with a book she'd bought from a city bookshop. It was a mammoth sex manual. Not pornographic in any way, but a serious educational tome, with helpful instructions, pictures, diagrams and illustrations, showing how to do it, what went where, and with various positions which really stretched the imagination.

I was greatly surprised. Not so much at the book but the fact that Betty had actually walked into a shop and bought it. I would never have had the nerve to buy a book like that. I was so prudish and timid that I could never even bring myself to go into a chemist or even a barber's shop and purchase a packet of condoms.

Nevertheless, we both browsed through the pages with avid interest. After all, she'd paid good money for the book.

The wooing game was not easy, and was certainly not helped by the permanent presence of George Stirrup and Irene, before they also later became engaged.

George and I still both lived in Loraine Street. Betty and Irene both lived with their mother in Newcombe Street, which was a 15-minute walk away.

And shortly after Betty and I became engaged, George and Irene decided to follow suit and do the same. Which was fine, except that it led to slight complications when it came to the kissing game.

It meant that every night I took Betty out, we'd return to her house and she'd invite me in. However, the same applied to Irene and George, and quite often we'd find that all four of us would be back at No.4 Newcombe Street around 10 pm or so for a "farewell cup of tea or cocoa."

Mrs. Bagot was always quite magnanimous. But she was also very strict. I never knew whether she enjoyed the situation or just put up with it because there was no alternative. She would insist on staying up until both George and I were off the premises. Until then, she sat stoically in the living room, listening to the radio, and keeping an eye on the clock.

This meant that, as soon as we'd had our farewell drink, I would thank Mrs. Bagot, say goodnight, and Betty would usher me into the front parlour for a brief kiss and cuddle. The trouble was, Irene had exactly the same idea with George. So it was a matter of who said their goodnights first and made a beeline for the parlour.

More often than not, I found myself being too slow, or too polite to be rushing in to the parlour, so that by the time we made our move, Irene and George had beaten us to it and were already in there.

It became a romantic game of who can get into the parlour first. Because the only alternative was the hall, or lobby as we called it. The couple who missed out on the parlour would have to do their bit of canoodling standing up against the wall in the lobby. It was a bit like a Brian Rix farce in the end, with doors opening and shutting, and lovers discreetly slipping in and out, trying not to bump into each other.

It was all very unfair. If we didn't manage to make it first into the parlour, where there was a comfortable sofa and a couple of arm chairs, the facilities for love making in the lobby were extremely confined.

It also meant that on the nights you lost out to the comforts of the parlour, we would be on tenterhooks out in the hall, anticipating that George and Irene might come out at any time and have to push past us in the lobby on the way to the front door.

The whole thing was fraught with danger. I did think at one time that perhaps George and I should have come to some kind of amicable and friendly gentleman's arrangement to occupy the parlour on alternate nights. Maybe he could even print out a rota system, just like he used to do when producing the team lists when we played football in Loraine Street.

The hard and fast rule was that it all had to be over in the Bagot household before midnight. That was the ultimate deadline for vacating the premises. Because if we were still there, Mrs. Bagot would poke her head through the living room door and shout, "I'm going to bed now. I want to lock the front door."

That was the final warning. It was her polite way of saying, 'Goodnight, you randy buggers!'

We all knew what we were doing of course. Which, to be honest, was not a lot. What Irene and George got up to, I could only guess. But as far as Betty and I were concerned it was a wonderful way of getting to know each other, even though physically we were both terrified of going too far.

We were determined to wait until our wedding day in September, but it was excruciatingly difficult not to experiment, particularly as we were both such innocents when it came to sex.

As it was, most of our time together was spent fumbling in the dark. Literally. Embracing and kissing led to what was then known as light petting. It was all so wonderful and new. But there were strict boundaries. Limits we could go to. Wandering hands were okay, but the wandering would stop at often crucial moments.

Eventually, however, our love for each other grew, and our passions became something much too strong to contain. And then it happened. A month or so before we were to be married. One Saturday night, when we had luckily claimed occupation of the front parlour for a whole evening, the electric fire was on, the lights were dimmed low, and we were snuggling up together in a very cosy position. Betty looked at me, quite seriously. No words were really needed. It was quite spontaneous. Nothing had been planned. She started to undress. I looked at her. "Are you sure?" I said. "Yes," she said quietly.

We were sitting on the floor in front of the fire, but as we both stripped off I held her close and we moved over to sit on the settee. As we held each other, we knew there was no going back. She lay down on the sofa and I moved gently on top of her.

We knew instinctively what to do. We didn't need that manual. I was massively excited and my heart was pounding. We wrestled together for a short while. No noise was made. It was all very discreet and lovely. I don't know how long it actually lasted. Not long. But the dynamic feeling of ecstasy that came over me as we climaxed was the most wonderful experience I had ever had in my life. And I knew it was the same for her, as we slowly separated, then lay quietly together, side by side, without saying a word.

We got dressed, sat for a while, and then kissed before I said goodnight and walked home. I was probably still in a daze. Surprised at what had happened. I wasn't regretful or annoyed with myself. I realised later that it was inevitable. Expecting us to wait until our wedding night was never really practical. And I knew that Betty thought the same. I was only hoping that she wouldn't regret it in any way.

The next day was Sunday, and I was looking forward to seeing her in church in the evening. But to my surprise, she didn't turn up. I was suddenly anxious and wondered what had happened to her. Then, after the service, Mrs. Bagot told me that Betty was not feeling very well. This made me even more worried, so I hurried down to her house to see her.

I dreaded the worst. Maybe she was upset at what had happened, I thought. Perhaps she was sorry we'd been so impetuous.

When I saw her, she was fine. She invited me in and we talked quietly together and had a cup of tea. She wasn't upset or angry with me, but just had a headache, she said.

When I thought about it afterwards, I realised that it must have been pretty traumatic. After all, she had suddenly lost her virginity overnight. It must be an awkward if not painful moment in any woman's life. Betty assured me that she was happy and would be okay for work next day. From then on, we couldn't wait for the day to come to get married.

There was one other occasion, however, when our passions took over again and we got carried away. With only a few weeks to go before our wedding, Betty and I went for a day out to Heswall on the bus. It was a beautiful summer's day, the sun was shining and we decided to walk to the beach. But on the way, tramping over the Heswall hills, we stopped to have a picnic.

It was deserted, very quiet, and we started fooling around. The next thing we knew we were lying in the deep grass, in each other's arms and fondling each other. It seemed like too good an opportunity to miss.

Nobody was around to see us. And it felt strangely liberating, having sex in the open air.   Kind of sex alfresco. And a picnic we'd never forget.

Away from the church, we started going regularly to the professional theatre, to the Liverpool Playhouse where they had an excellent repertory company, with brilliant actors all bound for bigger things in London's West End and films.

Every Saturday night, a group of us would go to the theatre to see the latest production. The gang was made up of Bill Fairhurst and his sisters Mary and Emily, some of the Culshaw family, Jim, Jean and Ted, Vic Lane, Betty and me, Les Davies, and Edna Thomas, who lived around the corner in Eyes Street and took a fancy to Les.

At one time, Les, Edna, Betty and I hung out together and became a regular foursome. We went to the pictures together, and once even went to Walton Hall Avenue Park for a game of tennis, which turned out to be disastrous. We paired off, with Les and Edna playing a doubles game against Betty and I.

The trouble was that Betty just didn't have a clue how to play. She couldn't hit the ball, and when she did manage to make contact with ball and racket, she'd whack it so hard that the ball went soaring high over the perimeter fence, and I'd have to go and fetch it. That was the night when I realised Betty had no kind of sporting talent whatsoever. She was one of life's spectators rather than a participant.

Then came the parting of the ways as far as Vic, Les and I were concerned. The Three Amigos were finally split up. Les was called up for National Service and went into the RAF for two years. Vic won a place at Liverpool University (the first person I ever knew who was clever enough to do that). And I was turned down for National Service because of my asthma and got married. Les would have been my best man but he was away on duty at the time, so my cousin Frank stepped in instead.

Our wedding day fast approaching, Betty and I tried to plan everything to perfection. We were getting married on a Saturday afternoon, with a reception to be held in the church hall immediately afterwards, and then we were going off on honeymoon.

On the evening before our wedding, for some reason we decided to go over to the church and check that everything was in order. It was just as well we did, because purely by coincidence that weekend happened to be the Harvest Festival celebrations, and we were both shocked to discover that the whole of the church altar had been submerged in a massive display of fruit and vegetables, ready for Sunday morning's Harvest service.

We were both speechless. I was angry and annoyed that someone could have been so thoughtless as to arrange all the harvest lay-out, knowing that there was going to be a wedding the day before.

Betty and I marched around to the manse, confronted Mr. Tanner and complained about the whole thing. He fully understood, put the blame on to someone else, and arranged for the caretaker to remove all the fruit and veg and put it in storage until after our wedding ceremony had been completed.

So at least, on our big day, when the bride walked down the aisle on the arm of her brother, it was a church we were in, and not a fruit and vegetable market stall.

We were married on Saturday, 22 September, 1956. And everything went like clockwork. Both our families were there, even my father and mother standing together in church, which was a rare if not unique event in itself.

Betty was given away by her brother Arnold, and her bridesmaids were sister Irene, her niece Pauline Hughes, and my young sister Joan. Pauline and Joan were the same age, both 12, and they looked lovely together. As for Betty, she looked quite radiant, dressed in a traditional full-length white silk wedding gown.

Immediately after the ceremony, we all went to the manse where our official photographer took lots of pictures in the garden, the only bit of greenery in the area.

Afterwards, lots of guests arrived for the reception which was held in the church hall. And there was plenty of tea, sandwiches, cakes and everything but no alcohol, of course. Remember, we were on Methodist premises. Though I dare say that my father, Uncle Joe and some of the other men may have slipped off to the nearest pub as soon as we had departed and gone off on honeymoon.

The wedding cake was cut, speeches made, and there was a pile of nicely-wrapped gifts from the guests stacked in a corner of the room, which we politely opened and checked out. All very gratefully received, of course, but nothing more expensive than the usual toasters, sets of crockery, cutlery, glassware and bedsheets.

When it was finally time to go, Betty and I were noisily waved off on our honeymoon. It was early evening and we had arranged to go by bus to Colwyn Bay in North Wales. Actually we stayed at nearby Old Colwyn where we'd booked in for a week at what we hoped would be a comfortable bed-and-breakfast accommodation.

By the time we arrived there, it was quite late. No time really to inspect the premises. We were made welcome by the woman who owned the house. And like most newly-married couples, I suppose, we were only interested in one thing – going to bed.

It was, of course, the first time we'd ever spent the night together. And we had been engaged for about nine months, so I guess there was a lot of anticipation involved. The good thing was that we could have a lie-in on the Sunday morning. We had no plans to rush down for breakfast or go to church. And I seem to remember that it all went very well. Betty and I were now finally married. It didn't seem strange at all. We were madly in love. We'd just have to get used to being Mr. and Mrs. Irwin.

When we eventually got up and found time to look around, we discovered that we were the only couple staying there that week. The place was quite spacious, clean and tidy and was run by a very nice woman who was warm and friendly. We had booked in for breakfast and dinner, and the meals were good. In fact, the whole atmosphere of the place was comfortable and cosy.

The weather was typical late September. Summer had gone, autumn was here, and there was a nip in the air, and Betty wore a long, below-the-knee coat for most of the week when we went out on casual walks to explore the local countryside.

We were about half a mile from the coast, and it was a pleasant stroll through the village and down to the sand. We had the whole week to do nothing but enjoy just being married.   And one evening, after dinner, we made our way casually down towards the beach, and came across a half hidden cave in the rocks. It was quiet and deserted. As we stopped to linger, we held hands, then one thing led to another. We fell into each other's arms. Next thing I knew we were intimate. We wanted each other right there. So we stood in the cave, against the wall, and celebrated our marriage all over again. It was another case of love alfresco style. Now all legal and above board.

Everything comes to an end of course, and after seven days we had packed our little suitcases and were having our final breakfast in the dining room before returning by coach to Liverpool.

Then the most surprising thing happened. The lady of the house came over to our table, sat down and asked us if we had enjoyed our stay because as far as she was concerned we had been the perfect guests.

We thanked her for a very pleasant week. Then she said, quite suddenly, "I was just thinking. You wouldn't like to buy this house, would you?"

Betty and I looked at her. Both puzzled. "I'm thinking of selling up," she said. "It's a lovely house. There's plenty of room, but it needs a family in it. I think it would make a wonderful home for a young married couple like yourselves. Are you interested?"

This was all such a surprise that we didn't quite know how to respond. It was indeed a wonderful old house and I had no idea how much it would have been worth. But later, on the bus home, Betty and I couldn't help laughing at the whole situation. Because, truthfully, after our honeymoon was paid for and we'd returned to our jobs in Liverpool, I had a bank account which would have been around £17 in credit. Hardly enough to buy a house anywhere, let alone a beautiful detached period place in Old Colwyn!

As it was, we politely told the woman that, much as we appreciated her kind offer, we couldn't afford it and now intended to start saving to maybe buy a house in Liverpool at some time in the future.

Only a couple of years ago, we returned to Old Colwyn on a day's drive, and that house where we spent our honeymoon is still standing. I don't know who lives there. It still looks substantial and elegant. But a new foot-bridge has been built over the coastal road, the nearby dual carriageway. Which meant that the quaint old walk-way through the rocks and the little cave which we found so romantic has now all gone. A pity really. I would have mischievously quite liked to see a blue plaque erected on the wall of that cave to mark our 60th anniversary of the honeymoon consummation of our marriage.

After that, it was back to work and a return to normal life.   Well it wasn't so normal any more. We were now a married couple, with new responsibilities and a long-term plan to make life better and more comfortable.

First, we had to find accommodation. The cheapest and easiest was to move into Newcombe Street where Betty was already living. Mrs. Bagot agreed that we could have the biggest bedroom and we shared all the facilities with Mrs. B and Irene, who was then training to be a midwife. For this, we paid an agreed weekly rent. This was only meant to be a temporary measure anyway, because I was not too enthusiastic about going through married life living with the mother-in-law, and Betty was as keen as I was to find our own place.

It lasted, in fact, only a few weeks. They still had no hot water in the house, except for a small gas-geyser contraption in the kitchen which we had to use to heat up water for a wash.

Irene recalls that she once had a row with me because I took too long in the kitchen, having a wash and a shave, and when she got in, there was no hot water left.

Betty and I then moved to a fully-furnished couple of rooms on the first floor of No.5 St. Domingo Vale, literally opposite the church. But we only stayed a short while before finding a really nice furnished flat in a semi-detached house in Warwick Avenue, Wallasey. The road sloped down to the river, which was a five-minute walk away. This meant that Betty and I both had to get the ferry over to Liverpool every day to get to work. She was still a telephone operator and I was a reporter on the Evening Express in Victoria Street.

We both liked it in Wallasey. The flat was comfortable and cosy, and the landlord who lived downstairs was friendly enough.

But then, Betty discovered she was pregnant. It didn't take long. Only about three months after we'd been married. Funny, but Betty reckoned later that she knew exactly the night it happened. It was one particularly amorous evening after dinner when we both became over excited, and I rose to the occasion in a very big way.

It wasn't planned, but as we had never used any kind of contraception or birth control, it wasn't really a surprise. It was all perfectly natural and we were both happy, even if it did mean that Betty would be leaving her job earlier than expected, and we now had only one source of income to live on.

Money never really worried us. I was doing quite well in my job on the Evening Express and earning enough to pay the bills. But then came the unexpected chance for us to move house. My father managed to win quite a large sum of money by winning on the football pools. Like most people, he filled in the football pools, sent off the coupon each week and hoped for the best. No one was more surprised than he was when, one week, Vernon's Pools told him he had won and they paid him out something in excess of £2,500.

This was a small fortune. He'd never had money like that in his life. Suddenly he was rich. The first thing he did was to invest most of it into buying a corner shop – a general store selling sweets, tobacco, drinks and foodstuffs. The shop was in Lance Street, Everton, and it came with living accommodation above the shop. So, my father and mother packed everything up and moved out of Loraine Street, with my brother and sister Eric and Joan. Dad was now a property owner for the first time in his life.

He also bought his very first car, a Ford Popular. The Irwin's were the only family in the street with a car.

Consequently, Betty and I decided to take over my mother's house in Loraine Street. After some tough negotiating with the landlord, we managed to sign a new agreement and were taken on as tenants.

I don't think Betty was ever over keen on Loraine Street. But it meant me moving back to the house I'd been brought up in for most of my life, and it made a lot of sense. It was a three-bedroom house, and it was ideal for a new family. It also meant that my mum and dad, and Mrs. Bagot and

Betty's family were all only about ten minutes' walk away. And St. Domingo church was at the end of our street.

Betty continued working right up to a couple of months before the expected date. When she finally quit her job, I was soppy enough to buy her a book, in which I wrote: "To Bette. July 15, 1957. From Ken. It's The End of a Very long Day." (The book was titled I Am Fifteen and I Do Not Want To Die, by Christine Arnothy. It cost me 10s.6d at the Charles Wilson bookshop in Church Alley, Liverpool). Betty was always a tremendously keen reader. We've still got the book.

We celebrated our first wedding anniversary on September 22, 1957. Exactly five days later, on September 27, Betty gave birth to our lovely little daughter. She went in to Mill Road maternity hospital, in Everton. Everything went more or less to plan. The timing was right. There were no complications. No histrionics. The baby weighed in at the average of around 7 lbs 6 oz. And Betty was out of hospital and back home within three days.

We called the baby Susan Elizabeth. We'd decided on the name very easily months before she arrived. If it was a boy, he was to be called Mark. If it was a girl, then it was Susan.

The one big blessing was that the baby was perfect in every way. Beautiful. Adorable. Cute. We thanked God, very sincerely, for the sheer happiness that baby brought to our lives. Just to hold her, pick her up out of her cot and cuddle her was pure joy. We were both so proud. Betty became the perfect mother. And Susan - or Suki, as we started calling her - was the perfect daughter.

But then, surprise, surprise, only seven months later, Betty revealed that she was pregnant again. It must have been something in the Loraine Street water, we thought. Again, we prepared for the birth of a new baby. Let's hope it's a boy, we said. That would be terrific.

But then, only two months before we were expecting our second child, disaster struck. I was in the office, as normal, and it was the usual busy day, when the News Editor Harry Walgrove came out looking very serious and announced to the reporting staff, "I'm sorry to have to tell you this, but the paper is closing down. From three o'clock today, we're out of business. You can stop working now. There won't be a late edition. The noon edition was the last."

The news came as a complete shock to everyone. At first there was a deadly silence. Then suddenly a babble of voices as we discussed it and tried to get our heads around what was happening. There were five or six of us in the office. Those reporters who were out on jobs were quickly told to drop everything and get back to the office.

Then, within the hour, someone came around and gave each of us a brown envelope. The letter, from the General Manager, read: "Dear Mr. Irwin. It is with the very greatest regret that I have to inform you that the Evening Express has, this afternoon, ceased publication and has been amalgamated with the Echo. The Express has been published for some years at a heavy loss and this has reached a level which has made closing inevitable.

"Regret is also expressed that it has not been possible for us to offer alternative employment to you. Details of the special financial consideration which has been arranged for you are enclosed."

Our complete editorial staff was made redundant, with the exception of only two journalists – George Harrison, who was the very popular gossip columnist who wrote the daily Over The Mersey Wall page (and for whom I stood in one day a week, when he was off), and Bill Rogers, who was a veteran news reporter only a few years off retirement age and who was considered too old to find a job elsewhere.

The Over The Mersey Wall column was so well read that it was taken over and transferred immediately to the pages of the Echo. So George Harrison was the lucky one. For the rest of us, it meant a month's pay in lieu of notice, and the Labour Exchange.

It was ironic that in that very last edition of the Evening Express, on Monday, October 13, 1958, it was me, not veteran George Harrison, who wrote that day's Over The Mersey Wall column.

The full-page column, which was one of the most popular features in the paper, was under my by-line. I still have a copy of it. And it was rather funny because one of the stories I had written that day was about a young boy called Billy Kenwright (who went on to become an actor, theatre impresario, and chairman of Everton football club).

The story, with the headline Happy (not angry) young man, read: "Meet Liverpool's keenest young author. No Angry Young Man this, but a jovial little character who gets a kick out of putting pen to paper...and he's only 12 years of age.

"Billy Kenwright, a pupil at Liverpool Institute, who lives in Mather Avenue, Allerton, wrote his first 'piece' at the age of five – a witty little one-act play which I am assured made plenty of sense. His first three-act play came two years ago, a comedy which Billy called 'Treasure for Three.'

"And now he's busy writing a book – a thriller which he tells me is all about a girl who uncovers a spy ring. Powerful stuff! But Billy's talents are not reserved to the literary field. As a pop singer, he recently 'stole the show' at a local open-air theatre talent contest and won the first prize of ten bob.

"'I want to be an actor though,' says Billy, and he wrote and told Sir Laurence Olivier the same thing. One of the lad's valued possessions is a letter from Sir Laurence, wishing him 'All the best.'"

Bill Kenwright certainly achieved his ambition in life and later, after making his name in Coronation Street, he became a friend of mine. And as chairman of Everton, once invited me for a grand tour of Goodison Park and dinner after a match.

When the Evening Express folded, I had been with the paper for just over two years, as a news reporter, feature writer, stand-in gossip columnist. The trouble was I was now in a desperate situation because I was not only married with one child, but was expecting a second in a couple of months' time. It wouldn't have been so bad if I had been single, but I felt I now had a tremendous responsibility with a wife and family to look after.

The day they announced the newspaper closure, most of the journalists just left the office and went to the nearest pub to drown their sorrows. One or two dashed over to Manchester and even down to London, hoping to pick up any spare jobs that happened to be going. It was panic stations for some.

Although I didn't drink in those days, I ended up with a few colleagues in the Liverpool Press Club, where the regular hard drinkers from the national papers were putting their hands in their pockets and generously buying drinks and offering words of sympathy to the out-of-work Evening Express lads. I had a few drinks myself. I think that may have been the date when I actually broke the Methodists' teetotal code for good.

When I eventually got home, I explained the whole situation to Betty. There was nothing we could do except sleep on it. And in the cold light of the next day, we sat down to discuss what we were going to do. At least we had a month's pay to come, so we were not going to starve.

It would mean me having to start looking for a job and moving to another city because there were clearly no more jobs to be had on Merseyside. Maybe – just maybe – there was the possibility of getting a job on a national paper. Through the grapevine, we were told that some of the national papers were sympathetically willing to take one or two reporters on to their staff. It felt a bit like The Titanic going down. Some would be rescued, but most of us were still floundering in the sea without a life jacket.

Then, we were told that the Editor of the Daily Express had decided to come up from London, and interviews would be held with any out-of-work journalists who might be interested in obtaining employment. I was invited along with several others to go to a Manchester hotel where the interviews were taking place.

We were ushered in separately, and each given about 20 minutes of interrogation from the big white chiefs from London. I had with me a briefcase full of sample cuttings of my work but was told these would not be necessary. I left with the promise that they would be in touch with me but could not guarantee any definite jobs at this stage.

I returned home, just hoping that I'd done enough to impress them into giving me a job. I had always liked the Daily Express as a newspaper and was brought up as a regular reader, particularly of its sports pages. It then became a waiting game.

Then, completely out of the blue came a phone call from an old colleague of mine from the Evening Express who now worked on the Daily Mirror in Manchester. He was a sub editor called Des Jones and he told me there was a job going on the Mirror for a TV critic. Was I interested? He'd be happy to recommend me, if I was. But I must act quickly. Of course, I said Yes, and I was invited to go for an interview with the Mirror's Northern Editor, Ted Fenna.

He was a man of very little charm. A tall, stout fellow who was very blunt and didn't mess about. They were looking, he said, for a Northern TV critic to replace their man who was leaving. He'd made enquiries about me, liked what he'd heard, and Des Jones had spoken very highly of me. He was prepared to offer me the job, he said. The salary was £19 a week, and it would be on a three-months trial period.

"I'll give you a week to think about it. Go home and discuss it with your wife," said Mr. Fenna. "Then I must have a definite decision from you."

I couldn't believe my luck. I sought out Des Jones, who I didn't really know very well, but thanked him for his recommendation and help.

But when I got home and discussed it with Betty, I was still rather hoping the Daily Express would come back to me with a job offer. I'd heard nothing at all from them.

Faced with the deadline from the Mirror, I left it a couple of days and then made a phone call to the Northern Editor's office at the Daily Express,

587

and asked them if any decision had been made about taking on staff following the recent interviews. I hinted that I might have another job offer. Without any hesitation, I was told very nicely but firmly that they could not guarantee any new jobs at all, and that if I had another offer, then I should take it.

That was it. The decision was made for me. I phoned Ted Fenna and accepted his job offer. I was now the new Northern TV Critic of the Daily Mirror. "Can you start next Monday?" he said.

"We'll have to buy a TV set," I said to Betty. "I think I'm going to need it."

CHAPTER 48: MOVING TO MANCHESTER

When I landed the job with the Daily Mirror, it meant a very hectic first few months. Betty was pregnant and had only about two months to go, so we decided it would be best for her to stay in Liverpool and give birth at home. With only a week's notice to starting my new job, I had to frantically find accommodation of some sort in Manchester. And I ended up having digs in the suburb of Chorlton-cum-Hardy, with a bed-and-breakfast arrangement in a little semi-detached. The trouble was - and I didn't know this until I'd moved in - the woman owner had a couple of cats. And I hate cats. And she was also not too clean in other ways. When she offered me a couple of boiled eggs for breakfast every day, I happily accepted. But then after a while discovered she was not very thorough with the washing-up and found myself being given egg-stained cutlery, which put me off the whole place.

Fortunately, I didn't stay there too long. I was there Monday to Friday, and then went back to Liverpool at weekends.

Betty gave birth to our second baby, on December 3, 1958, at home. And, fortunately, she had not only her mother there to help out, but also sister Irene, who was a fully-trained midwife. Again, no complications with the new arrival. This time a boy, with the name we had already decided upon - Mark.

Domestically, everything was looking rosy. But we had to quickly sort out what we were going to do about moving house.

The job of being a TV critic, I found, was not too taxing – but my very first night on duty was a real baptism of fire. I had been told to report for work at 2 pm, when my regular hours would be from 2 to around 10 pm every day. I was taking over from a chap called Bob Stoker, who had been the Mirror's Northern TV correspondent for about three years.

He was an amiable enough bloke, well into middle age, going bald and with a pencil-thin moustache which made him look like the spiv character played by old-time comedian Arthur English.

He showed me my new office, which was a small room with a desk, a chair and a TV set, and which we shared with the office lawyer, who had his own desk and filing cabinet in the corner, which I found a very odd arrangement. But apparently there was a lack of individual offices on the two floors which the Mirror occupied in the Withy Grove building.

Within the first hour of meeting him, the chatty Bob Stoker had given me almost his entire working history. He was a born and bred Geordie, had been deputy chief sub editor on the Sunderland Echo for three years, then moved to Manchester, was in charge of features on the Daily Dispatch, and had written a novel called Unfinished Symphony, before joining the Mirror.

Now, he was going back to his roots and joining Tyne Tees TV in Newcastle on the editorial staff of the programme magazine The Viewer. He was quick to point out that he had appeared on TV quite a lot and had also been on the BBC's What Makes A Star? radio programme dozens of times. And he was now hoping to make some appearances on Tyne Tees. He was clearly trying to impress me.

The plan was that I should sit in with Bob for his last week, before he left, so that he could show me how the job was done and exactly what was expected of me. This seemed reasonable enough. But after about an hour in the office, he looked at his watch and said to me, "Let's go and have a drink. There's a little place across the road we use."

We put on our coats and he took me across the road and into a club in a back street near Victoria Station. It was a rather seedy, run-down place, a private drinking club, and he was obviously a regular there. He introduced me to the owner behind the bar and several other drinkers. "You're supposed to sign in because it's a private members club. But you've no need to bother with all that stuff in future. Now they know you're a friend of mine and you work for the Mirror, you'll be okay here," he said. "What will you have?"

He was drinking Guinness. "I'll have a lager," I said. And before I could say Bob Stoker, a pint was put in front of me.

This went on for some time. It was all very friendly. The barman wanted to know where I'd come from, what my background was, and Bob regaled everyone with show business stories and jokes, most of which I'm sure they had all heard many times before.

The pints were being consumed at a rapid rate, and as I was not much of a drinker I began to look anxiously at my watch, wondering how long this was all going to last.

"Oh, don't worry about the time," Bob kept reassuring me. "There's no hurry to get back to the office. Let's have another. Lager okay? Or do you fancy going on to shorts?"

At about 7 o'clock, I really was getting a little worried. We'd now been drinking for about three hours, and although I didn't want to admit it, I was becoming a little drunk. "Hadn't we better get back?" I finally feebly suggested. My new colleague reluctantly relented, we collected our overcoats and returned to the office. Or staggered, in my case.

Once back in our little office, I was not only relieved to sit down but was also anxious to see exactly how Mr. Stoker got down to the job.

He switched on the TV set and then said, "Right, what are we going to write about tonight? Let's see what's on." Then he turned to me and said, "It's up to you. You can choose whatever programmes you want, there's no restriction. You just type out your crit, no more than 500 words, and deliver the copy to the Features subs. The deadline is 10 o'clock. Make sure it's in before then, or they'll go mad."

Then, to my horror, I realised that he was expecting me to write that night's column. "I'll leave you to it," he said. "I'm going to have a couple more on the way home. I'll see you tomorrow." And off he went, waving me goodnight.

For a few minutes, I just sat there, trying to take it all in. I was by now well and truly drunk. Not falling-over drunk, but certainly my-vision-is-impaired-and-I've-got-a-bit-of-a-headache drunk. I'd lost count of how many pints we'd consumed. Maybe I was being naive, but I was horrified that I should now have to sit down and write a sensible column for the paper in the state I was in. I honestly thought that Bob Stoker would be writing that night's column. At no point did he even warn me that the column was now my responsibility, and not his.

It was stupid of me, of course. I should never have gone out drinking with him, particularly on my very first day on the job. But I also thought that it was a dirty, and probably deliberate trick of Mr. Stoker's to suddenly land me in trouble. Or maybe he simply assumed I was a seasoned drinker, like him.

In the circumstances, I was lucky. As I sat there, wondering what to do, the first programme I watched was an edition of This Your Life, with Eamonn Andrews presenting the big red book to an up-and-coming rock n roll star called Tommy Steele. It was a terrific show, and I hurriedly bashed out a piece, no more than 500 words, which I hoped made sense.

Eventually, with some trepidation, I delivered my first TV crit to the subs. Eric Smith, the tall, elderly chief sub, took my copy from me, quickly read through it, and gave me a smile. I was so nervous that I didn't know what he was thinking. He must have smelled the alcohol on my breath, but was discreet enough not to mention it, or else accepted it as all part of the job.

When I checked with him later, before going home, he assured me that everything was fine.

Next morning, I picked up the Daily Mirror. There was my very first column in print. "Last Night's TV by Ken Irwin." It read quite well and all made sense. More by good fortune than anything else, I thought.

I went back into the office at 2 o'clock. Never would I ever get into that state of intoxication again, I decided. How could I have allowed myself to get drunk on my very first day in the job? I could have blown the whole thing. Crazy. Stupid. What a fool I was.

Fortunately, I didn't see much of Bob Stoker. He worked out the rest of his final week, popping his head briefly into the office each day, picking up his expenses, and then swanning off to his little drinking club to tell his jokes.

At the end of the week, he threw a farewell party for his Mirror pals, and then departed back to Tyneside. I don't think I ever saw him again. To be honest, I didn't particularly like him. There was only one thing I had to thank him for. His leaving had created a vacancy, and I now had a new job on a national paper. I was determined to make the most of it.

The first priority was to move Betty and the family to Manchester. I was fed up with living in digs, putting up with the smell of cats and egg-stained crockery, and travelling up and down by train from Liverpool to Manchester every weekend.   And once I had settled into the job, Betty was as keen as I was to make the break from Liverpool to start a new life together. We were still living on a tight budget, with very little savings in the bank. Could we afford to buy a new house, or would we have to find one to rent?

House-hunting was top of our list. This was made more difficult because we didn't have a car. I'd not even learned to drive yet, so we were dependent on public transport. We weren't sure which part of Manchester we wanted to live in, North or South. I then spotted an advert in the Houses for Sale pages of the local paper. It was for a brand-new semi-detached, part of a new build, in Woodley, about ten miles outside of Manchester, not far from Stockport. It was quite cheap and was described as one of a pair of semi-detached three-bedroomed houses being built on a site overlooking lovely countryside but with good transport links to Manchester.

There was something about it which appealed to me. When I went and looked at the location, I fell in love with it. It was in a higgledy-piggledy old road called Poleacre Lane, which was a mixture of ancient old terraced cottages at one end, and a group of more modern houses the other end, with a small farm in the middle. The plot on which the new pair of semis

592

was being built was opposite the farm, behind a high hedge, and at the back had a panorama of open countryside for a couple of miles.

The builder was an Irishman called Mr. Flaherty, who seemed very friendly and pointed out that he planned to build one detached house, next door to the pair of semis, on a little corner plot, which he intended to live in himself.

It all sounded too good to be true. The cost of the brand-new semi was only £1,950. Betty and I quickly did our sums, I applied to a building society for a mortgage, but the best I could get was a 90 per-cent mortgage over 25 years. This meant I had to find a 10 per-cent deposit. Unfortunately, we didn't have that much money in the bank. We only had enough to raise five per-cent. However, when I told Mr. Flaherty the jovial Irishman this, he came up with a ready-made solution. He was prepared to take only five per-cent deposit and arrange the other five per-cent as a personal loan on condition I paid him back over a 12-month period.

It was an extremely generous offer. Was there a catch in it somewhere? Was the new house going to be a Gerry-built affair which I'd regret? Surely not, if the builder himself was going to be living right next door in his detached mansion?

We decided to go for it. I arranged a mortgage with the building society, Mr. Flaherty drew up a private agreement for me to pay him £10 a month for a year, with a little receipt book he handed to me, and the deal was settled. We were ready to move in. The trouble was the house wasn't quite finished. Mr. Flaherty's labourers were still working on it.

But he gave us a completion date of a month or so, and I anxiously went over to Woodley every few days to see how the building was coming on.

Eventually, we were told it was finished. We could pick up the keys and move in as soon as we wanted.

Betty and I couldn't wait to inspect it. We finally took a train to Woodley, with the keys. And there was our new house. Pristine, red bricks, traditional style semi-detached, with a short path leading from the road to the front door. But we were a bit surprised to find that the house, which was built on the side of a hill, had only a 3ft wide single concrete pathway around the house from the front door to the back. And there was a drop of some 20 feet or more from the back door on to the field below, which was supposed to be our back garden.

Somewhat alarmed, when I called Mr. Flaherty and asked him to explain this, he came over to the house and pointed out that the builders were only responsible for providing the front garden and the narrow path around the house. The back garden, which would stretch for some 70 yards or more, was left for me develop however I wished.

When I pointed out that there was a steep drop of 20 feet between my back door and the field below, he looked at me, smiled and said, "Well, that's for you to decide what you want to do with it."

He said that his men would erect a wire fence onto poles marking my boundary from the field beyond. But that would be the completion of our house, as far as he was concerned.

It was only then that I fully realised how naïve I had been. When we were told originally that the house would have a back garden stretching some 70 yards, I had assumed that we would be able to walk out into the garden. Silly me! Instead, we had a piece of land which stretched for 70 yards, but there was no way of accessing it because it was all just fresh air.

When I asked Mr. Flaherty what I could do about this, he immediately saw my dilemma. "Well, what I'm going to do next door, with my house," he said, "is build a solid stone retaining wall at the end of my garden, and fill it with tons of landfill material and top soil, bringing it to the level of my back door. Why don't you do the same?"

He knew of course that this was a big job, far too much for me to tackle alone. So I sat down, drew a map of what I wanted to do with the back garden. Then I agreed, at a price, for his men to build me a stone retaining wall, and fill in with some top soil, so that I could create a rockery which sloped down to my part of the field.

It all cost me a lot of extra money, of course. I soon found out I could save money by doing some jobs myself. So, after they'd built me the extra stone wall, I then laboriously carved out a set of steps and put paving stones down to the level of the garden.

In the end I built a small patio from the back kitchen door, with a wall around it, a steep rockery filled with various plants and shrubs, and a set of steps down to a play area for the children, and even a small vegetable plot at the end.

No one was more surprised than I was at how good I became and how quickly you can adapt to becoming a builder, labourer and gardener when you have no money but only your own two hands to finish the job.

We lived there for some years. The back garden became quite an added attraction to the house. The field beyond our garden was owned by the local farmer, who used it to graze his cattle and sheep. So when you looked out of the windows from our kitchen, living-room or rear bedroom, all you could see, as well as the lazy cattle, was a wild meadow running down to a distant railway line. It was idyllic.

There was only one problem. Rabbits. No matter how thick the wire netting was at the end of our garden, it was impossible to grow vegetables. The local rabbits quickly regarded it as their own free food bank and I grew tired of feeding them. It was easier to put up a swing and give the kids a bigger play area, and forget the vegetables.

Once I'd solved the problem of our somewhat strange elevated back garden, there was one other dilemma we had to face which concerned our friendly neighbour Mr. Flaherty.

When he had built and completed his own house next door, it turned out to be a rather splendid Derbyshire stone detached pile. God knows what it must have cost him. At least three times the price of our little semi, I'd guess. The house included a large built-in garage on the far side, away from us. Which was something he needed, because although Mr. Flaherty himself was quite a small man, about 5ft 5ins tall, he drove a very large car, the biggest and most splendid Jaguar on the market, a Mark 10 saloon.

But when it came to this side of his house, the distance between his house and ours was only 10 feet. And according to the Deeds and Land Registry, eight feet belonged to me, and only two feet to him.

I don't know whether he had miscalculated this when he was building it. Or maybe he was simply using an Irish tape measure. But the result was that when I decided to widen my side path, from the mere three-feet he'd concreted for me in the original sale, it meant that I could extend my path to 8 ft. But this would leave my neighbour with only 2ft. And when I started work extending the width from my single path into a double drive, in anticipation of buying a car and having a garage erected on the back, I told him I was planning to put a fence up between our two houses.

Obviously, this would mean his 2ft path would be too narrow to even get his dustbin from the back of his house to the front. It was clearly a problem he had to face.

The man had built himself a beautiful house but it was at least two or three feet too close to my property. I held all the cards. There was nothing nasty about it. I wasn't trying to blackmail him or anything. But in the end he came to me and asked if I would agree to a compromise by not erecting a fence and having a shared drive. At least so that he could get his bins from the back to the front.

As a token of friendship and appreciation, I finally agreed with his suggestion. Though what would happen in future years, when I moved on, and a new owner would maybe not want to share their drive, that would be a matter for him to sort out.

Just to prove my newly developed building skills, I then set about laying my double drive, had tons of earth and landfill delivered, and prepared a concert surface suitable for a 16ft x 8ft asphalt garage to be erected. It finished up as a splendid addition to the house, and I was very proud of my own handiwork. Now all the garage needed was a vehicle to go in it. But that's another story.

I knew nothing about cars, except that I needed one, and I'd been fascinated with the various makes and models, ever since I was a kid of 13 who once spent the whole of four hours on board a boat to the Isle of Man on holiday sitting staring at a beautiful Jowett Javelin saloon parked on the boat deck. That became the car I secretly yearned for, but by the time I could afford one, they'd stopped making them.

First, I had to learn to drive. I was 23 and it was about time I got behind the wheel, so I booked myself a batch of 12 lessons with the British School of Motoring.   And with great trepidation, set forth to conquer the highways of Britain with a few nervous stop-start drives through the back streets of Manchester.

Even before I'd passed my test, I decided I had enough in the bank to buy my first car, so I asked my Uncle Billy to come with me. He knew all about cars, I thought. After all, her had a lovely big Ford Zodiac so he was bound to be an expert.

We met in Liverpool, and we went together to a car sales room in Prescot Road, West Derby, walked in and then inspected a dozen or so cars, all brightly polished and gleaming in the showroom. One that caught my eye was a green Hillman Minx. It was in beautiful condition, its chrome bumpers sparkling in the late afternoon sunshine. The price was about right. I fell in love with it immediately.

I sat in the driver's seat and admired the soft leather upholstery. It was unmarked and almost like new.

When the salesman came over, he asked if he could help. Would we like to see under the bonnet? he asked. Oh yes, insisted Uncle Billy. We must have the bonnet up. So the salesman released the catch on the bonnet, and for a full five minutes Billy and I stared ponderously at the engine and all its intricacies. To me, it was just an engine. But I'm sure to Uncle Billy it was something much more. He would know all the technicalities involved. Bound to.

He didn't touch anything however, but then went back to the driver's seat and banged on the horn. As the noise echoed around the showroom, Billy pronounced, "Nice horn, Ken."

That was it. We counted the four wheels, looked in the boot, made sure it had a spare wheel. "I think it's a bargain, Ken. I think you should buy it," said Billy. At the end of our session, I wasn't so sure whether Uncle Bill really knew any more about cars than I did. But he was right, it did have a lovely sounding horn.

The salesman didn't have to bother with any of the hard sales pitch, I'd already made up my mind. The price was £350. I signed the sales document and an HP agreement, paid over the necessary deposit, took possession of the car keys, and shook hands on the deal, before driving off, with Billy at the steering wheel, all the way to Manchester.

Billy stayed with us overnight, and we agreed that next morning he would take me out on a driving lesson in my new car. What an experience that proved to be.

It was a Sunday morning, after breakfast, about 10 am, and Billy suggested we set off on my first drive. Billy had carefully parked the car overnight in my brand-new garage, which on reflection was a mistake, because we now had to reverse it out on the drive and onto the road.

It was a tricky manoeuvre and it would have been far easier for Billy, with his experience, to drive the car out in reverse and put it at the kerbside.

Instead, he seemed keen to know just how good a driver I already was, and instructed me to get behind the wheel and put it in reverse, while he guided me from behind the vehicle. "Okay, come on. Straighten up. Come on, straight back. A bit to the left," whilst waving his arms around.

It all went well, but it was quite a long driveway and as I came to the gateposts, with the wrought iron gates both fully open, Billy instructed me, "Now turn the wheel, slowly. Slowly. Come on." I was almost through the gates when, unfortunately, I turned just a fraction too soon, and the front bumper caught on to one of the gates. And as I was still reversing, ever so slowly, I was horrified to see the gate come crashing out of the mortar in the stone built gatepost. It was dragged off its hinges and ended up on the bonnet of the car, with a loud wrenching noise.

When I slammed my foot on the brake, the car came to a halt. I got out and looked at the damage. Billy said nothing, but slowly removed the iron gate from off the car. He then placed the gate on to the front lawn, got into the car's passenger seat and said, "Don't worry. You've just had your first accident. Let's go for a run."

Whilst having to admire his coolness, my nerves were now shattered. Betty came dashing out of the house to see what had happened. And unfortunately my next door neighbour, Mr. Smith, who was mowing his front lawn, was a witness to the whole dreadful thing, and I was convinced was trying not to laugh. I was completely mortified. The last thing I wanted to do was casually go off for a drive. I felt so stupid and embarrassed.

Billy insisted however, "Just forget it. Let's go. You'll be all right when you get on to the open road." I didn't feel all right. I was now shaking with nerves. But eventually I drove off, very slowly, after making sure that the L-plate was still firmly in place and on display on the front bumper. Mr. Smith just smiled benevolently. But I felt sure that, inside, he was enjoying my erratic driving antics and was probably already wondering what I'd do for a party trick on the way back.

Fortunately, we managed to get through the rest of the morning without further mishap. After cruising around at no more than 20 miles an hour for a short while, I returned home with the car still in one piece.

We examined the damage. There was only the slightest of scratches on the car but the bumper was bent and twisted a little and would need mending. And of course the front gate would have to be re-cemented into the gate-post.

Billy calmly tried to reassure me that I'd make a good driver one day and told me not to worry, before going back home on the train to Wirral. That's what I liked about Uncle Billy. He was a cool customer who was also very wise and helpful. I mean, after all, he'd spotted that my new car had such a wonderful horn.

Within a few weeks, I got around to fixing the front gate and cemented it back into the gatepost.

Ironically, when I happened to go and look at that little house in Poleacre Lane, only a couple of years ago, I saw that it still had the same little stone front wall which I built with my own hands some 55 years ago. And the same pair of wrought iron gates, though they were looking a bit tired now and in need of a new coat of paint.

I passed my driving test in Manchester at the first attempt a few months after that nasty little encounter with the gatepost.   But I must confess that I was a very naughty boy during the build-up to taking the test. For whilst I was taking professional driving lessons, I still required a lot of practise sessions in between. My problem was that I didn't have anyone I knew as a qualified driver to sit in with me. So I'm afraid I occasionally decided to get extra driving experience simply by taking the L-plates off and driving to and from the office on my own. It was strictly illegal, of course, and not to be recommended. But on the day my test was due, I was quite a competent driver. I had one final lesson with the BSM instructor who seemed confident that I would pass. And when I returned from my test drive, the examiner gave me a smile, said I was now a fully qualified driver and shook hands. I walked around the corner, took off the L-plates and drove in to the office to start work. It was a great feeling.

That green Hillman Minx was my pride and joy. It put an end to all public transport as far as I was concerned. From then on, we could enjoy family outings all over the place. Betty loved it, and the kids too.

But the little Minx let me down. One day, we decided to go for a day out to North Wales and take Betty's mother with us. It was her first time in my car, and she was looking forward to it. So I gave it a good polish, we packed a picnic lunch, and off we went.

They call it Sod's Law, don't they, but it happened to me that day. Within an hour of being out on the road, we were driving up a rather steep hill, when the car began to shudder. There was a hissing noise, a bang and a clump, and we came to a standstill. I tried desperately to hit the accelerator, but there was no response. So I put the handbrake firmly on, got out and put up the bonnet lid, and looked fiercely at the engine as though I knew what I was doing.

It was no good. I tried a few more times to start it, but there was no reaction. The engine had died.

I had no idea where we were. We were on the side of the road, halfway up a steep hill in North Wales. Betty began to look concerned. Mrs. Bagot just sat there on the back seat, unimpressed with the car and with my attempts to re-start it. God, what had I ever done to deserve this?

It ended with me having to tramp down the hill, locate exactly what road we were on, and find the nearest telephone box so I could phone the AA. Fortunately, I was a member of the Automobile Association, but this was the first time I'd needed them.

Eventually, an AA patrol man arrived on the scene, put his head under the bonnet, got out his magic box of tools, and after a short while found and fixed the problem. "You should be okay for now," he said, "but I wouldn't drive too far in it today. Best get it home and into a garage to have it fully checked over."

"What was wrong with it?" asked Betty. It was no good asking me that, was it? All I knew was that the damn car had a very nice horn.

The kids ate all their sandwiches and we drove back home. It would be a long time before I'd risk taking my mother-in-law for a drive again.

The next big event in our lives came with another addition to the family. Betty was pregnant again. I blamed that bloody manual Betty had bought before we'd got married. Or maybe we were just practising too much.

The result was she gave birth in Stepping Hill Hospital, Stockport, on October 13, 1960. Another little boy. With a chubby face and a shock of fair curly hair. We called him Paul. Well, Paul Wesley, actually.

We both liked the name Paul. But I also liked the name Wesley. It had a certain ring to it. Betty went along with it because she approved of him being named after the Methodist founder John Wesley.

Paul, on the other hand, grew up thinking he was named after a West Indian cricketer, Wes Hall, and hated it. Still does.

Either way, we decided that three children in four years was enough. We'd better do something about it. Either I'd have to tie a knot in it, or we'd have to take urgent contraceptive action. Betty lost out. I was never very good at tying knots. Even when I was in the Boy Scouts.

Our family was now complete. Three lovely, healthy, adorable kids were all a man could ask for. Now we could get on with enjoying life.

There's a funny story I can recall which concerned our niece Pauline Hughes, daughter of Betty's sister Nancy, who lived in Wallasey.

Shortly after Paul was born, Pauline came over to stay with us at Woodley for a few days. She was keen to see Betty and help out, especially with baby-sitting and fussing over the new infant. It was lovely to have her there and we encouraged her to stay as long as she liked while she was on holiday from school.

Pauline was then 15 years old and an attractive young thing. But what we hadn't accounted for was the boy next door. Mr. Flaherty, our Irish building contractor, had a handsome young son who was two or three years older than Pauline. And they soon spotted each other across the fence that I didn't put up.

Before long, the two teenagers were chatting to each other. No harm in that, of course. But we then learned from Pauline that Mr. Flaherty was away for the week and the boy was looking after himself in the house.

At first, we thought nothing of it. But then Pauline came to us and told Betty she'd been invited over for the evening next door. Was it all right if she went? Of course, we said yes. She was a big girl, not a child, but we both had slight reservations.

This happened a couple of times. The lad next door was a nice enough bloke, but it soon became obvious that he fancied Pauline and couldn't get enough of her company.

On the second night, when Pauline told us she has been invited over again for the evening, Betty and I both voiced our concerns about whether it was a good idea or not. But she assured us that he was a very nice chap, they could have a few laughs together, and she would be perfectly all right.

She went, but we told her not to be too late, suggesting she be back with us well before ten o'clock.

We then spent the whole evening looking at the clock. I became more anxious as the hours ticked by. What would they be up to?   Probably just playing records and having some laughs together.   But you never know. She was only 15, and it didn't help when Betty suddenly suggested that she didn't think Nancy would have approved.

That was it. By ten o'clock we were pacing up and down. I told Betty to go and knock next door and bring Pauline home.

Pauline came back, giggling. She said she'd had a great time. We packed her off to bed.

A few days later, I took Pauline back home to Wallasey. She told me she'd enjoyed herself on her week's holiday, and would love to come over to stay with us again some time. Yes, I thought, but not too soon!

What she got up to with the young Master Flaherty only she will ever know. But as far as I was concerned, it was a premature lesson for me in fatherhood. The whole incident had taught me one thing - I'd better be prepared for the time when my own daughter would be reaching puberty.

The next thing to do was buy a new car. I had outgrown the old Hillman, so traded it in and swapped it for a lovely Singer Gazelle. A really sleek saloon. Two toned in green with a wide white stripe along either side. It was a remarkably sexy car to look at, and I kept it for a couple of years, until I could afford my very first brand-new car, which was a powder blue Morris 1100. Pristine in every way. And I started wearing bow ties to look like the bees' knees when I was out in it.

Once I'd established myself at the Mirror, I found the job rather easy. As well as just being the TV critic, I had to attend Press conferences at the BBC, do news stories on all broadcasting matters, and cover events at the ever-growing Granada TV company.

On December 2, 1960, Granada launched their new domestic drama series Coronation Street. It had been kept under wraps for a while and the scriptwriter Tony Warren had originally called it Florizel Street. But when one of the studio workers suggested it sounded like a lavatory cleaner, the producers quickly changed the title.

The first programme was aired on a Friday night and it was scheduled to be screened twice a week for a run of three months.

I found it a dreary, dark and dismal piece of drama, without much humour. And made the mistake of saying so.

My first crit in the Daily Mirror on the new show read: "Young Tony Warren claims to have spent a couple of months going around meeting the ordinary people of the North before he wrote the first episode of Granada's serial Coronation Street. Frankly, I can't believe it. If he did, he certainly spent his time with the wrong folk. For there is little reality in his new serial, which, apparently, we will have to suffer twice a week. The programme is doomed from the outset - with its dreary signature tune and grim scene of a row of terraced houses and smoking chimneys."

That short pithy critique has now gone down in television history, and I was saddled for life with being the TV critic who didn't know what he was talking about. Because of course the programme is still running today, after more than 55 years.

My clanger has since gone down in the Guinness Book of Records. And it's now one of those questions which still comes up occasionally on various quiz shows: Who was the critic who said Coronation Street would never last?

Mind you, if anyone had suggested, after those first few dreary episodes in 1960, that Coronation Street would still be on the screen 50 years later, they would have sent for the men in white coats to take you away.

Pat Phoenix, who played Elsie Tanner, used to laugh about it. Every year, for quite a few years, she'd send me a card at the Mirror on the anniversary of the programme, saying, "Remember that crit, Ken? Well, we're still here!"

It doesn't haunt me anymore. I've laughed it off a long time ago. And I quickly found that there was life after Coronation Street.

I then took up playing golf. As I didn't have to go into the office until 2pm every day, I was introduced to the game by Warwick Bedford, a freelance photographer who, with his father Harry, worked for the TV Times in Manchester. He was a smashing bloke, we became great pals, and he took me to the New Mills golf club in Derbyshire, a tough nine-hole course only a few miles from where I lived in Woodley.

On quiet days, when there were no Press conferences on, I would be out on the golf course by 10 am, sometimes with Warwick, but most days on my own. I'd have a couple of rounds, hacking away with my bag full of Sam Snead clubs, trying to improve my technique. Lunch would be a pie and a pint in the pleasant little club house, before driving in to the office mid- afternoon. I was so keen, that I even took up regular golf lessons from the club's professional coach.

It was wonderful just being out in the fresh air on those glorious hills of New Mills. It wasn't one of those snobby, posh golf clubs. I would never have joined anything like that. The membership here was made up of local farmers, policemen and such. And the only hard and fast rule was: No wearing studded golf shoes in the bar.

After a few years on the Mirror, I liked the job but found it not very demanding, so started looking around for other things to do. I was always interested in sport, and in my earlier days in Liverpool had covered football and boxing for the local papers.

Now, with nothing to do at weekends, I got my foot in the door at the BBC and applied to be a football correspondent. After an audition, they took me on in Manchester as a soccer reporter and invited me to do a match every Saturday for radio.

It was something I really enjoyed, even though I found it a bit hairy at times. Going off to cover matches around the North, and then tuning in to give a two or three-minute report from the Press Box on the telephone. It was all "live" of course, and sometimes you didn't have time to write notes, and had to be prepared to do spontaneous reports ad-lib.

They said I knew my stuff and had a good voice for radio and encouraged me to do more. Then, in the summer, when the football season finished, the BBC asked me if I could handle being anchor-man in the studio on their live broadcast which ran throughout the afternoon.

This meant sitting at the big studio desk in front of a microphone, editing and reading out snippets from various sports, and then bringing in outside correspondents on the phone with their reports.

It was a frantic affair, but once I got used to being on the air live, I found the adrenalin flowed and it was all very exhilarating.

Unfortunately, it all came to an end one day when my Northern Editor Ted Fenna called me into his office, closed the door, and asked me bluntly, "Do you want to work for the BBC or the Daily Mirror?"

When I pointed out to him that I was only doing the sports reports for the BBC on Saturdays in my spare time, he said it didn't matter. He'd heard me on the radio, and I was quite good, but thought I might be getting too close to the BBC, and as a TV critic he thought this might lead to a clash of interests. "It's up to you to decide," he said. "Go away and think about it."

He tried not to make it sound like an ultimatum, but that's what it was. I could see his point. So I quickly had to decide what to do. It was a no-contest decision really. The BBC was one day a week, and they were paying me something like seven guineas a game to cover a football match, and a little more as the anchor-man presenter of the Saturday sporting scene programme. The Mirror was my full-time job. I had no hesitation in deciding. I reluctantly told the BBC I couldn't work for them anymore, and they released me from my contract with the summer season sports show, and said they were sorry to lose me.

That was the end of my budding BBC sports career. It was back to watching telly for a living.

Round about the same time, I also started doing some TV shows for ABC Television in the North. They invited me to appear on a series called Personal Opinion, in which I had to write and perform a five-minute programme, talking direct to camera, each week. I could choose any subject to talk about, as long as it was entertaining and preferably also amusing.

This time, there was no problem with my office. The Editor didn't mind me doing these programmes, because it meant there was a regular free plug for the paper - on screen it was announced as "Personal Opinion by Ken Irwin of the Daily Mirror."

Then came the occasional appearance on TV as a judge in bathing beauty contests, which became amazingly popular as light entertainment in the 1960s and 70s.

All things considered, I was doing okay. Enjoying the job, but still feeling the need to do more. I was never really satisfied until I was fully stretched.

Despite the warning from the Editor, I simply felt I was capable of doing so much more.

So, in my spare time, I started to diversify. First, I wrote a full-length 60-minute play for radio, which I sent to the BBC under the name of Mark Irwin. It was called A Matter of Policy, and I was cock-a-hoop when they sent me a letter saying they liked it and wanted to produce it in their prestigious Afternoon Theatre slot.

The play, was broadcast on Saturday, May 18, 1963 on the BBC Home Service. I was rather chuffed at the idea of having my first play on the radio, and I made sure my Mum was tuned in. She loved listening to all the radio plays. She told me later how much she'd enjoyed it.

Then I tried my hand at writing comedy scripts and sending them off to one or two comedians to get their reaction. One was a sketch I dreamed up which I thought was quite funny, so sent it to Michael Bentine, the ex-Goon who then had his own whacky series called Square World on BBC TV.

To my surprise, the phone went at 8 o'clock one morning at home. It was Michael Bentine, saying, "I've got this script of yours. I like it very much and would like to use it. How much do you want for it?"

A little taken aback, I hesitated. He said, "I usually pay £25 a minute. This sketch runs for about three minutes, so I'll give you £75 for it. Is that okay?"

Yes, of course, I said. He used the sketch in his TV show the following week and I duly received a cheque from him. That was long before I ever met Michael Bentine, and he didn't know who I was.

Obviously, this encouraged me to write some more comedy. And for a while I was on cloud nine.

CHAPTER 49: BREAKING UP IS HARD TO DO

There weren't enough hours in the day as far as I was concerned. I worked for six years on the Mirror in Manchester, learning my trade and improving my skills as an interviewer as well as a reporter and feature writer.

There was a great drinking culture in newspapers at that time, and it was difficult not to be part of it.

Ted Fenna left (he retired, I think, to live in North Wales) and the new Northern Editor was a much younger man called Bernard Shrimsley, who came from the Daily Express. He was bubbling with fresh ideas, was energetic and obviously very ambitious, and he encouraged the staff to follow his example.

The first thing he did with me was walk into my little office one day and say, "I'd like you to start writing more features. I want much more television and show business in the paper. You produce the copy, and I'll get you much more space in the paper." It was a challenge I couldn't resist.

He even came up with one or two big-name showbiz stars he suggested I should pursue. One was Clifford Richard, an up and coming rock n roll star, and I managed to set him up for an interview and some exclusive pictures on Blackpool beach. Shrimsley loved it, and I found myself with my first double-page centre spread, which also went in the London editions.

Until then, the Mirror had always had quite separate editions, with Manchester office producing stories from the North, and the London office being responsible for the bulk of the paper from the South. It was very much a "them and us" situation.

Suddenly, Shrimsley changed all that. He was determined to get more stuff into the main London editions.

He then came to me and said, "I think you're wasted as a TV critic. I want you to do more feature writing. Forget about the nightly TV column."

I couldn't have been happier. This got me off the nightly treadmill of having to write a Northern crit. Instead, he arranged for us to print our London criticism column, to give me more time, working all day on features.

This worked fine. For some months I was spending more time out and about, doing interviews, producing some lively features and getting more in the London editions than I'd ever done before.

Then suddenly, for no apparent reason, Shrimsley told me that he wanted me to go back to writing our own Northern TV crit. He wasn't very impressed with the copy coming up from London each night, or so he said, and he wanted to revert back to the old system of working.

Naturally, I was disappointed. But there was nothing I could do about it. I was back as the TV critic. But I was still grateful to him. It had opened up new opportunities for me and I was now better known in London, and still doing some features as well as news stories.

It was about this time that the Beatles suddenly emerged, the new Mersey beat sound was born, and I became heavily involved in producing all the early stories on the Fab Four, Paul, John, George and Ringo. As well, of course, a Brian Epstein's string of other pop stars, Gerry and the Pacemakers, Billy J. Kramer, and Cilla Black.

Brian Epstein became very friendly with me after I gave him all his early national publicity, and he would ring me up with stories on all his up-and-coming artists.

My friendship and association with Epstein came to an abrupt end, however. (See Chapter 1 – The Beatles).

It wasn't long before Bernard Shrimsley left and moved to London. He was far too ambitious to hang around for long, and having come in and given the Manchester office a hefty kick up the backside, he now had bigger fish to fry. Destined for higher things, he became an assistant editor in the London office, having used Manchester as a giant stepping-stone.

In his place as Northern Editor came Derek Webster. He was a small, quiet, middle-aged, rather reserved and polite chap, far less flamboyant than Shrimsley.

As far as I was concerned, he was fine. He seemed to be happy with my output and let me get on with it, without any interference.

In fact, I had complete freedom to do more or less what I liked. With more time on my hands, I found myself getting involved in various freelance activities. I was constantly trying to find new ways of earning more money, on top of my Mirror salary, and the easiest and most lucrative solution to this was by producing features for TV programme magazines and provincial papers, who were always on the look-out for new material.

I had to be careful, of course. I didn't want to upset the Mirror or jeopardise my job in any way, but I knew there was also a freelance market out there, and I was determined to exploit it.

Then I began to dabble even further in show business circles and set myself up as a publicity agent, doing private publicity - and even personal management - for a number of Northern artists. These included singers Pat O'Hare, Julie Jones, Alberta Lane, and comedy-impressionist Peter Goodwright, as well as some up-and-coming pop groups. They didn't pay me much, but it helped me get what I regarded as valuable experience in that side of show business.

There was no stopping me now. I had my fingers into every new pie I could find. It wasn't just a matter of making more money, I simply felt that I had the potential to do more, and I hated wasting time.

Consequently, it came to the stage where I was working around the clock. I was going into the Mirror every day, covering whatever had to be done, flitting around with my various enterprises, doing the TV crits before leaving the office at 10 pm, then going home and working well into the night on the typewriter, bashing out freelance articles and still trying to do comedy scripts.

In the end, cracks began to appear in our home life. It was inevitable, I suppose. I was doing too much. Trying to prove I was a literary superman. Meanwhile Betty was just busy as a housewife, bringing up the children, which was more than a full-time job. She seemed quite content and although she was interested in a vague way in my career, she had no real ambitions. The result was that we were slowly growing apart.

It didn't help that I was now embroiled in show business, surrounded by glamorous people. There were obvious temptations, and it came to the stage where I began to think that maybe marriage was stifling my ambitions, that I could do much better in life. Sex reared its ugly head and I began to question my marriage.

Why was it so important that everyone should meet just one person and then spend the rest of their lives together? Was sex outside of marriage such a big sin? Why couldn't people go through life having new experiences without ruining what we already had? Was divorce and re-marriage such a big deal, anyway? And why was marriage necessary at all in order to have sex?

All these things were buzzing around in my brain. I still loved Betty very much, and the children were mine forever. Yet all the signs were there. We had been married for seven years and I somehow convinced myself that there was such a thing as the dreaded Seven Year Itch, the time when couples parted and found new partners. Or, less restricting, didn't bother with new partners at all, but just got on with life and whatever it threw at them.

I was flattered when other women showed an interest in me. And there were sudden offers there for the taking, if I had wished. It wasn't Betty's fault. But we began to row more and more at home. There were occasional screaming matches. Our domestic life became humdrum and boring. And it came to the stage, finally, where we had to sit down and discuss what we were going to do about it. Was our marriage over? Had we both had enough? Would a break-up affect the kids? How could we financially sort things out?

We tried to be reasonable with each other, to face the truth. I decided that I now wanted to move to London. For a year or two, I had been going down to work in the London office, sitting in for colleagues Clifford Davis and Jack Bell when they were on holiday, and doing other occasional stints. This meant I was already spending about three months of the year, on average, in London. And I was enjoying it. I was still ambitious enough to want to make it to the very top.

Betty, on the other, made it quite clear that she didn't want to move to London. She was quite happy staying with the children in the North.

In the end, we came to a decision. We'd sell the house in Woodley, buy a new house in Wallasey where Betty and the children would be happy, near Nancy and her family, and I would be over to see them at weekends.

It was like a split but not a complete split. A trial separation, if you like. I was more than a little surprised at how quickly Betty reacted once we had made the big decision. For a start, she lost no time in finding new friendships, and I discovered later that for a short while she had joined one of those singles' clubs for divorcees, etc., and even been out on a few dates.

When she told me some time later what she had got up to, I didn't know whether to be annoyed, shocked, or amused.

Betty and I went house-hunting in Wallasey and eventually bought a good solid, red-bricked semi-detached in Manville Road, with four bedrooms, an attic, a tiny walled garden at the front and a back yard to the rear. It was about ten minutes' walk down to the beach at New Brighton, and Susan, Mark and Paul were all enrolled at the nearby junior school in Vaughan Road. We put our house at Woodley on the market for a quick sale.

In the meantime, the Mirror made me a definite offer to move to London. And in all the circumstances, I took it. I joined the TV department, with Clifford Davis as my new boss.

Finally, I'd made it. Fleet Street. The Street of a thousand dreams I'd had for years. Full of eccentrics and big-name writers. And there I was, working alongside such legendary figures as William Connor (Cassandra), Marjorie Proops, and Donald Zec, on the daily paper with the biggest circulation in the world.

At first, the office put me up at The White House, near Regent's Park and paid all my hotel expenses for up to six months. It was the height of luxury living and I loved it.

But then I had to find a flat of my own, and I rented a little furnished apartment in the attic of a period terraced house in Highbury Gardens in trendy Highbury Village.

Every weekend, whatever the weather, I drove North to Wallasey to see Betty and the kids. They had now settled in at school, made new friends and seemed to be happy enough. Betty too was experiencing a new lease of life.

But it wasn't long before I was missing them. Although the job was taking up most of my time, and I was trying to establish myself, it wasn't the same without the family around me.

Within the year, I decided I couldn't go on like this. I loved the children too much to lose them, and desperately wanted them back with me. So I went to Betty, explained my feelings, and practically begged her to let's make up, and get back together again. I suggested we buy a house in London, and this time she agreed.

She had never really liked the idea of living in London, but now she finally realised that it was what I wanted, what I had always yearned for. And she also realised, just as I did, that we still loved each other and we had three wonderful children, and we should be together.

So it was back to the estate agents. I went house hunting in London. We figured it would be best to live in North London, to make it easier to drive back up North to see our families, so we concentrated on the Pinner and Harrow area. I viewed several properties and finally ended up with two. One was a nicely decorated and modernised semi-detached in Pinner, the other an attractive but rather run-down detached in North Harrow which required a lot doing to it.

Betty came down to London to join me to make a final choice. We viewed both houses. I liked the one in Pinner, which was cheaper and ready to walk into, but she preferred the one in Harrow. When I argued that it needed a lot of work doing on it, including fitting a central heating system which it didn't have, she insisted it had more potential. It was a detached, which meant more status, and once decorated it would make a lovely family home, she insisted. She won. She convinced me. I rang the estate agent. The deal was done.

Our new house - 219 The Ridgeway, North Harrow, Middlesex - cost us £6,900 in 1966. We lost no time in putting our house in Manville Road, Wallasey, back on the market. By the time we sold it, all the work on the house in Harrow was completed and it was ready to move in to.

Betty was right. It did look good after it was decorated and we'd bought new furniture. We were now the proud owners of a splendid double-fronted detached house in London, with three bedrooms, a nice front garden, a large back garden with detached garage. And a wonderful ancient plum tree which overhung the back garden fence, and produced more fruit than we could eat every summer.

When we finally moved, the children were all enrolled at their new junior school. It was called Vaughan Road, the same as the school in Wallasey. Now wasn't that a coincidence? It was a ten-minute walk from home. And when they were 11 years old, they would all move to Harrow Grammar School for Girls and Harrow Grammar School for Boys, two very prestigious colleges just at the bottom of the hill from the renowned public school of Harrow. But with no fees to pay.

All three of them enjoyed their school days. And they all went on to better things. Ask them now which school they liked best, and which house they consider the best home when growing up, and they all plump for Harrow.

CHAPTER 50: LIVING IN LONDON

London was a whole new world after Liverpool and Manchester. Unlike the Northern cities, it seemed to have no boundaries and the roads went on for ever.

Fleet Street was everything I'd imagined it to be. For years I'd dreamed of working there. Now, with all the time in the world, I spent every spare hour exploring its narrow little back alleys, discovering where Doctor Johnston had lived, and finding great delight in the historical pubs and inns such as the Cheshire Cheese and El Vino's wine bar.

There was an even greater drinking culture in Fleet Street than there was in Manchester. It was expected of journalists that they should be big drinkers. In fact, within a very short time, one had to get used to the idea that when a reporter said he was going out to lunch, it usually meant he would not be back in the office until the pubs closed in the afternoon. Two and three hour lunches were regarded as perfectly normal. And when the licensing laws were changed to allow all-day drinking, it was anybody's guess when some of the really hard drinkers would be back at their desks, if at all.

It was a wonder to me that we ever managed to get a paper out, but most journalists found it perfectly easy to function and carry out their duties even when totally inebriated. Though there was the odd occasion, I'd been told, when a particularly drunken reporter had been known to pick up a typewriter and hurl it through the plate glass window. This behaviour was frowned upon, however.

Working in the TV department, I shared an office with Clifford Davis, Jack Bell, and TV critic Kenneth Easthough, who later left for another paper and was replaced by Mary Malone.

Clifford marked the diary each morning and allocated which jobs we'd do. We had a rota system for who would write the TV preview page, and who would be on news duty.

News duty meant going around all the various Press conferences held by the BBC and ITV companies, picking up stories, and ending up back at the BBC Press Office building in Cavendish Square, where they had a TV correspondents' room, with telephones and a battery of typewriters for our use, and a canteen where we could get tea and coffee. There, we would meet up with the correspondents from all the other national papers, compare notes if necessary, and file our stories. Quite often, we'd all share taxis throughout the day to the various Press conferences.

Usually, our hours were 10 am in the office, finish at around 6 pm, but we'd still be "on call" from the news desk until 11 pm or midnight, when the last editions went to press.

I found the job pretty easy and I thoroughly enjoyed myself most of the time. I got on very well with Clifford Davis, and in fact after a while we would have lunch together at least once a week at his favourite restaurant, a little place called The Nosherie in a back street off Hatton Garden. The Nosherie was in the London Good Food Guide, and served delicious plates of chicken soup, salt beef and cucumber, and the best apple pie in the world. Just going in there for a meal was an experience in itself. Apart from a smattering of journalists, the regular customers were all boisterous Jewish jewellers, busy doing deals and buying and selling gold and other trinkets.

Harrow was exactly 11 miles from the office. So I had the option of going in by Tube (a ten-minute walk to North Harrow Station, a train to Baker Street, then change to a train for Fleet Street) which usually took me nearly an hour. Or I could drive in, which, with the heavy traffic, would also take me exactly an hour. But I had free parking in the Mirror underground car park, providing I was in by 10.30 am, when it would then be full, and this meant putting the car in a public stacker car-park around the corner which would cost ten quid a day.

As I've always had a fascination for cars. I preferred to drive in, even though it often meant being stuck in slow-moving traffic for the last three or four miles. I'd just put the radio on, sit back and enjoy the exhaust fumes! It also meant me changing cars quite frequently, which was an expensive hobby I grew to enjoy.

I then got an appetite to write more books. After the thrill of   my first paperback, The Real Coronation Street, published by Corgi, I then wrote a book on The Comedians, which was another Granada show, but this time they were happy to give me permission. In fact, they invited me to write it. TV Times published it as a paperback. And I sold the serial rights of that book to the Sunday People, and they ran extracts from it over three weeks, which of course helped to boost the sales.

With the success of the books, as a freelance side line away from the Mirror, I began to feel really comfortable, and assured myself that I could now do anything if I put my mind to it.

The BBC then came to me and asked me if I was interested in writing and producing a book on Top of the Pops. I jumped at it, spent time going down to the programme regularly, interviewed all the top stars, and came out with a book which not only pleased the BBC, but sold extremely well. And it developed into the Top of the Pops Annual, which I went on to produce for about seven years, before handing it over to an independent publisher.

At the Mirror, I was determined to get my feet on the promotion ladder. The chance finally came when Clifford Davis walked into the office one day and told us he'd had enough of writing about TV and he was going to see the Editor with a new idea he had. A few days later, he announced he was leaving us to set up a new department called the Daily Mirror Pop Club, which he had convinced the Editor would attract younger readers to the paper. With free offers, competitions, discount deals and tickets to concerts, the Pop Club did indeed prove to be a big success for a while. At the age of 58, Clifford had completely re-invented himself and found a new career. Even then, though, he sought my help and asked me to edit and produce the Pop Club Annual, which I happily did on a freelance arrangement.

As a result, there was a scramble to fill his old job. Clifford told me he was recommending me for the job of TV Editor. But instead, Bill Hagerty came in for a short while to replace Clifford, but he didn't stay long before being promoted to Editor of the Sunday Mirror. Then I made my bid for the top job, but was again disappointed when they brought in Alan Garratt, who was a former editor of the Reveille paper. When I complained and made my feelings known, they promoted me to be his deputy and gave me a rise in salary.

But Garratt was hopeless at the job. He was completely lost. He spent most of his time wining and dining TV stars and just liked the idea of mingling with the celebrities. In the end, they paid him off and he went to California to try his hand as a freelance.

With his departure, I finally got the job I wanted. First, I became TV Editor. Then we merged two departments into one, and I became TV and Show Business Editor, with a staff of 12 writers working under me, two secretaries, and a big budget to handle. And a cocktail cabinet which I inherited from Alan Garratt, and was kept well stocked with champagne and every other drink imaginable. It proved an ideal asset for when we were interviewing visiting celebrities.

When I took the whole of the showbiz staff to a lunch on the first day of my new appointment, in January 1980, I was determined that I was going to make a success of it. I was now in charge of the biggest department outside of the News Room. It included TV writers, showbiz reporters, film and theatre critics and pop music writers.

I'd finally made it to the top job. I happily settled for being TV and Show Business Editor. I didn't want anything else. I was like a cat who'd got the cream.

For three years I ran the showbiz department very successfully. But there must be something inside me which demands I have to make changes in my life because I gave up being Show Business Editor, quite voluntarily. I grew tired of running the office, signing expenses, sending other people out on jobs which often I knew I could do better. I just missed being "out on the road" and got itchy feet. I became disillusioned with London, was fed up being on the treadmill, and asked for a move back to Manchester.

Partly, this was due to domestic circumstances. My younger son Paul was suddenly taken seriously ill, and when we visited him in hospital, we thought we might actually lose him. He had to have an operation, and they took away half a lung.

Fortunately, he recovered. But I started to look at my own life and reflect on things. What was I doing - working around the clock? On call night and day, drinking far too much in the well-known watering holes of Fleet Street and in our office pub, which was ironically nicknamed the Stab in the Back. And for what?

There were times when I'd find the car perfectly parked in our garage at home in the morning, but I couldn't even remember driving home the night before or which route I had taken.

And there was one awful occasion, when I caught the last Tube train home, staggered down our road at midnight, and surprised Betty who was in bed by delivering her a massive load of beautiful assorted flowers, which practically filled the whole bedroom. Only for me to wake up next morning and be horrified walking to the station to find that not a single garden in The Ridgeway had any flowers in it. It looked like every garden from ours up to the traffic lights had been raided and vandalised overnight by a mysterious flower thief.

Then, to cap it all, I was stopped by police for drunk driving. Going home, about 10 pm after an evening drinking in the office pub with reporter Evil Sid Williams and others, I was caught in a radar trap, doing 50 mph just coming off the Westway motorway at Shepherds Bush. I was breath tested, was over the limit, and arrested by police right opposite the BBC studios.

I ended up being banned for the statutory 12 months, which meant I was without my car and had to get used to public transport from then on. I gave the car (a lovely blue Triumph 2-litre saloon) to my mate Mike Day, a reporter with the Press Association, on loan for him to run and look after for the 12 months. When he returned it to me a year later, the petrol tank was practically empty (but that's another story).

We sold our house in Harrow and moved to the lovely district of Disley, Cheshire. We bought a spacious dormer bungalow with magnificent views over the rolling Derbyshire hills and Kinder Scout, and we were only a short walk away from the famous Lyme Hall and park.

From the sale of our London house, I managed to give each of our grown-up children the 10 per-cent deposit to help buy their first homes and get them on the property ladder.

I still love London and enjoy going down to meet up with old chums for lunch. But my roots are in the North and that's where my heart will always be.

As well as later appearing regularly as a judge on ITV's top talent show New Faces (which I did in the mid-1970s) and also judging on bathing beauty contests, which were extremely popular on TV for many years, I was more than a little delighted when ABC TV in Manchester booked me for a series of short programmes they did called Personal Column.

Each programme ran for about five minutes. This involved writing my own script on any subject which appealed to me. I usually tried to be funny. I'd pick out something from that week's news and try and get laughs out of it.

It must have been okay, because they kept coming back and asking me to do more. I would record one show each week. The only trouble was, they screened the programmes on ITV in the North, usually around 11.45 pm. It was almost like doing the Epilogue!

Later, however, when I moved to London, I dealt a lot with a woman who was Press Officer for the BBC's religious programmes. When she heard that I had once been quite attached to the Methodist church, she asked me if I was interested in doing some radio programmes for them.

She took me to lunch and we talked about it. I told her frankly that I was not really keen to do religious stuff. But she then said, "What about 'Pause For Thought?' That hasn't got to be religious, but it has a moral theme. You can choose whatever you like to talk about. It lasts five minutes and you write your own script."

So I thought about it and agreed to have a go. As it turned out, I quite enjoyed it. The programmes were recorded in Broadcasting House and, in those days, transmitted every day, in a mid-morning slot.

I didn't want to sound preachy, so rather than be religious, I just stuck to one subject, such as Honesty, Integrity, or Courage, and rambled on in moralistic tones for five minutes. The BBC paid a fee of £12 for each programme. But I was really amazed at the reaction of the radio audiences because the programmes resulted in quite a lot of mail.

In fact, after one programme, among the letters I received was one from an old uncle of mine, Uncle Tommy, one of my father's brothers, in Liverpool. I hadn't seen him since I was a teenager. But he was very complimentary about the radio programme, asked how my mother was, and the rest of the family, and then went on to pour out his own troubles.

As for Pause For Thought, it's still very popular and still being broadcast on Radio 4. But they now call it Thought For The Day. I usually listen to it every morning over breakfast.

CHAPTER 51: OLD PALS

SCHOOL REUNION

A few years ago, I set out to try and find an old schoolteacher who had been a great influence on me in my last year at Breckfield Secondary School in Liverpool. He was Mr. S.R. Gardiner, and he was the master of Form 4A, a great teacher, who encouraged me to write and appointed me Editor of the first school magazine.

In my search to find if he was still alive, I wrote a letter to the Liverpool Echo's Old Pals column, asking for information about Mr. Gardiner's whereabouts, and trying to trace old pupils.

The following day I had a phone call from a chap who said he was a nephew of Mr. Gardiner, pointing out that his uncle had died some years ago. But I also got a call from a bloke who went to school with me. He remembered me being in the same class with him and he told me they had an old boys' get-together once a year at Christmas. Why didn't I join them, he suggested, they'd love to see me.

So I arranged to go to Liverpool for their next reunion - at a Wetherspoon's pub. It turned out that they had been meeting annually for the last four or fives years. There were eight of them, only three of whom I knew, who were in the same class as me from the age of 11 to 15.

It was amazing meeting up again with school mates I hadn't seen for 60 years. The reunions were all organised by David "Spud" Carter, and others who had been in my class were Frank Smith and John Tempest. But the others who also turned up regularly, and I soon became friendly with, were John Tempest's brother David, Ron Williams, Richard Phythian (who travelled from Kent every year), Sammy Gregory, George Williams, Jimmy Lawson and Norman Owens.

Exchanging stories, sharing schoolboy memories, finding out what jobs and careers they had all forged out for themselves, was quite fascinating. I've been happily meeting up with them every Christmas for the last half dozen years.

Some of them now have pace-makers and others have new hips and replacement knees, and we're all on pills. But it's still good to see each other and I enjoy the camaraderie. Sadly, one or two have fallen off their perches in recent years, but the rest of us keeping going. Somehow.

Here's to next year!

FRIENDS

How many friends do we have? Real friends, I mean? People we know, those we can trust, whom we can confide in, tell our innermost secrets to, go to if we are ever in trouble and need a shoulder to cry on. Or maybe just share a drink with and hope for a bit of sympathy if things go wrong.

Well, thinking very seriously about this, I've got five. Just five friends. I don't know whether that is sad or not. Something to boast about or perhaps be pitied or ridiculed for maybe not being more popular.

The important thing, to me anyway, is that they are all very good friends who have been around for many years, and hopefully we will remain friends for the rest of our lives, however long that may be.

Who are they, these precious friends? Well, there's Les Davies and Victor Lane, my two oldest buddies. They were both members of St. Domingo Church and the club which we frequented from about the age of 14. Vic lived in St. Domingo Vale, with his mother and sister Sheila. And Les lived with his mum and brothers Stan and George, about 300 yards away from Loraine Street, along Breckfield Road North.

The three of us went everywhere together. We all played in the table tennis team (Vic No.1, me No.2 and Les at No.3) and also in the football team, which was famous as the St. Domingo church team from which the mighty Everton Football Club had first been formed, back in 1888.

We were together right through our teenage years and split up only when Les was called up for National Service in the RAF, Vic won a place at Liverpool University, and I failed my medical for National Service and went off to get married.

Les would have been my best man, but he was away on RAF duty, so that job fell to my cousin Frank Jones, who was in the Royal Navy and turned up in the wedding pictures in his Admiral's uniform.

We didn't see much of each other after that. I moved away from Liverpool when I joined the Daily Mirror. Les joined the Liverpool Daily Post and Echo as a printing compositor. And Vic went off to do all sorts of wonderful things as a qualified Civil Engineer.

Once, when I was working in Fleet Street, Vic popped in to meet me at the office and we had lunch together at a local wine bar. But after that, we never saw each other for years. The same with Les. He went on to leave the Echo and launch his own printing company and became quite a successful businessman.

Les and I met up again about 20 years ago, when he invited my wife Betty and I, and my sister Louise and her husband Ernie to his house in

West Derby, Liverpool, for dinner and we had a jolly reunion with Les, his wife Val, and brothers. Les has lived in the same house for many years and says he'll never move.

Sadly, his wife died a few years ago, but Les and I are now back in touch on a regular basis and meet in Liverpool for lunch occasionally.

Vic and I had not met for years, until I decided it was time to catch up with him and renew our friendship. So last year I drove down to Goring-by-Sea, West Sussex, where he lives, and we had dinner in nearby Hove. He picked me up at my hotel in a very smart open-topped Mercedes sports car and zipped through the country lanes to a lovely restaurant where he was greeted: "Yes, Professor Lane, we have your table for two."

Professor? Oh yes, our Vic, my old football and table tennis mate from 65 years ago, has really been very successful in life. He's a couple of years older than me, and although now retired, he has an amazing career to look back on, having re-invented himself more than once and become a renowned academic who still dabbles in lectures and seminars around the world. I googled him recently just for fun, and I was staggered by his achievements. He's got more letters after his name than the Queen!

Vic too lost his wife a couple of years ago and now lives alone. But we are in regular touch, and I'd like to think we can get together for another lunch or dinner some time before one of us snuffs it.

Another guy whose friendship I greatly value is Pat O'Hare, a singer from Manchester I first met when I was a young reporter on the Mirror and he was struggling to make a name for himself in show business in the early 1960s. (See Chapter 38: Just Memories, Pat O'Hare).

He sang with the BBC's Northern Dance Orchestra, then got his own radio and TV series. I tried to help him by handling all his publicity and we became close friends.

We lost touch. But then, in the mid-1970s, when I was one of the judges on ITV's top talent show New Faces, Pat turned up as a contestant on one of the shows. He not only wowed the studio audience but also the panel. We voted him the winner and he went on to appear in the grand final of the series, when Terry Wogan, one of the judges, said that if there was a better ballad singer in Britain, then he had yet to hear him. Pat went on to have a very successful career.

We hadn't met for 40 years when I phoned him last year and we got together for a reunion lunch in Manchester. He was still doing the occasional show and he invited me to one of his monthly weekend gigs at a club in Batley, Yorkshire. When I went to see him, I was amazed at how well he was singing. He's still got a great voice and bags of personality. And his regular Sunday afternoon audiences love him.

He still lives near Manchester with his wife Christine. But he doesn't let the singing get in the way of his golf.

Then to round off my list of friends, I've got two journalist chums, John Stevenson and Tony Purnell.

John, I first met in the 1960s when he joined the Daily Mail in Manchester from his local Oldham paper, and became their Northern show business reporter. We immediately hit it off. We have the same sardonic sense of humour and he is the funniest man I know.

He left the Mail and became a TV scriptwriter, devising several comedy series - including Brass, Nearest and Dearest and The Brothers McGregor - and joined the Coronation Street writing team. He went on to write 447 episodes for The Street. And when Stan and Hilda Ogden, and then Jack and Vera Duckworth had all those wonderful moments of classic comedy, it was invariably big John whose name was on the scripts.

We've kept in touch and been mates for years, and still get together for lunch on a fairly regular basis. Whenever we meet, I look forward to the laughs even more than the steak and kidney pudding!

Tony Purnell was a reporter on the Sunday People when our paths first crossed. He was one of those investigative reporters you wouldn't want to cross swords with.

Our friendship started over the odd pint in the office pub, but we'd often meet at the same showbiz functions and it wasn't long before we became friends more than rivals. We also had the odd foreign trip together.

I remember once, when I was show business editor of the Mirror, Tony saying to me, "I wish I could work with you. I think we'd make a great team." Unfortunately, at that time there were no vacancies, otherwise I would have jumped at the chance to employ him and bring him into our department.

It was ironic that after I quit London and moved back to Manchester, Tony moved over from The People to join the Mirror. We did however work together later in the same department for a couple of years before I decided to leave and go freelance.

Tony and I think alike. We have the same tenacity for a good story. He has a great sense of humour and is a very likeable guy.

We like to meet at least once a year for lunch (which usually lasts all day and once even went over into a second). We keep in touch regularly by phone. It's just a pity that London and Manchester are so far apart.

But yes, it's great to have friends. Even though I'm down to five.

CHAPTER 52: EPILOGUE

HAVING A LAST LAUGH

When I hear people asking, "What would you like on your Epitaph?" it makes me smile. It's easy to get too serious about this kind of thing.

I still think that Spike Milligan came up with the best one. He insisted in having on his gravestone: "I Told You I Was Ill." That's a classic.

Or you could throw in a joke on the headstone. "Have you heard about the dyslexic agnostic insomniac? He couldn't sleep at nights, wondering if there really was a dog!"

What do I want on mine? I think I'd be happy with something like: "He Was Always Good For A Laugh." I'd certainly like to think I was. But that's for others to judge.

At the age of 82, however, and with many of my old friends and colleagues now having bitten the dust, I am growing increasingly wary about the future. How long is the future? Who knows? But with practically every new phone call from an old chum from Fleet Street telling me that so-and-so has just fallen off his perch or did I know that *whatsisname* had a heart attack and died without recovering but had a lovely funeral, I suppose it was inevitable that I recently began to think what I should do about making arrangement for my own final farewell.

I hate the idea of taking out one of those much-advertised insurance policies to pre-arrange and pay for all your funeral costs in advance. And I particularly and absolutely hate my old journalist colleague and pal Michael Parkinson (or SIR Michael Parkinson as he is now) for cashing in and making his own fortune out of presenting those never-ending TV adverts aimed at vulnerable pensioners, conning them into thinking they shouldn't die without first paying the full whack for their funeral costs. Even if they do get the promise of a cheap free pen for merely enquiring about it!

Having made out my Will some years ago, I began thinking recently whether it would now be sensible to make any tentative steps about arranging a funeral, or at least throw in one or two ideas or suggestions which might be helpful, instead of leaving it to my poor kids after I've gone to make all the morbid arrangements.

The first thing I want to make sure is that I end up in dear old Liverpool. I have always thought I want to be buried in Anfield Cemetery, within hearing distance of the roar of the crowd every Saturday at Goodison Park.

And have a headstone suitably erected to mark my sad demise, and hopefully inscribed with a funny quip or two.

And, after the funeral, my ideal plan would be for a reception held in the function room of Everton football club, with mourners able to go out and tread the hallowed turf, after stuffing themselves with food and drink, and then viewing the trophy room and picture gallery of The Blues' string of famous players over the years. (This is what they did for my late brother-in-law George Stirrup, a Baptist parson. And it went down very well with his children and family!).

So, I decided to make some enquiries about the possibility of maybe booking a plot for a grave and finding out how much it cost.

When I phoned the Liverpool city council, they put me through to the Parks and Cemeteries department, a woman took my name and phone number and said she would have to send an internal e-mail and that someone would phone me back. This might take between five and seven working days, she stressed.

"No hurry," I said. "I'm not going anywhere."

To my surprise, exactly half an hour later my phone rang and I got a call from a man with a very pronounced lilting Scouse accent. The phone conversation went something like this.

"My name is Colin and I'm from the Cemeteries department," he said. "Am I speaking to Mr. Irwin?" "You are," I said.

"Okay, well I gather you wanna know about reserving a burial plot at Anfield Cemetery. Is that right?"

"Yes, I just want to know how I go about this, and how much it costs," I said. "Is it for yourself?" he asked. "Yes."

"Right, I've got to ask you a few questions," said Colin "The first thing is, when are you going to die? Have you any idea?"

The question took me by surprise. I laughed awkwardly and said, "Well, no. Not really."

"We have to ask you that," said Colin in a very matter-of-fact way. "I mean, you're not going to go tomorrow? Or next week, say?"

"I hope not. I'm not planning to," I stammered.

"So, it's not one of those cases where you have only a few months to live?" he ventured undiplomatically. "You're not ill or nothin?"

No, I told him. But I suppose you could still say it was a matter of life or death. I was 82 and was just making enquiries.

"Fair enough," he said. "Well, first, do you live in Liverpool?"

"No," I said. "But I was born there and lived many years of my life on Merseyside. But I now live in Manchester."

There was a pause and I could hear Colin take a deep breath.

"Are you sittin' down?" he suddenly asked. "Why, do I need to?" I said.

"You might," he quipped, trying to stifle a chuckle. "For a non-residential – and that means if you don't live in Liverpool – to reserve a burial plot for yourself, it would cost you £1,980."

"Wow," I said. "And how much would it cost me if I did live in Liverpool?"

"Well, that doesn't apply, does it, cos you live in Manchester, don't you?" said Colin. And then he added, "And the other thing is this - if you reserved a plot and you didn't die within 12 months, but then applied again at a later date, you'd have to pay the same fee a second time."

"Blimey," I said. "It might be cheaper for me to move to Liverpool before I die."

He laughed loudly. "No, you'd have to be resident here and paying rates to Liverpool council before you could get buried on the cheap," he announced. "But there is a way around this, if you want to cheat. Have you any relatives living in Liverpool?

"No, but I have relatives living in Wirral, in Birkenhead, Upton, Wallasey. Why?"

"No, they've got to be resident rate-payers in Liverpool," he said. "Then, maybe one of them could make an application, offering to buy the burial plot for you. That would be a lot cheaper, instead of you buying it for yourself."

"Well, I'll have to go away and think about all this," I said.

"Yeah," said Colin. "It's an expensive business, dying, you know."

"You're telling me," I replied.

Then, quite suddenly, he said, "Why do you want to go to Anfield Cemetery, anyway? Surely it would be cheaper for you in Manchester."

"Well, because I'm a lifelong Evertonian and I've always said I wanted to be buried within hearing distance of Goodison Park on a match day. I suppose you're now going to tell me you are a staunch Red, a Liverpudlian?"

"You're bloody joking, aren't you?" he replied. "I'm Blue through and through. I've had a season ticket at Goodison – in the Bullens Road stand – for about 30 years."

I hesitated, and then said, "Thirty years? How old are you?"

"Fifty- seven," he said. "Why?"

"You sound about 28 or 29," I told him. "Well, I don't look it, mate," he said.

"What do you think about Wayne Rooney coming back to Everton?" I asked. "Bloody great," said Colin. "He was always too bleedin' good for Manchester United."

I told him I thought Rooney still had a good two years or more in him, and he agreed. "I trust our manager Ronald Koeman. If he wants him back, then that's good enough for me," he said.

Then, just as I was about to thank him, Colin laughed loudly down the phone and said, "Why have you got to get buried, anyway? Why don't you just throw yourself in the Mersey?"

"What?" I said.

"No, I mean after you've kicked the bucket," he hurriedly replied. "Bugger the cemetery. Get someone to throw your ashes in the Mersey. It's much cheaper. That's what I'm going to do."

"Are you serious?" I asked.

"Yeah. I can't afford to pay our burial rates, meself. Not on the money I earn."

"But surely you'll get it cheaper, living in Liverpool," I suggested.

"No. I live in Sefton. I don't pay Liverpool rates," he said. "I'd have to pay the full fee, like you, as a non-resident."

"So, you're going to have your ashes scattered in the Mersey?" I said. "What, near the Pier Head?"

"Oh no," said Colin the Scouse, now almost triumphantly looking forward to his own death. "I'm going in at the posh end, near all the super yachts parked in the marina. I want to be where the money is."

We both laughed. "Anyway, I hope I've been of some help, Mr. Irwin. And here's hoping for a good season at Everton."

I put down the phone. And it got me thinking. Colin from the Cemeteries department is probably right. It costs too much to die. I think I'll hang on as long as I can. And I might even change my mind. Tell them to have me cremated and scatter my ashes on the sand at New Brighton, near the lovely pink house on the Prom, where I used to live, and be gently swept away in the Mersey. It will certainly be cheaper.

INDEX

OTHER BOOKS BY KEN IRWIN

The REAL Coronation Street

Laugh with the Comedians

Top of the Pops Annuals

From Liverpool to Fleet Street ...And Back

The Pink House On The River

A Matter Of Policy – A Play For Radio

A Laugh A Day Keeps The Doctor Away

Printed in Great Britain
by Amazon

21635096R00363